CORNERSTONE
BIBLICAL
COMMENTARY

General Editor
Philip W. Comfort
D. Litt. et Phil., University of South Africa;
Tyndale House Publishers;
Coastal Carolina University.

Consulting Editor, Old Testament
Tremper Longman III
PhD, Yale University;
Robert H. Gundry Professor of Biblical Studies, Westmont College.

Consulting Editor, New Testament
Grant Osborne
PhD, University of Aberdeen;
Professor of New Testament, Trinity Evangelical Divinity School.

Associate Editors
Jason Driesbach
MA, Biblical Exegesis and Linguistics, Dallas Theological Seminary;
Tyndale House Publishers.

Mark R. Norton
MA, Theological Studies, Wheaton Graduate School;
Tyndale House Publishers.

James A. Swanson
MSM, Multnomah Biblical Seminary;
MTh, University of South Africa;
Tyndale House Publishers.

CORNERSTONE BIBLICAL COMMENTARY

Genesis
Allen Ross

Exodus
John N. Oswalt

GENERAL EDITOR
Philip W. Comfort

with the entire text of the
NEW LIVING TRANSLATION

TYNDALE HOUSE PUBLISHERS, INC. CAROL STREAM, ILLINOIS

Cornerstone Biblical Commentary, Volume 1

Visit Tyndale's exciting Web site at www.tyndale.com

Genesis copyright © 2008 by Allen Ross. All rights reserved.

Exodus copyright © 2008 by John N. Oswalt. All rights reserved.

Designed by Luke Daab and Timothy R. Botts.

Unless otherwise indicated, all Scripture quotations are taken from the *Holy Bible*, New Living Translation, copyright © 1996, 2004, 2007 by Tyndale House Foundation. Used by permission of Tyndale House Publishers, Inc., Carol Stream, Illinois 60188. All rights reserved.

TYNDALE, *New Living Translation, NLT,* Tyndale's quill logo, and the New Living Translation logo are registered trademarks of Tyndale House Publishers, Inc.

Library of Congress Cataloging-in-Publication Data

Cornerstone biblical commentary.
   p. cm.
  Includes bibliographical references and index.
  ISBN-13: 978-0-8423-3427-3 (hc : alk. paper)
  ISBN-10: 0-8423-3427-0 (hc : alk. paper)
  1. Bible—Commentaries. I. Oswalt, John N. II. Ross, Allen P.
  BS491.3.C67 2006
  220.7'7—dc22   2005026928

Printed in the United States of America

14 13 12 11 10 09 08
7   6   5   4   3   2   1

CONTENTS

Contributors to Volume 1
vi

General Editor's Preface
vii

Abbreviations
ix

Transliteration and Numbering System
xiii

GENESIS
1

EXODUS
259

CONTRIBUTORS TO VOLUME 1

Genesis: Allen Ross
BA, Barrington College;
ThM, Dallas Theological Seminary;
ThD, Dallas Theological Seminary;
PhD, Cambridge University;
Postdoctoral study at Tübingen University and Cambridge University;
Distinguished Professor of New Testament Studies at Dallas Theological Seminary.

Exodus: John N. Oswalt
BA, Taylor University;
BD, ThM, Asbury Theological Seminary;
MA, PhD, Brandeis University;
Research Professor of Old Testament at Wesley Biblical Seminary.

GENERAL EDITOR'S PREFACE

The *Cornerstone Biblical Commentary* is based on the second edition of the New Living Translation (2007). Nearly 100 scholars from various church backgrounds and from several countries (United States, Canada, England, and Australia) participated in the creation of the NLT. Many of these same scholars are contributors to this commentary series. All the commentators, whether participants in the NLT or not, believe that the Bible is God's inspired word and have a desire to make God's word clear and accessible to his people.

This Bible commentary is the natural extension of our vision for the New Living Translation, which we believe is both exegetically accurate and idiomatically powerful. The NLT attempts to communicate God's inspired word in a lucid English translation of the original languages so that English readers can understand and appreciate the thought of the original writers. In the same way, the *Cornerstone Biblical Commentary* aims at helping teachers, pastors, students, and laypeople understand every thought contained in the Bible. As such, the commentary focuses first on the words of Scripture, then on the theological truths of Scripture—inasmuch as the words express the truths.

The commentary itself has been structured in such a way as to help readers get at the meaning of Scripture, passage by passage, through the entire Bible. Each Bible book is prefaced by a substantial book introduction that gives general historical background important for understanding. Then the reader is taken through the Bible text, passage by passage, starting with the New Living Translation text printed in full. This is followed by a section called "Notes," wherein the commentator helps the reader understand the Hebrew or Greek behind the English of the NLT, interacts with other scholars on important interpretive issues, and points the reader to significant textual and contextual matters. The "Notes" are followed by the "Commentary," wherein each scholar presents a lucid interpretation of the passage, giving special attention to context and major theological themes.

The commentators represent a wide spectrum of theological positions within the evangelical community. We believe this is good because it reflects the rich variety in Christ's church. All the commentators uphold the authority of God's word and believe it is essential to heed the old adage: "Wholly apply yourself to the Scriptures and apply them wholly to you." May this commentary help you know the truths of Scripture, and may this knowledge help you "grow in your knowledge of God and Jesus our Lord" (2 Pet 1:2, NLT).

PHILIP W. COMFORT
GENERAL EDITOR

ABBREVIATIONS

GENERAL ABBREVIATIONS

b.	Babylonian Gemara	Heb.	Hebrew	NT	New Testament
bar.	baraita	ibid.	*ibidem*, in the same place	OL	Old Latin
c.	*circa*, around, approximately	i.e.	*id est*, the same	OS	Old Syriac
		in loc.	*in loco*, in the place cited	OT	Old Testament
cf.	*confer*, compare			p., pp.	page, pages
ch, chs	chapter, chapters	lit.	literally	pl.	plural
contra	in contrast to	LXX	Septuagint	Q	Quelle ("Sayings" as Gospel source)
DSS	Dead Sea Scrolls	𝔐	Majority Text	rev.	revision
ed.	edition, editor	m.	Mishnah	sg.	singular
e.g.	*exempli gratia*, for example	masc.	masculine	t.	Tosefta
		mg	margin	TR	Textus Receptus
et al.	*et alli*, and others	ms	manuscript	v., vv.	verse, verses
fem.	feminine	mss	manuscripts	vid.	*videur*, it seems
ff	following (verses, pages)	MT	Masoretic Text	viz.	*videlicet*, namely
fl.	flourished	n.d.	no date	vol.	volume
Gr.	Greek	neut.	neuter	y.	Jerusalem Gemara
		no.	number		

ABBREVIATIONS FOR BIBLE TRANSLATIONS

ASV	American Standard Version	NCV	New Century Version	NKJV	New King James Version
CEV	Contemporary English Version	NEB	New English Bible	NRSV	New Revised Standard Version
		NET	The NET Bible		
ESV	English Standard Version	NIV	New International Version	NLT	New Living Translation
GW	God's Word	NIrV	New International Reader's Version	REB	Revised English Bible
HCSB	Holman Christian Standard Bible	NJB	New Jerusalem Bible	RSV	Revised Standard Version
JB	Jerusalem Bible				
KJV	King James Version	NJPS	The New Jewish Publication Society Translation (*Tanakh*)	TEV	Today's English Version
NAB	New American Bible				
NASB	New American Standard Bible			TLB	The Living Bible

ABBREVIATIONS FOR DICTIONARIES, LEXICONS, COLLECTIONS OF TEXTS, ORIGINAL LANGUAGE EDITIONS

ABD *Anchor Bible Dictionary* (6 vols., Freedman) [1992]

ANEP *The Ancient Near East in Pictures* (Pritchard) [1965]

ANET *Ancient Near Eastern Texts Relating to the Old Testament* (Pritchard) [1969]

BAGD *Greek-English Lexicon of the New Testament and Other Early Christian Literature*, 2nd ed. (Bauer, Arndt, Gingrich, Danker) [1979]

BDAG *Greek-English Lexicon of the New Testament and Other Early Christian Literature*, 3rd ed. (Bauer, Danker, Arndt, Gingrich) [2000]

BDB *A Hebrew and English Lexicon of the Old Testament* (Brown, Driver, Briggs) [1907]

BDF *A Greek Grammar of the New Testament and Other Early Christian Literature* (Blass, Debrunner, Funk) [1961]

ABBREVIATIONS

BHS *Biblia Hebraica Stuttgartensia* (Elliger and Rudolph) [1983]
CAD *Assyrian Dictionary of the Oriental Institute of the University of Chicago* [1956]
COS *The Context of Scripture* (3 vols., Hallo and Younger) [1997–2002]
DBI *Dictionary of Biblical Imagery* (Ryken, Wilhoit, Longman) [1998]
DBT *Dictionary of Biblical Theology* (2nd ed., Leon-Dufour) [1972]
DCH *Dictionary of Classical Hebrew* (5 vols., D. Clines) [2000]
DJD *Discoveries in the Judean Desert* [1955–]
DJG *Dictionary of Jesus and the Gospels* (Green, McKnight, Marshall) [1992]
DOTP *Dictionary of the Old Testament: Pentateuch* (T. Alexander, D.W. Baker) [2003]
DPL *Dictionary of Paul and His Letters* (Hawthorne, Martin, Reid) [1993]
EDNT *Exegetical Dictionary of the New Testament* (3 vols., H. Balz, G. Schneider. ET) [1990–1993]
HALOT *The Hebrew and Aramaic Lexicon of the Old Testament* (L. Koehler, W. Baumgartner, J. Stamm; trans. M. Richardson) [1994–1999]
IBD *Illustrated Bible Dictionary* (3 vols., Douglas, Wiseman) [1980]

IDB *The Interpreter's Dictionary of the Bible* (4 vols., Buttrick) [1962]
ISBE *International Standard Bible Encyclopedia* (4 vols., Bromiley) [1979–1988]
KBL *Lexicon in Veteris Testamenti libros* (Koehler, Baumgartner) [1958]
LCL *Loeb Classical Library*
L&N *Greek-English Lexicon of the New Testament: Based on Semantic Domains* (Louw and Nida) [1989]
LSJ *A Greek-English Lexicon* (9th ed., Liddell, Scott, Jones) [1996]
MM *The Vocabulary of the Greek New Testament* (Moulton and Milligan) [1930; 1997]
NA[26] *Novum Testamentum Graece* (26th ed., Nestle-Aland) [1979]
NA[27] *Novum Testamentum Graece* (27th ed., Nestle-Aland) [1993]
NBD *New Bible Dictionary* (2nd ed., Douglas, Hillyer) [1982]
NIDB *New International Dictionary of the Bible* (Douglas, Tenney) [1987]
NIDBA *New International Dictionary of Biblical Archaeology* (Blaiklock and Harrison) [1983]
NIDNTT *New International Dictionary of New Testament Theology* (4 vols., C. Brown) [1975–1985]

NIDOTTE *New International Dictionary of Old Testament Theology and Exegesis* (5 vols., W. A. VanGemeren) [1997]
PGM *Papyri graecae magicae: Die griechischen Zauberpapyri.* (Preisendanz) [1928]
PG *Patrologia Graecae* (J. P. Migne) [1857–1886]
TBD *Tyndale Bible Dictionary* (Elwell, Comfort) [2001]
TDNT *Theological Dictionary of the New Testament* (10 vols., Kittel, Friedrich; trans. Bromiley) [1964–1976]
TDOT *Theological Dictionary of the Old Testament* (8 vols., Botterweck, Ringgren; trans. Willis, Bromiley, Green) [1974–]
TLNT *Theological Lexicon of the New Testament* (3 vols., C. Spicq) [1994]
TLOT *Theological Lexicon of the Old Testament* (3 vols., E. Jenni) [1997]
TWOT *Theological Wordbook of the Old Testament* (2 vols., Harris, Archer) [1980]
UBS[3] *United Bible Societies' Greek New Testament* (3rd ed., Metzger et al.) [1975]
UBS[4] *United Bible Societies' Greek New Testament* (4th corrected ed., Metzger et al.) [1993]
WH *The New Testament in the Original Greek* (Westcott and Hort) [1882]

ABBREVIATIONS FOR BOOKS OF THE BIBLE

Old Testament

Gen	Genesis	1 Sam	1 Samuel	Esth	Esther
Exod	Exodus	2 Sam	2 Samuel	Job	Job
Lev	Leviticus	1 Kgs	1 Kings	Ps, Pss	Psalm, Psalms
Num	Numbers	2 Kgs	2 Kings	Prov	Proverbs
Deut	Deuteronomy	1 Chr	1 Chronicles	Eccl	Ecclesiastes
Josh	Joshua	2 Chr	2 Chronicles	Song	Song of Songs
Judg	Judges	Ezra	Ezra	Isa	Isaiah
Ruth	Ruth	Neh	Nehemiah	Jer	Jeremiah

Lam	Lamentations		Amos	Amos		Hab	Habakkuk
Ezek	Ezekiel		Obad	Obadiah		Zeph	Zephaniah
Dan	Daniel		Jonah	Jonah		Hag	Haggai
Hos	Hosea		Mic	Micah		Zech	Zechariah
Joel	Joel		Nah	Nahum		Mal	Malachi

New Testament

Matt	Matthew		Eph	Ephesians		Heb	Hebrews
Mark	Mark		Phil	Philippians		Jas	James
Luke	Luke		Col	Colossians		1 Pet	1 Peter
John	John		1 Thess	1 Thessalonians		2 Pet	2 Peter
Acts	Acts		2 Thess	2 Thessalonians		1 John	1 John
Rom	Romans		1 Tim	1 Timothy		2 John	2 John
1 Cor	1 Corinthians		2 Tim	2 Timothy		3 John	3 John
2 Cor	2 Corinthians		Titus	Titus		Jude	Jude
Gal	Galatians		Phlm	Philemon		Rev	Revelation

Deuterocanonical

Bar	Baruch		1–2 Esdr	1–2 Esdras		Pr Man	Prayer of Manasseh
Add Dan	Additions to Daniel		Add Esth	Additions to Esther		Ps 151	Psalm 151
Pr Azar	Prayer of Azariah		Ep Jer	Epistle of Jeremiah		Sir	Sirach
Bel	Bel and the Dragon		Jdt	Judith		Tob	Tobit
Sg Three	Song of the Three Children		1–2 Macc	1–2 Maccabees		Wis	Wisdom of Solomon
			3–4 Macc	3–4 Maccabees			
Sus	Susanna						

MANUSCRIPTS AND LITERATURE FROM QUMRAN

Initial numerals followed by "Q" indicate particular caves at Qumran. For example, the notation 4Q267 indicates text 267 from cave 4 at Qumran. Further, 1QS 4:9-10 indicates column 4, lines 9-10 of the *Rule of the Community*; and 4Q166 1 ii 2 indicates fragment 1, column ii, line 2 of text 166 from cave 4. More examples of common abbreviations are listed below.

CD	Cairo Geniza copy of the *Damascus Document*	1QIsa^b	Isaiah copy ^{b}	4QLam^a	Lamentations
		1QM	War Scroll	11QPs^a	Psalms
1QH	Thanksgiving Hymns	1QpHab	Pesher Habakkuk	11QTemple^{a,b}	Temple Scroll
1QIsa^a	Isaiah copy ^{a}	1QS	Rule of the Community	11QtgJob	Targum of Job

IMPORTANT NEW TESTAMENT MANUSCRIPTS

(all dates given are AD; ordinal numbers refer to centuries)

Significant Papyri (𝔓 = Papyrus)

𝔓1 Matt 1; early 3rd
𝔓4+𝔓64+𝔓67 Matt 3, 5, 26; Luke 1–6; late 2nd
𝔓5 John 1, 16, 20; early 3rd
𝔓13 Heb 2–5, 10–12; early 3rd
𝔓15+𝔓16 (probably part of same codex) 1 Cor 7–8, Phil 3–4; late 3rd

𝔓20 James 2–3; 3rd
𝔓22 John 15–16; mid 3rd
𝔓23 James 1; c. 200
𝔓27 Rom 8–9; 3rd
𝔓30 1 Thess 4–5; 2 Thess 1; early 3rd
𝔓32 Titus 1–2; late 2nd
𝔓37 Matt 26; late 3rd

𝔓39 John 8; first half of 3rd
𝔓40 Rom 1–4, 6, 9; 3rd
𝔓45 Gospels and Acts; early 3rd
𝔓46 Paul's Major Epistles (less Pastorals); late 2nd
𝔓47 Rev 9–17; 3rd

ABBREVIATIONS

𝔓49+𝔓65 Eph 4-5; 1 Thess 1-2; 3rd
𝔓52 John 18; c. 125
𝔓53 Matt 26, Acts 9-10; middle 3rd
𝔓66 John; late 2nd
𝔓70 Matt 2-3, 11-12, 24; 3rd
𝔓72 1-2 Peter, Jude; c. 300

𝔓74 Acts, General Epistles; 7th
𝔓75 Luke and John; c. 200
𝔓77+𝔓103 (probably part of same codex) Matt 13-14, 23; late 2nd
𝔓87 Phlm; late 2nd
𝔓90 John 18-19; late 2nd
𝔓91 Acts 2-3; 3rd

𝔓92 Eph 1, 2 Thess 1; c. 300
𝔓98 Rev 1:13-20; late 2nd
𝔓100 James 3-5; c. 300
𝔓101 Matt 3-4; 3rd
𝔓104 Matt 21; 2nd
𝔓106 John 1; 3rd
𝔓115 Rev 2-3, 5-6, 8-15; 3rd

Significant Uncials

ℵ (Sinaiticus) most of NT; 4th
A (Alexandrinus) most of NT; 5th
B (Vaticanus) most of NT; 4th
C (Ephraemi Rescriptus) most of NT with many lacunae; 5th
D (Bezae) Gospels, Acts; 5th
D (Claromontanus), Paul's Epistles; 6th (different MS than Bezae)
E (Laudianus 35) Acts; 6th
F (Augensis) Paul's Epistles; 9th
G (Boernerianus) Paul's Epistles; 9th

H (Coislinianus) Paul's Epistles; 6th
I (Freerianus or Washington) Paul's Epistles; 5th
L (Regius) Gospels; 8th
Q (Guelferbytanus B) Luke, John; 5th
P (Porphyrianus) Acts—Revelation; 9th
T (Borgianus) Luke, John; 5th
W (Washingtonianus or the Freer Gospels) Gospels; 5th
Z (Dublinensis) Matthew; 6th
037 (Δ; Sangallensis) Gospels; 9th

038 (Θ; Koridethi) Gospels; 9th
040 (Ξ; Zacynthius) Luke; 6th
043 (Φ; Beratinus) Matt, Mark; 6th
044 (Ψ; Athous Laurae) Gospels, Acts, Paul's Epistles; 9th
048 Acts, Paul's Epistles, General Epistles; 5th
0171 Matt 10, Luke 22; c. 300
0189 Acts 5; c. 200

Significant Minuscules

1 Gospels, Acts, Paul's Epistles; 12th
33 All NT except Rev; 9th
81 Acts, Paul's Epistles, General Epistles; 1044
565 Gospels; 9th
700 Gospels; 11th

1424 (or Family 1424—a group of 29 manuscripts sharing nearly the same text) most of NT; 9th-10th
1739 Acts, Paul's Epistles; 10th
2053 Rev; 13th
2344 Rev; 11th

f^1 (a family of manuscripts including 1, 118, 131, 209) Gospels; 12th-14th
f^{13} (a family of manuscripts including 13, 69, 124, 174, 230, 346, 543, 788, 826, 828, 983, 1689, 1709—known as the Ferrar group) Gospels; 11th-15th

Significant Ancient Versions

SYRIAC (SYR)
syr^c (Syriac Curetonian) Gospels; 5th
syr^s (Syriac Sinaiticus) Gospels; 4th
syr^h (Syriac Harklensis) Entire NT; 616

OLD LATIN (IT)
it^a (Vercellensis) Gospels; 4th
it^b (Veronensis) Gospels; 5th
it^d (Cantabrigiensis—the Latin text of Bezae) Gospels, Acts, 3 John; 5th
it^e (Palantinus) Gospels; 5th
it^k (Bobiensis) Matthew, Mark; c. 400

COPTIC (COP)
cop^{bo} (Boharic—north Egypt)
cop^{fay} (Fayyumic—central Egypt)
cop^{sa} (Sahidic—southern Egypt)

OTHER VERSIONS
arm (Armenian)
eth (Ethiopic)
geo (Georgian)

TRANSLITERATION AND NUMBERING SYSTEM

Note: For words and roots from non-biblical languages (e.g., Arabic, Ugaritic), only approximate transliterations are given.

HEBREW/ARAMAIC

Consonants

א	aleph	= '	מ, ם	mem	= m
ב, ב	beth	= b	נ, ן	nun	= n
ג, ג	gimel	= g	ס	samekh	= s
ד, ד	daleth	= d	ע	ayin	= '
ה	he	= h	פ, פ, ף	pe	= p
ו	waw	= w	צ, ץ	tsadhe	= ts
ז	zayin	= z	ק	qoph	= q
ח	heth	= kh	ר	resh	= r
ט	teth	= t	שׁ	shin	= sh
י	yodh	= y	שׂ	sin	= s
כ, כ, ך	kaph	= k	ת, ת	taw	= t, th
ל	lamedh	= l			(spirant)

Vowels

	patakh	= a		qamets khatuf	= o
ח	furtive patakh	= a		holem	= o
	qamets	= a	ו	full holem	= o
ה	final qamets he	= ah		short qibbuts	= u
	segol	= e		long qibbuts	= u
	tsere	= e	ו	shureq	= u
	tsere yod	= e		khatef patakh	= a
	short hireq	= i		khatef qamets	= o
	long hireq	= i		vocalic shewa	= e
	hireq yod	= i		patakh yodh	= a

Greek

α	alpha	= a	ε	epsilon	= e
β	beta	= b	ζ	zeta	= z
γ	gamma	= g, n (before γ, κ, ξ, χ)	η	eta	= ē
			θ	theta	= th
δ	delta	= d	ι	iota	= i

κ	kappa	= k	τ	tau	= t
λ	lamda	= l	υ	upsilon	= u
μ	mu	= m	φ	phi	= ph
ν	nu	= n	χ	chi	= ch
ξ	ksi	= x	ψ	psi	= ps
ο	omicron	= o	ω	omega	= ō
π	pi	= p	ʽ	rough breathing mark	= h (with vowel or diphthong)
ρ	rho	= r (ῥ = rh)			
σ, ς	sigma	= s			

THE TYNDALE-STRONG'S NUMBERING SYSTEM

The Cornerstone Biblical Commentary series uses a word-study numbering system to give both newer and more advanced Bible students alike quicker, more convenient access to helpful original-language tools (e.g., concordances, lexicons, and theological dictionaries). Those who are unfamiliar with the ancient Hebrew, Aramaic, and Greek alphabets can quickly find information on a given word by looking up the appropriate index number. Advanced students will find the system helpful because it allows them to quickly find the lexical form of obscure conjugations and inflections.

There are two main numbering systems used for biblical words today. The one familiar to most people is the Strong's numbering system (made popular by the *Strong's Exhaustive Concordance to the Bible*). Although the original Strong's system is still quite useful, the most up-to-date research has shed new light on the biblical languages and allows for more precision than is found in the original Strong's system. The Cornerstone Biblical Commentary series, therefore, features a newly revised version of the Strong's system, the Tyndale-Strong's numbering system. The Tyndale-Strong's system brings together the familiarity of the Strong's system and the best of modern scholarship. In most cases, the original Strong's numbers are preserved. In places where new research dictates, new or related numbers have been added.[1]

The second major numbering system today is the Goodrick-Kohlenberger system used in a number of study tools published by Zondervan. In order to give students broad access to a number of helpful tools, the Commentary provides index numbers for the Zondervan system as well.

The different index systems are designated as follows:

TG Tyndale-Strong's Greek number   ZH Zondervan Hebrew number
ZG Zondervan Greek number   TA Tyndale-Strong's Aramaic number
TH Tyndale-Strong's Hebrew number   ZA Zondervan Aramaic number

So in the example, "love" *agapē* [TG26, ZG27], the first number is the one to use with Greek tools keyed to the Tyndale-Strong's system, and the second applies to tools that use the Zondervan system.

---

1. Generally, one may simply use the original four-digit Strong's number to identify words in tools using Strong's system. If a Tyndale-Strong's number is followed by a capital letter (e.g., TG1692A), it generally indicates an added subdivision of meaning for the given term. Whenever a Tyndale-Strong's number has a number following a decimal point (e.g., TG2013.1), it reflects an instance where new research has yielded a separate, new classification of use for a biblical word. Forthcoming tools from Tyndale House Publishers will include these entries, which were not part of the original Strong's system.

Genesis

ALLEN ROSS

INTRODUCTION TO
Genesis

THE TITLE "GENESIS" comes from the Greek translation of the Old Testament (called the Septuagint), which uses the Greek word *geneseōs* [TG1078, ZG1161] to render the key Hebrew word in the book, *toledoth* [TH8435, ZH9352] ("generations" in KJV; "account" in NLT). The Hebrew title of the book is the first word of the book, *bere'shith* [TH871.2/ 7225, ZH928/8040] (in the beginning).

Genesis is the book of beginnings, the beginning of mankind and his universe, the beginning of sin in the world and its catastrophic effects on the race, and the beginning of God's plan to restore blessing to the world through his chosen people. God's plan begins with the call of Abraham and the granting of a covenant to him. From this beginning of God's covenant program, the book of Genesis traces the promise of the blessings from generation to generation, up to the eve of the great redemption from Egypt.

Because Genesis lays the foundation for all of God's subsequent revelation and not just the law, it is no surprise that most of the other books of the Bible draw on the content of Genesis in one way or another. But beyond that, the subject matter of Genesis and the unembellished way in which it is written have captivated the minds of scholars and readers of the Bible for ages. As with all biblical truth in general, this book has been a stumbling block for those who approach it with biases that do not allow for the supernatural or for special revelation. But to those who accept that Genesis is part of the divinely inspired Word of God, the book is a source of comfort and edification.

As might be expected, different readers approach the questions and difficulties in Genesis differently. An overly skeptical approach to the material will exploit the difficulties and seek to explain them according to modern presuppositions that destroy the unity and integrity of the text; whereas an approach that accepts the integrity of the text, at the very least as good literature, will look for resolutions to the difficulties in a way that harmonizes the Scriptures. Along the way, there will be many questions that Genesis will simply leave unanswered. The believer must accept that and rather than spending the majority of his or her time trying to search those matters out, should spend the time trying to understand what God wants people to know. After all, the revelation did not come by the will of man—if it had, it would have been written very differently; it came by the will of God.

AUTHOR AND SOURCES

Given the fact that Genesis stands before us as a unified, fully developed theological treatise based on selected events and records (see discussion below), it is natural to ask, "Who wrote it?" The Bible does not say, other than to include it in the general description of "the law of Moses," which would cover the five books of the Pentateuch, or Torah. Both Scripture and tradition attribute the Pentateuch to Moses. This was sufficient to convince the vast majority of biblical scholars and readers down through the ages that Genesis, the first book of the Pentateuch, could safely be ascribed to Moses, allowing for minor additions and clarifications by later writers.

For those who accept that there was a Moses who received the law at Sinai, there is no one better qualified to have written this book. Moses was educated in all the wisdom of the Egyptians (Acts 7:22) so his literary skills would have enabled him to collect and edit Israel's traditions and records and to compose this theological treatise. His communion with God at Sinai and throughout his life would have given him the spiritual illumination and understanding that was needed to guide him into all truth—what we call inspiration. And the historical circumstances of the Israelites' bondage in Egypt, along with the task of delivering them and establishing a new nation in accordance with the promises made to the ancestors, provided a strong motivation to write this book: to establish the theological and historical foundation for the Exodus and the covenant at Sinai (Moberly 1992; Sailhamer 1992).

Most critical scholarship, however, does not accept the Mosaic authorship of the Pentateuch, and some do not accept the historicity of Moses or the Exodus. Doubts about Mosaic authorship are not necessarily recent. Early in the Christian era, theologians wondered if the work was written by Moses or Ezra. But the modern view that the Pentateuch was compiled from sources written by different groups of people over time seems to have developed as the product of rationalistic skepticism. Soon after the Reformation, writers like Baruch Spinoza (1632-1677) were attributing the work to Ezra, who he said utilized a mass of traditions (including some by Moses). But the first attempt to arrange a documentary theory came about a century later: Jean Astruc (1684-1766) in 1753 proposed that Moses compiled Genesis using two major and several minor documents. Over the next 124 years scholars debated and developed the idea and its component features until Julius Wellhausen (1844-1918), a historian, restated the theory boldly and with exacting detail in 1877.

Wellhausen's theory, along with its development and application, has been well documented and analyzed in commentaries on Genesis and introductions to the Old Testament. There is neither the need nor the space to review it at length. S. R. Driver's *Introduction to the Literature of the Old Testament* provides a formal presentation of the theory. The commentary by J. Skinner is a prime example of how it is worked out chapter by chapter. R. K. Harrison's *Introduction to the Old Testament* is a particularly thorough interaction with the theory from the conservative point of view. Umberto Cassuto's *Documentary Hypothesis and the Composition of the Pentateuch* also gives it a critical review. And Herman Wouk's *This Is My God* has a classic essay from a literary point of view.

Essentially the Documentary Hypothesis states that the Pentateuch was assembled from four literary sources, represented by four letters, J, E, D, and P. Passages classified as J material were supposedly from a source written or compiled in the southern kingdom of Judah about 850 BC (so named because of the constant use of the holy name "Yahweh," or "Jehovah"). This source was personal, biographical, and anthropomorphic. It included prophet-like ethics and theological reflection. The E material was supposed to have been written or compiled in the northern kingdom of Israel about 750 BC (so named because of its preference for calling God "Elohim" rather than "Yahweh"). In these passages the material is more objective, less concerned with ethical and theological reflection, and given more to concrete particulars. After these two documents were combined by an editor around 650 BC (forming what is called JE), the source called D (essentially the book of Deuteronomy) was added around 621 BC—during the reforms of Josiah (2 Kgs 22-23). The authors of this material, known as the Deuteronomic school, were responsible also for reworking the material that became the books of Joshua, Judges, 1-2 Samuel, and 1-2 Kings. Finally, the P source was added by later priests (hence, P); it came from the time of Ezra, or at least the Babylonian exile, and included a section of material focusing on holiness, called H. This material is dated anywhere between 570 and 445 BC. It is concerned with the origins and institutions of the theocracy, genealogies, and sacrifices.

What brought about this detailed approach and reconstructive theory was the realization that there are texts in the Pentateuch that differ greatly. The scholars observed changes in the divine name from passage to passage, parallel stories that seemed very similar (such as the three "sister" stories in chs 12, 20, and 26), different names and descriptions of the same things (like both Horeb and Sinai being used), and a number of diverse theological emphases that seemed to harmonize with these other observations. With the development of Wellhausen's theory, the task of the critical scholars was to analyze the text with these observations in mind and assign the passages, verses, or even the words as being specific to one of the sources. Two immediate difficulties with the theory surfaced: first, there was no complete agreement on which passages belonged to which sources, and second, additional sources were invented to cover passages that could not be placed into one of the major sources. Wellhausen worked it out in such detail that very few biblical scholars today would take the time to study each bit of evidence that he covered, let alone read the work.

This theory of the sources of the Pentateuch, meticulously developed and seemingly plausible, has captured the imagination of the scholarly world ever since. The modern critic might not speak of the sources as literary documents, but the same basic theory remains behind most source criticism today.[1]

The evaluation of this theory and of subsequent theories of source criticism by traditional scholars has been thorough and critical but often ignored. The major criticisms of the theory include its supposition that the book of Genesis cannot be treated any differently than any other literature from the ancient Near East, that it is merely a human book and therefore unreliable. The formulation of the approach came to be influenced strongly by anthropomorphic and evolutionary ideas, leaving little room for the supernatural and certainly no room for divine inspiration. For example, it is suggested that the monotheism found in the texts was of human origin and gradually evolved over the centuries until it was settled upon during the Babylonian exile under a number of external influences. Proponents of the theory were satisfied to say that the development of such ideas was due to the creative genius of the writers who carefully borrowed from incompatible predecessors material that they could harmonize with their faith. The difficulty here is that in the biblical history, every time the Israelites borrowed from their neighbors it was away from monotheism toward polytheism and idolatry. The critics were convinced, however, that the teachings evolved until they reached their final form. But the Pentateuch, they explain, preserves all the materials from along the way and weaves them together into a composite text.

Conservatives have used archaeological discoveries to show that many of the criteria used in the theory should be called into question. Indeed, the early proponents of the theory did not make any use of archaeology, although it was available, and yet it was called a literary and analytical approach to Scripture. From the documents of the ancient world there is evidence of such things as the use of multiple names, the early use of cultic terms that were thought to be late (as in the notion of P), the use of rare words that earlier had been called late Aramaisms (i.e., stemming from the Persian period), and the constant use of repetition in the literary style. These have been recorded and explained in the main Introductions to the Old Testament, and need not be referenced here. Not only do these discoveries argue against the criteria used in the theory, they actually give background and local color to the texts. When the traditions of the patriarchs, for example, are set against the background of the Hurrian customs found in texts from Nuzi and Mari (second millennium BC), there is a remarkable connection. The stories about the patriarchs fit that culture and would be out of place in the first millennium BC.

Of course, the findings of archaeology do not prove the existence of the patriarchs, or the early date of the narratives (for cautions, see Thompson 1974 and Coote and Ord 1989). But they do fit rather well with the material and the manner in which the narratives are presented in Genesis. With the ever-increasing finds, there is less and less reason to date the material or the compiling of it to the later periods, certainly not as late as the Babylonian exile.

Out of these considerations a number of scholars turned their attention to the form of the narratives. The pioneer of form criticism, Hermann Gunkel, recognized the antiquity of the traditions (e.g., that Gen 1–11 had to be compared to the Akkadian and Sumerian accounts and would be strangely out of place against an Assyrian background in the first millennium). Form criticism sought to determine the genre, the structure, the setting, and the intention of the literary unit that was behind the extant text. The purpose was to reconstruct the original material and trace the development of it as it related to the history of the faith. The method isolates the literary units, often following the division of the old sources (J, E, D, and P), identifies the literary forms by comparing common vocabulary, motifs, and structures, and then tries to identify the original setting for the material in the life of Israel. There is much in this approach that is helpful; but the identification of an original setting for the story behind the present form of the text is both unnecessary and generally impossible. It is unnecessary because the final form of the text is the holy Scripture that we study and live by; it is impossible because we do not have the evidence to confirm the preliterary stages, especially when they are determined by removing parts of the text thought to have been added later (such as supernatural motifs). But on the whole, form criticism takes a more cautious view of the text and recognizes the antiquity of the material in the ancient world. Moreover, its emphasis on literary types and ancient oral tradition points out Israel's ancient literary heritage.

However, form criticism scholarship is often plagued with the same weaknesses of the Documentary Hypothesis. The supposition that the literature developed naturally rather than supernaturally leads to very different interpretations: Monotheism developed out of polytheism, old pagan stories were borrowed and demythologized to be applied to the patriarchs, miracles were later explanations of early events, and the records do not give us real history. Not all who follow this method would agree with these ideas, but by and large they apply to the procedure.

The idea that there were oral traditions, called "sagas" by some, that existed before the written text and were collected and compiled later may be correct in some cases, but it is difficult to prove. It is possible that family stories and genealogies could have been handed down orally and then written down. But that idea does not tell us anything about the date of the literary composition, and it unnecessarily complicates the idea by suggesting that in the process of telling and writing, the material was edited and embellished a good deal. Too often, critical interpretation considers this embellishing to be an extensive reshaping and reinterpreting of the tradition. Consequently, many scholars spend their time trying to reconstruct the original tradition, an endeavor which is usually subjective and often impossible. Granted, there was editing of the material and a certain amount of interpretation to apply it to the Israelite experience, but it is not on the scale that modern critical scholarship proposes.

The emphasis on literary forms and structure, and the setting in life and in text is very helpful for biblical exegesis (see, e.g., McCarter 1988). Exegesis, however, is concerned with the interpretation of the final form of the text, not with supposed pre-literary stages of the tradition. If there is evidence that allows the exegete to see how the material was composed, then that can be very helpful (for example, ancient treaties, law codes, laments, and the like; see also Walton 1989; Carr 2005). But where the biblical text differs from similar genres of the ancient texts, it should be explained on the basis of the exegesis of the text, that is, understanding the purpose of the writer under the inspiration of God.

Out of a greater interest in the literary features of the text and comparative literature there emerged traditio-historical criticism. Some scholars who have followed this approach have criticized the old literary analytical approach (JEDP) from various perspectives. They believe that a complete analytical approach is needed—one that takes into account oral tradition, comparative mythology, and Hebrew psychology—for the purpose of discovering the formation and transmission of Israelite tradition in its preliterary stage.

Though the subjectivity involved in such an approach has led to great diversity among the proponents of the method, the essential elements in the theory are as follows: The story of Genesis was transmitted from memory; it was accompanied by an interpretation; it was reformulated in accordance with various forces (perhaps a redemptive motif in the historical period); and it finally found its fixed form in the text. Then similar stories were collected and redacted into literary units by a creative editor. These cycles of tradition then became normative for faith in the postexilic period. The two long-developing, contemporaneous tradition collections were the P and D collections. The former is largely Genesis through Numbers, and the latter is Deuteronomy through Kings. So even though the old documentary theory was rejected, a similar theory of sources was put in its place.

This approach puts too much emphasis on the oral tradition behind the texts and the development of the material from that tradition. No doubt there was oral tradition, but as Kitchen (1966:136) notes, for anything truly important in ancient cultures, written documents were used from the earliest ages. The emphasis on comparative mythology can be helpful, but if it is studied with the presupposition that Israel's faith was quite comparable to that of the pagans and was not a unique, revealed faith, then the conclusions will undermine the whole message of the Bible. Following such an approach leaves one without an explanation of the origin of the Hebrews' unique faith and without a meaningful understanding of its truth.

Finally, concentration on the supposed reforming of the traditions lacks any scientific controls, a fact evidenced by the lack of agreement among the critics. The reconstructions are often the product of the critic's presuppositions. And one is right to ask why those should be believed rather than what the Bible actually says. Even if one could find the sources and reconstruct their history with certainty, one would still be left with the question as to why the material was recorded in its current form.[2]

DATE OF WRITING

Today the study of the Pentateuch is even more complicated because most modern critics recognize the excesses and extremes in earlier approaches. But still, for them there is no going back to what is called a "precritical" view of the Mosaic authorship of the Pentateuch. They still will work with sources and dates in an effort to work through the difficulties in the text, some even allowing that some of the traditions go back to Sinai. But the Pentateuch is still seen as a complex compilation of different sources, most of which were added much, much later than the time of Moses.

More emphasis is put on the final fixed form of the text today than ever before among critical scholars. Repetition, diversity of style, variation in vocabulary, and the like are often considered part of the unity of the text (as opposed to their being considered evidence of different sources), which employs a large array of rhetorical devices. Structure and texture have finally been given a more appropriate place in the literary, analytical study of the material (see for example Fokkelman 1991).

All of the debates about the authorship of the Pentateuch have made conservative scholars more aware of the difficulties in the text. But with a totally different working presupposition, they have set about to resolve the questions in a way that harmonizes the material. In most cases an understanding of the structure and the purpose of the material has been useful in resolving tensions. Traditional scholars always acknowledged that sources were used in the writing of Genesis and other historical texts in the Bible (such as Kings or Luke); what they have not accepted is that the sources are incompatible with one another and with the rest of the Bible in many ways and that they were completed late. There would be no difficulty in saying that Moses used collections of family records, some oral traditions, ancient accounts of primeval events, and genealogies to write Genesis. Those sources could have been left pretty much the way they were received, thus exhibiting changes in style and wording, and stitched together with additional material added by Moses for his particular purposes. The historical material that largely makes up what the critic calls the J and E sources could have been the material used here (although even some conservatives would reject this because they have accepted the view that the name *Yahweh* was not known until the days of Moses; see Ross 2003). Sections that deal with the institutions of Israel, sacrifices, ritual worship, and the like, so necessary for the giving of the law at Sinai, could very well have been emphasized by Moses, the Levite, in tracing the foundation of the faith.

But there is still no compelling reason why Genesis should be dated so late as the exilic or postexilic periods. There is no reason why the book could not have reached its final form by the time of Samuel or David. There are passages and expressions that are obviously later editorial glosses (e.g., the names "Dan" in 14:14 and "Chaldeans" in 15:7); and there are sections (such as the list of Edomite kings; cf. 36:31) that could have been added to the work during the early days of the monarchy. Yet, there is no reason to say that the Book of Genesis was not essentially the work of Moses. It may have been edited by subsequent writers whose work was guided by the Holy Spirit; nonetheless, the suggestion of widespread reshaping and embellishing of the material is unfounded and unnecessary.

The conclusion that most modern conservative scholars arrive at is that given the fact that Moses may have used sources, and even allowing for some editing and clarification as well as a few additions to the Pentateuch after Moses, the biblical material, in the form we have it, records actual events and gives them correct theological interpretations. What is at stake is the nature of truth. Either the Bible tells the truth or it does not. The rest of Scripture attests to its trustworthiness; but too much skeptical criticism robs it of that quality and makes it merely a collection of ideas that pious people had over the ages. This in turn leads modern readers of the Bible to interpret the text however they wish or to write their own truth. Everyone who studies the book of Genesis must ask the fundamental question, "Is this the written Word of God or not?" The historical faith has consistently affirmed so. And because it is divine revelation, biblical scholars are constantly working on translations that will convey the precise meaning of the words in a way that each generation can understand and believe.

Even among those who accept the historicity of Moses and grant that at least the essence of the law came from him, there is disagreement over the date of the writing. The traditional view, which takes the dates and details of Scripture at face value, would place Moses in the fifteenth century BC, the Exodus at 1446 BC, and the giving of the law shortly after that (see the details in Merrill 1987:57-79). Those who accept a late date for Moses and the Exodus would place the giving of the law, and with it the writing of Genesis, somewhere in the thirteenth century BC. This date is preferred by many because it seems to harmonize better with the archaeological data of the conquest and settlement. Moreover, the reference to Rameses in Exodus 1:11 has been used (at least in the popular presentations) as a clue to the identity of the pharaoh of the Exodus. Those who hold to the earlier date in the fifteenth century reason that biblical passages such as 1 Kings 6:1 and Judges 11:26, if taken for what they say, point to an early date. Moreover, if Exodus 1:11 does refer to Rameses II, he could not be the pharaoh of the Exodus because there would not be enough time in his reign to cover whatever construction he had done, the time leading up to the infanticide, and Moses's 80 years before the Exodus. And, according to Exodus 2:23, the king from whom Moses fled died before Moses returned. So the city the Israelites built could not possibly have been named for Rameses II previous to the Exodus (Merrill 1987:71). If it is argued that the city was built for an earlier Rameses, say a son of Seti I, or that the city was renamed by Rameses II, the conclusion is still that Exodus 1:11 cannot be used to support a late date for the Exodus in the reign of Rameses II. It is also unlikely that the Exodus occurred during the reign of Rameses II's successor, Merneptah, who fought against Israel in the land of Canaan. This evidence points to an earlier date for Moses. Thus Genesis, for the most part, if written by Moses, would have been written in the late-fifteenth century, in part to encourage the Israelites to leave the land of Egypt (for further details about the chronology, see Merrill 1987:66-79). Parts of the work could have been added over the next few centuries, but there is no reason to suggest that all of it should be regarded as having been written centuries later.

OCCASION OF WRITING

Genesis provides the historical and theological basis for God's covenant with his people. The development of this covenant can then be traced through the entire Pentateuch; but it begins here with the promises made to the patriarchs and against the background of a world that is far from the blessing of God. If the central theme of the whole Pentateuch is the selection of Israel from among the nations and its consecration to the service of God and his laws in a Promised Land (Segal 1967:23), then the central theme of Genesis is the provision of a divine covenant with Abraham and his descendants with its promises to make them the people of God, heirs of the land of Canaan, and a blessing to the world.

Within the development of the message of the Pentateuch, Genesis forms the prologue to the drama that begins to unfold in Exodus. As a theological explanation for the command to Israel to go forth from Egypt to the Promised Land, Genesis affirms that such a command was in fulfillment of the covenant promises made to Abraham, Isaac, and Jacob. And the promises of the covenant—Abraham's descendants would be as numerous as the stars of the heavens (15:5), possess a rich land (Deut 8:7-9), and have dominion as a kingdom of priests (Exod 19:5-6)—all go back to the creation when God gave those privileges to the human beings he had made. Unfortunately, sin ruined God's creation and placed all life under the curse. After Genesis traces the extent of the curse throughout the world, it focuses on God's choice of Abraham and the promises made to him. Thus, the first book of the Bible would foreshadow the same themes that the descendants of Abraham, the people of Israel, would know after the Exodus, as they were being separated from all the others that lay under the curse—all in order that they, as recipients of the promises, might be the means by which the Creator's original plan might be carried forth (to bless the world and all that is in it; 12:2-3; cf. Gen 1:28, 31). Genesis then traces the developments from the beginning, from the account of creation where the divine plan is made known; it then accounts for what went wrong with the plan, how the curse of pain, conflict, and death came to dominate the human condition. Out of that hopeless condition it tells how God set about with a new creation, a people who would be his image in the world. Genesis 1–11 is designed to explain why God prepared and set apart a distinct people for a special purpose in a chosen land.

But from the very beginning, the path to the restoration of blessing in the earth was not easy. In the opening section of the book, chapters 1–11, two opposite progressions appear in the narratives: (1) God's amazing work of establishing his program and blessing it, and (2) the totally disruptive effects of sin that brought about major judgments from God, first with the Flood and then with the dispersion at Babel (Kidner 1967:13). And these two progressions set the tone for the whole book, indeed the whole Bible—God's constant work to bring about perfect order amid the corruption of the human race in rebellion against God. But it is the rebellion of mankind that necessitates God's constant work of redemption.

The moral deterioration recorded in the early chapters of the book is connected with the development of civilization. But that developing civilization chose evil continually and not the way of God, so that when it was corrupted beyond repair, it had to be destroyed in a severe judgment. But the judgment via the Flood was also a new beginning, a re-creation, because for a second time the world that had been covered with water began to emerge, appearing as a new creation, with a new Adam who was given the same basic instructions as the first (cf. 1:28; 9:1). Yet even after this new beginning, the heart of mankind remained evil, and people rebelled against God. The arrogance and ambition of the race in rebellion to God led to the confusion of languages and the dispersion of humanity across the face of the earth.

With these accounts of ancient events, the book of Genesis presents a theological picture of mankind's rebellion against the Creator and its terrible consequences. And this theological treatise prepares the reader for a solution, namely a covenant that God would make with one man to bring blessing to the whole world. Thus, in the Abrahamic covenant we have the work of creation renewed again, starting fresh, but this time in a world that was totally polytheistic and corrupt. By this the Israelites, for whom this message was first written, would see that there was hope for them as well.

With these first 11 chapters the reader is prepared for the family history, the record of the development of the divine plan through the patriarchal families (chs 12–50). Out of all the nations that were scattered throughout the world in darkness and chaos, the focus now would be on one man and his family. God's saving hand was extended to the scattered nations through this one who was loosed from his tribal ties and pagan ancestry and made the founder of a new nation, the people of God, the recipients of the promises. Only with the call of Abraham and its promises in Genesis 12:1-3 can the reader begin to understand why chapters 1–11 were written.

As the story of this family develops, we find the same tensions appearing, but in a vastly different way. As Abraham and his family find their way in their new-found faith, fears and failures within the family and opposition and threats from outside constantly surface to hinder the plan to bless the world. And yet the program of the covenant goes forward toward its intended end. But there is a gradual deterioration in the lives of the covenant people from age to age; Isaac is not the man that Abraham was, and Jacob is certainly not the man that his forebears were. And Jacob's sons are envious, hateful, and deceptive, ridding themselves of Jacob's special son. This was not a covenant people who could bless anyone. So with the story of Joseph the family moves to Egypt where it would not be subject to the corrupting influence of the Canaanites. In Egypt the family would have to endure bondage and growing hardship while it flourished and became the great nation that was promised to Abraham. Then God would deliver Israel from bondage in a display of his powerful redemption. The blessing would be given to the Israelites, but not until they were ready; and the curse on Canaan would be exacted to make room for Israel, but not until Canaan's sin had reached its full measure.

In sum, the family record tells the story of God's development of the covenant and the covenant people, a development that would overcome all the complications threatening it due to the weak faith and sinful acts of the descendants of Abraham. This account would also be a great encouragement to the Israelites in Egypt—namely, that in spite of their faithlessness and failures, if they followed God alone, his grace would see them through to the fulfillment of the promises. Genesis ends its narrative about the family with a coffin in Egypt, but also with a promise of divine visitation. Genesis would teach the Israelites that their future was not in Egypt but in Canaan. But to receive the promises they would have to respond by faith as their ancestors had done. This message set the tone for the message of the whole Bible, for God had a gracious plan to bless people and bless the world through them when they exercise faith in his word and follow him. Apart from that, the curse would continue to take its toll.

AUDIENCE

Because the book of Genesis is the foundation of the Pentateuch, the book of Exodus recalls frequently how God made the covenant promises to Abraham, Isaac, and Jacob. For example, the deliverance from bondage is explained this way: "God heard their groaning, and he remembered his covenant promise to Abraham, Isaac, and Jacob. He looked down on the people of Israel and knew it was time to act" (Exod 2:24-25). This is what Joseph anticipated when he promised, "God will surely come to help you and lead you out of this land of Egypt. He will bring you back to the land he solemnly promised to give to Abraham, to Isaac, and to Jacob" (50:24). This statement was reiterated by Moses when he took the bones of Joseph out of Egypt (Exod 13:19).

Genesis gives Israel the theological and historical basis for her existence as God's chosen people. Israel could trace her ancestry to the patriarch Abraham and her destiny to the promises made to the patriarchs. Out of all the nations of the earth, God had chosen one man, and from that one man had created a family, and that family he so blessed that it multiplied and became the promised great nation. With that heritage behind them, and with the realization of the promised blessing of the seed, the nation of Israel could turn its attention to the fulfillment of the promise of the land. It was time for the exodus from Egypt.

Because of the importance of the promise of a seed (i.e., a great nation) much of the material in Genesis is devoted to the family concerns of the patriarchs, their wives, their sons, their heirs, birthrights, and blessings. After Jacob gave his final oracle on the destiny of the tribes, the record fell silent for 400 years. But the message of this book would remain as a statement of the birthright of the tribes of Israel as they labored in Egypt and then were called to leave it. Knowing that they had become the great nation promised to Abraham, they knew that their future was not in Egypt, certainly not in slavery to another nation. The future was in Canaan, where they would live as a free nation, the people of the living God.

In many ways the contents of the book of Genesis would have been evangelistic. Moses would have reminded the Israelites of these traditions in order to assure them that God had promised them a glorious future and that he was able to provide it for them. They would be assured of these truths by hearing again how God had worked in the lives of their ancestors in Egypt and in Canaan to deliver them, provide for them, and bless them. And since the nation of Israel was evidence of that blessing, they would respond to Moses's message with faith and obedience, just as Abraham had believed the word of the Lord and had left Ur to become a great nation in the Promised Land. The message would have made it clear that the God who had begun a good work in their family would complete it (cf. Phil 1:6). After all, God did not call Abraham, make the promises, and provide the family so that they could all be slaves to the Egyptians. If the people would recognize that they owed their existence to divine election (the calling of Abraham), sovereign creation (providing children from barren wombs), and supernatural enablement through the blessings that had been given, they would respond in obedient faith.

Afterward, the traditions and records used by Moses would have been put together as a cohesive treatise to introduce the rest of the Pentateuch.

CANONICITY AND TEXTUAL HISTORY

As one of the five books that make up the law (or Torah), the canonicity of Genesis was never in question. Not only was the book seen as an integral part of the law but also Moses was acknowledged to be a prophet who received the law from God at Mount Sinai. The traditional view of Scripture, held by both Jewish and Christian scholars, is that these five books are a unit and as such form the foundation of all subsequent Scripture. Even among modern critical scholars who conclude that much of the material came from later writers, Genesis retains its place in the Canon, though it is not attributed to Moses. But Genesis is still recognized as the traditional foundation for the law and therefore a necessary part of the law. (See further Rendtorff 1993 and Moberly 1992).

Because Genesis is part of the law of Moses, the text was handled with great care by the scribes down through the ages. The received Hebrew text, the Masoretic Text, is clearly the superior text type for the book. Variant readings for the text occur with greater frequency in the poetic sections of Genesis, notably Genesis 49, where the Hebrew is obscure and difficult. Where significant variant readings occur in the manuscripts and versions, the commentary will evaluate the textual criticism (see also Campbell and O'Brien 1993).

LITERARY GENRE AND STRUCTURE

Over the years there has been a great deal of discussion about the nature of the contents of this book. Introductory books and study guides often list Genesis among the historical books, but many biblical scholars would be very hesitant to call it history or historical, unless they could redefine what that would mean. Classification of the book is made more difficult by the fact that it includes very different types of literature. Genesis 1-11, with its emphasis on universal events is not at all like the patriarchal narratives of chapters 12-36. And the descriptions of the patriarchal narratives do not apply to the story of Joseph (essentially chs 37-50). Over the years, several suggestions have been made as to the nature of the material.

Myth. Many writers have described the contents of Genesis as myth, especially material found in chapters 1-11 but also sporadically through the rest of the book. Mythological literature is designed to explain the origins of things via symbolic forms. Myth records what has often been called "sacred history" rather than actual history. It seeks to report how reality or realities came into existence, and it does so through the deeds of gods and supernatural creatures. It purports to establish reality, the nature of the universe, the function of the state, and the values of life, and to answer various questions about the world such as why people die, why they wear clothes, why snakes crawl on the ground, and the like. Since myths explained reality, they were not considered to be lies (contrary to the popular use of the word "myth" today). They were the beliefs of ancient people that explained life, so they had a reality of their own.

Scholars who pursue this course compare Genesis with pagan literature of the ancient Near East that has accounts of Creation, the Flood, or other divine interventions in the world. Here the degree of the influence of mythology will differ from scholar to scholar. Some see only a slight borrowing of certain elements with regard to creation or demons; others see a wholesale borrowing of myths by Israel, with a subsequent cleaning up of the material (demythologizing) to make it compatible with their particular beliefs. But this does not fit with what we know of mythology. Borrowing phrases and motifs from the pagan world is one thing, but borrowing a mythology completely requires buying into a whole worldview, and these other worldviews would have been totally incompatible with the faith of Israel.

Myths were not simply an array of symbolic expressions or reflections of primitive mentalities. They were the stuff of the ancient views of reality. At the heart of Semitic mythology is a full doctrine of correspondences between supernatural beings, gods and goddesses, and humans—a system that would never work in a strict monotheism. According to the ancient myths, what occurred on earth had a corresponding reality in the heavens (when the god dies, vegetation also dies). Accordingly, a whole system of ritual activities developed to be enacted in the sanctuaries in order to ensure that the forces of fertility, or life and death, would continue year by year. Some of these rituals became profane, as might be expected, giving rise to cult prostitution in the pagan temples along with other base activities.

The Old Testament makes a radical break with the pagan mentality of the ancient world. Pagan mythology worked with a multitude of gods and goddesses; Israel was completely monotheistic. Pagan mythology prompted fertility rituals in the sanctuary to induce the gods to act; Israel's cultus was to remain pure from all such defilement, especially sexual activities within its sacred precincts. Pagan mythology was concerned with the annual cycles of seasons; Israel had a history and an eschatology—it had a beginning and it was going somewhere in time; it was not merely concerned with another season of crops. It would be very difficult to classify the materials in Genesis as myths.

And yet there are numerous passages in the Old Testament that use language or motifs identical to mythological material in the ancient world. The use of these kinds of expressions has to be harmonized with the general faith of the Bible, that the one true and living God, the sovereign God, brought everything into existence by his decrees and also formed the nation of Israel and gave them his commands. This faith was not limited to the primeval world of supernatural beings but was actualized in history. Their worship was not cosmic, magical, or superstitious, but a reenactment of their redemption and a celebration of God's intervention in history. James Barr says that "the main battle of the Hebrew faith is fought against the confusion of human and divine, of God and nature," which was so prevalent in pagan myth (1959:3). If the writers of the Old Testament use any elements of mythological language, it is to show that Yahweh is sovereign over such ideas. The biblical writers used certain terms and motifs partly because some of them were common religious expressions and partly because the writers wanted to display a deliberate contrast with comparable pagan concepts. For example, Lotan (Leviathan) might be feared or venerated in the pagan world as a powerful spirit, but in the Bible it is just a large sea creature, a crocodile. Or the sun might be worshiped as a god in the ancient world, the giver of law; but in the Bible, Yahweh gives the law, and the sun, which is not a god, declares his glory (Ps 19). Or, to the Canaanites, Baal might be the storm god, but it is actually the voice of the Lord that brings the storms over Canaan (cf. Ps 29). In other words, the writers often used these ideas and images in a polemical way—to undermine false beliefs and establish the truth. The faith of Israel reflects very clearly a theological parting of the ways with the ancient world and its way of explaining reality. Thus, the Old Testament in general and the book of Genesis in particular are a cemetery for lifeless myths and dead gods. Genesis is not myth.

Etiology. Many of the narratives of Genesis have also been called etiological, that is, stories that explain some given phenomenon—a topographical, ethnological, customary or cultic reality (etiology is the study of causes). Here we have to be precise in how this description is used, because there is a sense in which this is true. But if the etiological narrative is the point of the tradition and not simply a motif, that is, if the narrative is primarily etiology, then doubt is cast over its historicity. For example, if one says that the story of Cain and Abel was told to explain why shepherds and farmers do not get along, then the account loses its integrity. Moreover, if this theory is scrutinized, then the matter is still not resolved because the event never happened. Not only does such an etiology not explain the reality but it is impossible to prove that an etiology is the creative force of the tradition (Bright 1956:90).

The narratives of Genesis record the traditions of the family and of antiquity, and there is no reason whatsoever to say that the stories were made up to explain later customs and beliefs. If there is an etiological element added to the story by the writer or editor, it usually refers to a single detail or application of the event. For example, the Creation account of Genesis 2 ends with the explanation, "This explains why a man leaves his father and mother" (2:24). The event was used to show why marriage was formed the way it was. To say a story explains something is one thing; to say the story was fabricated to explain it, or that it used some mythical episode to form the tradition, is quite another. Etiological elements certainly do occur in Genesis, because the book is giving the foundation and the rationale for almost everything that later Israel was to do. But these narratives should never be referred to as etiological tales that came into existence to answer or justify certain things in the society.

History. Debates about the nature of the accounts center on the question of the historicity of the records. Most modern scholars have been unwilling to use the word "history" to define the nature of Genesis, unless it is carefully defined as distinct from modern philosophies of history. Norman Porteous explains, "The fact that Israel's religious traditions made frequent reference to supernatural interventions is usually enough to make the historian look askance at them and assume that the actual course of events must have been very different" (1972:22). Many scholars also view the record of the events in Genesis as not historically reliable because they cannot be validated from outside sources. Without such verification, the historians must depend on biblical records themselves, and when they are filled with the supernatural it becomes more of a challenge. For them, even the many findings of archaeology, which always confirm the reliability of the material by providing the setting, the situation, and the specific details for the biblical event, do not make the existence of an Abraham, or a Joseph, or any of the family history any more likely. Moreover, the universal events (chs 1–11) and the patriarchal narratives (chs 12–36) do not give anything close to full histories—that is, a full tracing of the events with causes and effects included. Rather, little episodes are selected from the family traditions and put together in a sequence.

One must remember that the Bible is a unique work. Genesis was not meant to be a chronicle of the lives of the patriarchs, a history for history's sake, or even a complete biography of any one person. Rather, it is clearly a theological interpretation of selected ancestral records that is based on monotheism and not polytheism and one that develops historically toward a destiny and is not a mythological cycle of events. Moreover, the fact that Genesis (and the rest of biblical historical narratives) includes the failures of the people of Israel and the punishment from their God, often by means of other nations, sets the biblical records apart from most of the propaganda written in the records and on the monuments of the ancient Near East. As with all histories, Genesis explains the causes behind the selected events—causes that are both human and divine. Because Genesis is part of divine revelation and not a modern history or an ancient pagan mythology, both the events and the explanations are true. But the actual events, and certainly the divine causation, cannot be tested by outside sources. Nevertheless, the claims that the book makes about the lives of the patriarchs must also be allowed to stand unless proven completely false by similar tests.

For the people of Israel, the most important questions about life in general and their existence in particular were answered by the interpretation of the narratives in Genesis. Major issues such as life and death, and other matters such as possession of the land of Canaan or how the people ended up in Egypt, were explained by God's providential working in history. All of it was part of the divinely planned program of God in this world. That program had a starting point—Creation—and a finishing point—eschatology; in between is the biblical history. And since this came by revelation, it was accepted that faith was an integral part of understanding the real causes behind national and international events. The event could possibly be verified, but the divine cause could not be, apart from faith.

At the heart of this biblical history is God's covenant. It began with election, the call of Abraham. God's people could possibly prove that Abraham lived, that he moved from Ur to Canaan, and that he was their ancestor; but they would have to accept by faith that God called him and revealed himself to him, making the promises. Israelites could look back at the records, both the events and their interpretations, and see what God had done, and on that basis they could look to the future fulfillment of the promises. Even though promise and fulfillment are predominant motifs in the biblical history, the call for faith and obedience were uppermost in the minds of the writers. So the events were reported for apologetic, polemical, and didactic reasons. And what made the events and their interpretations believable to the Israelites were the many examples of the fulfilled promises that they had already experienced, some of them coming about in a supernatural way. They were not as troubled by supernatural events as modern critics, for they experienced them frequently enough to authenticate the reports of the events.

The fact that Genesis is a theological interpretation of ancient events does not destroy its historicity. As Porteous says, "It would seem reasonable to suppose that interpretation is a response to something that demands an interpretation" (1972:107). Interpretations of events can differ, even today, but the offering of interpretations is a good witness to the actuality of the event. Speiser (1957:202) says that while the material of Genesis may not be called history in the pure or conventional sense,

> it cannot be set down as fancy. The author retells the events in his own inimitable way; he does not invent them. What is thus committed to writing is tradition, in the reverent care of literary genius. Where the tradition can be independently checked, it proves to be authentic. This much has been evident for some time in respect to a number of incidental details. It now turns out that the main framework of the patriarchal account has been accurately presented.

For many believers it comes as no surprise that the narratives prove to be authentic. It is simply a confirmation of their faith that when all the archaeological and historical data are assembled around the events, the events fit perfectly in the setting, and the details of the narratives make perfectly good sense.

Tradition. Modern scholars prefer to use words like "traditions" or even "sagas" (von Rad 1961:31) to describe the narrative reports. That is, they preserve the events that are in the memory of the people of Israel. A word like "tradition" does not say the events happened, but neither does it say they did not happen. So when we look at the texts primarily as records and memories of the people, "traditions" or the like is workable. But if we add the biblical understanding that these have been recorded in the Bible under divine inspiration, that they are part of the revelation of God, then they must be taken more seriously. The biblical writers are capable of marking a story as a parable or rhetorical device, if in fact they do not mean it to be taken as having actually happened; but if the story is presented as an actual event in antiquity, then there is no reason to doubt that it occurred. The writer may have taken a certain amount of freedom in the way the story is cast or what in the event is emphasized—but he will not fabricate the event or embellish it with things that never occurred, not if he is writing the account to present the historical and theological foundation of the people of Israel, the covenant, the law, or God's plan of redemption.

In all probability the primeval accounts and the family genealogies would have been brought from Mesopotamia by the patriarchs. To these collections would have been added the stories about the family. All the traditions, both written and oral, could have been easily preserved by Joseph in Egypt along with his own records. Moses then could have compiled the works in essentially the same form that they appear in today, adding his editorial comments all along the way. Since he was a prophet, working under the inspiration and guidance of God at Sinai, he would have been kept from putting error or pagan intrusions in the records so that what was produced was the truth—that is, the true record of the events explained in a way that instructed the people about what God wanted them to believe and do (Kitchen 1971:1-10). So whether the narratives are called traditions, stories, or histories, they record exactly what God wanted written and therefore are true—meaning they correspond with reality. It may not be accurate to describe the book of Genesis as history, because it is essentially a theological treatise using a number of selected events; but it can be called historical.

Since Genesis is the first book of the Pentateuch, the law, it may be best to classify it as "Torah Literature" (*torah* [TH8451, ZH9368], "instruction, law"). It may not be legal literature in the sense that the Ten Commandments are (Exod 20), but it lays the foundation for the law. It is a theological interpretation of the historical traditions behind the formation of the covenant with Israel at Sinai. In the way it is written, one may discern throughout the book that Moses was preparing his readers for the revelation of the law, and for their call to go and receive the fulfillment of the promises made to the fathers. It is this shaping of the material that gives Genesis its didactic nature. Genesis is therefore a unique work; it is here that theology and history come together to prepare the people of God for the blessing of God.

The Literary Structure of Genesis. Genesis in its final form is a single literary composition; it arranges family traditions, genealogies, historical events, and editorial comments into a sustained argument. All this material is organized into sections with the heading "this is the account of" (or, "these are the generations of") which trace the development of the blessing of God against the threat of the curse. This plan of divine blessing on and through the family of Abraham is the basis for the covenant that God made with his people; as the blessing develops section by section, the covenant is clarified. By the end of the book the reader is ready for the fulfillment of the promises in Israel's redemption from bondage.

The structure of the book is arranged by sections that differ from the chapter and verse divisions that were added later. There is an initial introduction, the account of creation, and then 11 sections with headings. The formulaic word in the headings is the Hebrew word *toledoth* [TH8435, ZH9352], and the heading usually reads, "These are the *toledoth* of . . ." In all instances but the first, the formula is followed by a personal name. *Toledoth* is a feminine noun from the verb *yalad* [TH3205, ZH3528] (to bear, to generate) in the causative stem of the verb. Earlier versions translated this word as "generations," while more modern versions translate it as "records" or "accounts" (NLT, NIV). Driver paraphrases it somewhat more generally as the "particulars about a man and his descendants" (1904:19). It indicates that what follows will be the subsequent records or accounts of the person or thing (as in the case of the first use) named. It essentially explains "This is what became of [a given person or thing]," and the account that follows starts with the person and traces the records through subsequent generations, focusing on the most important people in that family record. The headings using this word (rendered "account" below) are as follows:

The account of the heavens and the earth (2:4–4:26)
The account of Adam (5:1–6:8)
The account of Noah (6:9–9:29)
The account of Shem, Ham, and Japheth (10:1–11:9)
The account of Shem (11:10-26)
The account of Terah (11:27–25:11)
The account of Ishmael (25:12-18)
The account of Isaac (25:19–35:29)
The account of Esau (36:1-8)
The account of Esau, father of the Edomites (36:9–37:1)
The account of Jacob (37:2–50:26)

The views on the use of this word in this clause vary. Speiser (1964:xxiv) takes it as a heading in all places except 2:4 and 37:2. In these places he suggests that *toledoth* means "story" or "history" and that it refers to the preceding material and not the following. Others go further and doubt that it ever is a heading; P. J. Wiseman and R. K. Harrison (1969:548) suggest that the expressions are equivalent to the colophons found on clay tablets. Their view is based on the theory that Genesis was originally written on separate clay tablets with a colophon giving the owner's name written at the end of each one. Wiseman argues that these expressions parallel the Babylonian colophons which give a title, date of the writing, serial number, and a statement of the completion of the series (1937:8; 1949:46). But the view is unconvincing. The colophons on the Babylonian tablets are nothing like these expressions in Genesis (see Heidel 1963:25, 30). In the cuneiform tablets, each title is a repetition of that tablet's first line and not a description of its contents. Also, the owner's name seems to refer to the present owner and not the original owner of the tablet. And no equivalent of *toledoth* [TH8435, ZH9352] is used. And of course, there is no evidence that Genesis was first written on separate clay tablets anyway.

Skinner (1930:39-40) doubts that the expression *toledoth* could be used in reference to what precedes it; it seems always to be a heading. In Genesis, if these expressions are references to what immediately precedes the phrase, then the statement in 5:1 should have come at 4:16, at the end of the story of Adam and not later after the intervening material in 4:17-26. Another placement that could scarcely be a concluding formula is 10:1, the account of the sons of Noah. It is unlikely that this concludes the account of the Flood and the curse at Babel, especially in view of 10:32. Then there is the difficulty of having the story about Abraham (11:27–25:11) preserved by Ishmael (25:12), or having Isaac keep Ishmael's records (25:19), Esau those of Isaac (36:1), and Jacob those of Esau (37:2). But when these expressions are taken as titles to what follows there is harmony in the material. In fact, nowhere in the Old Testament does *toledoth* [TH8435, ZH9352] clearly refer to the material that precedes it. In every place it can and often must refer to what follows. For example, in Ruth 4:18 the word introduces the line of Perez; and in Numbers 3:1 the "family line of Aaron and Moses" cannot refer to the census of Numbers 1 and 2. A similar idea may be reflected in the usage of the Greek *geneseōs* in Matthew 1:1.

As stated earlier, this word is derived from the verb *yalad* [TH3205, ZH3528] (to bear, generate) and refers to what is brought forth. As a formula word in Genesis, *toledoth* marks a starting point from which a combination of narrative and genealogy move the reader to the end of the account. It is Moses's way of moving along the historical lines from a beginning to an ending, including the product of the starting point. The starting point is identified by the word in the genitive that follows *toledoth*. The title then would be "these are the particulars about (such and such a man) and his descendants" (Driver 1891:19). A more interpretive paraphrase might be "This is what became of X" (see Woudstra 1970:187). So, for example, when we read "This is what became of Terah" in chapter 11, what follows is the family record beginning with Terah but moving directly to tell the particulars about Abraham and his family. Or, when we read "This is what became of Jacob" in chapter 37, what follows is the story of Jacob's family, mostly about Joseph and his brothers. Taken with this idea in mind, even the use in 2:4 is appropriate as a heading for what follows it. It is made up of two parallel lines that are difficult to separate into two sections of the book. Wiseman himself agrees that 2:1-3 forms a natural conclusion for the creation account. Genesis 2:4a would then be the heading, and 2:4b would be the beginning dependent clause (much like the beginning of the Babylonian account of creation that begins with "when above. . . ."). Genesis 2:4 would read, "These are the *toledoth* [TH8435, ZH9352] of the heavens and the earth when they were created. When Yahweh God made earth and heaven. . . ." The construction is similar to that in 5:1.

The fact that "Yahweh God" is used throughout 2:4–3:24 would also support the idea that 2:4 is the title of the section. If the meaning of the word conveys the idea of what became of the subject, then the section of 2:4–4:26 was intended to explain what became of creation when Yahweh God made it. What became of it was sin and the curse. When the arrangement of the material is looked at this way, this definition of *toledoth* is the most satisfactory. The translation of *toledoth* cannot be limited to "genealogy" because the contents of the sections go beyond that; nor does the word simply denote biographies or histories, because the narratives do not follow that through. The sections tell what became of a given person, and the content of the sections is selected to trace the relevant particulars about that line, which help develop the argument of the book. Thus, the best interpretive translation would perhaps be "this is the account of the succession from."

Two additional observations may be made here. One is that in the tracing of each line there is a narrowing process. After the new beginnings with Noah, the text records the *toledoth* [TH8435, ZH9352] of Shem, Ham, and Japheth. But immediately after that section comes the *toledoth* of Shem, the genealogy from Shem to Abram. The next section is that of Terah, but this part is concerned with the family of Abraham, out of the line of Shem. Abraham's family is then narrowed to the *toledoth* of Isaac, with the account of Ishmael being given first as a tidying up of the accounts. The same holds true of the next generation; the *toledoth* of Esau, the one not chosen, is given before the *toledoth* of Jacob (which is primarily about Jacob's sons).

A second observation is that the material within each *toledoth* section is a microcosm of the flow of the book as a whole, with the themes of blessing and cursing playing a major role. Within each of the first several sections of the book there is a deterioration which leads to a curse; then with 12:1-3 the message changes to the promise of blessing. From this point on there is a struggle for the blessing, but still there is a general deterioration with each successive section after the Abraham stories, although not as severe as in chapters 1-11. Isaac does not measure up to the faith of Abraham, and Jacob is even further away from the standard; then the sons of Jacob are even more base with their actions against Joseph and the family in general. Consequently, at the end of the book the family is not in the Promised Land, not in the place of blessing, but in Egypt. Kidner says that "man had traveled far from Eden to a coffin, and the chosen family far from Canaan to Egypt" (1967:224).

In summary, the *toledoth* [TH8435, ZH9352] sections are the "very fabric around which the whole of Genesis has been constructed" (Woudstra 1970:188-189). Each of these sections, explaining what became of a line, shows a narrowing and a deterioration in the development of God's plan to bring blessing to the world.

1. Creation (1:1-2:3). The first section does not have the *toledoth* heading and logically so—it is the account of creation in the beginning. Rather, its own heading in 1:1 depicts the content of the unit. The significance of this material is that the work of creation is wrapped in divine approval and blessing over the fulfillment of God's plan. Animal life (1:22-25), human life (1:27), and the Sabbath day (2:3) were all blessed specifically. This trilogy of blessed things highlights the Creator's plan: Mankind had a blessed beginning, made as the image of God, enjoying sovereign dominion over the creatures of the earth, and enjoying the Sabbath rest of God.

2. The toledoth of the heavens and the earth (2:4-4:26). This section reports what became of God's creation. It begins with a restatement of creation in specific detail about human life, and then records the sin of Adam and Eve, the curse on the sin, and the expansion of sin to their descendants. No longer enjoying the rest of God, mankind experienced guilt and fear, fleeing from God, making their way in the world, and developing civilization. As if in response to the blessings of creation, this section records a threefold cursing from God: on Satan (3:14), on the ground because of Adam (3:17), and on Cain (4:11). Yet in the increase of sin and the application of the curse, there is a token of grace (4:15) and a ray of hope when people begin to call on the name of the Lord (4:26).

3. The toledoth of Adam (5:1-6:8). Here too, in this genealogy from Adam to Noah, the downward drift of human life is noted. The section includes more than the genealogy; it starts with the genealogy and concludes with the report that the human race was so evil that it brought God great grief and sorrow. The contrast is heightened in the way the genealogy begins by recalling the creation of man as the image of God and the blessing given (5:1-2). But as the genealogy is traced panel by panel, the ominous note that they died, generation by generation, reminds the reader that the curse was indeed in place. But one exception to the rule, Enoch, provides a ray of hope to a dying world that the curse is not final (5:23-24). Verse 29 records the birth of Noah, which is seen as a token of grace that God would bring them comfort from the curse. But the way that comfort would be realized was far different than what they hoped for. The last part of the section tells how God was sorry he ever made man and would bring a judgment on the earth. But it ends on the hopeful note that Noah found grace (6:8).

4. *The toledoth of Noah (6:9–9:29).* This section is about the judgment via the Flood and the blessing of a new beginning, in which God promised never again to curse the ground with a flood (8:21). Nevertheless, the story line about Noah begins with his integrity, walking in righteousness and obeying the Lord, and ends with his lying drunk and naked in his tent, delivering an oracle of cursing on Canaan. Even after the great Flood, the human race exhibits the same sinful characteristics that warranted the judgment in the first place; but these would be dealt with differently.

The pattern of re-creation is most pronounced here. It is a new beginning out of a watery world, parallel in many ways to the beginning of Genesis 1: the covering of the whole earth with water and resultant chaos; the gracious provision of life to a family that would have the privilege of filling the whole earth; the covenant made by God (with Noah, a second Adam), reiterating the promises and instructions that were given in the beginning alongside his blessing on the family. Here the race began over again in a new creation, purged of some of the abominable evil that had invaded and ruined it. And from this beginning point the blessing motif becomes more prominent: the line of Shem would be blessed, and the line of Japheth would share in it; but the Canaanites would be cursed.

5. *The toledoth of the sons of Noah (10:1–11:9).* As the population of the world expands in line with Noah's oracle, the direction of the book focuses on the nations. The book's emphasis on people being bent on disobedience and chaos is displayed here on the international level. This section begins by surveying what seems to be the fruitful population of the earth by Shem, Ham, and Japheth. For the later Israelites, the Table of Nations would read like a Who's Who in ancient warfare, ethnic cleansings, and exiles. But there is something wrong: these people are all divided by languages and boundaries. Only when the second part of the section was read, the account of the dispersion of the nations at Babel (11:1-9), would the divisions begin to make sense. It is a stroke of genius to put such a powerful story at the end of the survey of nations, especially when the event preceded it chronologically. Here the reader discovers that the people were dispersed because of their pride and rebellion against God, and their dispersion and confusion of languages was both a prevention of greater wickedness and a punishment. But the whole section leaves the reader wondering what would become of the blessing, for the whole human race

was scattered and divided, and there was no nation that sought to do the will of God. This leads to Genesis's next point: God would have to build such a nation, from one man, if the blessing was to be restored to the world.

6. *The toledoth of Shem (11:10-26)*. From the chaos of the scattered nations in the preceding section, this brief unit forms another transition in the book, narrowing the choice to Abram. The list traces the line from Noah to Abram with an emphasis on the blessings of prosperity and posterity (in contrast to ch 5, which focuses on the death of the ancestors). God would not leave the expanding world, divided and confused under his judgment, without hope. He would select a man and build from him a nation that would bring blessing to all. A reader who knew anything about Abraham would have caught the importance of this genealogy immediately.

7. *The toledoth of Terah (11:27–25:11)*. Whereas Genesis 1–11 generally portrays the rebellion of the human race, chapters 12–50 detail God's bringing people into a place of blessing. This section tells what became of Terah—it is the story of his son Abraham and the covenant God made with him. This is the central point of the message of the book, and that of the Old Testament as well. God promised Abraham a great nation, a land, and a great name. The narratives trace—from Abram's call to his great test—the development of this covenant with its promises and the faith of the patriarch (ch 22). Thereafter the narratives are devoted to the transition of the covenant to the next generation.

8. *The toledoth of Ishmael (25:12-18)*. Before tracing the covenant to the next generation, Isaac, the book tells what became of Ishmael, the son not chosen. This little section completes the line of this son of Abraham through Hagar before focusing on the heir.

9. *The toledoth of Isaac (25:19–35:29)*. In this section we have the account of what became of Isaac, the son of promise. It tells the story of Jacob for the most part, the son of Isaac, brother of Esau, and nephew of Laban. Through the stories of the struggles of this patriarch in different settings, the "nation of Israel" (in seed form) emerged. The promises to Abraham (12:1-3) finally begin to unfold more fully; and the blessing that was at the heart of the covenant promises passed to Jacob (ch 27) in the end. Jacob also developed in his faith, but was crippled in the process (ch 32)—a constant reminder that these were spiritual blessings that could not be obtained by human endeavors. Jacob was not the man that his grandfather was, but he was a man of faith who produced the tribal chiefs of the nation that would bear his name, Israel.

10. *The toledoth of Esau (36:1-8)*. Once again the development from Isaac is recorded, this time through the family of Esau, the son of Isaac not chosen. True to the pattern of the book, Esau's line is dealt with before the line of the heir. It was also important to include the names of those who came from Esau because the later nation of Israel would have to interact with these tribes, the Edomites.

11. *The toledoth of Esau, father of the Edomites (36:9–37:1)*. An additional accounting of the descendants and affiliates of Esau was necessary for a complete report because of the impact of the Edomite, Amalekite, and Horite chieftains in the region that Israel was to occupy. All of these names, witnessing to the rapid expansion of

the family of Esau, are contrasted in the last verse (37:1) with Jacob, for whom the promises seemed to lag.

12. The toledoth of Jacob (37:2–50:26). What became of Jacob? His sons became the founding fathers of the tribes of Israel. This section is concerned with Jacob and his family, primarily centering on the life of Joseph, who would receive the double blessing from his father and the responsibility from God of saving the family. The writer used the events of the life of Joseph to trace the move of the family to Egypt, to the land of Goshen, where we find them at the beginning of the book of Exodus. In the land of Canaan the family had become corrupt, easily influenced by the Canaanites, to the point of merging with them. To preserve the line of blessing God sent the family into Egypt, where they could flourish and become a great nation, but where they would also be tested severely by the Egyptians. The book closes with the promise of a visitation from the Lord to deliver the people from Egypt.

MAJOR THEMES

It may be readily discerned that the entire message of the book turns on the motifs of blessing and cursing. The promised blessing would give innumerable descendants to the patriarchs and the land of promise to the descendants; it would also make them famous in the earth, enable them to flourish and prosper, and use them as the means to bring others into the covenant blessings as well. By contrast, the curse would alienate, deprive, and disinherit people from the blessings that God gave and would give. Later in the Bible, prophets and priests drew on Genesis and expanded these motifs, speaking of even greater blessings in future events and at the end of the age, as well as an even greater curse for those who refused God's gift of salvation and its attendant blessings.

The Old Testament verb for "to bless" (*barak* [TH1288A, ZH1385]) means basically "to enrich." It refers to a gift, an enrichment of some kind, whether material, physical, or spiritual. God is always the source of a blessing, even when humans offer it. In Genesis only those who are the leaders of the covenant family pronounce the blessings, and in those cases it is clear that they are declaring an oracle that came from God. It is not a magic formula. People do not have the power to bless; it is God who blesses.[3] As used in Genesis, the promise of blessing is largely concerned with the descendants in the land of Canaan. The promised blessing included prosperity with respect to fertility (of both the family and the land). But the blessing from God also included the faculty to gain the prosperity, whether the blessing was on the earth, the animals, or the people. And since the enablement came from God, reflecting divine approval, it was ultimately a spiritual blessing (see Westermann 1984:18-23). In Genesis, it is in the blessing of God that we see such a striking contrast with the pagan religions of antiquity. For them fertility of flock and family, fields and fortunes, came about through sympathetic magic in cultic observances at their shrines—profane customs that were designed to induce the deities to act on their behalf so that the cycle of life could be maintained. But in Genesis all of life and all of fertility comes by God's decree, for he is the only true and living God.

The word for "to curse" ('*arar* [TH779, ZH826]) has the sense of removing someone or something from the place of blessing, of imposing a ban or a barrier, a paralysis on movement or other capabilities (Brichto 1963:217). Again, such power belongs only to God, or an agent endowed by him with special power to effect a curse. Of course, many in the pagan world thought that they could curse other people, especially the Israelites, but their curses were turned to blessing (cf. Num 23–24). If the curse had a deleterious effect, it would have come only through the psychological impact of the curse and the fear that it engendered. Thus, the Bible reminds God's people to not fear what these people can do, but to fear God who has the power to bless and to curse. If God imposes a curse, it involves separation from the place of blessing or even from those who are blessed. The prologue of Genesis displays the curse frequently, but the word is used sparingly; concerning people, only Cain and later Canaan are said to be cursed. The effects of the curse, however, are felt by the whole race as death and pain and eventually the judgment of God are worked out in the world.

Along with these motifs of blessing and cursing, the corresponding motifs of good and evil run from the beginning to the end of the book. That which is good in Genesis produces life, enhances life, preserves life, and harmonizes with life; that which is good is blessed by God. But that which is evil interferes with life, causes pain to life, diverts life from what is good, and even destroys life; that which is evil is cursed. From the beginning the temptation was to gain the knowledge of good and evil, that is, the ability to alter what God had created for better or for worse. Whatever the humans sought to improve, they destroyed because they themselves were only evil continually. Humans simply do not have the knowledge and wisdom and power to change the order of creation or its institutions. The book, then, in many ways is a tracing of this perpetual struggle between good and evil which characterizes a fallen race. Only in the conclusion do we learn from the words of Joseph that what humans intend for evil, God can overrule because he has a plan for good (50:20); and, in fact, he will occasionally use the evil that people do to bring about the greater good and build his people's faith.

THEOLOGICAL CONCERNS
Genesis begins with the presupposition that God exists and that he has revealed himself in word and deed to the ancestors. The book does not argue for the existence of God; it simply starts with God and shows how everything falls into place when the sovereign God begins to develop his plan. And that plan is the theological center of the book: it is the work of God to establish Israel as the means of restoring blessing to the whole world. Thus Genesis provides the fitting introduction to the founding of the theocracy, the rule of God over all creation, a rule that would be developed through his chosen people. As an introduction to this message, Genesis primarily lays out the promises, and the rest of the books of the law show how these promises came to fulfillment. Exodus presents the redemption of the seed out of bondage and the granting of a constitution to them at Sinai. Leviticus provides the manual of ordinances and rituals enabling the holy God to dwell among them and

make them a holy nation. Numbers records the census of the tribes in the wilderness, their military and religious arrangements, and how the Lord preserved his people from threats to the promised blessing from without and within. Finally, Deuteronomy records the renewal of the covenant in prophetic form, focusing on the great king of the theocracy and the covenant he made with the people.

In the unfolding of this grand program of God to establish his theocracy, Genesis also lays down the initial and necessary revelation of God's sovereignty. He is the Lord of the universe who will move heaven and earth to bring about his plan. He desires to bless people, but he will not tolerate rebellion and unbelief. According to Genesis, the promises of God are great, and the power of God is fully able to bring them to fruition. But participation in God's program required faith, as it always does, for without faith it is impossible to please God (Heb 11:6).

OUTLINE
I. The Primeval Universal Events (1:1–11:26)
  A. The Creation of All Things (1:1–2:3)
    1. The beginning (1:1-2)
    2. The six days of creation (1:3-31)
    3. Sabbath rest (2:1-3)
  B. The Account of the Succession from the Creation (2:4–4:26)
    1. The creation of man (2:4-7)
    2. The creation of the garden (2:8-14)
    3. The first commandment (2:15-17)
    4. The creation of woman (2:18-25)
    5. The temptation (3:1-7)
    6. The results of sin (3:8-24)
    7. The advance of sin in the family (4:1-16)
    8. The spread of godless civilization and the faith (4:17-26)
  C. The Account of the Succession from Adam (5:1–6:8)
    1. The genealogy from Adam to Noah (5:1-32)
    2. The corruption of the human race (6:1-8)
  D. The Account of the Succession from Noah (6:9–9:29)
    1. The commission of Noah (6:9–7:5)
    2. The destruction of all life outside the ark (7:6-24)
    3. The end of the judgment and Noah's worship (8:1-22)
    4. God's covenant with Noah (9:1-17)
    5. Curse on Canaan; blessings on Shem and Japheth (9:18-29)
  E. The Account of the Succession from the Sons of Noah (10:1–11:9)
    1. The Table of Nations (10:1-32)
    2. The dispersion at Babel (11:1-9)
  F. The Account of the Succession from Shem (11:10-26)

II. The Patriarchal Narratives (11:27–37:1)
  A. The Account of the Succession from Terah (11:27–25:11)
    1. The Lord's call to Abram (11:27–12:9)
    2. Abram and Sarai in Egypt (12:10-20)
    3. Abram's separation from Lot (13:1-18)
    4. Abram's victory over the invading kings (14:1-16)
    5. The blessing of Melchizedek (14:17-24)
    6. The Lord's covenant promise to Abram (15:1-21)
    7. Abram's lack of faith (16:1-16)
    8. The confirmation of the promise by signs (17:1-27)
    9. The time of fulfillment guaranteed by divine visitation (18:1-15)
    10. Abraham's intercession for Sodom (18:16-33)
    11. God's judgment on the cities of the plain (19:1-38)
    12. Abraham's deception before Abimelech (20:1-18)
    13. The birth of Isaac and expulsion of Ishmael (21:1-21)
    14. The covenant at Beersheba (21:22-34)
    15. The testing of Abraham's faith (22:1-24)
    16. The burial of Sarah (23:1-20)
    17. God's provision of a wife for Isaac (24:1-67)
    18. The death of Abraham (25:1-11)
  B. The Account of the Succession from Ishmael (25:12-18)
  C. The Account of the Succession from Isaac (25:19–35:29)
    1. The births of Esau and Jacob (25:19-26)
    2. The sale of the birthright (25:27-34)
    3. Isaac's deception (26:1-11)
    4. The blessing on Isaac and failure of Esau (26:12-35)
    5. Jacob's deception of Esau for the blessing (27:1-40)
    6. The flight of Jacob (27:41–28:9)
    7. The confirmation of the blessing at Bethel (28:10-22)
    8. Jacob's marriages to Leah and Rachel (29:1-30)
    9. The births of the tribal ancestors (29:31–30:24)
    10. The increase of Jacob's possessions (30:25-43)
    11. Jacob's flight from Laban (31:1-42)
    12. The treaty on the border (31:43-55)
    13. Jacob's preparation for meeting Esau (32:1-21)
    14. Jacob becomes Israel (32:22-32)
    15. Reconciliation with Esau and settlement in Shechem (33:1-20)
    16. The defilement of Dinah (34:1-31)
    17. Jacob's return to Bethel (35:1-15)
    18. The completion of the family (35:16-29)
  D. The Account of the Succession from Esau (36:1-8)
  E. The Account of the Succession of the Edomites from Esau (36:9–37:1)

III. The Account of the Succession from Jacob: The Story of Joseph and His Brothers (37:2–50:26)
   A. The Selling of Joseph into Egypt (37:2-36)
   B. The Corruption of Judah and the Confirmation of God's Ways (38:1-30)
   C. Joseph's Rise to Power in Egypt (39:1–41:57)
      1. Joseph's temptation by Potiphar's wife (39:1-23)
      2. Joseph's interpretation of the prisoners' dreams (40:1-23)
      3. Joseph's interpretation of Pharaoh's dreams (41:1-40)
      4. The exaltation of Joseph (41:41-57)
   D. The Testing of Joseph's Brothers (42:1–45:15)
      1. The test of conscience (42:1-38)
      2. The test of jealousy (43:1-34)
      3. The test of loyal love (44:1-34)
      4. The reconciliation of Joseph and his brothers (45:1-15)
   E. The Move of the Family to Egypt (45:16–47:12)
   F. The Wisdom of Joseph's Rule (47:13-27)
   G. The Blessing of Joseph's Sons (47:28–48:22)
   H. Jacob's Oracle for the Tribes (49:1-28)
   I. The Death and Burial of Jacob (49:29–50:14)
   J. Reassurance of the Blessing (50:15-26)

ENDNOTES
1. For a survey of the approach see Friedman 1987; Blenkinsopp 1992; for an evaluation of it, see Rendtorff 1992 and especially Knierim 1985a. For a survey of subsequent views, see Carpenter 1986; and for discussions favoring the former consensus, see Nicholson 1989; Emerton 1987, 1988.
2. For further discussion of the various theories, see the introductory comments in Matthews 1996; Rendsburg 1986; Knierim 1985b; Garrett 1991; Kikawada and Quinn 1987:36-53; Nicholson 1989.
3. The word "bless" is used with a different sense throughout the Book of Psalms as one of several words for praise. But how can our words make God more blessed or more enriched? Or how can we glorify or exalt one who is all-glorious and exalted in the highest heaven? We can only do so by making him known throughout the world through praise. In this way we are enriching God by extending his reputation.

COMMENTARY ON
Genesis

◆ **I. The Primeval Universal Events (1:1–11:26)**
  A. The Creation of All Things (1:1–2:3)
    1. The beginning (1:1-2)

In the beginning God created the heavens and the earth.* ²The earth was formless and empty, and darkness covered the deep waters. And the Spirit of God was hovering over the surface of the waters.

1:1 Or *In the beginning when God created the heavens and the earth,* . . . Or *When God began to create the heavens and the earth,* . . .

NOTES

1:1-2 All expositors have to deal with the relationship between v. 1 and v. 2. The Hebrew text begins v. 2 with a Waw disjunctive, indicating that the verse is not in sequence with v. 1 and so should not be translated "and then the earth became. . . ." Rather, v. 2 provides a series of circumstantial clauses to describe the existing conditions when God said, "Let there be light." The NLT chose not to translate the Waw as "and" or "now"; and its marginal note attempts to capture the nature of the clauses as circumstantial, suggesting for v. 1 the translation "In the beginning when God created" or "When God began to create." This is probably too free, for it makes the first verse a temporal clause when the Hebrew is clearly an absolute statement. The Hebrew MT has a preposition "in" followed by the noun "beginning" in the absolute state (so, "in the beginning") and not in the construct state (which would mean "in the beginning of"). This is followed by the perfect tense and its subject, "God created," and then the compound direct object, "the heavens and the earth." In order to make the first verse a temporal clause, the noun "beginning" would properly be taken as a noun in construct, and the vowels of the verb changed to make an infinitive: "In the beginning of the creating of God," or "when God created." Most English translations have chosen the absolute as the preferred reading ("In the beginning God created"); some suggest in the margin that it could be taken as a temporal clause ("When God created/began to create"). But this suggestion does raise the question of the relationship between vv. 1 and 2. A number of commentators have taken v. 1 to be a report of the beginning of creation prior to the events of ch 1. Some of them take "waste," "void," "darkness," and "deep" in v. 2 to refer simply to the yet unformed nature of the universe, an initial stage of creation to be completed in the subsequent events of the chapter. The benefit of this view is that it makes 1:1 "the" beginning, and that fits nicely with the straightforward reading of the Bible. The difficulty is that it does not do justice to the meanings of the words in v. 2 and their connection to *bara'* [TH1254, ZH1343] (to create) in v. 1.

Older commentators had seen that the words in v. 2 are too strong to refer to unshaped matter, that they are corrected, not completed, in the rest of the chapter, and that *bara'*, "to create," usually produces something perfect and pristine, not waste and void. They also sensed a need to fit Satan's fall from heaven into the order of things as well. This led to what has been known as the "gap theory," that Satan fell after v. 1 and brought darkness and chaos to the earth, so that God had to set about to correct it. This view had the value of keeping 1:1 as original creation, accounting for Satan, and keeping v. 2 as a chaos. But it required translating the beginning of v. 2 as "and the earth became," which is not how the Waw disjunctive clause with the perfect tense would be normally translated.

Other scholars, however, have concluded that v. 1 serves well as a brief introductory statement of the message of 1:1-2:3, with the particulars to follow. This view makes the most sense of the grammar, syntax, and philology of the beginning verses. Moreover, this arrangement is paralleled by 2:4-7, which begins with the introductory statement, followed by three circumstantial clauses (the first two of which are also causal) and then the Waw consecutive form to begin the narrative proper. For 1:1-3, this view does justice to the terms and the syntax, but its potential difficulty is theological: It would mean that Genesis is describing the beginning of the creation as we know it, but not the original creation of matter, with the story assuming the earth was already there when God said "Let there be light." The Bible clearly affirms that God created everything out of nothing, including the angels who were already there when God laid the foundations of the earth (Job 38:4-7). This "re-creation" view would account for the creation of everything we know, but not the actual beginning of matter. Other statements in Scripture would embrace all of that. It would also allow for a greater age for the planets and the stars, even though life on our planet would be recent. (For more detailed discussions on the issue, see Waltke 1975; NIDOTTE 1.606-609; Tsumura 1994.)

1:2 *the Spirit of God was hovering over the surface of the waters.* It was by his Spirit that God sovereignly created everything. The Gospel of John clarifies that the God of creation is the living Word, the second person of the Trinity (John 1:3-4). In the darkness of the deep the Spirit hovered, preparing for the effectual, creative word of God. This is the pattern that fits all of God's works: The Spirit is at work when the word is given.

COMMENTARY

The first two verses of the Bible have received a good deal of attention over the years. The traditional understanding is that they refer to the actual beginning of matter, creation out of nothing (i.e., *creatio ex nihilo*), and are both therefore part of day one. That would mean that the first step involved making matter that at first was "formless and empty," and then a second step involved shaping it and filling it to make the world as we know it. But many biblical scholars have concluded that the vocabulary and grammar of the two verses pose difficulties for this interpretation. The language of the second verse with its "waste and void" seems to describe more of a ruined or dismantled state than merely a formless and empty mass; and the rest of the chapter provides the correction of the conditions in verse 2. That the universe is God's creation is perfectly expressed by the statement "God created the heavens and the earth" (1:1). This took place "in the beginning," not the beginning of God for there is none, but the beginning of our universe. The Bible is clear on this point. There is no room for atheistic alternative explanations. The sovereign work of creation is established by the verb that is used here—God "created." The word is *bara'* [TH1254, ZH1343] (to create); it can be used in sentences that declare creation that is made out of nothing; but it can also be used to indicate a refashioning or a renovation (e.g., God "created" the man from the dust; 1:27-28 and 2:7). This verb does not go well with the following statement in 1:2, in that *bara'* would not likely be said to produce formlessness and emptiness and darkness (cf. Isa 45:18). The point is that what God creates is perfect, new, and fresh.

How then do we relate these verses? If the expressions of verse 2 do describe a chaos and not simply unformed matter, then verse 1 should be interpreted as a general summary statement of what the entire chapter will tell about the creation of the heavens and the earth (an expression for the whole universe) as we know it. This would mean that verse 1 is not part of day one, that the account in Genesis begins with the state of things recorded in verse 2 and not with the original creation of matter, and that the earth specifically and the universe in general could be very old. Genesis does not explain how these conditions came about, only that they were there. The second verse is set off by the grammar (with a Waw disjunctive) to form three circumstantial clauses: "[1] The earth was formless and empty, [2] and darkness covered the deep waters. [3] And the Spirit of God was hovering over the surface of the waters." These clauses are circumstantial, explaining the condition of things when God said, "Let there be light" (1:3). They would not normally be the product of divine creation, but would describe a chaos that happened to the creation. Moreover, the chapter does not call them good, but sets about to correct them. First God corrects the darkness with light. Then the formlessness is corrected in the first three days, and the emptiness in the last three days. And all these things that God did were good.

Where did the chaos come from if the second verse is not an early stage of the creative process? An earlier theory posited that between verses 1 and 2 there is a gap of time, allowing for the fall of Satan and the entrance of evil into God's creation. The theory was put forward with the understanding that verse 1 was part of the first day; so God created the heaven and the earth, then the earth became waste and void, and then God created light. The conditions of waste and void and darkness may be the result of the fall of Satan, but the theory is not compelling. The second verse should not be translated "and the earth *became* waste and void," but "now the earth *was* waste and void."

If verse 1 is taken as a summary statement for the creation account, however, then it is not part of the first day. And whatever caused the chaos occurred before this account. The first day records the creation of light to dispel the darkness. In a sense, then, the account of creation has many aspects of re-creation in it, which fits with its later use in Scripture as a paradigm of redemption. The chapter details the creation of the universe as we know it, not the actual beginning of every form of matter. It begins with the clear proclamation that God created everything; then reports the chaos and how in six days God corrected the chaos by the creation. We know from the rest of Scripture that God created things before Genesis 1:1 because the angels were present to sing for joy at the wonderful work of creation (Job 38:4-7). Genesis is not interested in explaining the darkness or the formlessness or the emptiness, just what God did about it. But the expressions that are used lead one to suspect immediately that something ominous happened—darkness, throughout Scripture, suggests danger, and the verb "have dominion over" (1:28) implies putting down some opposition. The challenge comes in 3:1 when the tempter, using the form of a reptile, is introduced. He manages to convince Adam and Eve to disobey the Creator. The serpent is already there as part of creation, but the tempter simply speaks after God has finished his work of creation—he too is present in the garden. Later, Scripture will identify the tempter in this account as Satan (see Rev 12:9). The prophet Ezekiel seems to be hinting at the same thing, saying that the evil spirit behind the king of Tyre was in Eden (Ezek 28:11-14).

If this is the proper interpretation of these difficult expressions and constructions, nothing at all is taken away from God's sovereignty in creation. Rather, God's sovereignty is clear in the way that he made everything, and made it perfect. The Bible clearly teaches that everything that exists was made by him through his powerful decrees, leaving no room whatsoever for atheistic evolution. But Genesis may be indicating that something happened in the earliest stages of creation which God had to correct, and in the process, he put everything the way he wanted it to be. In fact, Genesis develops a pattern of creation—un-creation—re-creation several times to show God's sovereignty over all things.[1]

The account of creation is the logical starting point for Genesis, for it reports the beginning of all things. It is also the best theological way to begin the book, for it lays the foundation for the whole law in the decrees of the Creator.

The chapter portrays God as the sovereign creator of all life. As the prologue to the Pentateuch, it teaches Israel that the God who formed them into a people is the God who created the world, all that is in it, and everything in the cosmos beyond it. Thus, the theocracy is founded on the almighty God of creation. Israel's laws, customs, and beliefs were only as authoritative as the God who gave them; Israel would learn from the creation account that her God was the sovereign over all life, all matter, and all gods.

The implications of this are great. It means that everything that exists must be under God's dominion. The creation must be subject to the Creator. Forces of nature, all creatures, and all material objects are all part of his creation. The pagan nations may have venerated these things as gods, but none of them could pose a real threat to the plan of the one true God.

Second, the account of creation also lays the foundation for the law. If God was before all things and created all things, how foolish it would be to have any other gods before him (Exod 20:3). There were none! If God made people to be his image on earth representing him, how foolish it would be to make an image of God after the pattern of a human (Exod 20:4-6; Isa 44:9-20). If God set aside the seventh day for the enjoyment of his creation (Exod 20:8-11), how presumptuous it would be to treat the Sabbath day as any other day rather than enter into its celebration with the living God. The commandments of God find their rationale in creation, or rather, in the nature of the creator God.

A third implication is that if creation with all its richness and beauty and function came into existence by the word of the Lord (Ps 33:9-11), God's people certainly should realize that their lives will be ordered and blessed if they obey the word of the Lord. What better way to introduce the law (i.e., the five books of Moses) than to articulate the very first ten commands, by which God brought all things into existence.

And what a contrast between this account and the pagan accounts of creation in the ancient world. Myths about battles among the gods, carcasses being used for parts of creation, or the fusion of spirit and matter in a way so perplexing that it defies logic—there was nothing uplifting and purifying in them. The elegance and majesty of the sovereign God simply giving the command for things to come into existence and then blessing them by his powerful word shows all pagan myths and modern alternatives to be base and foolish. And it was this powerful word that would motivate God's people to put their trust in him and not in the perverse deities of the world around them.

Fourth, the account of creation also begins the revelation of the nature of God as a redeeming God. It tells how he brought the cosmos out of formlessness and emptiness, countered darkness with the creation of light, made divisions in what he had created, and in the end sanctified and blessed all that he had made. All this would have had a powerful impact on Moses's first audience, for in many ways the redemption from Egypt reflected many of the motifs of creation: God's deliverance of his people from the *chaos* of Egypt through the *waters* of the sea, granting them *light* for the way, forming them into a nation that would be his *image* on earth, and *blessing* them with all provisions of life as they became his holy nation. The prophets and the apostles saw in creation the patterns of redemption. And Paul certainly drew upon it by writing that the one who caused light to shine out of darkness has caused his light to shine in our hearts (2 Cor 4:6) so that we might become new creations (2 Cor 5:17).

ENDNOTES
1. For particular views see the following resources: For the older "gap theory," A. C. Custance, *Without Form and Void* (Brockville, Ontario: Doorway Papers, 1970); for the recent-creation view, H. Morris and J. Whitcomb, *The Genesis Flood* (Philadelphia: Presbyterian and Reformed, 1961); for progressive creationism, B. Ramm, *The Christian View of Science and Scripture* (Grand Rapids: Eerdmans, 1964); for theistic evolution, H. J. Van Till, *The Fourth Day* (Grand Rapids: Eerdmans, 1986); for the literary view, H. Blocher, *In the Beginning* (Leicester: Inter-Varsity, 1984).

◆ ## 2. The six days of creation (1:3-31)

³Then God said, "Let there be light," and there was light. ⁴And God saw that the light was good. Then he separated the light from the darkness. ⁵God called the light "day" and the darkness "night."

And evening passed and morning came, marking the first day.

⁶Then God said, "Let there be a space between the waters, to separate the waters of the heavens from the waters of the earth." ⁷And that is what happened. God made this space to separate the waters of the earth from the waters of the heavens. ⁸God called the space "sky."

And evening passed and morning came, marking the second day.

⁹Then God said, "Let the waters beneath the sky flow together into one place, so dry ground may appear." And that is what happened. ¹⁰God called the dry ground "land" and the waters "seas." And God saw that it was good. ¹¹Then God said, "Let the land sprout with vegetation—every sort of seed-bearing plant, and trees that grow seed-bearing fruit. These seeds will then produce the kinds of plants and trees from which they came." And that is what happened. ¹²The land produced vegetation—all sorts of seed-bearing plants, and trees with seed-bearing fruit. Their seeds produced plants and trees of the same kind. And God saw that it was good.

¹³And evening passed and morning came, marking the third day.

¹⁴Then God said, "Let lights appear in the sky to separate the day from the night. Let them be signs to mark the seasons, days, and years. ¹⁵Let these lights in the sky shine down on the earth." And that is what happened. ¹⁶God made two great lights—the larger one to govern the day, and the smaller one to govern the night. He also made the stars. ¹⁷God set these lights in the sky to light the earth, ¹⁸to govern the day and night, and to separate the light from the darkness. And God saw that it was good.

¹⁹And evening passed and morning came, marking the fourth day.

²⁰Then God said, "Let the waters swarm with fish and other life. Let the skies be filled with birds of every kind." ²¹So God created great sea creatures and every living thing that scurries and swarms in the water, and every sort of bird—each producing offspring of the same kind. And God saw that it was good. ²²Then God blessed them, saying, "Be fruitful and multiply. Let the fish fill the seas, and let the birds multiply on the earth."

²³And evening passed and morning came, marking the fifth day.

²⁴Then God said, "Let the earth produce every sort of animal, each producing offspring of the same kind—livestock, small animals that scurry along the ground, and wild animals." And that is what happened. ²⁵God made all sorts of wild animals, livestock, and small animals, each able to produce offspring of the same kind. And God saw that it was good.

²⁶Then God said, "Let us make human beings* in our image, to be like us. They will reign over the fish in the sea, the birds in the sky, the livestock, all the wild animals on the earth, and the small animals that scurry along the ground."

²⁷So God created human beings* in his own image.
In the image of God he created them;
male and female he created them.

²⁸Then God blessed them and said, "Be fruitful and multiply. Fill the earth and govern it. Reign over the fish in the sea, the birds in the sky, and all the animals that scurry along the ground."

²⁹Then God said, "Look! I have given you every seed-bearing plant throughout the earth and all the fruit trees for your food. ³⁰And I have given every green plant as food for all the wild animals, the birds in the sky, and the small animals that scurry along the ground—everything that has life." And that is what happened.

³¹Then God looked over all he had made, and he saw that it was very good!

And evening passed and morning came, marking the sixth day.

1:26 Or *man;* Hebrew reads *adam.*   1:27 Or *the man;* Hebrew reads *ha-adam.*

NOTES

1:3 *God said.* The first day establishes a literary pattern for each of the days of creation: There is a creative word, a report of its effect, an evaluation of the work as "good," at times a naming, and then a numbering of each day.

1:5 the first day. Concerning the word "day" (*yom* [TH3117, ZH3427]) in ch 1, it is well known that there are different interpretations based on the usage of the word. It could refer to a literal 24-hour day, or to an age, such as a geological age prior to the presence of human beings on the earth. In favor of the former, it should be noted that whenever numerals are joined with the word, it refers to a literal day (e.g., Lev 23:3, 6, 7, 8, 34, 35, 36, 39). Moreover, the Ten Commandments legislating the keeping of the Sabbath day assumes six days of creation (Exod 20:11), for the normal reading of the law would indicate a parallel between the six days of creation and the six days of labor each week. In addition, the literal understanding would harmonize with the presence of words like "night" and "years" and "seasons" in the passage. All of these would have to receive a different understanding if not taken literally.

If the day-age theory is accepted, it would simply mean that God's creative work ranged over extended periods of time, and the chronological order of those periods fits what one would expect in the development of the universe and life in it. This in no way teaches evolution since the passage reveals that the sovereign God created everything according to its kind. Development of species within their species is one thing, but evolution from a simple form to more complex forms over time does not fit the text. God is the sole creator of every individual species. In addition, as mentioned above, the vocabulary of the chapter would have to be adjusted to fit ages. If the word "day" is taken to be a long period of time, or an age, then similar interpretations must be given to "night" and "years" and "seasons," all of which appear in the chapter and appear to have a normal meaning. By the fourth day we read how the sun and the moon were established to rule over the day and the night; the day and the night already existed, and the sun and the moon dominated the heavens in each time period. All these exegetical details would have to be explained differently to harmonize with the day-age interpretation. It is easier to support the literal 24-hour-day interpretation exegetically; but the day-age theory seems to fit better with some of the findings of science. In either case we are talking about creation of all things by divine decree, and under those circumstances neither interpretation would pose a problem for God's sovereign work. In contrast to atheistic scientific theories, the biblical text declares again and again that God created everything by his powerful word.

1:22 God blessed them. While this translation conveys the definition of the word *barak* [TH1288A, ZH1385], it needs further clarification. The verb *barak* has the basic idea of giving a gift, of enriching someone or something in some way. When God blessed people (or animals, as here), it signified his giving them good gifts for their life. But the word also includes the sense of enablement as part of the enrichment. The decree to be fruitful comes as the blessing but also includes the ability to be fruitful.

1:27 God created human beings in his own image. The idea that man was created "in the image" here should not be understood to imply that God has a limiting shape (as in pagan conceptions)—God is spirit. "Image" is used figuratively here to indicate that humans share, although imperfectly, in the nature of God in his communicable attributes, such as intelligence, creativity, compassion, and the like.

COMMENTARY

The first creative word of God produced light: "Let there be light" (1:3). This is a majestic, sublime, and amazing decree. God spoke and immediately there was light. The light was natural, physical light. And its creation immediately dispelled and limited the darkness (1:4-5). Light and darkness in the Bible are also symbols of good and evil, of the nature of God and the nature of evil. This initial act of creation finds its final and complete parallel in the age to come when there will be no darkness (Rev 22:5). The Israelites would have appreciated this fact about God's first act of creation, for he had given them light in their dwellings in Egypt when there was darkness on the Egyptians and their sun-god (Exod 10:21-24), and it was his light that led them through the wilderness (Exod 13:21-22). They would know that God is light, and that in him they could know the way to life.

God named the light "day" and the darkness he named "night." In the culture of the ancient Near East, the act of naming was a sovereign act, an act of creation in its own right. The sovereign gives something true existence and identification by ascribing a name to it. The divine evaluation of this light is that it was "good." In Genesis, whatever produces life, preserves life, or enhances life, is "good." The light was the first element that God called good—not the darkness that it countered.

On the second day (1:6-8) God separated the atmospheric waters from the terrestrial waters by an arching expanse or "space" that God called "sky." This may suggest that previously there had been a dense moisture covering the earth. By making this area of atmospheric pressure, God was making further divisions and distinctions within his creation. First light as opposed to darkness, and now water and air as opposed to dense moisture over the whole planet—conditions were beginning to come about that would support life. So God gave the command, and it happened. The report in the text is that "that is what happened." The expression in Hebrew ("and it was so") has a stronger connotation: What God created took its fixed place in time and space and was made perfect in conjunction with all other aspects of creation.

On the third day (1:9-13), God formed dry land with its vegetation. The waters were gathered into reservoirs, called "seas"; and the dry land emerged and produced all kinds of vegetation. This report is uncomplicated and pure compared with the pagan accounts: The sea was not a god that had to be controlled, and vegetation was not the result of some cyclical seasonal myth in which the gods ensured annual fertility. No, God controlled the boundaries of the seas (Job 38:8-11), and God caused everything to grow by his creative decree.[1]

On day four (1:14-19), God made the sun appear and "govern" the day, and the moon to "govern" the night. And the stars appeared in the heavens as well. Either these things were created with apparent age (like Adam) or they had been created earlier and were made visible on earth after God separated light from darkness and the waters above from the waters below. If the latter, the language would be phenomenal, in that it appeared that these were made on the fourth day because that is when they could first be seen from the earth.

The text says that these heavenly bodies were "to separate the day from the night. . . . to mark the season, days, and years" (1:14). Literally, they were signs in the heavens that regulated time. Such terms assume the existence of the sun and the rotation of the planet earth with its moon in its present cycle. The pagan world used the sun, moon, and stars as signs for divination; but the Bible says they declare the glory of God the creator (Ps 19:1). How foolish it was to follow the astrological charts of the Babylonians or the sun-god of Egypt; these were part of God's creation. Divine revelation for guidance comes from the word of the Lord, the same word that made these things the pagans sought. But as Paul says, such people rejected the Creator to worship the creation (Rom 1:25).

In the ancient world, the pagans associated the stars with divinities that they worshiped, whether the sun-god or the moon-god, or the morning star or evening star. They would decide on a course of action based on the phenomena in the heavens. Israel was not permitted to do this for the very reason that Paul later stated (Col 3:5): Idolatry is covetousness, for it seeks to manipulate the deities for personal gain. Deuteronomy 18:14-22 made the prohibition absolute. Israel was not to attempt to divine the future by the stars, or by any other means the pagans used; rather, they were to seek to do the will of God, revealed at times with the Urim and Thummim, but more fully in the messages of the prophets. It was a matter of submission to the sole authority of the God of creation and of avoiding practices that challenged that authority. Later God would confound the stargazers and magicians of Babylon by his clear revelation through Daniel, showing the sovereignty of Yahweh over the deities that these people served (Dan 2:1-28; 5:7-28). It is true that at times God worked through the practices of such groups to reveal his sovereignty; he spoke a blessing through the pagan diviner Balaam who had been brought to curse Israel (Num 22-24), and drew the magi to Bethlehem with the sign of a star in the east (Matt 2:1-2). But God did not permit his people to become involved in such practices to obtain revelation that he had not given.

The great creatures of the sea and the air were created on the fifth day (1:20-23). Here we have the second use of the verb "created" (*bara'* [TH1254, ZH1343]; 1:21) in the chapter. Great sea creatures—whether referring to Leviathan the crocodile, or Behemoth the hippopotamus, or simply to whales or other large sea creatures—were venerated as dragons of the deep in the ancient world. But the use of this verb stresses that they were the creation of God alone, part of the animal world and not evil spirits or monsters at all. Moreover, their ability to be fruitful and multiply was given to them by God Almighty (1:22). This is emphasized by the statement that God "blessed them" (see note on 1:22).

The climax of the six days of creation is the creation of animal and human life (1:24-31). Everything created prior to this prepared for the final creation of human beings. And although man is the last creature mentioned in the days of creation, he did not evolve from earlier forms, but was separately formed by God. He was made from the dust of the ground, not from earlier life-forms; and he was given the breath of life from God and did not gradually develop the breathing and thinking faculties (see 2:7).

Only human life is called God's image. The term "image" applies equally to male and female, for that is what makes up the human race. It is used figuratively here, and does not refer to physical shape or outer appearance. Being the image of God means that humans share, although imperfectly, in the nature of God—that is, they were given the communicable attributes of intelligence, knowledge, spiritual understanding, creativity, wisdom, love, compassion, holiness, justice, and the like. As the text will explain (2:7), all these capacities were given by the inbreathing of the breath of life. Thus, humans have the capacity to commune with the living God, as well as with one another.

God's image in humans is functional: As God's representatives on earth, humans were to rule and have dominion over it (1:26, 28). The terminology may be borrowed from the Egyptian world where kings would set up colossal statues of themselves as signs of their authority over the region (cf. von Rad 1962:1.146). But God's image was alive—it was placed in living human beings, who would be responsible for carrying out that dominion. Unfortunately, when sin entered the human race, their capacities were greatly diminished. And because of sin, "all things" are not under mankind's dominion (Heb 2:8). By rebelling against God, the humans forfeited their right to rule and have dominion as God's representatives; they were expelled from the garden to scratch out a simple living from an unproductive ground, and outside the presence of God, life would be difficult and far more dangerous. Only in the victory of Christ over sin and Satan would there be the hope of the restoration of this dominion. Jesus will establish dominion over all the earth at his coming (Heb 2:5-8), and we will reign with him on earth (Rev 5:10).

God's blessing of the male and the female empowered them to be fruitful. This blessing could only come from God, for he alone can give life and make it productive. Later, the nation of Israel would come to realize how God had blessed them with descendants in fulfillment of his promises to Abraham (ch 15; 18:1-19; 22:1-19; Exod 1:7).

ENDNOTES
1. For detailed studies of the pagan myths, see W. G. Lambert and A. R. Millard, *Atrahasis* (Oxford: Clarendon, 1969); J. H. Grøndbaek, "Baal's Battle with Yam—A Canaanite Creation Fight," *Journal for the Study of the Old Testament* 33 (1985): 27-44; C. Kloos, *Yhwh's Combat with the Sea. A Canaanite Tradition in the Religion of Ancient Israel* (Leiden: E. J. Brill, 1986); John Day, *God's Conflict with the Dragon and the Sea* (Cambridge: Cambridge University Press, 1985); T. Jacobsen, "The Eridu Genesis," *Journal of Biblical Literature* 100 (1981): 513-529; J. D. Currid, "An Examination of the Egyptian Background of the Genesis Cosmogony," *Biblische Zeitschrift* (1991): 18-40; S. Dalley, *Myths from Mesopotamia: Creation, the Flood, Gilgamesh, and Others* (Oxford: Oxford University Press, 1991); J. H. Walton, *Ancient Israelite Literature in Its Cultural Context* (Grand Rapids: Zondervan, 1989).

◆ ## 3. Sabbath rest (2:1-3)

So the creation of the heavens and the earth and everything in them was completed. ²On the seventh day God had finished his work of creation, so he rested* from all his work. ³And God blessed the seventh day and declared it holy, because it was the day when he rested from all his work of creation.

2:2 Or *ceased*; also in 2:3.

NOTES

2:2 he rested. Critical to this section is the meaning of the verb *shabath* [TH7673, ZH8697]. It has traditionally been translated "to rest," but its basic meaning is "to cease." It is used in the OT to show how things ceased (like a war) or came to rest or stopped (like the ark on dry ground). The concept of refreshment on Sabbath day observance is expressed by the verb *napash* [TH5314, ZH5882] in Exod 23:12; 31:17.

2:3 declared it holy. The word *qadash* [TH6942, ZH7727] means "to be holy"—that is, set apart, unique, distinct. In the verbal stem used in this passage it is traditionally translated "sanctified"—that is, to make the day holy, or to set it apart for a special purpose. That is a little clearer than saying the day was declared holy.

COMMENTARY

The culmination of the account of creation is the seventh day, commonly referred to as the "Sabbath day." In a series of carefully constructed sentences designed to emphasize the number seven and stress the adjective "seventh," the account reports that God completed his work of creation and "rested," or better, "ceased" from his creating by the seventh day (see note on 2:2). The idea is more of a celebration of the completion of creation than a rest from labor because, unlike humans, God would not need to restore his energy by resting. According to the law, the people of God were to cease from their labors to devote the seventh day to the worship and service of God (Exod 20:8; 31:13). Keeping the Sabbath day would become the sign of the covenant at Sinai (Exod 31:13), for by it people would attest to their being in covenant with the God of creation.

"God blessed the seventh day and declared it holy" (or, more precisely, set it apart for special use—see note on 2:3) because it commemorated the completeness of his work. Those who participated in it by faith knew that it was not a mere holiday, but a true holy day. What was done on this day was to be set apart to the worship and service of the Lord, and it was to be a celebration because the people of God were to participate in the glory of creation that God had prepared for them.

The Sabbath day is a prominent motif throughout the Bible. Before sin entered the world, it represented the perfection of creation—complete, sanctified, and at rest. After the Fall, this sanctified rest became a goal to be sought. The celebration of the rest in the Promised Land after the conquest demanded faith and obedience by the people of God. But they often lacked this faith so that they never fully realized the promise of rest (Ps 95). In the fullness of time, however, Jesus declared that those who come to him by faith will receive this rest (Matt 11:28). Since then, all who believe in him enter into the Sabbath rest spiritually (Heb 4:8-11) and will certainly share in its full restoration at the end of the age.

The account of creation, seen through the eyes of the Israelites who were given the law, had great theological significance—as it does for the people of God in any age: God delivered his people out of the chaos and darkness of the pagan world, teaching them the truth, guaranteeing them victory over the powers of heaven and earth, commissioning them to be his representatives, and promising them theocratic rest—that is, they would live in peace and security in the abundance of the

◆ B. The Account of the Succession from the Creation (2:4–4:26)
1. The creation of man (2:4-7)

⁴This is the account of the creation of the heavens and the earth.

When the LORD God made the earth and the heavens, ⁵neither wild plants nor grains were growing on the earth. For the LORD God had not yet sent rain to water the earth, and there were no people to cultivate the soil. ⁶Instead, springs* came up from the ground and watered all the land. ⁷Then the LORD God formed the man from the dust of the ground. He breathed the breath of life into the man's nostrils, and the man became a living person.

2:6 Or *mist*.

NOTES

2:4 *This is the account of the creation.* The first part of this verse should not be divided from the next sentence in the verse; in the Hebrew it forms a beautiful parallel construction: "These are the generations of the heavens and the earth when they were created, when the LORD God made earth and heaven." The word "generations" (*toledoth* [TH8435, ZH9352]; NLT, "account") is used throughout Genesis as a heading, and never as a colophon (see Introduction, "The Literary Structure of Genesis"). So 2:4a should not be read as a summary of 1:1–2:3 but as the heading of the next section.

2:4b-7 The arrangement of the material in this brief introduction to the creation of the man follows the same pattern of clauses that was in 1.1-3. There is a title mentioning that God created the heavens and the earth (2:4), and three circumstantial clauses, two negative and one positive (lit., "before any shrub had yet appeared," "before any cultivated grain grew," and "a spring used to well up and water the surface of the ground"), parallel to 1:2 ("The earth was formless and empty," "darkness covered the deep waters," and "the Spirit of God was hovering"). And then follows the formal beginning of the narrative with the Waw consecutive form of the verb ("Then the LORD God formed") in v. 7 (parallel to 1:3). After the two negative circumstantial clauses, two causal clauses explain the circumstances: There were no wild shrubs *because it had not rained,* and there was no cultivated grain *because there was no man to work the ground.*

COMMENTARY

The expression "this is the account of" (lit., "these are the generations of") provides the heading for this second section of the book, 2:4–4:26. As the expression indicates, the section will tell "what became of" the heavens and the earth that God had made. The word *toledoth* [TH8435, ZH9352] ("account" or "generations") applies to narratives and genealogies alike. As a heading it marks a starting point, expressed by the following genitive, here "of the heavens and the earth." The story develops from the starting point of the creation of the heavens and the earth. It begins with a brief account of the creation of people, then moves to the temptation, sin, and the curse. In other words, what became of the creation of God is that sin entered it and changed it drastically. Thus, the material here is not a second and conflicting account of creation by a different source, as the old Documentary Hypothesis proposed, but a detailed account of how sin entered the world through the disobedience of Eve and Adam. The section includes a more detailed account of their creation in order to show the spiritual and intellectual capacities God had invested in them, and is not at odds with the general statement in Genesis 1 (for further comments on the use of such "doublets," see Doukhan 1978:78-79; Kikawada 1983). Because this passage begins with a more detailed explanation of the creation of the man and the woman and their immediate world, it will stress what God had invested in them as his servants on earth. Chapter 2, then, forms the basis for the account of the temptation and the disobedience in chapter 3.

Beginning with this section, the personal, covenant name of God, Yahweh, is used throughout (represented in most English Bibles as "LORD"). The repeated emphasis on "Yahweh God" ("the LORD God") is significant, for it makes it clear that the sovereign God of creation is indeed Israel's covenant God, Yahweh. Israel, whom Yahweh was forming into his covenant people, would be encouraged to know that their God had created everything and formed human beings by his special design.

The emphasis on creation by design comes from the use of the verb "to form" (*yatsar* [TH3335, ZH3670]). Forming human life involved the shaping of the man from the dust and the breathing of life into the man. This verb portrays God as an artist; its participle form is the word for "potter," an image of the Creator used elsewhere in the Bible (e.g., Jer 18:6). Memory of this divine work has been retained even in the pagan world of Egypt, which imagines the god Knum fashioning the person on a potter's wheel, and the goddess Hathor looking on and extending the ankh, the sign of life (Lurker 1974:74). It is clear that the ancient religions had preserved traditions about creation from generation to generation. With continual telling of the stories and the regular enactment of the ideas in their religious rituals, they kept alive the memory of the beginning of life, though gradually embellished with other religious ideas.

In the biblical account, the man was formed by the Lord God in accordance with a divine plan. He was made from the earth, as the wordplay between *'adam* [TH120, ZH132] (human) and *'adamah* [TH127, ZH141] (ground) emphasizes (2:7-9, 19; 3:17). Man is "earthy," in spite of his aspiration to be like God (3:5). God will remind him that he was dust, and would return to the dust (3:19).

God's breathing "the breath of life" into the man transformed him into a living being ("living person," 2:7, NLT). "Person" represents *nepesh* [TH5315, ZH5883] (soul, being), which refers here to the whole person. Since both animals and humans are referred to as *nepesh* (cf. 1:21, 24), the translation "being" works best.

It is the way in which the man came to be a living being that distinguishes him from the animals. God breathed into his nostrils "the breath of life" (2:7). This breath (*neshamah* [TH5397, ZH5972]) from God made man a living spiritual being, with the capacity for spiritual understanding, discerning right from wrong, and communing with God. With this special act of creation, the reader can appreciate the significance of the Fall. When sin entered the human race, the spiritual capacities were ruined, making a re-creation essential for fellowship with God. Since the Fall, regeneration by the divine Breath, the Holy Spirit, is essential for people to be restored to the life God had intended them to have from the beginning (cf. John 20:22).

2. The creation of the garden (2:8-14)

⁸Then the LORD God planted a garden in Eden in the east, and there he placed the man he had made. ⁹The LORD God made all sorts of trees grow up from the ground—trees that were beautiful and that produced delicious fruit. In the middle of the garden he placed the tree of life and the tree of the knowledge of good and evil.

¹⁰A river flowed from the land of Eden, watering the garden and then dividing into four branches. ¹¹The first branch, called the Pishon, flowed around the entire land of Havilah, where gold is found. ¹²The gold of that land is exceptionally pure; aromatic resin and onyx stone are also found there. ¹³The second branch, called the Gihon, flowed around the entire land of Cush. ¹⁴The third branch, called the Tigris, flowed east of the land of Asshur. The fourth branch is called the Euphrates.

NOTES

2:8 *a garden in Eden.* The garden was planted "in Eden," which seems to indicate that the whole region was a fruitful place of pleasure. Within Eden, the garden was the epitome of all creation.

in the east. The location of the garden is one of speculation. All we can say is that the names of the rivers give us a hint that it may have been in the middle of the Fertile Crescent, perhaps in the northern and central region (the area north of the Persian Gulf). If the rivers ran the same course then that they did in the days when this text was written, then the Tigris and the Euphrates flowed southeast from the region of Turkey and Syria which would put the source in the north. The first river, Pishon, went around Havilah, a term used later in the Bible for the regions of Arabia and Ethiopia. The second river, the Gihon, is unknown; but it went around Cush, a word related to the Kassites in the mountains east of Mesopotamia, although the word can be used for Ethiopia, too. If the Fertile Crescent is the approximate location of Eden, then much has changed since the days of its lush fertility.

2:9 *the tree of life.* The genitive after "tree" must be an objective genitive meaning "the tree that produced life." Interpreting it as "living tree" would not make it distinctive.

the tree of the knowledge of good and evil. This was a tree that God designated for the test so that eating from it would bring the knowledge of good and evil.

COMMENTARY

The man was placed in a perfect setting. God planted a garden, which would be a source of enjoyment as well as a place of testing. The description of the lavish garden (2:8) and the trees (2:9) and the river in it (2:10) leads up to the commandment that all of it could be enjoyed and used—if the word of God was obeyed and the forbidden fruit not eaten (2:17).

In this garden, God caused every kind of tree to grow. Among them was one that produced and preserved life ("the tree of life"), and another that produced knowledge ("the tree of the knowledge of good and evil") in those that ate it. The "knowledge" would be experiential; eating from this tree would enable the people to alter life for better or for worse. "Good and evil" effectively refers to all knowledge that would control life, whether promoting it or destroying it. The potential for disaster was enormous if mankind overstepped its bounds and tried to manipulate life. People might think that they were improving on what God had done, but in the process they would destroy it, for they did not have the wisdom of God necessary to make such changes. The tree of life, on the other hand, was apparently a means of preserving and enhancing the life of people in this blissful estate, for eating from it would keep them alive perpetually (3:22).

Verses 10-14 form a long parenthesis in the narrative; they describe the richness of the then-known world that God had made for mankind. The river was God's sustaining provision for life, not only in Eden but in the world. The trees (2:9), the river (2:10), and the pure gold and precious gems (2:11-12) emphasize what God had invested in this garden sanctuary. These elements would also be present in the heavenly sanctuary in the new creation (Rev 21:10-11, 21; 22:1-2), thus indicating that paradise will be restored on the new earth.

The story of Paradise has received a variety of interpretations over the years. Some scholars view it as an ancient Semitic myth, a story told to explain reality. But Semitic myths typically involve many gods and goddesses, follow a cyclical pattern of seasons and events, and seek to secure the cycle of life with a ritual of sympathetic magic. The Bible, on the other hand, has one God who is sovereign, follows a historical sequence from creation to redemption, and declares that all of creation is governed and controlled by God's decrees.

Others would approach the story as a literary device, presumably a parable, although seldom is the literary device in its particulars identified and explained. Here one must be careful of the implications of the interpretation. The Bible makes it clear that God created everything by his powerful word and that he created one man and one woman to begin the human race. It was by the disobedience of this one man, through the serpent's beguiling of the woman, that sin entered into the world. If God did not create human life, then there is no basis for morality and ethics; and if there was no historical fall of the human race into sin, then there is no need for redemption. If there was an Adam and an Eve at the very beginning, then there is little reason to doubt there was a garden with trees, water, and precious gems, especially when the text gives names and locations for the rivers and the garden. And there is little reason to doubt that Satan was there in disguise (see commentary on 1:1-2). Naturally, in Genesis these elements also include symbolic meanings which will be used throughout Scripture; and the record of the events includes a number of figures of speech. But in view of the way the narrative is detailed, and in view of the clear references to many of these details in the Bible, the burden of proof must rest with those who choose to interpret the material in a literary form that eliminates the reality of the people, places, and events, and asserts that the New Testament references were made to fictional records.[1]

ENDNOTES

1. For more information on the various literary approaches to the text, see, e.g., Gunn and Fewell 1993; Blocher 1984; Cohn 1983; and for an assessment, see Longman 1987:47-64.

◆ ## 3. The first commandment (2:15-17)

¹⁵The LORD God placed the man in the Garden of Eden to tend and watch over it. ¹⁶But the LORD God warned him, "You may freely eat the fruit of every tree in the garden—¹⁷except the tree of the knowledge of good and evil. If you eat its fruit, you are sure to die."

NOTES

2:15 to tend and watch. In Hebrew the two infinitives, "to work it" and "to take care of it," have feminine singular suffixes; however, "garden" is masculine. This is in itself not an insurmountable problem, but taken in conjunction with other considerations about the text, may call for a different interpretation. Cassuto (1964:1.122-123) observes that in similar constructions in the Bible the final He (ה) is added to the infinitive and has no *mappiq* (e.g., 1:29-30; Exod 29:29; 30:18). If the forms in this passage were taken as infinitives without a pronominal suffix, the sentence would then be saying "for serving and for keeping" without making a specific reference to the garden. This is the way that the rabbinic teaching took the line in *Genesis Rabbah* 16:5, "These denote the sacrifices, as it is said, You shall serve God [Exod 3:12], and as it is written, you shall take heed [lit., "keep"] to offer to Me in its due seasons [Num 28:2]." Cassuto concludes that there is no reason to emend the text to masculine pronouns, or to look for a feminine form earlier in the passage, for the forms are probably infinitives. Accordingly, Wenham (1986) concludes that the garden was a sanctuary and that the humans in it were to function as the later Levites would in the Tabernacle.

COMMENTARY

Man was created to be a spiritual servant in this perfect environment, as the subsequent descriptions and commandments indicate. He was "placed" (*nuakh* [TH5117, ZH5663], "set to rest"; 2:15) "in the Garden . . . to tend and watch over it." This traditional interpretation gives the impression that he was placed there to be a gardener. The verbs *'abad* [TH5647, ZH6268] and *shamar* [TH8104, ZH9068], however, are also two very important religious words in the Pentateuch. The verb "serve" (*'abad*) is used frequently in the Pentateuch for serving the Lord (Deut 28:47). With reference to the Tabernacle, the word was used for the duties of the Levites (see Num 3:7-8; 4:23-24, 26). And throughout Scripture the truly devout person is called "the servant of the Lord" (cf. Deut 34:5). The verb "keep" (*shamar*) also has a wide range of uses. But its religious use is that of observing spiritual duties or keeping the commandments (Lev 18:5). It is the word used for the duty of the Levites to guard the Tabernacle (see Num 1:53; 3:7-8 and elsewhere for the expression "they shall keep the charge": *weshameru 'eth-mishmereth* [TH4931, ZH5466]). In places where these two verbs are found together, we have the duties of the Levites (see Num 3:7-8; 8:26; 18:5-6). It is no surprise, then, that of the possible Hebrew verbs for "placed," the one chosen derives from *nuakh* [TH5117, ZH5663], "to rest," and here, "set to rest," for this word would be more appropriate to a context of sanctuary service than working the ground. The word is behind the usage of the noun *menukhah* [TH4496, ZH4957], which refers to the land as God's "rest" (Ps 95:11), a place that God would choose as a "resting place," a sanctuary (Ps 132:14). If the word refers to gardening here, it is hard to know what needed to be done. Besides, it was the result of sin that caused the man to be expelled from the garden to work the ground from which he was taken (3:23). The indications are that man was created to be a spiritual servant. When he sinned, his work became focused on serving the ground to survive, while the work of keeping the way to the tree of life was given over to the angels (3:24).

If this understanding is correct, verse 16 makes even more sense, and the choice of wording there has even greater significance. Here we find the first use in the Bible of *tsawah* [TH6680, ZH7422] (to command). The spiritual commandments begin here for the servant of the Lord. God's first order concerned life and death, good and evil. As with all God's subsequent commands, there were positive blessings and negative prohibitions. All earthly goods and pleasures were at the man's disposal, except one forbidden tree. The Hebrew wording in verses 16-17 states the command in the strongest terms: "You may freely eat" (*'akol to'kel* [TH398, ZH430]) from all the trees, but when you eat from the forbidden tree "you are sure to die" (*moth tamuth* [TH4191, ZH4637]).

Once again the primary point is made to the original readers/hearers, the people of God under Moses, the lawgiver. God had prepared mankind with the capacity for moral and spiritual responsibility. He set them in a beautiful garden to be his obedient servants, warning them that if they disobeyed his word, there would be death. Deuteronomy 30:11-20 set forth the same warning for Israel as they were poised to enter the Promised Land, using motifs that parallel Genesis 2:8-17: Obedience to the commandments of God brings life and blessing in the land God prepared, but disobedience brings expulsion from the land and death.

◆ ### 4. The creation of woman (2:18-25)

¹⁸Then the LORD God said, "It is not good for the man to be alone. I will make a helper who is just right for him." ¹⁹So the LORD God formed from the ground all the wild animals and all the birds of the sky. He brought them to the man* to see what he would call them, and the man chose a name for each one. ²⁰He gave names to all the livestock, all the birds of the sky, and all the wild animals. But still there was no helper just right for him.

²¹So the LORD God caused the man to fall into a deep sleep. While the man slept, the LORD God took out one of the man's ribs* and closed up the opening. ²²Then the LORD God made a woman from the rib, and he brought her to the man.

²³"At last!" the man exclaimed.

"This one is bone from my bone,
 and flesh from my flesh!
She will be called 'woman,'
 because she was taken from 'man.'"

²⁴This explains why a man leaves his father and mother and is joined to his wife, and the two are united into one.

²⁵Now the man and his wife were both naked, but they felt no shame.

2:19 Or *Adam*, and so throughout the chapter. 2:21 Or *took a part of the man's side*.

NOTES

2:18 I will make a helper. The word "helper" in this section is not a demeaning term at all; in the Bible it is used most frequently of God (Pss 33:20; 70:5; 115:9). When God helps people, it means he does for them what they cannot possibly do for themselves. In this context the word indicates that the woman would supply what man lacked and, by implication of the Hebrew behind the phrase, "just right for him," that he would provide what she lacked. Together they would be complete and completely able to produce life.

2:24 This explains. Lit., "for this reason" (*'al ken* [TH5921/3651A, ZH6584/4027]). These words are used frequently in Genesis to explain a given event as the basis of a later custom. For example, we find the expression used to explain the naming of Babel (11:9), the meaning of the name of Esau as Edom (25:30), and the Israelite custom of not eating the sinew of the hip (32:32).

why a man leaves. If the words in 2:24 are understood as spoken by God (or Adam) at the time of the events, then the verbs could be translated in the future tense: "will leave" (cf. KJV, NIV). But if the explanatory clause is understood as written by Moses (no less inspired), the verb stands in the present tense as in the NLT (cf. RSV, HCSB). The principle established here is that the man will initiate the separation from his parents and establish a new union with his wife. This was the normal and expected procedure for marriage; the fact that it was not always followed does not nullify the fact that from the beginning there was a design for marriage (in a similar way, polygamy became common but was not the plan of the Creator).

COMMENTARY

Adam was alone, and that was "not good." Everything else in creation was good, but this was not. By saying "not good" the text means that by himself the man could not fulfill the plan of God to be fruitful and multiply or rule and have dominion. As he began to function as God's representative, naming the animals (2:19-20), he was made even more aware that he was alone. God had made this human as a social being, and solitude was a serious problem on several levels. The man by himself could not produce life, and by himself he would not have everything he needed to serve the living God. God therefore put him into a deep sleep (2:21) and created the woman from his flesh and his bone, prompting the man to exclaim how she corresponded so well to him (2:21-23). Now with a partner, God's creation was "very good" (cf. 1:31).

The woman is described as a helper, which means that she supplied what he lacked (see note on 2:18), and by implication the reverse would also be true. That is why the woman as a helper is said to be "corresponding to him" (NLT, "just right for him"). In the Hebrew this phrase (*kenegdo* [TH3509.1/5048A, ZH3869/5584]) is very precise; it is literally "according to the opposite of him" and means that she corresponds perfectly to him. In other words, because God created the woman from the man, she has everything that God had invested in him (2:7). They both would have the same nature. They both were the image of God. Since the man and the woman were without sin, living in their perfect environment, there was no need for instruction on headship and authority at this point. That would come once sin entered the race; and Paul would discuss that need for Christians, reasoning in part from the order of creation (1 Cor 11:3; 1 Tim 2:13).

The culmination of the account says that these two became "one flesh"—one complete unity of man and woman in marriage ("united into one," 2:24, NLT). The phrase "one flesh" or "united into one" refers to their total life together—the physical, spiritual, intellectual, and emotional union. They came together in body and spirit, sharing everything in common as they enjoyed God's world together and sought to obey him as one.

The nakedness of the pair (2:25) suggests more than their physical condition; it stresses the fact that they were completely at ease with each other. There was no fear of exploitation, no potential for evil. Nakedness was a sign of their purity and integrity. Such communion was shattered by the Fall and is only restored in a measure in marriage as a couple becomes more at ease with each other. The physical aspect of the relationship between a man and a woman can only be pure and meaningful when the spiritual union is there and the couple is united in serving God with their lives daily.

Thus, in this section we have the account of the creation of the first woman and the institution of marriage; it has much to say about the mainstay of Israel's society and ours. God intended one man and one woman to be united in marriage to produce godly offspring. God intended that the man and the woman be a spiritual, functioning unity, walking in integrity, serving God together, and keeping his commandments. When this harmony is operative, society flourishes under God's blessing. Improper innovations only introduce chaos and ruin into society (see 4:19; 6:1-4).

◆ 5. The temptation (3:1-7)

The serpent was the shrewdest of all the wild animals the LORD God had made. One day he asked the woman, "Did God really say you must not eat the fruit from any of the trees in the garden?"

²"Of course we may eat fruit from the trees in the garden," the woman replied. ³"It's only the fruit from the tree in the middle of the garden that we are not allowed to eat. God said, 'You must not eat it or even touch it; if you do, you will die.'"

⁴"You won't die!" the serpent replied to the woman. ⁵"God knows that your eyes will be opened as soon as you eat it, and you will be like God, knowing both good and evil."

⁶The woman was convinced. She saw that the tree was beautiful and its fruit looked delicious, and she wanted the wisdom it would give her. So she took some of the fruit and ate it. Then she gave some to her husband, who was with her, and he ate it, too. ⁷At that moment their eyes were opened, and they suddenly felt shame at their nakedness. So they sewed fig leaves together to cover themselves.

NOTES

3:1 *serpent.* The tempter appears in this narrative as a serpent. The fact that Genesis says that the temptation came through a serpent, and that Rev 12:7 and 20:2 refer to the devil as a serpent, would suggest that Satan used the form of an actual reptile. This enhanced the shrewdness of the temptation—it came in disguise. It is not until the book of Revelation that we get a confirmation that this was Satan (Rev 12:7; 20:2). In the oracle delivered to the serpent after the Fall, part of it refers to the serpent (3:14) and part to the spiritual force behind it (3:15). But some interpretations suggest that the reference to a serpent is to Satan, who tempted Eve like a serpent (presumably meaning shrewdly, although the point of the implied comparison to a serpent is not clear). This would make sense as a polemic in the ancient world, where serpents were often venerated as mystical powers of life. Still others would simply describe it as storytelling or ancient mythology (see Day 1985), to explain how evil entered the world. Even if one of these were the case, the interpreter would still have to explain why a serpent was chosen and how these passages relate to prophetic oracles that depict the removal of the Curse with serpent figures (see Isa 11:8; 27:1).

3:6 *the tree was beautiful . . . looked delicious . . . wisdom it would give.* In Hebrew, these three clauses describe the appealing aspects of the tree with respect to three areas: It seemed good *for food,* pleasing *to the eyes,* and desirable *for wisdom.*

COMMENTARY

Genesis 3 provides the record of the historical fall of human beings into sin and death. It is also a picture of what temptation is like. The passage is about Adam and Eve to be sure, but it is also about all of us, every man and every woman, because the narrative is archetypal. The Fall appears as the result of temptation alone—the sin cannot be attributed to heredity nor the environment. And the tempter prompted them to sin. Thus, Paul could write that we are not ignorant of Satan's devices—we have them displayed right here (2 Cor 2:11; 11:1-4). Moreover, the pattern of the temptation in the garden has as its counterpart the temptation of Jesus in Matthew 4:1-11; there Jesus defeated Satan by his precise obedience to the commands of God. Later, Jesus identified Satan as a murderer and a liar from the very beginning (John 8:44) when he denounced his opponents as the "children of your father the devil."

In the first two chapters of Genesis, God had been the dominant speaker, not only in creation but in instructing his creation on what to do and what not to do. Now the serpent spoke. The word of the Lord brought life and order; the word of the serpent brought deception and death. By its very nature, truth is older than falsehood; God's words came before the serpent's words, but the serpent's words were more effective because the humans did not know God's words well enough.

The text begins with the report that the serpent was more shrewd than any of the creatures God had made. The text presents the temptation coming from what was clearly a reptile, for it states that the "serpent" spoke to the woman. We know that the tempter was Satan using the creature, but the woman did not, for temptation is most effective when it comes in disguise. After this event, the serpent became the symbol of the Curse and certainly one of danger. In Egypt, the people had seen the serpent venerated as either a force of life or of death, for the tombs were painted with snakes, and the king even wore a stylized serpent on his headdress. The Israelites would have regarded the serpent as an evil force because it was often a symbol of death, and its status as a symbol of life would have been rejected since only the Lord can produce life. Thus, in addition to its importance as the account of how evil entered the human race, this narrative also has a polemical force, showing the connection of the serpent with rebellion against God, which is death. In other words, divinity cannot be achieved (as promised in 3:5) by following the pagan beliefs and symbols, for they only bring death. The reason that Satan used a reptile in the first place helped conceal the temptation since it came through a subordinate creature, one over whom they were to have dominion (1:28). In short, Adam and Eve would have been less guarded against such an attack.

The text of Genesis gives no indication that the serpent had a different form or nature before the judgment decree other than perhaps its mobility. It is described as being more shrewd or wily than any other creature that God made, and so was cursed more than any other creature. Its restriction to crawling on its belly indicates it kept the same form but is now limited in the sphere of its movement. Moreover, crawling on its belly and eating dust are also symbolic of defeat. Ever after, the snake would be a physical reminder of the Curse, as it had been the physical representation of the tempter. In the promises of the new creation, the serpents will be rendered harmless as a sign that the curse is lifted (Isa 11:8).

The description of the serpent's shrewdness (*'arum* [TH6175, ZH6874]; 3:1) employs a wordplay with the description of the humans' nakedness (*'arummim*, [TH6174, ZH6873]; 2:25). The similar sounding words indicate that their integrity (see commentary on 2:25) was the target of his shrewd dealings. Shrewdness is not in itself an evil characteristic; the book of Proverbs is designed to train people to have this quality (Prov 1:4). The word denotes wariness, knowing where the traps and pitfalls are. Jesus instructed his disciples that in this world they needed to be as shrewd as serpents, but as harmless as doves (Matt 10:16). Satan was not harmless; Adam and Eve were. Satan was able to use his knowledge to ruin them. The nature of the temptation was a discussion about the word of God, not about an obscure meaning of a minor text, but about a clear-cut prohibition from God. Likewise today, when Satan wants to undermine the faith, it is the word of God that is attacked, the indisputably clear teachings of Scripture on doctrine and morality. In the narrative, Satan asked the woman about the commandment in a way that could not be answered with a yes or a no; it was designed to turn the word of God into a topic of debate. And it soon became clear that the woman did not know precisely what God had said. Whether this was her fault for getting it wrong or Adam's for telling it to her this way, we cannot know. By contrast, Jesus was able to defeat Satan in his temptation because he knew the word of the Lord better than Satan (Matt 4:4, 7, 10). Satan used passages from the Scripture, but Christ used passages in harmony with the whole revelation of God.

In answering the serpent, Eve made three changes in what God said, slight changes to be sure, but changes that opened the door to sin. First, God had said, "You may *freely* eat" but the woman simply said, "We may eat," minimizing the privileges (cf. 2:16-17; 3:2-3). Secondly, with her focus on the prohibition she added to it "or even touch it." Third, and most seriously, she lessened the emphasis on punishment by saying "lest you die" (rather than the stronger expression, "You shall surely die," which God had used). That this failure to preserve the exact words of God was at the heart of the temptation is clear from the response of the serpent, for when he heard what she said, he replied, "You won't die!" (The construction is unusual, with the negative particle placed blatantly in front of the very words God used of the penalty in 2:17.) Since she was not convinced of the certainty of death for sin, he was free to deny it (3:4). This is why Jesus explained that Satan was a liar from the beginning (John 8:44). The lie is that people can sin and get away with it. But death is the penalty of sin (2:17), as the man and the woman would immediately discover.

But the tempter went a step further and raised doubts about God's character. He implied that God was wrongly jealous, holding the humans back from their full potential which was to be like God, "knowing both good and evil" (3:5). So Satan held out for them the promise of divinity with the power to alter life.

With the penalty out of the way, and the character of God poisoned, the appeal of the forbidden fruit worked on the desires of the woman. When the text says that the tree was "desirable," (NLT, "she wanted") it uses a word that occurs later in the law: "You must not covet" (Exod 20:17). But the physical practicality (good for food), aesthetic beauty (pleasing to the eye), and the potential for gaining godlike wisdom (desirable to make one wise) were all too powerful for her (see note on 3:6). And they are too powerful for us as well if the barrier of punishment is removed and the goodness and wisdom of God in the prohibition is not trusted.

The temptation was over. The resistance was gone. So the narrative rapidly winds up: "She took . . . and ate it. Then she gave some to her husband, who was with her, and he ate it, too." But the results were not what they expected; they immediately were aware that they were naked—that is, guilty and vulnerable. They had been deceived; the promise of becoming divine did not come about, for one cannot become like God by defying God. Wisdom is never gained by disobeying the Lord; the fear of the Lord is the beginning of wisdom (Prov 1:7). Their eyes were opened to be sure, but everything they saw was spoiled. Adam and Eve were no longer at ease with each other. Mistrust and alienation in their relationship was a result of sin; and they were now afraid in the garden because they were alienated from God. Death had already immediately begun to work in them, because death is separation. Spiritual death is separation from God, and physical death is separation from life. Thus, we find that Adam and Eve were told that when they ate they would surely die (2:17). Similarly, the Scriptures describe death as being cut off from the land of the living or from the people (Lev 18:29; 20:6, 17; Isa 38:10-12). And this leads to the New Testament terminology of spiritual death for people who do not believe in the Lord (Eph 2:1), and a second death for them after the resurrection from the first death (Rev 20:6, 14; 21:8).

◆ ## 6. The results of sin (3:8-24)

⁸When the cool evening breezes were blowing, the man* and his wife heard the Lord God walking about in the garden. So they hid from the Lord God among the trees. ⁹Then the Lord God called to the man, "Where are you?"

¹⁰He replied, "I heard you walking in the garden, so I hid. I was afraid because I was naked."

¹¹"Who told you that you were naked?" the Lord God asked. "Have you eaten from the tree whose fruit I commanded you not to eat?"

¹²The man replied, "It was the woman

you gave me who gave me the fruit, and I ate it."

¹³Then the LORD God asked the woman, "What have you done?"

"The serpent deceived me," she replied. "That's why I ate it."

¹⁴Then the LORD God said to the serpent,

"Because you have done this, you are cursed
    more than all animals, domestic and wild.
You will crawl on your belly,
    groveling in the dust as long as you live.
¹⁵ And I will cause hostility between you and the woman,
    and between your offspring and her offspring.
He will strike* your head,
    and you will strike his heel."

¹⁶Then he said to the woman,

"I will sharpen the pain of your pregnancy,
    and in pain you will give birth.
And you will desire to control your husband,
    but he will rule over you.*"

¹⁷And to the man he said,

"Since you listened to your wife and ate from the tree
    whose fruit I commanded you not to eat,
the ground is cursed because of you.
All your life you will struggle to scratch a living from it.
¹⁸ It will grow thorns and thistles for you,
    though you will eat of its grains.
¹⁹ By the sweat of your brow
    will you have food to eat
until you return to the ground
    from which you were made.
For you were made from dust,
    and to dust you will return."

²⁰Then the man—Adam—named his wife Eve, because she would be the mother of all who live.* ²¹And the LORD God made clothing from animal skins for Adam and his wife.

²²Then the LORD God said, "Look, the human beings* have become like us, knowing both good and evil. What if they reach out, take fruit from the tree of life, and eat it? Then they will live forever!" ²³So the LORD God banished them from the Garden of Eden, and he sent Adam out to cultivate the ground from which he had been made. ²⁴After sending them out, the LORD God stationed mighty cherubim to the east of the Garden of Eden. And he placed a flaming sword that flashed back and forth to guard the way to the tree of life.

3:8 Or *Adam*, and so throughout the chapter.   3:15 Or *bruise*; also in 3:15b.   3:16 Or *And though you will have desire for your husband, / he will rule over you.*   3:20 *Eve* sounds like a Hebrew term that means "to give life."   3:22 Or *the man*; Hebrew reads *ha-adam*.

NOTES

3:15 *offspring.* Lit., "seed"; this has several applications. The "seed of the woman" must refer to those born of the woman, first Cain, but then the whole human race. "Seed" is normally used in connection with a man, not a woman (e.g., "the seed of Abraham," 15:5), so here it has a figurative use to refer to those who came from her and share her nature. Ultimately the apostle Paul would draw upon this and other biblical promises of the "seed" to declare their fulfillment in the Son who was "born of a woman" (Gal 4:4). The "seed of the woman," i.e., the human race, will have victory over evil finally in the representative of the race, Jesus Christ, who was born of a virgin, without a human father, so he was truly "the seed of the woman." The word "seed" is also used figuratively for the "seed of the serpent," but it is a different figure. The expression does not refer to baby snakes; it is referring to anyone who shares the nature of the evil one behind the serpent (such as the "sons of vipers," Matt 23:33). Such ungodly people, driven by spirits or demonic forces, would work to destroy life, and ultimately to destroy Christ. But the victory would be Christ's on behalf of the human race.

3:16 *desire to control*. The word "desire" is rightly translated in NLT as "desire to control." The word has often been assumed to mean physical desire, based on its use in the Song of Songs (Song 7:10). But that desire is not a result of sin; it is not a curse. Song of Songs is written in praise of the union of the sexes in marriage as God intended. Genesis 3 is an oracle declaring the effect of sin on the human race. The clue to the interpretation of this word comes from its use in 4:7, where God speaks to Cain, "Sin is crouching at the door, eager to control you [lit., "its desire is for you"]. But you must subdue it and be its master" (lit., "you can have the mastery over it"). It is that kind of struggle that is intended in 3:16, a struggle between desiring to control and mastering. This is not what God wants in a marriage; it is what sin looks like.

COMMENTARY

The remainder of this chapter recounts the results of the entrance of sin into the world; it falls into three sections: the confrontation with the Lord in which the two sinners confess (3:8-13); the oracle of the Lord in which new measures are decreed for the serpent, the woman, and the man (3:14-19); and the provision from the Lord for Adam and Eve (3:20-24). Whereas the pair had life, they now have death; where they had pleasure, they now have pain; where abundance, now a meager subsistence; and where perfect union and communion, now alienation and conflict.

It would take the suffering and death of Jesus to remove this curse. Thus, the motifs of death, toil, sweat, thorns, the tree, the struggle, and the promised seed were all later traced to Christ's passion by the writers of Scripture (Matt 26:36-46; 27:28-30; Gal 3:13). Christ is the last Adam, who became the curse for all of us, who sweat great drops of blood in bitter agony, who wore a crown of thorns, who was hanged on a tree until he was dead, and who was placed in the dust of death (Ps 22:15-18).

The guilty pair hid themselves among the trees when they heard the Lord God walking about in the cool part of the day. When he called for the man, it was not to locate him but to draw from him an explanation as to why he was hiding in fear. The second question, "Who told you that you were naked?" (3:11), was designed to draw a confession out of him. The wording of the sentence in the original text focuses on his disobedience of the command: "Did you, from the tree from which I commanded you not to eat, eat?" The point was that he had broken the commandment. Interestingly, while God asked the man if he disobeyed the command, he asked the woman what she had done. The implication is that the man knew the commandment and deliberately sinned against it, whereas the woman did not know it firsthand, only as Adam told her, and she was beguiled. The apostle Paul will declare, therefore, that it was by one man that sin entered the world (Rom 5:12). Both were responsible for their sin, but one sinned by willful disobedience and the other partly out of ignorance of the precise command and partly by being beguiled. In the end, the man acknowledged that he ate, but not without passing the blame. On the surface it appears that he was only blaming the woman, but the relative clause in the verse shows that ultimately he was trying to put it back on God: "The woman *you* gave me . . . gave me the fruit, and I ate it." But none of that reasoning counted. The question was simple: "Did you eat?"

God then asked the woman, "What have you done?" The force of this construction is something like "What in the world have you done?" And the woman tried to pass the blame to the serpent who beguiled her, but in the end the only thing that mattered was whether or not she ate. No question was asked of the serpent; there was no call for a confession from the tempter. God's word to the tempter simply began, "Because you have done this, you are cursed."

The Lord announced the new order of life that would exist now that sin had entered the human race. The sequence in the interrogation was first the man, then the woman; and then in the oracle of judgment the sequence is reversed, beginning with the serpent, then the woman, and finally the man. The serpent was central to the event; the man was the most responsible because he had received the commands, so his interrogation and his judgment bracket the whole section.

At the center is the pronouncement on the serpent who was cursed more than any other creature because of the evil he had wrought. While God's announcement focused on the serpent (3:14-15), it is clear from both the context itself and the rest of the Bible that part of this oracle addressed the spiritual force that used the reptile—Satan. The first part announced that the serpent would crawl on its belly and eat dust. The NLT correctly interprets this to mean grovel in the dust, a picture of defeat, but the idea of eating dust while crawling on the ground anticipates the fact that humans will become dust again and be the serpent's prey until the victory comes (cf. 2:7). This posture and performance of the serpent would be a perpetual reminder to people of the temptation and the Fall. Ultimate victory would come only when someone would conquer death and remove Satan's greatest weapon.

The oracle quickly turned to the real power behind the snake. God said there would be a perpetual conflict between the serpent and the woman, and between the seed of the serpent and the seed of the woman. The immediate offspring of the woman was Cain, and he did not fair so well in the struggle with evil. The more general offspring from the woman, the mother of all living, is the whole human race, and it has not done any better than Cain. But the apostles saw that the "seed" of the woman ultimately referred to Jesus Christ, who would deliver the crushing blow to Satan on behalf of the human race (Gal 3:16; 4:4). The "seed" of the serpent would ultimately refer to any who oppose the true word of God (John 8:44; see also Matt 3:7). The use of "seed" at first seems out of place in conjunction with the woman, but it would be one who was born of a woman and not of a human father that would gain the victory over sin and death on behalf of the human race (Gal 4:4). The seed of the serpent includes demons and forces of evil that try to destroy the human race (Eph 6:12).

In the immediate context of Genesis 4, a force of evil was crouching at the door to destroy Cain. But the seed of the serpent could also be human, including any person who opposes God and tries to destroy his people. Jesus said that the Pharisees who were trying to destroy him were of their father the devil, and not of their father Abraham as they had professed (John 8:44). According to the oracle in Genesis, the serpent would strike the seed of the woman in the heel, giving a crippling blow, but ultimately the seed of the woman would strike the serpent in the head—a fatal blow. Thus, the prophecy predicts final victory for the human race over the forces of evil. The victory would come through one who is qualified to do this, one born of a woman, one not contaminated with sin, one who is able to destroy sin and death.

In the next section God speaks to the woman (3:16). The oracle declared that God would multiply the pain—that is, physical and emotional pain along with anxiety—in conception. The word "conception" is figurative, for there is no pain in conception. It is a synecdoche, a part representing the whole, meaning that from the very beginning of the process (conception), the act of bringing children into the world will be painful. This is corroborated in the next line that clarifies: "In pain you will give birth." There is no reason to limit the pain to childbirth; it refers to the whole process of bearing and rearing children. Some of this certainly came to fulfillment when Mary brought the baby Jesus to the Temple and was told that a sword would pierce her soul (Luke 2:35).

The other half of the oracle about the effect of sin concerns the conflict the woman would experience with her husband. The clue for the interpretation of this text comes from the fact that God himself used these words to warn Cain about the conflict he was facing: "Sin is crouching at the door, eager to control you. But you must subdue it and be its master" (4:7; see note on 3:16). The words represent a struggle for control—sin wanted to have Cain (just as Satan desired to have Peter; Luke 22:31), but Cain could master it. That struggle would characterize life from now on, and in 3:16 we see that it would manifest itself in marriage too. Thus, the oracle is saying that the sinful nature of the woman, we would say at her worst, will "desire to control" the man, as Eve had done naively in the garden. And the sinful nature of the man, we would say at his worst, will try to dominate the woman. Human life, even in a marriage, will frequently display such a conflict or struggle.

We will see this tension work out in the marriages of the patriarchs, such as with Abraham and Sarah, and Isaac and Rebekah. It will be the challenge of godly people to remove such tension from a marriage and live above the Curse as far as possible. Marriage should not be a relationship characterized by manipulation and mastery—that is what sin will produce in a marriage. So this kind of desire and mastery are not ideals to live up to—they will be there naturally. The passage is not speaking of New Testament submission or headship—those are traits that have to be engendered by the Holy Spirit in the believer to take the sting out of the Curse. No, these oracles simply declare what life will be like now that sin is here; and try as one may, there will be pain, conflict, and death.

God then spoke to Adam, telling him that he would experience great pain (the same word for "pain" is used here as in 3:16), stressing physical and emotional pain. His work will be by the sweat of his brow, and he will have to contend with thorns and thistles that will spring up in his way. His life will be a long, laborious one until he returns to the ground (a gracious provision in view of the hard life he must lead), where he will return to dust, for that is what he is. So much for the ambition of divinity! So much for the promises of Satan! Man may desire to be like God, but in death his true nature is revealed—he is dust.

These punishments represent measure-for-measure justice. Adam and Eve sinned by eating, and so they would suffer in order to eat. The woman was the one used to prompt her husband to sin, so she would be dominated by him. The serpent destroyed the human race, and so he would be destroyed by one who represented the human race. This was the way that life was going to be. No matter how hard people try to do away with pain, conflict, male domination, manipulation, or death, the Curse will continue because of sin. Only when the presence of sin is removed at the end of the age will these effects be removed.

But God also made gracious provisions here. People would die, and not live on with this pain and conflict—a welcome relief. And children would be born, offsetting the constant drain of death and enabling the human race to endure and continue. Ultimately, victory would come through the seed of the woman (Gal 3:16; 4:4).

In the last verses (3:20-24) we see grace and faith working together. By grace God delivered the man and the woman from living in this state of guilty fear; he covered them with animal skins. Nothing is said of the animals or how this was done, but immediately in chapter 4, Abel knows to bring an animal sacrifice to God. And the Israelite reader would think of sacrifice, as well, because in the Tabernacle the skins of the animals went to the priests for clothing and additional income. God was not satisfied that a bunch of leaves snatched from a tree would cover the sinners' guilty fears. No, because of the seriousness of sin, a life would be relinquished instead (Ezek 18:20; Rom 6:23).

Adam's faith was expressed in the naming of his wife, now for the first time. He called her "Eve," which means "living" or more properly "life-giving." Under the sentence of death, Adam looked to the future, to life, and acknowledged that she would be the mother of all living. Eve's statement of faith comes in 4:1 in her acknowledgement that the blessing of God is on her.

All God's dealings with sinners are reflected in the motifs and principles in this chapter: People disobey God's word and then, because of their guilty fears, hide themselves. But God searches out the sinners, draws a confession from them, and then covers their guilt and shame with a symbol of his gracious provision. The gospel explains this symbol fully: In the fullness of time God accepted the death of Jesus for our sins, and on the basis of that sacrifice, he clothes us with righteousness (Rom 3:21-26).

And yet, even forgiven sinners could not remain in the presence of this holy God, in his garden sanctuary. They had now become aware of good and evil in a dangerous way—by disobedience. If they ate from the tree of life, they would live forever in that condition. If their desire was to be like God, then their rebellion against God could not possibly lead them to that divine level. In desiring the knowledge of good and evil, they had chosen evil; and so from this point on, it would be virtually impossible for humans to improve on God's creation and institutions without introducing pain and destruction at the same time. Apparently, if they had remained in the protective presence of God in the garden with all its supernatural provisions of life, they would have lived forever in that evil condition. And so God prevented that by expelling them from the garden so that death would take its decreed course and end the life of toil and trouble. So with severe mercy, the Lord drove them out of the garden and placed at its entrance the terrifying cherubim (see Ezek 1) with a flaming sword that flashed this way and that to guard the way to the tree of life. In the Tabernacle, shapes of cherubim were embroidered on the curtain that separated the people from the presence of God—that separation would remain in place until Jesus opened the way to God through his blood.

◆ ### 7. The advance of sin in the family (4:1-16)

Now Adam* had sexual relations with his wife, Eve, and she became pregnant. When she gave birth to Cain, she said, "With the LORD's help, I have produced* a man!" ²Later she gave birth to his brother and named him Abel.

When they grew up, Abel became a shepherd, while Cain cultivated the ground. ³When it was time for the harvest, Cain presented some of his crops as a gift to the LORD. ⁴Abel also brought a gift—the best of the firstborn lambs from his flock. The LORD accepted Abel and his gift, ⁵but he did not accept Cain and his gift. This made Cain very angry, and he looked dejected.

⁶"Why are you so angry?" the LORD asked Cain. "Why do you look so dejected? ⁷You will be accepted if you do what is right. But if you refuse to do what is right, then watch out! Sin is crouching at the door, eager to control you. But you must subdue it and be its master."

⁸One day Cain suggested to his brother, "Let's go out into the fields."* And while they were in the field, Cain attacked his brother, Abel, and killed him.

⁹Afterward the LORD asked Cain, "Where is your brother? Where is Abel?"

"I don't know," Cain responded. "Am I my brother's guardian?"

¹⁰But the LORD said, "What have you done? Listen! Your brother's blood cries out to me from the ground! ¹¹Now you are cursed and banished from the ground, which has swallowed your brother's blood. ¹²No longer will the ground yield good crops for you, no matter how hard you work! From now on you will be a homeless wanderer on the earth."

¹³Cain replied to the LORD, "My punishment* is too great for me to bear! ¹⁴You have banished me from the land and from your presence; you have made me a homeless wanderer. Anyone who finds me will kill me!"

¹⁵The LORD replied, "No, for I will give a sevenfold punishment to anyone who kills you." Then the LORD put a mark on Cain to warn anyone who might try to kill him. ¹⁶So Cain left the LORD's presence and settled in the land of Nod,* east of Eden.

4:1a Or *the man;* also in 4:25.   4:1b Or *I have acquired. Cain* sounds like a Hebrew term that can mean "produce" or "acquire."   4:8 As in Samaritan Pentateuch, Greek and Syriac versions, and Latin Vulgate; Masoretic Text lacks *"Let's go out into the fields."*   4:13 Or *My sin.*   4:16 *Nod* means "wandering."

NOTES

4:3-4 crops as a gift . . . a gift—the best of the firstborn lambs. In the law both types of offerings were acceptable for a gift (*minkhah* [TH4503, ZH4966]; Lev 1–2); so God looked at the heart to determine if the gift was acceptable. Nonetheless, it is most likely that there is a hint here of the superiority of the animal sacrifice. Abel would have learned about such a sacrifice from the fact that God had clothed Adam and Eve with the skins of animals.

4:7 *You will be accepted.* This is an attempt to capture the meaning of an extremely difficult word. The passage literally says, "If you do what is right, [there will be] uplift." The word "uplift" (*se'eth* [TH7613, ZH8420]) appears to be the infinitive of the verb *nasa'* [TH5375, ZH5951] (to lift up, lift away, carry). The word may contrast with the report that Cain's face fell, which is to say that if he did right things, his attitude and expression would begin to look up. God says that things will be fine if Cain simply tries to please him; he could be accepted like Abel. The word *nasa'* can be used in the Bible for forgiveness, but God is not condemning Cain yet, nor calling for a confession. He is simply telling him to do well.

eager to control you. God uses the language of 3:16 (see note) to warn Cain not to submit to sin. Thus, the meaning of "desire" is interpreted for us from the same section of the Bible.

4:8 *"Let's go out into the fields."* The Hebrew text is elliptical: "And Cain said to Abel his brother . . . and when they were in the field Cain rose up and slew his brother." As noted in NLT mg, some ancient versions supply what Cain said, "Let's go out into the fields." But the Hebrew text skips over any such expression and reports the murder in the field. The sudden silence here is a rhetorical device that breaks off with the dialogue to get to the more important part. The text is not interested in preserving what, if anything, was said; ithurries past that to the crime.

4:15 *a mark.* God put a mark on Cain to protect him from possible avengers. There is no clue in the passage or elsewhere in the Bible as to what this mark might have been. Gerhard von Rad guessed that the narrator was thinking of some kind of a tattoo, but there is no strong evidence to support the suggestion (see von Rad 1961:103; Mellinkoff 1981). Whatever it was, a visible mark or simply a symbol of God's protection, God was extending grace to Cain so that he could live on without fear. This is what we call common grace.

COMMENTARY

These verses introduce us to Cain and Abel and the circumstances behind the killing. The structure of the narrative alternates the descriptions of the two, beginning one sentence with the name that ended the previous sentence, and then contrasting him with the other man. The number of references in the chapter are nearly balanced, too: Cain is mentioned thirteen times, Abel seven, and "his/your brother" seven.

The true nature of Cain unfolds gradually. He had an auspicious beginning, a child born with the help of the Lord—a real godsend, a child of hope, perhaps the one who would crush the serpent's head. But the narrative gradually begins to unveil Cain—first associating him with the Curse because he worked the soil (see 3:17), whereas Abel's herding stood closer to God's original purpose that mankind have dominion. The text does not say that shepherds are more spiritual than farmers; it makes an observation in harmony with the preceding chapter: One man was living according to the original instruction of God, ruling over living creatures, but the other was living according to the decree of the Curse, working the ground from which they were taken. The alignment of their occupations does not mean that one was cursed and the other was not; it simply shows that they each had a different orientation to life, one with living animals, the other with the ground.

Then, these coincidental circumstances give way to a greater distinction—the way each of them worshiped the Lord. Abel brought to God the "best of the firstborn lambs from his flock" (4:4). In other words, he went out of his way to please God with the best and the first of his flock. Leviticus taught the Israelites that they were to bring the fattest of the firstborn of the flock. By contrast, the text simply says that Cain "presented some of his crops" (4:3) as an offering; he appears to be simply discharging a duty. Accordingly, God had accepted Abel and his offering, but not Cain or his offering (note that the person is placed first as the object, and then his offering). In other words, Abel was acting by faith, seeking to please God. By contrast, Cain was performing a ritual duty. One may observe that in all worship settings since then the same types appear: There are those who go out of their way to please God and those who simply show up and discharge a duty. Abel's actions were righteous, whereas Cain's were evil (1 John 3:12). But at the heart of the matter, it was faith that distinguished Abel from Cain (Heb 11:4).

Cain's lack of genuine faith begins to show more clearly in his reaction to his rejection and God's favor shown to his brother (4:5). Rather than being crushed in his spirit and concerned about God's rejection of his gift, he became very angry and his facial expression reflected it. Cain was so angry over the matter that he could not be talked into doing what was right, not even by God. It is as if he could not wait for the Lord to leave him alone so he could go and destroy his brother.

The Lord's question to Cain, "Why are you so angry?" (4:6), was intended as a mild corrective, like a father reasoning with an angry child. He told Cain that if he did well (meaning he should try his best to please God), then all things would be well (see note on 4:6). But if he did not, sin was crouching at the door, desiring to have him, but Cain could master it. The word "crouching" is a participle (*robets* [TH7257, ZH8069]), portraying sin as an animal ready to pounce. Its desire was to control Cain. Sin desired Cain, but Cain could have the mastery over it. How? By doing well—that is, by living to please God and giving no place to the tempter. So here is the perpetual struggle between good and evil taken to the next level: Anyone filled with envy and anger is vulnerable to Satan's temptation to evil.

As the Lord finishes speaking to Cain, the story moves swiftly to the murder and the next conversation. Cain rose up and killed his brother in the field, suggesting he was waiting for him or at least that it was premeditated. After murdering his brother, the Lord again came and asked Cain questions: "Where is your brother? Where is Abel?" He was not asking for directions to the body; God had seen it all. This was a rhetorical question seeking confession (as in 3:9-13). But he did not get one from Cain; in this we see another level of his rebellion. Cain denied any knowledge of the crime and repudiated any responsibility for his brother: "Am I my brother's guardian?" His question to God was defiant and was meant to be rhetorical; he was saying he had no responsibility for his brother's welfare. But his question actually had an answer: Yes, he was his brother's keeper. It was his duty to look out for the welfare of his brother, as his brother would have for him. But he had no intention of protecting the life of his brother.

God then declared a curse on Cain. The word *'arur* [TH779, ZH826] (cursed) essentially means to be removed or banished from the place of blessing. Cain was guilty because the blood of Abel was crying out against him. So because he was cursed, Cain had to be a ceaseless wanderer (*na' wanad* [TH5128/5110, ZH5675/5653]) on the earth (*'erets* [TH776, ZH824]), away from the fertile soil (*'adamah* [TH127, ZH141]). As he wandered off to the east he would find only a cropless soil to work, making life even more difficult than it had been before.

The picture of Cain's rebellion is not yet complete. He complains that the "punishment is too great" for him (4:13). The word translated "punishment," *'awon* [TH5771, ZH6411], has the basic meaning of "iniquity"; but it came to be used for the guilty feelings that went with the iniquity and the punishment for it. Cain was not confessing that his sin was great; he was complaining the punishment was too severe. He was concerned that someone would come after him to seek vengeance. It must be concluded that those whom Cain feared would be other sons of Adam and Eve because the issue is the right of the next of kin to avenge a murdered relative. We know from 5:4 that Adam had other sons and daughters after Seth. Cain was afraid that someone from the family, perhaps even Adam, might come after him seeking vengeance. The passage then reminds us of the primitive instinct that is in mankind to seek vengeance, even if the offense lies long in the past. But God sought to check this instinct with a mark on Cain, just as he would do later with the cities of refuge. To be sure, under the law there were many more rulings to be applied, but God used the same principle to prevent widespread, unchecked revenge killings. The stories are therefore about actual events in the beginnings of the family, but they are also archetypal as regards human nature in general.

So God in his grace protected Cain by some mark that would be a deterrent to an avenger (4:15). Here we see how God made himself Cain's protector. This is the beginning of common grace, the protection of the godless in the world, even though they do not trust the Lord. Even with that goodness of God, Cain defied him yet again and settled in the east, in the land of Nod (which means "wandering") and built a city.

The subject of chapter 4 is the spread of sin in the family and in society, producing a godless society. Here we find man in rebellion against God in ways that Adam and Eve never imagined—Cain destroying Abel, denying responsibility for it, and then demanding divine protection from the consequences of his act. The descendants of Cain, ungodly civilizations, are portrayed here as living on in the world with a protective mark of grace but not as becoming the people of God. Any sense of guilt they had was eased by their cultural development and geographical expansion.

The message of this chapter was critical for Israel. Under Moses's leadership the people would move into a world of pagan cultures. Civilizations with music, art, industry, enterprise, and expanding cities would be on every side. But these would all be antagonistic to Israel and would influence God's people to reject the Lord and his sacrifices. Such groups may enjoy God's common grace, but they were not to be emulated by God's special people.

This section is primarily the story of Cain. This seed of the woman met the seed of the serpent head-on (see 3:15), and he fell victim to the crouching evil. Cain had to leave the fertile land God had given him and go off into the world, where he formed what became godless society. The "way of Cain" (Jude 1:11, KJV), then, is a lack of faith that reveals itself in envy of God's dealings with the righteous, in murderous acts, in denial of responsibility, and in refusal to accept God's punishment.

In the story of Cain and Abel there are several theological ideas presented: (1) The worship of God must come from a heart of faith, and that faith will be demonstrated by the worshiper's giving the very best to God. (2) People do have responsibilities for one another, to ensure the well-being of other people. Certainly they must not kill one another (as the law would later state). (3) Homicidal blood polluted the land, crying out for vengeance. This blood cried out from the ground to condemn man as a brother killer from the beginning; but the blood of Christ in the New Testament cries out for the forgiveness of sin (Luke 23:34; Heb 12:24). (4) The instinct to take revenge was averted by God's putting the mark on Cain, but punishment for sin was at the heart of the theocracy. (5) Life without God is dangerous and terrifying in the world.

◆ ## 8. The spread of godless civilization and the faith (4:17-26)

¹⁷Cain had sexual relations with his wife, and she became pregnant and gave birth to Enoch. Then Cain founded a city, which he named Enoch, after his son. ¹⁸Enoch had a son named Irad. Irad became the father of* Mehujael. Mehujael became the father of Methushael. Methushael became the father of Lamech.

¹⁹Lamech married two women. The first was named Adah, and the second was Zillah. ²⁰Adah gave birth to Jabal, who was the first of those who raise livestock and live in tents. ²¹His brother's name was Jubal, the first of all who play the harp and flute. ²²Lamech's other wife, Zillah, gave birth to a son named Tubal-cain. He became an expert in forging tools of bronze and iron. Tubal-cain had a sister named Naamah. ²³One day Lamech said to his wives,

"Adah and Zillah, hear my voice;
　listen to me, you wives of
　　Lamech.
I have killed a man who attacked me,
　a young man who wounded me.
²⁴If someone who kills Cain is
　punished seven times,
　then the one who kills me
　will be punished seventy-seven
　　times!"

²⁵Adam had sexual relations with his wife again, and she gave birth to another son. She named him Seth,* for she said, "God has granted me another son in place of Abel, whom Cain killed." ²⁶When Seth grew up, he had a son and named him Enosh. At that time people first began to worship the LORD by name.

4:18 Or *the ancestor of*, and so throughout the verse.　**4:25** *Seth* probably means "granted"; the name may also mean "appointed."

NOTES

4:17-18 *Cain had sexual relations with his wife.* Eventually Cain married, presumably a sister from the rapidly growing population (5:4), and began a family in what became known as the land of Nod. This is the word translated "wanderer" in 4:14; Cain dwelt in the land of wandering, a fugitive from God.

gave birth to Enoch. Cain named his first child Enoch, and then named a city after him. This would be the "foundation" of his world, for Enoch means "foundation" or "dedication."

4:23 I have killed. The word Lamech uses, *harag* [TH2026, ZH2222] (to slay, to murder), is the same verb used for the murder of Abel (4:8, 25).

4:26 people first began to worship the LORD by name. Lit., "men began to call on the name of the LORD." The Hebrew expression is used several times in the Pentateuch (the next time is Abram in 12:8), and its use shows that it means people began to make proclamation of the person and works of Yahweh. A similar expression (identical to that in 12:8) occurs in Exod 34:5ff., where it is Yahweh himself who is proclaiming "his own name, Yahweh." This verse makes it clear that people knew the name *Yahweh* from the beginning and worshiped him by that name. In time they would come to know what this name truly meant, first as Moses explained it (Exod 3 and 6) and then as God revealed it through the fulfillment of the promises.

COMMENTARY

The narrative now traces the line of Cain to its full development. The seventh descendant from Adam through Cain was a man known as Lamech (probably a contemporary of the righteous Enoch, also the seventh from Adam—see 5:3-21). Lamech deviated from the divine institution of marriage by taking two wives. His descendants began to raise livestock and settle down in tents. They produced musical instruments (harp and flute) and implements (tools of bronze and iron) to make life bearable and in fact enjoyable. It appears from this that civilization began to develop in a number of ways prior to the great flood. This civilization prospered. But the righteous need not envy the wicked (Pss 49; 73), for their wealth and pomp are limited to this life. God in his grace allowed them to flourish—so that they produced music, weapons, agricultural implements, and cities. They produced culture; it was their only recourse in a dying and painful world. But their advances could not conceal that they were living in defiance of God—changing marriage, killing, bragging, and exacting revenge.

In spite of the prosperous good life, evil was also advancing in an ominous way. Lamech killed a youthful warrior who had apparently insulted or harmed him in some way. Showing no remorse over the act, he actually gloated about it, putting his boast into a taunting song. Not only did Lamech exact revenge—a fate Cain had feared—but he demanded greater leniency than that which was afforded to Cain (4:24), boasting that his killer would be punished seventy-seven times and not just seven. In contrast to this defiance, Jesus taught his disciples to forgive "seventy times seven" (Matt 18:22).

So here is a picture of a community of people, fast developing into a society with all the conveniences necessary for the good life; but it is one in which people are changing the divine institutions and defying the laws of God, seeking power, pleasure, and self-indulgence. Into this kind of world Israel (and later, the church) would come as a kingdom of priests to champion righteousness. It would always be a question of who would influence whom.

The chapter ends with a contrast. Some people, who traced their line through Seth, the replacement of Abel, were known for their worship of the Lord. They no doubt made use of the implements that civilization provided—but that is not what they are remembered for. They, like Enoch, Noah, Abram, and others, declared their faith in Yahweh to their generation (see note on 4:26). They were not caught up in the good life of the world but were concerned with things that were spiritual and eternal. The Israelites would be instructed to live like their great ancestor Enosh in their fast-developing world.

◆ C. The Account of the Succession from Adam (5:1–6:8)
　　1. The genealogy from Adam to Noah (5:1-32)

This is the written account of the descendants of Adam. When God created human beings,* he made them to be like himself. ²He created them male and female, and he blessed them and called them "human."

³When Adam was 130 years old, he became the father of a son who was just like him—in his very image. He named his son Seth. ⁴After the birth of Seth, Adam lived another 800 years, and he had other sons and daughters. ⁵Adam lived 930 years, and then he died.
⁶When Seth was 105 years old, he became the father of* Enosh. ⁷After the birth of* Enosh, Seth lived another 807 years, and he had other sons and daughters. ⁸Seth lived 912 years, and then he died.
⁹When Enosh was 90 years old, he became the father of Kenan. ¹⁰After the birth of Kenan, Enosh lived another 815 years, and he had other sons and daughters. ¹¹Enosh lived 905 years, and then he died.
¹²When Kenan was 70 years old, he became the father of Mahalalel. ¹³After the birth of Mahalalel, Kenan lived another 840 years, and he had other sons and daughters. ¹⁴Kenan lived 910 years, and then he died.
¹⁵When Mahalalel was 65 years old, he became the father of Jared. ¹⁶After the birth of Jared, Mahalalel lived another 830 years, and he had other sons and daughters. ¹⁷Mahalalel lived 895 years, and then he died.
¹⁸When Jared was 162 years old, he became the father of Enoch. ¹⁹After the birth of Enoch, Jared lived another 800 years, and he had other sons and daughters. ²⁰Jared lived 962 years, and then he died.
²¹When Enoch was 65 years old, he became the father of Methuselah. ²²After the birth of Methuselah, Enoch lived in close fellowship with God for another 300 years, and he had other sons and daughters. ²³Enoch lived 365 years, ²⁴walking in close fellowship with God. Then one day he disappeared, because God took him.
²⁵When Methuselah was 187 years old, he became the father of Lamech. ²⁶After the birth of Lamech, Methuselah lived another 782 years, and he had other sons and daughters. ²⁷Methuselah lived 969 years, and then he died.
²⁸When Lamech was 182 years old, he became the father of a son. ²⁹Lamech named his son Noah, for he said, "May he bring us relief* from our work and the painful labor of farming this ground that the LORD has cursed." ³⁰After the birth of Noah, Lamech lived another 595 years, and he had other sons and daughters. ³¹Lamech lived 777 years, and then he died.
³²By the time Noah was 500 years old, he was the father of Shem, Ham, and Japheth.

5:1 Or *man;* Hebrew reads *adam;* similarly in 5:2.　5:6 Or *the ancestor of;* also in 5:9, 12, 15, 18, 21, 25.
5:7 Or *the birth of this ancestor of;* also in 5:10, 13, 16, 19, 22, 26.　5:29 *Noah* sounds like a Hebrew term that can mean "relief" or "comfort."

NOTES

5:1 *This is the written account of the descendants of Adam.* Lit., "this is the book of the *toledoth* [TH8435, ZH9352] of Adam." See Introduction, "Literary Genre and Structure."

5:3-4 *Adam was 130 years old . . . Adam lived another 800 years.* The longevity of the people in the list finds literary support from extrabiblical literature: The Sumerian King List from Mesopotamia has exceedingly long ages for the antediluvians. The numbers recorded there are excessively large (e.g., kings who ruled for 36,000 years), but they do witness to the tradition of longevity. Apparently the environment before the Flood enabled people to live longer. This may have been part of God's design to fill up the earth (1:28).

5:29 *Lamech named his son Noah, for he said, "May he bring us relief."* The last word could also be rendered "comfort." The explanation of the name employs a wordplay, as if to say that the meaning of the name is "comfort." The name Noah is from *nuakh* [TH5117, ZH5663] (to rest); the word "comfort" (or "relief") is from a different word, *nakham* [TH5162, ZH5714]. Although some have tried to harmonize the two etymologically (suggesting an earlier form of the name), the two words simply sound alike and make the point memorably.

COMMENTARY

A new section of the book begins here, having the dual purpose of linking the history of the early people to the story of Noah and of showing the continuing effect of sin on the race. The genealogy in this chapter is a "vertical" list, tracing the line from Adam through Seth to Noah. The genealogy of the Cainites in chapter 4 had seven generations from Cain to Jubal; this list has 10 names from Adam to Noah. Both lists end with three sons being named as coming from the last person on the list: Jabal, Jubal, and Tubal-cain (4:20-22); and Shem, Ham, and Japheth (5:32). In each list there is a quotation from only one man—Lamech in the Cainite list (4:23-24) with a taunt song, and a different Lamech in the Sethite list (5:29) with a lament over the effects of the Curse and a desire for comfort through his son Noah. The text of Genesis is showing that their outlooks on life differ greatly.

The chapter begins by reiterating the creation of the man as the "likeness" (a synonym for "image") of God (cf. 1:26-27). Also repeated is the mention of the blessing of God at creation. The "image" of God was passed on seminally to the descendants, for the text states that Adam begat Seth in his image. In other words, the spiritual and intellectual capacities that God had given to the parents are passed from generation to generation by natural reproduction.

The genealogy may begin with the reminder of the blessing of God, but it quickly proceeds to show how everyone died as a result of sin—with one notable exception, Enoch. The rest of the chapter constantly repeats the depressing refrain "and he died." Indeed, the genealogy answers a question raised by the last section: If in spite of sin there is progress, civilization, and prosperity in the world, what happened to the Curse? The answer is clear: People die (5:5, 8, 11, 14, 17, 20, 27, 31). If any were to doubt the word of the Lord that said "You are sure to die" (2:17) or the words of the apostle that "the wages of sin is death" (Rom 6:23), they need only look at human history: All sin, and all die.

The exception of Enoch (5:22-24) is a bright spot in the list, like the reminder of God's image in vv. 1-2. In the other panels of the genealogy, the literary pattern is that a man lived a number of years and had a son; after he had the son, he lived a number of years and had other children; then the years of his life are added up and his death is reported. But the record of Enoch breaks this pattern in two places. The text does not say that after Enoch had his son he *lived* (although of course he did live); rather, it says that he *walked* with God, a walk that lasted 300 years (5:22, 24). To walk with God is to live a life in obedience and fellowship with God. There is a difference, then, between just living with God and walking with God. It is this latter lifestyle of perfect harmony with the Lord that was required of Israel (17:1; Lev 26:3, 12).

The second break in the pattern is that Enoch did not die. His walk with God would have continued longer if it were not for the fact that God "took him." So, not only did he not merely "live"—in place of this the text says he walked with God—he also did not die, for God took him. This little panel, then, tells us that death's authority is not absolute; it can be overruled by God.

The third bright spot in the chapter comes with the birth of Noah (5:28-31). At the end of the chapter, it is reported that Lamech had a son and called him Noah, hoping that this one would bring them relief from the painful toil of the ground that the Lord had cursed (5:29). God would fulfill the wish of Lamech, but in a very different way than the man likely imagined. Noah would be the dominant force in the chapters to come, and the verb "to rest," related to his name (see note on 5:29), would play a significant role in the establishment of a new order—after the judgment on the race. So with the birth of Noah, Lamech had a glimmer of hope that life under the Curse could change.

The chapter, then, reveals that even though death reigns over the whole human race because of sin, humans are still the image of God and the blessing is still available if they walk with God in obedience and devotion. Death is not the final authority, for God can overrule it instantly; but until he does, each generation awaits the relief to come from God, who alone can change darkness to light, cursing to blessing, and death to life. The hope of the human race will be realized in the age to come, but as in Noah's day, that rest will come only after the judgment of the world.

◆ ## 2. The corruption of the human race (6:1-8)

Then the people began to multiply on the earth, and daughters were born to them. ²The sons of God saw the beautiful women* and took any they wanted as their wives. ³Then the LORD said, "My Spirit will not put up with* humans for such a long time, for they are only mortal flesh. In the future, their normal lifespan will be no more than 120 years."

⁴In those days, and for some time after, giant Nephilites lived on the earth, for whenever the sons of God had intercourse with women, they gave birth to children who became the heroes and famous warriors of ancient times.

⁵The LORD observed the extent of human wickedness on the earth, and he saw that everything they thought or imagined was consistently and totally evil. ⁶So the LORD was sorry he had ever made them and put them on the earth. It broke his heart. ⁷And the LORD said, "I will

wipe this human race I have created from the face of the earth. Yes, and I will destroy every living thing—all the people, the large animals, the small animals that scurry along the ground, and even the birds of the sky. I am sorry I ever made them." ⁸But Noah found favor with the LORD.

6:2 Hebrew *daughters of men;* also in 6:4.   6:3 Greek version reads *will not remain in.*

NOTES

6:3 My Spirit will not put up with humans. The verb is *yadon,* which occurs only here in the Bible. Earlier translations rendered it "strive" because it appeared to be from the verb *din* [TH1777, ZH1906] (judge, vindicate, contend). But that verb would be written *yadin.* The LXX used "remain"—"My Spirit will not always remain with mankind." The Akkadian language offers a better solution for the rare word; it has a verb *dananu* (the pattern of the Hebrew verb fits a geminate verb pattern perfectly) and related nouns that have the sense of "protect" and "shield." God says that his Spirit will not always protect mankind; in about 120 years he would destroy them.

6:6 the LORD was sorry he had ever made them. God "repented" (lit.) that he had ever made man because he was so evil. This is an anthropomorphic expression that is used to convey the intensity of the grief that God felt over the sin on earth. It does not mean that God changed his mind, for God does not change (Mal 3:6). Rather, it uses a human expression to communicate to humans the sorrow of God. It is "as if" he was sorry for having made human beings.

COMMENTARY

This short paragraph has been the subject of extensive studies over the centuries, often leaving the obvious point undeveloped—that the human race was completely corrupt and deserved the judgment of God. This report is part of the *toledoth* [TH8435, ZH9352] section that began in 5:1. This part of it brings the discussion to a culmination: Not only was the race dying under the Curse, it became so corrupted that God determined to terminate all things with the Flood.

It is unlikely that a completely satisfactory explanation can be given for the first four cryptic verses (6:1-4), at least one that would find widespread acceptance. To start, there are hints in the lines that lead us to the understanding that the times were not simply evil but grotesque and dangerous. Some have suggested that the passage is referring to unions between *Homo sapiens* and a pre-Adamic race of people. Others, more cautiously, have suggested that the "sons of God" were the godly line of Seth, and the "daughters of men" the Cainites. But this does not do justice to the terminology and does not make much sense because the "godly" line would then be guilty of taking all the women they wanted (a reference to the beginnings of harems perhaps), which is an act of hubris in light of the story of creation and appears here as a criticism of these "sons of God." God had made one man and one woman to produce a godly seed, as Malachi explained later (Mal 2:15), but almost immediately Lamech sought to improve on God's institution of marriage by taking two wives (4:19), and here the powerful sons of God took all the women they wanted. Immediately the text affirms that everything they desired and did was only evil continually (6:5). In any event, how could intermarriage between believers and unbelievers (even if we could be sure the lines neatly divide that way) produce giants in the world (cf. Num 13:32-33)? And would such marriages be sufficient reason for God to destroy the human race?

In the Old Testament the expression "sons of God" primarily refers to angels (see Job 1:6, NLT mg). But since spirit beings such as angels cannot cohabit with mortal flesh (see Matt 22:30), "sons of God" cannot merely refer to angelic spirits in this passage. If angelic spirits possessed certain powerful people, the despots of the ancient world, they would be able to cohabit with humans and claim the lofty title, "sons of God" as well. These may be the angels referred to in Jude 1:6 and the spirits mentioned in 1 Peter 3:19-20. The ancient men of renown would owe more to the spirit world than they realized, unless they believed that they were the offspring of gods and demigods as many in the pagan world believed. (These brief descriptions in Genesis certainly do sound similar to what the pagan religions believed about kings and warriors—but in Genesis they are said to be mortal, mere humans who would be destroyed in the Flood.) Such a chaos in the order of creation would be a more sufficient reason for a judgment like the Flood (see further, Hendel 1987; VanGemeren 1981).

Thus, it may be that "sons of God" here denotes fallen angels who invaded or possessed human life. Similar expressions using "gods" can refer to human judges and leaders (cf. Ps 82:6). What the text may be describing is hubris on a grand scale, the arrogant overstepping of boundaries in defiance of the will of God. The "sons of God" would be powerful leaders, people who became military conquerors or rulers over the whole world, who were enabled to do this because of the spirit forces within them. The prophets often refer to spirit forces behind the great kingdoms. The kings of Tyre (Ezek 28:11-19) and Persia (Dan 10:13), for example, had "princes" dominating them and driving them to their unimaginable deeds. It is no surprise that in Canaanite literature, as well as in that of other ancient countries, kings were thought to have been gods or demigods. The ancient myths even describe these powerful individuals as being the offspring of the gods. In fact, in Canaanite texts, the term "sons of god" (*bn'lm*) refers to the lesser gods of the pantheon or great rulers on the earth. So in mythology these demigods or heroes, possibly demon-possessed or demon-driven powerful people, became the terrifying tyrants of the ancient world.

In the Ugaritic legend of Dawn and Dusk (COS 1.274), the chief god of the pantheon, El, seduces two human women.[1] This union of a spirit and two humans produced "Dawn" and "Dusk" who seem to have been deities associated with the planet Venus. Thus for the pagans, gods and demigods had their origins in copulations between humans and gods. Any superhuman or herculean individual in a myth or any actual giant or powerful tyrant would suggest a divine origin to the ancient mind. In the thinking of the time, the way to achieve immortality involved a divine marriage. And a whole cult arose to allow people the opportunity to engage in this quest for immortality.

The spirit force in their character may then be the angels who did not keep their first habitation (Jude 1:6) but rebelled and desired to enter into the human race in some way. Because of this these spirits have been kept in prison since the days of the Flood, awaiting the final judgment (1 Pet 3:19-20). Accordingly, when Jesus says in the days of the Flood people were marrying and giving in marriage, something far more grotesque was going on than ordinary lifestyles—something for which the race had to be brought to a halt (see Matt 24:38-39).

Genesis 6:1-4, then, describes how corrupt the world had gotten when this violation was rampant. It provides a polemic against the worldwide pagan belief that these "giant Nephilites" (cf. Num 13:32-33) and the "heroes and famous warriors" (6:4) were of divine origin. These ancient cults included fertility rites involving sympathetic magic, based on the assumption that people are supernaturally affected through an object that represents them. Israel was prohibited from involvement in pagan ritual or the occult because it was completely corrupt and contrary to the true faith.

The passage then refutes pagan beliefs by declaring the truth. There was a time when such confusion existed. But the "sons of God" were not divine, nor were they demigods; they were human beings who were overstepping the boundaries God had instituted, and the powerful despots on the earth were mere mortals. Their marrying as many women as they wished was more to satisfy their basic lusts and to demonstrate their greater power over people than to become immortal, but their myths and ritual held out that prospect too. They were just another group of sinful people, although empowered by supernatural beings, who corrupted the race completely. Children of these marriages were not god-kings, despite what people thought or said. Though they were "heroes" and "famous warriors," they were flesh and would all die in due course like the rest of the human race. When God would judge the world (as he was about to with the Flood in 120 years), no giant, no false deity, no human would have any power to resist. God simply allotted the time of grace and then brought the end.

The sinfulness of the human race grieved the heart of God greatly. The text says that the wickedness of the people was great, and that every inclination (*yetser* [TH3336, ZH3671]) of their hearts was only evil continually. One could hardly express the depravity of the people in stronger terms, or in terms that contrast more with the design of creation. God had formed (*yatsar* [TH3335, ZH3670], "form by design"; 2:7) man from the ground and given him the spiritual and intellectual capacity to serve God on earth, but mankind used that intelligence (*yetser*) to devise evil continually. The next chapter will add that mankind was corrupt and full of violence (6:11, 13).

Some of the words used in 6:5-8 form a striking play on the words of Lamech in the last chapter, which in turn echo the curse in Genesis 3. We are told that God "was sorry" (*nakham* [TH5162, ZH5714]) that he had "made" (*'asah* [TH6213, ZH6913]) man because the sin of the race "broke" (*'atsab* [TH6087A, ZH6772]) his heart. Lamech longed for "relief" (*nakham*) from the "work" (*ma'aseh* [TH4639, ZH5126]) and "painful labor" (*'itsabon* [TH6093, ZH6779]) under the Curse (5:29). This helps us to understand the extent of pain in the world, the inevitable increase of suffering as a result of sin. Sin is painful, bringing pain to even God himself. So there is an ironic twist to the words of Lamech: God would indeed do something about the painful toil on earth. He would judge the world, purge it of its great wickedness, and start over with a new creation through Noah.

The judgment was certain because the Spirit of God would not always shield mankind (6:3). Once the divine protection was removed, then the judgment would come in full force. That, according to the text, would be delayed for about 120 years (6:3). During all that time Noah was a preacher of righteousness (2 Pet 2:5). What this must mean is that while Noah was building the ark and preparing for the Flood he was telling people what God had revealed to him—that because of ungodliness and violence in the world, judgment was going to come and bring an end to the world and all wickedness in it (6:11-13). His message would have been a warning of judgment from the righteous God, delivered in the hope of calling people to escape the judgment—but only he and his family escaped the judgment; there were none that listened outside Noah's immediate family.

The little section ends with a ray of light: "Noah found favor with the LORD" (6:8). Because Noah was a recipient of grace, he was spared from the judgment (in contrast to those who thought they had achieved immortality). Grace is unmerited favor; in fact, when the word "grace" or "favor" is used, it usually means that the recipient deserves the opposite of the favor. It is not that Noah was the most righteous person on the earth and so God decided to save him. No, he was a sinner, and God saved him from the judgment by his grace. The note in 6:9 about his righteousness begins the next *toledoth* [TH8435, ZH9352] of the book; it describes the life of the man who received grace.

In the time of Moses the Israelites would also know that by the grace of God they had been chosen to walk in righteousness and serve him as a kingdom of priests (Exod 19:5-6). They too were delivered from the judgment on their world in Egypt as they walked through the waters that would flood the Egyptians. But they, as God's people, would still meet extremely wicked Canaanites, and giant Nephilites, Anakites (Num 13:33), and Rephaites (Deut 2:11; 3:13; Josh 12:4) when they entered the land. But Israel was not to fear any giants or self-proclaimed demigods; neither should they live like the wicked Canaanites, for God would judge the corrupt world for its idolatry and fornication. If Israel became entangled in their lifestyle, she too would be judged. And this theme is brought forward to the New Testament as well, for in the latter days it will be as in the days of Noah when the wicked will suddenly be swept away by judgment and the Lord will establish his theocratic kingdom of blessing (Matt 24:36-39).

ENDNOTES
1. Cassuto (1973:23) says, "*The poem on the pleasant and beautiful gods* [i.e., The Dawn and Dusk] is, it is true, obscure in detail, yet it is at any rate clear that it speaks of the father of the deities, El, who took to wife two daughters of men and begat by them two sons, Šḥr and Šlm, who both became gods."

D. The Account of the Succession from Noah (6:9–9:29)
1. The commission of Noah (6:9–7:5)

⁹This is the account of Noah and his family. Noah was a righteous man, the only blameless person living on earth at the time, and he walked in close fellowship with God. ¹⁰Noah was the father of three sons: Shem, Ham, and Japheth.

¹¹Now God saw that the earth had become corrupt and was filled with violence. ¹²God observed all this corruption in the world, for everyone on earth was corrupt. ¹³So God said to Noah, "I have decided to destroy all living creatures, for they have filled the earth with violence. Yes, I will wipe them all out along with the earth!

¹⁴"Build a large boat* from cypress wood* and waterproof it with tar, inside and out. Then construct decks and stalls throughout its interior. ¹⁵Make the boat 450 feet long, 75 feet wide, and 45 feet high.* ¹⁶Leave an 18-inch opening* below the roof all the way around the boat. Put the door on the side, and build three decks inside the boat—lower, middle, and upper.

¹⁷"Look! I am about to cover the earth with a flood that will destroy every living thing that breathes. Everything on earth will die. ¹⁸But I will confirm my covenant with you. So enter the boat—you and your wife and your sons and their wives. ¹⁹Bring a pair of every kind of animal—a male and a female—into the boat with you to keep them alive during the flood. ²⁰Pairs of every kind of bird, and every kind of animal, and every kind of small animal that scurries along the ground, will come to you to be kept alive. ²¹And be sure to take on board enough food for your family and for all the animals."

²²So Noah did everything exactly as God had commanded him.

CHAPTER 7

When everything was ready, the LORD said to Noah, "Go into the boat with all your family, for among all the people of the earth, I can see that you alone are righteous. ²Take with you seven pairs—male and female—of each animal I have approved for eating and for sacrifice,* and take one pair of each of the others. ³Also take seven pairs of every kind of bird. There must be a male and a female in each pair to ensure that all life will survive on the earth after the flood. ⁴Seven days from now I will make the rains pour down on the earth. And it will rain for forty days and forty nights, until I have wiped from the earth all the living things I have created."

⁵So Noah did everything as the LORD commanded him.

6:14a Traditionally rendered *an ark*. 6:14b Or *gopher wood*. 6:15 Hebrew *300 cubits* [138 meters] *long, 50 cubits* [23 meters] *wide, and 30 cubits* [13.8 meters] *high*. 6:16 Hebrew *an opening of 1 cubit* [46 centimeters]. 7:2 Hebrew *of each clean animal;* similarly in 7:8.

NOTES

6:15 *450 feet long, 75 feet wide, and 45 feet high*. These are the measurements of the ark, which was a rectangular, flat-bottomed vessel with a displacement of some 43,400 tons and three decks (Unger 1954:59-60). The boat used to escape the flood in the Babylonian account of Gilgamesh was cubical and five times as big as Noah's ark; such dimensions would have made the Babylonian boat totally unseaworthy.

COMMENTARY

The narrative begins with a description of Noah as a righteous and blameless man—he stood in sharp contrast to his generation. In fact, the human race had become so "corrupt" (6:11-12) and the earth so filled with violence (6:11, 13) that

God revealed to Noah that he was about to destroy all life, except for Noah, his family, and what Noah saved (6:18-19). It is clear from this that the Flood was a moral judgment. The arrangement that God made with Noah includes the main features of a unilateral covenant. The Lord announced what he was going to do for and through Noah and made stipulations for Noah to follow. The announcement of God was sure; but Noah's participation in the plan required faith, faith demonstrated by obedience. After the Flood, Noah offered a sacrifice of thanksgiving to God, who had fulfilled his promise of salvation in the face of judgment. And then God expanded his covenant with Noah, who would now be the new Adam. The promise of preservation from judgment through such a flood was also a unilateral covenant promise, requiring nothing from the human race for its fulfillment. But God did stipulate that humans did not have the right to take the life of another person, or eat blood (9:4-6).

The deliverance from the judgment would come in the form of a large boat traditionally called an "ark," about which Noah would receive instructions. He would also be instructed to take two of every kind of animal into this ark, as well as enough food for them all to survive. The section closes with the repeated theme of the chapter: Noah did exactly as the Lord commanded him (6:22; 7:5, 9, 16).

When Noah was told to go into the ark, he was told to take seven pairs of all clean animals (7:1-5). Here already there was a distinction made between clean and unclean animals. To preserve life, Noah had to take on board two of every kind of animal, but for food and for sacrificing, he had to have seven pairs of clean animals (7:2). The distinction between clean and unclean animals was fully explained later in the law (Lev 11:2-23). Again, Noah was completely obedient, doing just as the Lord commanded him (7:5).

◆ ## 2. The destruction of all life outside the ark (7:6-24)

⁶Noah was 600 years old when the flood covered the earth. ⁷He went on board the boat to escape the flood—he and his wife and his sons and their wives. ⁸With them were all the various kinds of animals—those approved for eating and for sacrifice and those that were not—along with all the birds and the small animals that scurry along the ground. ⁹They entered the boat in pairs, male and female, just as God had commanded Noah. ¹⁰After seven days, the waters of the flood came and covered the earth.

¹¹When Noah was 600 years old, on the seventeenth day of the second month, all the underground waters erupted from the earth, and the rain fell in mighty torrents from the sky. ¹²The rain continued to fall for forty days and forty nights.

¹³That very day Noah had gone into the boat with his wife and his sons—Shem, Ham, and Japheth—and their wives. ¹⁴With them in the boat were pairs of every kind of animal—domestic and wild, large and small—along with birds of every kind. ¹⁵Two by two they came into the boat, representing every living thing that breathes. ¹⁶A male and female of each kind entered, just as God had commanded Noah. Then the LORD closed the door behind them.

¹⁷For forty days the floodwaters grew deeper, covering the ground and lifting the boat high above the earth. ¹⁸As the waters rose higher and higher above the

ground, the boat floated safely on the surface. ¹⁹Finally, the water covered even the highest mountains on the earth, ²⁰rising more than twenty-two feet* above the highest peaks. ²¹All the living things on earth died—birds, domestic animals, wild animals, small animals that scurry along the ground, and all the people. ²²Everything that breathed and lived on dry land died. ²³God wiped out every living thing on the earth—people, livestock, small animals that scurry along the ground, and the birds of the sky. All were destroyed. The only people who survived were Noah and those with him in the boat. ²⁴And the floodwaters covered the earth for 150 days.

7:20 Hebrew *15 cubits* [6.9 meters].

NOTES

7:6 *Noah was 600 years old.* His sons were about 100 years old (cf. 5:32).

7:11-12 *all the underground waters erupted from the earth. . . . The rain continued to fall for forty days and forty nights.* The judgment began with a torrential rain that lasted for 40 days and nights, something the world in its protected environment apparently had not seen. But with the rain there were corresponding upheavals and shiftings of the earth's crust which caused the oceans to rise and break up their reservoirs of subterranean waters, probably, as some suggest, forming greater mountain ridges in the process. The passage indicates that there was nowhere for the people or animals to go to escape the deluge—it had no bounds. A flood of this magnitude would have changed the surface of the earth, the manner of life, and apparently the longevity of life.

7:21 *All the living things on earth died.* Everything living on earth was destroyed. Only marine life survived the Flood. Sin had infected every aspect of life, and so nothing short of a new beginning would suffice. Thus will it also be at the end of this age (Matt 24:37-39).

7:24 *the floodwaters covered the earth.* The word "earth" can mean "land" (i.e., a local area) and not the entire globe. But the language of the judgment speaks of such worldwide devastation that the straightforward reading of this passage is that the writer meant the whole world as he knew it. Still, there is much debate about whether the Flood was a local flood or a universal flood. The fact that the Flood covered all the highest mountains by a good 20 feet has led many to argue for a local flood because the amount of rain that fell and the water from the deep would not cover the mountains as we know them. But even if the Flood was local, the mountains in the region are rather high, Mount Hermon in Syria being 9,000 feet high. And the ark came to rest on Mount Ararat. That would still suggest an enormous flood which could not be restricted to the region of the Middle East if it had that amount of water. Moreover, if it was to be a local flood, Noah had plenty of time to gather the animals and move away. In addition, some who argue for a universal flood suggest that the great mountains were formed in this universal catastrophe because of the shifting of the earth's crust and the breaking up of the deep.

COMMENTARY

Why did God use a flood to judge the world? There are several reasons that come to mind. First, God is the sovereign Lord of creation and frequently uses nature's forces for his blessings or curses. This judgment used water, the rains and the deep, showing that God alone controls these forces—not the pagans and their deities. Second, water was the natural way of purging and cleansing. The water would not only destroy wickedness, but it would wash the world clean so that it could begin afresh. Third, the Flood was used by God to replicate the situation at creation.

This is part of the creation—un-creation—re-creation development found in Genesis. The new life after the Flood parallels the original creation in a number of ways. In the beginning, the world was covered with the deep (1:2), and here the fountains of the deep were broken up to cover the land with water (7:11). In the beginning, the dry land began to emerge (1:9), and here the waters abated until the land dried and the ark came to rest on Mount Ararat (8:4). When Noah came out of the ark, God commissioned him to be fruitful and multiply and to have dominion over the earth (9:1-2), the very instructions he had given to Adam (1:26, 28). Noah then planted a vineyard (9:20), whereas God had planted a garden for Adam and Eve (2:8). But this garden was also an occasion for sin. In Eden nakedness was a sign of Adam's integrity (2:25), but Noah's nakedness was one of degradation (9:21), and it led to the disruption of the family (9:25-27).

In this narrative, we see God revealed as the judge of the whole earth and as the savior who provides for the recipients of his grace to escape the judgment. The redeemed will worship the Lord with thanksgiving for being delivered from the judgment. This theme is repeated in the days of Moses: Just as God had judged the world in Noah's day and brought Noah's family through the Flood, compelling them to worship the Lord with a sacrifice, so he judged Egypt and brought Israel through the waters of the Red Sea to worship and serve him on the other side. Instructions for that worship are distinctly spelled out in Leviticus and Numbers. This parallelism goes a long way to explain why so many Levitical terms were used in telling the story of the great Flood (e.g., "clean" and "unclean"; 7:2). It was first written for the Israelites who were learning to worship God.

The severe judgment on the world was designed to make an impact on subsequent generations. It was a warning for all to flee the wrath to come. It also made it clear to what lengths God would go to prevent evil from destroying his creation completely. The catastrophe of the Flood did not alter God's plan for his creation; that plan would now work through Noah, the second Adam. God would still have his image on the earth, and with it the hope of ultimate victory over evil.

The story of the Flood should make people aware of the wrath of God. Such a judgment for sin shows that God's gracious provision of redemption is meaningful, and that his grace is not to be taken lightly. The ultimate cause of the Flood is stressed clearly from the outset—the monstrous acts of sin that controlled life. The account of the Flood in Genesis is very different from the pagan accounts of the Flood that we have (*Gilgamesh* and *Atrahasis*). In the Babylonian account the gods brought on the Flood because of the noise that the humans made. Pettiness and capriciousness often characterize the gods in ancient myths. Only the Bible has a reason serious enough to warrant such a judgment. Can human beings get away with living in moral abandon and enjoying the pleasures of their evil inclinations forever? Is there a God who has something to say about the way people live? Genesis 6–9 answers these questions.

This often seems harsh to many modern readers. We hear nothing of the terror of the people who died, even though Noah must have felt it. The only emphases the passage leaves are that God will not tolerate wicked rebellion forever and that good will ultimately replace evil. God judged the world with a severe judgment in order to purge it of great evil and begin anew with a worshiping community and a binding covenant. In the midst of this great catastrophe, God's servant Noah and his family, the recipients of grace, sailed through the Flood to become the "new creation" of God.

◆ 3. The end of the judgment and Noah's worship (8:1-22)

But God remembered Noah and all the wild animals and livestock with him in the boat. He sent a wind to blow across the earth, and the floodwaters began to recede. ²The underground waters stopped flowing, and the torrential rains from the sky were stopped. ³So the floodwaters gradually receded from the earth. After 150 days, ⁴exactly five months from the time the flood began,* the boat came to rest on the mountains of Ararat. ⁵Two and a half months later,* as the waters continued to go down, other mountain peaks became visible.

⁶After another forty days, Noah opened the window he had made in the boat ⁷and released a raven. The bird flew back and forth until the floodwaters on the earth had dried up. ⁸He also released a dove to see if the water had receded and it could find dry ground. ⁹But the dove could find no place to land because the water still covered the ground. So it returned to the boat, and Noah held out his hand and drew the dove back inside. ¹⁰After waiting another seven days, Noah released the dove again. ¹¹This time the dove returned to him in the evening with a fresh olive leaf in its beak. Then Noah knew that the floodwaters were almost gone. ¹²He waited another seven days and then released the dove again. This time it did not come back.

¹³Noah was now 601 years old. On the first day of the new year, ten and a half months after the flood began,* the floodwaters had almost dried up from the earth. Noah lifted back the covering of the boat and saw that the surface of the ground was drying. ¹⁴Two more months went by,* and at last the earth was dry!

¹⁵Then God said to Noah, ¹⁶"Leave the boat, all of you—you and your wife, and your sons and their wives. ¹⁷Release all the animals—the birds, the livestock, and the small animals that scurry along the ground—so they can be fruitful and multiply throughout the earth."

¹⁸So Noah, his wife, and his sons and their wives left the boat. ¹⁹And all of the large and small animals and birds came out of the boat, pair by pair.

²⁰Then Noah built an altar to the LORD, and there he sacrificed as burnt offerings the animals and birds that had been approved for that purpose.* ²¹And the LORD was pleased with the aroma of the sacrifice and said to himself, "I will never again curse the ground because of the human race, even though everything they think or imagine is bent toward evil from childhood. I will never again destroy all living things. ²²As long as the earth remains, there will be planting and harvest, cold and heat, summer and winter, day and night."

8:4 Hebrew *on the seventeenth day of the seventh month;* see 7:11. 8:5 Hebrew *On the first day of the tenth month;* see 7:11 and note on 8:4. 8:13 Hebrew *On the first day of the first month;* see 7:11. 8:14 Hebrew *The twenty-seventh day of the second month arrived;* see note on 8:13. 8:20 Hebrew *every clean animal and every clean bird.*

NOTES

8:1 God remembered Noah. The turning point in this drama comes with the key word "remember." The verb "to remember" (*zakar* [TH2142, ZH2349]) most often means far more than a mental recollection. It signifies action based on what is remembered. This is certainly what one would mean in praying, "Lord, remember me" (cp. Luke 23:42). Here the point is that God began to act on what he had promised Noah. Everything up to this point is the increase of the Flood on the earth; everything after this will trace its cessation and the return to the dry land.

COMMENTARY

The torrential rains lasted 40 days (7:4, 12), but the waters continued to rise for 110 days (cf. 7:24). Thus, the waters flooded the earth for 150 days, exactly five months of 30 days each for the lunar calendar. The 40 days were part of the 150 days, and apparently lighter rain fell or subterranean water upheavals continued for another 110 days.

When the waters began to recede, the ark came to rest on Mount Ararat 150 days after the rains began. The theme of "rest," based on Noah's name, runs throughout the account. The name "Noah" (*noakh* [TH5146, ZH5695]) is almost certainly related to the verb "to rest" (*nuakh* [TH5117, ZH5663]). But in the naming of Noah in 5:29, the explanation of the name is, "He will comfort us," as if the name were from the verb *nakham* [TH5162, ZH5714]. Hebrew seldom presents exact etymologies for names, especially in the early parts of the Bible; it is more interested in providing wordplays on the names, what scholars call popular etymologies. Such a wordplay, *paronomasia* to be precise, is satisfied with a connection between the name and the sentiment based on sound and sometimes meaning. "Noah" included the sounds of *nakham*, "comfort," and expressed the hopes of Lamech for the boy. The word *nakham* is given an ironic twist in 6:6 where it expresses the Lord's sorrow for making man. The hoped for relief would come only after the ark came to "rest" on dry land.

The ark rested on the mountain (8:4). At first the dove could not find a "resting place" for its feet (8:9), and then finally it was safe to leave the ark. When the ark came to rest on the mountain, this was more than just the docking of the ark; it was a new beginning, for the world was clean and at rest. The precise location of Mount Ararat is as yet unknown, even though Assyrian records and tradition identify such a name in Armenia or eastern Turkey. After it was clear that the earth was again suitable for habitation, the eight people and all the animals left the ark. This was 370 days after they had entered it (cf. 7:11 with 8:13-14).

Once the family had left the ark, Noah worshiped the Lord by making a sacrifice of animals and birds (8:20-22), which sent up a pleasing aroma to God. In this act of worship Noah was expressing his gratitude to God for the gift of life. He was acknowledging that God was the sovereign Lord of the whole earth and that their lives were in his hand. Thus, from the dawn of civilization, it is clear that the redeemed people of God have been a worshiping people, submitting themselves to God and his program, acknowledging his lordship over them, and offering some token of gratitude to him for the grace they have received.

Israel would be reminded that the form of worship that would please God would be to give to him the best that they had. But giving a gift to God was not in and of itself sufficient; by giving it, they had to be offering themselves to him. Then when they offered their gifts to God and the fruit of their lips in praise (Heb 13:15), they would be pleasing to God. So Noah received God's grace, walked with him in obedience and righteousness, became a preacher of righteousness, was preserved through the judgment, entered a new age with the gross wickedness of that generation removed, and afterward offered his gratitude to God with pleasing worship.

After Noah made the sacrifice, God responded by promising two things: First, he would never again curse the ground because of man; second, he would never again destroy all living creatures as he had done here (8:21). This does not mean that there will be no judgment to come at the end of the age; rather, it means that God will not again destroy life and curse the ground as he did here. The continuity of the seasons was to be the evidence of God's forbearance: As long as the earth endures, the cycle of life would continue. God would later reveal that in the final judgment he will make a new heaven and a new earth, and this life as we know it will be transformed.

◆ ### 4. God's covenant with Noah (9:1-17)

Then God blessed Noah and his sons and told them, "Be fruitful and multiply. Fill the earth. ²All the animals of the earth, all the birds of the sky, all the small animals that scurry along the ground, and all the fish in the sea will look on you with fear and terror. I have placed them in your power. ³I have given them to you for food, just as I have given you grain and vegetables. ⁴But you must never eat any meat that still has the lifeblood in it.

⁵"And I will require the blood of anyone who takes another person's life. If a wild animal kills a person, it must die. And anyone who murders a fellow human must die. ⁶If anyone takes a human life, that person's life will also be taken by human hands. For God made human beings* in his own image. ⁷Now be fruitful and multiply, and repopulate the earth."

⁸Then God told Noah and his sons, ⁹"I hereby confirm my covenant with you and your descendants, ¹⁰and with all the animals that were on the boat with you—the birds, the livestock, and all the wild animals—every living creature on earth. ¹¹Yes, I am confirming my covenant with you. Never again will floodwaters kill all living creatures; never again will a flood destroy the earth."

¹²Then God said, "I am giving you a sign of my covenant with you and with all living creatures, for all generations to come. ¹³I have placed my rainbow in the clouds. It is the sign of my covenant with you and with all the earth. ¹⁴When I send clouds over the earth, the rainbow will appear in the clouds, ¹⁵and I will remember my covenant with you and with all living creatures. Never again will the floodwaters destroy all life. ¹⁶When I see the rainbow in the clouds, I will remember the eternal covenant between God and every living creature on earth." ¹⁷Then God said to Noah, "Yes, this rainbow is the sign of the covenant I am confirming with all the creatures on earth."

9:6 Or *man*; Hebrew reads *ha-adam*.

NOTES

9:9 confirm my covenant. The common Hebrew word for "covenant" is *berith* [TH1285, ZH1382]. A covenant is an agreement, a treaty, or a pact between parties, which both parties swear by oath to observe. Covenants that the Lord makes with people are therefore binding; he guarantees them with an oath. They usually begin with a historical statement declaring what the Lord has done for people, then add a section of stipulations for the participants of the covenant to abide by, and conclude with a series of promises telling what God will do for them. Covenants usually have a sign that serves as a perpetual reminder for both sides that the covenant is being kept. In this chapter the covenant is unconditional, God simply promising what he will do, and it is universal, for it includes all of creation. The sign of this covenant is the rainbow.

9:16 rainbow. Lit., "bow," the same word as for the "battle bow" (*qesheth* [TH7198, ZH8008]). Elsewhere in the OT, God referred to his acts of judgment with the images of bows and arrows (Pss 7:10-13; 18:14; 38:2; 64:7; 144:6; Ezek 5:16). The rainbow arcs like a bow in the sky, hung up against the clouds; it was as if God had hung up his battle bow because the battle was over.

COMMENTARY

After the great flood was over, God instructed Noah, as he had instructed Adam, to be fruitful, increase in number, and fill the earth (9:1, 7; cf. 1:28). Noah, like Adam, was also instructed to have dominion over the animals (9:2; cf. 1:26, 28). Also, both were given food to eat (9:3; cf. 1:29; 2:16) and prohibitions—not partaking of the tree of knowledge (for Adam, 2:17) and not taking a human life or eating blood (for Noah, 9:4-6).

With the new beginning through Noah after the judgment, God made a covenant which included his promises and the stipulations for humans. Because of the devastation of the Flood, the Israelites in Egypt might have come to the conclusion that life was cheap and expendable, that taking a life was a small matter in God's eyes. But God's covenant with Noah shows people for all time that human life is sacred and that people are not to destroy other people, for they are all the image of God. Only God, the righteous judge of the whole earth, has such authority.

The Noachian covenant, then, was installed to ensure the stability of life and of nature. It recorded God's guarantee of the order of the world. People would also learn here that law was necessary for preserving life and punishing wickedness if social order was to survive. So a basic principle of human government was established with this covenant.

This covenant that God confirmed (9:9, 11-13, 15-17) was a universal covenant in that it extended to every living creature (9:9-10, 12,15-16) and all life (9:11, 15, 17). And it was cosmic in nature because the sign of the covenant was a rainbow in the sky (9:12-13, 17). After the Flood, when the earth began to dry and blue sky had driven away the dense atmosphere held in place by the firmament (see commentary on 1:6-8), the light of the rainbow shone in the heavens as God's sign that the judgment was over. Whenever the rainbow arches over the horizon after a rainfall, it is God's sign of grace. Covenant signs remind the participants to keep their word; here God, who needs no such reminder, makes this a perpetual reminder that he would never flood the whole world again (9:15-16). This is said for the benefit of humans. Since apparently no rain had fallen before the Flood (2:5-6), no rainbow had appeared previously. Now when clouds cleared, light refraction showed this marvelous display of colors in the shape of a bow. The rainbow speaks of peace (see note on 9:16).

In the ancient world, covenant treaties were made after wars as a step toward lasting peace. After judging the wickedness of those who had rebelled against him, God set forth this covenant of peace with all people. People in general, and Israel in particular, would have been encouraged again and again when they saw the rainbow because it was a reminder that God is a covenant God who keeps his promises, in this case, his continued peace with the earth and its inhabitants, whom he would never again destroy with a flood (9:11). And they would also remember the stipulations. After all, humans were still sinful after the Flood; nonetheless, God initiated this covenant through Noah with sinful humanity. He always does, for covenants come from his grace and draw people to his love.

Judgment will come again on the whole earth in the end times (Zech 14:1-3; Rev 19:15) before there can be lasting peace and righteousness on the earth. This passage may have reminded Israel to anticipate that in some glorious future day the righteous would be beating their swords into plowshares (Isa 2:4; Mic 4:3). In the meantime, life goes on in a new order; and the divine provision of common grace assures that the cycle of life continues and that people are preserved alive for the time being.

◆ 5. Curse on Canaan; blessings on Shem and Japheth (9:18-29)

¹⁸The sons of Noah who came out of the boat with their father were Shem, Ham, and Japheth. (Ham is the father of Canaan.) ¹⁹From these three sons of Noah came all the people who now populate the earth.

²⁰After the flood, Noah began to cultivate the ground, and he planted a vineyard. ²¹One day he drank some wine he had made, and he became drunk and lay naked inside his tent. ²²Ham, the father of Canaan, saw that his father was naked and went outside and told his brothers. ²³Then Shem and Japheth took a robe, held it over their shoulders, and backed into the tent to cover their father. As they did this, they looked the other way so they would not see him naked.

²⁴When Noah woke up from his stupor, he learned what Ham, his youngest son, had done. ²⁵Then he cursed Canaan, the son of Ham:

"May Canaan be cursed!
 May he be the lowest of servants
  to his relatives."

²⁶Then Noah said,

"May the LORD, the God of Shem,
  be blessed,
 and may Canaan be his
  servant!
²⁷May God expand the territory of
  Japheth!
 May Japheth share the prosperity of
  Shem,*
 and may Canaan be his servant."

²⁸Noah lived another 350 years after the great flood. ²⁹He lived 950 years, and then he died.

9:27 Hebrew *May he live in the tents of Shem.*

NOTES

9:18 *The sons of Noah . . . were Shem, Ham, and Japheth. (Ham is the father of Canaan.)* Those who came out of the ark are identified again, but now with a special editorial note that "Ham was the father of Canaan"—a note probably more concerned with the continuity of character qualities than lineage.

9:20 *Noah began to cultivate the ground.* Noah is identified here as "the man of the soil" (*'adamah* [TH127, ZH141]; cf. 2:7). This may be designed to identify him as the new Adam, the head of the family; it may also mean that he was "a man of the soil" because he began to plant a vineyard.

9:21 *he drank some wine.* Though wine is said to cheer the heart of God and man (Judg 9:13; Ps 104:15) and alleviate the pain of suffering and death (Prov 31:6-7), it is also clear that it can have disturbing effects ("Wine is a mocker," Prov 20:1, KJV).

9:26 *May the LORD, the God of Shem, be blessed.* The oracle for Shem first blesses the God of Shem and then announces the subjugation of Canaan. The blessing of the God of Shem involves a wordplay to make the blessing more memorable: The word *Shem* means "name," and the divine name Yahweh has just been identified as Shem's God. The God of this name, Yahweh, is the God of Shem. Thus, Shem and his descendants are now identified with the covenant God, Yahweh.

COMMENTARY

This little passage has several interpretive problems that have captured the imagination of Bible students for some time. At the outset it is important to remember the purpose and focus of this section of the book: the record of world events under the Curse. From the world God will gradually narrow his choice from the line of Seth through Noah to Shem, and the Japhethites along with him; but the Canaanites will be cursed. The descendants of Shem were the Shemites, from whom Abraham descended (cf. 10:21-31; 11:10-26). So this passage sets forth the nature and the destiny of the Canaanite people, Israel's antagonists. And the Table of Nations in the next chapter will identify who they are.

The chapter begins with an account of Noah planting a vineyard, making wine, and drinking it to the point of intoxication. Noah lay drunk in his tent, and under the influence of the wine became warm and "uncovered himself" (9:21; the text uses *wayyithgal* [TH1540, ZH1655], an important term in understanding Ham's actions later). Intoxication along with nakedness became part and parcel of the cultic practices of the pagan cultures that Israel faced, and both are traced back to this event in Noah's life. Man had not changed. With the opportunity to start a new order of life, Noah appeared in a base condition—like the later pagans would (cf. 6:5; 8:21). That is how his son Ham (a fully grown man) found him, and that is what he reported to his brothers.

The basic question concerns what Ham did (9:22, 24) and why Noah cursed Ham's "son" Canaan (9:25-27). Many fanciful ideas have been put forward over the years. One is that Ham actually castrated his father, thus explaining why Noah had no more children. (This view is drawn from Greek mythology.) Another claims that Ham slept with his mother, thus "uncovering his father's nakedness" (an expression common to Lev 18) and that the offspring of that union, Canaan, was therefore cursed. Still another claims that Ham committed a homosexual act on his father. But these and similar views require some significant rewriting of the text. The Hebrew expression is clear. It simply says that Ham saw that his father was naked and went outside and told his brothers. There is not a hint that he did anything physically or sexually to his father. If that were the case, the text would have said that Ham uncovered his father's nakedness (that is the idiom used in Lev 18). But the text says that Noah "uncovered himself" (a reflexive form of the verb, 9:21) and Ham saw him that way.

Although not many scholars are satisfied with the obvious, in this case it seems obvious that the text means what it says. This may be hard for people in the modern secular world to understand, for nakedness is fairly commonplace. But to the ancients, and to religious cultures in the Middle East today, nakedness is disgraceful, and to see the nakedness of one's father would be a breach of family ethic (see Lev 18; and see the account in Herodotus which tells how Gyges saw the nakedness of Candaules's wife, something that was a shame among the Lydians, and so either he had to be put to death, or Candaules had to be to allow Gyges to marry his wife [Herodotus 1.8-13]). This "event" may seem trivial to us today, but it was not trivial to the family of Noah. The sanctity of the family was destroyed, and the dignity of the father had been made a mockery. Ham apparently stumbled on this accidentally, but rather than respect his father and cover him up, he went out and told his two brothers. The text suggests that he may have taken the robe out to show his brothers, perhaps as an act of triumph over the old man.

Whatever Ham did, the text reports that Shem and Japheth reversed it by their act. They took "the garment" (which is literally what the text says, so it was probably Noah's garment), backed into the tent, and covered their father. They had the filial respect for their father and the dignity of his position in the family. They acted responsibly. Thus, what seems to us to have been a trivial incident turned out to be a rather telling event in the family; in fact, it was at a time in human history when no event was trivial. The whole episode prompted an oracle from Noah wherein he declared that the nature of each of his three sons would be perpetuated in their respective descendants. Specifically, the negative traits of Ham would show up in Canaan.

The Canaanites that Israel encountered in the land descended from Ham, but more to the point, they had the same basic character qualities as their ancestor. This is why the text reminds us that Ham was the father of Canaan (9:25). The advancement of their moral abandonment is found in passages like Leviticus 18:6-19 which warns the Israelites not to follow the abominable practices of Canaan. In all but one of the verses of this section of Leviticus, Moses used the causative form of the verb "to uncover" (*gillah* [TH1540, ZH1655]) to warn Israel to avoid those pagan practices, and so the verb describes their practices—they uncovered the nakedness of close family members, meaning they took advantage of their situation and forced their sexual acts on them. A number of modern versions (e.g., NIV, NLT) translate the idiom as "have sexual relations." This rendering is accurate enough, but it does not capture the emphasis on the forcefulness of the activity, nor the graphic imagery. The phrase expresses the actual licentiousness and repulsively immoral behavior of the Canaanites. What happened, then, is that over the centuries the disposition of Ham toward moral abandon bore fruit in the immoral acts of his descendants, the Canaanites (Lev 18:3). The law said that the sins of the fathers would be visited on the children—among those who reject the Lord (Exod 20:5).

Because of this incident, Noah prophesied what would become of the descendants of his three sons. This little oracle is broad in scope, dealing with the course of nations (9:25). Ham's act of hubris and moral abandon would necessarily have extensive repercussions. A humiliation in like measure would be the outcome, according to the principle of measure-for-measure justice. Ham made an irreparable breach in his father's family, thus a curse would be on his descendants, so that they would reflect badly on their father. Was Ham thinking that he now would seize the leadership of the clan? It is impossible to say, but the curse plunged his descendants into abject slavery. Only one line in Ham's family—the Canaanites (cf. 10:6)—was singled out for this curse because they would be the most corrupt and contaminating of all the people that Israel had to deal with as they entered the land.

Noah began with the direct words, "May Canaan be cursed." Noah was not punishing Ham's son for something that Ham did. Noah used the occasion to prophesy how the descendants of Ham, the Canaanites, would act given this impetus to immorality. His words referred to the Canaanite tribes of the future because his words about Shem and Japheth look to the future with their expanding civilizations. Canaan would be in slavery to the tribes of Shem and Japheth (9:26-27). This was not because of something their ancestor did but because they would live the same way their ancestor did. The point is that nationally, at least, drunkenness and debauchery enslave people, and the pattern of debauchery continues unless halted by faith. The Canaanites were to be judged by God through the conquest of Canaan. For a people to be enslaved would require defeat in battle and subjugation in the land under new rulers. Many Canaanites were killed in the major wars, but most of them were left in the land to test Israel. Individual Canaanites like Rahab, of course, could turn to the Lord in faith and escape the judgment that hung over the sinful tribes of the land of Canaan.

The oracle began to be fulfilled early in the history of the tribes. The Canaanites' enslavement to Shemites and Japhethites may be witnessed in a number of early events in the Old Testament. One was the enslavement of Canaanites from the region of Sodom by the eastern kings (ch 14). Another was the more peaceful servitude of the Gibeonites who escaped death to become water carriers and wood choppers for the sanctuary (Josh 9:27). If the subjugation of the Canaanites to the lines of Japhethites is traced historically, then it comes to an end in 146 BC at the Battle of Carthage, where the Carthaginians (who were Phoenicians—Canaanites) were finally destroyed as a people. But Noah's oracle seems to be more general; it sets the direction for the great sweep of human history: The line of Shem will be blessed, and the line Canaan will be cursed.

According to Genesis 10, the descendants of Ham were Cush, Mizraim, Put, and Canaan. Over the centuries people have assumed that Ham was cursed, and with him, the black African peoples. If that were the case, Cush and Mizraim, the source of many tribes in North Africa, would have been named in the curse of chapter 9, for the descendants of Cush were the people of the Arabian peninsula as well as Ethiopia; the people who had their source in Egypt were the numerous tribes that lived to the south of Egypt. But the curse is on the line of Canaan, meaning the various tribes living in the land that Israel was to inherit (see 10:15). After the Canaanite people met their end at the Battle of Carthage in 146 BC, there was no longer any application to be made of this ancient oracle. (For a full study of the passage, see Ross 1980.)

The motifs of blessing and cursing in Genesis are crucial to the argument of the book. God's creation was blessed by God because it was perfect. But the creation was early on ruined by sin, and so a curse replaced the blessing in the working out of the history of the human race. But now the word of God through Noah announced that the blessing would come through the line of Shem, the ancestor of Abram, and that the land of Canaan would be given to the descendants of Abraham. In other words, the Canaanites in that land would have to be subjugated and dispossessed before the blessing could work out for Shem's descendants, the Israelites (9:26), and for the Japhethites to dwell in the tents of Shem and share the blessing (9:27). And in God's providence, it was the wickedness of the Canaanites that warranted the judgment of God on them to make room for the chosen people.

So verses 24-29 provide a little oracle from God through Noah, based on an incident that was most telling. The oracle set in motion the plan of God for the nations of the world; and it even provided the foundation for Israel's foreign policy in the land (Deut 20:16-18). As Israel entered the land to dispossess the Canaanites, they would know that the Canaanites were cursed. And the Table of Nations in chapter 10 would provide a road map of the peoples of the world, so that Israel, and others, might discern on whom the blessing and the curse would land.

The culmination of this episode is the oracle announcing a blessing and a curse. This is not simply something Noah said. As an oracle it was divine revelation through him. It was prophecy. The oracle should be compared to that of 3:13-19 and chapter 49. In all these passages, the characteristics and actions of the individuals form the basis of the prophecies about their descendants. Unless there was a concerted effort by faith to break the pattern, the sins and the nature of the ancestors would be perpetuated from generation to generation. Noah's oracle concerns all the races; Jacob's oracle in chapter 49 concerns the tribes of Israel.

◆ **E. The Account of the Succession from the Sons of Noah (10:1–11:9)**
   1. The Table of Nations (10:1–32)

This is the account of the families of Shem, Ham, and Japheth, the three sons of Noah. Many children were born to them after the great flood.

²The descendants of Japheth were Gomer, Magog, Madai, Javan, Tubal, Meshech, and Tiras. ³The descendants of Gomer were Ashkenaz, Riphath, and Togarmah. ⁴The descendants of Javan were Elishah, Tarshish, Kittim, and Rodanim.* ⁵Their descendants became the seafaring peoples that spread out to various lands, each identified by its own language, clan, and national identity. ⁶The descendants of Ham were Cush, Mizraim, Put, and Canaan. ⁷The descendants of Cush were Seba, Havilah, Sabtah, Raamah, and Sabteca. The descendants of Raamah were Sheba and Dedan.

⁸Cush was also the ancestor of Nimrod, who was the first heroic warrior on earth. ⁹Since he was the greatest hunter in the world,* his name became proverbial. People would say, "This man is like Nimrod, the greatest hunter in the world." ¹⁰He built his kingdom in the land of Babylonia,* with the cities of Babylon, Erech, Akkad, and Calneh. ¹¹From there he expanded his territory to Assyria,* building the cities of Nineveh, Rehoboth-ir, Calah, ¹²and Resen (the great city located between Nineveh and Calah).

¹³Mizraim was the ancestor of the Ludites, Anamites, Lehabites, Naphtuhites, ¹⁴Pathrusites, Casluhites, and the Caphtorites, from whom the Philistines came.*

¹⁵Canaan's oldest son was Sidon, the ancestor of the Sidonians. Canaan was also the ancestor of the Hittites,* ¹⁶Jebusites, Amorites, Girgashites, ¹⁷Hivites, Arkites, Sinites, ¹⁸Arvadites, Zemarites, and Hamathites. The Canaanite clans eventually spread out, ¹⁹and the territory of Canaan extended from Sidon in the north to Gerar and Gaza in the south, and east as far as Sodom, Gomorrah, Admah, and Zeboiim, near Lasha.

²⁰These were the descendants of Ham, identified by clan, language, territory, and national identity.

²¹Sons were also born to Shem, the older brother of Japheth.* Shem was the ancestor of all the descendants of Eber.

²²The descendants of Shem were Elam, Asshur, Arphaxad, Lud, and Aram. ²³The descendants of Aram were Uz, Hul, Gether, and Mash. ²⁴Arphaxad was the father of Shelah,* and Shelah was the father of Eber. ²⁵Eber had two sons. The first was named Peleg (which means "division"), for during his lifetime the people of the world were divided into different language groups. His brother's name was Joktan.

²⁶Joktan was the ancestor of Almodad, Sheleph, Hazarmaveth, Jerah, ²⁷Hadoram, Uzal, Diklah, ²⁸Obal, Abimael, Sheba, ²⁹Ophir, Havilah, and Jobab. All these were descendants of Joktan. ³⁰The territory they occupied extended from Mesha all the way to Sephar in the eastern mountains.

³¹These were the descendants of Shem, identified by clan, language, territory, and national identity.

³²These are the clans that descended from Noah's sons, arranged by nation according to their lines of descent. All the nations of the earth descended from these clans after the great flood.

10:4 As in some Hebrew manuscripts and Greek version (see also 1 Chr 1:7); most Hebrew manuscripts read *Dodanim.*   10:9 Hebrew *a great hunter before the Lord;* also in 10:9b.   10:10 Hebrew *Shinar.*   10:11 Or *From that land Assyria went out.*   10:14 Hebrew *Casluhites, from whom the Philistines came, and Caphtorites.* Compare Jer 47:4; Amos 9:7.   10:15 Hebrew *ancestor of Heth.*   10:21 Or *Shem, whose older brother was Japheth.*   10:24 Greek version reads *Arphaxad was the father of Cainan, Cainan was the father of Shelah.* Compare Luke 3:36.

NOTES

10:1 *the account of the families of Shem, Ham, and Japheth.* Our knowledge of many of names in the table of 10:2-30 comes from ancient records, especially Assyrian lists (from the time of 840 BC), as well as information in the Bible. But the fact that they are attested in Assyrian lists does not mean that the table and its lists are late. If the table was compiled later, such as during the Babylonian exile, as critical scholarship holds, it would be strange that the name Persia is not on the list, for it was the dominant world power.

10:2 *descendants of.* Lit., "sons of." The basic framework of the table is the listing of names with the simple expression "the sons of" (*bene* [TH1121, ZH1201]). This Hebrew construction occurs 13 times in the table (10:2-4, 6-7, 20-23, 29, 31-32).

Japheth. The first section of the table (10:2-5) gives the 14 names descended from Japheth. For the most part these were tribes of northern and western peoples who were remote from Israel.

Gomer. This represents the Cimmerians who were of the same stock as the Scythians (see next note).

Magog. This name is associated with the land of Gog between Armenia and Cappadocia (Ezek 38:2; 39:6). The name represents the Scythian hordes southwest of the Black Sea.

Madai. These are the Medes east of Assyria and southwest of the Caspian Sea.

Javan. This was the general word for the Hellenic race, the "Ionians" of western Asia Minor.

Tubal, Meshech. These were northern militaristic states. They seem to have been located between Pontus and the Armenian mountains.

Tiras. This may refer to the seafaring Pelasgians of the Aegean coasts.

10:3 *descendants of Gomer.* From the seven in 10:2, seven more were derived. Three northern tribes came from Gomer: "Ashkenaz" (related to the Scythians), "Riphath," and "Togarmah" (both northern tribes). The sons of Javan include two geographical names and two tribal names; they are all related to the Greeks.

10:4 *Elishah.* This is known from Akkadian and Hittite inscriptions to indicate Cyprus (cf. Holmes 1971).

Tarshish. This was most likely a distant coast in Asia Minor. In the Bible, Tarshish designates a distant coast reached by sea (Ps 72:10; Isa 66:19; Jer 10:9; Ezek 27:12). Of the several places it has been connected with, Sardinia (see Albright 1941), Spain (Herodotus 1.163; Strabo 3.151), and the coast of Anatolia are the best possibilities. The meaning of the word *Tarshish* is thought to be "foundry" (Neiman 1965). Based on its sources of iron ore, it seems that one of the Anatolian locations is meant, even possibly Tarsus.

Kittim. They lived in Cyprus and on other smaller islands as well. This name is preserved in the ancient name *Kition* or *Kettion* on the island of Cyprus, and remained a designation of the Greeks in later Jewish literature (1 Macc 1:1; 8:5; *b. Ta'anit* 5b).

Rodanim. Most Hebrew mss read "Dodanim" here (cf. NLT mg). "Dodanim" may refer to the people of Dodona, Greece. Alternatively, "Dodanim" may be a textual variant of "Rodanim," refering to the people of Rhodes (cf. 1 Chr 1:7).

10:5 *Their descendants became the seafaring peoples.* The northern tribes did not figure prominently in Israel's history apart from the coming of the Philistines, a seafaring people from the Aegean. Nonetheless, they do appear frequently in prophetic writings (Ezek 27; 38–39).

10:6 *The descendants of Ham.* These descendants (10:6-20) formed the eastern and southern peoples of the region.

10:7 descendants of Cush. These settled in south Arabia, and in present-day southern Egypt, Sudan, and northern Ethiopia. They became mingled with Semitic tribes dwelling in the same region; hence there is repetition of some of the names in other lines.

Seba. This was in Upper Egypt (i.e., southern Egypt) on the Nile. It has been connected with the ancient city of *Meroe,* which is between Berber and Khartoum. Cf. Ps 72:10; Isa 43:3; 45:14.

Havilah. Meaning "sand-land," this could refer to northern and eastern Arabia on the Persian Gulf, or to the Ethiopian coast.

Sabtah. This was ancient Hadhramaut on the western shore of the Persian Gulf.

Raamah, and Sabteca. These were in southern Arabia, with Raamah indicating a tribe of Sabaeans in southwest Arabia (near modern Yemen) and Sabtekah located east toward the Persian Gulf.

Sheba. This was in southwest Arabia, with its metropolis in Ma'rib, 75 miles east of Sana'a in modern Yemen (cf. the queen of Sheba in 1 Kgs 10:1-13).

Dedan. This was in northern Arabia. Some of the people of these ancient kingdoms traced their lineage to Joktan and Shem (10:29), so there was a mixing of lineage in the settlement.

10:8 Cush was also the ancestor of Nimrod. Lit., "Cush begot Nimrod." This is the first use of "begot" (*yalad* [TH3205, ZH3528]) in the chapter and forms a major stylistic break from the listing of tribal names before it. In several places the chapter uses *yalad* to introduce sections—10:8, 13, 15, 21, 24-26. Different versions render the verb *yalad* as "became the father of" or as the NLT often has it, "was the ancestor of." This allows for direct generational gaps in the genealogical table (i.e., the genealogy may skip over some generations).

Nimrod. Inserted into this Table of Nations is the short report of Nimrod. Attempts to identify or date Nimrod have proven unsuccessful; they usually follow the writer's basic presupposition about the origin and date of the composition, whether early or late. If it is legitimate to give his name a Hebrew etymology, it appears to be connected with the verb "to rebel" (*marad* [TH4775, ZH5277]). This has led tradition to identify him with tyrannical power. He was the founder of what became the earliest imperial world powers: Babylon and Assyria.

10:9 the greatest hunter in the world. The table presents Nimrod as a "mighty hunter," a tradition carried on among Assyrian kings in their lion hunts. But what did Nimrod hunt? The word for "hunt" is an unusual word; related verbs are often used for hunting people (1 Sam 24:11 [12]; Jer 16:16; Lam 3:52) as well as animals. Also, the text does not seem interested in identifying Nimrod as famous for his acts of "derring-do," but rather as the first tyrant in what became the ancient centers of power for the known world: He was the founder of several powerful cities of the east; and those cities became major enemies of Israel. So Nimrod became a symbol of the powerful empires that would eventually destroy Israel and punish Judah.

10:13 Mizraim. This is the Hebrew word for Egypt (*mitsrayim* [TH4714, ZH5213]). Mizraim "developed into" (*yalad* [TH3205, ZH3528] "begot," see note on 10:8) tribes that ranged from North Africa to Crete.

10:14 the Caphtorites, from whom the Philistines came. The placing of the Philistines here represents their migration and not their origin (similar to Israel's being "from Egypt"). The Philistines migrated from their Aegean homelands through Caphtor (which has traditionally been identified with Crete) into the Delta of Egypt and finally to what would later be called Palestine (because of their presence it was called Palestine, first by Hadrian in AD 135). This table, however, appears to refer to an earlier ethnic group of Pelasgo-Philistine tribes, distinct from those of the 13th century BC. For more on the Philistines, see Wainwright 1959; Hestrin 1970; Kitchen 1973:53-54; Grintz 1945.

10:15 Canaan. The final Hamite line that was significant for Israel was the Canaanite group. Once again this entry uses *yalad* [TH3205, ZH3528] (begot) to introduce the beginnings of the tribes and cities in the Promised Land.

Sidon. This was the predominant Canaanite/Phoenician city to the north.

Hittites. From the Hebrew word *kheth* [TH2845, ZH3147], which probably refers to a pocket of Hittite tribes that migrated, early on, to the south of eastern Asia Minor.

10:16 Jebusites. These were the people who dwelt in and around Jerusalem (cf. 2 Sam 5:6).

Amorites. This was a small ethnic group in the mixed Canaanite population; the name means "western" Semite and is usually connected to the great western migration at the end of the Early Bronze Age. The name is often interchangeable with Canaanites but here is referring to a smaller group among the Canaanite population. The other seven Canaanite tribal names are a little easier to identify; they were tribes that settled in Lebanon, Hamath on the Orontes River, and all through the land. Their listing is significant after the passage announcing the curse on Canaan (9:25-27).

10:22 Elam. Elamites, descendants of Shem's first son, dwelt in the highlands east of Babylonia.

Asshur. This was the name of the region and people of Assyria, where Nimrod, a Hamite, had founded several major cities (10:11).

Arphaxad. He resided north of Nineveh. This is known through the later mention of *Arapha* in Assyrian texts.

Lud. This is a reference to the *Ludbu* of the Assyrian texts, situated on the banks of the Tigris, even though the word itself can be used for other locations.

Aram. This was an ancestor of the Aramaean tribes in the steppes of Mesopotamia. His descendants listed here (10:23) are not well known. Abraham was an Aramean, and Laban and Jacob are both called Aramaeans (25:20; Deut 26:5).

10:25 Eber. The line then traces Arphaxad to Eber and his sons, using *yalad* [TH3205, ZH3528] (beget) to introduce this additional information.

Peleg. The note on Eber's son Peleg—that in his time the earth was divided—seems to link this record with the Babel experience at his time (11:1-9).

"division." The verb "divide" (*palag* [TH6385, ZH7103]) can refer to a number of things, among them the division of languages. This would mean that the event at Babel occurred five generations after the Flood.

10:26-29 Joktan. The table turns to trace the tribes from Peleg's brother Joktan, most of whom lived in the Arabian peninsula. The Israelites would find ancient blood ties with these 13 tribes of "Joktanites" in the desert.

10:32 These are the clans that descended from Noah's sons. Here is a colophon-type ending for the table. It reminds the readers that all families came from Noah, but some were of special interest to the nation of Israel as they prepared to leave the land of Egypt and enter a land possessed by Canaanites and threatened by the empires of the east.

COMMENTARY

After the Flood, God commanded the survivors to "fill the earth" (9:1). This chapter is the evidence that they did so, for it tells how Noah's three sons, Shem, Ham and Japheth, scattered throughout the known world and began to populate it. It is as if they obeyed the Lord. But there is one glaring problem throughout the whole chapter: They were divided by languages (10:5, 20, 31). Since 11:1 tells us that the whole world had the same language, something is not right here. Moreover, for anyone who knows the history of the ancient world, this list reads like a who's who in the wars of antiquity. So when we begin Genesis 11 and read how the whole world had the same language, we can only conclude that the chapters were not put in chronological order. The narrator surveyed the nations of the ancient world before explaining how they divided and ended up speaking different languages. As such, 11:1-9 falls historically within the generations recorded in chapter 10, where the nations with different languages are scattered throughout the world (see note on 10:25). It is clear, then, that the people did not fill the earth by obedience, but were forced to do so by the divine judgment at Babel; God had to disperse them and change their languages to forestall their effort to unite in rebellion against God. This arrangement of the chapters is rhetorically powerful. Similarly, in the story of Jacob's crossing the Jabbok, the narrative gives the conclusion or outcome first (32:22) and then provides the explanation (32:23-32).

The table seems to include the known nations of the world prior to the time of the conquest of the land; the fact that Israel is not on the list is particularly strong evidence of this. Seventy descendants of Noah's three sons were selected for the list: 14 from Japheth, 30 from Ham, and 26 from Shem. And these names are arranged into patterns. First, there are seven "sons" listed for Japheth. Then, two names are selected from these seven, and seven more sons are listed from each of these two—yielding fourteen. The other sons had sons, of course, but only these were selected, perhaps being the best known. The design for 70 tribes, families, or nations is intended to emphasize the completeness of the three branches of the race.

This material may have originally been part of an old list that was the base for the table. Perhaps the compiler, possibly even Moses, had an old list and inserted various elaborations into it. For example, 10:5 says that the descendants of Javan became the seafaring people. Additions, such as this, into the basic "sons of" structure, explaining or describing persons and events, are in harmony with the title of the chapter, the *toledoth* [TH8435, ZH9352] of the sons of Noah. Other explanatory notes appear in 10:8-12, 19, 25, 30. These provide information about the Egyptians, descendants from Ham, the great kingdoms in the East, such as Babylon and Assyria, and the Canaanites—all of special interest to Israel's future. Also of special interest are verses 15-19 in which Canaan's descendants are listed and even the boundaries of the Promised Land—Canaan—are included (10:19). The writer was apparently using the ancient table to identify who would experience the blessing of God and who would be under the curse that was declared upon Canaan. And the way that the names are arranged on the table points to the Promised Land from all geographical directions.

The Table of Nations is a horizontal genealogy rather than a vertical one, showing tribal affiliations rather than lineage alone (chs 5 and 11 contain vertical genealogies). This table is designed to show political, geographical, and ethnic affiliations among tribes for various reasons, the most common being treaties and covenants. Tribes shown to be "kin" to each other would be in league with each other. But the table is also quite fluid; it includes names of towns and countries as well as tribes and clans, all in the language of "begetting" or "sonship."

The fluid use of genealogical terms to describe political and social alliances demands that the table be read with some flexibility. For example, the basic structure of the chapter uses "the sons of" as its formula. But in several places these "sons" are nations (the Medes [Madai] and the Greeks [Javan] are sons of Japheth; 10:2) places (Cyprus [Elishah] and Egypt [Mizraim]; 10:4, 6); or an individual is said to have begotten (fathered) a place (Sidon; 10:15), or a place to have fathered tribes (Egypt [Mizraim] fathered tribes; 10:13-14). While it is possible that all the names were at first names of individuals, it is more probable that they were the names of cities, lands, and tribes (especially when they end with the Hebrew plural -*im*). A horizontal genealogy like this one is designed to show tribal affiliations, but it retains the normal terminology of vertical genealogies that trace lineage.

A certain unity of the human race is stressed here, even though the chapter prepares the reader for the history of these groups, which are divided and often antagonistic to one another. Be that as it may, the fact remains that they all came from one man, Noah. They were therefore one people, although some were more closely related than others. But the plight of the human race, here on the eve of the call of Abram, is that the families of the earth were hopelessly divided, speaking different languages, living in their lands, and following their own cultural affiliations. Wars and conflicts inevitably resulted from this situation. God's calling of Abraham makes the point that, of all the families and tribes on the earth, none were deemed worthy to be the people of God; God would have to make a new nation to serve him.

◆ ## 2. The dispersion at Babel (11:1-9)

At one time all the people of the world spoke the same language and used the same words. ²As the people migrated to the east, they found a plain in the land of Babylonia* and settled there.

³They began saying to each other, "Let's make bricks and harden them with fire." (In this region bricks were used instead of stone, and tar was used for mortar.) ⁴Then they said, "Come, let's build a great city for ourselves with a tower that reaches into the sky. This will make us famous and keep us from being scattered all over the world."

⁵But the LORD came down to look at the city and the tower the people were building. ⁶"Look!" he said. "The people are united, and they all speak the same language. After this, nothing they set out to do will be impossible for them! ⁷Come, let's go down and confuse the people with different languages. Then they won't be able to understand each other."

⁸In that way, the LORD scattered them all over the world, and they stopped building the city. ⁹That is why the city was called Babel,* because that is where the LORD confused the people with different languages. In this way he scattered them all over the world.

11:2 Hebrew *Shinar.* 11:9 Or *Babylon. Babel* sounds like a Hebrew term that means "confusion."

NOTES

11:1-9 This account falls chronologically within the time span narrated in ch 10 (see commentary above). The account in ch 11 is structured in an antithetical parallelism known as a chiasm. At the beginning, the people are united and speaking one language; at the end, they are scattered and speaking different languages. The material in between explains this reversal. Everything that mankind proposes in the first half (11:1-4) is disposed of in the second half (11:5-9). This undoing or reversing of what the humans did is stressed by the reversal of sounds in the words that are used: The people say, "Come, let's *make bricks*" (*laban* [TH3835A, ZH4236]); and "Come, let's *build*" (*banah* [TH1129, ZH1215]). But God reverses their plans and mocks their words, saying, "Come, let's go down and confuse" (*balal* [TH1101, ZH1176]). The repetition of the Hebrew letters Beth, Lamedh, and Nun are used in the parallel sections to underscore the reversal; and they prepare the reader for the final contrast, the name *babel* [TH894, ZH951] and the explanatory verb "confuse" (*balal* [TH1101, ZH1176]). (For a detailed look at this chiastic structure and all the sound plays in the passage, see Ross 1981.) The turning point in the story, and so in the parallel structure, is found in the statement "But the LORD came down" (11:5).

11:9 *That is why the city was called Babel.* The name Babel (*babel* [TH894, ZH951]) sounds like the Hebrew verb "confuse" (*balal* [TH1101, ZH1176]). The Babylonians spoke of their city with immense pride; in the Babylonian language the name meant "the gate of god"; but in this wordplay on the name, an interpretation of "confusion" is given to the name. Gradually the name and its interpretation came to refer to people who spoke with a strange language—barbarians.

COMMENTARY

This account explains how the nations came to be scattered around the world, speaking different languages. It is an account of divine judgment for disobedience; the unity the people prided themselves in became their downfall, and what they feared the most, being scattered, came upon them (cf. Prov 10:24a).

The narrative begins with the migration of the people down to the region of Shinar, the area later known as Babylon. They settled there and began to build their city and tower to make a name for themselves. From their motive and from their actions it becomes clear that these "Shinarites" had immense pride—what one could call hubris. They had been commanded to spread out and fill the earth (9:7), but they came together and strengthened their identity. This was open rebellion against the command of God; more than that, it was independence from God. In the Bible, humility is often equated with trust and obedience, and pride with independence and disobedience. Here they came together to strengthen themselves with their building and to become famous. They were driven by the fear of being scattered and the pride of becoming famous. They tried to avoid the very thing God wanted; and the way they chose to avoid it would make them famous, but not as they thought.

They certainly had ingenuity. They were in an area that had no stones for building and nothing with which to cement the bricks together. So they first had to make the bricks, then build the city. The passage introduces these two steps with the hortatory verb *yahab* [TH3051, ZH3364]: "*Let's* make bricks and harden them with fire"; "*Come, let's* build a great city for ourselves" (11:3-4). They believed this would give them fame and protection against being scattered everywhere (11:4).

But the Lord recognized that their desire to gain strength in their unity had potential for great evil (11:6).

The narrative turns with the Lord's coming down "to look at the city and the tower the people were building" (11:5). The words of the Lord deliberately mimicked their words, "*Come, let's* go down and confuse" (11:7) to show that their work was going to be undone. The reason for the divine judgment on the people of Shinar is expressed in terms of the threat that their unity posed. The Lord said, "If this people, having one language, have begun to do this, then nothing they set out to do will be impossible for them" (11:6, my translation). Thus, what they would not do in obedience, God did through the judgment, and what they would have done in disobedience, God prevented by confusing and dispersing them (11:8). The work of God was preventive as well as punitive.

That the region of Shinar refers to Babylon is clear because of the play on the name at the end of the episode. The name Babel (*babel* [TH894, ZH951]) sounds like the Hebrew verb "confuse" (*balal* [TH1101, ZH1176]). Thus, the narrative forms a polemic against the traditions about the city of Babylon, referring even to the texts and the architecture of those traditions. The Babylonian accounts of the origin of the city place its construction in the heavens by the gods as a celestial city, an expression of immense pride (see *Enuma Elish* VI, lines 50-64). The accounts say that its construction first involved a ceremony of brick-making (as described in 11:3), with every brick inscribed with the name of the Babylonian god Marduk. They then used these products to build the city and its tower. The gods then brought the celestial city down to earth. (Note how the tables are turned in Rev 18–22, where Babylon is destroyed, and afterward the heavenly city of Jerusalem descends.) But in Genesis, Babylon is the work of humans, "sons of man," and not of gods.

The building of a tower recorded in Genesis refers to the original building of the tower of stairs (known as a *ziggurat*) so common in the cities of the East such as Babylon. The Babylonians described their temple tower as the tower with its top in the heavens (cf. 11:4). This artificial mountain became the center of worship in the city, with a temple to the high god situated at the very top of the pyramid. But according to Genesis, no matter how high they ascended, the Lord still had to descend to see what they were building. And the many languages that were spoken in the city, considered by some to be evidence of the richness of its diverse cultures, were actually the result of judgment from God.

The biblical records view this city as the predominant force in the world for the "anti-kingdom," the epitome of ungodly powers, where the seed of the serpent would move with terrifying freedom. This passage shows that God is sovereign over even this, and that his judgment is swift. What the people considered their greatest and indispensible strength, their unity, God easily destroyed by confusing their language (11:7, 9). And what they considered their greatest fear, being scattered abroad (11:4), came upon them as they went their separate ways over all the earth (11:8-9). What they desired the most, to make a name for themselves (11:4), ironically came about by their receiving the name Babylon, negatively interpreted through a

Hebrew wordplay. All that the Lord had to do was alter their communication slightly, perhaps even dialectically, so that they could not understand each other. After they were scattered and banded together in language groups, they developed their own full languages, cultures, and characteristics.

This narrative provides a fitting conclusion for the primeval events of Genesis 1–11. It leaves the families of the earth hopelessly scattered throughout the then-known world. At this point there was no mark to protect the dispersed fugitives (cf. 4:15), no rainbow in the clouds to signal the that this judgment was over (cf. 9:13), no token of grace to give them hope (6:8). The ending leaves the reader looking for a solution. And so, after a genealogy connecting these events to later ones (11:10-26), that solution is recounted: Out of the scattered nations God chose one man to form a completely new nation that would become his channel of blessing to the whole world. God was not through with the human race. He simply scattered them abroad, to different languages and cultures and lands, where they would war with one another. This activity on their part would keep all of them in check. God knew that the consequent nationalism and warfare were lesser problems than that of collective apostasy.

For the first readers of Genesis, this story not only explained the many nations listed in chapter 10, it also taught an important theological lesson. Israel was to be united as the people of God, unique in all the world. The one simple requirement for them was to obey the word of the Lord. If they did, God would establish them firmly in the land; if they rebelled against the Lord and his institutions, then they too would be scattered across the whole face of the earth and speak different languages. And that is what happened. Israel followed the same disastrous path as the ancient Babylonians and actually ended up in exile in Babylon. Thus, the theme of arrogant rebellion is central to the story. God puts down those who exalt themselves. God's plan will be established, if not with man's cooperation and obedience, then in spite of his disobedience.

This event at Babylon was used by the prophet Zephaniah to prophesy the great regathering and unification of God's people at the end of the age. Zephaniah reversed the motifs of this account, telling how the scattered people would be regathered from places like Cush (a name perhaps also used for Babylon or places in the East) and come to the holy mountain (not a *ziggurat*) and worship in one accord, everyone speaking one purified language (Zeph 3:9-11, ESV). The miracle of tongues at Pentecost was a harbinger of this future reversal of the dispersion that will occur at the end of the age (Acts 2:6-11).

◆ F. The Account of the Succession from Shem (11:10-26)

¹⁰This is the account of Shem's family.

Two years after the great flood, when Shem was 100 years old, he became the father of* Arphaxad. ¹¹After the birth of* Arphaxad, Shem lived another 500 years and had other sons and daughters.

¹²When Arphaxad was 35 years old, he became the father of Shelah. ¹³After

the birth of Shelah, Arphaxad lived another 403 years and had other sons and daughters.* ¹⁴When Shelah was 30 years old, he became the father of Eber. ¹⁵After the birth of Eber, Shelah lived another 403 years and had other sons and daughters. ¹⁶When Eber was 34 years old, he became the father of Peleg. ¹⁷After the birth of Peleg, Eber lived another 430 years and had other sons and daughters. ¹⁸When Peleg was 30 years old, he became the father of Reu. ¹⁹After the birth of Reu, Peleg lived another 209 years and had other sons and daughters. ²⁰When Reu was 32 years old, he became the father of Serug. ²¹After the birth of Serug, Reu lived another 207 years and had other sons and daughters. ²²When Serug was 30 years old, he became the father of Nahor. ²³After the birth of Nahor, Serug lived another 200 years and had other sons and daughters. ²⁴When Nahor was 29 years old, he became the father of Terah. ²⁵After the birth of Terah, Nahor lived another 119 years and had other sons and daughters. ²⁶After Terah was 70 years old, he became the father of Abram, Nahor, and Haran.

11:10 Or *the ancestor of;* also in 11:12, 14, 16, 18, 20, 22, 24. 11:11 Or *the birth of this ancestor of;* also in 11:13, 15, 17, 19, 21, 23, 25. 11:12-13 Greek version reads ¹²*When Arphaxad was 135 years old, he became the father of Cainan.* ¹³*After the birth of Cainan, Arphaxad lived another 430 years and had other sons and daughters, and then he died. When Cainan was 130 years old, he became the father of Shelah. After the birth of Shelah, Cainan lived another 330 years and had other sons and daughters, and then he died.* Compare Luke 3:35-36.

NOTES

11:10-26 Are there gaps in this genealogy, or is this a closed chronological record of the ancestors? The symmetry of the genealogies in chs 5 and 11 suggests that their compiler wanted to show a harmony and a contrast between the two: Both lists have 10 names, and the last name on each list has three sons. To allow gaps in the genealogy, one must posit ellipses in formula "X lived so many years and begot [the line that culminated in] Y." Such ellipses are very hard to prove without some notification from the writer. Moreover, gaps are not possible in two places: Shem was literally the son of Noah, and Abram was literally the son of Terah. Taking these two panels as a guide, vv. 10-26 would also seem to present a tight chronology. But that is not an indisputable conclusion, for each relationship in the list need not be understood in the sense that these two are. People who deal with history and archaeology often argue for gaps, otherwise the Flood and the confusion of languages would come quite late in history, later than known languages and kingdoms.

COMMENTARY

This vertical genealogy (cf. ch 5) traces the line from Shem, who survived the great Flood, to Abram. The symmetry of the genealogies in Genesis 5 and 11 (each lists 10 fathers, the last having three sons) indicates selectivity in composition. This is all part of the design to bring the greatest attention to the three sons, first Shem, Ham and Japheth, and now Abram, Nahor and Haran. In Genesis 10 the Table of Nations was a horizontal genealogy, showing how the descendants of Noah's sons were related. Here all the attention is given to the Shemites. And if the purpose of a vertical genealogy is to trace someone's authenticity to the ancestors and the history of the faithful, this genealogy shows the straight line of the blessing (9:26) from Shem to Abram, thus authenticating God's handing down the blessing to Abram.

The main contribution of this passage is the linkage of Abram with the line of Shem and the divine blessing. Whether there are gaps or not on the list, the ancestry of Israel lies here in God's blessing. But unlike the genealogy of chapter 5, the list in 11:10-26 does not total the number of years of each person, and does not end with "and he died." Genesis 5:1-32 stresses death before the great Flood; Genesis 11:10-26 stresses life and expansion, even though longevity was declining. The mood of this passage is different; 5:1-32 led to Noah and judgment, but 11:10-26 leads to Abram and blessing.

◆ **II. The Patriarchal Narratives (11:27–37:1)**
  A. The Account of the Succession from Terah (11:27–25:11)
  1. The Lord's call to Abram (11:27–12:9)

²⁷This is the account of Terah's family. Terah was the father of Abram, Nahor, and Haran; and Haran was the father of Lot. ²⁸But Haran died in Ur of the Chaldeans, the land of his birth, while his father, Terah, was still living. ²⁹Meanwhile, Abram and Nahor both married. The name of Abram's wife was Sarai, and the name of Nahor's wife was Milcah. (Milcah and her sister Iscah were daughters of Nahor's brother Haran.) ³⁰But Sarai was unable to become pregnant and had no children.

³¹One day Terah took his son Abram, his daughter-in-law Sarai (his son Abram's wife), and his grandson Lot (his son Haran's child) and moved away from Ur of the Chaldeans. He was headed for the land of Canaan, but they stopped at Haran and settled there. ³²Terah lived for 205 years* and died while still in Haran.

CHAPTER 12

The LORD had said to Abram, "Leave your native country, your relatives, and your father's family, and go to the land that I will show you. ²I will make you into a great nation. I will bless you and make you famous, and you will be a blessing to others. ³I will bless those who bless you and curse those who treat you with contempt. All the families on earth will be blessed through you."

⁴So Abram departed as the LORD had instructed, and Lot went with him. Abram was seventy-five years old when he left Haran. ⁵He took his wife, Sarai, his nephew Lot, and all his wealth—his livestock and all the people he had taken into his household at Haran—and headed for the land of Canaan. When they arrived in Canaan, ⁶Abram traveled through the land as far as Shechem. There he set up camp beside the oak of Moreh. At that time, the area was inhabited by Canaanites.

⁷Then the LORD appeared to Abram and said, "I will give this land to your descendants.*" And Abram built an altar there and dedicated it to the LORD, who had appeared to him. ⁸After that, Abram traveled south and set up camp in the hill country, with Bethel to the west and Ai to the east. There he built another altar and dedicated it to the LORD, and he worshiped the LORD. ⁹Then Abram continued traveling south by stages toward the Negev.

11:32 Some ancient versions read *145 years;* compare 11:26 and 12:4. 12:7 Hebrew *seed.*

NOTES

11:27 *the account of Terah's family.* We should read 11:27 as the title for the whole section about Abram and verses 28-32 as the complete summary of Terah's move and death—

almost a parenthesis to the main point of the story, bringing closure to the topic of Terah's life. The narrative then actually begins with the report of the call in 12:1. The strict sequence, then, could be read: "Now this is the record of Terah; Terah begot Abram, Nahor and Haran . . . And the Lord said to Abram. . . ." The note about the marriages and the move to Haran is then incidental to the main flow of the narrative. The text offers no further details about the chronology; its main interest is the call.

11:31 *moved away from Ur of the Chaldeans.* The Bible is clear that the call of Abram occurred in Ur of the Chaldeans (15:7; Acts 7:3-4), but the sequence from Genesis 11 to 12 suggests that he received the call after the family moved to Haran. It does not help to attempt to locate a place named Ur near Haran, because the Bible clarifies that it was Ur of the Chaldeans, the great city of Ur near the mouth of the Persian Gulf. One would have to conclude that once again the style of the writer does not follow a strict chronological sequence. In fact, Genesis often will tidy up one part of the family before focusing on the chosen line. The chronological order should be understood with God's call coming to Abram in Ur before the family moved to Haran; the notes about the sons' marriages and the family's move would then be incidental to the overall emphasis on the call.

It seems likely that the family had moved down to Ur, the main city of Sumer, sometime before Abram's call, perhaps even generations before, for their ancestral home was in the region of Haran. Support for this comes from the designation of the family as wandering Arameans (Deut 26:5) and from the location of the Shemites in the genealogy in 11:10-26 in that area. It was in Ur that Terah's youngest son, Haran, died. With a call that promised an inheritance of land (12:1-3), the natural thought may have been to go to Haran. But in Haran, Terah died; and since no word of confirmation came to Abram (i.e., God had not yet shown him the place, 12:1), he continued west looking for the Promised Land. Others, no doubt, were migrating westward, but Abram had a reason, a call.

12:1-3 The first three verses record the call of God in poetic form; and then 12:4-9 records the response of Abram by faith. The structure of the first three verses lays out two commands and the promises that follow each of them, but this is sometimes lost in the translations. The first imperative cannot be missed: "Get out" (NLT, "Leave"). It is followed by three promises that God made to Abram if he would get out: He would make Abram "a great nation," he would bless him, and make him famous. The next imperative is often subordinated to the preceding as a purpose clause, "that you may be a blessing," and that captures the sequence of the verbs nicely: God promised to do these three things "so that" Abram would be a blessing. But Abram still was commanded to be a blessing—it is still an imperative. This imperative is followed by three more promises. Because of the sequential construction of the clauses, the entire call of Abram follows a chain reaction, beginning with his getting out of Ur. This structure also emphasizes that his call had a purpose—to be a blessing.

12:3 *I will bless those who bless you and curse those who treat you with contempt. All the families on earth will be blessed through you.* The wording of these promises is precise. The first uses the cohortative construction of the verb that stresses God's determination or resolve, and the object, the participle, is a plural form: "I am determined to bless all those who bless you." But the second clause makes some changes. The verb is not a cohortative but a simple imperfect, probably expressing obligation (since he was binding himself to Abram), and the participle is singular, perhaps indicating a hesitancy to curse as opposed to the desire to bless. Moreover, the Hebrew words in the two halves of the second clause are different (see NLT): The participle means "the one who treats you lightly" (from *qalal* [TH7043, ZH7837]), but the verb is the normal word for "curse," that is, to remove someone from the place of blessing. Thus, it would read: "But the one who treats you lightly I must curse."

COMMENTARY

The brief beginning section (11:27-32) accounts for the births of the sons of Terah and their marriages; it also accounts for Lot, Abram's nephew, who will figure prominently in some of the stories. Terah, or his family, was apparently idolatrous, worshiping other gods on the other side of the Fertile Crescent (see Josh 24:2). But with the call of Abram there seemed to be a change in the family, at the very least, a willingness to leave Ur and go back to Haran.

The stories about Abram, which begin in 11:27, come under the heading of "the *toledoth* [TH8435, ZH9352] of Terah," that is, they are "what became of Terah." What follows this heading are the particulars about the family descended from Terah, notably about Abram and the covenant. The narrative begins with the report of Terah's move to Haran where he died, and then turns immediately to the call of Abram. The account comes to an end after Abraham finally has a son, Isaac, the child of promise, to carry forward the line and the blessing to the next generation.

With this passage the focus of the book narrows from the wider history of the human race to that of one family. It records how God called Abram out of a pagan world and made amazing promises to him, promises that later became the Abrahamic covenant. The passage also extols the faith of Abram, teaching that faith obeys the word of the Lord. Here was a man who was middle-aged, settled, prosperous, aristocratic, and probably pagan (although it is possible that among the gods he revered there was a remembrance of the ancestral God Yahweh). Then suddenly the word of the Lord came to him, although it is not known exactly how. He obeyed the word, turned his back on the old ways, and obediently left Ur to follow God's direction (see note on 11:31; cf. 15:7). That is why Abram is the epitome of faith in the Bible, and believers are referred to as "the seed of Abraham" (cf. Rom 4:1-3, 16-24; Gal 3:6-9; Heb 11:8-19; Jas 2:21-23).

The story of God's calling of Abram to begin a new nation that would bring blessing to the world was a history lesson for Israel. Israel would realize through this event that her very existence was God's work, carried out through a man who lived by faith. It would therefore be a message to convince Israel of the divine call they had in Egypt. And later, when the Israelites were in exile in Babylon, this record of the very beginning of God's plan for them as a nation would remind them that their future was not in Babylon but in the Promised Land.

The nature of the life of faith is clearly displayed in God's call to Abram, who was told to leave his country, his people, and his father's household. It was very clear what he should leave; it was not clear where he would be going. That is where the faith comes in. All that God said was that it would be a land that he would show him.

Once Abram left, God was then bound to do the three things he had promised (see note on 12:1-3): make from him a great nation, bless him, and make him famous (make his name great). All three of these promises have been fulfilled because of the faithful response of Abram. And the fulfillment of these promises enabled Abraham to be the blessing that God wanted him to be. Then, according to his obedience to the command to be a blessing, God promised to do three more things for him: bless those who bless him, curse anyone who would treat him lightly, and bless the families of the earth through him (see note on 12:3). Abram's blessing was a blessing that would extend to all the families of the earth; it included all the ways that the blessing was spread—through Israel, the Scriptures, the prophets, the covenants, and ultimately the Messiah, its greatest fulfillment (Gal 3:8, 16; cf. Rom 9:5). People who, by faith, revered the covenant that God was making with Abram and therefore blessed Abram would be blessed in return. If people treated Abram lightly, that is, saw no importance for him or his covenant, they would be rejecting God, his choice, and his plan. God would be bound to separate such people from the blessing—although these persons actually would have already removed themselves.

The themes of blessing and cursing that are highlighted here run through the entire book of Genesis. This passage forms the central episode of the book; here God begins his program to restore the blessing that was there in the beginning. Everything before this chapter lays down the need for blessing, and everything following it traces its development in the faith and family of Abram. Because Abram responded by faith, these promises of God could be confirmed in a binding covenant (15:8-21).

The second part of the narrative (12:4-9) simply reports that Abram got out. His obedience to the call was demonstrated in two ways, corresponding to the two imperatives of the previous section: He left (12:4) and he was a blessing (12:5-9). In Haran, a good number of "people" (*nephesh* [TH5315, ZH5883], "souls") were acquired (lit., "made") by Abram. This "making of living beings" cannot refer to having children since Abram and Sarai had none; nor is it the typical way to refer to acquiring servants. In the same passage God has already used the verb "make" in the sense of "make you into a great nation." That is not just a promise for numerous descendants but for the formation of a nation by covenant. Thus, "making souls" here refers to proselytizing—that is, to Abram's influence on people to join him in following Yahweh's call in this new venture.

But how would this influence be expressed? The answer comes from the next verses, which report how Abram continued to be a blessing: He made altars, first at Shechem (12:6-7) and then east of Bethel (12:8). One may safely assume that he made animal sacrifices on these altars (see 22:8). But at the second location of his worship, the Hebrew text says that "he made proclamation of Yahweh by name." Some translations render 12:8 as "[Abram] called on the name of the LORD [Yahweh]," and the NLT interprets the verse to mean "he worshiped the LORD." But the usage of the expression in the Pentateuch points to a more specific meaning; this is the same kind of expression found in Genesis 4:26 where the worship of Yahweh began. The most helpful passage for understanding the expression is Exodus 34:5-7, where the same clause is found, but with Yahweh as the speaker—Yahweh proclaimed the name of Yahweh. And in that passage, we have exactly what Yahweh proclaimed as he passed by—a long list of the divine attributes. This explanation of Yahweh's nature is what the text means by "the name of Yahweh." We see this very clearly in passages such as Isaiah 9:6 ("His name will be called Wonderful . . .";

NASB). In time, Israel's creeds developed out of passages such as Exodus 34, for the formulation of their faith in the Lord required that they affirm that Yahweh is "the God of compassion and mercy . . . slow to anger and filled with unfailing love and faithfulness," who lavishes unfailing love on thousands and forgives iniquity, rebellion, and sin. When Abram built an altar, in order to distinguish his worship from Canaanite worship, he proclaimed the person and the nature of his God, Yahweh.

Apparently Abram was in the custom of making an altar to sacrifice to God; but to distinguish that ritual act from similar acts of the Canaanites, he proclaimed the nature of the Lord whom he was worshiping. Luther translated this verb "preached"; he was not far off. God thus had a worshiper and a witness in the land, in the midst of the Canaanites. In fact, it appears that Abram camped near one of their shrines, a place called "the oak of Moreh" (12:6). In Hebrew, a "Moreh" (*moreh* [TH4175B, ZH4621]) was a teacher. Groves of trees were considered sacred spots to the Canaanites because of their fertility. Judging by the name given here, this may have been a place where Canaanite priests gave instruction in their ritual and myth. Thus, Abram proclaimed the name of Yahweh next to a Canaanite holy place, a place of pagan worship and instruction. This is what he probably had been doing in Haran to gain the proselytes who came with him.

It was at Shechem that the Lord appeared to Abram to confirm that this was indeed the Land of Promise: "I will give this land to your descendants" (12:7). Abram had arrived in Canaan, and God showed it to him. But it would not be given to him as a possession; it would be given to his descendants. That, however, would constitute a continuing blessing from God, for it meant that the land would belong to Abram's family long after he was gone. Abram dwelt in the land as a temporary settler (a "sojourner"), waiting for the promises. But since the Canaanites had all the good, fertile lands, Abram had to keep moving his camp (by stages) down toward the Negev, the dry south desert (12:9).

For Israel in Moses's time, the call of Abram made it clear that the covenant promises came from God: promises of a land, a divine blessing, a great nation, and sovereign protection. Yahweh's appearance and confirmation (12:7) proved that Canaan was to be their destiny. But as always, God demanded faith in his word if they or any other generation were to share in the promises.

◆ ## 2. Abram and Sarai in Egypt (12:10-20)

¹⁰At that time a severe famine struck the land of Canaan, forcing Abram to go down to Egypt, where he lived as a foreigner. ¹¹As he was approaching the border of Egypt, Abram said to his wife, Sarai, "Look, you are a very beautiful woman. ¹²When the Egyptians see you, they will say, 'This is his wife. Let's kill him; then we can have her!' ¹³So please tell them you are my sister. Then they will spare my life and treat me well because of their interest in you."

¹⁴And sure enough, when Abram arrived in Egypt, everyone noticed Sarai's beauty. ¹⁵When the palace officials saw her, they sang her praises to Pharaoh, their king, and Sarai was taken into his palace. ¹⁶Then Pharaoh gave Abram many gifts

because of her—sheep, goats, cattle, male and female donkeys, male and female servants, and camels.

17But the LORD sent terrible plagues upon Pharaoh and his household because of Sarai, Abram's wife. **18**So Pharaoh summoned Abram and accused him sharply. "What have you done to me?" he demanded. "Why didn't you tell me she was your wife? **19**Why did you say, 'She is my sister,' and allow me to take her as my wife? Now then, here is your wife. Take her and get out of here!" **20**Pharaoh ordered some of his men to escort them, and he sent Abram out of the country, along with his wife and all his possessions.

NOTES

12:10 *At that time.* The chronology that the Bible presents in its notation of years for events and ages for the patriarchs would put the call of Abram at 2091 BC. The birth of Isaac, coming 25 years later (cf. 12:4; 21:5), occurred in 2066 BC. Thus, when Abram went into Egypt, many of the pyramids including the Great Pyramid, were already hundreds of years old. Since Abram went to Egypt very shortly after his arrival in Canaan, the Egyptian king he lied to would have been Wahkare Achthoes III (c. 2120–2070) of Dynasty 10. Interestingly, this Egyptian king wrote wisdom literature including advice concerning the treachery of Asiatics. Could this be related in some way to Abram's duplicity? For a discussion of these dates and all the related possibilities, see Merrill 1987:35.

12:11 *you are a very beautiful woman.* Sarai's beauty has perplexed many people because she was 65 years old when they went down into Egypt. But two things need to be remembered. She may have been 65, but she lived to be about 127. In other words, in the eyes of men at the time she would probably be like a modern woman of about 35, and one who had never had children. Secondly, if she and Abram had come from a noble family, as the Bible suggests, she would have been very well groomed and very regal in her person. One would be surprised if the Pharaoh did not take an interest.

12:13 *tell them you are my sister.* The claim that "she is my sister" occurs three times in the patriarchal narratives, twice by Abraham and once by Isaac (12:13; 20:2; 26:7). The first occurence (ch 12) is outside the land, and the second (ch 20) occurs inside the land, showing that God protects his promise in both regions despite the way Abram endangers it. The thesis that these stories are variants of one tradition has always been part of the literary critical analysis of the text (see Skinner 1930:240-241), and even now, when Pentateuch criticism has been greatly modified, it remains a standard view (see Westermann 1986:161).

COMMENTARY

This little episode has much more to it than a lesson on honesty, although it does warn against the foolishness of trying to lie to escape a difficulty. Abram seems to have profited from the lie, but the wealth and servants (including probably Hagar) he accumulated would create even greater problems later. The narrative reveals how the Lord would not allow the patriarch to jeopardize the promise through his deception of the king of Egypt. God would deliver Abram and his family in spite of his foolishness. As a typical narrative, the story is traced through an arc of tension—the famine and the fear of a threat to the marriage—to its inglorious resolution. But in its solution are the seeds of further crises.

One cannot miss the fact that the way the story is told shows deliberate parallelism with the later bondage of the Israelites in Egypt: There was a famine in the land (12:10; 47:13); they went down to sojourn in Egypt (12:10; cf. 47:27); there was an attempt to kill the males and save the females (12:12; cf. Exod 1:22); God plagued Egypt (12:17; cf. Exod 7:14–11:10); they spoiled Egypt (12:16; cf. Exod 12:35-36); they were expelled from Egypt (12:20; cf. Exod 14, 15, where the same verb is used: *shalakh* [TH7971, ZH8938]); and they escaped to the Negev (13:1; cf. Num 13:17, 22). This story had significant import for the book's Israelite audience in Egypt before and after the Exodus. The great deliverance out of bondage in Egypt that Israel was to experience had already been accomplished for her ancestor, the one to whom the promises were given. This fact was probably a source of comfort and encouragement to the Israelites. So God was doing more than promising deliverance for the future nation; it was as if in anticipation of the Exodus event he acted out their deliverance in Abram.

In relation to the message of the book, 12:10-20 is significantly placed right after the obedience of Abram to the call. The famine in the land was designed to test Abram; and the test showed him to be weak in his faith.

Abram's scheme, born out of fear, turned out badly, and God's promises to him were thrown into jeopardy. He put his family in a position that he could not resolve. Faced with a famine, he decided to go to Egypt temporarily. One cannot fault Abram for doing this; after all, he needed water for his large household and his animals. But there is no sign that he was walking by faith when he went. His custom of building altars ceases, and his deception takes center stage. The scheme he concocted was to speak a half-truth about his wife, who happened to be his half-sister (20:12). This lie was clever, because while it was clearly intended to deceive the Pharaoh, it was also worded in such a way that Abram could salve his own conscience—he did not technically lie, after all. Besides, he could rationalize, in a foreign land they might kill the man to get to his wife. He could die, and Sarai's life would be very bad if she was left alone there. So he would convey to the Egyptians what he wanted them to know. His plan was probably based on the social customs of the day in which the brother would arrange the marriage of his sister (cf. 24:29-61). He may have thought that if someone was attracted to her, that person would have to deal with him, and that would give him time to get away. So he instructed Sarai to say she was his sister in order that things would go well for him. But the one thing he did not count on was Pharaoh—a person who did not need to negotiate.

When they entered Egypt the young princes saw that Sarai was extremely beautiful, and so they praised her to Pharaoh (12:14-15). Almost immediately, Sarai was taken into the harem of the palace to be made ready for the king. And here is where the ironic twist to the story comes: It went well with Abram because of Sarai. The king gave him animals and servants so that he became even more wealthy. But all this wealth bound Abram to an agreement about Sarai that he did not want but that he could not stop. Here he was in Egypt, without Sarai, and hence without a hope for the blessings of the promise.

The Lord intervened; he plagued the residents of the palace with very serious diseases, sufficient to make them realize that the addition of Sarai to the harem was a misstep. Divine intervention alone could deliver Sarai and keep the marriage together for the fulfillment of covenant. But the restoration of Sarai to Abram came with a rebuke (from Pharaoh but on God's behalf): "Why didn't you tell me she was your wife?" (12:18-19). Pharaoh was an honorable man, and adultery was considered a great sin. There was no need for an answer. The rebuke was followed by an expulsion from the land (12:20).

One can see in this story how the Lord delivered the family from the Egyptians by plagues and how that foreshadowed the future Exodus experience. But this story is also the record of the developing faith of Abram. The deliverance was made necessary because of Abram's deception, a trait that would plague the family, as recorded throughout the entire book of Genesis. Abram, and his descendants after him, thought that deception was the easiest way out of a threatening situation, but all it did for Abram was to put him and Sarai in danger. Still, God was faithful to his word and did not let this foolishness of man throw the whole covenant into jeopardy. The people of God would learn from his mistake that they should trust the Lord and fear no man.

At the time, it appeared that Abram prospered from his deception because he came away with great wealth. It is true that he got rich, but those riches would always remind him how he nearly lost his wife. Moreover, two subsequent crises were about to develop because of these new possessions. In chapter 13, Abram and Lot have so many things that their men almost come to blows; they must separate. And in chapter 16, an Egyptian maid named Hagar causes strife between Abraham and Sarai. In giving away his wife, Sarai, Abram likely acquired the slave Hagar as a gift from the Egyptians, and she would become the mother of the Ishmaelites, the perennial enemies of the Israelites. So the deception of Abram in Egypt immediately brought him additional possessions, but the abundance of his possessions would occasion new troubles in his future.

◆ ### 3. Abram's separation from Lot (13:1-18)

So Abram left Egypt and traveled north into the Negev, along with his wife and Lot and all that they owned. ²(Abram was very rich in livestock, silver, and gold.) ³From the Negev, they continued traveling by stages toward Bethel, and they pitched their tents between Bethel and Ai, where they had camped before. ⁴This was the same place where Abram had built the altar, and there he worshiped the LORD again.

⁵Lot, who was traveling with Abram, had also become very wealthy with flocks of sheep and goats, herds of cattle, and many tents. ⁶But the land could not support both Abram and Lot with all their flocks and herds living so close together. ⁷So disputes broke out between the herdsmen of Abram and Lot. (At that time Canaanites and Perizzites were also living in the land.)

⁸Finally Abram said to Lot, "Let's not allow this conflict to come between us or our herdsmen. After all, we are close relatives! ⁹The whole countryside is open to you. Take your choice of any section of the land you want, and we will separate. If you want the land to the left, then I'll take the land on the right. If you prefer the land on the right, then I'll go to the left."

¹⁰Lot took a long look at the fertile plains of the Jordan Valley in the direction

of Zoar. The whole area was well watered everywhere, like the garden of the LORD or the beautiful land of Egypt. (This was before the LORD destroyed Sodom and Gomorrah.) ¹¹Lot chose for himself the whole Jordan Valley to the east of them. He went there with his flocks and servants and parted company with his uncle Abram. ¹²So Abram settled in the land of Canaan, and Lot moved his tents to a place near Sodom and settled among the cities of the plain. ¹³But the people of this area were extremely wicked and constantly sinned against the LORD.

¹⁴After Lot had gone, the LORD said to Abram, "Look as far as you can see in every direction—north and south, east and west. ¹⁵I am giving all this land, as far as you can see, to you and your descendants* as a permanent possession. ¹⁶And I will give you so many descendants that, like the dust of the earth, they cannot be counted! ¹⁷Go and walk through the land in every direction, for I am giving it to you."

¹⁸So Abram moved his camp to Hebron and settled near the oak grove belonging to Mamre. There he built another altar to the LORD.

13:15 Hebrew *seed*; also in 13:16.

NOTES

13:5 *Lot, who was traveling with Abram, had also become very wealthy.* Crucial to the introductory paragraph is the stress on the wealth of Abram (13:2): He was rich (lit., "heavy") in livestock and silver and gold. But Lot was also wealthy; he had flocks and herds and tents (13:5). It is not that Abram had no tents; but tents are mentioned for Lot because they would figure prominently in the story about him.

13:8 *Let's not allow this conflict to come between us.* Abram's concern was that there be no strife between them because they were relatives. The wording of the statement must have struck a nerve with the later Israelite audience who heard it: "Let there be no *meribah* [TH4808, ZH5312]." This wording clearly foreshadows the incident on the way to Sinai where the people strove with the Lord over the water (Exod 17:7). Ever after Massah and Meribah became watchwords for testing the Lord and striving with him (Ps 95). As a result of this tendency, the people of Israel were condemned to wander in the wilderness until they all died, not receiving the Promised Land (Ps 95:8-10). Their selfishness exhibited unbelief (Ps 95:10), so that they did not enter the Lord's rest (Ps 95:11).

13:10 *the fertile plains of the Jordan Valley . . . like the garden of the LORD or the beautiful land of Egypt. (This was before the LORD destroyed Sodom and Gomorrah.)* The fertile plains (lit., "the circle or region") of the Jordan probably refers to the southern end of the Dead Sea, based on ancient records and the frequent descriptions of the location of the cities of the plain (see Fields 1997). The whole Jordan Valley and the area of the Dead Sea have undergone major changes over the ages, even in very early times being one huge inland sea. But in the days of Abraham, the valley was extremely fertile, judging from the lavish descriptions in this chapter. The Jordan Valley is still fertile with abundant produce, but not at the southern end—that area is desolate. That is why the text explains that the area was rich and fertile before the Lord destroyed it.

COMMENTARY

The first few verses of this section record the return of Abram to the place where he had been before but more importantly, to the place where he had built the altar—a return to where he had been spiritually. One cannot miss the emphasis placed on "before" and "again" in describing his return to the land (13:3-4). Back in the land, Abram renewed his worship and proclamation of the name of the Lord (cf. 12:8).

Soon, though, Abram's company found that they had too many possessions to stay together—the land could not sustain their dwelling together. The text then supplies the ominous note that the Canaanites and the Perizzites were at that time dwelling in the land (13:7; cf. 34:30; Deut 7:1; Judg 1:4; 3:5). These tribes held the good land with the water, and they were observing the men of Abram and Lot quarreling. In spite of this vulnerable position, the two sides continued to quarrel over the water and the land.

The situation was getting so tense that Abram realized that they would have to separate. And so he gave Lot the first choice. One might have expected that Abram, being the man to whom the land was promised, might have told Lot to go find his own place. But he magnanimously offered Lot the choice of land. And Lot made his choice purely from the human perspective, satisfying himself with the best of all the land. Abram's gesture was obviously an act of faith, for he knew that the promise was his, and that he did not have to cling to things. And he knew that even if he gave the whole land away, God would still give it to him and his descendants.

The motivation for Abram's concern must not be overlooked: They were close relatives (13:8). Their common bond shared over a long period of time was something that Abram did not want to lose. To keep that relationship intact required that they part company.

Abram offered Lot the choice of the whole land that was before him, the land that rightfully would belong to him. Lot lifted up his eyes and saw the whole plain of the Jordan Valley. The text then goes out of its way to describe it: It was lush and fruitful, well watered, "like the garden of the Lord," like the land of Egypt on the way to Zoar (13:10). (Zoar was a small town in the plain to which Lot and his daughters would later flee, 19:18-22; before then it was called Bela, 14:2.) But in the middle of this lavish description an ominous note is struck with the addition of a temporal clause: "before the LORD destroyed Sodom and Gomorrah" (13:10). The reader would know that what appealed to Lot was going to be short-lived. Also, the reader looking for that garden land would no longer find it, for it was desolate (the verb "destroyed" is a strong one, meaning "to completely ruin"—from *shakhath* [TH7843, ZH8845]).

Without a concern for Abram at all, Lot made his choice—the greatest mistake of his life. But then, he was walking by sight. Lot's choice was totally selfish—he "chose for himself" the best land (13:11). So Lot went off toward Sodom (13:12), and pitched his tents next to Sodom. The text then has another parenthetical clause to explain the danger; it says literally: "Now the men of Sodom were wicked sinners against the Lord—exceedingly" (13:13). The events of chapter 19 will demonstrate how wicked the people of this city were.

The final section of the chapter provides the reassurance that the Lord provided very good land for Abram (13:14-18). These verses explain why Abram could give the choice land away to Lot: Abram had the sure promise from God that it would still all be his. These verses also show a contrast between Abram and Lot. Earlier, Lot had been active in examining the land and taking what was the best for himself. Now the Lord instructed Abram in similar terms to lift up his eyes and look (13:14;

cf. 13:10) in every direction, for everything that he saw would be his. Abram was waiting for God to give him the land; Lot took the land he wanted. Better that God give it than that man take it. Repeating his promise, God told Abram that his descendants would be as numerous as the dust of the earth (cf. 22:17; 28:14). He then was invited by God to walk to and fro in all the land, to reconnoiter the land that would be his possession. The chapter closes the way that it began, with Abram settling down and making an altar to the Lord (this time near the great trees of Mamre [cf. 14:13], at Hebron, 22 miles south of Jerusalem).

Hardly any other chapter in the Bible portrays the reality of faith so marvelously. Here was the patriarch as a genuine believer in and worshiper of the Lord—one whose faith functioned in the midst of conflict. Lot's choice was self-seeking and self-gratifying. Such a choice was dangerous and short-lived, for all was not as it appeared to be on the surface. It would take spiritual discernment, not physical sight, to see what was wrong with the place. Abram, on the other hand, walking by faith, generously gave up the choice land to Lot. Generosity is the evidence of a living faith, for faith does not selfishly seek its own desires but is self-denying and magnanimous. Since Abram was trusting the Lord, he was not selfish. He had learned that it was not by his own plan or by jealously guarding what was his that he would come into his possessions. He acted righteously and generously.

◆ **4. Abram's victory over the invading kings (14:1-16)**

About this time war broke out in the region. King Amraphel of Babylonia,* King Arioch of Ellasar, King Kedorlaomer of Elam, and King Tidal of Goiim ²fought against King Bera of Sodom, King Birsha of Gomorrah, King Shinab of Admah, King Shemeber of Zeboiim, and the king of Bela (also called Zoar).

³This second group of kings joined forces in Siddim Valley (that is, the valley of the Dead Sea*). ⁴For twelve years they had been subject to King Kedorlaomer, but in the thirteenth year they rebelled against him.

⁵One year later Kedorlaomer and his allies arrived and defeated the Rephaites at Ashteroth-karnaim, the Zuzites at Ham, the Emites at Shaveh-kiriathaim, ⁶and the Horites at Mount Seir, as far as El-paran at the edge of the wilderness. ⁷Then they turned back and came to En-mishpat (now called Kadesh) and conquered all the territory of the Amalekites, and also the Amorites living in Hazazon-tamar.

⁸Then the rebel kings of Sodom, Gomorrah, Admah, Zeboiim, and Bela (also called Zoar) prepared for battle in the valley of the Dead Sea.* ⁹They fought against King Kedorlaomer of Elam, King Tidal of Goiim, King Amraphel of Babylonia, and King Arioch of Ellasar—four kings against five. ¹⁰As it happened, the valley of the Dead Sea was filled with tar pits. And as the army of the kings of Sodom and Gomorrah fled, some fell into the tar pits, while the rest escaped into the mountains. ¹¹The victorious invaders then plundered Sodom and Gomorrah and headed for home, taking with them all the spoils of war and the food supplies. ¹²They also captured Lot—Abram's nephew who lived in Sodom—and carried off everything he owned.

¹³But one of Lot's men escaped and reported everything to Abram the Hebrew, who was living near the oak grove belonging to Mamre the Amorite. Mamre and his relatives, Eshcol and Aner, were Abram's allies.

¹⁴When Abram heard that his nephew Lot had been captured, he mobilized the 318 trained men who had been born into his household. Then he pursued Kedorlaomer's army until he caught up with them at Dan. ¹⁵There he divided his men and attacked during the night. Kedorlaomer's army fled, but Abram chased them as far as Hobah, north of Damascus. ¹⁶Abram recovered all the goods that had been taken, and he brought back his nephew Lot with his possessions and all the women and other captives.

14:1 Hebrew *Shinar*; also in 14:9.   14:3 Hebrew *Salt Sea.*   14:8 Hebrew *Siddim Valley* (see 14:3); also in 14:10.

NOTES

14:1-2 *King Amraphel of Babylonia, King Arioch of Ellasar, King Kedorlaomer of Elam, and King Tidal of Goiim.* Archaeology has not identified these particular kings, but similar names from antiquity indicate the general accuracy of the report. The kings in the east were confederate under a sovereign lord, apparently Amraphel, king of Shinar (so NLT mg), because he is mentioned first and this is said to have happened in his days. But it was Kedorlaomer's war. Kedorlaomer was the Elamite king; his name fits the name *Kudur* of that time and place. Elam was just east of Shinar, which has already been located as Babel (10:10). The name *Arriyuk*, similar to the name Arioch, was found in the city of Mari on the Euphrates. And Tidal, similar to the early Hittite name *Tudhaliyas*, apparently had a number of city states under his dominion, and so he was called the king of "Goiim," which here should be understood as "nations" (*goyim* [TH1471, ZH1580]) rather than a place called Goiim (*goyim* [TH1471A, ZH1582]; cf. Josh 12:23). This system, either of tribal affiliations or feudalism, informs the chapter. It was Kedorlaomer's war, but those in covenant with him had to go. Likewise in the chapter it is Abram's war to rescue Lot, but those he had a treaty with had to go with him.

14:7 *the Amorites.* This term is often used interchangeably for Canaanites, but it can also refer to smaller ethnic groups of "westerners" living in the Transjordan kingdoms and the hill country of Canaan. Here it probably refers to a small ethnic group and not the later waves of "western Semites" (called *Amurru*).

14:14 *he caught up with them at Dan.* This is an editorial modernization of the Hebrew text, for Dan, a son of Jacob, had not been born by Abram's time, and the tribe of Dan migrated north in the days of the Judges, after the time of Moses. But "Dan" was substituted for the original name so that the readers would know where the location was.

COMMENTARY

The record of the battle of the four kings against the five is fascinating on several levels. First, it gives us a window on international policies in the ancient world. Here is a typical "international" skirmish in which powerful kings (of cities and of groups of cities) formed a coalition to plunder some smaller city states, which just happened to be on the edge of the land promised to Abram. Second, it presents Abram the Hebrew as a force to be reckoned with in that ancient world. He was known as "the Hebrew" (14:13), apparently a description used of him by the various kings and tribal chieftains of the day. Third, the passage had a warning for the later Israelites: The land would from time to time be invaded by the tyrants of Mesopotamia, but the Lord would enable them to drive them away. And fourth, it is part of the outworking of God's promise to make Abram great and to bless those who blessed him and curse those who cursed him (12:3).

The first part of the story lays the foundation for the great victory of Abram (14:1-12). It tells how foreigners invaded the land and carried off the people of the Jordan Valley, Lot included. The text explains that the city-states of the valley served Kedorlaomer for 12 years, but in the thirteenth year they rebelled. This means that the easterner had apparently defeated these folk at an earlier time and put them under tribute—much as the Assyrian kings would do later to Israel. So for 12 years these local kings sent the tribute—perhaps asphalt, olive oil, or copper—to keep the tyrants away. But in the thirteenth year they refused to send it, and so in the fourteenth year the invaders came again to put them down.

These kings invaded the region of the Jordan Valley near the Dead Sea (lit., "the Salt Sea"; 14:3). There were five Jordanian kings of city-states that were defeated in the battle: those of Sodom, Gomorrah, Admah, Zeboiim, and Bela (which is Zoar). These all came out and prepared for battle in order to defend against the invaders.

These invaders came down the east side of the Jordan Valley all the way down to the Gulf of Elath, and then came back up on the west side. We can trace their route by the names listed here. Ashteroth and Karnaim are in Hauran, ancient Bashan, east of the Sea of Galilee. Ham was in eastern Gilead, just south of Bashan. Shaveh-kiriathaim is east of the Dead Sea. And the hill country of Seir was southeast of the Dead Sea, the region later known as Edom. El-paran was the site of modern Eilat on the Gulf of Aqaba. Kadesh and Tamar were southwest of the Dead Sea, on the way back to the north. The conquerors' southward route was known from antiquity as the King's Highway (Num 20:17; 21:22). So the invaders went down the eastern side of the Jordan Valley, on the high plateau, turned around in the Arabah (the rift valley south of the Dead Sea), went up to Kadesh, over to Tamar, and then to the region of Sodom and Gomorrah in the Valley of Siddim (14:8-10). The five cities of the plain were apparently all very close together at the south end of the Dead Sea. It was there that the four kings defeated the frail coalition, looted the cities of Sodom and Gomorrah, and carried Lot off with the rest of the captives.

A fugitive fled to tell Abram that his relative had been taken captive (14:13). Abram immediately mustered his force, 318 trained men who could fight and who had been born in his household. (That means Abram's clan would probably have been over 1,000 people in total.) Abram had other help; he had a treaty with the Amorite chieftain Mamre and his two brothers (or allies), Aner and Eshcol (14:13, 24). Under the agreements of the day, if one tribe went to war, the allies went too. These men with their fighters joined Abram's fight. Here the treaty system worked in Abram's favor.

With a sizeable force, Abram pursued the invaders far to the north, to the location that would later be known as Dan (see note on 14:14). The distance was about 150 miles from Abram's home in Hebron, depending on the route they took. The city of Dan was at that time named Leshem (Josh 19:47) or Laish (Judg 18:29). Dividing the troops and springing a surprise attack at night, Abram was able to rout the enemy. He then pursued them another 100 miles north to Hobah. There Abram was able to rescue the prisoners, including his nephew Lot and his family. Because it was Abram's war, the victory was attributed to him (14:17).

Abram was recognized as "the Hebrew" (14:13), the first occurrence of the word in the Bible. It should not be equated with the later term "Habiru" from the Egyptian texts, which refers to bands of mercenaries who roamed the land in the times of the judges. Abram's victory in this chapter shows that he was well known as a force to be reckoned with. Still, Abram's strength alone does not fully explain the victory. Later in the narrative, Melchizedek rightly attributes the victory to God (14:20).

Through this narrative, Israel could see that God was able to give his people victory over any forces that invaded the Promised Land. This would have encouraged God's people in the difficult days of the judges and the kings. Of course, faithfulness to God was the prerequisite for victory. Warfare would have been a constant threat for people in antiquity. In the Old Testament, warfare was also a spiritual battle because it required faith in the Lord.

According to the New Testament, a Christian's battle and weapons are said to be spiritual, and God's promises are eternal. Using military figures, Paul portrayed Christ's death as a victory (Eph 4:8) in which he conquered sin, death, and the grave. Accordingly, the gifts from our mighty king are spiritual. With these spiritual gifts, and armed with spiritual weapons, Christians are to champion righteousness, truth, and equity (Eph 6:10-19). God gives his people victory over the world in accord with his promises to bless, using his servants who know his calling and who can use the weapons of warfare with skill.

The Israelites would also be reminded from this that living too closely with Canaanites could lead to being ensnared in such conflicts. To live next to them was dangerous, as Lot came to realize. To be like them would be even worse.

◆ ### 5. The blessing of Melchizedek (14:17-24)

17After Abram returned from his victory over Kedorlaomer and all his allies, the king of Sodom went out to meet him in the valley of Shaveh (that is, the King's Valley). 18And Melchizedek, the king of Salem and a priest of God Most High,* brought Abram some bread and wine. 19Melchizedek blessed Abram with this blessing:

"Blessed be Abram by God Most High,
 Creator of heaven and earth.
20And blessed be God Most High,
 who has defeated your enemies for
 you."

Then Abram gave Melchizedek a tenth of all the goods he had recovered.

21The king of Sodom said to Abram, "Give back my people who were captured. But you may keep for yourself all the goods you have recovered."

22Abram replied to the king of Sodom, "I solemnly swear to the LORD, God Most High, Creator of heaven and earth, 23that I will not take so much as a single thread or sandal thong from what belongs to you. Otherwise you might say, 'I am the one who made Abram rich.' 24I will accept only what my young warriors have already eaten, and I request that you give a fair share of the goods to my allies—Aner, Eshcol, and Mamre."

14:18 Hebrew *El-Elyon;* also in 14:19, 20, 22.

NOTES

14:18 *Melchizedek.* Some interpreters have thought that this important biblical figure was a pre-incarnate appearance of Christ because of the way the book of Hebrews describes him (cf. Heb 7:1-3, 15-25). It is more likely that he was an actual Jebusite priest and king of Salem, the old name for Jerusalem. In a book that gives genealogies of all the significant people, this man appears on the scene with no reference to father or mother, and disappears just as quickly (Heb 7:3); but he stands out in biblical memory as a royal priest in the holy city. Thus he provided the writer of Hebrews with a perfect type of Christ. That typology was solidified in the prophecy of David in Psalm 110. Under divine inspiration David foresaw that his royal descendant would be both his Lord and a priest after the order of Melchizedek. David, of course, was the first Israelite to occupy the royal city of Melchizedek, for the city was not taken until Joab captured it for David. It was here that David acquired the threshing floor for the future location of the Temple and offered the first sacrifices to the Lord on the site. His prophecy is remarkable in that no Israelite king could occupy the office of high priest, for they were from different lines—the king from Judah and the priest from Levi. Therefore, David's descendant could not be a priest in the line of Aaron—he would have to be identified with a different order of priesthood, one that was a royal priesthood. Only with the fulfillment of prophecy in the New Testament could this be entirely understood: Christ would satisfy the law by being the perfect sacrifice, bringing the need for the Temple, the priesthood, and the sacrifices to fulfillment. His role as our high priest is greater than the Aaronic priests because he has made the perfect sacrifice, entered into the heavenly sanctuary, and remains forever making intercession for us. The writer of Hebrews saw the superiority of the line of Melchizedek already in the fact that Abram paid tithes to Melchizedek, the only person on earth considered to be his spiritual superior (cf. Heb 7:1-19).

Christ the King would be a priest according to the order of Melchizedek (Ps 110:4), indicating that when the line of Aaron had ended, when there was no longer a Temple or sacrifices, Jesus would take up the priestly ministry in conjunction with his kingship. When Hebrews says that this man was without father and without mother, he was probably drawing upon the fact that in a book that gives the genealogies of everyone, this mysterious figure comes on the scene without any such record, and disappears as quickly (Heb 7:3). He remains forever in the reader's mind as a royal priest, but one who is superior to Levi because Abram, from whom Levi descended, paid tithes to him (Heb 7:4-10).

COMMENTARY

Abram would meet two more kings before returning to his home. On his way back from the battle, two kings went out to meet him, and they could not have been more different. On one hand, there was Bera, the king of Sodom who had been defeated in the battle (14:2, 21); on the other hand there was Melchizedek, the king of Salem (Jerusalem; cf. Ps 76:2), a priest of the Most High God (14:18). Furthermore, since Melchizedek's name means "king of righteousness," it suggests at least the desire of this ruler to be righteous.

Melchizedek came out to meet Abram in the Valley of Shaveh, probably the Kidron Valley (2 Sam 18:18), bringing him bread and wine. He also brought a blessing to the patriarch, a blessing of the Most High God (*'el 'elyon* [TH410A/5945B, ZH446/6610], 14:19). Abram recognized in this man a true spiritual brother, one who believed in a sovereign God who created the heaven and the earth. Normally pagans would not make that clear a division, for there was a confusion of spirit with matter in their beliefs. They would worship the sun-god, or the moon-god, or the sea, which for them were physical objects as well as gods. The idea of an invisible Spirit God who made the sun and the moon and the sea as natural parts of the physical world would have been foreign to them.

Abram also saw Melchizedek as his spiritual superior, for he paid tithes to him (14:20). This was not an ordinary use of tithes; the tithes came from the goods that Abram retrieved from the invaders. (The King of Sodom, then, became an unwilling tither.) But the act was a public acknowledgment of the truth of the words of this priest, that God had given Abram the victory. It shows that Abram recognized that divine revelation had come to others as well as to him. His gift shows how humble and unthreatened Abram was. While he was occupied with the deliverance of his relative and all the people of the cities of the plain, there emerged out of this obscure Jebusite city a man who ministered to the Most High God on his holy mountain.

Note the chiastic arrangement of the interactions with the kings of Sodom and Salem here: First the *king of Sodom* came out (14:17), then the *king of Salem* met Abram (14:18); then the *king of Salem* blessed Abram (14:19-20), and finally the *king of Sodom* made an offer (14:21). After the blessing of Melchizedek and all that this holy moment entailed for Abram, the king of Sodom's offer to get his power back must have seemed so banal. No doubt the blessing of the priest helped Abram keep everything in perspective, for it was the Lord who would bless Abram, not some pagan king offering to give him the possessions in exchange for the people.

Abram swore before the Lord, God Most High, Creator of heaven and earth (14:22), that he would take nothing that belonged to Sodom, lest the king of Sodom take credit for making Abram rich (14:23; the Hebrew text is forceful, "lest you say, *I* have made Abram rich"). In the wording of this oath, Abram may have been clarifying to all that his God, Yahweh, was the same as the Most High God who Melchizedek had invoked. Perhaps Melchizedek had not heard the name Yahweh before.

The incident with these two kings was another test of Abram's faith. Bera, Sodom's king, offered a most appealing deal to the patriarch. But Abram, knowing what he did about Sodom and its king, thought that keeping Sodom's loot that he had retrieved might make him allied to, if not subject to, Bera. But beyond that, Abram wanted something far more enduring than possessions and wealth—for these he already had. He wanted the fulfillment of the promises of God. Faith looks beyond the riches of the world to the greater blessings that God has in store.

Abram knew that he would become more prosperous, but he also knew who it was who would make him prosperous. He wanted to receive everything from God, and not so much as a thread from Sodom. (He would allow his confederates to take their share, though.) Devout believers order their lives so that they know that all their successes, joys, comforts, and prosperity come from God. Abram could have agreed to taking Sodom's possessions and then explained that "the Lord works in mysterious ways." But he knew that doing that would confuse those who looked to him for spiritual leadership. He could not bring himself to equate the blessing of God with the best that Sodom had to offer.

◆ ## 6. The Lord's covenant promise to Abram (15:1-21)

Some time later, the LORD spoke to Abram in a vision and said to him, "Do not be afraid, Abram, for I will protect you, and your reward will be great."

²But Abram replied, "O Sovereign LORD, what good are all your blessings when I don't even have a son? Since you've given me no children, Eliezer of Damascus, a servant in my household, will inherit all my wealth. ³You have given me no descendants of my own, so one of my servants will be my heir."

⁴Then the LORD said to him, "No, your servant will not be your heir, for you will have a son of your own who will be your heir." ⁵Then the LORD took Abram outside and said to him, "Look up into the sky and count the stars if you can. That's how many descendants you will have!"

⁶And Abram believed the LORD, and the LORD counted him as righteous because of his faith.

⁷Then the LORD told him, "I am the LORD who brought you out of Ur of the Chaldeans to give you this land as your possession."

⁸But Abram replied, "O Sovereign LORD, how can I be sure that I will actually possess it?"

⁹The LORD told him, "Bring me a three-year-old heifer, a three-year-old female goat, a three-year-old ram, a turtledove, and a young pigeon." ¹⁰So Abram presented all these to him and killed them. Then he cut each animal down the middle and laid the halves side by side; he did not, however, cut the birds in half. ¹¹Some vultures swooped down to eat the carcasses, but Abram chased them away.

¹²As the sun was going down, Abram fell into a deep sleep, and a terrifying darkness came down over him. ¹³Then the LORD said to Abram, "You can be sure that your descendants will be strangers in a foreign land, where they will be oppressed as slaves for 400 years. ¹⁴But I will punish the nation that enslaves them, and in the end they will come away with great wealth. ¹⁵(As for you, you will die in peace and be buried at a ripe old age.) ¹⁶After four generations your descendants will return here to this land, for the sins of the Amorites do not yet warrant their destruction."

¹⁷After the sun went down and darkness fell, Abram saw a smoking firepot and a flaming torch pass between the halves of the carcasses. ¹⁸So the LORD made a covenant with Abram that day and said, "I have given this land to your descendants, all the way from the border of Egypt* to the great Euphrates River— ¹⁹the land now occupied by the Kenites, Kenizzites, Kadmonites, ²⁰Hittites, Perizzites, Rephaites, ²¹Amorites, Canaanites, Girgashites, and Jebusites."

15:18 Hebrew *the river of Egypt*, referring either to an eastern branch of the Nile River or to the Brook of Egypt in the Sinai (see Num 34:5).

NOTES

15:1 *I will protect you.* Lit., "I am your shield." This word "shield" is from the same verbal root (*mgn* [TH4042, ZH4481]) that was used by Melchizedek for "defeated" (14:20).

15:2 *Since you've given me no children, Eliezer of Damascus, a servant in my household, will inherit all my wealth.* Abram's concern about remaining childless is expressed here in a wordplay on the origin of his household servant. Eliezer was from Damascus (*dammeseq* [TH1834, ZH1966]), and Abram was concerned that according to social custom he might be the heir apparent (*ben-mesheq* [TH1121/4943, ZH1201/5479], "son of possession") should Abram die childless. The wordplay suggests that the omen might be in the nomen—the Damascene would be the heir.

15:6 *And Abram believed the LORD, and the LORD counted him as righteous because of his faith.* The construction of this Hebrew sentence requires precise analysis. The verb "believe" used with its conjunction (a Waw disjunctive) is clearly not to be interpreted as in sequence with the verses that came before it. If the text had wanted to say that this faith came about after the object lesson of the stars (15:5), it would have used the Waw consecutive construction ("And then Abram believed"). But this sentence begins with a Waw on a perfect and could not be a Waw consecutive or the tense would be put into the future. Here we have instead a form of the Waw disjunctive to mark a parenthetical clause. For those who argue that Abram came to faith here after seeing the stars in the object lesson, there remains the question of what kind of faith prompted him to leave Ur (Heb 11:8). They end up saying it was faith but not true saving faith because it was here that God declared him righteous. But that interpretation is untenable. It does not do justice to the way the text is written, and it is theologically problematic. The Bible says that it was by faith that Abram left Ur.

What the writer is doing here is simply stating that Abram believed in the Lord and the Lord reckoned righteousness to him, but not indicating it was a result of the revelation from God just mentioned. The statement is made at this point to affirm that the patriarch was a believer because the rest of the chapter records the making of the covenant—it will be made with Abram the believer, the one to whom righteousness was credited. Verse 6 then serves more as an introduction to the cutting of the covenant than as a result of the object lesson in vv. 1-5. It could be translated simply with "And [Abram] believed" if it was set apart from the previous paragraph; it could also be rendered "Now [Abram] believed" or simply "[Abram] believed." Because Abram first came to faith when he left Ur, this verse could even indicate that he continued to believe, or that he was a believer. The emphasis here, though, is more on the result of Abram's faith: "And the LORD counted him as righteous"—the Lord credited Abram with righteousness because of his faith.

15:13 *oppressed.* In Hebrew this word (*'anah* [TH6031, ZH6700]) is the same word used in Exod 1:11-12 to describe Egypt's oppression of Israel.

400 years. Exodus 12:40 and Gal 3:17 state that the bondage in Egypt lasted 430 years. Apparently Gen 15:13 and Acts 7:6 with their references to 400 years are using round figures. According to the chronology that is presented in the Bible, the family moved to Egypt in 1876 BC, and the Exodus occurred in 1446 BC, accounting for 430 years. Most critical scholars, however, discard the biblical numbers and dates, and come out with a later Exodus and a shorter time of bondage.

COMMENTARY

Abram the conqueror, Abram the man who gave all the possessions and people back to their king, now stood very much alone, and perhaps began to be overcome with a sense of fear. But the Lord brought his fears to an end with words of comfort: "Do not be afraid . . . I will protect you" (15:1, see note). God was Abram's protection. God was also the one who would provide for him. But when the Lord said, "Your reward will be great," Abram immediately thought of the promises and responded: "What good are all your blessings when I don't even have a son?" Abram's vision had not been blinded by Bera's offer (14:22-24); he still had one dominant hope, the promise of a seed (12:2-3). (It may be that this word "reward" in God's promise is what inspired the psalmist to think of children as a reward from the Lord in Ps 127:3). But without a child, Abram was concerned that the inheritance would go to his household servant, Eliezer. That was the custom of those days, but God would have none of it. He did not even use the servant's name, but said,

"No, your servant will not be your heir." Instead, a son would be coming from the loins of Abram. To underscore the extent of the fulfillment of the promise, God then showed Abram the stars, pointing out that Abram's descendants would be as numerous as they were (22:17; 26:4). The divine word that created the stars also promised to Abram innumerable descendants.

The text then says that "Abram believed the LORD, and the LORD counted him as righteous because of his faith" (15:6, see note). This is the central statement about Abram's saving faith. More than that, this statement is quoted three times in the New Testament (Rom 4:3; Gal 3:6; Jas 2:23) as the foundational passage for the doctrine of justification by faith. Righteousness was credited to him for faith alone, and not for works. Genesis 15:6 therefore makes an important statement about Abram; and it has been strategically placed here as an introduction to the formal cutting of the covenant—God cut the covenant with Abram the believer, the one to whom he had reckoned righteousness (15:10).

Using a solemn ceremony, God "cut the covenant" (*karath berith* [TH3772/1285, ZH4162/1382]) with Abram (15:7-10, 18). In making such a binding covenant, God was guaranteeing to the patriarch the fulfillment of the promises (15:7, 18-21). Abram obeyed God's instructions and gathered the animals for the ceremony; he severed (15:10) three animals, a heifer, a goat, and a ram (15:9), and also set out a dove and a young pigeon. The idea of "cutting a covenant" literally involved cutting the animal as the symbolism of the oath, indicating that the maker of the covenant was staking his own life on his word. During the ceremony a sudden horror came upon Abram, as unclean birds of prey swooped down on the offering's animals—clearly a bad omen in anybody's book. Then Abram was covered with a terrifying darkness (15:11-12). God's announcement of the enslavement (15:13-14) clarified the meaning of the attacking birds. There would be a period of 400 years of bondage for Abram's descendants before the complete fulfillment of the covenant. But Abram could be assured that nothing could interfere with the plan to fulfill the covenant, not his death, not even a long enslavement. Egypt, like the birds of prey, would oppose the covenant Israel had, and try to destroy them or hinder its fulfillment. But ultimately the covenant would be fulfilled. When Abram got up and drove the birds of prey away, this symbolized his task to protect the covenant as much as possible.

One of the reasons for the Israelites' long term of bondage in Egypt had to do with God's justice toward the Amorites. God told Abram that the sins of the Amorites had not yet warranted their destruction (lit., "were not yet full"—15:16). In order to give the Promised Land to Israel, the inhabitants of the land had to be dispossessed—it was part of the curse on Canaan (9:25). God would give Israel the land, but not one day before the justice of God allowed it. God would tolerate the sins of the Amorites until they were fully deserving of judgment. Thus, the fulfillment of the promises to Abram involved a retributive judgment on the people of the land. Until then, God would send the family to Egypt, where it could become a great nation and where God could discipline them to make them fit to receive the promises. Abram's seeing all this in advance was horrible on the one hand, but on the other hand it was comforting, for nothing could interfere with God's plan to fulfill his promise.

Then, after sunset, God revealed himself with the image of a smoking firepot and a flaming torch (15:17), two objects that were connected with sacrificial ritual in the ancient world. Fire represents the consuming, cleansing zeal of the Lord, as well as his unapproachable holiness—two things that are interrelated (cf. Isa 6:3-7). Abram saw nothing else in the vision except these fiery elements as they passed between the pieces of the slaughtered animals. Thus, the holy God came down and cut the covenant with Abram. Since God could not swear by anyone greater, he swore by his own life (Heb 6:13). In other words, this was a unilateral covenant; its promises were absolutely sure because they did not depend on what Abram or his descendants might do. Of course, people would have to believe if they were to participate in the blessings of this covenant.

At the end of his proclamation, God specified the boundaries of the Promised Land—from the River of Egypt (probably the Wadi el-Arish) to the great river (the Euphrates). Israel has never possessed all this land in its entirety. In the days of the conquest, the Canaanite tribes listed (15:19-21) were largely dispossessed, but not completely. In the days of David and Solomon, Egypt still controlled the coastal region, and the Philistines and other groups remained a hindrance in the land promised to Israel. So the promise of the land was never fulfilled; it remained a hope for the believing Israelites and was carried forward in the royal psalms and messianic passages (Ps 72:8-17). And at Israel's darkest moment, when it was being expelled from the land, the New Covenant reiterated the old promise of their dwelling in a land in complete peace and prosperity (Isa 54:1-14; Jer 31:31-37; Ezek 36:24-36). The restoration to the land after the Exile would not fulfill the promises made to the fathers, not without the coming of the Messiah, the forgiveness of sins, or the pouring out of the Spirit on all flesh. This hope will find ultimate fulfillment in the creation of a new heaven and a new earth where everlasting peace and righteousness will exist.

For Abram, God's message was clear: In spite of the prospects of death and suffering (enslavement in bondage), he and his descendants would eventually receive the promises, for God had sworn to it. So Israel could be encouraged by this at the time of the Exodus and in subsequent times of distress. They would be encouraged, just as we are, that nothing can separate us from the love of God. God's solemn covenant assures his chosen people of the ultimate fulfillment of all his promises, and those promises are bound to be fulfilled in a far more glorious way than anyone could have even imagined.

The Israelites under Moses would also notice the significant parallel wording at the beginning of this chapter and the beginning of the law: "I am Yahweh who brought you out of Ur" (15:7) parallels Exodus 20:2, "I am Yahweh your God, who brought you out of the land of Egypt." This would have assured the Israelites that in spite of their bondage, in spite of the attempt to kill all the males, in spite of the armies of Egypt, God would judge their oppressors and deliver them.

This passage is an encouragement for New Testament believers as well. God affirms solemnly that he will fulfill all his promises to us that concern salvation and all his blessings that pertain to this life and the life to come (cf. 2 Pet 1:3-4) despite suffering, persecution, and even death. God has promised us eternal life, and death cannot nullify that promise. But because of the suffering and death in this world, for the promises of God to be fulfilled there must be a resurrection; otherwise our faith is in vain (1 Cor 15:12-19). The Bible is clear: God will keep his promises to us, even if, like Abram, we die without receiving all the promises. Ultimately all the promises will be fulfilled in the life to come.

◆ 7. Abram's lack of faith (16:1-16)

Now Sarai, Abram's wife, had not been able to bear children for him. But she had an Egyptian servant named Hagar. ²So Sarai said to Abram, "The LORD has prevented me from having children. Go and sleep with my servant. Perhaps I can have children through her." And Abram agreed with Sarai's proposal. ³So Sarai, Abram's wife, took Hagar the Egyptian servant and gave her to Abram as a wife. (This happened ten years after Abram had settled in the land of Canaan.)

⁴So Abram had sexual relations with Hagar, and she became pregnant. But when Hagar knew she was pregnant, she began to treat her mistress, Sarai, with contempt. ⁵Then Sarai said to Abram, "This is all your fault! I put my servant into your arms, but now that she's pregnant she treats me with contempt. The LORD will show who's wrong—you or me!"

⁶Abram replied, "Look, she is your servant, so deal with her as you see fit." Then Sarai treated Hagar so harshly that she finally ran away.

⁷The angel of the LORD found Hagar beside a spring of water in the wilderness, along the road to Shur. ⁸The angel said to her, "Hagar, Sarai's servant, where have you come from, and where are you going?"

"I'm running away from my mistress, Sarai," she replied.

⁹The angel of the LORD said to her, "Return to your mistress, and submit to her authority." ¹⁰Then he added, "I will give you more descendants than you can count."

¹¹And the angel also said, "You are now pregnant and will give birth to a son. You are to name him Ishmael (which means 'God hears'), for the LORD has heard your cry of distress. ¹²This son of yours will be a wild man, as untamed as a wild donkey! He will raise his fist against everyone, and everyone will be against him. Yes, he will live in open hostility against all his relatives."

¹³Thereafter, Hagar used another name to refer to the LORD, who had spoken to her. She said, "You are the God who sees me."* She also said, "Have I truly seen the One who sees me?" ¹⁴So that well was named Beer-lahai-roi (which means "well of the Living One who sees me"). It can still be found between Kadesh and Bered.

¹⁵So Hagar gave Abram a son, and Abram named him Ishmael. ¹⁶Abram was eighty-six years old when Ishmael was born.

16:13 Hebrew *El-roi*.

NOTES

16:9 *The angel of the* LORD. This is the first mention of the angel of the Lord (lit., "the Angel of Yahweh"). The angel is identified with Yahweh in 16:13, as well as in 22:11-12;

31:11, 13; 48:16; Judg 6:11, 16, 22; 13:22-23; Zech 3:1-2. And yet the angel is distinct from Yahweh (24:7; 2 Sam 24:16; Zech 1:12). Most commentators see him as a manifestation of Yahweh in some way. Driver (1891:184) notes that older commentators saw in this figure a preview of the incarnation of the Lord, but he adds that the OT writers would have had no such conception. Westermann (1985:242-244) tries to explain the development of the idea of this "messenger of Yahweh" as a softening of an older idea of God's coming to visit people; he concludes that what is most important is not the divine presence but the message. Von Rad (1961:188) also prefers the translation "messenger" rather than angel, although that is a small point; he describes the messenger as an instrument of Yahweh's grace, concluding that the messenger is a form in which Yahweh appears, because Yahweh and the messenger are one and the same.

The evidence in the text leads to no other conclusion but that "the angel of LORD" refers to a manifestation of Yahweh. And although this was not even a consideration in the OT, it seems probable from the perspective of complete revelation that this was a preincarnate appearance of the second person of the Trinity. It is the work of the second person of the Trinity to reveal the Godhead, and the NT confirms that many of the passages that refer to appearances or visions of Yahweh refer to God the Son (John 8:54-59; Heb 1:10-12). If the angel was not the Lord in some form, he at least spoke with all the authority of the Lord.

COMMENTARY

The next series of narratives present the struggle that Abram and Sarai underwent while waiting for God's promise to be fulfilled (ch 21). At times their faith stumbled, but eventually it was rewarded and even proved (ch 22). As part of the testing of their faith, the promise was delayed. And in waiting for the promise to be fulfilled, there were attempts to follow alternative plans, plans that were out of harmony with the newly found faith. Human efforts to assist the fulfillment of the divine promise have to be divinely instructed or in harmony with the divine instructions.

The narrative in chapter 16 begins with the tension that Abram and Sarai his wife faced—she was barren and getting older. (This chapter about her being barren parallels chapter 12 and the land having a famine; the two main promises of land and descendants are thus confronted with immediate problems.) By all human calculations the heir could not come through her. And besides, the promise had not yet specifically said it would, just that he would be from Abram's loins. This reasoning set in motion an alternative approach which led to greater problems. In the end the couple would be rebuked and learn that God's promises, even if they seemed unreasonable, would not be fulfilled in the way of the world. Unfortunately, the world has had to bear the consequences of this mistake ever since because of the tribal conflicts in the Middle East between the different sons of Abraham.

Ishmael was born to Abram first, through the slave wife Hagar. Ishmael figures prominently in Islamic thought today because he was the firstborn son; and even though most of the Arab population derives from different ancestors, Ishmael has become the focal point of their heritage. According to their tradition, Abraham and Ishmael established the holy shrine in Mecca, and Ishmael was to be the heir of the promise of the land. Interestingly, the prophecy in Genesis 16 predicted that he and his descendants would lift their hand against everyone, and that everyone would lift their hand against them, and that they would live in hostility to all their brothers (16:12). Under the customs of the day, Ishmael could have been the heir if Sarai remained barren and if Abram declared him to be the heir. But that never happened, according to the Bible (which Islam rejects). God told Abram that Isaac would be the heir, and so Abram was instructed to send Ishmael away (21:11-13). God promised to make Ishmael into a great nation as well—but the line for the covenant and the Messiah would come through Isaac.

In many ways the ancient conflicts between the Israelites and the Ishmaelites are being played out today. God has blessed both lines with numerous descendants, just as he promised. But both claim their right to the land of Canaan as the heir of Abram. God did not promise that Ishmael would be the heir of the promise; but neither did God allow the Israelites to stay in the land if they did not demonstrate their faith by obedience. The only true harmony between Palestinian Arabs and Israelis today comes when individuals put their faith in Christ Jesus; and ultimately, peace can only come with the coming of the Messiah to judge the world. Until then there will be wars, rumors of wars, terror and violence, not only in that land, but throughout the world. And so until Christ returns, we must try to promote peace and justice in that troubled part of the world without naively choosing sides, for we have two nations, very closely related, who are forced to live together in one land.

In the legal custom of the day, a barren woman could give her maidservant to her husband as a slave wife and the child that would be born to that union would be regarded as the first wife's child. If the husband then declared in public that the child of the slave wife was his son, then that son would be adopted as the heir. So Sarai's suggestion was unobjectionable according to the customs of the day, but God often repudiates social customs, especially if they interfere with his wonderful works.

Sarai's plan, with Abram's approval, turned sour. When the slave, an Egyptian girl named Hagar, got pregnant, she began to despise her mistress, probably anticipating that according to the social custom she would become the favored wife in place of Sarai if Sarai were to remain barren. The child of the slave wife could have been counted as Sarai's child, as in the cases of the children born to Rachel and Leah through slave wives. But it appears that Hagar had higher ambitions, and Sarai reacted harshly to them, eventually demanding that Hagar and Ishmael leave (ch 21).

Because of the tension that was growing, Sarai turned on Abram to affix the blame for what had happened. The NLT translates her words to fit her intent: "The LORD will show who's wrong—you or me" (16:5). An even more pointed translation may be justified; since she now believed the situation was Abram's fault, she may have meant, "God will get you for this." Abram, not knowing how to deal with the matter, simply gave it over to Sarai to handle as she saw fit. After all, Hagar was her servant. And so Sarai began to mistreat Hagar, most likely to let her know who was in charge. The mistreatment was so severe that Hagar fled to the wilderness (16:6). Abram, who had "obeyed his wife" (the precise wording of 16:4; cf. 3:17), was caught weakly in the middle. He would have a son, but it was not going to be the fulfillment he had been waiting for.

The story has both a dark side (Sarai's mistreatment of Hagar) and a bright side—the angel of the Lord found Hagar in the wilderness. It is not hard to see what went wrong in the dark side of the episode. When the way of faith (which involves patient waiting) was abandoned and the way of the world's custom was followed, Abram was caught in a situation with causes and effects that would trouble him for years to come. Ishmael and his descendants, the Ishmaelite tribes, would become the perennial enemies of the Israelites.

But God turned it into something positive for Hagar and instructive for the family. The angel of the Lord appeared to Hagar; he found her in the desert at a spring beside the road to Shur (cf. 25:18) on the way back to her homeland, Egypt. The angel asked Hagar two questions: "Where have you come from, and where are you going?" (16:8). These, like the questions asked of others so far in the book, were rhetorical, for God knew the answers already. These questions were designed to get Hagar to pour out her heart to God. And when she did, God gave her two sure words: One was hortatory—return and submit (16:9), and the other was promissory—she would give birth to a boy, but more than that, innumerable descendants (16:10-12). But in all the conversation with Hagar, the Lord never referred to her as Abram's wife, only as Sarai's maidservant. She would have a child of Abram's, but she would not have a part in the covenant with Abram.

Hagar responded by faith to the divine provision, first in her words, and then in her obedience. She called God "the God who sees me" (*'el ro'i* [TH410A/7210, ZH446/8024]; 16:13), meaning the God who knows her plight and watches over her. Then, to commemorate the event she named the well at that unknown spot Beer-lahai-roi, which means "well of the Living One who sees me" (cf. 24:62; 25:11).

Frequently in Genesis, etymologies of names capture the message of the passage they appear in. These are rhetorical devices that explain the names from the events in the account, using wordplays on the sounds and meanings of the name. The name then functions as a mnemonic device for remembering the events and their significance in the history of the faith. In this passage, two popular etymologies not only form the climax of the section but capture the point of the whole unit. One we have seen, the naming of God as "the God who sees me." It was God who saw Hagar's dilemma and looked after her. The other is the name she was to give to the boy: Ishmael, which means "God hears." God then explained the meaning of this name for Hagar: "The LORD has heard your misery" ("your cry of distress," 16:11, NLT). This name with its explanation would have been a great comfort for Hagar, along with the name she gave to God: Not only did God see her but God heard her as well. "Ishmael" would be a reminder of that, every time the name was pronounced.

Hagar was told to return and submit to her mistress, and then she would undoubtedly tell Sarai and Abram that the Lord had rescued her, given her a promise, and instructed that the child be named "God hears"—Ishmael. She became the messenger of the Lord to the patriarch. The message was "God sees" and "God hears." God sees distress and affliction; he hears the cries of those in distress and in need. Sarai and Abram should have known this. Since God knew that Sarai was barren, they should have cried out to the Lord. Instead, they learned this truth the hard way, through the experience of a despised slave wife who, ironically, came back with word of her marvelous experience in the wilderness.

God provided for the pregnant woman who was thrust out into the wilderness. God promised that Hagar would be a matriarch. Her son would become the father of a great tribe of wild, hostile people (cf. 25:18) living in the Arabian desert (25:12-18). But they would not be the chosen line from Abram; in fact, they would complicate matters. For example, Joseph, Sarai's grandson, was later taken to Egypt by the Ishmaelites (37:28). So when God blessed Hagar and her descendants, he did so in a way that would preserve the preeminent blessing for Abram's true heir.

In times of great distress, or when the future seems impossible, one must turn to the Lord because he hears the afflicted, sees them in their need, and will miraculously meet their needs. The impossible difficulties Abram's household faced could not be resolved by human intervention—giving children to the barren is God's work (Ps 113:9). Later, Leah would also reflect on the fact that God noticed her affliction, for she named Reuben and Simeon to reflect that (29:32-33). Sarai and Abram still had a way to go in their faith. God's people are to trust God's word and to wait for its fulfillment, even if it sounds impossible. Human effort may be part of the life of obedience to God, but not if it turns to the world for a solution to the plan of God, especially if that solution violates the institutions of God. But the good news for the people of God is that God can turn even false starts into something useful. God blessed Hagar and he blessed her descendants; but he did so in a way to preserve the covenant with Abram and his true heir.

◆ ## 8. The confirmation of the promise by signs (17:1-27)

When Abram was ninety-nine years old, the LORD appeared to him and said, "I am El-Shaddai—'God Almighty.' Serve me faithfully and live a blameless life. ²I will make a covenant with you, by which I will guarantee to give you countless descendants."

³At this, Abram fell face down on the ground. Then God said to him, ⁴"This is my covenant with you: I will make you the father of a multitude of nations! ⁵What's more, I am changing your name. It will no longer be Abram. Instead, you will be called Abraham,* for you will be the father of many nations. ⁶I will make you extremely fruitful. Your descendants will become many nations, and kings will be among them!

⁷"I will confirm my covenant with you and your descendants* after you, from generation to generation. This is the everlasting covenant: I will always be your God and the God of your descendants after you. ⁸And I will give the entire land of Canaan, where you now live as a foreigner, to you and your descendants. It will be their possession forever, and I will be their God."

⁹Then God said to Abraham, "Your responsibility is to obey the terms of the covenant. You and all your descendants have this continual responsibility. ¹⁰This is the covenant that you and your descendants must keep: Each male among you must be circumcised. ¹¹You must cut off the flesh of your foreskin as a sign of the covenant between me and you. ¹²From generation to generation, every male child must be cir-

cumcised on the eighth day after his birth. This applies not only to members of your family but also to the servants born in your household and the foreign-born servants whom you have purchased. ¹³All must be circumcised. Your bodies will bear the mark of my everlasting covenant. ¹⁴Any male who fails to be circumcised will be cut off from the covenant family for breaking the covenant."

¹⁵Then God said to Abraham, "Regarding Sarai, your wife—her name will no longer be Sarai. From now on her name will be Sarah.* ¹⁶And I will bless her and give you a son from her! Yes, I will bless her richly, and she will become the mother of many nations. Kings of nations will be among her descendants."

¹⁷Then Abraham bowed down to the ground, but he laughed to himself in disbelief. "How could I become a father at the age of 100?" he thought. "And how can Sarah have a baby when she is ninety years old?" ¹⁸So Abraham said to God, "May Ishmael live under your special blessing!"

¹⁹But God replied, "No—Sarah, your wife, will give birth to a son for you. You will name him Isaac,* and I will confirm my covenant with him and his descendants as an everlasting covenant. ²⁰As for Ishmael, I will bless him also, just as you have asked. I will make him extremely fruitful and multiply his descendants. He will become the father of twelve princes, and I will make him a great nation. ²¹But my covenant will be confirmed with Isaac, who will be born to you and Sarah about this time next year." ²²When God had finished speaking, he left Abraham.

²³On that very day Abraham took his son, Ishmael, and every male in his household, including those born there and those he had bought. Then he circumcised them, cutting off their foreskins, just as God had told him. ²⁴Abraham was ninety-nine years old when he was circumcised, ²⁵and Ishmael, his son, was thirteen. ²⁶Both Abraham and his son, Ishmael, were circumcised on that same day, ²⁷along with all the other men and boys of the household, whether they were born there or bought as servants. All were circumcised with him.

17:5 *Abram* means "exalted father"; *Abraham* sounds like a Hebrew term that means "father of many." 17:7 Hebrew *seed;* also in 17:7b, 8, 9, 10, 19. 17:15 *Sarai* and *Sarah* both mean "princess"; the change in spelling may reflect the difference in dialect between Ur and Canaan. 17:19 *Isaac* means "he laughs."

NOTES

17:1 *I am El-Shaddai*—"God Almighty." Heb. *'el shadday* [TH410A/7706, ZH446/8724]. There is no certain explanation of the meaning of this epithet. It is used several times in the book (28:3; 35:11; 43:14; 48:3; see also 49:25). Some scholars connect the epithet to an Akkadian word that means "mountain" or "breast" (some words describing parts of the body were used for geographical descriptions; e.g., "mouth" of a river, or "foot" of a mountain, or "lip" as the bank of a river). If these suggestions are correct, then the title would depict his sovereignty (i.e., the high God, the mountain God) or his ability to supply abundantly (the breasts symbolizing him as the abundant one). But these attempts to explain the name have been far from compelling. Perhaps it is best to stay with the traditional understanding of the name, although a sure etymology is lacking: Jerome translated it as "Almighty God," and that has remained as the traditional understanding. For the sake of clarity, the NLT puts both a translation and the transliteration "El-Shaddai" in the text.

17:5 *you will be called Abraham, for you will be the father of many nations.* The new name is a wordplay on the promise: *'abraham* [TH85, ZH90] sounds similar to the expression "father of a multitude," *'ab hamon* [TH1/1995, ZH3/2162] (see NLT mg). Every time the new name was used, he and his household would be reminded of the multitude of nations that would come from him.

17:14 *will be cut off.* This is a punishment that is frequently mentioned in the law, but it is never clearly defined. It seems to have several applications: The person could be excommunicated, cut off from the society (and this would apply to lesser crimes, or unprovable crimes); the person could be put to death by the community, if there was sufficient evidence for a serious crime; or, the person might die prematurely, God cutting him off from the land of the living. The use of the threat at least would tell people how serious this matter was. In fact, in Exodus 4:24, the Lord met Moses on his return to Egypt to kill him because he had not circumcised his sons.

COMMENTARY

In this section, we see that God gave signs to Abram's family of the fulfillment of the promises. He changed the name of Abram to Abraham (17:1-8), he instituted the rite of circumcision as the sign of the covenant (17:9-14), and he assured Sarai of the fulfillment of the promises by changing her name to Sarah (17:15-22). By faith, Abraham then complied with the ritual of circumcision (17:23-27).

The promises to Abram grew more and more magnificent each time God spoke; the requirements on Abram also increased. God Almighty spoke to Abram. He commanded him, "Walk before me and be blameless" (NLT, "serve me faithfully"). The commands were demanding, but then God commands nothing less. Moreover, the task of being a blessing to the nations would require obedience in Abram. And the name for God used in this passage certainly stresses God's power and ability. Abram would be "walking before" the Almighty God.

In this passage the word from God declared that Abram would be the father of many nations (17:4). Earlier it had been promised that he would be the father of a great nation (cf. 12:2). But here not only would there be many nations but kings as well (17:6, 16). Then God added that the covenant would be an everlasting covenant (17:7) and the land of Canaan would be an everlasting possession for the descendants of Abram.

God gave a personal sign to Abram to guarantee this promise; he changed his name from Abram to Abraham. If the name Abram, which means "exalted father," refers to Abram's father Terah (cf. 11:27) and not to a god, it would indicate that Abram came from nobility. It did not refer to Abram himself (no one would call a baby "exalted father"). But from now on, the name of the patriarch would be Abraham because the focus of the promise would be on his descendants and not his background (see note on 17:5). One can well imagine how this would have played out in his household. Abram probably encountered disbelief and concealed smiles when he instructed his servants to call him "father of a multitude"—Abraham was in his nineties and had no children by his wife, Sarai (cf. 17:1, 24). Yet Abraham knew that God had not deceived him. His new name was a perpetual reminder of God's sure word. Every time someone addressed him he would be reminded of the promise, until one day his son would call him "father."

Another confirming sign was circumcision. This one was not a personal promise to Abraham but a sign for all households in the covenant. Circumcision was practiced in ancient Egypt, usually as a rite of passage. But here it carried a new meaning:

It would remind Abraham and his descendants of the promises of the everlasting covenant, that God would make them into a great nation (17:13; cf. 17:7, 19). By this rite, God was also impressing upon them the importance of purity and their dependence on God for the production of all life. By this sign, Israel would recognize and remember that native impurity must be laid aside, that human nature alone is unable to produce the promised seed, and that intermarriage with people who were not in the covenant, not circumcised, was a violation of the covenant. They had to be loyal to the covenant, to the family, and to the marriage. Anyone who refused to be circumcised (cut physically in this symbolic way) would be cut off (at the least separated) from the covenant people because of his disobedience to God's command (see note on 17:14).

Elsewhere in Scripture the significance of the rite of circumcision is explained more fully. It is a symbol of purity, of loyalty to the covenant, and of separation from the life of the world. Moses said that God would circumcise the hearts of his people so that they might be devoted to him (Deut 30:6). Paul added that circumcision of the heart (being inwardly set apart to God by the Spirit) evidences salvation and fellowship with God (Rom 2:28-29; cf. Rom 4:11). One must turn in confidence to God and his promises, laying aside the natural strength and the customs of the world. In contrast, unbelief is sometimes described as having an uncircumcised heart (Jer 9:26; Ezek 44:7-9).

God also announced that Sarai was now to be called Sarah (17:15). This new name, meaning "princess" or "queen," involved only a slight change in spelling, perhaps reflecting a change in the dialect of the language. It was a fitting name for one who was going to be the mother of kings (17:16). Hearing this promise from God to Sarah, Abraham laughed (*wayyitskhaq* [TH6711, ZH7464]; 17:17), for it all seemed so incredible. (The NLT explains that he laughed to himself in disbelief). A barren woman of 90 would give birth to a son—and kings! Abraham had begun to believe that his line would come through Ishmael. This was not so. Ishmael would not be forgotten or abandoned, however, for God said that he would have many descendants as well. Even the number of Ishmael's sons was predicted—12! Their names are recorded in 25:13-15. The point is that the Ishmaelite league of 12 tribes came from Abraham just as the Israelite tribes did. It was a blessing from God for Ishmael and his descendants. Whether or not they responded by faith would be another matter.

God assured Abraham that Sarah would have a son, whose name was to be Isaac (17:19). This name means "he laughs" or "may he laugh"; it recalls the fact that Abraham laughed when he heard the promise put so specifically. His name would be a constant reminder that a word from God was laughed at; but it would also be a constant reminder of the divine favor, for the name would normally signify that God laughs, that is, that God was pleased with the birth.

Having received God's word about Isaac, Abraham immediately set about complying with God's instructions (17:23-26). He began to implement the rite of circumcision as an act of faith in the promises. He was circumcised at the age of 99, and his son Ishmael was circumcised at the age of 13. Then, every male in the household was circumcised, whether born there or brought there as a servant. Everyone would come to know that the promises of God were to be taken seriously, and that the ritual was the sign of their participation in the covenant.

The modern Christian lives under the new covenant which has different signs: baptism as the ritual of initiation, and communion as the repeated sign in worship. Circumcision becomes a medical decision by the parents and doctors at the birth of a male; but it does not carry the same importance as it did for the covenant with Abraham. Participation in the covenant by faith, however, remains the important requirement behind all ritual and signs (Rom 2:28-29). Thus, circumcision of the heart, what we call sanctification to the Lord, remains a fundamental requirement, even though the physical rite may not.

◆ ### 9. The time of fulfillment guaranteed by divine visitation (18:1-15)

The LORD appeared again to Abraham near the oak grove belonging to Mamre. One day Abraham was sitting at the entrance to his tent during the hottest part of the day. ²He looked up and noticed three men standing nearby. When he saw them, he ran to meet them and welcomed them, bowing low to the ground.

³"My lord," he said, "if it pleases you, stop here for a while. ⁴Rest in the shade of this tree while water is brought to wash your feet. ⁵And since you've honored your servant with this visit, let me prepare some food to refresh you before you continue on your journey."

"All right," they said. "Do as you have said."

⁶So Abraham ran back to the tent and said to Sarah, "Hurry! Get three large measures* of your best flour, knead it into dough, and bake some bread." ⁷Then Abraham ran out to the herd and chose a tender calf and gave it to his servant, who quickly prepared it. ⁸When the food was ready, Abraham took some yogurt and milk and the roasted meat, and he served it to the men. As they ate, Abraham waited on them in the shade of the trees.

⁹"Where is Sarah, your wife?" the visitors asked.

"She's inside the tent," Abraham replied.

¹⁰Then one of them said, "I will return to you about this time next year, and your wife, Sarah, will have a son!"

Sarah was listening to this conversation from the tent. ¹¹Abraham and Sarah were both very old by this time, and Sarah was long past the age of having children. ¹²So she laughed silently to herself and said, "How could a worn-out woman like me enjoy such pleasure, especially when my master—my husband—is also so old?"

¹³Then the LORD said to Abraham, "Why did Sarah laugh? Why did she say, 'Can an old woman like me have a baby?' ¹⁴Is anything too hard for the LORD? I will return about this time next year, and Sarah will have a son."

¹⁵Sarah was afraid, so she denied it, saying, "I didn't laugh."

But the LORD said, "No, you did laugh."

18:6 Hebrew *3 seahs*, about 15 quarts or 18 liters.

NOTES

18:3 *My lord.* There is a question concerning Abraham's awareness of who his visitors were. The difficulty is that the Hebrew text does not have *'adoni* [TH113/2967.1, ZH123/3276] (my lord) but *'adonay* [TH136, ZH151] (the Lord), the title that is usually reserved for Yahweh.

The consonants in the two words are the same, but different vowel points are used. The NLT properly renders the expression with "My lord," for it is unlikely that Abram at first recognized these visitors to be manifestations of the Lord God. Still, in the MT the word was vocalized in a way that indicated it was the Lord, perhaps to alert the reader to the supernatural nature of the visitors. As the chapter unfolds, Abraham becomes aware that this is the Lord.

18:12 *pleasure.* The Hebrew word here means "pleasure, delight, luxury" (it is related to the word "Eden"). The context suggests that Sarah, recognizing she and her husband are old, asks if she is to have sexual pleasure. If she had only referred to having a child, the phrase would have been worded differently. Of course, she has in mind that the pleasure will bear fruit; but her words focus on the pleasure she will have with Abraham.

18:14 *Is anything too hard for the LORD?* The verb translated "[be] hard" (*pala'* [TH6381, ZH7098]) literally means "impossible, wonderful, surpassing, marvelous." This rhetorical question was designed to state that God is fully able to do amazing and marvelous things.

COMMENTARY

This narrative records the visit of "three men" to Abraham near the great trees of Mamre at Hebron (18:1; cf. 13:18; 14:13). The story is often used to remind people how important it is to receive strangers with hospitality because they might be entertaining angels (Heb 13:2). This may be true, but the narrative has a greater purpose than teaching hospitality. It records a visitation of the Lord to Abraham and Sarah, wherein God announced the time of the birth of Isaac for the following spring (18:10; lit., "when the season comes alive").

The three visitors have been the subject of much inquiry; it seems likely that they are the Lord (18:1, 10, 13; cf. notes and commentary on 16:7 about the "angel of the LORD") and two angels. As the three left, the Lord told Abraham that he intended to go see Sodom, and then the two angels showed up in the city (18:22; 19:1). This would make the visitation a theophany—the Lord appearing in human form.

Why did the Lord approach Abram in this manner? Could not the word have been given from heaven or in a dream? Yes it could, but the manner of this communication was probably meant to underscore that Abraham had a personal, intimate relationship with the Lord through the covenant. In the ancient world, and especially in Israel, to eat together was important for the making of treaties or confirming covenants. Thus, when the Lord was ready to specify the fulfillment of the promise of a son, he came in person and ate a meal in Abraham's tent. Nothing could have communicated the close relationship of the covenant better than this. Likewise, down through the ages in worship, fellowship with God has been signified by a communal meal, first the Israelites eating the peace offering in the presence of God (cf. Lev 3; 7), and then later the church celebrating Holy Communion at the Lord's Table.

Abraham hurried out to meet the visitors and bowed down before them (18:2). He had water brought to wash their feet (18:4); he then hurried back to the tent to arrange freshly baked bread for them (18:6), ran to the herd and had his servant hurry as well, so that he was able to serve them a choice calf (18:7), along with yogurt and milk (18:8). He then stood by while they were eating (18:8; cf. 18:1-2). All this indicates that Abraham considered his visitors as very important guests, perhaps messengers. It may also suggest that he perceived them to be from God, if not the angel of the Lord himself.

After the meal, one of the visitors announced that a son would be born to Sarah in a year (18:10). The way the statement was made indicated that this visitor, this angel of the Lord, was clearly the Lord himself. His announcement foretold a dramatic change that was coming, but the thought seemed incredible to Sarah, who laughed in her heart ("silently to herself," 18:12, NLT). She was no longer having sexual pleasure with Abraham (18:12; see note). Were they now going to have sexual relations and within the year have a child?

The mysterious visitor reveals his omniscience and identity when he asks Abraham, "Why did Sarah laugh?" (18:13). How would anyone but the Lord have known that she had just laughed silently to herself? And so she denied it. But the Lord's response was a correction of that denial: "No, you did laugh" (18:15). The Lord thereby rebuked her doubt and Abraham's.

This section of Genesis is a call to believe that God can do the impossible. He confirmed his promise with Abraham through a personal visit—and ate with him—to announce that the time was at hand. It was the annunciation of a humanly impossible birth. When something as incredible as this is promised, the human response is consistent. Like Sarah here, and Abraham earlier, people are taken off guard, laugh inwardly at the thought, and then, out of fear, deny that they doubted. But God knows human hearts, when they stagger at the promises, and when they embrace them by faith. Is bringing a child from a "dead" womb too difficult for the one who called all things into existence by his powerful word? It was no laughing matter. He could do it. Nothing is too difficult for him.

The apostle Paul tells us that Abraham did not grow weak in his faith; in spite of the fact that he and Sarah were too old to have children, he was able to produce Isaac, the child of promise (Rom 4:18-19). Even though he and his wife at first laughed at the specific promise of a child within a year, they embraced the word by faith and had the child. Paul compares this kind of faith (in a dead womb) with the faith that we have in the new covenant in the Lord Jesus Christ, who against all the laws of nature, rose from the dead. Truly, nothing is too marvelous, too extraordinary for God. Likewise the writer of Hebrews affirms that by faith Sarah was enabled to become a mother, even though Abraham was past the age, and she was barren (Heb 11:11-12). This is why their faith is so exemplary; it is easy to believe the word of the Lord in general, but when that word promises something that seems totally impossible, it will take a strong and growing faith to believe it and act upon it. The Bible is filled with stories of how God did the impossible, worked miracles, overcame seemingly great odds, and finally conquered death. And God expects the believer today to take him at his word, even though it may seem to be laughable folly.

In the fullness of time, the Lord came into the world in human flesh to establish the new covenant through his blood. And when the Lord Jesus ate the Last Supper with his disciples, he confirmed what he had been preaching, that through faith in him there would be forgiveness of sin, resurrection from the dead, and life everlasting. God delights in doing the impossible, and he delights in the faith of his people.

◆ 10. Abraham's intercession for Sodom (18:16-33)

16Then the men got up from their meal and looked out toward Sodom. As they left, Abraham went with them to send them on their way.

17"Should I hide my plan from Abraham?" the LORD asked. 18"For Abraham will certainly become a great and mighty nation, and all the nations of the earth will be blessed through him. 19I have singled him out so that he will direct his sons and their families to keep the way of the LORD by doing what is right and just. Then I will do for Abraham all that I have promised."

20So the LORD told Abraham, "I have heard a great outcry from Sodom and Gomorrah, because their sin is so flagrant. 21I am going down to see if their actions are as wicked as I have heard. If not, I want to know."

22The other men turned and headed toward Sodom, but the LORD remained with Abraham. 23Abraham approached him and said, "Will you sweep away both the righteous and the wicked? 24Suppose you find fifty righteous people living there in the city—will you still sweep it away and not spare it for their sakes? 25Surely you wouldn't do such a thing, destroying the righteous along with the wicked. Why, you would be treating the righteous and the wicked exactly the same! Surely you wouldn't do that! Should not the Judge of all the earth do what is right?"

26And the LORD replied, "If I find fifty righteous people in Sodom, I will spare the entire city for their sake."

27Then Abraham spoke again. "Since I have begun, let me speak further to my Lord, even though I am but dust and ashes. 28Suppose there are only forty-five righteous people rather than fifty? Will you destroy the whole city for lack of five?"

And the LORD said, "I will not destroy it if I find forty-five righteous people there."

29Then Abraham pressed his request further. "Suppose there are only forty?"

And the LORD replied, "I will not destroy it for the sake of the forty."

30"Please don't be angry, my Lord," Abraham pleaded. "Let me speak—suppose only thirty righteous people are found?"

And the LORD replied, "I will not destroy it if I find thirty."

31Then Abraham said, "Since I have dared to speak to the Lord, let me continue—suppose there are only twenty?"

And the LORD replied, "Then I will not destroy it for the sake of the twenty."

32Finally, Abraham said, "Lord, please don't be angry with me if I speak one more time. Suppose only ten are found there?"

And the LORD replied, "Then I will not destroy it for the sake of the ten."

33When the LORD had finished his conversation with Abraham, he went on his way, and Abraham returned to his tent.

NOTES

18:17 *"Should I hide my plan from Abraham?" the* LORD *asked.* The revelation about the pending judgment on Sodom is put into the form of a divine soliloquy, drawing the reader into God's considerations in revealing his plan to Abraham.

COMMENTARY

In this account of Abraham's intercession for Sodom, the predominant theme is righteousness, specifically the righteousness of God. Exercising his justice, God would unleash his wrath on the cities of the plain, the major city being Sodom, where Lot went to live. But before doing so, he would tell Abraham his plan.

God had a double motivation for revealing the plan to Abraham. First, if all nations were to be blessed because of Abraham, God was compelled to tell the patriarch that one group of families was to be removed before it had exhausted its opportunities to be blessed through him. Besides, these were the people that Abraham had rescued (ch 14); he had special interest in them. Second, Abraham was going to be responsible to teach his descendants righteousness and justice (18:19) so that they might enjoy God's blessings. Therefore, it was important for Abraham to know how the righteousness of God works in judgment.

At the outset what was conveyed to Abraham was God's caution in judgment. The Lord said that the outcry from Sodom and Gomorrah (because of the grievous sins of those cities) was so great that he, God, had to go down and see if it was as bad as he had heard. If the sin of that place was so bad, God would know it and they would be judged. The language is anthropomorphic to be sure, for divine omniscience knew all about the sins of Sodom and Gomorrah. But this close scrutiny of God was a way of communicating his careful justice; he would not destroy the people of the plain unless he was absolutely sure they were wicked enough for severe punishment.

Abraham's concern was over the righteous people who were living in those cities. So he appealed to God with a series of questions: Would God sweep away both the righteous and the wicked (18:23)? Abraham seems to be using the language of the faith: In 15:6 righteousness was imparted to him because of his faith. "Righteous" then became a description of those who were members of the covenant by faith and who were seeking to please the Lord. It is on this basis that the New Testament can call Lot "righteous" (2 Pet 2:7). He was a believer; but his life did not always show it. Yet, faced with great evil and the need to make a choice, he opposed the wicked. In the Bible, the term "wicked" (or as other versions have it more precisely, the "ungodly") refers to unbelievers, not to members of the covenant. They might be fairly good people, but they had given themselves over to sin and to the opposition of the righteous and their God. But since there were also righteous people in Sodom, Abraham appealed for Sodom on the basis of God's justice—he did not pray only for Lot.

Abraham's great character is revealed by his persistent but humble intercession. He prayed that all in the cities, the wicked as well as the righteous, be spared for the sake of the righteous (18:23-25). Earlier he had personally rescued these people in battle (14:14-16). Now he pleaded for them with the same boldness, perseverance, and generosity with which he had fought for them. Abraham's prayer seems too bold to us—like he was bargaining with God. But he approached God with genuine humility and reverence. Again and again he found God conceding the numbers to him—50, 45, 40, 30, 20, and even 10 righteous people (18:24-32). Abraham was not trying to talk God into doing something against his will, for he was convinced of the righteousness of God. Finally the matter was settled: If there were 10 righteous people in the city, God would not destroy it.

The theme of righteousness predominates: Those who will enjoy God's blessing (1) will teach justice (18:19); (2) may intercede for just judgment to preserve the righteous; and (3) know that God may preserve the ungodly for the sake of the righteous. Certainly the people of God learned from this that God is a righteous judge, that righteousness exalts a nation (Prov 14:34), and that righteous people help preserve society (cf. Matt 5:13). In fact, in Israel's own history, the Exile was postponed for decades because there was a righteous remnant, a holy seed. These truths should have been as great a concern for the Israelites in their historical period as they were for Abraham. Likewise, the believers today in the church are a restraining and preserving element in the world. The point of the prophets and apostles is clear: God will deliver his righteous people from the world before he destroys it (2 Pet 2:9).

◆ ### 11. God's judgment on the cities of the plain (19:1-38)

That evening the two angels came to the entrance of the city of Sodom. Lot was sitting there, and when he saw them, he stood up to meet them. Then he welcomed them and bowed with his face to the ground. ²"My lords," he said, "come to my home to wash your feet, and be my guests for the night. You may then get up early in the morning and be on your way again."

"Oh no," they replied. "We'll just spend the night out here in the city square."

³But Lot insisted, so at last they went home with him. Lot prepared a feast for them, complete with fresh bread made without yeast, and they ate. ⁴But before they retired for the night, all the men of Sodom, young and old, came from all over the city and surrounded the house. ⁵They shouted to Lot, "Where are the men who came to spend the night with you? Bring them out to us so we can have sex with them!"

⁶So Lot stepped outside to talk to them, shutting the door behind him. ⁷"Please, my brothers," he begged, "don't do such a wicked thing. ⁸Look, I have two virgin daughters. Let me bring them out to you, and you can do with them as you wish. But please, leave these men alone, for they are my guests and are under my protection."

⁹"Stand back!" they shouted. "This fellow came to town as an outsider, and now he's acting like our judge! We'll treat you far worse than those other men!" And they lunged toward Lot to break down the door.

¹⁰But the two angels* reached out, pulled Lot into the house, and bolted the door. ¹¹Then they blinded all the men, young and old, who were at the door of the house, so they gave up trying to get inside.

¹²Meanwhile, the angels questioned Lot. "Do you have any other relatives here in the city?" they asked. "Get them out of this place—your sons-in-law, sons, daughters, or anyone else. ¹³For we are about to destroy this city completely. The outcry against this place is so great it has reached the LORD, and he has sent us to destroy it."

¹⁴So Lot rushed out to tell his daughters' fiancés, "Quick, get out of the city! The LORD is about to destroy it." But the young men thought he was only joking.

¹⁵At dawn the next morning the angels became insistent. "Hurry," they said to Lot. "Take your wife and your two daughters who are here. Get out right now, or you will be swept away in the destruction of the city!"

¹⁶When Lot still hesitated, the angels seized his hand and the hands of his wife and two daughters and rushed them to safety outside the city, for the LORD was merciful. ¹⁷When they were safely out of the city, one of the angels ordered, "Run for your lives! And don't look back or stop anywhere in the valley! Escape to the mountains, or you will be swept away!"

¹⁸"Oh no, my lord!" Lot begged. ¹⁹"You have been so gracious to me and saved my life, and you have shown such great kindness. But I cannot go to the mountains. Disaster would catch up to me there, and I would soon die. ²⁰See, there is a small village nearby. Please let me go there instead; don't you see how small it is? Then my life will be saved."

²¹"All right," the angel said, "I will grant your request. I will not destroy the little village. ²²But hurry! Escape to it, for I can do nothing until you arrive there." (This explains why that village was known as Zoar, which means "little place.")

²³Lot reached the village just as the sun was rising over the horizon. ²⁴Then the LORD rained down fire and burning sulfur from the sky on Sodom and Gomorrah. ²⁵He utterly destroyed them, along with the other cities and villages of the plain, wiping out all the people and every bit of vegetation. ²⁶But Lot's wife looked back as she was following behind him, and she turned into a pillar of salt.

²⁷Abraham got up early that morning and hurried out to the place where he had stood in the LORD's presence. ²⁸He looked out across the plain toward Sodom and Gomorrah and watched as columns of smoke rose from the cities like smoke from a furnace.

²⁹But God had listened to Abraham's request and kept Lot safe, removing him from the disaster that engulfed the cities on the plain.

³⁰Afterward Lot left Zoar because he was afraid of the people there, and he went to live in a cave in the mountains with his two daughters. ³¹One day the older daughter said to her sister, "There are no men left anywhere in this entire area, so we can't get married like everyone else. And our father will soon be too old to have children. ³²Come, let's get him drunk with wine, and then we will have sex with him. That way we will preserve our family line through our father."

³³So that night they got him drunk with wine, and the older daughter went in and had intercourse with her father. He was unaware of her lying down or getting up again.

³⁴The next morning the older daughter said to her younger sister, "I had sex with our father last night. Let's get him drunk with wine again tonight, and you go in and have sex with him. That way we will preserve our family line through our father." ³⁵So that night they got him drunk with wine again, and the younger daughter went in and had intercourse with him. As before, he was unaware of her lying down or getting up again.

³⁶As a result, both of Lot's daughters became pregnant by their own father. ³⁷When the older daughter gave birth to a son, she named him Moab.* He became the ancestor of the nation now known as the Moabites. ³⁸When the younger daughter gave birth to a son, she named him Ben-ammi.* He became the ancestor of the nation now known as the Ammonites.

19:10 Hebrew *men;* also in 19:12, 16.   **19:37** *Moab* sounds like a Hebrew term that means "from father."
19:38 *Ben-ammi* means "son of my kinsman."

NOTES

19:5 have sex with them. Lit., "know them." The NLT's translation is the correct denotation, as is clear from Lot's rebuke of their wicked plans and his offer of his two daughters to them.

19:24 the LORD rained down fire and burning sulfur from the sky. Some have suggested that deposits of sulfur erupted from the earth (cf. the "tar pits" of 14:10) and then showered down out of the heavens in flames of fire (cf. Luke 17:29). Another plausible guess is that an earthquake caused the release of combustible gas (see further, Barton and Muddiman 2001:52). The account of the eruption of Vesuvius and the destruction of Pompeii in the first century AD illustrates how quickly and thoroughly a catastrophe like this could destroy a place. However it happened, the Lord was the one who caused it to happen in judgment on the cities.

19:37 she named him Moab. The name *mo'ab* [TH4124, ZH4565] sounds like a Hebrew term that means "from his father" (cf. NLT mg).

19:38 she named him Ben-ammi. The name *ben-'ammi* [TH1151, ZH1214] means "son of my kinsman" (cf. NLT mg).

COMMENTARY

This chapter records God's judgment on a morally bankrupt Canaanite civilization; but it also provides a severe warning against becoming like them—it was difficult to get Lot and his family out of Sodom, but it was also difficult to get Sodom out of Lot's family. The Canaanites, the antagonists of the book, are here portrayed as an evil, corrupting people. Israel would be reminded of their threat by this and also of the threat of the tribes spawned under their influence, the Moabites and the Ammonites.

No longer dwelling in tents next to Sodom, Lot had become an upright citizen in the city of Sodom, hospitable and generous (19:2-3), and a leader of the community. The fact that Lot was sitting in the gate (19:1; cf. 19:9) may very well indicate that he had found a consistent role of resolving issues and making decisions in the city. Judges (i.e., jurors or elders) usually sat in the gate to make such decisions; gates of ancient cities were public places where legal and business transactions were finalized (cf. 23:18; see also Job 29:7, 12-17). As a judge, Lot sought to screen out the wickedness of the townsfolk and to give advice on good living. He knew truth and justice, righteousness and evil. He was a righteous man (2 Pet 2:7-8). Yet in spite of his denunciation of gross evil, he himself liked the lifestyle of Sodom, "the good life" as it were. He preferred making money off the citizens to staying in the hills (cf. 13:10-11) where there would be no filthy living, but also no good life either.

The hour of truth came with the visit of the two angels from the Lord. Lot seemed godly and pure, but he was hypocritical, and that became evident when he was forced to choose life away from Sodom or death with it. Because he was a hypocrite, his words of warning for the people were not taken seriously (19:14). The "saint" had at first pitched his tent next to Sodom, but later Sodom controlled his life. He was moral, for he opposed sodomy and homosexuality—he knew flagrant evil when he saw it. But ironically, he was willing to sacrifice his daughters' virginity to fend off the vice of the men of the town (19:8). He escaped judgment by the grace of God, but his heart was in Sodom. His wife was just too attached to the place to follow the call of grace; and his daughters had no qualms about having sexual intercourse with their drunk father (19:30-35) when they thought the tribes were all destroyed.

As long as the Lord had left Lot and his family alone in Sodom, Lot managed to live comfortably there and hold to his personal belief in God. But ultimately he could not hold to both. Sodom would have destroyed Lot if the Lord had not destroyed Sodom.

The story begins with two angels warning Lot about the coming destruction. These two angels, who had been with the Lord at Mamre (cf. 18:2, 22), were reluctant visitors to Sodom, knowing what kind of people lived there. In spite of Lot's hospitality, they preferred lodging outside in the city square to entering Lot's house. Nonetheless, Lot eventually persuaded them to come home with him. While the visitors were inside Lot's house, the men of the town started to gather around outside. They wanted to have sex with Lot's visitors (see note on 19:5). The men's wickedness showed Lot to be hypocritical. He had been living comfortably in Sodom, but now tried to prevent the men from having their way with his visitors by offering them his daughters. Lot's pleas for righteousness were ignored (19:7); in fact, the people were incensed that "now" he was trying to judge them (19:9). The implication is that they now saw a different side of Lot, a side that attempted to forestall wickedness in a wicked city. As things got more and more out of hand, the two angels pulled Lot back into the house and blinded the men outside (19:10-11). They warned Lot of the impending destruction (19:12-13), but his daughters' fiancés did not believe (19:14). It appeared that there were not even 10 righteous people in the city (cf. 18:32).

Early in the morning the angels had to drag Lot and his family from Sodom (19:16). Once the family of Lot was out, the Lord overthrew the cities of the plain with burning sulfur in a great devastation (see note on 19:24). The Lord was being merciful in sparing Lot for Abraham's sake (cf. 18:23; 19:29). This means that Lot also deserved judgment for the way he had been living, but because he was a believer at heart, the Lord rescued him. Even after Lot was delivered, he still wrung a concession out of the angels: He wanted to go to the small town of Zoar, which means "little place" (19:18-22). Before this it had been called Bela (14:2). Lot was pressing his luck, for it was by God's mercy he was alive at all. Israel would remember this glimpse of Lot, the father of Moab and Ammon, lingering and halting, being dragged to safety by the angels (cf. Luke 17:32). But Lot is not alone in this conflicted lifestyle. Down through the ages countless believers have fallen in with a corrupt world rather than willingly flee a society destined for destruction.

The narrative says that Lot's wife looked back and turned into a pillar of salt, a monument to her disobedience, for the family was explicitly instructed not to look back at all. It was no casual glance or curiosity. The verb for her looking indicates a prolonged, intense gazing at the world she had grown to love. She became part of the judgment as she lingered there on the slopes of the valley.

Abraham saw dense smoke (19:28), caused by burning sulfur (19:24), ascending from the deep valley like the smoke of some great furnace. When God judged the cities of the plain, he honored the request that Abraham had made in the intercession (cf. 18:23-32). Thus, he saved Lot from the judgment. But Lot's entire world was gone, as well as all that good land he had selfishly chosen for himself.

The chapter ends with the sordid story of Lot and his daughters in the cave (19:30-38). Lot had been afraid to flee to the mountains; he had gone to Zoar instead (19:22). But now, ironically, he left Zoar and sought safety in a little cave (19:30). What a stark contrast with the good life he had enjoyed in Sodom.

Lot's two daughters took stock of the situation and reasoned that their family would die out because there were no available husbands and their fiancés had died in the catastrophe (19:31). As far as they knew, the three of them were the only people left. The two daughters then got their father drunk enough to have sexual intercourse with him so that they could conceive (19:32-35). In sum, Lot is portrayed as a buffoon: In the city he was a fool and a hypocrite to the people of the town, on the journey he was a malingerer, still working the angles. Now to be made drunk and impregnate his two daughters, one on each night, reveals even more of his character. But the plan of the daughters worked, and they each got pregnant by their father. The first was named "Moab," a name that would raise no suspicions in the land (see note on 19:37); but the people who knew the account would know the sordid side of the event. The second daughter named her son "Ben-ammi" (see note on 19:38). No one would suspect that the kinsman was the father of the mother. From these two sons born of incestual relations came the Moabites and the Ammonites, two perennial enemies of the Israelites. The etymologies on the names in this account perpetuated the memory of the ignominious beginnings of these tribes. It is as if they were saying that the grotesque wickedness of those enemies was due in part to the way they began.

Four major motifs come to the fore in this chapter: God's swift judgment on the Canaanites, Lot's close attachment to the wicked society, God's merciful sparing of Lot from the fate of Sodom, and the rebirth of Sodom in the cave. Through these points, Israel could see that if God judges a people so severely, it is because they are guilty of great evil. After all, he is the righteous judge of the whole earth.

How then should the people of God live in a pagan, doomed world? The lesson is quite clear: "Do not love this world nor the things it offers you . . . [for] this world is fading away, along with everything that people crave" (1 John 2:15, 17). It is dangerous and foolish to become attached to the present corrupt world system because it awaits God's judgment. The people of society might laugh at the warnings, but the judgment will be sudden and swift.

Jesus referred to 19:26 to warn of the destruction to come on unbelieving Israel: "Remember what happened to Lot's wife!" (Luke 17:32). When Christ comes to judge the world, the events will be as sudden and devastating as at Sodom. People will be warned to flee and not look back (Luke 17:30-31). If an unbeliever craves the best of this world, he will lose both this world (since it is passing away) and his life in the next (Luke 17:33-37).

Jesus also said that if the miracles he did in Capernaum had been done in Sodom and Gomorrah, the people there would have repented long ago (Matt 11:23). As it is, "even Sodom will be better off on judgment day" than the cities of Galilee who heard Jesus' teachings and saw his miracles (Matt 11:24). This signifies that God judges according to the amount of knowledge possessed by the sinners—an indication of his just judgment. It also signifies that there will be a judgment to come that will be far greater than the physical destruction of the cities of Sodom and Gomorrah.

◆ 12. Abraham's deception before Abimelech (20:1-18)

Abraham moved south to the Negev and lived for a while between Kadesh and Shur, and then he moved on to Gerar. While living there as a foreigner, ²Abraham introduced his wife, Sarah, by saying, "She is my sister." So King Abimelech of Gerar sent for Sarah and had her brought to him at his palace.

³But that night God came to Abimelech in a dream and told him, "You are a dead man, for that woman you have taken is already married!"

⁴But Abimelech had not slept with her yet, so he said, "Lord, will you destroy an innocent nation? ⁵Didn't Abraham tell me, 'She is my sister'? And she herself said, 'Yes, he is my brother.' I acted in complete innocence! My hands are clean."

⁶In the dream God responded, "Yes, I know you are innocent. That's why I kept you from sinning against me, and why I did not let you touch her. ⁷Now return the woman to her husband, and he will pray for you, for he is a prophet. Then you will live. But if you don't return her to him, you can be sure that you and all your people will die."

⁸Abimelech got up early the next morning and quickly called all his servants together. When he told them what had happened, his men were terrified. ⁹Then Abimelech called for Abraham. "What have you done to us?" he demanded. "What crime have I committed that deserves treatment like this, making me and my kingdom guilty of this great sin? No one should ever do what you have done! ¹⁰Whatever possessed you to do such a thing?"

¹¹Abraham replied, "I thought, 'This is a godless place. They will want my wife and will kill me to get her.' ¹²And she really is my sister, for we both have the same father, but different mothers. And I married her. ¹³When God called me to leave my father's home and to travel from place to place, I told her, 'Do me a favor. Wherever we go, tell the people that I am your brother.' "

¹⁴Then Abimelech took some of his sheep and goats, cattle, and male and female servants, and he presented them to Abraham. He also returned his wife, Sarah, to him. ¹⁵Then Abimelech said, "Look over my land and choose any place where you would like to live." ¹⁶And he said to Sarah, "Look, I am giving your 'brother' 1,000 pieces of silver* in the presence of all these witnesses. This is to compensate you for any wrong I may have done to you. This will settle any claim against me, and your reputation is cleared."

¹⁷Then Abraham prayed to God, and God healed Abimelech, his wife, and his female servants, so they could have children. ¹⁸For the LORD had caused all the women to be infertile because of what happened with Abraham's wife, Sarah.

20:16 Hebrew *1,000 [shekels] of silver*, about 25 pounds or 11.4 kilograms in weight.

NOTES

20:1 *Gerar*. This town was near the coast in the land of the Philistines, about 12 miles south of Gaza and about 50 miles southwest of Hebron.

20:7 *prophet*. This is the first occurrence of the word in the OT. A prophet speaks for God and has direct communication with him. People could go to a prophet to enquire of the Lord (e.g., 1 Sam 9:6). Even though Abraham had acted wrongly, he was God's chosen mediator for this pagan king. By using Abraham as a prophet, God was demonstrating his authority through Abraham over the people of Gerar.

COMMENTARY

This is the second "sister story" in Genesis. The first episode was Abraham's deception before Pharaoh in Egypt, and this one concerns Abimelech in Gerar. Both end with God's sovereign protection of the marriage of Abraham and Sarah for the sake of the covenant promises—the first one outside the land and the second inside it, the first one almost immediately after they arrived in Canaan and the second just on the eve of the fulfillment of the promise of the birth of Isaac. This story not only records God's providential protection of his people, but also emphasizes purity, specifically the preservation of Sarah's purity. For the fulfillment of the promise, the purity of the marriage was essential.

God had previously delivered Abram and Sarai from Egypt, bringing plagues on the household of Pharaoh after Abram had lied about Sarai being his sister (12:10-20). Here Abraham told the same lie to Abimelech (20:2), the king of Gerar, out of fear once again that he would kill him to take his wife (20:11). (Later, Isaac would play the same trick with the king of Gerar [26:1-11], probably learning it from his father.) Even at the age of 89 Sarah was attractive. She died at the age of 127, so at 89 she would be comparable to a woman in her fifties today, a woman who had not yet had children. But she was also regal, being the "sister" of this great prince (23:6), and this would also make her appealing to the king.

When Abimelech took Sarah, God warned him in a dream (20:3) and brought barrenness to his wife and slave girls, perhaps suggesting that some time passed while Sarah was in his custody (20:17-18). The warning was very clear.

Abimelech was innocent. His appeal to God sounded a familiar note, at least to the readers of these stories. He asked God, "Will you destroy an innocent nation" (20:4)? Abraham had prayed that the righteous would not be destroyed with the wicked (18:23-32); now Abimelech's words echoed the same concern as he appealed to God. When Abraham heard of this king's appeal, the rebuke he felt would have been forceful.

When Abimelech assured God of his clear conscience in this matter, God told him to return Sarah and to have Abraham, the prophet, pray for him (see note on 20:7). Only the patriarch's prayer saved the king's life and restored the well-being of his family. It was a way of teaching the king that Abraham's God was sovereign and that Abraham was God's chosen servant, even if he did not always live up to it.

God did not rebuke Abimelech, but he certainly gave him the sternest of warnings: He must not commit adultery because it is a capital offense (20:7). This was the accepted law in the entire ancient Near East—adultery was *the* great sin because it destroyed another man's family and created serious financial complications. When a man married, he had to pay a bride price and a dowry. If that marriage was violated, one's possessions and status would be jeopardized. In antiquity, having children was a priority, and so on occasion there would be more than one wife, and the same situation would apply to polygamy and harems, as well. Most commoners, however, could not afford more than one wife, and after the birth of Samuel we have no cases of polygamy in the Old Testament except among some of the kings.

Both of Abraham's deliverances preserved Sarah's purity and kept the promise intact. God had made Abraham and Sarah one in marriage so that they could produce the godly seed, the promised seed in this case. The first incident (ch 12) was outside the land and reflected more clearly the life-and-death struggle for the survival of the nation under the domination of Egypt. The later Israelites who were in bondage in Egypt would have been encouraged that God could deliver them by plagues and preserve them as the covenant people. This second incident (ch 20) in the land of promise was an event that showed how God would continue to protect them as they encountered new threats from other tribes. They would also learn how God sovereignly intervenes in the lives of people to bring about his plan. He controls births; he opens and closes wombs (20:17-18); he reveals his word even to pagan kings (20:3-7). But the passage would also teach Israel that God uses Israelites, especially the prophets, to mediate his intervention among the nations.

God may not have rebuked Abraham, but Abimelech certainly did, and rightly so. The king spoke of the great guilt that Abraham's deception had brought on him (20:9), and he spoke to Sarah of his (Abimelech's) offense against her (20:16). He realized that his plan to take her into his harem was wrong. So he made amends by giving the patriarch livestock (cf. 21:27) and slaves (20:14), allowing him to live in the region (20:15), and giving Abraham, whom he sarcastically called Sarah's "brother," a thousand shekels of silver to compensate for any wrong done to her (20:16).

God's preventing the destruction of Abraham's marriage by adultery reinforced the fact that the Israelites must not destroy their marriages by adultery and not even allow the opportunity for the threat to occur. To take the wife of another man was not only a capital offense—it would eventually destroy the covenant people and the covenant itself. Here there was also a warning about intermarriage with pagans. So the message to Israel was clear: God did not want his people to destroy their marriages by such foolish acts or by adultery or by intermarriage with pagans. But Israel seldom remembered this warning (see Mal 2:10-17).

◆ 13. The birth of Isaac and expulsion of Ishmael (21:1-21)

The LORD kept his word and did for Sarah exactly what he had promised. ²She became pregnant, and she gave birth to a son for Abraham in his old age. This happened at just the time God had said it would. ³And Abraham named their son Isaac. ⁴Eight days after Isaac was born, Abraham circumcised him as God had commanded. ⁵Abraham was 100 years old when Isaac was born.

⁶And Sarah declared, "God has brought me laughter.* All who hear about this will laugh with me. ⁷Who would have said to Abraham that Sarah would nurse a baby? Yet I have given Abraham a son in his old age!"

⁸When Isaac grew up and was about to be weaned, Abraham prepared a huge feast to celebrate the occasion. ⁹But Sarah saw Ishmael—the son of Abraham and her

Egyptian servant Hagar—making fun of her son, Isaac.* ¹⁰So she turned to Abraham and demanded, "Get rid of that slave woman and her son. He is not going to share the inheritance with my son, Isaac. I won't have it!"

¹¹This upset Abraham very much because Ishmael was his son. ¹²But God told Abraham, "Do not be upset over the boy and your servant. Do whatever Sarah tells you, for Isaac is the son through whom your descendants will be counted. ¹³But I will also make a nation of the descendants of Hagar's son because he is your son, too."

¹⁴So Abraham got up early the next morning, prepared food and a container of water, and strapped them on Hagar's shoulders. Then he sent her away with their son, and she wandered aimlessly in the wilderness of Beersheba.

¹⁵When the water was gone, she put the boy in the shade of a bush. ¹⁶Then she went and sat down by herself about a hundred yards* away. "I don't want to watch the boy die," she said, as she burst into tears.

¹⁷But God heard the boy crying, and the angel of God called to Hagar from heaven, "Hagar, what's wrong? Do not be afraid! God has heard the boy crying as he lies there. ¹⁸Go to him and comfort him, for I will make a great nation from his descendants."

¹⁹Then God opened Hagar's eyes, and she saw a well full of water. She quickly filled her water container and gave the boy a drink.

²⁰And God was with the boy as he grew up in the wilderness. He became a skillful archer, ²¹and he settled in the wilderness of Paran. His mother arranged for him to marry a woman from the land of Egypt.

21:6 The name *Isaac* means "he laughs." **21:9** As in Greek version and Latin Vulgate; Hebrew lacks *of her son, Isaac.* **21:16** Hebrew *a bowshot.*

NOTES

21:9 *making fun.* The word *metsakheq* [TH6711, ZH7464] is etymologically related to the word for laughter, which has been a theme throughout these narratives. Here the word could refer to something as harmless as playing or teasing, or something more serious like mocking, ridicule or scorn.

21:10 *Get rid of that slave woman and her son.* A number of critical scholars have seen ch 21 and ch 16 as a doublet that crept into the text, i.e., there originally was one story, but in the retelling the details were changed, giving rise to two accounts of the same event. This understanding was an integral part of the Documentary Hypothesis (see Skinner 1930:285), but it remains even today as a part of the critical analysis of the text (see Barton and Muddiman 2001:51). Anyone reading these narratives in their contexts would find that theory terribly flawed. The differences between the two stories are far greater than the similarities. The circumstances surrounding the life of Hagar would have created constant tension in Abraham's family, and her instinct to flee was simply postponed until the child Isaac was born.

COMMENTARY

At the very time he had promised, God provided a child to Sarah and to Abraham (cf. 18:10). Abraham responded in faith by naming him Isaac, as the Lord had commanded (21:3), and then by circumcising him according to the covenant (21:4; cf. 17:9-14); Sarah was filled with joy and praise at this amazing event (21:6-7). It was God alone who had enabled this couple to have a child.

The laughter of unbelief, when the promise was made (18:12), now changed to the laughter of joy through the provision of the son (21:5-6). In fact, this motif of rejoicing is more closely connected to the meaning of the name than the motif of disbelief, for names usually reflect positive and blessed experiences. The name Isaac (*yitskhaq* [TH3327, ZH3663]) is also a verb, "he laughs" (from *tsakhaq* [TH6711, ZH7464]); it could refer to both God's pleasure at the birth and the parents' joy as well. Sarah knew that everyone who heard about the birth of her son in old age would laugh with her, that is, they would certainly be amused by the experience, but in a way that rejoiced along with her. But the theme of laughter is given a sour twist when Ishmael turns the laughter into a ridicule and mockery (21:9).

Nonetheless, God used the incident of Ishmael's mocking Isaac to separate the boy Ishmael and his mother Hagar from the family and the child of promise (21:10), for they would be a constant threat to the promised seed if they remained with the family. At the festival for the weaning of Isaac, probably when he was about three, Sarah saw Ishmael "making fun of her son," perhaps mocking the boy (see note on 21:9), so she complained to Abraham (21:10). Earlier Sarah had mistreated Hagar (16:6); now Hagar's son was mistreating Isaac. Earlier Sarah pressured the pregnant Hagar to flee; now she demanded that Hagar and her 16-year-old son leave. When Abraham became distressed (NLT, "upset") because of Sarah's request to oust Hagar and Ishmael (21:11), God told him to do what she said, assuring him that Ishmael would have a future because he too was Abraham's seed (21:11-13).

The first 13 verses relate two episodes: the birth of Isaac in which the naming commemorated the fulfillment of the promise and the circumcising confirmed the covenant (21:1-7), and the expulsion of Ishmael as the removal of a threat to Isaac so that the child of promise could flourish as the heir (21:8-13). One son was joyfully received; the other was angrily dismissed. This was because once the promised child was born, Abraham and Sarah, rejoicing in God's miraculous provision, had to avoid any possible interference with Isaac's place and prospects. And because God had chosen one son, his choice had to be protected. Therefore, the slave wife and her son had to be sent away.

But God did not abandon Hagar and Ishmael. The next few verses record a second encounter of Hagar with God in the wilderness when she ran out of water. The angel of God met her at the place of despair (21:17-18), as before (cf. 16:7), and provided water from a well (21:19) as before. God told Hagar, as he had told Abraham, that from Ishmael would come a great nation (21:18). After this rescue, Ishmael lived in the wilderness and became an archer (21:20; cf. 16:12). He later married an Egyptian (21:21) and lived in the Wilderness of Paran in the northeast portion of the Sinai Peninsula.

Paul's use of this account in the book of Galatians is insightful (Gal 4:21-31). He reminds the readers that Ishmael was born by the flesh through the slave wife (Gal 4:29-30), whereas Isaac was born as the fulfillment of the promise and was therefore the heir. He suggests that these historical figures illustrate a truth about the new covenant: That which represented the bondage of the law at Sinai had to give way to that which represented the freedom of the promise fully realized. Accordingly, when Christ, the promised seed, came, the old covenant with its law was fulfilled in him and no longer binding. To go back under the law would be to threaten and even undo the fulfillment of God's promise. Just as Ishmael and Isaac were in conflict—just by who they were (Gal 4:29)—so the flesh and the Spirit do not harmonize. The flesh struggles against the Spirit, often mocking it (Gal 5:16-18). Therefore, believers are to get rid of the "slave and her son" (Gal 4:30)—that is, remove the threat of fleshly striving and live by the Spirit (Gal 5:16). In his analogical application, Paul was not addressing the question of whether or not Hagar and Ishmael had faith in the Lord; rather, he was only using them and the incident to support his point about removing things that threaten the fulfillment of the promise in Christ Jesus. Those adopted into the covenant through the Seed, Christ, are like Isaac; they are to live in freedom from the bondage of the law (Gal 5:1).

◆ 14. The covenant at Beersheba (21:22-34)

²²About this time, Abimelech came with Phicol, his army commander, to visit Abraham. "God is obviously with you, helping you in everything you do," Abimelech said. ²³"Swear to me in God's name that you will never deceive me, my children, or any of my descendants. I have been loyal to you, so now swear that you will be loyal to me and to this country where you are living as a foreigner."

²⁴Abraham replied, "Yes, I swear to it!" ²⁵Then Abraham complained to Abimelech about a well that Abimelech's servants had taken by force from Abraham's servants.

²⁶"This is the first I've heard of it," Abimelech answered. "I have no idea who is responsible. You have never complained about this before."

²⁷Abraham then gave some of his sheep, goats, and cattle to Abimelech, and they made a treaty. ²⁸But Abraham also took seven additional female lambs and set them off by themselves. ²⁹Abimelech asked, "Why have you set these seven apart from the others?"

³⁰Abraham replied, "Please accept these seven lambs to show your agreement that I dug this well." ³¹Then he named the place Beersheba (which means "well of the oath"), because that was where they had sworn the oath.

³²After making their covenant at Beersheba, Abimelech left with Phicol, the commander of his army, and they returned home to the land of the Philistines. ³³Then Abraham planted a tamarisk tree at Beersheba, and there he worshiped the LORD, the Eternal God.* ³⁴And Abraham lived as a foreigner in Philistine country for a long time.

21:33 Hebrew *El-Olam.*

NOTES

21:30 *seven lambs . . . Beersheba.* The number "seven" (*sheba'* [TH7651, ZH8679]) occurs three times in this passage (21:28-30). The name "Beersheba" (*be'er* [TH884, ZH937] *shaba'*), meaning "well of the oath" or "well of seven," also occurs three times (21:31-33).

21:31 *sworn the oath.* This word for "to swear, take an oath" (*shaba'* [TH7650, ZH8678]) occurs three times in the passage (21:23-24, 31). Certainly the stress of the passage is on the oath and its significance, commemorated by the naming of the place.

21:32 *Philistines.* These peoples are best known from the time of the judges and the early kings. They are believed to have been of Greek origin, having migrated from the Aegean region to the Delta of Egypt around 1200 BC. When the Pharaoh drove them out, they settled up the coast in the region of Gaza. Their customs reflected the Greek culture more than the Semitic. But the Philistines that appear in the patriarchal times do not appear to be of the same stock, for their names (like Abimelech) are Semitic. It may be that early groups of Aegean sea traders settled in the region as early as Abraham's time, roughly 2166–1991 BC. But would they have been settled in the land with established kings? It seems more likely that the later name was simply used to describe an earlier, unrelated people who had lived in the same region.

COMMENTARY

This story fits well in the context that is building up to the sacrifice of Isaac in chapter 22. The birth of Isaac was clearly promised (18:1-15), and a year later the child was born (21:1-7). In time the rival heir, Ishmael, was sent away and the rights of the son Isaac were preserved (21:8-21). Earlier, in the incident of Abraham's deception (ch 20), Abimelech had learned that God's hand was on this man (cf. 21:22). Now a covenant was to be made that would allow Abimelech to share in the blessings and allow Abraham to live in the land in peace.

The narrative in 21:22-34 reveals that the patriarch was blessed by God and that the pagans recognized this to be so. The motif of the well appears again as in previous narratives (cf. 16:14; 21:19). God provided water, a symbol of blessing, in the wilderness, the barren land (and later even out of the rock for later Israel; Exod 17). Abimelech recognized this, for any provision of water in this land was a sign of divine presence. But he knew Abraham, and he knew about Abraham's God. After some controversy over seizing the well (21:25), the two men made a treaty so that the pagan king could share in the blessing (cf. 12:1-3). Abimelech pressed for the treaty so that Abraham would not deal falsely with him (21:23). All Abimelech knew about this man was that God was blessing him (21:22) and that Abraham could not be trusted completely (cf. 20:9-10; 21:23). The sad contradiction made the treaty necessary.

In making the treaty Abraham gave Abimelech both sheep and cattle (21:27; cf. the reverse in 20:14), including seven ewe lambs (21:28-30). These secured Abraham's legal right to dwell in the land in peace, and it legally forced Abimelech to acknowledge that the well at Beersheba belonged to Abraham (21:30-31). The patriarch thus secured his right to the well and to the portion of land at Beersheba, which were additional provisions of the blessings of God.

After the agreement was sealed, Abraham named the place Beersheba (see note on 21:31). The climactic feature about this passage is the explanation of the name of Beersheba, the home of Abraham (21:33). This name would always reflect the covenant the patriarch made with the residents of the land, a covenant that allowed him to dwell there in peace and prosperity.

Abraham planted a tree there and lived there as a sojourner for a good number of days (21:33-34). To plant a tree in the region of Beersheba presupposed a constant supply of water and indicated his determination to stay in the region. The tree may have been planted in one of the usually dry river beds where the water table was near the surface. But Abraham still had to rely on God's provision of water for it, or anything, to survive in the region. Here Abraham would stay settled in the land, even if it was without permanent rights. And here Abraham continued to acknowledge that the Lord was blessing him because he worshiped the Lord, who is also known as the Eternal God (*'el 'olam* [TH410A/5769, ZH446/6409]; 21:33, NLT mg).

The story would have been encouraging for Israel's future peaceful coexistence in the land with other tribes who would respond to the revelation of the one true and living God, Yahweh, and to his gracious provision of life and thereby desire to have a share in the blessing. Israel was also instructed here to keep any oaths and treaties she made and to avoid all deceptive practices and falsehood. Today believers are instructed to speak the truth without using oaths (Matt 5:37; Jas 5:12). Truthful and faithful dealings that preserve such peaceful relations enhance the work of God. After all, to be a blessing to the world requires that the people of God demonstrate that they have received God's grace and are living by it.

◆ ### 15. The testing of Abraham's faith (22:1-24)

Some time later, God tested Abraham's faith. "Abraham!" God called.

"Yes," he replied. "Here I am."

²"Take your son, your only son—yes, Isaac, whom you love so much—and go to the land of Moriah. Go and sacrifice him as a burnt offering on one of the mountains, which I will show you."

³The next morning Abraham got up early. He saddled his donkey and took two of his servants with him, along with his son, Isaac. Then he chopped wood for a fire for a burnt offering and set out for the place God had told him about. ⁴On the third day of their journey, Abraham looked up and saw the place in the distance. ⁵"Stay here with the donkey," Abraham told the servants. "The boy and I will travel a little farther. We will worship there, and then we will come right back."

⁶So Abraham placed the wood for the burnt offering on Isaac's shoulders, while he himself carried the fire and the knife. As the two of them walked on together, ⁷Isaac turned to Abraham and said, "Father?"

"Yes, my son?" Abraham replied.

"We have the fire and the wood," the boy said, "but where is the sheep for the burnt offering?"

⁸"God will provide a sheep for the burnt offering, my son," Abraham answered. And they both walked on together.

⁹When they arrived at the place where God had told him to go, Abraham built an altar and arranged the wood on it. Then he tied his son, Isaac, and laid him on the altar on top of the wood. ¹⁰And Abraham picked up the knife to kill his son as a sacrifice. ¹¹At that moment the angel of the LORD called to him from heaven, "Abraham! Abraham!"

"Yes," Abraham replied. "Here I am!"

¹²"Don't lay a hand on the boy!" the angel said. "Do not hurt him in any way, for now I know that you truly fear God. You have not withheld from me even your son, your only son."

¹³Then Abraham looked up and saw a ram caught by its horns in a thicket. So he took the ram and sacrificed it as a burnt offering in place of his son. ¹⁴Abraham named the place Yahweh-Yireh (which means "the LORD will provide"). To this day, people still use that name as a proverb: "On the mountain of the LORD it will be provided."

¹⁵Then the angel of the LORD called again to Abraham from heaven. ¹⁶"This is what the LORD says: Because you have obeyed me and have not withheld even

your son, your only son, I swear by my own name that [17]I will certainly bless you. I will multiply your descendants* beyond number, like the stars in the sky and the sand on the seashore. Your descendants will conquer the cities of their enemies. [18]And through your descendants all the nations of the earth will be blessed—all because you have obeyed me."

[19]Then they returned to the servants and traveled back to Beersheba, where Abraham continued to live.

[20]Soon after this, Abraham heard that Milcah, his brother Nahor's wife, had borne Nahor eight sons. [21]The oldest was named Uz, the next oldest was Buz, followed by Kemuel (the ancestor of the Arameans), [22]Kesed, Hazo, Pildash, Jidlaph, and Bethuel. [23](Bethuel became the father of Rebekah.) In addition to these eight sons from Milcah, [24]Nahor had four other children from his concubine Reumah. Their names were Tebah, Gaham, Tahash, and Maacah.

22:17 Hebrew *seed;* also in 22:17b, 18.

NOTES

22:2 *go to the land of Moriah.* This is explained by the Chronicler (2 Chr 3:1) as the place of the later Temple Mount in Jerusalem. Abraham was instructed to go to the region of Moriah, which could have been any of the hills around the Jebusite city. The normal route from Beersheba to the region of Moriah would be to go northeast about 30 miles to Hebron, and then about 19 miles north to the designated region, roughly 50 miles depending on the exact path taken. Abraham saw the place on the third day, so the journey could have been finished in less than three full days, but Abraham's pace seems to have slowed the nearer he got to the location (see commentary).

22:8 *God will provide.* The verb is literally "see" (*ra'ah* [TH7200, ZH8011]), but here it has the connotation of seeing to something or providing.

22:14 *Yahweh-Yireh (which means "the Lord will provide").* The motivation for this name comes early in the passage, in 22:8, where Abraham answered Isaac with "God will provide" (lit., "God will see to it"). Two things are to be noted here. First, the text uses two names of God: *'elohim* [TH430, ZH466], in the motivation (22:12), and *yhwh* [TH3068, ZH3378] in the name Yahweh-Yireh. This is problematic for scholars adhering to the Documentary Hypothesis, which posits that passages that use the name *'elohim* can be classified as belonging to an original source called E, and passages that use the name *yhwh* belong to an originally separate source called J (the J comes from the German spelling *Jahweh*). The second thing to note is that Abraham's use of the holy name Yahweh in the commemorative naming shows that the patriarchs did know the name. They just did not know what it would come to mean when the promises were fulfilled. The revelation to Moses in Exod 3 would explain that.

"On the mountain of the Lord it will be provided." This little motto that accompanies the commemorative name is deliberately ambiguous. It does not specify the mountain, which would be the mountain God chose, first Sinai, but once in the land, Mount Zion. The verb *ra'ah* [TH7200, ZH8011] in the niphal stem could mean "it will be seen," "he will be seen" (i.e., appear), or "it will be provided." There is support from several passages of Scripture that "he will be seen" is the most appropriate, for the Lord would be seen in the way he made provisions for his people and his powerful interventions in their lives (see, e.g., Ps 63; Isa 38:9-20).

22:20-24 Chapter 22 ends with a report from the east that the family of Abraham's brother, Nahor (cf. 11:27-29) was flourishing. Among those born to him was Bethuel, who is identified as the father of Rebekah, the future wife of Isaac (22:23; cf. 24:15, 67). Bethuel was the youngest of Nahor's eight sons by Milcah (Nahor's niece). This notice is recorded here even though one would expect it closer to ch 24. But it serves as a tie-in with ch 23, which records Sarah's death and burial. In burying Sarah in Canaan, Abraham turned his back on the ancestral home, not going back there for her burial. The future would be in Canaan, and the promise with his family. And Rebekah would replace Sarah as the matriarch of the clan.

COMMENTARY

The greatest test in the life of Abraham came after he had received the long-awaited promised child; even more difficult, it came after Abraham had grown to love him and enjoy his presence for a good number of years. Then God "tested" (*nissah* [TH5254, ZH5814]) Abraham. The test was severe: He was to give Isaac back to God. As a test it was designed to prove his faith: Would he still obey God when God seemed to be working against him and against the covenant? For it to be a real test, it had to push the limits of logic and Abraham's understanding of God. It had to be something Abraham would naturally want to resist. God wanted to see if Abraham would obey, and so the instruction was severe and out of harmony with the revealed plan of God. Because it was a test of the man's faith, it was not simply a command to sacrifice his son. But Abraham did not know that, not until the Lord stopped him and approved his faith. Then it was clear to Abraham that God had not intended for him to sacrifice his son (and never would have, cf. Lev 18:21; Jer 32:35).

The passage begins with the expression "some time later" (lit., "after these things"), which points specifically to the events in the last chapter where Abraham had sent Ishmael away and then had settled in the land. Even though he loved Ishmael and was reluctant to send him away until God confirmed the decision, he nonetheless did dismiss him because he was the son of the slave wife. Now God tested him by telling him to give up the other son as well.

It is one thing to claim to trust God's word when waiting for something; it is quite another thing to trust with the same intensity after receiving the promise. This was a test to see how much Abraham would obey God's word. Would he cling to the boy now that he had him, or would he surrender him to God? In other words, would he still obey God when it meant giving up the dearest possession he had? Did he truly believe that God would still keep his word and bless the world through the seed of Abraham?

The way that the command of God is worded made the test very hard: "Take your son, your only son—yes, Isaac, whom you love so much" (22:2). It was as if God was making it as difficult as possible. In this way he was not only reminding Abraham that this young man was his beloved son but he was also intensifying the cost of the sacrifice. And yet the words of the command also recall the original call recorded in 12:1-3, which instructed Abraham to go to a land that God would show him. This would have reminded Abraham that his obedience to that call had been rewarded with great blessing; now he had the opportunity to show an even greater act of obedience. God was helping him obey by recalling the former call.

The command to go and offer Isaac as a sacrifice would have seemed totally unreasonable to Abraham. The pagans may have offered human sacrifice, but it was out of harmony with the nature of God. Beyond that, how could God fulfill the promises he had made earlier if the promised seed was now to be destroyed? And at Abraham's age there would not likely be another child, at least not one through Sarah. The cost to the covenant would be enormous, not to mention the emotional loss to Abraham and Sarah.

Abraham's response was almost as amazing as the test: He responded with instant, unquestioning obedience to the command of God. He even got an early start! However, the three-day journey (22:4) probably became more and more difficult as he drew near to the place, for the Hebrew narrative slows down the action with a more deliberate manner of telling the story (using more *and*s than needed—a rhetorical device called *polysyndeton*). When Abraham saw the place in the region of Moriah, he took only Isaac with him and left the two servants and the donkey behind. He said, "We will worship there, and then we will come right back" (22:5). This could also be translated, "We will worship there in order that we may return." His statement is amazing, and raises all kinds of questions regarding what was going through his mind at this moment. All that Abraham knew was that God had planned the future of the covenant around Isaac and that God wanted him to sacrifice Isaac. He could not reconcile these two things in his own mind, but could only do what God commanded him to do, leaving the future to God. That is faith. In response to Isaac's question, "Where is the sheep for the burnt offering?" (22:7), Abraham again revealed his faith in the Lord, "God will provide a sheep for the burnt offering, my son" (22:8). This statement of Abraham's would become the motive for the naming to follow (see 22:14 and note) and the theme of the entire narrative for the household of faith.

God's intervention was dramatic and instructive; it revealed that he had never intended for the boy to be sacrificed; child sacrifice was never to be practiced in Israel. What God wanted from Abraham was actually for Abraham to sacrifice his own will, to surrender his will to God by giving up his dearest possession. And when that happened, God intervened. So in a way Isaac was brought from the dead twice, once from the dead womb of Sarah by divine intervention, and once from the altar where he was essentially sacrificed to God (Heb 11:17-19). The angel of the Lord stopped Abraham just as he was ready to plunge the knife into his son (22:10-11). God then knew that Abraham would hold nothing back from him, that he did in fact fear God (22:12). This usage harmonizes with the biblical meaning, for to fear God means to revere him as sovereign, trust him implicitly, and obey him without question or protest.

This passage not only records the great test of Abraham, the pinnacle of his life of faith, but it also sets forth the pattern for sacrificial worship down through the ages. Like Abraham, a true worshiper of God holds nothing back from God, but obediently gives him what he asks, trusting that God will provide all his needs. A true worshiper knows that everything belongs to God anyway—it all came from God, and therefore must be acknowledged as God's own possession. The key idea of the whole passage is summarized in the commemorative name that Abraham gave to the place: "The LORD will provide" or "The LORD will see to it" (*yhwh yir'eh* [TH3068/ 7200, ZH3378/8011]; see note on 22:14). This truth is at the heart of faithful worship: The Lord was to be worshiped by his people on his holy mountain. Three times a year the people were to appear (*yera'eh* [TH7200, ZH8011], "be seen") before the Lord to worship him, bringing their sacrifices and offerings to him (Exod 23:17; Deut 16:16). They were to bring to God the best sacrifice they had, trusting that he would continue to provide for their needs—but they had to offer the sacrifice to God first and then expect his provision. Thus, they went to the sanctuary to "see" (*ra'ah*) the Lord, to behold his power and glory in the way he answered prayers and provided for his people (Ps 63:2-5). And God would "see" (*ra'ah*) the needs of those who came before him with their sacrifices, and would bless them with provisions for life. Thus in providing for them he would be seen. So a motto grew up for Israel's worship: "On the mountain of the LORD it will be seen" (or "it will be provided," or "he will be seen"; see note on 22:14). Faith first surrenders the dearest and the best to God, believing that God will provide.

In naming the place Abraham was commemorating his own experience of sacrifice to the Lord. But an animal (a ram, not a "sheep"; 22:8), caught by its horns in a thornbush, was the divine provision for the sacrifice. By his grace God allowed Abraham to offer a substitute sacrifice, an animal in the place of Isaac (22:13). Later all Israel would offer animals to the Lord, knowing that God's grace had provided for a substitute sacrifice to be made for the worshiper. Out of this event, Israel developed a major theological teaching: Whenever an animal was offered on the holy mountain of God, God remembered Isaac (this is seen in rabbinic writings on the Akedah). In other words, the believer knew that the sacrifice he was offering was a substitute, and that the true sacrifice that was pleasing to God was a broken heart, his heart broken of self-will and surrendered to God. And that surrender would be expressed by offering the best that could be given to God.

The passage also anticipates God's substituting his only son for all humanity, making the perfect sacrifice once and for all. John certainly had this in mind when he introduced Jesus as the Lamb of God who takes away the sin of the world (John 1:29). Yet the focus of Genesis 22 is not on the doctrine of atonement. Rather, it is portraying an obedient servant worshiping God in faith at great cost and then receiving God's provision. Abraham did not withhold his son from God. Similarly Paul wrote that God "did not spare (*epheisato* [TG5339, ZG5767]) even his own Son but gave him up for us all" (Rom 8:32). A form of the same word is used in the Greek version of Genesis 22:12: "You have not spared (*epheisō*) your beloved son." And based on this motif, Paul gets to the point, both of Genesis 22 and of his own argument: "Won't he also give us everything else?" If God gave us the dearest possession he has, he will surely provide all things for us.

This passage reveals the greatness of Abraham's faith: He was willing to obey God by sacrificing his son. It also says something about the spirit and faith of Isaac in submitting to his father—he had everything in the world to live for, but willingly did what his father told him to do, believing that God would provide a lamb.

Could Abraham and Isaac have even imagined what this event at this location anticipated? We cannot know what they thought. But Jesus said that Abraham saw his day, and rejoiced to see it (John 8:56). This "day" may have been a reference to the coming of the Messiah to make the perfect sacrifice. It may be that at that moment at Moriah God allowed Abraham to see more of the divine plan than the text has put into words.

After the event, God again confirmed his covenant with Abraham (22:15-19; cf. 15:5, 18-21; 17:3-8). His descendants would be numerous like the stars of the heavens (cf. 15:5; 26:4), like the sand of the seashore (cf. 32:12; and also like the dust of the earth, cf. 13:16; 28:14). God then added another element to the promise: Abraham's descendants would be victorious over the cities of their Canaanite enemies. This was fulfilled in great measure by Joshua during the conquest.

The lessons of this passage for devout worshipers are timeless: (1) Faith obeys the word of God even if it conflicts with our understanding and our preferences; (2) faith surrenders the best to God, holding nothing back; and (3) faith waits on the Lord to provide all one's needs. But God does not provide until the will has been surrendered and the offering given. True worship is costly. This was always the case for Israel as they came to the sanctuary. But if they were faithful—and if we are faithful—the Lord will provide.

◆ 16. The burial of Sarah (23:1-20)

When Sarah was 127 years old, ²she died at Kiriath-arba (now called Hebron) in the land of Canaan. There Abraham mourned and wept for her.

³Then, leaving her body, he said to the Hittite elders, ⁴"Here I am, a stranger and a foreigner among you. Please sell me a piece of land so I can give my wife a proper burial."

⁵The Hittites replied to Abraham, ⁶"Listen, my lord, you are an honored prince among us. Choose the finest of our tombs and bury her there. No one here will refuse to help you in this way."

⁷Then Abraham bowed low before the Hittites ⁸and said, "Since you are willing to help me in this way, be so kind as to ask Ephron son of Zohar ⁹to let me buy his cave at Machpelah, down at the end of his field. I will pay the full price in the presence of witnesses, so I will have a permanent burial place for my family."

¹⁰Ephron was sitting there among the others, and he answered Abraham as the others listened, speaking publicly before all the Hittite elders of the town. ¹¹"No, my lord," he said to Abraham, "please listen to me. I will give you the field and the cave. Here in the presence of my people, I give it to you. Go and bury your dead."

¹²Abraham again bowed low before the citizens of the land, ¹³and he replied to Ephron as everyone listened. "No, listen to me. I will buy it from you. Let me pay the full price for the field so I can bury my dead there."

¹⁴Ephron answered Abraham, ¹⁵"My lord, please listen to me. The land is worth 400 pieces* of silver, but what is that between friends? Go ahead and bury your dead."

¹⁶So Abraham agreed to Ephron's price and paid the amount he had suggested—400 pieces of silver, weighed according to the market standard. The Hittite elders witnessed the transaction.

¹⁷So Abraham bought the plot of land belonging to Ephron at Machpelah, near

Mamre. This included the field itself, the cave that was in it, and all the surrounding trees. ¹⁸It was transferred to Abraham as his permanent possession in the presence of the Hittite elders at the city gate. ¹⁹Then Abraham buried his wife, Sarah, there in Canaan, in the cave of Machpelah, near Mamre (also called Hebron). ²⁰So the field and the cave were transferred from the Hittites to Abraham for use as a permanent burial place.

23:15 Hebrew *400 shekels*, about 10 pounds or 4.6 kilograms in weight; also in 23:16.

NOTES

23:4 *sell me a piece of land so I can give my wife a proper burial.* The event described here includes many features that can be found in ancient Canaanite and Hittite treaties concerning land. Under one such treaty we learn that the system was an ancient form of feudalism and that buying a portion of a field would obligate one to certain responsibilities (cf. ANET 188-196, paragraphs 46-48, 169). Other laws from Ugarit (in Syria) are also relevant to the interpretation of this passage. Although these laws come from a later period, the customs and laws were no doubt in existence in the culture before they were written down.

COMMENTARY

Sarah lived to be 127 (Isaac was 37 at her death; cf. 17:17). And so Abraham sought to acquire a place for her burial, a cave near Mamre (23:19; cf. 13:18; 14:13; 18:1). This was the first indication that a permanent transition had taken place, for normally one would be buried in the ancestral homeland. But after mourning for his wife at Hebron (23:2), Abraham began bargaining with some Hittites for a portion of the land for a burial site.

In the text the owners of the field were a small group of Hittites who apparently had migrated south to Canaan. Even though the great Hittite empire (centered in what is now eastern Turkey) never extended this far south (Josh 1:4), pockets of Hittites apparently migrated, settled here, and continued in many of their customs while appropriating a Semitic language.

It appears that Abraham was held in high regard by the people around him—unless this was merely a polite way to appeal to his generosity. The Hittites acknowledged that he was a mighty prince among them (cf. 23:6-11). They would be willing to accommodate his request—especially if they could pass a few legal obligations on to him.

Abraham wanted to buy the cave that was owned by Ephron (23:9), but Ephron wanted him to buy the entire field. When Ephron said he would "give" the field and the cave to Abraham (two times in 23:11), he did not mean it was a free gift. This was the form of bargaining in ancient Near Eastern culture (and sometimes in the modern Near East as well). Ephron said, "I will give you the field and the cave" with the understood question being, "What are you going to give me?" Abraham did not want the whole field, but he was willing to take it (23:12-13) at a very high price (400 shekels of silver, which is about 10 pounds) to get the cave (23:15-16). Ephron's politeness was typical of the process: "The land is worth 400 pieces of silver, but what is that between friends?" So Abraham paid the amount, and the transaction was finalized in the presence of all the Hittites at the city gate, the place of legal and business dealings (cf. 19:1). The contract stated that the land and the field and even the trees (which were quite important in the ancient transactions of lands) passed into Abraham's possession.

This would be a permanent burial place for the family of Abraham. In this cave, the cave of Machpelah, Sarah was buried, and later Abraham (25:9), Isaac and his wife Rebekah, and Jacob and his wife Leah (49:29-31; 50:13). It was their permanent place in the Promised Land. Abraham was not presumptuous; in faith he waited for the Lord to give him the land, but in the meantime he bought the land, taking no gift from any of the people there (cf. 14:21-24). And so the first portion of the land was a burial site—a significant possession at a time when people were to be buried in their native lands and with their ancestors. Though Abraham was a foreigner among the people of the land (23:4), his hope was in the land that God had promised. When Abraham bought this cave he was renouncing his former homeland in Paddan-aram, that is, northwest Mesopotamia (cf. 25:20). The link to Mesopotamia had just been brought to the readers' attention indirectly by mentioning the relatives of Abraham who remained there (22:20-24; cf. 11:27-32).

Canaan was now the native land for Abraham's descendants. It was to this place that his descendants would come to bury their dead. But interestingly, the only part of the Promised Land Abraham ever possessed for himself was what he bought—and that was this field for a burial cave. But it was the start. This burial cave bound the patriarchs and their families to this land. This was the real Promised Land. There would be no return to Mesopotamia. Later patriarchs would die and be buried with their ancestors in Canaan.

Abraham knew that he could not exhaust God's promise, so he made plans for the future. By buying the land for his dead, he was declaring that God's promises did not end with this life. God would yet do far more than he had done in this life, and that is the hope of all who die in the faith.

The promise of the land to Abraham and his descendants is one of the great themes of the Old Testament. But so is death. Death entered the race by sin and brought ruin to it; and death comes suddenly, bringing mourning and an apparent end to hopes and dreams. In this passage, however, death is joined with hope by faith.

In life the patriarchs were sojourners (temporary residents with alien status); in death they were the heirs of the promise and the occupied land. Scripture says that the patriarchs and all the others died, not receiving the promises (Heb 11:39-40). But that was not the end of the promises. The promises were not all fulfilled because it was not God's plan to give them the promised rest without us, the believers yet to be born. The point is that God's promises to people in this life are not exhausted within their lifespans, for God makes promises that demand a resurrection. The time of death is a time of great mourning, but it should also be the time of the greatest demonstration of faith, for the recipients of God's promises have hope beyond the grave.

17. God's provision of a wife for Isaac (24:1-67)

Abraham was now a very old man, and the LORD had blessed him in every way. ²One day Abraham said to his oldest servant, the man in charge of his household, "Take an oath by putting your hand under my thigh. ³Swear by the LORD, the God of heaven and earth, that you will not allow my son to marry one of these local Canaanite women. ⁴Go instead to my homeland, to my relatives, and find a wife there for my son Isaac."

⁵The servant asked, "But what if I can't find a young woman who is willing to travel so far from home? Should I then take Isaac there to live among your relatives in the land you came from?"

⁶"No!" Abraham responded. "Be careful never to take my son there. ⁷For the LORD, the God of heaven, who took me from my father's house and my native land, solemnly promised to give this land to my descendants.* He will send his angel ahead of you, and he will see to it that you find a wife there for my son. ⁸If she is unwilling to come back with you, then you are free from this oath of mine. But under no circumstances are you to take my son there."

⁹So the servant took an oath by putting his hand under the thigh of his master, Abraham. He swore to follow Abraham's instructions. ¹⁰Then he loaded ten of Abraham's camels with all kinds of expensive gifts from his master, and he traveled to distant Aram-naharaim. There he went to the town where Abraham's brother Nahor had settled. ¹¹He made the camels kneel beside a well just outside the town. It was evening, and the women were coming out to draw water.

¹²"O LORD, God of my master, Abraham," he prayed. "Please give me success today, and show unfailing love to my master, Abraham. ¹³See, I am standing here beside this spring, and the young women of the town are coming out to draw water. ¹⁴This is my request. I will ask one of them, 'Please give me a drink from your jug.' If she says, 'Yes, have a drink, and I will water your camels, too!'—let her be the one you have selected as Isaac's wife. This is how I will know that you have shown unfailing love to my master."

¹⁵Before he had finished praying, he saw a young woman named Rebekah coming out with her water jug on her shoulder. She was the daughter of Bethuel, who was the son of Abraham's brother Nahor and his wife, Milcah. ¹⁶Rebekah was very beautiful and old enough to be married, but she was still a virgin. She went down to the spring, filled her jug, and came up again. ¹⁷Running over to her, the servant said, "Please give me a little drink of water from your jug."

¹⁸"Yes, my lord," she answered, "have a drink." And she quickly lowered her jug from her shoulder and gave him a drink. ¹⁹When she had given him a drink, she said, "I'll draw water for your camels, too, until they have had enough to drink." ²⁰So she quickly emptied her jug into the watering trough and ran back to the well to draw water for all his camels.

²¹The servant watched her in silence, wondering whether or not the LORD had given him success in his mission. ²²Then at last, when the camels had finished drinking, he took out a gold ring for her nose and two large gold bracelets* for her wrists.

²³"Whose daughter are you?" he asked. "And please tell me, would your father have any room to put us up for the night?"

²⁴"I am the daughter of Bethuel," she replied. "My grandparents are Nahor and Milcah. ²⁵Yes, we have plenty of straw and feed for the camels, and we have room for guests."

²⁶The man bowed low and worshiped the LORD. ²⁷"Praise the LORD, the God of my master, Abraham," he said. "The LORD has shown unfailing love and faithfulness to my master, for he has led me straight to my master's relatives."

²⁸The young woman ran home to tell her family everything that had happened.

29Now Rebekah had a brother named Laban, who ran out to meet the man at the spring. 30He had seen the nose-ring and the bracelets on his sister's wrists, and had heard Rebekah tell what the man had said. So he rushed out to the spring, where the man was still standing beside his camels. 31Laban said to him, "Come and stay with us, you who are blessed by the LORD! Why are you standing here outside the town when I have a room all ready for you and a place prepared for the camels?"

32So the man went home with Laban, and Laban unloaded the camels, gave him straw for their bedding, fed them, and provided water for the man and the camel drivers to wash their feet. 33Then food was served. But Abraham's servant said, "I don't want to eat until I have told you why I have come."

"All right," Laban said, "tell us."

34"I am Abraham's servant," he explained. 35"And the LORD has greatly blessed my master; he has become a wealthy man. The LORD has given him flocks of sheep and goats, herds of cattle, a fortune in silver and gold, and many male and female servants and camels and donkeys.

36"When Sarah, my master's wife, was very old, she gave birth to my master's son, and my master has given him everything he owns. 37And my master made me take an oath. He said, 'Do not allow my son to marry one of these local Canaanite women. 38Go instead to my father's house, to my relatives, and find a wife there for my son.'

39"But I said to my master, 'What if I can't find a young woman who is willing to go back with me?' 40He responded, 'The LORD, in whose presence I have lived, will send his angel with you and will make your mission successful. Yes, you must find a wife for my son from among my relatives, from my father's family. 41Then you will have fulfilled your obligation. But if you go to my relatives and they refuse to let her go with you, you will be free from my oath.'

42"So today when I came to the spring, I prayed this prayer: 'O LORD, God of my master, Abraham, please give me success on this mission. 43See, I am standing here beside this spring. This is my request. When a young woman comes to draw water, I will say to her, "Please give me a little drink of water from your jug." 44If she says, "Yes, have a drink, and I will draw water for your camels, too," let her be the one you have selected to be the wife of my master's son.'

45"Before I had finished praying in my heart, I saw Rebekah coming out with her water jug on her shoulder. She went down to the spring and drew water. So I said to her, 'Please give me a drink.' 46She quickly lowered her jug from her shoulder and said, 'Yes, have a drink, and I will water your camels, too!' So I drank, and then she watered the camels.

47"Then I asked, 'Whose daughter are you?' She replied, 'I am the daughter of Bethuel, and my grandparents are Nahor and Milcah.' So I put the ring on her nose, and the bracelets on her wrists.

48"Then I bowed low and worshiped the LORD. I praised the LORD, the God of my master, Abraham, because he had led me straight to my master's niece to be his son's wife. 49So tell me—will you or won't you show unfailing love and faithfulness to my master? Please tell me yes or no, and then I'll know what to do next."

50Then Laban and Bethuel replied, "The LORD has obviously brought you here, so there is nothing we can say. 51Here is Rebekah; take her and go. Yes, let her be the wife of your master's son, as the LORD has directed."

52When Abraham's servant heard their answer, he bowed down to the ground and worshiped the LORD. 53Then he brought out silver and gold jewelry and clothing and presented them to Rebekah. He also gave expensive presents to her brother and mother. 54Then they ate their meal, and the servant and the men with him stayed there overnight.

But early the next morning, Abraham's servant said, "Send me back to my master."

⁵⁵"But we want Rebekah to stay with us at least ten days," her brother and mother said. "Then she can go."

⁵⁶But he said, "Don't delay me. The LORD has made my mission successful; now send me back so I can return to my master."

⁵⁷"Well," they said, "we'll call Rebekah and ask her what she thinks." ⁵⁸So they called Rebekah. "Are you willing to go with this man?" they asked her.

And she replied, "Yes, I will go."

⁵⁹So they said good-bye to Rebekah and sent her away with Abraham's servant and his men. The woman who had been Rebekah's childhood nurse went along with her. ⁶⁰They gave her this blessing as she parted:

"Our sister, may you become
the mother of many millions!
May your descendants be strong
and conquer the cities of their
enemies."

⁶¹Then Rebekah and her servant girls mounted the camels and followed the man. So Abraham's servant took Rebekah and went on his way.

⁶²Meanwhile, Isaac, whose home was in the Negev, had returned from Beer-lahai-roi. ⁶³One evening as he was walking and meditating in the fields, he looked up and saw the camels coming. ⁶⁴When Rebekah looked up and saw Isaac, she quickly dismounted from her camel. ⁶⁵"Who is that man walking through the fields to meet us?" she asked the servant.

And he replied, "It is my master." So Rebekah covered her face with her veil. ⁶⁶Then the servant told Isaac everything he had done.

⁶⁷And Isaac brought Rebekah into his mother Sarah's tent, and she became his wife. He loved her deeply, and she was a special comfort to him after the death of his mother.

24:7 Hebrew *seed;* also in 24:60.   24:22 Hebrew *a gold nose-ring weighing a half shekel* [0.2 ounces or 6 grams] *and two gold bracelets weighing 10 shekels* [4 ounces or 114 grams].

NOTES

24:12 *unfailing love.* The key motif in the chapter is found in the word *khesed* [TH2617, ZH2876], "faithful covenant love" (24:12, 27, 49). It is active both divinely and humanly speaking—the figures in this story were all faithful to the covenant, working together to ensure that the program would continue into the next generation. Here the Lord providentially guided Abraham's servant in acquiring a bride for Isaac.

24:60 *mother of many millions.* This nicely captures the expression "thousands of ten thousands" (*'alpe rebabah* [TH505/7233, ZH547/8047]).

COMMENTARY

This event emphasizes the providence of God through the faithfulness of the people to bring about the marriage of Isaac and Rebekah. Abraham, confident in the Lord's promise, had his chief servant swear to find a wife from Abraham's relatives back east, some 450 miles away. Eliezer's putting his hand under Abraham's thigh (24:2; cf. 47:29) was a solemn oath that he would find a bride for Isaac so that the seed could be continued to the next generation. Taking the oath put the burden on the servant to complete the commission. If the woman he found was not willing to return with him, then he was free from the oath. But by no means was he to take Isaac out of the land in the process. Abraham was thereby ensuring that Isaac would be safe, both physically and in terms of perpetuating the covenant.

The servant, who remains anonymous in the passage but was most likely Eliezer (cf. 15:2), obeyed the instructions of his master and trusted the Lord to grant him specific leading to the right woman. He prayed that the woman who was to be Isaac's future bride would give him and his camels water to drink. That would be the sign he would look for when he arrived in the area—to provide water for 10 thirsty camels involved a good deal of work, for camels drink a lot of water. A woman who would do this for a stranger would certainly not be lazy—she would be generous and hospitable.

At the town of Nahor in Aram-naharaim (northwest Mesopotamia, 24:10; cf. 25:20), the servant received a precise answer to his prayer for guidance. The woman who came out to the well gave him water and provided it for the camels as well. That was far above what might normally be expected. And so the servant showed his gratitude by giving the girl expensive jewelry—a gold nose ring weighing about a half a shekel (one-fifth of an ounce) and two gold bracelets weighing 10 shekels (about four ounces). He soon discovered she was a relative of Abraham's (24:24-27) and she further revealed her kindness by offering him not only a place to stay but also food for the camels. The servant bowed to the ground and worshiped the Lord for his loyal love and faithfulness in guiding him to the exact place.

After this, we are introduced to Laban, the brother of Rebekah (24:29). And while he is not yet portrayed in all his craftiness, when he sees the gold the servant has given Rebekah, he rushes out to meet the visitor. Laban invited Eliezer and his men into his dwelling to show him hospitality. But the servant would not be diverted from his mission; he insisted first on telling his story to Laban and the whole household before he would even eat (24:33). He recounted his mission and God's providence in directing him to Rebekah. On the basis of all this, he was able to get their permission and blessing to take the girl to Isaac. For, as Laban said, the Lord had obviously brought him to this place (24:50).

In that society the eldest son would begin to take over the clan as he aged, and so here it was Laban, Rebekah's brother, who negotiated the marriage contract and gave his sister to Isaac as a wife. The servant gave gold and expensive gifts to her and her mother and brother to conclude the arrangements (24:53).

The next morning when it was time to leave, the family stalled a bit, wanting Rebekah to remain a few days (24:55). But it was her decision to leave immediately to be with her new husband (24:58). There is no explanation of her eagerness to go, other than what might be normally expected from a young girl who was waiting to marry. Later accounts of Jacob's dealing with Laban could suggest that she preferred leaving to staying under Laban's control. So Rebekah returned with the servant to the area where Isaac was dwelling—in the Negev, the south of the land of Canaan. Then she became his wife. Isaac was 40 years old when he married Rebekah, which means that Abraham had by then turned 140.

In this chapter the participants were all acting with faithfulness and loyalty to God and his covenant with Abraham. Abraham was faithful to the covenant by preparing for the future for Isaac. The servant was faithful in carrying out the mission perfectly, without diversion, and ensuring that God got all the glory. Rebekah already began to display faithful love to the servant, his family, and ultimately to Isaac by going to be his wife and be a part of this blessed family. But behind it all, God was displaying his faithful covenant love for the family and his plan by bringing all these things together. In his providence and by his faithful love, God sovereignly worked behind the scenes.

This hidden working of God is stressed in three ways in the chapter. First, God was the sole cause of all the events of the story. Eliezer wanted to make sure everyone understood that, even before he sat down to eat. His words, "The LORD has shown unfailing love and faithfulness . . . for he has led me" (24:27; see note), form the theological message of the chapter. And this message is revealed throughout the Bible. Even Laban had to acknowledge that this was the Lord's doing (24:50-51). Believers can trust in the leading of the Lord because he is sovereign in all things, and he never leaves his people to their own devices to carry on the work of the covenant.

Second, God was hidden behind the scene, deliberately directing the events. This event in Abraham's life is similar to the story of Ruth (see Hals 1969). The narrative of Genesis 24 records no word from God, no miracle, no prophetic oracle; it does not even restate the Abrahamic covenant. It is different than most of the book of Genesis, but it is very true to life. It is the way that the life of faith works for most believers. The anticipatory role of faith, expressed in personal prayer and obedience, looks for evidence of God's working. For most of their lives believers have to make wise choices and remain faithful to the covenant, trusting that through the circumstances of life God will guide them to that proper place in his will, whether for a marriage or some other decision.

Third, the story reveals more than God's providence; it is also part of his plan to bless mankind. Many potential missteps were avoided here: The servant could have failed (24:5-9), the "sign" could have been missed (24:14, 21), Laban might have refused (24:49-51), or Rebekah might have been unwilling (24:54-58). But everything worked together according to God's plan.

While one may marvel at God's providence in the event, one must also acknowledge the human faithfulness here. The servant faithfully carried out his assignment: (1) He was loyal to his holy commission to further God's program to bless all mankind; (2) he trusted God implicitly, looking for God's leading through prayer; (3) his predominant motivation was covenant loyalty (24:9, 12, 27, 49); and (4) he praised God even before his assignment was complete (24:27, 48-49). This praise is an important part of the story. Modern readers of the Bible may be tempted to skip over the entire section because it repeats all the details of the event preceding it. To do so is to miss the point: It was such a marvelous story that it had to be repeated—God had to be given credit—and all this before the servant's personal needs were attended to. The servant was bound to make sure everyone knew this was a work of God, not a chance meeting, not cleverness or human wisdom. The marriage, then, was truly made in heaven.

18. The death of Abraham (25:1-11)

Abraham married another wife, whose name was Keturah. ²She gave birth to Zimran, Jokshan, Medan, Midian, Ishbak, and Shuah. ³Jokshan was the father of Sheba and Dedan. Dedan's descendants were the Asshurites, Letushites, and Leummites. ⁴Midian's sons were Ephah, Epher, Hanoch, Abida, and Eldaah. These were all descendants of Abraham through Keturah.

⁵Abraham gave everything he owned to his son Isaac. ⁶But before he died, he gave gifts to the sons of his concubines and sent them off to a land in the east, away from Isaac.

⁷Abraham lived for 175 years, ⁸and he died at a ripe old age, having lived a long and satisfying life. He breathed his last and joined his ancestors in death. ⁹His sons Isaac and Ishmael buried him in the cave of Machpelah, near Mamre, in the field of Ephron son of Zohar the Hittite. ¹⁰This was the field Abraham had purchased from the Hittites and where he had buried his wife Sarah. ¹¹After Abraham's death, God blessed his son Isaac, who settled near Beer-lahai-roi in the Negev.

NOTES

25:3 *Sheba and Dedan*. This record lists Sheba and Dedan as descendants of Abraham, but they were already listed in 10:7. The text probably means that many of Abraham's descendants settled in those regions and became identified by those names, along with people who traced their lineage from a different source.

25:7 *Abraham lived for 175 years*. The narrative records the death of Abraham (25:1-11) before it reports the birth of Jacob and Esau (25:19-26). However, if Abraham was 100 when Isaac was born, and Isaac was 60 when the twins were born, Abraham would have lived into the first 15 years of their lives. The arrangement completes the Abraham story, and begins to focus on Isaac's family.

COMMENTARY

With these last comments, the life of Abraham comes to a close, and God's blessing is transferred to Isaac, his "only" son (22:2). The passage includes three sections: (1) the births of other sons to Abraham (25:1-4), (2) the safeguarding of Isaac's inheritance (25:5-6), and (3) the death and burial of Abraham (25:7-10). A brief closing note reminds us of the transfer of the blessing to Isaac (25:11).

Exactly when Abraham married Keturah is unknown (cf. 1 Chr 1:32), but the comment that he took another wife suggests that it happened after the death of Sarah. This would give a span of 37 years at most for the births of Keturah's six sons (Abraham was about 137 when Sarah died, and he died at 175). Tribes in Arabia (25:3), as well as the Midianites (25:4) came from Abraham. This was a part of the fulfillment of the promise to Abraham that he would become great (12:2) and be the father of many nations (17:4).

Abraham loved the sons of Keturah, for they too were his children. So before he died he gave them gifts and sent them away as he had done with Ishmael (21:8-14). They and their descendants at the least would have complicated things for Isaac and at the most may have posed a threat as Ishmael had. So Abraham sent them east, thus preserving Isaac's primacy and his right as the main heir.

When Abraham sent away all his other sons, he provided for transferring the blessing to Isaac who waited on the Lord. Abraham would be gone, but God's plan would continue. No leader of the covenant community is indispensable, for God's program to bless the world continues to grow and expand with each new generation. Each of God's servants must do all he can to ensure the ongoing work of God, but the work is bigger than any one person.

When Abraham died at the age of 175, Isaac and Ishmael came together to bury him in the cave of Machpelah next to Sarah his wife (25:9; cf. 23:19). Ishmael's presence may have posed a threat to Isaac now that the father was dead, but the text declares that the blessing was clearly on Isaac (25:11). Isaac was then living in Beer-lahai-roi. This was the place where God had heard Hagar and had delivered her (16:14). Thus it was known as a place where God was known to respond to the needs of his people. Isaac had been meditating there while waiting for his future wife (24:62-63). Thus he lived at a special place, a place where God had answered prayer.

◆ B. The Account of the Succession from Ishmael (25:12-18)

¹²This is the account of the family of Ishmael, the son of Abraham through Hagar, Sarah's Egyptian servant. ¹³Here is a list, by their names and clans, of Ishmael's descendants: The oldest was Nebaioth, followed by Kedar, Adbeel, Mibsam, ¹⁴Mishma, Dumah, Massa, ¹⁵Hadad, Tema, Jetur, Naphish, and Kedemah. ¹⁶These twelve sons of Ishmael became the founders of twelve tribes named after them, listed according to the places they settled and camped. ¹⁷Ishmael lived for 137 years. Then he breathed his last and joined his ancestors in death. ¹⁸Ishmael's descendants occupied the region from Havilah to Shur, which is east of Egypt in the direction of Asshur. There they lived in open hostility toward all their relatives.*

25:18 The meaning of the Hebrew is uncertain.

NOTES

25:18 *they lived in open hostility toward all their relatives.* The Hebrew is uncertain (see NLT mg) because the verb *napal* [TH5307, ZH5877] (to fall) may have a different meaning than previously thought. Traditionally the last clause has been translated "and he died [i.e., fell] in the presence of all his brothers." But the verb could be taken to mean either "settle" or "dwell in hostility."

COMMENTARY

Ishmael also was a son of Abraham, and so God had made promises to bless him as well as Isaac, although not as the line chosen for the covenant obligations. In the order of the book, then, the record of Ishmael is completed before the record of the chosen line is traced.

Here we have, then, the succession (*toledoth* [TH8435, ZH9352]) of Ishmael—that is, a record of what became of Ishmael. Ishmael had 12 sons, as God had predicted (17:20), and then died at the age of 137. The number 12 may have been a distinct way of grouping the families and their relatives together; it clearly reflects the later tribal organization of the family of Jacob, which had more than 12 names to arrange but managed to keep the number 12 for its organization with the addition of Ephraim and Manasseh in place of Joseph and Levi.

The descendants from Ishmael settled in the region of the Arabian peninsula from Havilah (in north central Arabia) to Shur (between Beersheba and Egypt). The Ishmaelites lived as a law to themselves, in hostility toward all their brothers—a fulfillment of God's words to Hagar (16:12).

◆ C. The Account of the Succession from Isaac (25:19–35:29)
1. The births of Esau and Jacob (25:19-26)

¹⁹This is the account of the family of Isaac, the son of Abraham. ²⁰When Isaac was forty years old, he married Rebekah, the daughter of Bethuel the Aramean from Paddan-aram and the sister of Laban the Aramean.

²¹Isaac pleaded with the LORD on behalf of his wife, because she was unable to have children. The LORD answered Isaac's prayer, and Rebekah became pregnant with twins. ²²But the two children struggled with each other in her womb. So she went to ask the LORD about it. "Why is this happening to me?" she asked.

²³And the LORD told her, "The sons in your womb will become two nations. From the very beginning, the two nations will be rivals. One nation will be stronger than the other; and your older son will serve your younger son."

²⁴And when the time came to give birth, Rebekah discovered that she did indeed have twins! ²⁵The first one was very red at birth and covered with thick hair like a fur coat. So they named him Esau.* ²⁶Then the other twin was born with his hand grasping Esau's heel. So they named him Jacob.* Isaac was sixty years old when the twins were born.

25:25 *Esau* sounds like a Hebrew term that means "hair." 25:26 *Jacob* sounds like the Hebrew words for "heel" and "deceiver."

NOTES

25:22 *the two children struggled with each other in her womb.* This account of the birth of Esau and Jacob is a fitting introduction to the following chapters because the struggle for supremacy began while the twins were yet in the womb (cf. Hos 12:3). The story of their births and the sale of the birthright are strategically placed at the fore because the whole section will be about Jacob primarily. The digression from Jacob in ch 26 records how the blessing of God rested on Isaac, not only showing that the covenant passed from one generation to another, but also displaying what it was that Jacob so desperately wanted.

COMMENTARY

The book now returns to relate the record of the chosen line through Isaac. What follows is an account of Isaac's prosperity (showing that the blessing had indeed passed to him) and of Jacob's struggle for the right to the blessing. That struggle will first focus on Jacob's dealings with Esau within the land (chs 25, 27), then Jacob's dealings with Laban outside the land (chs 29–31), and then with Esau again back in the land (chs 32–33). The final parts of this *toledoth* [TH8435, ZH9352] section will deal with dangers and difficulties for the family back in the land (chs 34–35), preparing for the transition to the next section of the book, the story of Joseph.

Because Isaac had married his cousin, Rebekah (cf. 24:15), his marriage tied him and his family to Abraham's ancestors (25:20), Arameans in northwest Mesopotamia (cf. 24:10), later known as Syria. Had he married a Canaanite, the covenant, indeed the faith itself, would have been imperiled by such a corrupt people, as the later history of Israel sadly reports.

As with Abraham and Sarah, God supernaturally provided children for Isaac and Rebekah. Rebekah was also barren—not for 25 years, but for 20 (25:21). This condition was a test of their faith, as it had been for the previous couple: How could they be childless when the promise of God said that nations would come from them? But Isaac must have learned from his father's sad experience: There would be no slave wife here to produce rival sons—there would be prayer. After all, God had sent the message to Abraham through Hagar that "God hears." Isaac and Rebekah pleaded with the Lord (lit., "entreated, prayed intently") for children. And God honored their prayers. The children would be a provision from God, an answer to prayer.

But there was difficulty with the pregnancy—the two children struggled with each other in her womb (25:22). And so Rebekah went to inquire about this from the Lord. She may have gone to a priest like Melchizedek (although he would probably have been too far away, if he was still alive), or she may have gone to Abraham, who was himself a prophet (20:7). Wherever she went, she received an oracle from the Lord: Two nations were in her womb struggling, and the younger would come to dominate the elder (25:23). Of course, this meant that the progenitors of two nations were in the womb (Jacob and Esau). In the course of history, the Israelites (Jacob's descendants) and the Edomites (Esau's descendants) fought continuously. But in their many conflicts, Israel achieved supremacy over them.

When the twin boys were born, there were some interesting conditions and acts that were noted by the parents and preserved in the naming of the boys (25:24-26). The unusual circumstances would have been enough to take note of, but against the background of the oracle, all these circumstances seemed significant and had to be preserved in memory. The first child was born very red and covered with thick hair—like a little animal. They named him "Esau" (*'esaw* [TH6215, ZH6916]; 25:25), a name that captured the sounds in the description "hairy" (*se'ar* [TH8181, ZH8552]). For each of the boys the text makes mention of the significance of the circumstances by means of clever wordplays. Describing Esau as red and hairy provided a clear connection to what would become of him. The word "red" anticipated the rugged nature of the man Esau (25:27-34) and the place where he would live—Edom. Edom lies to the southeast of the Dead Sea (32:3; 36:8). The word "reddish" (*'admoni* [TH122, ZH137]) is related to the name Edom (*'edom* [TH123, ZH121]; cf. 25:30), a name that may have been given to the region because of the red color of the soil. The boy was also described as being hairy (*se'ar*); the word is similar to the name for the region in Edom known as Seir (*se'ir* [TH8165, ZH8541]; cf. 32:3), perhaps because it was well wooded (and looked "hairy"). Those descriptive words were carefully chosen to foreshadow the nature of Edom, a later rival of Israel. The Hebrews could not have read these descriptions of baby Esau without thinking about the Edomites in Mount Seir.

The second child was born "grasping Esau's heel" (25:26). It is worth noting that Esau is described as red and hairy—static conditions—but Jacob is described as active. Their lives, as described in the narratives, would continue in these ways. With this strange birth of the younger son, the parents would have thought of the oracle that had been given, and therefore chose a name to reflect that connection in some way. The name "Jacob" (*ya'aqob* [TH3290, ZH3620]) was selected because of its connection to the word for "heel" (*'aqeb* [TH6119, ZH6811]). The name probably means "may he [God] protect," referring to the protection of a rearguard—someone who follows at the heels to protect. But as with Esau, Jacob's name would take on a different connotation later in life as his deceptive nature became clearer: Because he "tripped up" his brother twice, his name would have the sense of "heel grabber" or "deceiver."

God's fulfillment of his promise to Abraham would continue with his election of Jacob (later the nation of Israel) even before the birth. At the same time, on the human side, prayer played an important part in the discernment of God's provision. God later gave Israel (Jacob) the promise, but it did not come without a struggle. And much of that struggle was caused by Jacob's refusal to wait for God to do it. The oracle said the younger nation would have superiority over the other, but Jacob applied it to himself right away.

From the outset the births of Jacob and Esau were supernaturally prepared. They both were an answer to prayer; but that answer manifested a conflict that would lead to the descendants of one serving the descendants of the other. God's choice of the younger over the elder ran against the natural order of things. Paul noted that before the twins were born, God had chosen the younger (Rom 9:10-12; cf. Mal 1:1-5). Jacob himself would not fully learn this principle until he crossed his arms when blessing Ephraim and Manasseh (cf. 48:13-14).

◆ ## 2. The sale of the birthright (25:27-34)

²⁷As the boys grew up, Esau became a skillful hunter. He was an outdoorsman, but Jacob had a quiet temperament, preferring to stay at home. ²⁸Isaac loved Esau because he enjoyed eating the wild game Esau brought home, but Rebekah loved Jacob.

²⁹One day when Jacob was cooking some stew, Esau arrived home from the wilderness exhausted and hungry. ³⁰Esau said to Jacob, "I'm starved! Give me some of that red stew!" (This is how Esau got his other name, Edom, which means "red.")

³¹"All right," Jacob replied, "but trade me your rights as the firstborn son."

³²"Look, I'm dying of starvation!" said Esau. "What good is my birthright to me now?"

³³But Jacob said, "First you must swear that your birthright is mine." So Esau swore an oath, thereby selling all his rights as the firstborn to his brother, Jacob.

³⁴Then Jacob gave Esau some bread and lentil stew. Esau ate the meal, then got up and left. He showed contempt for his rights as the firstborn.

NOTES

25:27 *preferring to stay at home.* The NLT offers a good interpretive expression for the literal "dwelling in tents" to capture the significance of the description. But "stay at home" does not fully capture the idea, which is that he was a more civilized, even-tempered man than his brother Esau.

25:29 Jacob was cooking some stew. When the narrative says that Jacob was cooking lentil stew, it uses words (*wayyazed . . . nazid* [TH2102/5138, ZH2326/5686]) that sound like the word for hunter (*tsayid* [TH6718, ZH7473]). So the choice of these words tells the reader that he was boiling the stew; but it also indicates that he was hunting. He was satisfied to lay a trap and wait for the red, hairy animal (Esau) to come and eat. But this word for "boil" also was used in the language for acting presumptuously (apparently like water boiling over the rim of the pot).

COMMENTARY

Things of great spiritual value are often handled in profane or manipulative ways. Some people treat spiritual and eternal things with contempt, for they see them as of no value; others, though regarding such things highly, attempt to benefit from them through craft and manipulation. Esau and Jacob are examples of these types.

Jacob and Esau grew up, each developing in accordance with his initial characteristics. Esau, the reddish, hairy man, was finally overcome by his physical appetites (25:30) and sold his birthright. Jacob, the heel grabber, cunningly took advantage of his brother and gained the birthright. The story has some powerful humor in it; and so we may think of it as the story of Hairy and Grabby.

Though Jacob was not righteous, he was not deceptive—this time. He was open and obvious, but ruthless. He must be given credit for knowing what was worth having and going after it. But he also knew his brother and how he could force the birthright from him. Esau, on the other hand, did not care for things of lasting or spiritual value; he lived for the moment. He was profane (cf. Heb 12:16).

Several significant expressions are used in describing the two men. Esau was a "skillful hunter" (lit., "a man knowing hunting," *'ish yodea' tsayid* [TH376/3045/6718, ZH408/3359/7473]). He was also a man of the open country (25:27). He was the outdoorsman, the skillful hunter, who could not always find game as it turns out (25:29). Jacob, on the other hand, "had a quiet temperament" (NLT's rendering of *tam* [TH8535, ZH9447], "blameless," which does not have its moral sense in this passage). He was "dwelling in tents" (NLT, "preferred to stay at home"), a way of saying that he was civilized (25:27). He was the one that would do things properly, say things in the right way, and value the things that made life good.

We are also told that the parents were guilty of favoritism—one of the main problems for the patriarchal families throughout the book. Isaac loved Esau because he loved the taste of meat (25:28). In other words, Isaac liked Esau's nature and occupation because he enjoyed eating the wild game Esau brought home. This was an unhealthy love because it was conditional—as long as the son performed, the father's love was there. Rebekah's love for Jacob on the other hand was constant (the text uses a participle to express its durative nature). After all, he was a more civilized, quiet, even-tempered man, but more than that, the oracle had singled him out as the chosen one. This explains her reaction when she heard that her husband was going to bless the wrong son (ch 27).

Ironically, Jacob, the homebody, proved to be the craftier hunter (see note on 25:29). Here we can see the change in character between an Abraham and a Jacob—Abraham knew the promise was his and was comfortable in giving it away to Lot, but Jacob, knowing the promise was his, would not wait to secure it for himself.

After these descriptions we have the main event of the narrative—the exchange. At the beginning Esau had the birthright and Jacob the stew; in the end Esau got the stew, and Jacob, the birthright. The final comment on the passage explains why Esau did this—he despised the birthright (25:34). This simply means that he considered it worthless (NLT, "showed contempt")—especially since he felt he was about to die (25:32).

As the exchange approaches, Jacob is presented as this quiet, calculating, and cunning man standing there stirring the stew. He may have been waiting for this opportunity for some time. Esau is portrayed as emotional and carefree: He was fainting and gasping ("famished," 25:29, NASB), gulping the food down and rushing out. In this instance he was not like the cunning hunter but like trapped prey. And he was too preoccupied with his appetite to realize it. To live on such a base level, to be driven by one's appetites, is certainly the profane life—it leaves no place for spiritual things of value.

Esau came rushing in starved, near death as he claimed, pointing to the stew and blurting out: "Give me some of that red stew" (25:30). The narrative at this moment reminds the reader that this is Edom, "red," indicating that the Edomites are driven by natural passions and not spiritual things. Jacob, of course, refused to give him the food until he gave the birthright to Jacob under an oath. Esau eagerly complied in order to eat. He ate quickly, got up, and ran out, showing he was nowhere near death.

Certainly the profane nature of Esau was a warning for Israel and for all the people of God. It is foolish to sacrifice spiritual blessings and provisions in order to satisfy one's immediate physical appetites. It is a question of priorities—what one wants more than anything, and what one is willing to give up in order to get it. Esau saw food, and he did what was necessary to get what he wanted (cf. Eve and the fruit on the tree of the knowledge of good and evil, 3:6).

Jacob proved to be the better hunter on this occasion, but that is not the way God had designed the plan. Great danger also lies in such strong ambition. The Lord would deal with Jacob severely to purge him of his natural tendencies; he would not receive the promise as the heel grabber, as crafty Jacob, but as one whose name was changed to Israel.

◆ ### 3. Isaac's deception (26:1-11)

A severe famine now struck the land, as had happened before in Abraham's time. So Isaac moved to Gerar, where Abimelech, king of the Philistines, lived.

²The LORD appeared to Isaac and said, "Do not go down to Egypt, but do as I tell you. ³Live here as a foreigner in this land, and I will be with you and bless you. I hereby confirm that I will give all these lands to you and your descendants,* just as

I solemnly promised Abraham, your father. ⁴I will cause your descendants to become as numerous as the stars of the sky, and I will give them all these lands. And through your descendants all the nations of the earth will be blessed. ⁵I will do this because Abraham listened to me and obeyed all my requirements, commands, decrees, and instructions." ⁶So Isaac stayed in Gerar.

⁷When the men who lived there asked Isaac about his wife, Rebekah, he said, "She is my sister." He was afraid to say, "She is my wife." He thought, "They will kill me to get her, because she is so beautiful." ⁸But some time later, Abimelech, king of the Philistines, looked out his window and saw Isaac caressing Rebekah.

⁹Immediately, Abimelech called for Isaac and exclaimed, "She is obviously your wife! Why did you say, 'She is my sister'?"

"Because I was afraid someone would kill me to get her from me," Isaac replied.

¹⁰"How could you do this to us?" Abimelech exclaimed. "One of my people might easily have taken your wife and slept with her, and you would have made us guilty of great sin."

¹¹Then Abimelech issued a public proclamation: "Anyone who touches this man or his wife will be put to death!"

26:3 Hebrew *seed;* also in 26:4, 24.

NOTES

26:1 *Abimelech.* This is probably not the same man as in ch 20, for the events could have been as much as 90 years apart. It is possible that the name was a dynastic name or a title (note that Achish in 1 Sam 21:10-15 and Ps 34 is also called Abimelech).

26:7 *he said, "She is my sister." He was afraid to say, "She is my wife."* Critics have supposed that the story of the deception by Isaac was confused in the tradition with the stories of Abraham's deception (12:10-20; 20:1-18), that is, that the stories are doublets of one original story. But the repetition of the event is natural—the son learning from the father— and its telling is deliberate. It shows that even when the son acted like the father and jeopardized the covenant, God prevented the disaster and preserved the marriage.

The parallels to Abraham here are numerous: (1) a famine (cf. 12:10); (2) a plan to go to Egypt (cf. 12:11); (3) the stay in Gerar (cf. 20:1); (4) calling his wife his sister out of fear (cf. 12:12-13; 20:2); (5) the wife's great beauty (12:11, 14); (6) Abimelech's concern about committing adultery (20:4-7); and (7) Abimelech's rebuke (20:9-10).

COMMENTARY

Since Abraham was now gone, what would happen to God's promise to him? Very simply, the promise would continue from generation to generation. Chapter 26 stresses this by showing the parallels with Abraham. The basic idea in 26:1-11 is that the descendants of the obedient servant Abraham would be blessed because of Abraham, but they too had to exercise faith in order to enjoy the blessings. Genuine faith in God's promises engenders a fearless walk with him. To cower in fear endangers the blessing and makes a mockery of the faith. Isaac at first was afraid, but he soon grew to act in faith.

The narrative begins by assuring Isaac that the promises would go to him: the divine presence, the blessing, possession of the land, and posterity as numerous as the stars (26:2-5; cf. 12:2-3; 15:5-8; 17:3-8; 22:15-18; 28:13-14). All of this, God said, was "because Abraham listened to me and obeyed all my requirements, commands, decrees, and instructions" (26:5). These are standard terms from the law, primarily the book of Deuteronomy, that describe the full legal covenant made with Israel. Later Israelite readers would immediately think of the full Torah when hearing this list of words, and thereby be prompted to obey the law as Abraham had done. But Abraham did not have the full law; he had only a few commands from the Lord. By using these terms, the Lord was saying that Abraham had the kind of faith that obeys, such that he would have obeyed the later commands, if he had had them, because he was an obedient servant of the Lord. As further revelation is given, true believers like Abraham would obey them as well.

While staying in Gerar, Isaac, like his father, deceived the local king into believing his wife was his sister. He too was rebuked by this Abimelech, who knew that the penalty for adultery was death (26:10-11). This legal wording would have reminded Israel of the importance of preserving the purity of marriage. When that mainstay of society goes, the society cannot long endure—if Isaac's marriage had ended here, there would have been no Israelite society at all.

In telling how Abimelech discovered the deception, the narrative uses an interesting play on Isaac's name. After deceiving the king into thinking that Rebekah was his sister, Isaac was seen caressing her (*metsakheq* [TH6711, ZH7464]; 26:8—a figurative use of the idea of laughing or playing). This participle plays on the name "Isaac" (cf. the name with the verb *tsakhaq* [TH3327/6711, ZH3663/7464]), but it also recalls Ishmael's playing with Isaac as if mocking him (21:9; *metsakheq*). The choice of words is interesting. It is as if Moses was writing that Isaac's lapse of faith—going to Gerar and calling his wife his sister—made a mockery of the great promise embodied in his name, and that the activity was also a mockery of Abimelech. The realization that this was his wife made Abimelech aware of great danger. He issued a decree that anyone touching the woman would be put to death (26:11).

◆ ## 4. The blessing on Isaac and failure of Esau (26:12-35)

12When Isaac planted his crops that year, he harvested a hundred times more grain than he planted, for the LORD blessed him. 13He became a very rich man, and his wealth continued to grow. 14He acquired so many flocks of sheep and goats, herds of cattle, and servants that the Philistines became jealous of him. 15So the Philistines filled up all of Isaac's wells with dirt. These were the wells that had been dug by the servants of his father, Abraham.

16Finally, Abimelech ordered Isaac to leave the country. "Go somewhere else," he said, "for you have become too powerful for us."

17So Isaac moved away to the Gerar Valley, where he set up their tents and settled down. 18He reopened the wells his father had dug, which the Philistines had filled in after Abraham's death. Isaac also restored the names Abraham had given them.

19Isaac's servants also dug in the Gerar Valley and discovered a well of fresh water. 20But then the shepherds from Gerar came and claimed the spring. "This is our water," they said, and they argued over it with Isaac's herdsmen. So Isaac named the well Esek (which means "argument"). 21Isaac's men then dug another well, but again there was a dispute over it. So Isaac named it Sitnah (which means "hostility"). 22Abandoning that one, Isaac moved on and dug another well. This time there was no dispute over it, so Isaac named the place Rehoboth (which means "open space"), for he said, "At last the LORD has created enough space for us to prosper in this land."

²³From there Isaac moved to Beersheba, ²⁴where the LORD appeared to him on the night of his arrival. "I am the God of your father, Abraham," he said. "Do not be afraid, for I am with you and will bless you. I will multiply your descendants, and they will become a great nation. I will do this because of my promise to Abraham, my servant." ²⁵Then Isaac built an altar there and worshiped the LORD. He set up his camp at that place, and his servants dug another well.

²⁶One day King Abimelech came from Gerar with his adviser, Ahuzzath, and also Phicol, his army commander. ²⁷"Why have you come here?" Isaac asked. "You obviously hate me, since you kicked me off your land."

²⁸They replied, "We can plainly see that the LORD is with you. So we want to enter into a sworn treaty with you. Let's make a covenant. ²⁹Swear that you will not harm us, just as we have never troubled you. We have always treated you well, and we sent you away from us in peace. And now look how the LORD has blessed you!"

³⁰So Isaac prepared a covenant feast to celebrate the treaty, and they ate and drank together. ³¹Early the next morning, they each took a solemn oath not to interfere with each other. Then Isaac sent them home again, and they left him in peace.

³²That very day Isaac's servants came and told him about a new well they had dug. "We've found water!" they exclaimed. ³³So Isaac named the well Shibah (which means "oath"). And to this day the town that grew up there is called Beersheba (which means "well of the oath").

³⁴At the age of forty, Esau married two Hittite wives: Judith, the daughter of Beeri, and Basemath, the daughter of Elon. ³⁵But Esau's wives made life miserable for Isaac and Rebekah.

NOTES

26:23, 33 *Beersheba.* The naming of Beersheba at the end of this passage (26:33) is sometimes regarded as a doublet of 21:31, where the same place is named. Moreover, the appearance of Abimelech and Phicol in both chapters has been used to support the idea. But the narrative explains that Isaac was reopening Abraham's wells, so it makes perfectly good sense to see this as a renaming of this settlement with the same name Abraham gave it. As is clarified by the parenthetic additions of the NLT, Isaac's name for the place, "Shibah" confirmed his father's earlier naming of the place based on the fact he had sworn an oath. See notes on 21:30-31.

COMMENTARY

Isaac lived in the land as a temporary settler, enjoying abundant prosperity; his crops flourished and he became rich. But the people of the land, the Philistines, became envious of his prosperity (26:14) and filled his wells with dirt. The king then ordered him to leave that region because he was too powerful for them.

He moved to the Gerar Valley and reopened his father's wells. Once again, wells of water provide the dominant motif for a story—in this wilderness area, they were tangible evidence that God was blessing his people (cf. Abraham's dispute with these people over a well; 21:25, 30). No matter where Isaac reopened a well, and no matter how often the people caved them in, he found water (26:18). God was blessing Isaac, and that blessing could not be hindered.

Isaac also dug fresh wells in the valley and camped there. He faced opposition here as well, however. The men of Gerar seized the first two wells Isaac dug (26:20-21), but did not contest the third one (26:22). Because of the conflict, Isaac called the first wells "argument" ("Esek," 26:20) and "hostility" ("Sitnah," 26:21). Finally, he could call the third, uncontested well "open space" ("Rehoboth," 26:22). In these conflicts Isaac chose not to fight back; he simply relinquished one well after another until God's blessing outdid human opposition. Finally, the frustrated Philistines left him alone.

After Isaac moved to Beersheba, God appeared to him to confirm again the Abrahamic covenant (26:23-24). Isaac responded in faith, as his father had done, by building an altar to the Lord and proclaiming there, for all to hear, who the Lord was and what he was like (26:25; cf. 12:7-8; 21:33).

Once the conflict over the wells had died down, Abimelech requested that he and Isaac make a treaty. As the earlier king had acknowledged that God was blessing Abraham (21:22), so this one acknowledged that God was blessing Isaac. The king realized that if he made a treaty with Isaac he would no doubt benefit in some way from that blessing, just as Isaac would benefit from him by living at peace in the land. And so they made the treaty with an oath (26:28-33), similar to the treaty that Abraham had made earlier when he named the place Beersheba (21:23-24, 31). Since the treaty was renewed with Isaac, the name of the well was also renewed by the oath. And Isaac called the well Shibah, which means "oath" or "seven." This naming commemorated the treaty he had to make with Abimelech to be able to live in the area and dig wells there. Both the making of the covenant and the naming of the place confirmed what Abraham had done previously. And so the name Beersheba was retained after Abraham had passed off the scene.

So God's blessing was on Abraham's heir, and those who blessed him would also enjoy God's blessing on them. The passage makes it clear that for the people of God who walk by faith in the light of his promises, no amount of opposition can hinder God's blessing. The blessing would flourish in time, and other nations would see it and seek peace with Israel if they were to share in it.

The chapter concludes by telling the reader that Esau's marriages to two Hittite women (Judith and Basemath) were a source of grief for his parents (26:34-35). This little note in the chapter demonstrates how unfit Esau was to lead the covenant people into the blessings of God, and how foolish Isaac's later attempt to bless Esau actually was (27:1-40). In spite of all evidence to the contrary, Isaac still followed his baser instincts and favored his profane son. Esau later married a third wife, Mahalath (28:9).

◆ ### 5. Jacob's deception of Esau for the blessing (27:1-40)

One day when Isaac was old and turning blind, he called for Esau, his older son, and said, "My son."

"Yes, Father?" Esau replied.

²"I am an old man now," Isaac said, "and I don't know when I may die. ³Take your bow and a quiver full of arrows, and go out into the open country to hunt some

wild game for me. ⁴Prepare my favorite dish, and bring it here for me to eat. Then I will pronounce the blessing that belongs to you, my firstborn son, before I die."

⁵But Rebekah overheard what Isaac had said to his son Esau. So when Esau left to hunt for the wild game, ⁶she said to her son Jacob, "Listen. I overheard your father say to Esau, ⁷'Bring me some wild game and prepare me a delicious meal. Then I will bless you in the LORD's presence before I die.' ⁸Now, my son, listen to me. Do exactly as I tell you. ⁹Go out to the flocks, and bring me two fine young goats. I'll use them to prepare your father's favorite dish. ¹⁰Then take the food to your father so he can eat it and bless you before he dies."

¹¹"But look," Jacob replied to Rebekah, "my brother, Esau, is a hairy man, and my skin is smooth. ¹²What if my father touches me? He'll see that I'm trying to trick him, and then he'll curse me instead of blessing me."

¹³But his mother replied, "Then let the curse fall on me, my son! Just do what I tell you. Go out and get the goats for me!"

¹⁴So Jacob went out and got the young goats for his mother. Rebekah took them and prepared a delicious meal, just the way Isaac liked it. ¹⁵Then she took Esau's favorite clothes, which were there in the house, and gave them to her younger son, Jacob. ¹⁶She covered his arms and the smooth part of his neck with the skin of the young goats. ¹⁷Then she gave Jacob the delicious meal, including freshly baked bread.

¹⁸So Jacob took the food to his father. "My father?" he said.

"Yes, my son," Isaac answered. "Who are you—Esau or Jacob?"

¹⁹Jacob replied, "It's Esau, your firstborn son. I've done as you told me. Here is the wild game. Now sit up and eat it so you can give me your blessing."

²⁰Isaac asked, "How did you find it so quickly, my son?"

"The LORD your God put it in my path!" Jacob replied.

²¹Then Isaac said to Jacob, "Come closer so I can touch you and make sure that you really are Esau." ²²So Jacob went closer to his father, and Isaac touched him. "The voice is Jacob's, but the hands are Esau's," Isaac said. ²³But he did not recognize Jacob, because Jacob's hands felt hairy just like Esau's. So Isaac prepared to bless Jacob. ²⁴"But are you really my son Esau?" he asked.

"Yes, I am," Jacob replied.

²⁵Then Isaac said, "Now, my son, bring me the wild game. Let me eat it, and then I will give you my blessing." So Jacob took the food to his father, and Isaac ate it. He also drank the wine that Jacob served him. ²⁶Then Isaac said to Jacob, "Please come a little closer and kiss me, my son."

²⁷So Jacob went over and kissed him. And when Isaac caught the smell of his clothes, he was finally convinced, and he blessed his son. He said, "Ah! The smell of my son is like the smell of the outdoors, which the LORD has blessed!

²⁸ "From the dew of heaven
and the richness of the earth,
may God always give you abundant harvests of grain
and bountiful new wine.
²⁹ May many nations become your servants,
and may they bow down to you.
May you be the master over your brothers,
and may your mother's sons bow down to you.
All who curse you will be cursed,
and all who bless you will be blessed."

³⁰As soon as Isaac had finished blessing Jacob, and almost before Jacob had left his father, Esau returned from his hunt. ³¹Esau prepared a delicious meal and brought it to his father. Then he said, "Sit up, my father, and eat my wild game so you can give me your blessing."

³²But Isaac asked him, "Who are you?"

Esau replied, "It's your son, your firstborn son, Esau."

³³Isaac began to tremble uncontrollably and said, "Then who just served me wild game? I have already eaten it, and I blessed him just before you came. And yes, that blessing must stand!"

³⁴When Esau heard his father's words, he let out a loud and bitter cry. "Oh my father, what about me? Bless me, too!" he begged.

³⁵But Isaac said, "Your brother was here, and he tricked me. He has taken away your blessing."

³⁶Esau exclaimed, "No wonder his name is Jacob, for now he has cheated me twice.* First he took my rights as the firstborn, and now he has stolen my blessing. Oh, haven't you saved even one blessing for me?"

³⁷Isaac said to Esau, "I have made Jacob your master and have declared that all his brothers will be his servants. I have guaranteed him an abundance of grain and wine—what is left for me to give you, my son?"

³⁸Esau pleaded, "But do you have only one blessing? Oh my father, bless me, too!" Then Esau broke down and wept.

³⁹Finally, his father, Isaac, said to him,

"You will live away from the richness
  of the earth,
and away from the dew of the
  heaven above.
⁴⁰You will live by your sword,
  and you will serve your brother.
But when you decide to break free,
  you will shake his yoke from your
  neck."

27:36 *Jacob* sounds like the Hebrew words for "heel" and "deceiver."

NOTES

27:27 he blessed his son. Isaac blessed Jacob unwittingly. Jacob had already obtained the birthright, the legal right to be the primary heir, but he had pressured his brother into selling it. He had not received the blessing that went with it, and until he received that, the right of the firstborn would not be his. Through deception Jacob received the blessing that he thought rightfully belonged to him, and Esau had to settle for an inferior blessing from his father. So when Esau found out, he realized that his brother was a deceiver, as the sound of the name "Jacob" suggested (the name means "may he protect" as a rear guard; but Esau said he tripped him twice).

the LORD has blessed! The word "bless" (*barak* [TH1288A, ZH1385]) means "to enrich"—physically (as with children), materially (as with possessions), or spiritually (as with power or influence). The verbs used in such blessings are volitional forms (jussives), but they are not prayers or wishes—they are oracles from God. Thus, Isaac could not change what he had said, for the oracle that declared that Jacob would be blessed over his brother had come from God. That blessing included material abundance from the land (27:28), headship over other tribes who would serve him (27:29), and divine intervention and protection on his behalf (27:29; cf. 12:1-3). Jacob received a token of these promises in his lifetime, for God blessed him and protected him, first with Laban and then with Esau. But these promises were to be realized in Jacob's descendants. Thus, at the time that the Israelites were poised to enter the Promised Land, they were reminded that all the good things in it came from God (Deut 8:7-10) and would be given to them (Deut 28:1-8)—if they obeyed. If they did not obey, the land would be cursed (Deut 28:15-44), and God would not intervene on their behalf (Deut 28:25-29). The blessing, therefore, was given to Israel, but it would not be realized if they rebelled—which they did. And when they did, the prophets began to predict that a future Israel, who would be regathered to the land, would receive the material blessings in abundance (Joel 3:17-21) and would see nations coming to serve them and bringing their wealth to them (Isa 60; 61:5). These promises would only be fulfilled when the Messiah had come and the house of David had been rebuilt to exercise authority over Edom (Amos 9:11-15). The apostles rightly saw the extension of the gospel of Jesus Christ to the nations as the beginning of bringing the nations under the authority of the Messiah (Acts 15:12-21), and the complete fulfillment of the promised blessings as awaiting the Second Coming, when Christ will reign and there will be a new heaven and a new earth. Only those who believe in Jesus the Messiah will share in those blessings.

27:39-40 The oracle given to Esau is anticlimactic, for it predicts that his line will dwell far from abundance, live by the sword, and serve his brother's line—until it is able to throw off that yoke. This was a general prediction of how the descendants of Esau would live. They dwelt in the desert region of Mount Seir, in Edom (ch 36), quite likely in what is today Petra (see Obad 1:3). That was not a fruitful region, but it was inhabitable, probably well wooded in those days, as the name Mount Seir indicates (related to "hairy" in the birth narrative of 25:25). They became a warrior tribe; they confronted the Israelites and warned them that if they came through the area they would attack (Num 20:14-20). The Edomites became a perennial enemy of Israel (e.g., 2 Kgs 14:7) and because of their opposition to Israel, were cursed by God (see 27:29; Obad 1). Malachi declared that their destruction was proof that God had chosen Israel and rejected Esau.

COMMENTARY

God expects his people to carry out their spiritual responsibilities with understanding and integrity. When it is otherwise, then matters become complicated. This chapter portrays an entire family trying to carry out their responsibilities by their physical senses, not with faith. This is the familiar story of how Jacob got the blessing of his father Isaac through deception.

All members of the family participated; all were at fault. Isaac certainly knew of God's oracle (25:23), and yet he set out to thwart it by trying to bless Esau. Esau, in agreeing to the plan, broke the oath he had sworn to Jacob (25:33). Rebekah and Jacob, though having a just cause, each tried to achieve God's blessing by deception, without faith or love. (Whether Jacob would have even thought of this without the instigation and pressure of his mother is unlikely.) Theirs would be the victory, but they would reap hatred from Esau and separation from each other—Rebekah would never see Jacob again. So the conflict between Jacob and Esau was greatly deepened by Jacob's pursuit of what belonged to the firstborn, the blessing. Yet the story is not just about Jacob. He did not destroy this family alone—parental favoritism did.

The narrative is presented in a series of scenes. In each scene, two members of the family are together on stage, but in no scene are all the members of the family together. In this way the narrative underscores the favoritism and separation that characterized this family.

The first scene sets up the crisis for the chapter (27:1-4). Isaac offered to bless Esau, his favored son, if Esau would bring him some of the venison he loved (cf. 25:28). Isaac's palate was governing his heart. Interestingly, important notes are given here about Isaac's weak eyesight and increasing age. He was losing his senses, but he was intending to give the blessing to Esau because of the tasty food. Here was the dilemma that prompted Rebekah to spring into action.

In scene two Rebekah and Jacob are on stage (27:5-17). Rebekah sent Jacob into action to stop the blessing from going to the wrong son. Rebekah's plan was to deceive the old man into thinking he was blessing Esau, when he would be blessing Jacob. She seemed certain that she could duplicate the meal that Esau would make for his father by using a goat instead (27:9). But Jacob was not so sure that this was going to work, for Esau was hairy, and he was smooth-skinned. If Isaac touched him, he would know the difference right away. Jacob had no qualms about this deception, only fear that it might not work and that he would be cursed for trying it. But the blessing seemed to be in jeopardy, so Rebekah persuaded him that it would work if he dressed up with Esau's clothes and put animal skins around his arms. She was willing to take a risk that even left her open for a curse (27:12-13). So Jacob obeyed his mother, put on Esau's best clothes, and went in to obtain the blessing.

Scene three, with Jacob and Isaac, relates how Jacob deceived his father and received the blessing (27:18-19). Prodded by his mother, Jacob lied twice to his father: first, about his identity ("It's Esau," 27:19), and second, that God had given him success in hunting (27:20). It was one thing to lie, but to bring God into it came close to blasphemy. Three times the old man voiced his suspicion (27:20, 22, 24). But deceived by his senses of touch (27:16, 23) and smell (27:27), he finally accepted that this was Esau and gave him the blessing (27:27-29). The blessing included the prosperity of the crops (27:28), domination over other nations and over his brothers, cursing on those who cursed him, and blessing on those who blessed him (27:29).

In scene four, everything is discovered, and the family becomes even more divided (27:30-40). When Esau came in from the field, brought the food to Isaac and stated he had done what his father requested in preparing the meal, Isaac realized something was terribly wrong. When it was clear to him what had happened, he began to tremble uncontrollably, and Esau let out a loud and bitter cry—he was hurt and angry enough to kill (27:34, 41). Isaac trembled because he now knew that he had been tampering with God's plan and had been overruled by God. There was no going back—what he had declared was an oracle from God. He had made Jacob Esau's master.

Esau began to realize Jacob's true nature now—he had cheated (or "overreached" or "deceived") him twice (see commentary on 25:26; NLT mg at 27:36), first by taking the birthright (25:27-34) and then by deceiving the father to receive the blessing. All that was left for Esau was a common blessing, a blessing without spiritual emphases for a profane person (27:39-40). Esau would not enjoy the earth's riches or heaven's dew (27:28). The descendants of Esau, the Edomites, would live in an unfertile land outside of Canaan. Also, Esau's descendants would live by force, be controlled by Jacob's descendants, and remain restless (cf. Ishmael, 16:12) until they eventually broke free (27:40).

On the surface it appeared that Rebekah and Jacob had won. They got what they went after. But they gained nothing from it that God would not have given to them anyway. Instead, they lost a good deal in the way that they went about things. Jacob would have to flee for his life from the land he thought he had won, and Rebekah would never see him again.

All the natural senses were at play in the drama, especially the sense of taste in which Isaac had prided himself, but which gave him the wrong answer. Reliance on the senses to discern spiritual choices not only proves fallible but can also foul up one's life unduly. Most importantly, however, the story is about deception in pursuing the plan of God. Jacob's only hesitancy had been that he would be caught in his trickery. He would have to learn that God's blessings come by faith, not deceit. Yet God would work through the scheming to bring about the blessing on Jacob, though Jacob would not realize it until God had disciplined him.

◆ ## 6. The flight of Jacob (27:41–28:9)

⁴¹From that time on, Esau hated Jacob because their father had given Jacob the blessing. And Esau began to scheme: "I will soon be mourning my father's death. Then I will kill my brother, Jacob."

⁴²But Rebekah heard about Esau's plans. So she sent for Jacob and told him, "Listen, Esau is consoling himself by plotting to kill you. ⁴³So listen carefully, my son. Get ready and flee to my brother, Laban, in Haran. ⁴⁴Stay there with him until your brother cools off. ⁴⁵When he calms down and forgets what you have done to him, I will send for you to come back. Why should I lose both of you in one day?"

⁴⁶Then Rebekah said to Isaac, "I'm sick and tired of these local Hittite women! I would rather die than see Jacob marry one of them."

CHAPTER 28

So Isaac called for Jacob, blessed him, and said, "You must not marry any of these Canaanite women. ²Instead, go at once to Paddan-aram, to the house of your grandfather Bethuel, and marry one of your uncle Laban's daughters. ³May God Almighty* bless you and give you many children. And may your descendants multiply and become many nations! ⁴May God pass on to you and your descendants* the blessings he promised to Abraham. May you own this land where you are now living as a foreigner, for God gave this land to Abraham."

⁵So Isaac sent Jacob away, and he went to Paddan-aram to stay with his uncle Laban, his mother's brother, the son of Bethuel the Aramean.

⁶Esau knew that his father, Isaac, had blessed Jacob and sent him to Paddan-aram to find a wife, and that he had warned Jacob, "You must not marry a Canaanite woman." ⁷He also knew that Jacob had obeyed his parents and gone to Paddan-aram. ⁸It was now very clear to Esau that his father did not like the local Canaanite women. ⁹So Esau visited his uncle Ishmael's family and married one of Ishmael's daughters, in addition to the wives he already had. His new wife's name was Mahalath. She was the sister of Nebaioth and the daughter of Ishmael, Abraham's son.

28:3 Hebrew *El-Shaddai.* 28:4 Hebrew *seed*; also in 28:13, 14.

NOTES

28:3 *May God Almighty bless you and give you many children. And may your descendants multiply and become many nations!* The entire section of the Jacob–Laban stories parallels the later sojourn of Israel in the land of Egypt. In the east, Jacob would struggle, serving his uncle, but in the final analysis, he would emerge with a large family—the tribal chiefs of Israel (as it would turn out)—and great wealth. In Egypt the Israelites would suffer under the hand of their oppressor, but there they would flourish, become a great nation, and finally escape with great wealth.

COMMENTARY

This section begins the transition from the Jacob–Esau stories to the Jacob–Laban stories. Because of Jacob's deception, Esau planned to kill him. So Jacob had to flee from home. The occasion introduces the motif of taking a wife from relatives in the east. Whereas Isaac had remained in the land while his father's servant went to procure a wife, Rebekah (ch 24), Jacob's journey was necessitated by the imminent danger of being killed by his angry brother (27:41-42). Moreover, God would deal with Jacob under the hand of Laban, his uncle. In Laban, Jacob would meet his match for deception, and thereby his means of discipline.

Rebekah alerted Jacob about Esau's anger, and placed all the blame squarely on Jacob's back ("what you have done," 27:45, NLT). But she urged him to go immediately to her brother Laban in Haran, several hundred miles to the northeast. Rebekah also shared her disgust over the marriages of Esau to two Hittite women (27:46; cf. 26:34-35) and the fear that Jacob would marry one like them. She used this circumstance to urge Isaac to let Jacob go and get a wife from her own people. In that way, Jacob could get away from Esau and leave with a legitimate blessing from his father (28:1).

Once again Isaac blessed Jacob, but this time with the full knowledge of what he was doing (28:1-5). He told his son not to marry a Canaanite woman. The inhabitants of Canaan had incorporated dozens of groups and clans into their society by wars, treaties, and marriages. The family of Abraham was to resist such mixing (cf. Abraham's refusal to give a Canaanite wife to Isaac, 24:3). The reason for marrying within the clan was a desire for maintaining the purity of the line and the faith that identified Abraham's descendants as the chosen seed. The surest way to lose that distinctiveness was to intermarry with people from numerous tribal backgrounds and beliefs.

Before Jacob departed, Isaac gave him a pure and legitimate blessing. There was no holding back now because Isaac knew what God wanted him to do. Isaac clearly passed on the blessing God had given to Abraham and to him. He reiterated the blessing of God Almighty (see 17:1) pertaining to prosperity and the land (28:3-4; cf. 15:5, 18-21) and then sent his son to Paddan-aram. The message for Israel was clear: To inherit the blessings of the covenant, they were to remain separate from the Canaanites. In fact, the point applies to believers of all ages that spiritual purity has to be maintained and that marriages outside the faith are a detriment to the passing on of the faith.

Esau, still trying to please his father, married another woman whom he thought would be more acceptable, a daughter of a descendant of Abraham through Ishmael, Mahalath. Poor Esau, the unchosen son of Isaac, was trying to gain his parents' approval by marrying a daughter of the unchosen line of Ishmael. God had said to Abram that he should let Ishmael go because it would be in Isaac that the seed would be called (21:12), a clear word that the line of the promise would descend through Isaac. Esau had no understanding of the uniqueness of the covenant family. The scene is pathetically anticlimactic.

◆ 7. The confirmation of the blessing at Bethel (28:10-22)

¹⁰Meanwhile, Jacob left Beersheba and traveled toward Haran. ¹¹At sundown he arrived at a good place to set up camp and stopped there for the night. Jacob found a stone to rest his head against and lay down to sleep. ¹²As he slept, he dreamed of a stairway that reached from the earth up to heaven. And he saw the angels of God going up and down the stairway.

¹³At the top of the stairway stood the LORD, and he said, "I am the LORD, the God of your grandfather Abraham, and the God of your father, Isaac. The ground you are lying on belongs to you. I am giving it to you and your descendants. ¹⁴Your descendants will be as numerous as the dust of the earth! They will spread out in all directions—to the west and the east, to the north and the south. And all the families of the earth will be blessed through you and your descendants. ¹⁵What's more, I am with you, and I will protect you wherever you go. One day I will bring you back to this land. I will not leave you until I have finished giving you everything I have promised you."

¹⁶Then Jacob awoke from his sleep and said, "Surely the LORD is in this place, and I wasn't even aware of it!" ¹⁷But he was also afraid and said, "What an awesome place this is! It is none other than the house of God, the very gateway to heaven!"

¹⁸The next morning Jacob got up very early. He took the stone he had rested his head against, and he set it upright as a memorial pillar. Then he poured olive oil over it. ¹⁹He named that place Bethel (which means "house of God"), although it was previously called Luz.

²⁰Then Jacob made this vow: "If God will indeed be with me and protect me on this journey, and if he will provide me with food and clothing, ²¹and if I return safely to my father's home, then the LORD will certainly be my God. ²²And this memorial pillar I have set up will become a place for worshiping God, and I will present to God a tenth of everything he gives me."

NOTES

28:12-13 *he dreamed.* The Hebrew includes a particle before this phrase to express surprise (*hinneh* [TH2009, ZH2180] "look, behold"). It points out the parts of the dream as if the reader were seeing it all for the first time with Jacob. To capture some of this one might translate: "There, there's a staircase; and look, the angels of God ascending and descending on it; and oh—at the top, there stood the LORD!"

COMMENTARY

Jacob's vision at Bethel was a demonstration of pure grace, for God appeared to assure him of his promise of protection and provision—in spite of the way that Jacob had secured the blessing. And here, Jacob responds in a worshipful manner by vowing his devotion to the Lord. This was a vow that God would have to call to Jacob's memory later (ch 35).

The narrative answers the question of Jacob's relationship to the Lord. God was the God of Abraham and of Isaac—would he also be the God of Jacob? And then the narrative shows how Jacob's outlook on things was dramatically changed by the revelation. It would take some time to put this perspective into practice, but at least his direction in life was now one in which faith played a clearer role.

The first half of the narrative records the revelation (28:10-15). Jacob set out on his journey and by day's end came to a place where he could spend the night. It was apparently a protected area at the foot of some hill. There he took a stone to set at the place where his head would lie, more for protection than for a "pillow" (contra NLT, "to rest his head against"). The expression indicates that he put the stone at the place of his head. It could have been used to lean against; but it would have provided a secure place for his head. The narrative unfolds the events in a subtle manner—it was just one of the stones, taken from some place on the way—nothing extraordinary. But before the night was over this "place" would be known by everyone as a holy place, and to later Israel as Bethel—the stone would become an altar to the Lord.

At this spot Jacob dreamed, and the dream unfolded to him in dramatic fashion (see note on 28:12-13). The point of the vision was that God and his angels were with Jacob on his journey. This was symbolized by the staircase, the communication between heaven and earth, and by the angels who were with Jacob, ascending to heaven and returning, and it was explained in words by God (28:13-15). This is one of the two places in all of Genesis where "the angels of God" appear, the other being in Genesis 32, in which they meet Jacob returning from Laban. Two nocturnal revelations involving the angels occurred with the patriarch, one when he was leaving the land, guaranteeing protection outside the land, the other when he was returning, forcing a personal change before he reentered the land.

The heart of this vision was the word from the Lord. God reiterated to Jacob the promises of the covenant made to Abraham and to Isaac, promising him the land, descendants as numerous as the dust (cf. 13:16; 22:17), and universal blessing through him (cf. 12:2-3; 15:5, 18; 17:3-8; 22:15-18; 35:11-12). God also promised to be with Jacob and to watch over him until he returned. Here the promise of the divine presence is first expressed directly in that God said to Jacob, "I am with you" (28:15). For God to be with someone means that God will intervene in a special way in that person's life to protect them and provide for them.

The second half of the passage records Jacob's response to the revelation (28:16-22). Here we see not only specific acts of worship that would become normative for Israel but we also see the naming of the place as Bethel, a place that would be the center of Israelite worship for a period of time. Jacob's immediate response in the night was fear—reverential fear and awe in the presence of the Lord. He said, "[This] is none other than the house of God, the very gateway to heaven" (28:17). Then, in the morning, he stood up the stone for a commemorative pillar, consecrated it by pouring oil on top of it (the top corresponded to the presence of the Lord at the top of the stairway), named the place Bethel ("house of God") to commemorate the place, and made a vow to the Lord. He vowed that if God did all this for him and truly was his God, then he would make this place a place of worship and give tithes to God (28:21-22).

All of these are proper responses in faith to the divine revelation of the Lord whose presence guaranteed protection and provision. Several motifs pertaining to later worship are established here. The most memorable is the naming of the place as "Bethel." Later the Israelites who settled in the land would regard this as a holy place, a place where God chose to reveal himself to the patriarch. The Tabernacle would be located in the vicinity of Bethel for a good while before worship was centralized in Jerusalem; here the Israelites would go to appear before the Lord (see Judg 21:2, 19; 1 Sam 7:16; 10:3). Later, of course, the site was corrupted when Jeroboam set up a golden calf there (1 Kgs 12:28-29). Anointing with oil for consecration would also become a major feature of the worship of Israel. It was a form of setting something apart for special use, but it was also a gift that was given to God like any other sacrifice on the altar.

Jacob's vow is also important to the development of the idea of making commitments to God in worship. He could only vow what he could do for God, not what God would do for him. He vowed to serve God and worship him in this place and offer tithes. This reintroduces another motif for worship, paying tithes (first seen with Abram in 14:20). To give a tithe was an act whereby a person acknowledged that everything he had was a gift from God, and thus, in the final analysis, it all belonged to God.

All these important religious acts declare this to be a holy place, a place of worship, because God revealed his presence there. The parallel structure between the two halves of the passage (28:10-13, 16-19) shows that the worship was a direct response to the revelation. For example, "head" is repeated, first for Jacob's head as the place of the stone (28:11), then for the top ("head") of the stairway (28:13), and then for the top ("head") of the stone pillar that he anointed (28:18). Another repetition occurs with the word "stood," used first as a participle to describe the Lord's presence at the top of the stairway (28:13), and then used as a derived noun for "standing stone" ("memorial pillar," 28:18, NLT). Truly, Jacob's miniature altar represented what he saw in the vision.

God's promise to be with his people is a strong theme repeated throughout Scripture (cf. 26:24). The assurance of God's presence should bring about in every believer the same response of worship and confidence that it prompted in Jacob. This is the message from the beginning: God by grace visits his people and promises to be with them so that they might be a blessing to the world; they in turn are to respond in faith with reverential fear, worshiping him, offering to him, vowing to him, and preserving their faith in memory for future worshipers. This event at Bethel, then, is an archetype for Israel's worship. The vision of the stairway was a vision of grace, God himself providing access into his presence by it. Accordingly, Jesus drew upon this revelation to reveal himself as the means of access to heaven. Just as the angels of God were ascending and descending on the stairway that Jacob saw, so Jesus said they would be ascending and descending on the Son of Man (John 1:51). Moreover, just as Jacob had responded to the revelation by worshiping the Lord, now all worship is centered on Jesus, who is the only way to the Father.

8. Jacob's marriages to Leah and Rachel (29:1-30)

Then Jacob hurried on, finally arriving in the land of the east. ²He saw a well in the distance. Three flocks of sheep and goats lay in an open field beside it, waiting to be watered. But a heavy stone covered the mouth of the well.

³It was the custom there to wait for all the flocks to arrive before removing the stone and watering the animals. Afterward the stone would be placed back over the mouth of the well. ⁴Jacob went over to the shepherds and asked, "Where are you from, my friends?"

"We are from Haran," they answered.

⁵"Do you know a man there named Laban, the grandson of Nahor?" he asked.

"Yes, we do," they replied.

⁶"Is he doing well?" Jacob asked.

"Yes, he's well," they answered. "Look, here comes his daughter Rachel with the flock now."

⁷Jacob said, "Look, it's still broad daylight—too early to round up the animals. Why don't you water the sheep and goats so they can get back out to pasture?"

⁸"We can't water the animals until all the flocks have arrived," they replied. "Then the shepherds move the stone from the mouth of the well, and we water all the sheep and goats."

⁹Jacob was still talking with them when Rachel arrived with her father's flock, for she was a shepherd. ¹⁰And because Rachel was his cousin—the daughter of Laban, his mother's brother—and because the sheep and goats belonged to his uncle Laban, Jacob went over to the well and moved the stone from its mouth and watered his uncle's flock. ¹¹Then Jacob kissed Rachel, and he wept aloud. ¹²He explained to Rachel that he was her cousin on her father's side—the son of her aunt Rebekah. So Rachel quickly ran and told her father, Laban.

¹³As soon as Laban heard that his nephew Jacob had arrived, he ran out to meet him. He embraced and kissed him and brought him home. When Jacob had told him his story, ¹⁴Laban exclaimed, "You really are my own flesh and blood!"

After Jacob had stayed with Laban for about a month, ¹⁵Laban said to him, "You shouldn't work for me without pay just because we are relatives. Tell me how much your wages should be."

¹⁶Now Laban had two daughters. The older daughter was named Leah, and the younger one was Rachel. ¹⁷There was no sparkle in Leah's eyes,* but Rachel had a beautiful figure and a lovely face. ¹⁸Since Jacob was in love with Rachel, he told her father, "I'll work for you for seven years if you'll give me Rachel, your younger daughter, as my wife."

¹⁹"Agreed!" Laban replied. "I'd rather give her to you than to anyone else. Stay and work with me." ²⁰So Jacob worked seven years to pay for Rachel. But his love for her was so strong that it seemed to him but a few days.

²¹Finally, the time came for him to marry her. "I have fulfilled my agreement," Jacob said to Laban. "Now give me my wife so I can sleep with her."

²²So Laban invited everyone in the neighborhood and prepared a wedding feast. ²³But that night, when it was dark, Laban took Leah to Jacob, and he slept with her. ²⁴(Laban had given Leah a servant, Zilpah, to be her maid.)

²⁵But when Jacob woke up in the morning—it was Leah! "What have you done to me?" Jacob raged at Laban. "I worked seven years for Rachel! Why have you tricked me?"

²⁶"It's not our custom here to marry off a younger daughter ahead of the firstborn," Laban replied. ²⁷"But wait until the bridal week is over, then we'll give you Rachel, too—provided you promise to work another seven years for me."

²⁸So Jacob agreed to work seven more years. A week after Jacob had married Leah, Laban gave him Rachel, too. ²⁹(Laban gave Rachel a servant, Bilhah, to be

her maid.) ³⁰So Jacob slept with Rachel, too, and he loved her much more than Leah. He then stayed and worked for Laban the additional seven years.

29:17 Or *Leah had dull eyes*, or *Leah had soft eyes*. The meaning of the Hebrew is uncertain.

NOTES
29:1 *Jacob hurried on.* The Hebrew text says that "he picked up his feet," as if he felt the wind was at his back. Here was a man who had received a marvelous revelation that God was going to protect him and bless him. So he continued on his journey with a fresh enthusiasm.

29:11 *Jacob kissed Rachel.* Kissing relatives was a proper greeting, as in 29:13 where we see Laban kissing his nephew, Jacob.

COMMENTARY
Jacob now focused his attention on finding a wife. This change in outlook was the direct result of the vision he received at Bethel. His quest now was the fulfillment of the promises that God had made to him there and not simply escaping from Esau. Moreover, Jacob's attitude was now positive and magnanimous, to the point of being naive and vulnerable.

His meeting with Rachel at the well was providential, of course, although the text does not stress that he was led by God, as it did for the servant of Abraham. Certainly Laban, Rebekah's brother, would have remembered the account of how the Lord had led Eliezer to their place. But in this narrative we read that Jacob saw a well and later found out that he just happened to be near Haran, where Laban and his family lived (29:5). After he began to ask about Laban, Laban's daughter Rachel just happened to be coming out to the well (29:6). The timing was the work of the sovereign God who was leading Jacob to the fulfillment of the promises. And the fact that the meeting took place at a well was also a sign of God's blessing (cf. 16:13-14; 21:19; 26:19-25, 33).

At first, Jacob tried to get the lazy shepherds to move the stone on the well so that they could water the animals. So when Rachel came, because she was his cousin and the animals were Laban's, Jacob moved the stone and watered them. This note of Jacob watering Laban's flocks anticipates chapters 30–31, where Laban's flocks would flourish under the care of Jacob. But at this point, in contrast to the lazy shepherds who would not help (29:7-8), Jacob is portrayed as generous, industrious, and energetic (29:10)—but then, he was on a mission. When he finished watering the animals, he kissed Rachel and wept aloud (see note on 29:11). Then he explained who he was and why he had come. Through this meeting he was invited to Laban's house, just as Eliezer had been a generation earlier. When Laban heard his story, he acknowledged that he truly was his own flesh and blood (29:14). This indicated that Jacob would be welcomed into his house and treated almost as a son.

But in the next section of this chapter (29:15-30), we see how Jacob's joyful prospect of being married to the lovely Rachel turned into an unimaginable nightmare, thanks to Laban's shrewdness. Laban's deception on Jacob's wedding night struck an ominous note for the patriarch. Jacob had deceived his own father and his brother to gain the blessing; now he was deceived by his mother's brother. What would follow would be 20 years of labor, affliction, and deception in the service of Laban (31:38). Through Laban, Jacob received a dose of his own duplicity, whereby he would come to realize that God was disciplining him. But his tenacity shows that he considered this a minor setback. In the time of his service to Laban, God blessed him abundantly with a large family and many possessions. In the end Laban was glad to see him go.

As the story unfolds, Jacob was willing to serve Laban for seven years for Rachel, a high price for a bride in the ancient world. But Rachel was beautiful (as indeed were Sarah and Rebekah), and Jacob loved her. The text says that these seven years passed quickly because of the love that Jacob had for Rachel (29:20).

When the time for the wedding came (29:21-22), Laban put on quite a feast. But somewhere along the line, Leah, the older sister of Rachel, was substituted for the bride. We can only imagine what Rachel was going through—not being allowed near the wedding tent. And we must also fault Leah for her part in the deception because she had to cooperate to make it work. This shameless treachery must have given Laban and his circle a good laugh—the unloved Leah being married off to the man who loved Rachel. Jacob did not laugh. In the morning when Jacob discovered it was Leah, he was angry to say the least. But it was to no avail, for the marriage had been consummated. Perhaps now he could understand a little of the pain that Esau had felt. He certainly would have remembered this when Laban said to him: "It's not our custom here to marry off a younger daughter ahead of the firstborn" (29:26). Jacob, the younger son, had pretended to be his older brother, to gain the blessing (ch 27); now Leah, the older sister, pretended to be the younger sister, to get a husband. Laban's words are left without any comment—as if they are God's decree against Jacob.

Here we have a classic example of the biblical teaching that a man reaps what he sows (Gal 6:7). This was more than poetic justice; it was divine justice. God orders the affairs of people to set things right. This deception was perfectly fitted for Jacob, designed to bring his own craftiness before his eyes. It was the only way to get through to such a deceiver. Jacob is not the only person to ever need a Laban in his life. God often brings people into the lives of believers as a means of discipline.

After the marriage week was completed (29:27-28), he was also given Rachel as a wife—provided he would serve another seven years. He loved her much more than Leah; there was no question in his mind. So Jacob married the two women within seven days, but he worked for 14 years for the two of them. Laban seemed to have gained the upper hand because for the next seven years, Jacob had to work for Laban to fulfill the agreement (29:30; cf. 31:38, 41).

◆ ## 9. The births of the tribal ancestors (29:31-30:24)

31When the LORD saw that Leah was unloved, he enabled her to have children, but Rachel could not conceive. 32So Leah became pregnant and gave birth to a son.

She named him Reuben,* for she said, "The LORD has noticed my misery, and now my husband will love me."

33She soon became pregnant again and gave birth to another son. She named him Simeon,* for she said, "The LORD heard that I was unloved and has given me another son."

34Then she became pregnant a third time and gave birth to another son. She named him Levi,* for she said, "Surely this time my husband will feel affection for me, since I have given him three sons!"

35Once again Leah became pregnant and gave birth to another son. She named him Judah,* for she said, "Now I will praise the LORD!" And then she stopped having children.

CHAPTER 30

When Rachel saw that she wasn't having any children for Jacob, she became jealous of her sister. She pleaded with Jacob, "Give me children, or I'll die!"

2Then Jacob became furious with Rachel. "Am I God?" he asked. "He's the one who has kept you from having children!"

3Then Rachel told him, "Take my maid, Bilhah, and sleep with her. She will bear children for me,* and through her I can have a family, too." 4So Rachel gave her servant, Bilhah, to Jacob as a wife, and he slept with her. 5Bilhah became pregnant and presented him with a son. 6Rachel named him Dan,* for she said, "God has vindicated me! He has heard my request and given me a son." 7Then Bilhah became pregnant again and gave Jacob a second son. 8Rachel named him Naphtali,* for she said, "I have struggled hard with my sister, and I'm winning!"

9Meanwhile, Leah realized that she wasn't getting pregnant anymore, so she took her servant, Zilpah, and gave her to Jacob as a wife. 10Soon Zilpah presented him with a son. 11Leah named him Gad,* for she said, "How fortunate I am!" 12Then Zilpah gave Jacob a second son. 13And Leah named him Asher,* for she said, "What joy is mine! Now the other women will celebrate with me."

14One day during the wheat harvest, Reuben found some mandrakes growing in a field and brought them to his mother, Leah. Rachel begged Leah, "Please give me some of your son's mandrakes."

15But Leah angrily replied, "Wasn't it enough that you stole my husband? Now will you steal my son's mandrakes, too?"

Rachel answered, "I will let Jacob sleep with you tonight if you give me some of the mandrakes."

16So that evening, as Jacob was coming home from the fields, Leah went out to meet him. "You must come and sleep with me tonight!" she said. "I have paid for you with some mandrakes that my son found." So that night he slept with Leah. 17And God answered Leah's prayers. She became pregnant again and gave birth to a fifth son for Jacob. 18She named him Issachar,* for she said, "God has rewarded me for giving my servant to my husband as a wife." 19Then Leah became pregnant again and gave birth to a sixth son for Jacob. 20She named him Zebulun,* for she said, "God has given me a good reward. Now my husband will treat me with respect, for I have given him six sons." 21Later she gave birth to a daughter and named her Dinah.

22Then God remembered Rachel's plight and answered her prayers by enabling her to have children. 23She became pregnant and gave birth to a son. "God has removed my disgrace," she said. 24And she named him Joseph,* for she said, "May the LORD add yet another son to my family."

29:32 Reuben means "Look, a son!" It also sounds like the Hebrew for "He has seen my misery." 29:33 Simeon probably means "one who hears." 29:34 Levi sounds like a Hebrew term that means "being attached" or "feeling affection for." 29:35 Judah is related to the Hebrew term for "praise." 30:3 Hebrew bear children on my knees. 30:6 Dan means "he judged" or "he vindicated." 30:8 Naphtali means "my struggle." 30:11 Gad means "good fortune." 30:13 Asher means "happy." 30:18 Issachar sounds like a Hebrew term that means "reward." 30:20 Zebulun probably means "honor." 30:24 Joseph means "may he add."

NOTES

29:32 Reuben. This name (*re'uben* [TH7205, ZH8017]) means something like "Look, a son" (*ra'ah* [TH7200, ZH8011] + *ben* [TH1121, ZH1201]). But the sentiment Leah gives along with the name simply captures the sounds of the name in the sentence *ra'ah yhwh be'onyi* [TH6040/5204.1, ZH6715/5761], "the Lord has seen my misery."

29:33 Simeon. The name *shim'on* [TH8095, ZH9058] means "hearing," related to the verb "to hear" *shama'* [TH8085, ZH9048]. This name has an etymological connection with the saying concerning it: The Lord "heard."

29:34 Levi. The name *lewi* [TH3878, ZH4290]) is a difficult word to explain. The study of its etymology and meaning is inevitably tied up in the study of the Levites and the priesthood. It may be an old name for a priestly family, meaning something like "client of God," if the explanation of "being joined" (*yillaweh* [TH3867, ZH4277]) is drawn from the idea of being connected to the altar—as is implicit in Num 18:2, 4. But Leah wanted her husband "to be joined" to her (NLT, "feel affection").

29:35 Judah. This name (*yehudah* [TH3063, ZH3373]) matches a verbal form precisely, "may he be praised." Leah's sentiment uses the same verbal root, but in a different form: "I will praise" (*'odeh* [TH3034A, ZH3344]).

30:6 Dan. The name *dan* [TH1835, ZH1968] is equivalent to a verbal form that means "judge"; it is closely connected etymologically with the sentiment expressed by Rachel in this verse: "God has vindicated me"—*dananni* [TH1777/5204.1, ZH1906/5761], the same verb with a pronominal suffix added.

30:8 Naphtali. The name *naptali* [TH5321, ZH5889] probably means "my struggle." Its meaning is explained by Rachel's comment, lit., "great struggles I have fought" (*naptule 'elohim niptalti* [TH5319/430/6617, ZH5887/466/7349]). In this phrase, the word for "God" is used to signify the superlative "great," as elsewhere in the Bible (e.g., Jonah 3:3).

30:10-13 Gad . . . Asher. Though these names (*gad* [TH1410, ZH1514] and *'asher* [TH836, ZH888]) reflect a pagan background, they were probably adapted to this situation without any pagan significance. The name of the deity called *gad* [TH1408/9, ZH1513] could be translated "Fortune," and that of the deity called *'asher* as "Luck." Leah's description of her "joy" in 30:13 comes from the same root: *'shr* [TH833A, ZH887].

30:14 mandrakes. A mandrake is a stemless herb with large green leaves that grows in uncultivated areas. A legend grew in antiquity that its small, plum-like berry and fleshy root could induce human fertility (and so it is called the "love apple"). Its fragrance is referred to in Song 7:13. Rachel apparently was willing to try anything to have a son; ironically, it was Leah who got pregnant, showing that childbirth was by divine intervention and not by popular superstition and magic. See J. Sasson, "Love's Roots: On the Redaction of Genesis 30:14-24," in *Love and Death in the Ancient Near East* (Guilford, CT: Four Quarters Publishing, 1987), pp. 205-209.

30:16 I have paid for you. Lit., "I have hired you." The word for "hire," *sakar* [TH7939, ZH8510], ties the story of the mandrakes to the name Issachar (see next note).

30:18 Issachar. The name *yissakar* [TH3485, ZH3779] could mean "man of reward" or "there is a reward." It is a strange name, but does capture the sense of Jacob's being hired (see note on 30:16) and Leah receiving Issachar as her wages (*sekari* [TH7939/2967.1, ZH8510/3276], "my hire").

30:20 Zebulun. The name *zebulun* [TH2074, ZH2282] is an abstract noun connected to the verb *zabal* [TH2082, ZH2290], meaning both a "gift" such as a dowry, as well as "to honor" as with a gift or tribute (cf. NLT, "treat me with respect").

30:24 Joseph. This name (*yosep* [TH3130, ZH3441]) is the Hebrew verbal form that Rachel used in her comments at the birth: "May the Lord add (*yosep* [TH3254, ZH3578]) yet another son."

A secondary wordplay was made first, using the similar sounding word *'asap* [TH622, ZH665], "to take away," in the expression "God has removed my disgrace" (30:23).

COMMENTARY

The desire for affectionate approval is apparent in the story of Leah, but it led down a dangerous path. The contest of childbearing between Leah and Rachel may have been won by Leah, but it would not gain Jacob's love for her. Here again we have a family torn apart by favoritism—understandable in this case—and manipulation. The desire for love and recognition would not easily be fulfilled after the start of this marriage, but leaving Leah so unloved and favoring Rachel so much would have lasting results: The "tribes" would hardly ever be united in this family. Nevertheless, the narrative reveals how through the tension and the jealousy, and even by means of the manipulation and trading of things that should have been held sacred, God was still able to build the family of tribal ancestors.

The story begins with a reminder that Jacob was cool towards Leah, his unwanted wife (29:31). Leah—and God—were painfully aware of this. Jacob should have treated Leah better now that they were husband and wife, but we simply hear that Jacob fathered children by Leah over the first few years. Rachel, on the other hand, was barren—like Sarah and Rebekah before her (29:31; cf. 16:1; 25:21). And her condition was made more painful because Leah was not barren.

Leah's first four sons were born in rapid succession, which contrasts remarkably with the long periods of waiting that Jacob's father and grandfather had to endure before having a son. But the story of these births is bittersweet, not filled with joy as the births of Isaac and Jacob had been.

The significance of each name in this passage is provided by a wordplay on the name. As we have seen before, these are popular etymologies; they are related by sound and some sense to the name but are not usually exact etymologies. This unit has more of them than any other passage in Genesis; they fix in the reader's memory the founding of the nation through its patriarchs.

Leah named her firstborn son Reuben, explaining that the Lord had seen her misery. With an additional wordplay, Leah hoped that now her husband would love her (see note on 29:32). This birth gave her hope for Jacob's love—and consolation from God. Jacob seems not to have seen her misery, but God did (compare God's care for Hagar at Beer-lahai-roi in 16:14; 24:62; 25:11).

The second son was named Simeon because, as Leah explained, the Lord had heard that she was not loved. The name suggests that she had cried out to the Lord, and he heard her cries (see note on 29:33)—much as Hagar had done in the wilderness, when the Lord gave her the name Ishmael, "God hears," for her son (16:11, 15).

Levi was named for her hope that her husband would become attached to her now that she had given him three sons (see note on 29:34). But it was not to be fulfilled. And so Leah reconciled herself to the fact that nothing would turn Jacob's affections and considerations toward her. So the fourth son was named Judah, with the sentiment, "I will praise the Lord" (see note on 29:35). It is as if she was giving up on Jacob and therefore considered the Lord to be her sole consolation.

The naming of the sons of Rachel through Bilhah did not reflect the faith that Leah's namings did. Rachel felt wronged over the marriage and her being barren. Her decision to have children through her maid servant recalls Sarai's use of Hagar (16:1-4). The names given to the sons reflect the bitter struggle that Rachel was having with her sister and the feeling of some victory. The first son was named Dan because she felt vindicated by his birth (see note on 30:6). And her second son was named Naphtali to recall her great struggle with her sister (see note on 30:8).

When Leah saw that she had stopped bearing children, she matched Rachel's effort by giving her maidservant to Jacob as a wife; this was totally unnecessary since she already had four sons, but she did it to overshadow her sister. To Zilpah was born Gad, meaning "fortune," and then Asher, meaning "blessed luck" (see note on 30:10-13). Leah saw that with God's blessing she was flourishing—everything was turning her way.

Then follows the episode of Reuben and the mandrakes: Reuben found some mandrake plants, believed to be aphrodisiacs, while he was out in the field. Rachel thought they would help her conceive, so she traded with Leah to get them (30:14-15). What she traded was a night with Jacob, and in the process it was Leah who got pregnant—not Rachel—with another son. His name was Issachar, meaning "man of reward," (see notes on 30:16-18). The name of Leah's sixth son was Zebulun; it has the double meaning of a "gift," such as a dowry, as well as "honor" (see note on 30:20). Leah thought that God gave her Zebulun as a gift so that her husband would honor her and so with the birth of this child her hope was renewed. Finally, a daughter was born to Leah, named Dinah (cf. ch 34).

Finally, Rachel gave birth to a son of her own, Joseph. His birth shows that births are given by God—not by superstitious practices or by force of social customs. Joseph's name, like Zebulun's, had a double significance. Rachel said, "God has removed my disgrace" (see note on 30:24). Then she prayed that God would add (*yosep*) another son—a wordplay using Joseph's name precisely. Rachel was filled with joy over the birth of Joseph and looked for another son from God.

With the birth of Joseph the section is complete. It is a combination of small narratives, accenting the puns on the names of the sons. Each name was interpreted by the mothers to reflect the situations in the family and in their own lives. All too frequently, what was lost amid this competition was the idea that God is the giver of life.

Certainly the passage records how God gave Jacob sons who would become the tribal ancestors. (Benjamin would be added when Jacob was back in the land.) The people of Israel could therefore look back and see the conflict of these women in their ancestry. As brothers, the "sons of Israel" were not to become envious and divided against one another as their mothers had been. Unfortunately, the division and strife came early in the history of the tribes and never disappeared.

To Israel these narratives were not just interesting stories or bits of family lore. The rivalry that occurred here explains much of the rivalry between the brothers and later between the tribes (just as the rivalry between Jacob and Laban was to foreshadow the conflicts between Israel and the Arameans of Damascus). But God champions the cause of the poor and oppressed; thus the despised woman Leah, the unloved wife, was exalted to be the first mother. The kingly tribe of Judah and the priestly line of Levi came through her, in spite of Jacob's love for Rachel and the assignment of a double portion of the blessing to Joseph in his sons Ephraim and Manasseh.

◆ 10. The increase of Jacob's possessions (30:25-43)

25Soon after Rachel had given birth to Joseph, Jacob said to Laban, "Please release me so I can go home to my own country. 26Let me take my wives and children, for I have earned them by serving you, and let me be on my way. You certainly know how hard I have worked for you."

27"Please listen to me," Laban replied. "I have become wealthy, for* the LORD has blessed me because of you. 28Tell me how much I owe you. Whatever it is, I'll pay it."

29Jacob replied, "You know how hard I've worked for you, and how your flocks and herds have grown under my care. 30You had little indeed before I came, but your wealth has increased enormously. The LORD has blessed you through everything I've done. But now, what about me? When can I start providing for my own family?"

31"What wages do you want?" Laban asked again.

Jacob replied, "Don't give me anything. Just do this one thing, and I'll continue to tend and watch over your flocks. 32Let me inspect your flocks today and remove all the sheep and goats that are speckled or spotted, along with all the black sheep. Give these to me as my wages. 33In the future, when you check on the animals you have given me as my wages, you'll see that I have been honest. If you find in my flock any goats without speckles or spots, or any sheep that are not black, you will know that I have stolen them from you."

34"All right," Laban replied. "It will be as you say." 35But that very day Laban went out and removed the male goats that were streaked and spotted, all the female goats that were speckled and spotted or had white patches, and all the black sheep. He placed them in the care of his own sons, 36who took them a three-days' journey from where Jacob was. Meanwhile, Jacob stayed and cared for the rest of Laban's flock.

37Then Jacob took some fresh branches from poplar, almond, and plane trees and peeled off strips of bark, making white streaks on them. 38Then he placed these peeled branches in the watering troughs where the flocks came to drink, for that was where they mated. 39And when they mated in front of the white-streaked branches, they gave birth to young that were streaked, speckled, and spotted. 40Jacob separated those lambs from Laban's flock. And at mating time he turned the flock to face Laban's animals that were streaked or black. This is how he built his own flock instead of increasing Laban's.

41Whenever the stronger females were ready to mate, Jacob would place the peeled branches in the watering troughs in front of them. Then they would mate in front of the branches. 42But he didn't do this with the weaker ones, so the weaker lambs belonged to Laban, and the stronger ones were Jacob's. 43As a result, Jacob became very wealthy, with large flocks of sheep and goats, female and male servants, and many camels and donkeys.

30:27 Or *I have learned by divination that.*

NOTES

30:27 I have become wealthy. Or, "I have learned by divination that" (NLT mg). The verb that is used in this sentence, *nikhashti* [TH5172, ZH5727], is traditionally understood to mean "to take omens, learn by divination" (see 1 Kgs 20:33; see also Gen 44:5, 15). The meaning of the word is clear in the listed biblical passages, notably within Genesis itself, and it makes very good sense in the passage, meaning essentially that Laban was observing the signs; after all, Laban did mix whatever thoughts he had of the Lord with superstition and divination (as he was later anxious to retrieve his *teraphim*; ch 31). Laban knew he was getting wealthy, but it was through his religious instincts that he concluded the Lord was blessing him because of Jacob. Some commentators, however, think it unlikely that Laban would use divination to determine the source of the blessings, and so they translate it in accord with a proposed Akkadian cognate word *nahashu*, "to become wealthy, prosper" (Sarna 1966:211; Wenham 1994:251, 255). The NLT has adopted this view.

COMMENTARY

This rather bizarre story tells how Jacob acquired wealth—or at least how Jacob thought he acquired wealth, for he would later acknowledge that it was God who prospered him. But as the story unfolds, the point becomes clear that Jacob was outwitting his opponent and becoming rich.

After the 14 years were up, Jacob sought permission from Laban to go home (30:25-26). But Laban pleaded with him to stay because Laban thought there was more that he could get out of this man (30:27-28, 31). Here we see ancient Near Eastern bargaining at work: two bedouin leaders cautiously on their guard as they negotiate. Laban claimed that he had learned by divination (see note on 30:27) that God had prospered him because of the presence of Jacob. He may have looked for omens, or he may have simply perceived what was happening. But it was no secret; the Abrahamic covenant promised this kind of blessing. Dark-colored sheep (30:32) were rare and Laban may have viewed the inordinate number of them in his flock (which he had no doubt noticed) as an omen of God's blessing. Jacob agreed that God had blessed Laban because he (Jacob) was there (30:30). Jacob then proposed a plan whereby he believed he would gain even more for himself. He proposed that he would take as wages for his work the black and multicolored goats—the rarer kind—and the speckled and spotted sheep which would be born. Laban thought this over and then quickly agreed (30:34). He could only think that this would benefit him.

Jacob's plan was risky. Part of his success was due to selective breeding, but the larger part of it, he thought, was due to his special breeding method (30:37-39). Laban, however, added to Jacob's difficulty by removing all the animals of abnormal coloring and giving them to his sons and not to Jacob. Then, as an additional precaution, he put three-days' distance between them. He was obviously seeking to ensure that Jacob would have a difficult time acquiring a large flock of those animals for his wages.

But God blessed Jacob anyway, even through the unusual and difficult circumstances of this deal. Jacob took sticks and peeled off the bark, exposing streaks of the white wood; he then stuck these sticks in the ground at the watering trough so that when the animals copulated there the stick would influence the color of the animal that was born. There is a clever wordplay here that captures the meaning of the whole section: When Jacob peeled back the bark on the sticks he exposed the "white" (*laban* [TH3836, ZH4237]) streaks of the wood underneath (30:37); in other words, he played the "white" game (the Laban game) and won.

As Jacob later acknowledged (31:7-12), God had told him that he had intervened when the animals were at the trough and had fulfilled the expectations that Jacob had in placing the branches at the troughs. The peeled branches appeared to make his animals reproduce in the desired colors and patterns as they mated in front of the troughs, but in the final analysis it had nothing to do with sticking sticks in front of them. Some benefit was derived, of course, in Jacob's custom of mating the stronger animals for himself and the weaker animals for Laban (30:41-42), but it was God who prospered Jacob, for if the strong animals were not the right color, they would go to Laban.

So Jacob became very prosperous (30:43) in fulfillment of the promises of God to him. His prosperity came at the expense of Laban, who now received the recompense he deserved for his treatment of Jacob. A fascinating struggle had been at work between Jacob and Laban, just as in the earlier struggle to claim the birthright Esau had ceded to Jacob, which had prompted Jacob's deception. In both cases the attempt to defraud Jacob was overcome by Jacob. In both cases, Jacob came to realize God's plan was at work in his life.

◆ ## 11. Jacob's flight from Laban (31:1-42)

But Jacob soon learned that Laban's sons were grumbling about him. "Jacob has robbed our father of everything!" they said. "He has gained all his wealth at our father's expense." ²And Jacob began to notice a change in Laban's attitude toward him.

³Then the LORD said to Jacob, "Return to the land of your father and grandfather and to your relatives there, and I will be with you."

⁴So Jacob called Rachel and Leah out to the field where he was watching his flock. ⁵He said to them, "I have noticed that your father's attitude toward me has changed. But the God of my father has been with me. ⁶You know how hard I have worked for your father, ⁷but he has cheated me, changing my wages ten times. But God has not allowed him to do me any harm. ⁸For if he said, 'The speckled animals will be your wages,' the whole flock began to produce speckled young. And when he changed his mind and said, 'The striped animals will be your wages,' then the whole flock produced striped young. ⁹In this way, God has taken your father's animals and given them to me.

¹⁰"One time during the mating season, I had a dream and saw that the male goats mating with the females were streaked, speckled, and spotted. ¹¹Then in my dream, the angel of God said to me, 'Jacob!' And I replied, 'Yes, here I am.'

¹²"The angel said, 'Look up, and you will see that only the streaked, speckled, and spotted males are mating with the females of your flock. For I have seen how Laban has treated you. ¹³I am the God who appeared to you at Bethel,* the place where you anointed the pillar of stone and made your vow to me. Now get ready

and leave this country and return to the land of your birth.'"

¹⁴Rachel and Leah responded, "That's fine with us! We won't inherit any of our father's wealth anyway. ¹⁵He has reduced our rights to those of foreign women. And after he sold us, he wasted the money you paid him for us. ¹⁶All the wealth God has given you from our father legally belongs to us and our children. So go ahead and do whatever God has told you."

¹⁷So Jacob put his wives and children on camels, ¹⁸and he drove all his livestock in front of him. He packed all the belongings he had acquired in Paddan-aram and set out for the land of Canaan, where his father, Isaac, lived. ¹⁹At the time they left, Laban was some distance away, shearing his sheep. Rachel stole her father's household idols and took them with her. ²⁰Jacob outwitted Laban the Aramean, for they set out secretly and never told Laban they were leaving. ²¹So Jacob took all his possessions with him and crossed the Euphrates River,* heading for the hill country of Gilead.

²²Three days later, Laban was told that Jacob had fled. ²³So he gathered a group of his relatives and set out in hot pursuit. He caught up with Jacob seven days later in the hill country of Gilead. ²⁴But the previous night God had appeared to Laban the Aramean in a dream and told him, "I'm warning you—leave Jacob alone!"

²⁵Laban caught up with Jacob as he was camped in the hill country of Gilead, and he set up his camp not far from Jacob's. ²⁶"What do you mean by deceiving me like this?" Laban demanded. "How dare you drag my daughters away like prisoners of war? ²⁷Why did you slip away secretly? Why did you deceive me? And why didn't you say you wanted to leave? I would have given you a farewell feast, with singing and music, accompanied by tambourines and harps. ²⁸Why didn't you let me kiss my daughters and grandchildren and tell them good-bye? You have acted very foolishly! ²⁹I could destroy you, but the God of your father appeared to me last night and warned me, 'Leave Jacob alone!' ³⁰I can understand your feeling that you must go, and your intense longing for your father's home. But why have you stolen my gods?"

³¹"I rushed away because I was afraid," Jacob answered. "I thought you would take your daughters from me by force. ³²But as for your gods, see if you can find them, and let the person who has taken them die! And if you find anything else that belongs to you, identify it before all these relatives of ours, and I will give it back!" But Jacob did not know that Rachel had stolen the household idols.

³³Laban went first into Jacob's tent to search there, then into Leah's, and then the tents of the two servant wives—but he found nothing. Finally, he went into Rachel's tent. ³⁴But Rachel had taken the household idols and hidden them in her camel saddle, and now she was sitting on them. When Laban had thoroughly searched her tent without finding them, ³⁵she said to her father, "Please, sir, forgive me if I don't get up for you. I'm having my monthly period." So Laban continued his search, but he could not find the household idols.

³⁶Then Jacob became very angry, and he challenged Laban. "What's my crime?" he demanded. "What have I done wrong to make you chase after me as though I were a criminal? ³⁷You have rummaged through everything I own. Now show me what you found that belongs to you! Set it out here in front of us, before our relatives, for all to see. Let them judge between us!

³⁸"For twenty years I have been with you, caring for your flocks. In all that time your sheep and goats never miscarried. In all those years I never used a single ram of yours for food. ³⁹If any were attacked and killed by wild animals, I never showed you the carcass and asked you to reduce the count of your flock. No, I took the loss myself! You made me pay for every stolen

animal, whether it was taken in broad daylight or in the dark of night.

⁴⁰"I worked for you through the scorching heat of the day and through cold and sleepless nights. ⁴¹Yes, for twenty years I slaved in your house! I worked for fourteen years earning your two daughters, and then six more years for your flock. And you changed my wages ten times! ⁴²In fact, if the God of my father had not been on my side—the God of Abraham and the fearsome God of Isaac*—you would have sent me away empty-handed. But God has seen your abuse and my hard work. That is why he appeared to you last night and rebuked you!"

31:13 As in Greek version and an Aramaic Targum; Hebrew reads *the God of Bethel.* 31:21 Hebrew *the river.* 31:42 Or *and the Fear of Isaac.*

NOTES

31:19-20 *Rachel stole her father's household idols . . . . Jacob outwitted Laban.* A wordplay in the narrative shows Rachel to be very much like Jacob in their parallel thefts: She stole (*wattignob* [TH1589, ZH1704]) Laban's household gods, and he "stole away the heart of Laban" (*wayyignob . . . leb* [TH1589/3820, ZH1704/4213]), which means he deceived him (thus the NLT's "outwitted Laban").

31:35 *household idols.* These were household gods (*terapim* [TH8655, ZH9572]) and were highly valued by their owner. They would apparently be transferred to the chief heir of the family, in this case one of Laban's sons, and would be retained by him exclusively. They were part of the world of divination and may have been thought to provide protection or give power in some way. They could be large or small, as in this case, where Rachel has hidden them in her saddle (see IDB 4.574; for the proposal that possession of these gods might have given Rachel's son primacy, see K. Spanier, "Rachel's Theft of the Teraphim: Her Struggle for Family Primacy," *Vetus Testamentum* 42 [1992]:404-412).

31:36 *he challenged.* In the dispute between the two men, the language is that of legal controversies and lawsuits, as is marked by the use of the word *rib* [TH7378, ZH8189], meaning "to dispute, to challenge."

COMMENTARY

God kept his word to Jacob: In the east he flourished, and on the journey home, he was protected. This chapter records the return journey and the protection from Laban in a confrontation that set a lasting boundary between "Israel" and "Syria."

There were two reasons why Jacob returned to his homeland. First, animosity by Laban's sons was growing against Jacob because his flocks were multiplying faster than Laban's. The blessing of God on Jacob had made them jealous and afraid that he would completely overtake them (31:1-2). Second, God told Jacob to return to his own land and that he would be with him on the journey (31:3). Here was another divine call for a patriarch to go to the land of Canaan, but this time it was Jacob (Israel) and his sons, the ancestors of 11 of the future tribes.

In telling his wives about his call to return, Jacob delivered an excellent speech (31:4-13). At his request they met him out in the fields, safely away from the dwellings. His words were not only a self-defense, but also an explanation of how God had blessed him in spite of Laban's efforts. Since he wanted to take with him a willing family, he had to make an effective appeal. He was not sure they would be willing to break free from Laban's control or even want to go to Canaan. So he rehearsed God's leading and God's provision over the years; then he told them that he had to keep his vow that he had made at Bethel (28:20-22). In view of this presentation, the women responded immediately and with faith to go with him because God had blessed him (31:14-16). They explained that Laban had lost their goodwill, squandered their wealth (any substance that he would have provided them), and agreed that he had mistreated Jacob. They knew that what God had given to Jacob also belonged to them and to their children. They were willing to leave Laban (31:14-16).

Jacob, his family, and all his flocks stole away from Laban in secret (31:17). But the escape would be more risky than Jacob had thought because Rachel, no doubt out of seething revenge, stole her father's household gods (*terapim* [TH8655, ZH9572]). Their existence shows Laban's acceptance of pagan elements along with whatever belief he had in the Lord. Perhaps Rachel told herself that since Laban had turned the tables on her and deprived her of her right to marry Jacob, she would deprive him of his gods. Whatever reason she had, her theft almost brought disaster to the fleeing family when Laban caught them. To have the idols may have meant rights as the primary heir, as customs in subsequent periods clearly show; their absence certainly would have left Laban feeling alarmed and vulnerable.

The theft of the idols was probably the main reason why Laban and his men chased after Jacob. It was one thing for Jacob to take Laban's family and flocks—and Laban probably still believed they were all his—but it was another matter entirely to take his household gods. The fact that Laban wanted to make a treaty that would keep Jacob apart from him (31:43-53) after Laban failed to find the gods may indicate his fears that Jacob would return someday and claim all of his estate.

The journey took Jacob's family from Haran southwest to the land of Gilead, just east of the Jordan River in the northern part of today's kingdom of Jordan. It took Laban seven days of pursuit to catch up with Jacob. On the way, he was warned by God in a dream not to interfere with Jacob—literally, to say neither "good or evil" to him. Here the narrative reiterates the key theological motif of the book, which began in the garden with the knowledge of good and evil. In other words, Laban was warned by God not to do anything to Jacob. The character of Laban as portrayed in the preceding narratives shows that this warning was necessary, for even if he tried to do something that he thought was good, it would only make matters worse for Jacob. That is so often the nature of the knowledge of good and evil, for evil contaminates almost everything people do. God had called Jacob to leave and return to his land; Laban would not be permitted to interfere with that, even if he wanted to assist Jacob's family.

After several days Laban finally caught up with them in the hills of Gilead, and the dispute between Laban and Jacob began (see note on 31:36). In his first argument Laban accused Jacob of robbing him (31:26-27, 30). In making this charge Laban presented himself as the wounded party, the hurt father (31:28), and baffled avenger (31:29). When he demanded that his household gods be returned to him, Jacob insisted that they did not have them. Then when Jacob used an oath, he unwittingly put Rachel under a death sentence (31:32).

As Laban searched from tent to tent he found nothing. In the search, Rachel deceived her father to prevent him from retrieving his gods (31:33-35). She put the idols in her camel saddle and sat on the saddle in the tent, claiming that she was experiencing her period and could not get up (31:35). Laban never dreamed that anyone would sit on the idols in that condition; in later Israel a woman having her period was not even to enter the Holy Place. Had Rachel been having her period, such a contact would have contaminated the gods (cf. Lev 15:20).

The second accusation came from Jacob in retaliation (see note 31:36). Here Jacob really took Laban to task. Laban the accuser now became Laban the defender, for his charges had been demeaning and "proven" baseless as Rachel's theft remained undiscovered. Jacob made his counterattack: He recounted the hardships of his service to Laban for the past 20 years (cf. 29:27-30), taking the losses on himself while caring for Laban's flocks during the hot days and the cold nights. But the God that Isaac feared (lit., "the fear of Isaac"; NLT, "fearsome God of Isaac") was with him and had seen his hard work and his faithfulness and had rewarded him (31:42). Jacob concluded that this was why the Lord appeared to Laban and warned him (31:42).

◆ ## 12. The treaty on the border (31:43-55)

⁴³Then Laban replied to Jacob, "These women are my daughters, these children are my grandchildren, and these flocks are my flocks—in fact, everything you see is mine. But what can I do now about my daughters and their children? ⁴⁴So come, let's make a covenant, you and I, and it will be a witness to our commitment."

⁴⁵So Jacob took a stone and set it up as a monument. ⁴⁶Then he told his family members, "Gather some stones." So they gathered stones and piled them in a heap. Then Jacob and Laban sat down beside the pile of stones to eat a covenant meal. ⁴⁷To commemorate the event, Laban called the place Jegar-sahadutha (which means "witness pile" in Aramaic), and Jacob called it Galeed (which means "witness pile" in Hebrew).

⁴⁸Then Laban declared, "This pile of stones will stand as a witness to remind us of the covenant we have made today." This explains why it was called Galeed— "Witness Pile." ⁴⁹But it was also called Mizpah (which means "watchtower"), for Laban said, "May the LORD keep watch between us to make sure that we keep this covenant when we are out of each other's sight. ⁵⁰If you mistreat my daughters or if you marry other wives, God will see it even if no one else does. He is a witness to this covenant between us.

⁵¹"See this pile of stones," Laban continued, "and see this monument I have set between us. ⁵²They stand between us as witnesses of our vows. I will never pass this pile of stones to harm you, and you must never pass these stones or this monument to harm me. ⁵³I call on the God of our ancestors—the God of your grandfather Abraham and the God of my grandfather Nahor—to serve as a judge between us."

So Jacob took an oath before the fearsome God of his father, Isaac,* to respect the boundary line. ⁵⁴Then Jacob offered a sacrifice to God there on the mountain and invited everyone to a covenant feast. After they had eaten, they spent the night on the mountain.

⁵⁵*Laban got up early the next morning, and he kissed his grandchildren and his daughters and blessed them. Then he left and returned home.

31:53 Or *the Fear of his father, Isaac.* 31:55 Verse 31:55 is numbered 32:1 in Hebrew text.

NOTES

31:47 *Laban called the place Jegar-sahadutha (which means "witness pile" in Aramaic), and Jacob called it Galeed (which means "witness pile" in Hebrew).* The names given for the stone marker reflect the two parties making the treaty. Laban called it *yegar sahaduta'*, which is the Aramaic form (Laban was an Aramaean or Syrian), but Jacob used a Canaanite dialect (more closely related to biblical Hebrew, which came after it) and named it *gal'ed* [TH1567, ZH1681]. Jacob was more used to the Canaanite dialects and used that for the name since this would be a monument for later Israel to observe. Both words mean "heap of witness." It was given a third name as well (31:49): the *mitspah* [TH4709, ZH5207], which means the "watchtower."

COMMENTARY

It was Laban who pushed for a treaty to settle the dispute. Jacob had no need of a treaty, for God had provided for him and delivered him. But Laban felt vulnerable and wanted to secure his borders (31:44, 52). Jacob set up a tall standing stone and then piled a heap of stones around it. It was called "Witness Pile" by the men, Laban using his native Aramaean (later Aramaic) dialect, and Jacob using his language. Another name was added to the marker: "Watchtower" (31:49). The point of this name was that God would watch over the two of them while they were apart—to keep them apart, for they could not trust each other.

Then Laban added some stipulations to the treaty; these were more face-saving items than necessary stipulations, for he demanded that Jacob take care of his daughters (31:50) and that Jacob would stay on his own side (31:52). In making these stipulations, Laban used many words to cover up his own untrustworthiness. The man was trying to portray Jacob as the slippery, untrustworthy party who had to be bound by a whole series of stipulations. He came close to trying to terrify Jacob, as though he needed to be threatened. The truth was that the women and the children would be much safer and better cared for with Jacob than they ever could have been with Laban.

Both the treaty at the border and the rights of the women show that the two men wanted to preserve the status quo. But this border treaty also marked a major break between Israel and the familial ancestry in the East. It would remain the perpetual border area between later Israel and the kingdom of Syria (Heb. *'aram* [TH758A, ZH806]) with its capital in Damascus. These are two nations (from close relatives) that have been at war with each other on and off throughout history—even as it is today (Judg 3:8-10; 2 Sam 8:5-6; 1 Kgs 20; 22; 2 Kgs 5–8).

Before this last confrontation, God had appeared to Jacob (31:13) and to Laban (31:24) in dreams for the purpose of separating them. The entire event was complicated, though, by Rachel's personal revenge and self-interest, as well as Laban's self-seeking animosity. But in the end, God himself was invoked to watch over them (31:53). So God protected "Israel" (i.e., Jacob) as he brought the family back to the land that was promised to them. This was typological for later Israel in that God brought them back to the land of Canaan after long years of service in Egypt. In that great return, Israel would see God defeat foreign gods and beliefs, God's use of dreams for deliverance and protection, God's victory over those who tried to threaten them, and in the settlement, God's establishing of boundaries with neighboring tribes according to the number of Israelites (cf. Deut 32:8).

◆ 13. Jacob's preparation for meeting Esau (32:1-21)

¹*As Jacob started on his way again, angels of God came to meet him. ²When Jacob saw them, he exclaimed, "This is God's camp!" So he named the place Mahanaim.*

³Then Jacob sent messengers ahead to his brother, Esau, who was living in the region of Seir in the land of Edom. ⁴He told them, "Give this message to my master Esau: 'Humble greetings from your servant Jacob. Until now I have been living with Uncle Laban, ⁵and now I own cattle, donkeys, flocks of sheep and goats, and many servants, both men and women. I have sent these messengers to inform my lord of my coming, hoping that you will be friendly to me.'"

⁶After delivering the message, the messengers returned to Jacob and reported, "We met your brother, Esau, and he is already on his way to meet you—with an army of 400 men!" ⁷Jacob was terrified at the news. He divided his household, along with the flocks and herds and camels, into two groups. ⁸He thought, "If Esau meets one group and attacks it, perhaps the other group can escape."

⁹Then Jacob prayed, "O God of my grandfather Abraham, and God of my father, Isaac—O LORD, you told me, 'Return to your own land and to your relatives.' And you promised me, 'I will treat you kindly.' ¹⁰I am not worthy of all the unfailing love and faithfulness you have shown to me, your servant. When I left home and crossed the Jordan River, I owned nothing except a walking stick. Now my household fills two large camps! ¹¹O LORD, please rescue me from the hand of my brother, Esau. I am afraid that he is coming to attack me, along with my wives and children. ¹²But you promised me, 'I will surely treat you kindly, and I will multiply your descendants until they become as numerous as the sands along the seashore—too many to count.'"

¹³Jacob stayed where he was for the night. Then he selected these gifts from his possessions to present to his brother, Esau: ¹⁴200 female goats, 20 male goats, 200 ewes, 20 rams, ¹⁵30 female camels with their young, 40 cows, 10 bulls, 20 female donkeys, and 10 male donkeys. ¹⁶He divided these animals into herds and assigned each to different servants. Then he told his servants, "Go ahead of me with the animals, but keep some distance between the herds."

¹⁷He gave these instructions to the men leading the first group: "When my brother, Esau, meets you, he will ask, 'Whose servants are you? Where are you going? Who owns these animals?' ¹⁸You must reply, 'They belong to your servant Jacob, but they are a gift for his master Esau. Look, he is coming right behind us.'"

¹⁹Jacob gave the same instructions to the second and third herdsmen and to all who followed behind the herds: "You must say the same thing to Esau when you meet him. ²⁰And be sure to say, 'Look, your servant Jacob is right behind us.'"

Jacob thought, "I will try to appease him by sending gifts ahead of me. When I see him in person, perhaps he will be friendly to me." ²¹So the gifts were sent on ahead, while Jacob himself spent that night in the camp.

32:1 Verses 32:1-32 are numbered 32:2-33 in Hebrew text. **32:2** *Mahanaim* means "two camps."

NOTES

32:1-2 [2-3] *As Jacob started on his way again, angels of God came to meet him.* In several ways, the description of this encounter parallels the incident at Bethel (28:10-22), when Jacob was going out of the land 20 years earlier. First, the narrative verb *halak* [TH1980, ZH2143] (walk) is used in 28:10 and 32:1, both times in a construction that gives the idea of "go on one's way" or "take a journey" (used with *yatsa'* [TH3318, ZH3655] in 28:10 and with *derek* [TH1870, ZH2006] in 32:1). Second, the expression "angels of God" occurs only in 32:1 and 28:12 in the OT. Third, in both passages the verb *paga'* [TH6293, ZH7003] with its object taking the preposition *be-* [TH871.2, ZH928] is used, translated "arrived" in 28:11 and "came to meet" in 32:1. Fourth, the word "this" (*zeh* [TH2088, ZH2296]) is used four times in the Hebrew of 28:16-17 and occurs with the important note in 32:2—compare "[This is] the very gateway to heaven" (28:17) with "This is God's camp" in 32:2. And finally, in both events Jacob interpreted what he had seen, and then he made the commemorative name.

he named the place Mahanaim. This name means "two camps." By this he must have meant his own company and the company of angels (32:1), together at one place.

32:20 [21] *I will try to appease him by sending gifts.* The verb for "appease," is *kapar* [TH3722, ZH4105], the word for atonement and the appeasement of wrath. In order to appease his brother Esau, Jacob took a large portion of the blessing God had given him and prepared a gift (*minkhah* [TH4503, ZH4966]) for Esau. This word is also used for the meal or grain offering described in Lev 2.

32:21 [22] *the gifts were sent on ahead, while Jacob himself spent that night in the camp.* This section closes with a wordplay that shows how contrary Jacob's actions were to the vision he had received. He had just received the vision of the angels of God coming out to meet him, a sign that this was the "camp" (*makhaneh* [TH4264, ZH4722]) of God, which he named Mahanaim, "two camps"—his and that of the angels. But then he turned around and sent an enormous gift (*minkhah* [TH4503, ZH4966]) to appease his brother Esau because he was afraid of him. Jacob would have to learn that God would fight for him and that his cleverness would not do. And that is why the Lord would now meet him and cripple him.

COMMENTARY

God's preparation for the meeting between Jacob and Esau took the form of another visitation of angels at the border of the land (cf. 28:12). Jacob had just left Laban at the border and was about to return to his homeland, and to Esau, when "angels of God came to meet him." At this moment God's invisible world opened to Jacob. The encounter is mentioned with brevity—four Hebrew words describe it, followed by a sentence recounting Jacob's response—to declare the place as "God's camp" (see note on 32:2). There is no interpretation given, whether this was a warning or an encouragement from God. But Jacob must have seen the "angels" as a sign of protection from God as at the earlier vision of Bethel (see note on 32:1-2). This assurance of divine protection came at a time when Jacob truly needed such assurance. By revealing his presence to Jacob this way, God indicated that the journey was not just physical but spiritual. What was true for Jacob was also true for later Israel and is true for all believers who follow God's call. No mere human effort is ever sufficient to meet all the challenges inherent in the mission God has designed. Both the protection and the performance of God's program come from God's presence.

Jacob sent messengers into Edom to meet Esau, apparently inspired by the vision (32:2; the word for "messengers," *mal'akim* [TH4397, ZH4855], is the same word as "angels"). This section of the chapter employs wordplays to connect its ideas—the words for "camp" and "messenger" sound alike. He had recognized the angels as the "camp of God" and so named the place "two camps," for his own camp and the angels' (32:2). And then, out of fear of Esau, who was coming to meet him with 400 men, he divided his who company into two groups or "camps" (*makhanoth* [TH4264, ZH4722]; 32:7). After dividing his family into two groups, Jacob offered a prayer. Out of fear, he prayed for God to deliver him because he was thinking about Esau's threat to kill him (27:41). Jacob would still be afraid, even with the promises from God; but he would see his prayer for deliverance answered in a truly marvelous way.

Jacob's prayer is brief but powerful. He addressed God as the God of his grandfather Abraham and of his father Isaac, appealing to God's covenant promises. He reminded God of his command to return to the land and his promise to bless him, indicating to God that he was obeying that call. God wants people to rehearse his words when they pray to him because it is a motivation of faith in the one praying. Then Jacob confessed his unworthiness of God's lovingkindness and faithfulness and blessings. He had the correct attitude in prayer, a genuinely honest humility, and total dependence on God. Finally, he made his petition, that God deliver (*natsal* [TH5337, ZH5911]; NLT, "rescue") him from his brother because he was afraid of him (32:11 [12]). Then, to build his confidence further, Jacob repeated God's promise to make his descendants as innumerable as the sand of the sea (cf. 22:17)—he would have to rescue the family to fulfill that.

All of this, along with the evidence of God's past dealings with him, should have calmed his fears. But his fear, and probably his guilt, still controlled him and left him uncertain about the outcome of his prayer. Guilty fears will do this to prayer, for somewhere in the back of the mind is the idea that the answer to the prayer is not deserved and that justice will be meted out instead.

After his prayer, Jacob prepared a gift so as to appease Esau and gain his favor (see note on 32:20). Was he, consciously or subconsciously, trying to appear to Esau as though he were restoring the blessing? His words to Esau in 33:11 indicate this: "Please take this gift" (*birkathi* [TH1293/2967.1, ZH1388/3276], "my blessing"). The gift he sent was 550 animals—goats, sheep, camels, cattle, and donkeys, not counting the young camels. He thought that these herds and flocks sent in five separate groups would impress his brother and appease his anger, if it was still there after all the years (32:20). He would learn later that God would have answered his prayer and delivered him from his brother without these gifts. The nation of Israel would also have to learn that they could not buy off their enemies, but God would deliver them.

◆ ### 14. Jacob becomes Israel (32:22-32)

²²During the night Jacob got up and took his two wives, his two servant wives, and his eleven sons and crossed the Jabbok River with them. ²³After taking them to the other side, he sent over all his possessions.

²⁴This left Jacob all alone in the camp, and a man came and wrestled with him until the dawn began to break. ²⁵When the man saw that he would not win the match, he touched Jacob's hip and wrenched it out of its socket. ²⁶Then the man said, "Let me go, for the dawn is breaking!"

But Jacob said, "I will not let you go unless you bless me."

²⁷"What is your name?" the man asked.

He replied, "Jacob."

²⁸"Your name will no longer be Jacob," the man told him. "From now on you will be called Israel,* because you have fought with God and with men and have won."

²⁹"Please tell me your name," Jacob said.

"Why do you want to know my name?" the man replied. Then he blessed Jacob there.

³⁰Jacob named the place Peniel (which means "face of God"), for he said, "I have seen God face to face, yet my life has been spared." ³¹The sun was rising as Jacob left Peniel,* and he was limping because of the injury to his hip. ³²(Even today the people of Israel don't eat the tendon near the hip socket because of what happened that night when the man strained the tendon of Jacob's hip.)

32:28 *Jacob* sounds like the Hebrew words for "heel" and "deceiver." *Israel* means "God fights." 32:31 Hebrew *Penuel*, a variant spelling of Peniel.

NOTES

32:22 [23] *the Jabbok River*. This river (now known as *Nahr ez-Zerqa* in modern-day Jordan) flows down to the Jordan Valley and divides the region into northern and southern Gilead.

COMMENTARY

Before Jacob returned to the land promised to him, he was met by God who blessed him, but crippled him as well. This episode was an important turning point in the patriarch's life—and in the history of "Israel."

Several features of this event help us appreciate its significance. First, it occurred just as Jacob was crossing the river Jabbok from the wooded and mountainous northern region to the southern region where there would be easier access to the Promised Land. He would not get to the Promised Land under his own strength. Second, it was here that Jacob was renamed—where he indeed became "Israel." It mattered a great deal to the people of Israel to know where "Israel" came from and what it signified. Third, the account is linked to a place name, Peniel, which also preserves the memory of the event. If the patriarch truly saw God face-to-face and survived, there was no reason to fear what man might do to him. Fourth, the story includes the origin of an ancient dietary tradition in Israel: not eating the tendon of an animal's hip. This became a custom for the people but was not made part of the law. Observant Jews still refuse to eat the tendons of the hindquarters of animals. This practical custom helped preserve the memory of the whole story in a natural way.

The focus of the passage is certainly on the wrestling, but its purpose was the changing of Jacob into Israel. One cannot read this passage without recalling the nature of Jacob and the meaning his name came to have. That connection is strengthened by the wordplays here: At the outset are the name "Jacob" (*ya'aqob* [TH3290, ZH3620], 32:24 [25]), the place "Jabbok" (*yabboq* [TH2999, ZH3309]; 32:22 [23]), and the fight itself (*wayye'abeq* [TH79, ZH84], "he wrestled"). These words attract the reader's attention immediately and imply that something is going to happen to the nature and the name of Jacob. Once again Jacob would have to fight, and he would almost defeat his adversary, this mysterious visitor who encountered him on the border—*almost*. He was instead defeated rather easily as it turned out, and yet, the Lord said Jacob had prevailed ("won," 32:28, NLT).

In typical Hebrew style, the passage opens with a summary statement recounting the crossing of the river Jabbok (32:22); then it starts the story over, giving the details that he sent his family and his possessions across first and that he was left alone in the camp. Before he could cross the river, he was grabbed by an unknown assailant and forced into a fight that lasted all night (32:24).

No details of the fight are given because the important material is the dialogue that follows it. Yet the fight was real. And no details are given about the assailant; he is simply called "a man." This anonymity is appropriate to the revelation that comes later, for there the assailant refused to identify himself. The fact that the fight took place at night is significant. The darkness fit Jacob's situation, adding to the fear and uncertainty that seized him. If Jacob had known who his assailant was from the outset, he would have never engaged in the combat, let alone fight so tenaciously. But in the darkness he had no idea who it was—possibly one of Esau's men, or Laban's. Since he had many enemies, he could only imagine the worst. And the fact that the fight lasted until daybreak indicates how persistent Jacob was. The assailant could not defeat him until he resorted to something extraordinary. The text says "he touched Jacob's hip and wrenched it out of its socket" (32:25). Clearly the assailant gave himself the advantage with this blow. Jacob, the deceitful fighter, could fight no more. Like so many of his own rivals, he had now more than met his match. The supernatural blow crippled him and made him realize he could never have won.

With the approaching dawn, the identity of his assailant and the significance of the fight began to dawn on Jacob. So he quit fighting and began to cling to his assailant in hopes of a blessing. When the scrappy patriarch refused to let go until his assailant blessed him, the man asked, "What is your name?" Obviously the assailant was not trying to find out who Jacob was. He was asking for more than a simple name. When we remember that in the Old Testament one's name is linked to his character or actions, the point becomes clear: By giving his name, Jacob was confessing his nature, his way of doing things. He was the heel-grabber, the deceiver, the crafty opponent. All that had to be radically changed before he would be blessed. He had to acknowledge who he was.

That this was the intent of the question is clear from the form that the blessing took: "Your name will no longer be Jacob. . . . From now on you will be called Israel" (32:28). This new name, like so many others in the Old Testament, is built from a verb with a theophoric element (*'el* [TH410A, ZH446], "God") added to the end as its subject. It means "God fights." Then the explanation of the name is given with a wordplay: "You have fought" (*sarita* [TH8280, ZH8575]) with God and with men and have won." Popular etymologies do not give the exact etymology of the name but memorable sayings based on the event. Here the name "God fights" is explained by "you have fought with God and with men." It is easy to see how Jacob fought with men, but his fighting with God is more difficult to understand. Throughout his entire life, Jacob had been seizing God's blessing by any means that would work, by his own abilities. He knew the importance of the blessing, but he was not the kind of person to wait for it. He was too self-sufficient and proud to let the blessing be given to him. In that sense, he had been fighting God long before this encounter.

But now his name would be "God fights." It was to be a reminder first that God had to fight him, and then it would also be a motto to live up to, that God would now fight for him. Only in this sense could it be said that "he won," for he came away from the fight crippled. His new name, however, was full of promise for the patriarch and his descendants, the people of "Israel." Their conflicts would be successful because, and only because, God would fight for them.

Jacob immediately wanted to know the name of his assailant. It was not that he had no idea who this was, for his naming of the place clearly shows that he knew the person was divine. The request was an attempt to gain some power; having the name would enable him to manipulate this powerful visitor. But God would not reveal his name; it cannot be had on demand. So all Jacob could do was to name the place. He called it Peniel (32:30 [31]; *peni'el* [TH6439C, ZH7161]—"face of God"—*panim* [TH6440, ZH7156] + *'el* [TH410A, ZH446]) because he had seen God "face to face," and as a result, his life had been delivered. He had prayed for deliverance (*natsal* [TH5337, ZH5911], 32:11 [12]), and now he was delivered (*natsal*; 32:30 [31]). His prayer for deliverance was answered by an encounter with the Lord in which he came away blessed. If he could meet God this way and walk away, he had nothing to fear from Esau.

When God touched Jacob's hip, it shriveled, and with it Jacob's self-sufficiency. He could no longer take a step without limping. From this point on, he would be reminded that his natural strength had been restricted by the Lord. He was forced to accept that his life and his destiny were in the hands of the one against whom it is useless to struggle. Now he would have to rely on the Lord with greater faith. He had thought that returning to his land was going to be a matter of outwitting his brother once again, but here as he was preparing to enter the land he met the real proprietor of the land. He would get the land, but only if God fought for him.

The message of the encounter for Jacob, and for his descendants, the Israelites, and also for us, is that the blessing of God is the work of God. He wants to fight for us, but he might have to fight us to get us to the point of surrendering our wills to him. Self-sufficiency, trying to achieve the blessing by our own strength, will not be successful. If we persist in thinking that it will, God may have to "cripple" our self-sufficiency to make us trust him more.

◆ 15. Reconciliation with Esau and settlement in Shechem (33:1-20)

Then Jacob looked up and saw Esau coming with his 400 men. So he divided the children among Leah, Rachel, and his two servant wives. ²He put the servant wives and their children at the front, Leah and her children next, and Rachel and Joseph last. ³Then Jacob went on ahead. As he approached his brother, he bowed to the ground seven times before him. ⁴Then Esau ran to meet him and embraced him, threw his arms around his neck, and kissed him. And they both wept.

⁵Then Esau looked at the women and children and asked, "Who are these people with you?"

"These are the children God has graciously given to me, your servant," Jacob replied. ⁶Then the servant wives came forward with their children and bowed before him. ⁷Next came Leah with her children, and they bowed before him. Finally, Joseph and Rachel came forward and bowed before him.

⁸"And what were all the flocks and herds I met as I came?" Esau asked.

Jacob replied, "They are a gift, my lord, to ensure your friendship."

⁹"My brother, I have plenty," Esau answered. "Keep what you have for yourself."

¹⁰But Jacob insisted, "No, if I have found favor with you, please accept this gift from me. And what a relief to see your friendly smile. It is like seeing the face of God! ¹¹Please take this gift I have brought you, for God has been very gracious to me. I have more than enough." And because Jacob insisted, Esau finally accepted the gift.

¹²"Well," Esau said, "let's be going. I will lead the way."

¹³But Jacob replied, "You can see, my lord, that some of the children are very young, and the flocks and herds have their young, too. If they are driven too hard, even for one day, all the animals could die. ¹⁴Please, my lord, go ahead of your servant. We will follow slowly, at a pace that is comfortable for the livestock and the children. I will meet you at Seir."

¹⁵"All right," Esau said, "but at least let me assign some of my men to guide and protect you."

Jacob responded, "That's not necessary. It's enough that you've received me warmly, my lord!"

¹⁶So Esau turned around and started back to Seir that same day. ¹⁷Jacob, on the other hand, traveled on to Succoth. There he built himself a house and made shelters for his livestock. That is why the place was named Succoth (which means "shelters").

¹⁸Later, having traveled all the way from Paddan-aram, Jacob arrived safely at the town of Shechem, in the land of Canaan. There he set up camp outside the town. ¹⁹Jacob bought the plot of land where he camped from the family of Hamor, the father of Shechem, for 100 pieces of silver.* ²⁰And there he built an altar and named it El-Elohe-Israel.*

33:19 Hebrew *100 kesitahs;* the value or weight of the kesitah is no longer known.   33:20 *El-Elohe-Israel* means "God, the God of Israel."

NOTES

33:11 *this gift.* Lit., "my blessing" (*birkathi* [TH1293/2967.1, ZH1388/3276]). This indicates that Jacob wanted to give part of God's blessing to his brother, Esau. Perhaps in what would appear to be a restoration of what he had taken from his brother earlier, he thought that Esau's anger would be pacified.

33:17 *Succoth.* This name means "booths" or "sheds." Jacob made this name for the place because of the stalls he built for all his livestock.

COMMENTARY

Jacob's long-anticipated meeting with his brother Esau turned out far better than the patriarch could have imagined. It is a classic example of how "God fights" (see discussion of the name "Israel" in the commentary on 32:22-32). God so changed the heart of Esau that he was eager to be reconciled with his brother. Earlier he had cared little about the birthright (25:32-34); now he cared little for old grudges. That was Esau—he lived for the moment! But there was more to it than that, or Jacob would not have been so afraid. Once again Jacob had to recognize that more was due to God's intervention than he realized.

In the preparation to meet Esau, Jacob still showed a weakness of faith—that old favoritism that splits families apart. He lined up his family and his possessions in order of their importance to him, with the slave wives and their children out front (to be killed first), Leah's group behind them, and Rachel and Joseph in the back where they would be the safest. One can only imagine what was running through the minds of the family members as they watched Jacob line them up.

Then Jacob went on ahead to meet his brother, bowing seven times to the ground in homage (33:3), halting along on his way to his brother. Some have seen this as true humility and a gracious attempt to be reconciled, but it is more likely that Jacob was groveling in fear. These fears were dispelled immediately as Esau eagerly ran to meet Jacob, hugged him, and kissed him—and they both wept (33:4). This was an answer to prayer: God delivered Jacob from Esau's revenge. In talking with his brother, Jacob continued to refer to himself as Esau's servant (33:5, 14), and Esau as his lord (33:8, 13-15), whereas Esau called Jacob "my brother" (33:9). Jacob's words seem to reverse his father's blessing, which made Jacob Esau's lord (27:29). He was definitely playing down any of that, as he cautiously tried to ward off any possible retaliation.

Esau was surprised by the animals his brother had sent, but Jacob continued to press Esau to accept them as a gift. Jacob's statement that seeing the face of his brother Esau was like seeing the face of God shows that he knew this deliverance from harm was the work of God, secured at Peniel where he saw God face-to-face (32:30). Esau's favorable action was God's gracious work. Jacob would not take "no" for an answer, as he told his brother to accept the gift.

Even with Esau's apparent magnanimity, Jacob was wary. Going to dwell with Esau in Mount Seir would have been problematic in a number of ways. So Jacob cleverly avoided traveling with his brother, explaining that the little ones could not go very fast (33:13). He promised to follow Esau to Seir down south, but instead he headed in the opposite direction to Succoth, east of the Jordan River and north of the Jabbok. He was wise in avoiding further dealings with Esau, but he need not have deceived his brother again.

By the end of the chapter, one can see that miraculous changes had begun to take place in both men. Esau was changed from seeking revenge to desiring reconciliation. And Jacob was forced to depend on the Lord to deliver him, which prompted in him a spirit of humility and generosity, even if guilty fears and deceptive practices remained.

The final verses of the chapter (33:17-20) form an epilogue to Jacob's adventures outside of the land. He returned to the Promised Land in peace with a large family and many possessions; he camped near Shechem, directly west of the Jabbok, about 20 miles into Canaan from the Jordan River. Shechem was between Mount Ebal and Mount Gerizim. This was the place where Abraham had first camped when he arrived in Canaan (12:6). At that time, the text indicates that the Canaanites were in the land. Soon Jacob's family would realize the danger of this.

In this section, Jacob names two more places (he had already named Bethel, 28:19; Galeed, 31:47; Mahanaim, 32:2; Peniel, 32:30). He named his first settlement "Succoth" (see note on 33:17). Then he traveled on to Canaan and arrived at Shechem. Jacob, like Abraham, purchased a portion of the land, and there, like

Abraham, he set up an altar, which he named El-Elohe-Israel, or "El is the God of Israel." In this way he publicly acknowledged that the Lord God was his God, and that he had led him back to the land he would inherit. And the name of the altar commemorated his relationship to God. God had prospered and protected him, as he had promised. Jacob was now Israel.

◆ ## 16. The defilement of Dinah (34:1-31)

One day Dinah, the daughter of Jacob and Leah, went to visit some of the young women who lived in the area. ²But when the local prince, Shechem son of Hamor the Hivite, saw Dinah, he seized her and raped her. ³But then he fell in love with her, and he tried to win her affection with tender words. ⁴He said to his father, Hamor, "Get me this young girl. I want to marry her."

⁵Soon Jacob heard that Shechem had defiled his daughter, Dinah. But since his sons were out in the fields herding his livestock, he said nothing until they returned. ⁶Hamor, Shechem's father, came to discuss the matter with Jacob. ⁷Meanwhile, Jacob's sons had come in from the field as soon as they heard what had happened. They were shocked and furious that their sister had been raped. Shechem had done a disgraceful thing against Jacob's family,* something that should never be done.

⁸Hamor tried to speak with Jacob and his sons. "My son Shechem is truly in love with your daughter," he said. "Please let him marry her. ⁹In fact, let's arrange other marriages, too. You give us your daughters for our sons, and we will give you our daughters for your sons. ¹⁰And you may live among us; the land is open to you! Settle here and trade with us. And feel free to buy property in the area."

¹¹Then Shechem himself spoke to Dinah's father and brothers. "Please be kind to me, and let me marry her," he begged. "I will give you whatever you ask. ¹²No matter what dowry or gift you demand, I will gladly pay it—just give me the girl as my wife."

¹³But since Shechem had defiled their sister, Dinah, Jacob's sons responded deceitfully to Shechem and his father, Hamor. ¹⁴They said to them, "We couldn't possibly allow this, because you're not circumcised. It would be a disgrace for our sister to marry a man like you! ¹⁵But here is a solution. If every man among you will be circumcised like we are, ¹⁶then we will give you our daughters, and we'll take your daughters for ourselves. We will live among you and become one people. ¹⁷But if you don't agree to be circumcised, we will take her and be on our way."

¹⁸Hamor and his son Shechem agreed to their proposal. ¹⁹Shechem wasted no time in acting on this request, for he wanted Jacob's daughter desperately. Shechem was a highly respected member of his family, ²⁰and he went with his father, Hamor, to present this proposal to the leaders at the town gate.

²¹"These men are our friends," they said. "Let's invite them to live here among us and trade freely. Look, the land is large enough to hold them. We can take their daughters as wives and let them marry ours. ²²But they will consider staying here and becoming one people with us only if all of our men are circumcised, just as they are. ²³But if we do this, all their livestock and possessions will eventually be ours. Come, let's agree to their terms and let them settle here among us."

²⁴So all the men in the town council agreed with Hamor and Shechem, and every male in the town was circumcised. ²⁵But three days later, when their wounds were still sore, two of Jacob's sons, Simeon and Levi, who were Dinah's full brothers, took their swords and entered the town

without opposition. Then they slaughtered every male there, ²⁶including Hamor and his son Shechem. They killed them with their swords, then took Dinah from Shechem's house and returned to their camp.

²⁷Meanwhile, the rest of Jacob's sons arrived. Finding the men slaughtered, they plundered the town because their sister had been defiled there. ²⁸They seized all the flocks and herds and donkeys—everything they could lay their hands on, both inside the town and outside in the fields. ²⁹They looted all their wealth and plundered their houses. They also took all their little children and wives and led them away as captives.

³⁰Afterward Jacob said to Simeon and Levi, "You have ruined me! You've made me stink among all the people of this land—among all the Canaanites and Perizzites. We are so few that they will join forces and crush us. I will be ruined, and my entire household will be wiped out!"

³¹"But why should we let him treat our sister like a prostitute?" they retorted angrily.

34:7 Hebrew *a disgraceful thing in Israel*.

NOTES

34:2 raped her. Heb., *'anah* [TH6031, ZH6700], meaning "to afflict, to oppress, to humble." It is used frequently of oppressing a woman by means of sexual activity (see Deut 21:14; 22:24; Judg 19:24). A literal rendering would be "he lay with her and humbled her," giving the idea that it was in fact a rape but not a physically violent rape, as the subsequent story indicates.

34:5 defiled. Heb. *timme'* [TH2930, ZH3237], meaning "to pollute, defile, make unclean."

34:7 a disgraceful thing against Jacob's family. Lit., "a disgraceful thing in Israel" (cf. NLT mg). This is the first mention of the nation Israel by name. The story uses it to refer to Jacob's family, but in using it the text is already anticipating the nation Israel that will come from this family and warning them about the danger the Canaanites will pose. The word translated "disgraceful thing" (*nebalah* [TH5039, ZH5576]) could also be rendered as "folly."

COMMENTARY

As far as we know, Dinah was Jacob's only daughter (30:21). So it would be understandable for her to wonder how other young women lived. She went out to visit some of them, an innocent enough action that proved to be catastrophic for her, for her family, and for the family of the young man who became infatuated with her. Jacob had made a commercial arrangement with Hamor, the father of Shechem (33:19), but Dinah's attempt to establish a social relationship had serious consequences. It was far better to avoid the Canaanites, as many sons of Israel before and after this came to realize.

A young man named Shechem, the up-and-coming ruler of the area, took Dinah and raped her. After a woman was debased in this way, she had no chance for a proper and joyful marriage. But the text says that Shechem loved her—he wanted her for his wife.

Jacob's response to this crime is surprising. When he heard that Dinah had been defiled (see note on 34:5), he said nothing about it until his sons came home. Why was he so passive? Could it be that he was too shaken by the whole thing to act, or was it because this was Leah's daughter? The reaction of Dinah's real brothers was very different, and appropriate—they were absolutely incensed that such a disgraceful thing had been done against Israel (see note on 34:7). Such a sexual crime was an outrage, incriminating a whole community. While Jacob was silent, the sons were filled with fury and grief; and when the leader of the clan did nothing, the young and immature members took matters into their own hands.

In the meantime, the Canaanites approached Jacob with an offer. Old Hamor, Shechem's father, made a diplomatic speech, wherein he proposed that great advantages would be gained by both sides if they made an agreement to intermarry (34:8-10). He poignantly offered Israel a chance to buy more land (34:10). But God, not the Canaanites, would give them the land (recall that Abraham believed that God, not the king of Sodom, would give him the blessing). Shechem pressed for the deal, offering to pay Jacob and Dinah's brothers whatever price for the bride they wanted. He was trying to buy his way out of trouble. But Hamor was being deceptive, as his private appeal to his own people reveals—they would soon possess everything that Jacob's family had (34:23). No good could possibly come from trusting the defiling Canaanites.

The brothers of Dinah, and not Jacob, responded to the proposal. But the narrative explains they did so "deceitfully" (*mirmah* [TH4820, ZH5327]; 34:13). They refused it on the grounds that Shechem was not circumcised, and intermarriage with his clan would be a disgrace (34:14; *kherpah* [TH2781, ZH3075], "a reproach, a scorn"). The expressions "not circumcised" and "disgrace" were appropriate, for they fit the Canaanites very well. So the brothers demanded the outward conforming to the rite of circumcision before they would approve the proposal of marriage. But, of course, this would not make the Canaanites members of the covenant; they were still pagans. The brothers of Dinah may not have thought that Shechem and his people would ever agree to the rite. But the Canaanites accepted the stipulation and had every male in town circumcised, not only so that Shechem could marry the girl, but so that they eventually could acquire everything that belonged to Israel.

The outworking of the brother's plot was tragic and unnecessary. Simeon and Levi, and no doubt their households, went and slaughtered all the males in the town while they were incapacitated and in pain from the circumcision. And then Simeon and Levi rescued Dinah. The rest of the brothers came and plundered the city and the fields for the Shechemites' property, livestock, wealth, women, and children. This was not justice; it was brutal and excessive revenge. Ironically, the defilement of one woman, Dinah, led to the painful capture of many women and children. Their presence would be a perpetual reminder of the cruelty of the tribes.

All of this struck fear in the heart of Jacob, for it could bring him and his family serious repercussions. But the brothers were defiant: "Why should we let him treat our sister like a prostitute?" (34:31). The answer, of course, is that they should not allow it. But there was a better way to deal with the problem. The leader of the tribes, Jacob, should have dealt with the problem directly, demanding justice with restitution. But Jacob did nothing, and the sons dealt deceitfully and excessively in killing many people in the community.

The instincts of Simeon and Levi were correct—a sense of moral outrage and a desire for righting the wrong. But because of their unbridled passion, a whole group of people were slaughtered. Worse than that, they dangled the covenant before the Canaanites to deceive them. It is one thing to trick the Canaanites (as they themselves were deceptive), but it was another matter to use the covenant and its rites deceitfully—that is sacrilege.

This story is a skein of good and evil, as are most of the narratives about the patriarchs. But this one is far more serious than most because it ended in slaughter. The account was a stern warning for the Israelites leaving Egypt regarding the defiling effects of dealing with the Canaanites on any level. The nation of Israel was commanded not to intermarry with them, or make treaties with them, for they were a corrupt and corrupting people. This chapter would even warn against investigating the way they lived (34:1). Moreover, the narrative would remind the Israelites to keep holy things holy—the covenant must not be used for deception (34:13) because the reputation of Israel was at stake in the land (34:30). For this sham, Simeon and Levi were passed over in the blessing with the birthright as Reuben was, so the leadership would be with Judah (49:5-7).

Finally, it should be noted that this chapter is often explained as an example of a tribal story set in the language of a family narrative because the names in the chapter are also the names of places and tribes. Westermann argues for its classification as a combination of a settlement of land account from the time of the Judges and a family history (1985:535-537; see also von Rad 1961:329-330).

The young man is Shechem, the name of the Canaanite town. Jacob's family is called Israel, the nation. The avengers are the tribes Simeon and Levi. The narrative uses actual participants, but in so doing describes the defilement and the retaliation in terms of tribal conflicts that would certainly characterize the later historical period. Frequently in Genesis the nature and character of a person foreshadows that of his descendants.

◆ 17. Jacob's return to Bethel (35:1-15)

Then God said to Jacob, "Get ready and move to Bethel and settle there. Build an altar there to the God who appeared to you when you fled from your brother, Esau."

²So Jacob told everyone in his household, "Get rid of all your pagan idols, purify yourselves, and put on clean clothing. ³We are now going to Bethel, where I will build an altar to the God who answered my prayers when I was in distress. He has been with me wherever I have gone."

⁴So they gave Jacob all their pagan idols and earrings, and he buried them under the great tree near Shechem. ⁵As they set out, a terror from God spread over the people in all the towns of that area, so no one attacked Jacob's family.

⁶Eventually, Jacob and his household arrived at Luz (also called Bethel) in Canaan. ⁷Jacob built an altar there and named the place El-bethel (which means "God of Bethel"), because God had appeared to him there when he was fleeing from his brother, Esau.

⁸Soon after this, Rebekah's old nurse, Deborah, died. She was buried beneath the oak tree in the valley below Bethel. Ever since, the tree has been called Allon-bacuth (which means "oak of weeping").

⁹Now that Jacob had returned from Paddan-aram, God appeared to him again at Bethel. God blessed him, ¹⁰saying, "Your name is Jacob, but you will not be called Jacob any longer. From now on your name will be Israel."* So God renamed him Israel.

¹¹Then God said, "I am El-Shaddai—'God Almighty.' Be fruitful and multiply. You will become a great nation, even many nations. Kings will be among your descendants! ¹²And I will give you the land I once gave to Abraham and Isaac. Yes, I will give it to you and your descendants after you." ¹³Then God went up from the place where he had spoken to Jacob.

¹⁴Jacob set up a stone pillar to mark the place where God had spoken to him. Then he poured wine over it as an offering to God and anointed the pillar with olive oil. ¹⁵And Jacob named the place Bethel (which means "house of God"), because God had spoken to him there.

35:10 *Jacob* sounds like the Hebrew words for "heel" and "deceiver." *Israel* means "God fights."

NOTES

35:8 *Rebekah's old nurse, Deborah, died.* This death marks the passage of a generation of people from the scene; the narrative is going to focus increasingly on the story of the sons. Deborah had been given to Rebekah as a nurse and companion.

Allon-bacuth (which means "oak of weeping"). The naming of the place of burial commemorated the sorrow over the loss of someone greatly loved. Deborah had probably been with Rebekah for Rebekah's entire life (24:59-61).

35:11 *I am El-Shaddai—'God Almighty.'* For the sake of clarity, the NLT puts both a transliteration of the Hebrew *'el shadday* [TH410A/7706, ZH446/8724] and an English translation of the name in the text. Although there is no certain explanation of the meaning of this epithet (see note on 17:1), the following words here, "be fruitful and multiply," point to God's abundant supply and correspond to the suggestion of some that the name speaks of God's ability to provide.

COMMENTARY

Two themes run through this chapter: completion and correction. Jacob was back home, the victories over Laban and Esau were won, and the promise to return safely was fulfilled. But the family had not kept to the faith perfectly: Idols had to be destroyed and Reuben's hubris (35:22) did not go unnoticed.

The first part of the chapter records Jacob's return to Bethel, about 15 miles south of Shechem, where he had to complete his vows. Those vows were made when he saw the vision at Bethel; they included making Yahweh his God, making Bethel God's house, and giving tithes to God (28:20-22). Jacob's pilgrimage back to the land had not been uncomplicated, but now he was back. God then reminded him to return to Bethel—to keep his promise (35:1). Apparently his indifference to doing that had provided the occasion for Dinah's defilement (ch 34); Jacob should have traveled straight back to Bethel as he vowed, without stopping at Shechem.

To complete his vows there had to be a sanctifying procedure (35:2-5). Jacob made the family remove all household idols, the foreign gods they had. God permits no rivals; he does not allow images or magical charms. In Bethel, only the Lord was to be their God. All this getting rid of idols and washing and changing clothes was thorough; and it was instructive for subsequent Israelites who would also need such consecration when they came into the land (see Josh 5:1-9), especially when they went to the house of God. After burying the idols and the earrings associated with pagan worship, Jacob and his family left Shechem and set out for Bethel. People in the towns along the way had heard of the massacre of Shechem; consequently, they were afraid of Jacob's group (cf. 34:25-29).

When Jacob arrived at Bethel (formerly Luz), he built an altar there, as God had instructed (35:1)—he called it El-bethel, the God of Bethel (35:7). At Bethel, God confirmed the promise he had made there earlier and reiterated the change of his name from Jacob to Israel as proof that the blessing had been given (35:10). God's reference to himself as "El-Shaddai—God Almighty" (see note on 35:11) was an assurance that his promise could and would be fulfilled. Now that Jacob was back in the land, the promise of the seed and the land was repeated (35:12). During both experiences at Bethel, God promised Jacob descendants in the land (28:13-14; 35:11-12), but here he adds that kings would be born. Jacob's actions here are almost identical to his actions in the earlier experience at Bethel: He set up the stone pillar, poured wine on it and anointed it with oil, and reestablished it as a place of worship, naming it again as "Bethel," the house of God (28:16-19; 35:6-7, 14-15).

◆   **18. The completion of the family (35:16-29)**

¹⁶Leaving Bethel, Jacob and his clan moved on toward Ephrath. But Rachel went into labor while they were still some distance away. Her labor pains were intense. ¹⁷After a very hard delivery, the midwife finally exclaimed, "Don't be afraid—you have another son!" ¹⁸Rachel was about to die, but with her last breath she named the baby Ben-oni (which means "son of my sorrow"). The baby's father, however, called him Benjamin (which means "son of my right hand"). ¹⁹So Rachel died and was buried on the way to Ephrath (that is, Bethlehem). ²⁰Jacob set up a stone monument over Rachel's grave, and it can be seen there to this day.

²¹Then Jacob* traveled on and camped beyond Migdal-eder. ²²While he was living there, Reuben had intercourse with Bilhah, his father's concubine, and Jacob soon heard about it.

These are the names of the twelve sons of Jacob:

²³The sons of Leah were Reuben (Jacob's oldest son), Simeon, Levi, Judah, Issachar, and Zebulun.

²⁴The sons of Rachel were Joseph and Benjamin.

²⁵The sons of Bilhah, Rachel's servant, were Dan and Naphtali.

²⁶The sons of Zilpah, Leah's servant, were Gad and Asher.

These are the names of the sons who were born to Jacob at Paddan-aram.

²⁷So Jacob returned to his father, Isaac, in Mamre, which is near Kiriath-arba (now called Hebron), where Abraham and Isaac had both lived as foreigners. ²⁸Isaac lived for 180 years. ²⁹Then he breathed his last and died at a ripe old age, joining his ancestors in death. And his sons, Esau and Jacob, buried him.

35:21 Hebrew *Israel;* also in 35:22a. The names "Jacob" and "Israel" are often interchanged throughout the Old Testament, referring sometimes to the individual patriarch and sometimes to the nation.

NOTES

35:19 Rachel died and was buried on the way to Ephrath (that is, Bethlehem). Rachel's grave site was between Bethel and Bethlehem. Ephrath was an older name for Bethlehem (cf. Mic 5:2; see also 1 Chr 2:50-51; Ruth 1:2; 4:11).

35:21-22 Jacob. Significantly, Jacob is called Israel three times in these verses. The NLT changes it to "Jacob," "he," and "Jacob" and notes in the margin that the Hebrew reads "Israel." The writer was beginning to draw more attention to Israel as a people.

COMMENTARY

The family was completed with the birth of Benjamin, but it was a birth filled with sorrow—Rachel died in giving birth to the child. Her death is the second transitional death recorded in the chapter. As she was dying she gave a name to the boy, "Ben-oni," meaning "son of my sorrow" (35:18a). But that name would not do, so Jacob changed it to something more positive. He named him Benjamin, meaning "son of my right hand" (35:18b). Jacob thereby turned this day of sorrow into a day of triumph, the birth of a son with the prospect of success. After all, the child was an answer to Rachel's prayer (cf. 30:24), and so he wanted the name to be positive.

Several short reports help to close out this section about Isaac's family. The first describes Reuben's violation of Jacob's family by having sexual relations with Bilhah, Jacob's concubine and Rachel's maidservant by whom Jacob had two sons, Dan and Naphtali (35:22; cf. 30:3-8). This transgression took place near Migdal Eder between Bethlehem and Hebron. It may be that Reuben, the oldest son, was trying to replace his father as the head of the clan by a pagan procedure, but in doing so he lost the birthright (cf. 49:3-4). The text says that Jacob heard about it; and again he did nothing—not yet anyway.

A second report lists the 12 sons who became the heads of the 12 tribes of Israel (35:22b-26). This was another assurance that the promises of God were good. The names are firstfruits, as it were, of the great nation to follow.

The chapter's last report concerns Jacob's return to his father, Isaac, which was soon followed by the death of Isaac at the age of 180 (35:27-29). This is the third transitional death in the chapter. Isaac was living at the time near Hebron. Jacob and Esau came together to bury him. Perhaps this was the first time the two had met since the reconciliation (33:16-17).

In the events of this chapter, Jacob learned that while his return to the land was a completion of promises God had made, he could not be complacent about his religious duties, for it was a new beginning. Deborah, Rachel, and Isaac all died, marking the end of an era. Reuben forfeited his right to inherit the prime blessing. But idols were removed and everyone was consecrated in order for Jacob's vow of pure worship to be completed. The "nation" was completed with the birth of the twelfth "tribe," Benjamin, in the land. During this time of transition, the faith had to be revitalized so that the covenant could be carried forward to the sons of Jacob, the focus of the last main section of the book. For this reason, the chapter emphasizes God's promises and Jacob's vow.

◆ D. The Account of the Succession from Esau (36:1-8)

This is the account of the descendants of Esau (also known as Edom). ²Esau married two young women from Canaan: Adah, the daughter of Elon the Hittite; and Oholibamah, the daughter of Anah and granddaughter of Zibeon the Hivite. ³He also married his cousin Basemath, who was the daughter of Ishmael and the sister of Nebaioth. ⁴Adah gave birth to a son named Eliphaz for Esau. Basemath gave birth to a son named Reuel. ⁵Oholibamah gave birth to sons named Jeush, Jalam, and Korah. All these sons were born to Esau in the land of Canaan.

⁶Esau took his wives, his children, and his entire household, along with his livestock and cattle—all the wealth he had acquired in the land of Canaan—and moved away from his brother, Jacob. ⁷There was not enough land to support them both because of all the livestock and possessions they had acquired. ⁸So Esau (also known as Edom) settled in the hill country of Seir.

NOTES

36:1 *the account*. The Hebrew word is *toledoth* [TH8435, ZH9352], the central term on which the literary structure of Genesis is based (see the Introduction).

36:2 *Oholibamah*. This wife of Esau's was a great-granddaughter of Seir the Horite (cf. 36:14, 18, 25), whose descendants were living in Edom when Esau went to live there (36:20, 25). Seir fathered Zibeon (36:20), who fathered Anah (36:24), whose daughter was Oholibamah.

36:7 *There was not enough land to support them both because of all the livestock and possessions they had acquired*. This statement reminds us of Lot (cf. 13:5-6); Esau, like Lot, left for the east and greener land (36:8).

COMMENTARY

This chapter is complicated and difficult, and the details quite baffling—and to the casual reader, very tedious. The *toledoth* [TH8435, ZH9352] of Isaac (25:19–35:29) has closed, so the book will turn to the accounts of the successions of his sons, following the practice of first wrapping up the lineage not chosen (ch 36) before proceeding to the chosen lineage (ch 37).

The first eight verses of the chapter give the *toledoth* of Esau. He had three wives: Adah, Oholibamah, and Basemath. Since two of these wives' names are not the same as those listed earlier (26:34; 28:9), either the others died or Esau favored these three among the five he took, or these were just different names. There is not enough information to decide. From the three wives named, Esau had five sons.

The short account stresses two points. First, Esau's sons were born in the land of Canaan (36:5) before he moved to Seir (36:8). This contrasts with Jacob, whose children for the most part were born outside the land but then moved into it. Second, Esau was Edom. In fact, all through the chapter the reader is reminded of this. Certainly Israel would understand the import of this because they often struggled with the Edomites (see e.g., Num 20:14-20; Obad 1)—they were Esau's descendants. And even though the Edomites were judged by God, remnants of the old national conflict with Israel remained even in New Testament times when the Jews had to endure the reign of Herod the Great, an Idumean, a descendant of Esau.

◆ E. The Account of the Succession of the Edomites from Esau (36:9–37:1)

⁹This is the account of Esau's descendants, the Edomites, who lived in the hill country of Seir.

¹⁰These are the names of Esau's sons: Eliphaz, the son of Esau's wife Adah; and Reuel, the son of Esau's wife Basemath. ¹¹The descendants of Eliphaz were Teman, Omar, Zepho, Gatam, and Kenaz. ¹²Timna, the concubine of Esau's son Eliphaz, gave birth to a son named Amalek. These are the descendants of Esau's wife Adah. ¹³The descendants of Reuel were Nahath, Zerah, Shammah, and Mizzah. These are the descendants of Esau's wife Basemath. ¹⁴Esau also had sons through Oholibamah, the daughter of Anah and granddaughter of Zibeon. Their names were Jeush, Jalam, and Korah.

¹⁵These are the descendants of Esau who became the leaders of various clans:

The descendants of Esau's oldest son, Eliphaz, became the leaders of the clans of Teman, Omar, Zepho, Kenaz, ¹⁶Korah, Gatam, and Amalek. These are the clan leaders in the land of Edom who descended from Eliphaz. All these were descendants of Esau's wife Adah.

¹⁷The descendants of Esau's son Reuel became the leaders of the clans of Nahath, Zerah, Shammah, and Mizzah. These are the clan leaders in the land of Edom who descended from Reuel. All these were descendants of Esau's wife Basemath.

¹⁸The descendants of Esau and his wife Oholibamah became the leaders of the clans of Jeush, Jalam, and Korah. These are the clan leaders who descended from Esau's wife Oholibamah, the daughter of Anah.

¹⁹These are the clans descended from Esau (also known as Edom), identified by their clan leaders.

²⁰These are the names of the tribes that descended from Seir the Horite. They lived in the land of Edom: Lotan, Shobal, Zibeon, Anah, ²¹Dishon, Ezer, and Dishan. These were the Horite clan leaders, the descendants of Seir, who lived in the land of Edom.

²²The descendants of Lotan were Hori and Hemam. Lotan's sister was named Timna.
²³The descendants of Shobal were Alvan, Manahath, Ebal, Shepho, and Onam.
²⁴The descendants of Zibeon were Aiah and Anah. (This is the Anah who discovered the hot springs in the wilderness while he was grazing his father's donkeys.)
²⁵The descendants of Anah were his son, Dishon, and his daughter, Oholibamah.
²⁶The descendants of Dishon* were Hemdan, Eshban, Ithran, and Keran.
²⁷The descendants of Ezer were Bilhan, Zaavan, and Akan.
²⁸The descendants of Dishan were Uz and Aran.

²⁹So these were the leaders of the Horite clans: Lotan, Shobal, Zibeon, Anah, ³⁰Dishon, Ezer, and Dishan. The Horite clans are named after their clan leaders, who lived in the land of Seir.

³¹These are the kings who ruled in the land of Edom before any king ruled over the Israelites*:

³²Bela son of Beor, who ruled in Edom from his city of Dinhabah.
³³When Bela died, Jobab son of Zerah from Bozrah became king in his place.
³⁴When Jobab died, Husham from the land of the Temanites became king in his place.
³⁵When Husham died, Hadad son of Bedad became king in his place and

ruled from the city of Avith. He was the one who defeated the Midianites in the land of Moab. ³⁶When Hadad died, Samlah from the city of Masrekah became king in his place. ³⁷When Samlah died, Shaul from the city of Rehoboth-on-the-River became king in his place. ³⁸When Shaul died, Baal-hanan son of Acbor became king in his place. ³⁹When Baal-hanan son of Acbor died, Hadad* became king in his place and ruled from the city of Pau. His wife was Mehetabel, the daughter of Matred and granddaughter of Me-zahab.

⁴⁰These are the names of the leaders of the clans descended from Esau, who lived in the places named for them: Timna, Alvah, Jetheth, ⁴¹Oholibamah, Elah, Pinon, ⁴²Kenaz, Teman, Mibzar, ⁴³Magdiel, and Iram. These are the leaders of the clans of Edom, listed according to their settlements in the land they occupied. They all descended from Esau, the ancestor of the Edomites.

CHAPTER 37

So Jacob settled again in the land of Canaan, where his father had lived as a foreigner.

36:26 Hebrew *Dishan*, a variant spelling of Dishon; compare 36:21, 28. 36:31 Or *before an Israelite king ruled over them*. 36:39 As in some Hebrew manuscripts, Samaritan Pentateuch, and Syriac version (see also 1 Chr 1:50); most Hebrew manuscripts read *Hadar*.

NOTES

36:9 *the account of Esau's descendants.* The latter part of the chapter (36:9-43) also begins with the heading of *toledoth* [TH8435, ZH9352] (cf. 36:1). Although this section could be joined with the previous one to be one major account of what became of Esau, this section traces the family to subsequent generations and alliances.

36:16 *Korah.* The Hebrew text lists him here as a son of Eliphaz, but not in 36:11 or in 1 Chr 1:36. It appears that there may be a textual problem: perhaps the name Korah was copied by mistake from 36:14 (see Driver 1891:318).

COMMENTARY

The sons of Esau also had sons; Esau had five sons and ten grandsons (either literal sons or tribes founded by descendants of Esau). He had eleven grandsons if Korah of 36:16 is included (see note). In the text, the 10 grandsons and three of the sons, thirteen in all, are called *'allup* [TH441B, ZH477]—a "leader of a clan," a head of a tribe (36:15, 17-18). Thus, a picture of Esau as a grand overlord of tribes begins to emerge (cf. 36:40-43).

Verses 20-30 list the sons (sons and grandchildren) of Seir the Horite—early inhabitants of the land. These were probably aboriginal Edomites conquered or controlled by Esau (Deut 2:12). Seir's seven sons (36:20-21) became Horite clan leaders (cf. 36:29), and from those came 20 tribes ("sons" or "daughters").

Following this there is a listing of the kings of Edom (36:31-39). It is not clear how the kings of Edom were related to Esau, but they were kings who ruled in Edom—and Esau is Edom (36:8). The organization of the clans in Edom followed the same pattern as the later tribes of Israel. They ultimately chose a king from one of their tribes and carried on a line of succession from him. Whether or not the line of eight kings in succession mentioned here extended beyond the time of Jacob and Esau is unclear. The point is comparative, though; the text states that there were kings in Edom before any king reigned in Israel (36:31).

Verses 40-43 list the names of the clan leaders who descended from Esau, according to their families, places, and names. Esau was thus a great and powerful overlord, the father of the Edomites (36:43), ruling over clans and regions (36:40), with 11 clan leaders who descended from him. In accord with Isaac's promises to Esau, Esau was separating from Jacob and beginning to shake the yoke of his brother from his neck (cf. 27:39-40).

In dramatic contrast to this entire chapter, which records the expanding, powerful line of Esau, 37:1 notes that Jacob was dwelling in the land of his father's sojourning, in the land of Canaan. (While this verse begins chapter 37 in English translations, it actually goes with chapter 36, for the heading of the next section is 37:2.) Jacob was still a temporary resident; "Israel" was still just a family. This contrast points out that unlike Esau, Jacob had no clan leaders or kings yet (35:11), no lands to govern, and no expanding tribes yet. Delitzsch (1889:2.238) pertinently remarks that secular, worldly greatness often comes swifter than spiritual greatness. The promised spiritual blessing demanded patience and faith. Waiting while others prosper, especially a brother like Esau, was a test of Jacob's personal faith and perseverance.

◆ III. The Account of the Succession from Jacob: The Story of Joseph and His Brothers (37:2–50:26)
   A. The Selling of Joseph into Egypt (37:2-36)

²This is the account of Jacob and his family. When Joseph was seventeen years old, he often tended his father's flocks. He worked for his half brothers, the sons of his father's wives Bilhah and Zilpah. But Joseph reported to his father some of the bad things his brothers were doing.

³Jacob* loved Joseph more than any of his other children because Joseph had been born to him in his old age. So one day Jacob had a special gift made for Joseph—a beautiful robe.* ⁴But his brothers hated Joseph because their father loved him more than the rest of them. They couldn't say a kind word to him.

⁵One night Joseph had a dream, and when he told his brothers about it, they hated him more than ever. ⁶"Listen to this dream," he said. ⁷"We were out in the field, tying up bundles of grain. Suddenly my bundle stood up, and your bundles all gathered around and bowed low before mine!"

⁸His brothers responded, "So you think you will be our king, do you? Do you actually think you will reign over us?" And they hated him all the more because of his dreams and the way he talked about them.

⁹Soon Joseph had another dream, and again he told his brothers about it. "Listen, I have had another dream," he said. "The sun, moon, and eleven stars bowed low before me!"

¹⁰This time he told the dream to his father as well as to his brothers, but his father scolded him. "What kind of dream is that?" he asked. "Will your mother and I and your brothers actually come and bow to the ground before you?" ¹¹But while his brothers were jealous of Joseph, his father wondered what the dreams meant.

¹²Soon after this, Joseph's brothers went to pasture their father's flocks at Shechem. ¹³When they had been gone for some time, Jacob said to Joseph, "Your brothers are pasturing the sheep at Shechem. Get ready, and I will send you to them."

"I'm ready to go," Joseph replied.

¹⁴"Go and see how your brothers and the flocks are getting along," Jacob said. "Then come back and bring me a report." So Jacob sent him on his way, and Joseph traveled to Shechem from their home in the valley of Hebron.

¹⁵When he arrived there, a man from the area noticed him wandering around the countryside. "What are you looking for?" he asked.

¹⁶"I'm looking for my brothers," Joseph replied. "Do you know where they are pasturing their sheep?"

¹⁷"Yes," the man told him. "They have moved on from here, but I heard them say, 'Let's go on to Dothan.'" So Joseph followed his brothers to Dothan and found them there.

¹⁸When Joseph's brothers saw him coming, they recognized him in the distance. As he approached, they made plans to kill him. ¹⁹"Here comes the dreamer!" they said. ²⁰"Come on, let's kill him and throw him into one of these cisterns. We can tell our father, 'A wild animal has eaten him.' Then we'll see what becomes of his dreams!"

²¹But when Reuben heard of their scheme, he came to Joseph's rescue. "Let's not kill him," he said. ²²"Why should we shed any blood? Let's just throw him into this empty cistern here in the wilderness. Then he'll die without our laying a hand on him." Reuben was secretly planning to rescue Joseph and return him to his father.

²³So when Joseph arrived, his brothers ripped off the beautiful robe he was wearing. ²⁴Then they grabbed him and threw him into the cistern. Now the cistern was empty; there was no water in it. ²⁵Then, just as they were sitting down to eat, they looked up and saw a caravan of camels in the distance coming toward them. It was a group of Ishmaelite traders taking a load of gum, balm, and aromatic resin from Gilead down to Egypt.

²⁶Judah said to his brothers, "What will we gain by killing our brother? We'd have to cover up the crime.* ²⁷Instead of hurting him, let's sell him to those Ishmaelite traders. After all, he is our brother—our own flesh and blood!" And his brothers agreed. ²⁸So when the Ishmaelites, who were Midianite traders, came by, Joseph's brothers pulled him out of the cistern and sold him to them for twenty pieces* of silver. And the traders took him to Egypt.

²⁹Some time later, Reuben returned to get Joseph out of the cistern. When he discovered that Joseph was missing, he tore his clothes in grief. ³⁰Then he went back to his brothers and lamented, "The boy is gone! What will I do now?"

³¹Then the brothers killed a young goat and dipped Joseph's robe in its blood. ³²They sent the beautiful robe to their father with this message: "Look at what we found. Doesn't this robe belong to your son?"

³³Their father recognized it immediately. "Yes," he said, "it is my son's robe. A wild animal must have eaten him. Joseph has clearly been torn to pieces!" ³⁴Then Jacob tore his clothes and dressed himself in burlap. He mourned deeply for his son for a long time. ³⁵His family all tried to comfort him, but he refused to be comforted. "I will go to my grave* mourning for my son," he would say, and then he would weep.

³⁶Meanwhile, the Midianite traders* arrived in Egypt, where they sold Joseph to Potiphar, an officer of Pharaoh, the king of Egypt. Potiphar was captain of the palace guard.

37:3a Hebrew *Israel;* also in 37:13. See note on 35:21.   37:3b Traditionally rendered *a coat of many colors.* The exact meaning of the Hebrew is uncertain.   37:26 Hebrew *cover his blood.*   37:28 Hebrew *20 shekels,* about 8 ounces or 228 grams in weight.   37:35 Hebrew *go down to Sheol.*   37:36 Hebrew *the Medanites.* The relationship between the Midianites and Medanites is unclear; compare 37:28. See also 25:2.

NOTES

37:2 *the account of Jacob and his family.* After the heading introduces this section as the *toledoth* [TH8435, ZH9352] of Jacob, the account of Joseph and his brothers begins, for this is what became of Jacob. Jacob will still figure prominently in the section, but the focus will be on Joseph.

Joseph reported to his father some of the bad things his brothers were doing. Joseph is introduced as a 17-year-old son who was obedient to his father. He worked for his half-brothers, the sons of the concubines, and had to bring back a bad report about their activities. It is fairly common for popular interpreters to make Joseph out to be a tattletale and spoiled brat, but such an interpretation misses the point entirely. Although bringing a bad report has never been a popular thing to do (even though it is sometimes the right thing to do), it shows that Joseph was faithful from the beginning. Before people can be given greater responsibilities, they have to prove faithful in the little things, the routine things of life. The content of the report is not known, and there is no word that the brothers even knew that he brought back the report.

37:8 *Do you actually think you will reign over us?* The construction of this response in the Hebrew stresses the brothers' amazement and contempt: "You don't mean to say that you will actually rule over us, do you?"

37:14, 17 *Joseph traveled to Shechem from their home in the valley of Hebron . . . Joseph followed his brothers to Dothan.* Based on the place names in the story, it appears that the brothers ranged far and wide. If Jacob was still living in the south, in the valley of Hebron, about 19 miles south of Jerusalem, Shechem would have been about 50 miles from home, and Dothan another 15 miles.

37:25, 28, 36 *Ishmaelite traders . . . Midianite traders.* In this section, there is a difficulty in the text as to whether it was the Ishmaelites or the Midianites who bought Joseph. This apparent discrepancy is often looked at as evidence of two different traditions being brought together. The text of 37:28 says that Midianite traders were passing by and that Joseph was sold to Ishmaelites on their way to Egypt (Ishmaelites were descendants of Ishmael by Hagar, 16:15; and Midianites were in part descendants of Abraham through Keturah, 25:1-2). The text only indicates that Midianites were with them, not that they were the same group. It is possible that the term Ishmaelite may have become a general description of bedouin tribes. But we have an additional bit of information in v. 36. There, the Hebrew text says that "Medanites" (*hammedanim* [TH4091, ZH4527]) sold Joseph to Potiphar, not "Midianites" (*hammidyanim* [TH4084, ZH4520]). Translations and commentaries have followed the LXX and assumed that the word in v. 36 should be "Midianites," to harmonize with v. 28 (see NLT mg on 37:36). But "Medanites" (*hammedanim*) is rare and therefore the more difficult reading by the standards of textual criticism; and according to 25:2 they are distinct from the Midianites. If "Midianites" (*hammidyanim*), which is not so rare, had been the intended word, it would be difficult to explain how the spelling *hammedanim* was accepted. It is more likely that "Medanites," the word that is in the Hebrew text, was the original reading. Because the chapter uses both "Midianites" in v. 28 and "Medanites" in v. 36, it is likely that the term "Ishmaelites" in this chapter is a broad term for various bedouin tribes and not just the tribes from Ishmael. If that were the case, we would have some unknown smaller tribe within the Ishmaelites, not the Midianites at all. They may have been some unknown tribe that was part of the bedouin or that traveled with the Ishmaelites.

COMMENTARY

The story of Joseph forms a unique unit in the book (37:2–50:26). It is not written like the patriarchal narratives, but traces one continuous development from episode to episode with Joseph at the center. The story is tied together by the repetition of several motifs. The fact that there are these repeated elements militates against the theory that the material was handed down in different traditions and combined by an editor because repetition is a key component of Hebrew rhetoric; it is used effectively here. There are three sets of dreams, four sets of parallel relationships (Joseph and his family, Joseph and Potiphar's household, Joseph and the prisoners, Joseph and Pharaoh's household), two episodes in a pit or prison that involved false accusation and use of Joseph's clothing for evidence, and two repeated visits of the brothers to Egypt. These cycles form the structure of the whole account.

The material differs in tone and emphasis from all the preceding material in the book as well. The themes are more closely related to those found in wisdom books like Proverbs and Ecclesiastes, such as avoiding the foreign woman (ch 39; cf. Prov 5), or storing up in times of plenty for future needs (ch 41; cf. Prov 6:6-8), as well as incidental comments, such as the note that Joseph was a wise ruler (41:39).

Another theme is that of suffering as a test of character, both for Joseph and his brothers. Though Joseph was righteous, he was not kept from suffering; he was instead preserved by his faith through it. And in the end he could acknowledge that God had intended it for good (50:20). Wisdom literature in the Bible assures the faithful that God brings good out of evil and joy out of pain, if not in this life, certainly in the life to come. It teaches that though the wicked may prosper for a time, the righteous are to hold fast to their integrity because there is a higher, more enduring principle of life that comes with obedience to God. Since the Lord is sovereign over all life, one cannot hope to fulfill his God-given destiny by disobeying him. At times God's ways seem unfair, but if endured to their end, they bring greater blessings to the righteous. And as the Joseph story will show, leaders cannot hope to rule with wisdom unless they have overcome opposition and suffering themselves.

So the story of Joseph is a short story written with the main themes of wisdom literature in mind. In short, it reveals how wisdom rules. That is why the book never faults Joseph. It is not that he was sinless, for no one is. Rather, it is the purpose of the story to focus on wisdom as exemplified in Joseph. Every king in Israel—indeed, everyone who aspires to leadership in God's program—must observe in Joseph how wisdom leads to success in God's plan. Christ Jesus himself lived out the life of wisdom portrayed here as no one else could, for he is the wisdom of God (1 Cor 1:30).

As with the story of Cain and Abel in chapter 4, the story of Joseph begins slowly, with only a brief word about the brothers' bad deeds (37:2). As the chapter progresses we see more of their wickedness displayed until, like Cain, they try to get rid of the brother who is pleasing to God. It was Jacob's favoritism that began to complicate things (37:4). He loved Joseph more than any of his other sons because he was the son of his old age (born when Jacob was about 90). He gave Joseph a richly ornamented robe, possibly a multicolored tunic (37:3). This clearly demonstrated to the brothers that Jacob favored Joseph above them all and had the full intention of granting him the larger portion of the inheritance. Not that this should have been a surprise to them, for they had seen Jacob's favoritism to Rachel's sons before.

Jacob should have perceived the mounting tension and been more cautious in the way he displayed his favoritism. He surely must have recalled what favoritism had done to his own family, how it had separated him from his mother. Sadly, it would also separate him from his son Joseph.

Because Jacob flaunted his favoritism of Joseph, the brothers hated Joseph and would not speak kindly to him. And yet God confirmed the choice of this faithful son as the eventual leader of the whole family by means of dreams. (It was no doubt God's perfect timing to reveal this amid his brothers' animosity in order to test Joseph and effect his transfer to Egypt.) In the Old Testament, God's revelation is given in various ways; here it came through symbolic dreams. God used this method when his people were going to other nations (28:12), when they were in other lands (31:10), or when the revelation was given to pagan kings (20:3). Dreams needed interpretations, and these were made known to the world through Israelites—a Joseph before Pharaoh, or a Daniel before the king of Babylon. Throughout the ancient world, dreams were considered to be ominous and thought to carry the most weight as a form of divine communication—especially if the dream revelation was given twice. In Genesis, God had already announced the bondage in Egypt through a dream given to Abraham (15:13); in another dream, God promised protection and provision for Jacob as he was heading for Paddan-aram (28:12-15); and God had warned both Abimelech, the king of Gerar (20:3), and Laban, the Syrian (31:24), by dreams to not do anything against the patriarchal families. So when God revealed his choice of Joseph through two symbolic dreams, everyone would have taken them very seriously.

But when Joseph spoke of his dreams, his brothers, who already hated him, hated him all the more (37:5, 8). He did not taunt them in any way about the dreams he had but simply told them to the family. The text explains that they hated him because they were jealous of him (37:11). They believed the dreams but wished they had received these prophecies rather than their hated brother. If any of Joseph's brothers had received these dreams, they too would have shared them because divine revelations that involved everyone had to be shared. Jacob pondered it all in his heart (37:11). He in particular knew how God worked; Jacob himself had received visions in dreams. He was well aware that God would choose the next leader. He also knew that God could choose the younger son to rule over the older sons; and he knew that God could reveal all this ahead of time in dreams.

The symbols of the first dream were agricultural (37:6-7). In them, there may have been a hint of the way in which his authority over the family would be achieved (cf. 42:1-3). In the dream, Joseph's sheaf of grain stood upright while all the sheaves of his family bowed down to his. The symbols of the second dream were celestial (37:9). The sun, moon, and 11 stars all bowed down to him. In the ancient world such astrological symbols often represented rulers. The dream, then, predicted the elevation of Joseph to a position of authority over his father, mother, and brothers—over the whole clan of Israel.

The brothers realized what the dreams appeared to be saying, but they could hardly believe it. Their angry response to the revelation, in contrast to Joseph's honesty and faithfulness, demonstrated very clearly why none of them was God's choice as future leader of the family, for those who would also be leaders cannot be consumed with jealousy and hatred over God's choice. But in their jealousy and anger they missed an important part of the revelation—they too would be stars, that is, rulers. But that did not register with them. All they heard was that they would bow down to him.

God's sovereign choice of a leader, especially if the one chosen is young, often brings out the true colors of those who have to submit to that leader's authority. Rather than recognize the hand of God, the brothers set out on a course to try to prevent the dream from happening—they plotted to kill Joseph. These actions again showed that they were not fit to lead the household of faith, and in fact, that they were on the very brink of not even being included in God's covenant program. What they would learn eventually was that there was no way to prevent God's plan from being fulfilled. And they would also learn that for them to share in that plan (and for them to be "stars"—exalted leaders) they would have to be dramatically changed.

So in the first part of the story, we learn that Joseph was faithful in his household responsibilities, that his father designated him as the heir, and that God chose him to be the ruler. None of that was acceptable to the brothers, for they were blinded to it by their envy. They represent the scores of people down through history who were driven by malice and envy because they were not committed to doing the will of the Lord.

The occasion for selling Joseph came when he again obeyed his father and went to Dothan to find his brothers (37:17). Even though he was being obedient to his father, his father was being foolish in sending him to check up on men who were obviously jealous of him. In spite of the hatred they had for him, Joseph went anyway as his father wished.

It took Joseph some time to find his brothers, but with help he located them in Dothan, far in the north. Did the brothers go all the way up into the hills because that was lush grazing land or because they wanted to be far from the watchful eye of their father, or possibly because they wanted to check out Shechem, the place where two of them had avenged Dinah's rape? The text does not say; it only says that Joseph eventually found them and that they were eager to use his visit to get rid of him (37:20).

When the brothers saw Joseph approaching, they devised a plot to kill the dreamer and end his dreams (their words were full of biting sarcasm). Earlier they had been incensed over their sister's rape, and two of them had avenged the crime by killing the Shechemites (ch 34), but now the brothers plotted to kill their own brother because he was faithful to their father and destined for greatness.

But Joseph's life was spared by the intervention of Reuben (37:21-22), who was trying to find a way to restore the boy to their father Jacob. His intention was perhaps to get back into Jacob's good graces after his violation of his father's concubine (cf. 35:22), which was probably an attempt to assume control of the clan. (In the end, however, Jacob effectively passed over Reuben in the blessings, 49:2-4). Reuben warned them not to shed blood because they were brothers. Instead, he suggested that they throw him into a cistern, with the thought that he would return later and rescue him. The brothers stripped the lad of his tunic and threw him into a cistern to die. They then callously sat down to eat.

Judah was not happy with leaving the boy there to die (37:26). Instead, he suggested that they sell the lad to some passing Ishmaelites who were on their way down from Gilead. So he would sell his brother, but he would not shed his brother's blood. The best we can say about Judah is at this time he was not faithful to the family covenant and sought his own way of living (see ch 38). The Ishmaelites had come from the child of the slave who was cast out for mocking Isaac. Whether the traders knew who these brothers were or not, it is ironic that they were the ones to enslave the heir of the leadership of the chosen people. Joseph had been treated very harshly by his brothers. Still, when he was sold for 20 shekels of silver (8 ounces) and carried off to Egypt, he was at least preserved alive.

When Reuben returned he was distressed over the turn of events, and tore his clothes in grief. What were they to do now? The old family propensity for deception seized the brothers' imaginations. Jacob was to be deceived again, this time by his own sons. They dipped Joseph's coat in goat's blood to deceive the father into thinking that his son was dead, probably devoured by a ferocious animal. They sent it to their father and coldly asked him to identify the coat—whether it was Joseph's or not. There is an interesting parallel with Jacob's own deception of his father in Genesis 27. There he used the clothes of his brother and the skins of the goats Rebekah had just slaughtered to deceive Isaac and to get Esau out of the way for the blessing (27:16); he even had his father feel the skins and the clothes to recognize him as Esau.

Jacob was devastated. He tore his clothes, dressed in sackcloth, and mourned for his son. Tearing one's clothes and wearing sackcloth were signs of great grief and mourning (cf. 44:13; Job 1:20; 16:15). Jacob refused to be comforted (37:35). Thus, the treachery was beginning to take its toll on everyone in the family. The sadness in Hebron is contrasted with the scene in Egypt. Hebron must have seemed so far away from Joseph now. He was sold to Potiphar, the captain of Pharaoh's guard (37:36). Joseph was alive and well, and he was about to begin his rise to authority, although it would not be by a direct route.

The story, then, is one of hatred and deception enacted against the faithfulness and goodness of one man. The brothers tried to improve their standing in the family by wicked means, by getting rid of this favored son. They all would have to learn that God does not give his promised blessing to people who act in such ways. If they would not learn this, if they would not change, there would be no nation through them. Here was the beginning of the suffering of Joseph. God was beginning to test his character, for he would have to learn obedience through the things he suffered (cf. Heb 5:8) before he would be a wise ruler.

B. The Corruption of Judah and the Confirmation of God's Ways (38:1-30)

About this time, Judah left home and moved to Adullam, where he stayed with a man named Hirah. ²There he saw a Canaanite woman, the daughter of Shua, and he married her. When he slept with her, ³she became pregnant and gave birth to a son, and he named the boy Er. ⁴Then she became pregnant again and gave birth to another son, and she named him Onan. ⁵And when she gave birth to a third son, she named him Shelah. At the time of Shelah's birth, they were living at Kezib.

⁶In the course of time, Judah arranged for his firstborn son, Er, to marry a young woman named Tamar. ⁷But Er was a wicked man in the LORD's sight, so the LORD took his life. ⁸Then Judah said to Er's brother Onan, "Go and marry Tamar, as our law requires of the brother of a man who has died. You must produce an heir for your brother."

⁹But Onan was not willing to have a child who would not be his own heir. So whenever he had intercourse with his brother's wife, he spilled the semen on the ground. This prevented her from having a child who would belong to his brother. ¹⁰But the LORD considered it evil for Onan to deny a child to his dead brother. So the LORD took Onan's life, too.

¹¹Then Judah said to Tamar, his daughter-in-law, "Go back to your parents' home and remain a widow until my son Shelah is old enough to marry you." (But Judah didn't really intend to do this because he was afraid Shelah would also die, like his two brothers.) So Tamar went back to live in her father's home.

¹²Some years later Judah's wife died. After the time of mourning was over, Judah and his friend Hirah the Adullamite went up to Timnah to supervise the shearing of his sheep. ¹³Someone told Tamar, "Look, your father-in-law is going up to Timnah to shear his sheep."

¹⁴Tamar was aware that Shelah had grown up, but no arrangements had been made for her to come and marry him. So she changed out of her widow's clothing and covered herself with a veil to disguise herself. Then she sat beside the road at the entrance to the village of Enaim, which is on the road to Timnah. ¹⁵Judah noticed her and thought she was a prostitute, since she had covered her face. ¹⁶So he stopped and propositioned her. "Let me have sex with you," he said, not realizing that she was his own daughter-in-law.

"How much will you pay to have sex with me?" Tamar asked.

¹⁷"I'll send you a young goat from my flock," Judah promised.

"But what will you give me to guarantee that you will send the goat?" she asked.

¹⁸"What kind of guarantee do you want?" he replied.

She answered, "Leave me your identification seal and its cord and the walking stick you are carrying." So Judah gave them to her. Then he had intercourse with her, and she became pregnant. ¹⁹Afterward she went back home, took off her veil, and put on her widow's clothing as usual.

²⁰Later Judah asked his friend Hirah the Adullamite to take the young goat to the woman and to pick up the things he had given her as his guarantee. But Hirah couldn't find her. ²¹So he asked the men who lived there, "Where can I find the shrine prostitute who was sitting beside the road at the entrance to Enaim?"

"We've never had a shrine prostitute here," they replied.

²²So Hirah returned to Judah and told him, "I couldn't find her anywhere, and the men of the village claim they've never had a shrine prostitute there."

²³"Then let her keep the things I gave her," Judah said. "I sent the young goat as we agreed, but you couldn't find her. We'd be the laughingstock of the village if we went back again to look for her."

²⁴About three months later, Judah was told, "Tamar, your daughter-in-law, has acted like a prostitute. And now, because of this, she's pregnant."

"Bring her out, and let her be burned!" Judah demanded.

²⁵But as they were taking her out to kill her, she sent this message to her father-in-law: "The man who owns these things made me pregnant. Look closely. Whose seal and cord and walking stick are these?"

²⁶Judah recognized them immediately and said, "She is more righteous than I am, because I didn't arrange for her to marry my son Shelah." And Judah never slept with Tamar again.

²⁷When the time came for Tamar to give birth, it was discovered that she was carrying twins. ²⁸While she was in labor, one of the babies reached out his hand. The midwife grabbed it and tied a scarlet string around the child's wrist, announcing, "This one came out first." ²⁹But then he pulled back his hand, and out came his brother! "What!" the midwife exclaimed. "How did you break out first?" So he was named Perez.* ³⁰Then the baby with the scarlet string on his wrist was born, and he was named Zerah.*

38:29 *Perez* means "breaking out."   38:30 *Zerah* means "scarlet" or "brightness."

NOTES

38:8 *marry Tamar, as our law requires of the brother of a man who has died. You must produce an heir for your brother.* The custom that informs this episode is the law for levirate marriage (*levir* is the Latin term for a woman's husband's brother). According to this custom, which was incorporated into the law of God (Deut 25:5-10), if a man died without children, his brother (or nearest relative) would marry his widow for the purpose of having a child who would carry on the family name of the deceased and who would inherit his property. Apparently the near kinsman could refuse to do this, as did the near kinsman in the book of Ruth (Ruth 4:1-8). That was his right, but he would be disgraced in the family because he refused to carry on his brother's name. In this passage, Tamar does not act on the basis of this custom until Judah's wife has died (38:12) and the family line appears to be coming to an end. Under the customary law of the times, which was later confirmed by its inclusion in the law of Moses, Tamar had a right to be the mother of Judah's child.

38:9 *whenever he had intercourse with his brother's wife, he spilled the semen on the ground.* This text is not addressing birth control per se; and neither is it addressing masturbation, although the term Onanism came to be used for that. The text is describing a man who took advantage of the levirate law (see note on 38:8) for his own sexual pleasure. He would have sexual intercourse with the woman, but would not fulfill the intent of the law that allowed him to do that, i.e, to raise up a child for the deceased relative.

38:18 *your identification seal and its cord.* The seal was an identification marker that was usually worn around the neck. A seal was rolled onto clay documents, leaving a unique impression. (For a helpful discussion of the identification seals used in the ancient Near East along with pictures of them, see IDB 5.254-260.)

38:21 *the shrine prostitute.* In the corrupt religious practice of the Canaanite fertility ritual, there were male and female cult prostitutes. The word for the female "shrine prostitute" in Hebrew, as well as in the Canaanite texts from Ugarit, is from *qadash* [TH6942, ZH7727], "to be holy,"—a *qedeshah* [TH6945, ZH7728] (female shrine prostitute) is a "holy one." In Genesis, the Hebrew word "holy" does not indicate morality or integrity; it simply means "set apart." The shrine prostitute was a woman who would not marry, but was set apart to the fertility ritual at the shrine (i.e., the sexual acts, which were intended to bring fertility by inducing the gods to act similarly). That the word is used here suggests that the event was connected with a festival.

There seems to be a hint in the passage about the individual scruples of the two men. Judah had sex with Tamar thinking her to be a regular prostitute, a *zonah* [TH2181B, ZH2390] (38:15). His friend Hirah was looking for a cult prostitute (*qedeshah* [TH6945, ZH7728]). Tamar could never have passed for a cult prostitute because she would have had to have been at the festival or at a shrine, not in the street. Was Judah only willing to go to the type that was not connected to religion? And did Hirah think that Judah would never have gone to a regular prostitute? These perceptions mattered in ancient Canaan.

COMMENTARY

This bizarre event seems out of place in the developing drama of the life of Joseph. It is an interlude to be sure, but when it is studied carefully, its place in the larger framework can be appreciated. In an earlier section that recorded events centered on Jacob, there was an interlude as well—namely, Genesis 26. It reported how God was blessing Isaac in order to show that God's plan was confirmed for the next generation, even though the men of Gerar tried to prevent it. Then the narrative returned to the stories about Jacob and Esau. This interlude (ch 38) tells what was happening in the family of Judah, which was far from the working out of a blessing. The strange events come together at the end to signify that God's plan (that the younger would have the preeminence over the older brothers) was confirmed in spite of their attempt to change it. As Genesis comes to an end (ch 49), Joseph's family will receive the blessing of the double portion in the inheritance, but the promise of leadership that normally goes with the firstborn would belong to Judah (Reuben, Simeon, and Levi being passed over).

Judah, who had come up with the idea to sell their brother into slavery (37:26-28), went to live in Adullam, about 15 miles northwest of Hebron. There he married a Canaanite woman and had three sons by her: Er, Onan, and Shelah (38:1-5). This marriage to a Canaanite woman contrasted sharply with what Isaac had told Jacob. Here it almost ruined Judah's family. Intermarriage with the Canaanites had been avoided earlier (ch 34), but not here. This episode of the assimilation of the family with the people of the land helps the reader understand why God sent the family to Egypt for a long period of growth: The Egyptians were strict separatists who would not intermarry with the Israelites. Therefore, the Israelites would be better able to keep their unique identity there than they would in Canaan.

Sufficient time passed for the sons to grow up and get married, so Judah got a wife for Er, a woman named Tamar (38:6). The text reports that Er was wicked, so the Lord took his life—we do not know what he did, or how he died (38:7). Then, by the custom of the levirate marriage (see note on 38:8), the second son, Onan, was to marry Tamar to have an heir for his brother. Onan, however, was not willing to provide an heir for his brother. Instead, he used the law for sexual gratification. He would have sex with Tamar, but not for its intended purpose, which is procreation. Since he refused the responsibility of providing an heir for his brother, God also took the life of Onan.

After this, Judah told Tamar to remain a widow until his youngest son was old enough to marry her (38:11). But he never intended that to happen, for even when he was old enough Judah still refused to give Tamar to him (38:12-14). What begins to emerge is the picture of a family in which the men were unfaithful, irresponsible, and far too Canaanite in their ways. It is interesting to contrast the story of Ruth, another widow, with this one: Ruth was dealing with a faithful, righteous man, Boaz; his virtue both continued the line of his dead relative and brought God's blessing.

Without a marriage, the future of Judah's family would be greatly restricted, especially when Judah's wife died a few years later. We hear nothing about Shelah except that in Numbers 26:20 he is the father of a clan of Judahites—the other two clans being from Tamar's sons. In order to continue the line of Judah through his firstborn son Er (deceased), Tamar pursued her right to be the mother of the heir.

As time passed, Tamar realized that she would have to take matters into her own hands if there was to be a future for the family. When Judah and Hirah went off to a sheep sheering event in Timnah, Tamar dressed up like a prostitute (*zonah* [TH2181B, ZH2390]; 38:15) and sat at the entrance to Enaim, a village on the way to Timnah. Judah was lured in and propositioned her (38:15-16). As a pledge that he would send the payment to this woman, Judah gave her his seal (see note on 38:18), its cord, and his staff. Later, when he sent his Canaanite friend Hirah to pay the woman and retrieve his things, she was nowhere to be found (38:20). Hirah had looked for a cult or shrine prostitute (*qedeshah* [TH6945, ZH7728]; see note on 38:21), but the villagers said they never had one there. Again Jacob's family experienced deception, this time by a Canaanite daughter-in-law.

Judah lacked integrity (38:16), and now in the climactic scene of the episode he is seen as a hypocrite (38:24-25). After three months, when word reached him that Tamar was pregnant, he condemned her to death as a prostitute. (This has to be one of the earliest examples of the double standard!) But when she produced the seal and the cord and the staff, proving that he was the father, he withdrew the condemnation. Judah acknowledged that she had been more righteous than he (38:26). She had won the right to be the mother of Judah's child, even though the way she did it was very risky. She was desperate because there were no responsible men around to ensure that there was an heir.

So here we have the account of sexual intercourse between Judah and Tamar. For Judah it was a sinful and irresponsible act, but for Tamar, it was not a sin because according to the law she had the right to be the mother of his child. Accordingly, in the book of Ruth, when the elders bless the marriage of Boaz and Ruth, they pray that God would make Ruth like Tamar (Ruth 4:12; cf. Matt 1:3, 5).

The last part of the chapter tells the outcome of this pregnancy and in so doing gives the reader the reason for this interlude being placed at this point in the narrative (38:27-30). God gave Tamar twins, and the line of Judah continued because of her. But the birth of the boys was unusual, paralleling the birth of Jacob and Esau in some ways. One twin's hand came out first, and the midwife tied a scarlet string around it, saying "This one came out first" (38:28). But the other twin pushed out instead, so he was named Perez (38:29; *perets* [TH6557/6555, ZH7289/7287], "breaking out" or "breach") to preserve the memory of this event. When the other twin was finally born, he was called Zerah (meaning "scarlet") because of the scarlet thread that the midwife tied on his wrist.

This episode is a mirror of the one wherein Jacob gained the right to rule over his older brother (27:29). What is so significant about this is the connection to Judah's dealing with his younger brother Joseph. He and his brothers had sold Joseph to Egypt, thinking that they could thwart God's plan that the younger would rule over the older brothers. Yet here in Judah's own family, despite his attempts to prevent Tamar from having a husband and children, God's will was manifest in a poignant confirmation of his plan: Twins were born, and the younger pushed past the older. Judah's line would carry on through Perez and not the first child Zerah (cf. Matt 1:3).

◆ **C. Joseph's Rise to Power in Egypt (39:1–41:57)**
   1. Joseph's temptation by Potiphar's wife (39:1-23)

When Joseph was taken to Egypt by the Ishmaelite traders, he was purchased by Potiphar, an Egyptian officer. Potiphar was captain of the guard for Pharaoh, the king of Egypt.

²The LORD was with Joseph, so he succeeded in everything he did as he served in the home of his Egyptian master. ³Potiphar noticed this and realized that the LORD was with Joseph, giving him success in everything he did. ⁴This pleased Potiphar, so he soon made Joseph his personal attendant. He put him in charge of his entire household and everything he owned. ⁵From the day Joseph was put in charge of his master's household and property, the LORD began to bless Potiphar's household for Joseph's sake. All his household affairs ran smoothly, and his crops and livestock flourished. ⁶So Potiphar gave Joseph complete administrative responsibility over everything he owned. With Joseph there, he didn't worry about a thing—except what kind of food to eat!

Joseph was a very handsome and well-built young man, ⁷and Potiphar's wife soon began to look at him lustfully. "Come and sleep with me," she demanded.

⁸But Joseph refused. "Look," he told her, "my master trusts me with everything in his entire household. ⁹No one here has more authority than I do. He has held back nothing from me except you, because you are his wife. How could I do such a wicked thing? It would be a great sin against God."

¹⁰She kept putting pressure on Joseph day after day, but he refused to sleep with her, and he kept out of her way as much as possible. ¹¹One day, however, no one else was around when he went in to do his work. ¹²She came and grabbed him by his cloak, demanding, "Come on, sleep with me!" Joseph tore himself away, but he left his cloak in her hand as he ran from the house.

¹³When she saw that she was holding his cloak and he had fled, ¹⁴she called out to her servants. Soon all the men came running. "Look!" she said. "My husband has brought this Hebrew slave here to make fools of us! He came into my room to rape me, but I screamed. ¹⁵When he heard me scream, he ran outside and got away, but he left his cloak behind with me."

¹⁶She kept the cloak with her until her husband came home. ¹⁷Then she told him her story. "That Hebrew slave you've brought into our house tried to come in

and fool around with me," she said. ¹⁸"But when I screamed, he ran outside, leaving his cloak with me!"

¹⁹Potiphar was furious when he heard his wife's story about how Joseph had treated her. ²⁰So he took Joseph and threw him into the prison where the king's prisoners were held, and there he remained. ²¹But the LORD was with Joseph in the prison and showed him his faithful love. And the LORD made Joseph a favorite with the prison warden. ²²Before long, the warden put Joseph in charge of all the other prisoners and over everything that happened in the prison. ²³The warden had no more worries, because Joseph took care of everything. The LORD was with him and caused everything he did to succeed.

NOTES

39:1 *When Joseph was taken to Egypt.* Following a chronology based on the dates and ages given in the Bible, Joseph was born in 1916 BC, entered Egypt in 1899 BC, and rose to power in 1886 BC (Merrill 1987:49). The events with these dates may be matched with the rulers of Egypt: Joseph was sold into Egypt when Amenemhet II was on the throne of Egypt (1929–1895 BC), and then the subsequent events took place under the reign of Senusret II (1897–1878 BC), and Joseph's administration would have continued into the reign of Senusret III (1878–1843 BC).

COMMENTARY

After the important interlude about Judah (ch 38), the story returns to Joseph, who had by then arrived in Egypt. The layout of this chapter is important: it begins with a paragraph telling how God was with Joseph (39:2) and enabled him to prosper; it then tells of Joseph's faithfulness to God to resist temptation and, in spite of that, how he ended up imprisoned again; it ends with a paragraph repeating that God was with him (39:21) and enabled him to prosper there. The first evidence of God's blessing gave Joseph the foundation to resist the temptation; the last gave him the confirmation that he did the right thing.

The important theological point, then, is the twice-stated fact that God was with Joseph so that he prospered in everything he did. In this chapter, he became the steward over the household of Potiphar. And because God was blessing Joseph, God also was blessing Potiphar (39:5).

Nevertheless, Joseph faced another test in the temptation by Potiphar's wife. Here we find one of the major motifs of wisdom literature being worked out in a dramatic form. Proverbs 5–7 warn the youth to avoid going with the foreign ("strange") woman because that is the way of disaster and death. The descriptions of the strange woman in Proverbs are personifications of evil, but Potiphar's wife was the real thing.

Joseph was able to resist the temptation because he had godly wisdom; he was convinced that God had a plan for his life and was determined to realize it. When the woman tried to seduce him, he refused to have sex with her because it would have been a sin against both God and his master (39:9). He knew that if he was to see the dreams of the sheaves and the stars fulfilled, if he was going to receive what God had in store for him, he could not sin against God. Besides that, wisdom would say that a woman like this could not be trusted anyway.

Joseph deliberately and wisely sought to avoid the woman's daily advances by keeping out of her way (39:10). His determination to resist this evil had been strengthened by the blessing of God in his life, his recent rise from being a captive to a place of authority. God had been at work in his life; he was not going to jeopardize that now.

One day she tried again. When he resisted her by running out of the house, she grabbed his cloak to be presented as evidence of a sexual assault. Humiliated by Joseph's refusal, Potiphar's wife fabricated a story that Joseph had tried to rape her. She showed the coat to the household and to her husband. In her accusation against Joseph, she claimed that this slave had come into their household to mock them (*letsakheq* [TH6711, ZH7464]; 39:14; cf. the same word used in 21:9). Potiphar was so furious that he had Joseph thrown into prison. (Whether he believed her story or not is hard to say—he did not have Joseph put to death). This was the second time that Joseph, while faithfully doing the right thing, was thrown into prison (cf. 1 Pet 2:11-25; 3:13-4:19). And this was the second time his clothing was used as evidence (cf. 37:31-33).

Joseph prospered in prison because God was with him. As a result, the jailor put Joseph in charge of the prison (39:22). Each time that Joseph prospers in this chapter, he is put in charge of something, first the household, and now the jail. These were signs to Joseph that God still had something wonderful for him to do. But would being thrown into prison discourage him in his faith? The events recorded in the next chapter (ch 40) answer this.

Chapter 39 shows that Joseph was a faithful and wise servant of God. Remembering the dreams of a future rule and seeing the evidence of divine blessing with him, he remained loyal to God rather than yielding to temptation at the first glimpse of his rise to power. Wisdom recognizes that allegiance to God is the first requirement of the ideal ruler. And what was true for rulers was also true for the people: They had to learn that they had to remain faithful to the Lord in spite of the circumstances and the consequences. No one can expect the blessings of God when he or she disobeys the word of God. Adam and Eve were the first to learn that.

◆ ## 2. Joseph's interpretation of the prisoners' dreams (40:1-23)

Some time later, Pharaoh's chief cup-bearer and chief baker offended their royal master. ²Pharaoh became angry with these two officials, ³and he put them in the prison where Joseph was, in the palace of the captain of the guard. ⁴They remained in prison for quite some time, and the captain of the guard assigned them to Joseph, who looked after them.

⁵While they were in prison, Pharaoh's cup-bearer and baker each had a dream one night, and each dream had its own meaning. ⁶When Joseph saw them the next morning, he noticed that they both looked upset. ⁷"Why do you look so worried today?" he asked them.

⁸And they replied, "We both had dreams last night, but no one can tell us what they mean."

"Interpreting dreams is God's business," Joseph replied. "Go ahead and tell me your dreams."

⁹So the chief cup-bearer told Joseph his dream first. "In my dream," he said, "I saw a grapevine in front of me. ¹⁰The vine had three branches that began to bud and blossom, and soon it produced clusters of ripe grapes. ¹¹I was holding Pharaoh's wine cup in my hand, so I took a cluster of grapes and squeezed the juice into the cup. Then I placed the cup in Pharaoh's hand."

¹²"This is what the dream means," Joseph said. "The three branches represent three days. ¹³Within three days Pharaoh will lift you up and restore you to your position as his chief cup-bearer. ¹⁴And please remember me and do me a favor when things go well for you. Mention me to Pharaoh, so he might let me out of this place. ¹⁵For I was kidnapped from my homeland, the land of the Hebrews, and now I'm here in prison, but I did nothing to deserve it."

¹⁶When the chief baker saw that Joseph had given the first dream such a positive interpretation, he said to Joseph, "I had a dream, too. In my dream there were three baskets of white pastries stacked on my head. ¹⁷The top basket contained all kinds of pastries for Pharaoh, but the birds came and ate them from the basket on my head."

¹⁸"This is what the dream means," Joseph told him. "The three baskets also represent three days. ¹⁹Three days from now Pharaoh will lift you up and impale your body on a pole. Then birds will come and peck away at your flesh."

²⁰Pharaoh's birthday came three days later, and he prepared a banquet for all his officials and staff. He summoned* his chief cup-bearer and chief baker to join the other officials. ²¹He then restored the chief cup-bearer to his former position, so he could again hand Pharaoh his cup. ²²But Pharaoh impaled the chief baker, just as Joseph had predicted when he interpreted his dream. ²³Pharaoh's chief cup-bearer, however, forgot all about Joseph, never giving him another thought.

40:20 Hebrew *He lifted up the head of.*

NOTES

40:13 *Pharaoh will lift you up.* Lit., "Pharaoh will lift up your head." This lifting up signifies restoration, in contrast to the lifting up in 40:19, which signifies execution (see note on 40:19).

40:19 *Pharaoh will lift you up.* Lit., "Pharaoh will lift up your head" (cf. 40:22). In Hebrew these are the same words as in 40:13, but in this context they signify execution in a general sense, leaving the precise means of execution somewhat uncertain.

COMMENTARY

While Joseph was taking care of the prison, two of Pharaoh's top officials offended the king in some way and were consequently sent to prison. These two were Pharaoh's chief cup-bearer and his chief baker (40:1-4). After a while they were put in Joseph's care (40:4). One night they each had a troubling dream that they could not interpret. When Joseph noticed they were depressed and troubled, he discovered what their problem was—their dreams. Without even hesitating for a moment, Joseph agreed to interpret their dreams. He explained that the interpretation of dreams belonged to God—especially since, once again, God was beginning to reveal himself through two more dreams. Joseph's eagerness to hear and explain their dreams tells us that he knew he was still able to interpret them, and most importantly, that he knew he had not misinterpreted his own dreams.

Joseph listened to them explain their dreams, then he offered the interpretations. The cup-bearer's dream reflected his occupation, but with accelerated activity (40:9-11). His dream had a favorable interpretation according to Joseph. The three vine branches of ripening grapes signified that within three days Pharaoh "would lift up the head of this man" (see note on 40:13), meaning Pharaoh would restore him to his office with all the honor due him. To this interpretation Joseph added his own request that when he was restored he would remember him and seek his release from prison (40:12-15).

The dream of the chief baker was not favorable at all. His dream also reflected his profession: He was carrying three baskets of bread on his head, and the birds came and were eating them. Joseph then explained that Pharaoh would also "lift up his head" (meaning "lift it off"—kill him; see note on 40:19) and within three days execute him, and afterwards the birds would eat his flesh. The interpretations Joseph gave the prisoners proved to be true, for in three days, on the Pharaoh's birthday, the cup-bearer was restored to his duties (40:20-21), but the chief baker was impaled (40:22). Joseph, however, was forgotten in prison (40:23).

There are two significant points that this chapter is making. First, the faith of Joseph had not faded. As mentioned before, his readiness to interpret the dreams indicates he still believed, not only in his ability, but also in the message of his own dreams. He had not abandoned the hope that they would be fulfilled. Second, when the dreams were fulfilled exactly as he had said, it would have been a tremendous confirmation from God of his understanding of dreams, and especially of his own. So Joseph now was even more certain that he did not misunderstand the dreams. He might not have foreseen his prison experience, but he knew what God was going to do.

Joseph would have been greatly encouraged to hear about the fulfillment of these dreams, although saddened by the death of the one man. The death speaks of the harsh realities of life in ancient Egypt with a king who was a law to himself. But the two dreams harmonize with Pharaoh's dreams (ch 41) that both good and bad days lay ahead. The dreams these people had were not trivial; they were messages from God, sounding an ominous warning about what each one was facing.

The cup-bearer may have forgotten Joseph, but God did not. Joseph's faith had not been destroyed by his circumstances. There were sufficient reasons for him to have been discouraged and to have abandoned all hope of ever rising to any position of authority. But he was still convinced that God's revelation to him in his own two dreams was true.

◆ ### 3. Joseph's interpretation of Pharaoh's dreams (41:1-40)

Two full years later, Pharaoh dreamed that he was standing on the bank of the Nile River. ²In his dream he saw seven fat, healthy cows come up out of the river and begin grazing in the marsh grass. ³Then he saw seven more cows come up behind them from the Nile, but these were scrawny and thin. These cows stood beside the fat cows on the riverbank. ⁴Then the scrawny, thin cows ate the seven healthy, fat cows! At this point in the dream, Pharaoh woke up.

⁵But he fell asleep again and had a second dream. This time he saw seven heads of grain, plump and beautiful, growing on a single stalk. ⁶Then seven more heads of grain appeared, but these were shriveled and withered by the east wind. ⁷And these thin heads swallowed up the seven plump, well-formed heads! Then Pharaoh woke up again and realized it was a dream.

⁸The next morning Pharaoh was very disturbed by the dreams. So he called for all the magicians and wise men of Egypt. When Pharaoh told them his dreams, not one of them could tell him what they meant.

⁹Finally, the king's chief cup-bearer spoke up. "Today I have been reminded of my failure," he told Pharaoh. ¹⁰"Some time ago, you were angry with the chief baker and me, and you imprisoned us in the palace of the captain of the guard. ¹¹One night the chief baker and I each had a dream, and each dream had its own meaning. ¹²There was a young Hebrew man with us in the prison who was a slave of the captain of the guard. We told him our dreams, and he told us what each of our dreams meant. ¹³And everything happened just as he had predicted. I was restored to my position as cup-bearer, and the chief baker was executed and impaled on a pole."

¹⁴Pharaoh sent for Joseph at once, and he was quickly brought from the prison. After he shaved and changed his clothes, he went in and stood before Pharaoh. ¹⁵Then Pharaoh said to Joseph, "I had a dream last night, and no one here can tell me what it means. But I have heard that when you hear about a dream you can interpret it."

¹⁶"It is beyond my power to do this," Joseph replied. "But God can tell you what it means and set you at ease."

¹⁷So Pharaoh told Joseph his dream. "In my dream," he said, "I was standing on the bank of the Nile River, ¹⁸and I saw seven fat, healthy cows come up out of the river and begin grazing in the marsh grass. ¹⁹But then I saw seven sick-looking cows, scrawny and thin, come up after them. I've never seen such sorry-looking animals in all the land of Egypt. ²⁰These thin, scrawny cows ate the seven fat cows. ²¹But afterward you wouldn't have known it, for they were still as thin and scrawny as before! Then I woke up.

²²"Then I fell asleep again, and I had another dream. This time I saw seven heads of grain, full and beautiful, growing on a single stalk. ²³Then seven more heads of grain appeared, but these were blighted, shriveled, and withered by the east wind. ²⁴And the shriveled heads swallowed the seven healthy heads. I told these dreams to the magicians, but no one could tell me what they mean."

²⁵Joseph responded, "Both of Pharaoh's dreams mean the same thing. God is telling Pharaoh in advance what he is about to do. ²⁶The seven healthy cows and the seven healthy heads of grain both represent seven years of prosperity. ²⁷The seven thin, scrawny cows that came up later and the seven thin heads of grain, withered by the east wind, represent seven years of famine.

²⁸"This will happen just as I have described it, for God has revealed to Pharaoh in advance what he is about to do. ²⁹The next seven years will be a period of great prosperity throughout the land of Egypt. ³⁰But afterward there will be seven years of famine so great that all the prosperity will be forgotten in Egypt. Famine will destroy the land. ³¹This famine will be so severe that even the memory of the good years will be erased. ³²As for having two similar dreams, it means that these events have been decreed by God, and he will soon make them happen.

³³"Therefore, Pharaoh should find an intelligent and wise man and put him in charge of the entire land of Egypt. ³⁴Then Pharaoh should appoint supervisors over the land and let them collect one-fifth of all the crops during the seven good years.

35Have them gather all the food produced in the good years that are just ahead and bring it to Pharaoh's storehouses. Store it away, and guard it so there will be food in the cities. 36That way there will be enough to eat when the seven years of famine come to the land of Egypt. Otherwise this famine will destroy the land."

37Joseph's suggestions were well received by Pharaoh and his officials. 38So Pharaoh asked his officials, "Can we find anyone else like this man so obviously filled with the spirit of God?" 39Then Pharaoh said to Joseph, "Since God has revealed the meaning of the dreams to you, clearly no one else is as intelligent or wise as you are. 40You will be in charge of my court, and all my people will take orders from you. Only I, sitting on my throne, will have a rank higher than yours."

NOTES

41:3 *scrawny.* The word used to describe the "scrawny" (*ra'oth* [TH7451, ZH8273]) appearance of the cows can also mean "bad," "ugly," or "evil."

41:5 *plump and beautiful.* The word for "beautiful" (*toboth* [TH2896, ZH3202]) can also be rendered "good" or "flourishing." "Plump" could also be rendered "healthy." I suspect that the two words form a hendiadys.

41:6 *east wind.* This may refer to the khamsin or sirocco (from Arabic *sherkiyeh*, meaning "eastern"). From February to June, this wind can come suddenly, blowing clouds of sand and burning like a furnace (see Skinner 1930:466).

41:14 *he shaved and changed his clothes.* The Egyptian nobility customarily shaved their heads and faces and wore artificial beards for ceremony. On their monuments, only foreigners and inferiors have beards. Joseph apparently had to be properly prepared to enter into the palace (see Driver 1891:341).

41:38 *this man so obviously filled with the spirit of God.* It is difficult to know exactly what Pharaoh meant by this. He at least recognized that there was a supernatural force at work in Joseph to enable him to interpret the dreams so readily. Since the Egyptians worshiped numerous gods, the reference at best could be to Joseph's god. The same question concerns Nebuchadnezzar's response to Daniel (Dan 2:47). In both events, a Hebrew was able to do what the wise men of the land could not do, and that indicated a divine spirit at work.

COMMENTARY

God had used two dreams to single Joseph out as the leader of Israel (37:5-9). He had used two dreams to test Joseph's faith in the prison (40:5-23). And now he would use two dreams to elevate Joseph from the horrible prison to the glory of the court. Joseph had proven himself faithful in the little things again and again; now he would be put in charge of great things.

Pharaoh's two dreams troubled him greatly, and none of the wise men of Egypt could explain them (41:8), so God used an Israelite slave to confound the wisdom of the world. Later, in the days of Moses, another Pharaoh would be at the mercy of God's power. And in the days of the Babylonian captivity, when Daniel was called on to interpret the dream of the king, this event in ancient Egypt must have been a source of confidence that "there is a God in heaven" who reveals the meaning of dreams (cf. Dan 2:28).

Naturally, Egyptian symbols are present in the dreams. The first dream had to do with cows. Cows liked to stand half-submerged in the Nile River among its reeds in order to take refuge from the heat and the flies. They then would come out of the water to find pasture. The disturbing part of the first dream was that seven ugly and gaunt cows (see note on 41:3) came up and devoured the seven fat cows. The second dream carried a similar message: Seven plump (see note on 41:5) ears of grain on a single stalk were swallowed up by seven thin and scorched ears of grain that sprouted after them.

None of the experts knew what to make of it. The magicians belonged to a guild that was supposed to be expert in handling the rituals of magic and priestcraft. But they could not interpret these dreams. Likewise, a later guild of wise men in Babylon would not be able to interpret Nebuchadnezzar's symbolic dream of the sweep of history. But Daniel would. In Egypt and in Babylon, a Hebrew captive would interpret the dreams, showing that no matter how powerful these nations became, they were still not beyond God's sovereign control. In both events the interpreters were rewarded: Joseph came to be ruler, and Daniel ascended to a high post in government.

Seeing the inability of the wise men to interpret the Pharaoh's dreams, the cupbearer remembered Joseph (41:8-9) and then told Pharaoh that Joseph was an accurate interpreter of dreams (41:11-13). When Joseph was summoned from the prison to stand before Pharaoh and interpret the dreams, Joseph declared that the interpretation was beyond his power, but not God's, who would interpret the dreams (41:16). After Pharaoh recounted both dreams to him (41:17-24; cf. 41:1-8), Joseph reiterated his conviction that God was making known to Pharaoh what he was about to do (41:25-27).

Both dreams predicted that seven years of abundant crops would be followed by seven years of famine so severe that the abundance would be forgotten. Moreover, the fact that Pharaoh had two similar dreams was evidence that the dreams came from God and would be fulfilled soon. As Joseph explained this pair of dreams, several things must have come to his mind: his own two dreams (37:5-9), his two imprisonments (37:24, 36; 39:20), and the two dreamers in the jail (40:5-23).

God's revelation demanded a response. So Joseph advised Pharaoh to choose an intelligent and wise man (41:33) to oversee the storage of 20 percent of the kingdom's grain during each of the years of plenty as rations for the coming years of famine. Wisdom literature teaches exactly this principle of wisely planning ahead rather than living for the moment (see, for example, Prov 6:6-11; 20:4; 31:21, 25, 27).

The man whom Pharaoh recognized as capable for such a task was Joseph himself, in whom was the spirit of God (see note on 41:38). Joseph had been faithful over small things and through the severe tests that God had sent him; now he would become ruler over all the land of Egypt under the Pharaoh.

God was showing his sovereignty to the world through this event. And the record of it would inspire confidence in his people when they were in bondage in Egypt (see Introduction, "Occasion of Writing"). He would again reveal his sovereignty over the nations when he gave another pagan king, Nebuchadnezzar, dreams that had to be interpreted by an Israelite.

♦ ## 4. The exaltation of Joseph (41:41-57)

⁴¹Pharaoh said to Joseph, "I hereby put you in charge of the entire land of Egypt." ⁴²Then Pharaoh removed his signet ring from his hand and placed it on Joseph's finger. He dressed him in fine linen clothing and hung a gold chain around his neck. ⁴³Then he had Joseph ride in the chariot reserved for his second-in-command. And wherever Joseph went, the command was shouted, "Kneel down!" So Pharaoh put Joseph in charge of all Egypt. ⁴⁴And Pharaoh said to him, "I am Pharaoh, but no one will lift a hand or foot in the entire land of Egypt without your approval."

⁴⁵Then Pharaoh gave Joseph a new Egyptian name, Zaphenath-paneah.* He also gave him a wife, whose name was Asenath. She was the daughter of Potiphera, the priest of On.* So Joseph took charge of the entire land of Egypt. ⁴⁶He was thirty years old when he began serving in the court of Pharaoh, the king of Egypt. And when Joseph left Pharaoh's presence, he inspected the entire land of Egypt.

⁴⁷As predicted, for seven years the land produced bumper crops. ⁴⁸During those years, Joseph gathered all the crops grown in Egypt and stored the grain from the surrounding fields in the cities. ⁴⁹He piled up huge amounts of grain like sand on the seashore. Finally, he stopped keeping records because there was too much to measure.

⁵⁰During this time, before the first of the famine years, two sons were born to Joseph and his wife, Asenath, the daughter of Potiphera, the priest of On. ⁵¹Joseph named his older son Manasseh,* for he said, "God has made me forget all my troubles and everyone in my father's family." ⁵²Joseph named his second son Ephraim,* for he said, "God has made me fruitful in this land of my grief."

⁵³At last the seven years of bumper crops throughout the land of Egypt came to an end. ⁵⁴Then the seven years of famine began, just as Joseph had predicted. The famine also struck all the surrounding countries, but throughout Egypt there was plenty of food. ⁵⁵Eventually, however, the famine spread throughout the land of Egypt as well. And when the people cried out to Pharaoh for food, he told them, "Go to Joseph, and do whatever he tells you." ⁵⁶So with severe famine everywhere, Joseph opened up the storehouses and distributed grain to the Egyptians, for the famine was severe throughout the land of Egypt. ⁵⁷And people from all around came to Egypt to buy grain from Joseph because the famine was severe throughout the world.

41:45a *Zaphenath-paneah* probably means "God speaks and lives." 41:45b Greek version reads *of Heliopolis;* also in 41:50. 41:51 *Manasseh* sounds like a Hebrew term that means "causing to forget." 41:52 *Ephraim* sounds like a Hebrew term that means "fruitful."

NOTES

41:42 *Pharaoh removed his signet ring from his hand and placed it on Joseph's finger.* The signet ring Joseph was given was a ring with a seal used for signing documents. The seal was impressed in soft clay, which then hardened and left a permanent impression of the ruler's seal and thereby carried the authority of the government.

41:45 On. This city was a center for the worship of the sun; it was seven miles north of modern Cairo and came to be known as "Heliopolis" (which is how "On" is rendered in the LXX), that is, "Sun City."

COMMENTARY

When Pharaoh installed Joseph in power, he gave him his personal signet ring (see note on 41:42), dressed Joseph in linen clothes and a gold chain, declared him second in command, and had him ride in the second chariot so that all the people could do homage to him. As a token of Joseph's new status, Pharaoh gave Joseph an Egyptian name: Zaphenath-paneah (the meaning is uncertain, but it may mean "God speaks and lives"—see NLT mg). Pharaoh also gave him a wife, Asenath, from the priestly family of On (see note on 41:45). All this happened 13 years after his brothers had sold him into slavery, for he was now 30 years old. God's sovereignty was evident in this turnabout (Ps 105:16-22).

The text then reports that Pharaoh's dreams were fulfilled as Joseph had interpreted (41:53-57). For seven years the land produced abundantly, and Joseph had a portion of the crops gathered into storage in the cities of Egypt, for he had absolute authority over all the land. But in spite of his high position and authority, Joseph never abandoned his heritage. He gave Hebrew names to his two sons: Manasseh (41:51; *menasheh* [TH4519, ZH4985], "causing to forget"), for he said, "God has made me forget" (*nashani* [TH5382, ZH5960]) the misery of separation from his family; and Ephraim (41:52; *'eprayim* [TH669, ZH713]), meaning "fruitful," for God had "made [him] fruitful" (*hiprani* [TH6509, ZH7238]) in the land of Egypt.

Joseph's wisdom paid off, for the seven years of plenty were followed by seven years of severe famine. The Egyptians, as well as people from other countries, came to buy grain from Joseph's storehouses. At last Joseph was in power in Egypt; God's revelations to him all those years ago were now beginning to be fulfilled.

◆ D. The Testing of Joseph's Brothers (42:1–45:15)
   1. The test of conscience (42:1-38)

When Jacob heard that grain was available in Egypt, he said to his sons, "Why are you standing around looking at one another? ²I have heard there is grain in Egypt. Go down there, and buy enough grain to keep us alive. Otherwise we'll die."

³So Joseph's ten older brothers went down to Egypt to buy grain. ⁴But Jacob wouldn't let Joseph's younger brother, Benjamin, go with them, for fear some harm might come to him. ⁵So Jacob's* sons arrived in Egypt along with others to buy food, for the famine was in Canaan as well.

⁶Since Joseph was governor of all Egypt and in charge of selling grain to all the people, it was to him that his brothers came. When they arrived, they bowed before him with their faces to the ground. ⁷Joseph recognized his brothers instantly, but he pretended to be a stranger and spoke harshly to them. "Where are you from?" he demanded.

"From the land of Canaan," they replied. "We have come to buy food."

⁸Although Joseph recognized his brothers, they didn't recognize him. ⁹And he remembered the dreams he'd had about them many years before. He said to them, "You are spies! You have come to see how vulnerable our land has become."

¹⁰"No, my lord!" they exclaimed. "Your servants have simply come to buy food. ¹¹We are all brothers—members of the same family. We are honest men, sir! We are not spies!"

¹²"Yes, you are!" Joseph insisted. "You have come to see how vulnerable our land has become."

¹³"Sir," they said, "there are actually twelve of us. We, your servants, are all brothers, sons of a man living in the land of Canaan. Our youngest brother is back there with our father right now, and one of our brothers is no longer with us."

¹⁴But Joseph insisted, "As I said, you are spies! ¹⁵This is how I will test your story. I swear by the life of Pharaoh that you will never leave Egypt unless your youngest brother comes here! ¹⁶One of you must go and get your brother. I'll keep the rest of you here in prison. Then we'll find out whether or not your story is true. By the life of Pharaoh, if it turns out that you don't have a younger brother, then I'll know you are spies."

¹⁷So Joseph put them all in prison for three days. ¹⁸On the third day Joseph said to them, "I am a God-fearing man. If you do as I say, you will live. ¹⁹If you really are honest men, choose one of your brothers to remain in prison. The rest of you may go home with grain for your starving families. ²⁰But you must bring your youngest brother back to me. This will prove that you are telling the truth, and you will not die." To this they agreed.

²¹Speaking among themselves, they said, "Clearly we are being punished because of what we did to Joseph long ago. We saw his anguish when he pleaded for his life, but we wouldn't listen. That's why we're in this trouble."

²²"Didn't I tell you not to sin against the boy?" Reuben asked. "But you wouldn't listen. And now we have to answer for his blood!"

²³Of course, they didn't know that Joseph understood them, for he had been speaking to them through an interpreter. ²⁴Now he turned away from them and began to weep. When he regained his composure, he spoke to them again. Then he chose Simeon from among them and had him tied up right before their eyes.

²⁵Joseph then ordered his servants to fill the men's sacks with grain, but he also gave secret instructions to return each brother's payment at the top of his sack. He also gave them supplies for their journey home. ²⁶So the brothers loaded their donkeys with the grain and headed for home.

²⁷But when they stopped for the night and one of them opened his sack to get grain for his donkey, he found his money in the top of his sack. ²⁸"Look!" he exclaimed to his brothers. "My money has been returned; it's here in my sack!" Then their hearts sank. Trembling, they said to each other, "What has God done to us?"

²⁹When the brothers came to their father, Jacob, in the land of Canaan, they told him everything that had happened to them. ³⁰"The man who is governor of the land spoke very harshly to us," they told him. "He accused us of being spies scouting the land. ³¹But we said, 'We are honest men, not spies. ³²We are twelve brothers, sons of one father. One brother is no longer with us, and the youngest is at home with our father in the land of Canaan.'

³³"Then the man who is governor of the land told us, 'This is how I will find out if you are honest men. Leave one of your brothers here with me, and take grain for your starving families and go on home. ³⁴But you must bring your youngest brother back to me. Then I will know you are honest men and not spies. Then I will give you back your brother, and you may trade freely in the land.'"

³⁵As they emptied out their sacks, there in each man's sack was the bag of money he had paid for the grain! The brothers and their father were terrified when they saw the bags of money. ³⁶Jacob exclaimed, "You are robbing me of my children! Joseph is gone! Simeon is gone! And now you want to take Benjamin, too. Everything is going against me!"

³⁷Then Reuben said to his father, "You may kill my two sons if I don't bring Benjamin back to you. I'll be responsible for him, and I promise to bring him back."

³⁸But Jacob replied, "My son will not go down with you. His brother Joseph is dead, and he is all I have left. If anything should happen to him on your journey, you would send this grieving, white-haired man to his grave.*"

42:5 Hebrew *Israel's*. See note on 35:21.   42:38 Hebrew *to Sheol*.

NOTES

42:5 *Jacob's sons.* Lit., "Israel's sons." Jacob's sons are frequently called "Israel's sons," using the new name that was given to the patriarch, in order to prepare the reader to think of the tribes of Israel and not just the sons of the patriarch.

42:15 *I swear by the life of Pharaoh.* Joseph was attempting to convince his brothers that there would be no change in his warning to them. He swore by the life of Pharaoh, meaning that as surely as Pharaoh lived, they would find his words to be true. Such oaths solemnized what was being said as certain, whether based on the life of God or the life of a person.

42:18 *I am a God-fearing man.* The word "fear" (*yare'* [TH3373, ZH3710]) is the common OT word used for a devout and obedient worshiper of God. For Joseph to use the expression would affirm that he was obedient to a higher power. Joseph's use of it in this context is likely to have eased his brothers' fears. They may have even understood him to mean that he worshiped the same God as they did.

42:37 *You may kill my two sons if I don't bring Benjamin back to you.* Reuben's statement here took responsibility and set him up to share the suffering of a father for the loss of a son. Should he fail in his responsibility, he would have to go through life grieving over his sons as Jacob had for Joseph, and as he would have for Benjamin.

42:38 *grave.* The Hebrew word here is *she'ol* [TH7585, ZH8619]; it is used to refer to several things in the Bible: (1) the grave, (2) death, (3) the realm of departed souls in an afterlife, or (4) extreme danger, a life-threatening experience. There is no clear occasion of the word being used of the righteous going to a realm in the afterlife—that place seems to be for the ungodly. Here Jacob would simply mean either the grave or death. (For a thorough study of this word, see Heidel 1954, in which there is an entire chapter devoted to death and afterlife in the OT world.)

COMMENTARY

According to Genesis 42–44, Joseph did several unusual things to his brothers when they came looking for grain. A casual reading might lead to the conclusion that Joseph was simply making life difficult for them. But there is more to it than that. Because of his dreams Joseph knew that his brothers were destined to be stars (i.e., leaders) under his authority. They were to play an important role in the future of God's program. But the last time Joseph was with them, they were filled with jealousy, hatred, and anger, so much so that they attempted to destroy their brother and deceive their father. That is not the stuff of leadership, spiritual or otherwise. Joseph's purpose, then, was to test them to see if they had changed. He could not simply ask them, or even be satisfied with observing them. He devised a plan whereby he could put them into situations that were similar to past events to see if they would act differently. If they did act differently, he would bring them to Egypt with him; if they did not, they would not be fit to lead the covenant community, and they would not be part of God's program to bring blessing to the world. It is the task of a wise leader to ensure that those who will have leadership responsibilities be qualified to do them.

The first test was a test of conscience. Joseph arranged things to see if the brothers remembered what they did to him and had any regrets about doing it. If they had no conscience about it, there would be no reason for pursuing any of the other necessary qualifications of leadership.

Genesis 42 opens with a note that the famine was widespread, reaching even Canaan where the family lived (42:1). So Jacob sent his sons down to Egypt to buy food for them. He sent all his sons except Benjamin (42:4) because he did not want to risk losing him. His refusal to send the boy suggests that he did not think his son would be safe with the brothers. Though Jacob did not know the details of Joseph's life, Jacob could not have been blind to the characteristics of these men (especially since he had gotten Joseph's reports about them years ago; cf. 37:2). Jacob's refusal to let Benjamin go likely had another effect as well—it would have opened an old wound by reminding the brothers of what happened to Joseph. Thus, even before Joseph could begin to probe their feelings of guilt or remorse, Jacob inadvertently pricked their consciences.

When the brothers arrived in Egypt, they came to Joseph and bowed down before him. Joseph recognized them right away. It must have been reassuring for Joseph to see his brothers bowing before him, for that is exactly what his dream had foretold. But he could not yet reveal himself and inform them of the fulfillment of God's revelation, for he had to bring all the family to Egypt under his rulership. Joseph "pretended to be a stranger and spoke harshly to them" (42:6-7). Speaking through an interpreter, he accused them of being spies—not once, but four times (42:9, 12, 14, 16). His rough treatment of them was designed to awaken their memory and prick their consciences. It was he, Joseph, whom they had considered a spy for their father, and it was he whom they treated roughly, even throwing him into a cistern. Joseph was putting them in a similar situation to see how they would react. When they protested that they were innocent men (42:10-11), they mentioned that there was another brother (42:13), something this Egyptian governor already knew. Joseph decided that he would keep them in prison until one of them went and got the younger brother—then he would know they were telling the truth. Retaining them in prison was a clever thing to do because it gave them time to think and react. It was also an interesting turn of the tables, a fact they may have caught as well, since they had thrown Joseph into a cistern prison while they decided what to do with him.

After a three-day custody of the brothers, Joseph altered his plan a bit: He would keep one of them there in custody, Simeon, and the other nine could go home with the grain they bought (42:19, 24). But if they did not return with the younger brother to prove that they were not spies, Simeon would be killed. With this new arrangement, the brothers began to sense that something powerful was happening to them. A sense of divine retribution began to awaken feelings in them that Joseph's cries for mercy (42:21) and their father's tears (37:34-35) had failed to awaken. They sensed that having to bring Benjamin back to Egypt against the wishes of their father was some kind of punishment for having sold Joseph to the traders. They began to accuse one another for the way Joseph had been treated. Reuben said, "Didn't I tell you not to sin against the boy? . . . Now we have to answer for his blood" (42:22). When Joseph heard this, he turned away and wept (42:24 cf. 43:30; 45:2, 14; 50:1, 17).

As a further means of putting the fear of God in them (42:18, 28, 35), Joseph had their silver (with which they had purchased the grain) put into their sacks of grain. At a way station one of them opened his bag and discovered the money. The sense of guilt that had already been awakened through the whole ordeal took on a different dimension with this discovery. They saw the hand of God in the governor's actions. They said, "What has God done to us?" (42:28). Actually, it was clear from their preceding feelings and words that they knew exactly what God was doing to them. But their question, as far as it went, was a fruitful reaction to their dilemma. They knew that the ruler would accuse them of theft, which would confirm that they were not to be trusted and were spies as suspected. And if God was doing this, then they faced a greater day of reckoning for their sins. They must have felt awfully uncomfortable, for once again they were going home to Jacob without a brother but with pieces of silver (cf. 37:28).

When the brothers told Jacob everything that had happened, he was filled with grief, thinking that another son—Simeon—was as good as dead as well. He was resolute: Benjamin would not go with them. Reuben stepped forward to try to assure their father that he would bring Benjamin back. This was not very convincing; after all, he failed to deliver Joseph out of the hands of his brothers (37:21-22). Jacob would not budge; he said that if anything happened to his youngest son he would sorrow the rest of his days, just as he had when he had heard of Joseph's "death" (37:35). Jacob's words must have also stung their guilty consciences: "You are robbing me of my children" (42:36). Jacob may not have known of their treachery when he said this, but they certainly did. Jacob probably was thinking of how they brought back the report of Joseph's death, and now might do the same if Benjamin were lost, but his words were strong and accusatory—they must have hit home.

The first stage in the reconciliation of the family comes to an end here. It was the test of conscience. The bad news was that another brother had been abandoned to Egypt, and the life of Benjamin would have to be put at risk if they were to see Simeon again. All of this was too much for Jacob. His grief must have weighed heavily on the sons. Nonetheless, the good news was that they had consciences (which had just been awakened rather harshly). As a result they were filled with guilty fears, knowing that God was beginning to deal with them.

◆ 2. The test of jealousy (43:1-34)

But the famine continued to ravage the land of Canaan. ²When the grain they had brought from Egypt was almost gone, Jacob said to his sons, "Go back and buy us a little more food."

³But Judah said, "The man was serious when he warned us, 'You won't see my face again unless your brother is with you.' ⁴If you send Benjamin with us, we will go down and buy more food. ⁵But if you don't let Benjamin go, we won't go either. Remember, the man said, 'You won't see my face again unless your brother is with you.' "

⁶"Why were you so cruel to me?" Jacob* moaned. "Why did you tell him you had another brother?"

⁷"The man kept asking us questions about our family," they replied. "He asked, 'Is your father still alive? Do you have

another brother?' So we answered his questions. How could we know he would say, 'Bring your brother down here'?"

⁸Judah said to his father, "Send the boy with me, and we will be on our way. Otherwise we will all die of starvation—and not only we, but you and our little ones. ⁹I personally guarantee his safety. You may hold me responsible if I don't bring him back to you. Then let me bear the blame forever. ¹⁰If we hadn't wasted all this time, we could have gone and returned twice by now."

¹¹So their father, Jacob, finally said to them, "If it can't be avoided, then at least do this. Pack your bags with the best products of this land. Take them down to the man as gifts—balm, honey, gum, aromatic resin, pistachio nuts, and almonds. ¹²Also take double the money that was put back in your sacks, as it was probably someone's mistake. ¹³Then take your brother, and go back to the man. ¹⁴May God Almighty* give you mercy as you go before the man, so that he will release Simeon and let Benjamin return. But if I must lose my children, so be it."

¹⁵So the men packed Jacob's gifts and double the money and headed off with Benjamin. They finally arrived in Egypt and presented themselves to Joseph. ¹⁶When Joseph saw Benjamin with them, he said to the manager of his household, "These men will eat with me this noon. Take them inside the palace. Then go slaughter an animal, and prepare a big feast." ¹⁷So the man did as Joseph told him and took them into Joseph's palace.

¹⁸The brothers were terrified when they saw that they were being taken into Joseph's house. "It's because of the money someone put in our sacks last time we were here," they said. "He plans to pretend that we stole it. Then he will seize us, make us slaves, and take our donkeys."

¹⁹The brothers approached the manager of Joseph's household and spoke to him at the entrance to the palace. ²⁰"Sir," they said, "we came to Egypt once before to buy food. ²¹But as we were returning home, we stopped for the night and opened our sacks. Then we discovered that each man's money—the exact amount paid—was in the top of his sack! Here it is; we have brought it back with us. ²²We also have additional money to buy more food. We have no idea who put our money in our sacks."

²³"Relax. Don't be afraid," the household manager told them. "Your God, the God of your father, must have put this treasure into your sacks. I know I received your payment." Then he released Simeon and brought him out to them.

²⁴The manager then led the men into Joseph's palace. He gave them water to wash their feet and provided food for their donkeys. ²⁵They were told they would be eating there, so they prepared their gifts for Joseph's arrival at noon.

²⁶When Joseph came home, they gave him the gifts they had brought him, then bowed low to the ground before him. ²⁷After greeting them, he asked, "How is your father, the old man you spoke about? Is he still alive?"

²⁸"Yes," they replied. "Our father, your servant, is alive and well." And they bowed low again.

²⁹Then Joseph looked at his brother Benjamin, the son of his own mother. "Is this your youngest brother, the one you told me about?" Joseph asked. "May God be gracious to you, my son." ³⁰Then Joseph hurried from the room because he was overcome with emotion for his brother. He went into his private room, where he broke down and wept. ³¹After washing his face, he came back out, keeping himself under control. Then he ordered, "Bring out the food!"

³²The waiters served Joseph at his own table, and his brothers were served at a separate table. The Egyptians who ate with Joseph sat at their own table, because Egyptians despise Hebrews and refuse to eat with them. ³³Joseph told each of his brothers where to sit, and to their

amazement, he seated them according to age, from oldest to youngest. ³⁴And Joseph filled their plates with food from his own table, giving Benjamin five times as much as he gave the others. So they feasted and drank freely with him.

43:6 Hebrew *Israel*; also in 43:11. See note on 35:21.   43:14 Hebrew *El-Shaddai*.

NOTES

43:14 God Almighty. The title that is used for God is El-Shaddai (*'el shadday* [TH410A/7706, ZH446/8724]). There have been many proposals for the etymology and meaning of this epithet for God, but none have been convincing. The older explanation of the name as "powerful one" or "overpowering God" may be the closest to the meaning. It would be a description of God as one who manifests himself in might, one who rules by might (see note on 35:11). In Jacob's words, it would describe God as fully able to protect his family and preserve the blessing (Driver 1891:404-406).

mercy. This word (*rakham* [TH7356, ZH8171]) means "tender mercies" and even "brotherly love."

COMMENTARY

As the famine continued in all the land, Jacob's family needed more grain. When Jacob prodded the sons to go and buy grain, they refused to go without Benjamin. Judah reminded their father that the man had said he would not deal with them if the younger brother was not with them. But Jacob was still reluctant; he wanted to know why they had told the ruler that there was a younger brother. This question was just an effort to delay the decision he had to make—Benjamin had to go with them or they would all die of starvation.

Judah broke the deadlock with a personal initiative by offering to take the blame if Benjamin did not return. Little comfort that would be for Jacob if this last son of Rachel's was lost. Nevertheless, Judah succeeded where Reuben had failed, and Benjamin went down to Egypt with his brothers. Judah's display of responsibility is heartwarming, especially since he was the one who came up with the idea to sell Joseph to the Ishmaelites (37:26-27). He seems to have changed.

Jacob instructed them to take all kinds of gifts to the man, the best products of the land, including balm, honey, spices, myrrh, pistachio nuts, and almonds (cf. 37:25). They also took double the money that was in their sacks. And Jacob had to resign himself to the high risk of losing a third son—first Joseph, then Simeon, and maybe Benjamin. All Jacob could do was pray that God would give them mercy (see note on 43:14).

The brothers hurried down to Egypt to get things settled, not knowing what to expect. They were quickly taken to the governor's (Joseph's) house. They were terrified, thinking they were going to be imprisoned and made slaves. They tried to explain the situation about money to the steward, but the steward told them not to be afraid because their God must have put that money in their sacks—the steward had received their payment in full. This delicately worded answer was true in a number of ways, but its effect was to bring God to their minds once again. How could God be doing these good things when they felt so guilty? God indeed had put the money in their sacks—through the wise dealings of Joseph. There was no need for the men to protest that they were innocent men; no one was accusing them of stealing.

They must have been delighted to be reunited with their brother Simeon (43:23). But then they were surprised to hear that they were going to eat with this ruler at noon. And when they came before him they were perplexed because he no longer treated them harshly but treated them kindly. They presented their gifts to him and bowed down to the ground before him, thus fulfilling Joseph's dreams precisely (37:7). When Joseph saw his brother Benjamin, he asked if this was the younger brother, the one of whom they had spoken. Then he blessed Benjamin, saying, "May God be gracious to you, my son" (43:29). Then Joseph was moved with compassion (43:30; *rakham* [TH7356, ZH8171]) and had to leave the room. By its description of the words and feelings of Joseph, the text is showing that the prayer of Jacob was being answered in a way that he could not have imagined, for he had prayed, "May God Almighty give you mercy [*rakham*] as you go before the man . . ." (43:14). Joseph could not hold back his tears; he had to leave their presence to compose himself (43:30; cf. 42:24). Joseph's tears were a mixture of painful memory along with joy and compassion.

At the meal, the brothers realized something else very troubling had happened—they were all seated according to their ages, from the firstborn to the youngest (43:33). It was clear to them that someone knew a whole lot more about them than they were comfortable with—they may have assumed it was God, or perhaps the ruler's powers of divination. Joseph may have wanted his brothers to think he had some supernatural power concerning them, whereas in fact, he simply knew them.

Even though they were likely uneasy, they enjoyed the meal, eating and drinking freely (43:34). At the meal Benjamin was highly favored—he received five times more food than all the others. Joseph was trying to see if there was a hint of jealousy in them, but there did not seem to be any, for they all were comfortable with the fact that Benjamin was being given special treatment (43:34). This was a second test, like the test of conscience earlier (42:1-38).

What a difference this trip made. The brothers were perplexed, but they were also confronted with generous and gracious dealings from God through this "Egyptian" (43:16, 27, 29, 34). By the end of their meal, they had passed the second test as well: They were not jealous of the gifts given to Benjamin.

In the household of faith, it is essential that people not only accept the fact that God gives different gifts to different people, but that they rejoice in those gifts. Envy and malice have no place in the family of God; they have to be purged like leaven at Passover. Each individual ought to be thankful for what God has given him or her, and not be concerned if someone else receives more. God is sovereign; he decides what each one receives.

◆   ### 3. The test of loyal love (44:1-34)

When his brothers were ready to leave, Joseph gave these instructions to his palace manager: "Fill each of their sacks with as much grain as they can carry, and put each man's money back into his sack. ²Then put my personal silver cup at the top of the youngest brother's sack, along with the money for his grain." So the manager did as Joseph instructed him.

³The brothers were up at dawn and were sent on their journey with their loaded donkeys. ⁴But when they had gone only a short distance and were barely out of the city, Joseph said to his palace manager, "Chase after them and stop them. When you catch up with them, ask them, 'Why have you repaid my kindness with such evil? ⁵Why have you stolen my master's silver cup,* which he uses to predict the future? What a wicked thing you have done!'"

⁶When the palace manager caught up with the men, he spoke to them as he had been instructed.

⁷"What are you talking about?" the brothers responded. "We are your servants and would never do such a thing! ⁸Didn't we return the money we found in our sacks? We brought it back all the way from the land of Canaan. Why would we steal silver or gold from your master's house? ⁹If you find his cup with any one of us, let that man die. And all the rest of us, my lord, will be your slaves."

¹⁰"That's fair," the man replied. "But only the one who stole the cup will be my slave. The rest of you may go free."

¹¹They all quickly took their sacks from the backs of their donkeys and opened them. ¹²The palace manager searched the brothers' sacks, from the oldest to the youngest. And the cup was found in Benjamin's sack! ¹³When the brothers saw this, they tore their clothing in despair. Then they loaded their donkeys again and returned to the city.

¹⁴Joseph was still in his palace when Judah and his brothers arrived, and they fell to the ground before him. ¹⁵"What have you done?" Joseph demanded. "Don't you know that a man like me can predict the future?"

¹⁶Judah answered, "Oh, my lord, what can we say to you? How can we explain this? How can we prove our innocence? God is punishing us for our sins. My lord, we have all returned to be your slaves—all of us, not just our brother who had your cup in his sack."

¹⁷"No," Joseph said. "I would never do such a thing! Only the man who stole the cup will be my slave. The rest of you may go back to your father in peace."

¹⁸Then Judah stepped forward and said, "Please, my lord, let your servant say just one word to you. Please, do not be angry with me, even though you are as powerful as Pharaoh himself.

¹⁹"My lord, previously you asked us, your servants, 'Do you have a father or a brother?' ²⁰And we responded, 'Yes, my lord, we have a father who is an old man, and his youngest son is a child of his old age. His full brother is dead, and he alone is left of his mother's children, and his father loves him very much.'

²¹"And you said to us, 'Bring him here so I can see him with my own eyes.' ²²But we said to you, 'My lord, the boy cannot leave his father, for his father would die.' ²³But you told us, 'Unless your youngest brother comes with you, you will never see my face again.'

²⁴"So we returned to your servant, our father, and told him what you had said. ²⁵Later, when he said, 'Go back again and buy us more food,' ²⁶we replied, 'We can't go unless you let our youngest brother go with us. We'll never get to see the man's face unless our youngest brother is with us.'

²⁷"Then my father said to us, 'As you know, my wife had two sons, ²⁸and one of them went away and never returned. Doubtless he was torn to pieces by some wild animal. I have never seen him since. ²⁹Now if you take his brother away from me, and any harm comes to him, you will send this grieving, white-haired man to his grave.*'

³⁰"And now, my lord, I cannot go back to my father without the boy. Our father's life is bound up in the boy's life. ³¹If he sees that the boy is not with us, our father will die. We, your servants, will indeed be

responsible for sending that grieving, white-haired man to his grave. ³²My lord, I guaranteed to my father that I would take care of the boy. I told him, 'If I don't bring him back to you, I will bear the blame forever.'

³³"So please, my lord, let me stay here as a slave instead of the boy, and let the boy return with his brothers. ³⁴For how can I return to my father if the boy is not with me? I couldn't bear to see the anguish this would cause my father!"

44:5 As in Greek version; Hebrew lacks this phrase. 44:29 Hebrew *to Sheol*; also in 44:31.

NOTES

44:5 my master's silver cup, which he uses to predict the future. This description of the divining cup was intended to make the men understand that Joseph could know things others could not. There have been a number of attempts to explain how this divining worked. It may have been hydromancy, in which water was poured into a cup and then pieces of silver, gold, or precious stones were thrown in and interpreted. Or it may have been lecanomancy, a form of divination in which oil was poured into a cup to give psychic insight, not unlike reading tea leaves (see Cryer 1994:145-147, 285).

44:16 God is punishing us for our sins. Or, "God has uncovered your servants' guilt." The words of Judah reveal that the events had uncovered their unresolved guilt. Their dealing with the Egyptians in trade, returning home with money in their bags, abandoning a brother to Egypt, and now the risk of losing Benjamin to Egypt all reminded them of what they had done to Joseph. The only conclusion they could come to was that God was now dealing with them for their sin, and since Joseph had already said that he feared God, they appealed to him on this basis.

COMMENTARY

Joseph's tests had proven successful so far. The brothers appeared to have changed: They showed remorse over what they had done to Joseph, they did care for their brothers, they were very concerned over what might happen to their father, and they showed signs of integrity in returning the money. But one more test was necessary: Given a chance to get rid of Rachel's other son, Benjamin, would they do it? And, by testing their care for Benjamin, Joseph was also getting them to remember once again the evil they had done to him. If they failed this test, if they had no regard for Rachel's young son, then they would have no part in the leadership of God's covenant people. God could start over again very easily and make Joseph into a great nation—as he told Moses he could do with him (cf. Exod 32:10).

The final test from Joseph involved not only putting the men's silver back in their sacks, as at the first trip, but also placing Joseph's silver cup in the sack of Benjamin. The men left Egypt for Canaan feeling very good about the situation; they had both Simeon and Benjamin with them, they had the grain they came for, and they were going home. But before they got very far Joseph's steward rushed after them and arrested them. He accused them of repaying his master's goodness (*tobah* [TH2896D, ZH3208]) with evil (*ra'ah* [TH7451B, ZH8288]), of having stolen his master's divining cup (44:4-5; see note on 44:5). The steward then created more tension by opening the sacks, beginning with the oldest before ending with the youngest. He knew, of course, that the cup was in Benjamin's sack. When the cup was found, the men were beside themselves (44:13). The sudden threat to Benjamin was like a sword thrust through their hearts. The steward had said that the culprit had to return to be his master's slave, and the rest could leave (44:10). Here was their best chance to be rid of Benjamin if they so wished: All they had to do was leave, and they could always say that they had no choice. Instead, they tore their clothes in grief, an act which they had earlier caused their father to commit over Joseph's apparent death (37:34). Judging from their reactions to this crisis, it is clear that the chastening had done its work. There was no way they would walk away and abandon the boy.

The brothers immediately returned to Joseph and once again bowed down before him (44:14; cf. 37:7; 43:26, 28). They were so filled with grief and fear that they hardly knew what to say. Judah again spoke for the group; he confessed that God had found out their iniquity and was punishing them, so that now they would all be Joseph's slaves. But Joseph reiterated what he had told the servant to say (44:10, 17)—that only the guilty person would remain; the rest were free to go.

Then Judah interceded for Benjamin with greater urgency. His lengthy plea to be enslaved in place of the boy (44:18-34) is one of the finest and most moving of all petitions. It demonstrated his concern for their father who would surely die if Benjamin did not return with them (44:31, 34; cf. 42:38), and it showed his willingness to give up his freedom, his family, and his future—to give up everything for the sake of his brother. Jesus said that there was no greater love than this, that a man was willing to give up his life for others (John 15:13). With this kind of integrity, Judah showed himself qualified to lead. Consequently, Jacob blessed Judah with kingship (49:10).

The brothers had demonstrated that they had repented of their sin against their brother (see note on 44:16), had concern for their father, and love for their brother. This is the stuff of spiritual leadership. God could use these men to build the covenant people so they would be a holy nation and kingdom of priests (Exod 19:6). Because of their change, Joseph could make himself known to them (45:1-15) and arrange for the family to join him in Egypt where there was food (45:16-47:12).

◆ ### 4. The reconciliation of Joseph and his brothers (45:1-15)

Joseph could stand it no longer. There were many people in the room, and he said to his attendants, "Out, all of you!" So he was alone with his brothers when he told them who he was. ²Then he broke down and wept. He wept so loudly the Egyptians could hear him, and word of it quickly carried to Pharaoh's palace.

³"I am Joseph!" he said to his brothers. "Is my father still alive?" But his brothers were speechless! They were stunned to realize that Joseph was standing there in front of them. ⁴"Please, come closer," he said to them. So they came closer. And he said again, "I am Joseph, your brother, whom you sold into slavery in Egypt. ⁵But don't be upset, and don't be angry with yourselves for selling me to this place. It was God who sent me here ahead of you to preserve your lives. ⁶This famine that has ravaged the land for two years will last five more years, and there will be neither plowing nor harvesting. ⁷God has sent me ahead of you to keep you and your families alive and to preserve many survivors.* ⁸So it was God who sent me here, not you! And he is the one who made me an adviser* to Pharaoh—the manager of his entire palace and the governor of all Egypt.

⁹"Now hurry back to my father and tell him, 'This is what your son Joseph says: God has made me master over all the land of Egypt. So come down to me immediately! ¹⁰You can live in the region of Goshen, where you can be near me with all your children and grandchildren, your flocks and herds, and everything you own. ¹¹I will take care of you there, for there are still five years of famine ahead of us. Otherwise you, your household, and all your animals will starve.'"

¹²Then Joseph added, "Look! You can see for yourselves, and so can my brother Benjamin, that I really am Joseph! ¹³Go tell my father of my honored position here in Egypt. Describe for him everything you have seen, and then bring my father here quickly." ¹⁴Weeping with joy, he embraced Benjamin, and Benjamin did the same. ¹⁵Then Joseph kissed each of his brothers and wept over them, and after that they began talking freely with him.

45:7 Or *and to save you with an extraordinary rescue.* The meaning of the Hebrew is uncertain.
45:8 Hebrew *a father.*

NOTES

45:7 *to preserve many survivors.* See NLT mg.

45:8 *an adviser to Pharaoh.* Lit., "a father to Pharaoh," which is probably an honorific title for the chief minister of the realm. It is used elsewhere for the advisor and administrator (see Isa 22:21).

COMMENTARY

In what is surely one of the most dramatic scenes of Genesis, if not the Bible as a whole, Joseph reveals his identity to his brothers. There is no way that Joseph could have done this without a burst of emotions; in fact, this is the third of five times in the story that he weeps (cf. 42:24; 43:30; 45:14; 50:1, 17). His brothers were absolutely stunned at this news, and they were afraid of what might happen next. But in that moment, as indeed throughout the testing of the brothers, Joseph's strong feelings were tempered by sound spiritual judgment. And so the reconciliation was able to happen because Joseph's tests showed that his brothers were reconcilable. It had been a task for a wise man, and Joseph had accomplished the task marvelously.

Joseph told his brothers that God had sovereignly brought him to Egypt to prepare for their deliverance from the famine (45:5). His words form some of the classic statements on providence: "It was God who sent me here ahead of you to preserve your lives" (45:5) and "It was God who sent me here, not you" (45:8). Joseph could look back on it all and know that God had been working through all the circumstances to bring him to this point. That he thought this when he was in the cistern or an Egyptian jail is unlikely. But the certainty that God's will, not any human's, is the controlling reality in every event comes through here as the basis for reconciliation. If it was not God at work, then one might feel free to affix blame on others. But the one who is spiritual can perceive the hand of God in every event, and therefore is able to forgive those who wrong him. It is essential that people who serve the Lord cultivate a healthy understanding and application of the sovereignty of God.

The brothers were reunited—first Joseph and Benjamin, then all of them—in an emotion-filled reunion. The brothers' previous hatred and jealousy of Joseph (37:4, 8, 11) had now come to an end, thanks to Joseph's magnanimity. Among those who seek to participate in the covenant plan of God, there is no room for revenge. With a generous spirit of reconciliation, Joseph fully welcomed his brothers. Then he instructed them to hurry home to Jacob without delay and inform him of his son's power as ruler and master of all Egypt (45:9-11). The whole family was to move to Egypt and live in the region of Goshen, a fertile area in the Nile Delta (cf. 47:1-12). According to God's provision for their circumstances, they were to dwell under Joseph's care. If they did not come to Egypt, they would not survive the five years of famine that remained.

◆ E. The Move of the Family to Egypt (45:16–47:12)

16The news soon reached Pharaoh's palace: "Joseph's brothers have arrived!" Pharaoh and his officials were all delighted to hear this.

17Pharaoh said to Joseph, "Tell your brothers, 'This is what you must do: Load your pack animals, and hurry back to the land of Canaan. 18Then get your father and all of your families, and return here to me. I will give you the very best land in Egypt, and you will eat from the best that the land produces.' "

19Then Pharaoh said to Joseph, "Tell your brothers, 'Take wagons from the land of Egypt to carry your little children and your wives, and bring your father here. 20Don't worry about your personal belongings, for the best of all the land of Egypt is yours.' "

21So the sons of Jacob* did as they were told. Joseph provided them with wagons, as Pharaoh had commanded, and he gave them supplies for the journey. 22And he gave each of them new clothes—but to Benjamin he gave five changes of clothes and 300 pieces* of silver. 23He also sent his father ten male donkeys loaded with the finest products of Egypt, and ten female donkeys loaded with grain and bread and other supplies he would need on his journey.

24So Joseph sent his brothers off, and as they left, he called after them, "Don't quarrel about all this along the way!" 25And they left Egypt and returned to their father, Jacob, in the land of Canaan.

26"Joseph is still alive!" they told him. "And he is governor of all the land of Egypt!" Jacob was stunned at the news—he couldn't believe it. 27But when they repeated to Jacob everything Joseph had told them, and when he saw the wagons Joseph had sent to carry him, their father's spirits revived.

28Then Jacob exclaimed, "It must be true! My son Joseph is alive! I must go and see him before I die."

CHAPTER 46

So Jacob* set out for Egypt with all his possessions. And when he came to Beersheba, he offered sacrifices to the God of his father, Isaac. 2During the night God spoke to him in a vision. "Jacob! Jacob!" he called.

"Here I am," Jacob replied.

3"I am God,* the God of your father," the voice said. "Do not be afraid to go down to Egypt, for there I will make your family into a great nation. 4I will go with you down to Egypt, and I will bring you back again. You will die in Egypt, but Joseph will be with you to close your eyes."

5So Jacob left Beersheba, and his sons took him to Egypt. They carried him and their little ones and their wives in the wagons Pharaoh had provided for them. ⁶They also took all their livestock and all the personal belongings they had acquired in the land of Canaan. So Jacob and his entire family went to Egypt—⁷sons and grandsons, daughters and granddaughters—all his descendants.

⁸These are the names of the descendants of Israel—the sons of Jacob—who went to Egypt:

Reuben was Jacob's oldest son. ⁹The sons of Reuben were Hanoch, Pallu, Hezron, and Carmi.

¹⁰The sons of Simeon were Jemuel, Jamin, Ohad, Jakin, Zohar, and Shaul. (Shaul's mother was a Canaanite woman.)

¹¹The sons of Levi were Gershon, Kohath, and Merari.

¹²The sons of Judah were Er, Onan, Shelah, Perez, and Zerah (though Er and Onan had died in the land of Canaan). The sons of Perez were Hezron and Hamul.

¹³The sons of Issachar were Tola, Puah,* Jashub,* and Shimron.

¹⁴The sons of Zebulun were Sered, Elon, and Jahleel.

¹⁵These were the sons of Leah and Jacob who were born in Paddan-aram, in addition to their daughter, Dinah. The number of Jacob's descendants (male and female) through Leah was thirty-three.

¹⁶The sons of Gad were Zephon,* Haggi, Shuni, Ezbon, Eri, Arodi, and Areli.

¹⁷The sons of Asher were Imnah, Ishvah, Ishvi, and Beriah. Their sister was Serah. Beriah's sons were Heber and Malkiel.

¹⁸These were the sons of Zilpah, the servant given to Leah by her father, Laban. The number of Jacob's descendants through Zilpah was sixteen.

¹⁹The sons of Jacob's wife Rachel were Joseph and Benjamin.

²⁰Joseph's sons, born in the land of Egypt, were Manasseh and Ephraim. Their mother was Asenath, daughter of Potiphera, the priest of On.*

²¹Benjamin's sons were Bela, Beker, Ashbel, Gera, Naaman, Ehi, Rosh, Muppim, Huppim, and Ard.

²²These were the sons of Rachel and Jacob. The number of Jacob's descendants through Rachel was fourteen.

²³The son of Dan was Hushim.

²⁴The sons of Naphtali were Jahzeel, Guni, Jezer, and Shillem.

²⁵These were the sons of Bilhah, the servant given to Rachel by her father, Laban. The number of Jacob's descendants through Bilhah was seven.

²⁶The total number of Jacob's direct descendants who went with him to Egypt, not counting his sons' wives, was sixty-six. ²⁷In addition, Joseph had two sons* who were born in Egypt. So altogether, there were seventy* members of Jacob's family in the land of Egypt.

²⁸As they neared their destination, Jacob sent Judah ahead to meet Joseph and get directions to the region of Goshen. And when they finally arrived there, ²⁹Joseph prepared his chariot and traveled to Goshen to meet his father, Jacob. When Joseph arrived, he embraced his father and wept, holding him for a long time. ³⁰Finally, Jacob said to Joseph, "Now I am ready to die, since I have seen your face again and know you are still alive."

³¹And Joseph said to his brothers and to his father's entire family, "I will go to Pharaoh and tell him, 'My brothers and my father's entire family have come to me from the land of Canaan. ³²These men are shepherds, and they raise livestock. They have brought with them their flocks and herds and everything they own.' "

³³Then he said, "When Pharaoh calls for you and asks you about your occupation, ³⁴you must tell him, 'We, your servants, have raised livestock all our lives, as our ancestors have always done.' When you tell him this, he will let you live here in the

region of Goshen, for the Egyptians despise shepherds."

CHAPTER 47

Then Joseph went to see Pharaoh and told him, "My father and my brothers have arrived from the land of Canaan. They have come with all their flocks and herds and possessions, and they are now in the region of Goshen."

²Joseph took five of his brothers with him and presented them to Pharaoh. ³And Pharaoh asked the brothers, "What is your occupation?"

They replied, "We, your servants, are shepherds, just like our ancestors. ⁴We have come to live here in Egypt for a while, for there is no pasture for our flocks in Canaan. The famine is very severe there. So please, we request permission to live in the region of Goshen."

⁵Then Pharaoh said to Joseph, "Now that your father and brothers have joined you here, ⁶choose any place in the entire land of Egypt for them to live. Give them the best land of Egypt. Let them live in the region of Goshen. And if any of them have special skills, put them in charge of my livestock, too."

⁷Then Joseph brought in his father, Jacob, and presented him to Pharaoh. And Jacob blessed Pharaoh.

⁸"How old are you?" Pharaoh asked him.

⁹Jacob replied, "I have traveled this earth for 130 hard years. But my life has been short compared to the lives of my ancestors." ¹⁰Then Jacob blessed Pharaoh again before leaving his court.

¹¹So Joseph assigned the best land of Egypt—the region of Rameses—to his father and his brothers, and he settled them there, just as Pharaoh had commanded. ¹²And Joseph provided food for his father and his brothers in amounts appropriate to the number of their dependents, including the smallest children.

45:21 Hebrew *Israel;* also in 45:28. See note on 35:21.   45:22 Hebrew *300 shekels,* about 7.5 pounds or 3.4 kilograms in weight.   46:1 Hebrew *Israel;* also in 46:29, 30. See note on 35:21.   46:3 Hebrew *I am El.*   46:13a As in Syriac version and Samaritan Pentateuch (see also 1 Chr 7:1); Hebrew reads *Puvah.*   46:13b As in some Greek manuscripts and Samaritan Pentateuch (see also Num 26:24; 1 Chr 7:1); Hebrew reads *Iob.*   46:16 As in Greek version and Samaritan Pentateuch (see also Num 26:15); Hebrew reads *Ziphion.*   46:20 Greek version reads *of Heliopolis.*   46:27a Greek version reads *nine sons,* probably including Joseph's grandsons through Ephraim and Manasseh (see 1 Chr 7:14-20).   46:27b Greek version reads *seventy-five;* see note on Exod 1:5.

NOTES

46:1 Because this is a transition section, it is helpful to keep the chronology of the patriarchs in mind. The dates are calculated by beginning with the later fixed dates in Israel's history (the building of the Temple, certain wars, and the captivities) and working back to the birth of Abram in 2166 BC. The call to leave Ur came in 2091 when Abram was 75. Isaac was born when Abraham was 100 (21:5; 2066 BC). Jacob was born when Isaac was 60 (25:26; 2006 BC). Abraham died at the age of 175 (25:7; 1991 BC). Joseph was born late in Jacob's life, when Jacob was about 91 years of age (1915 BC). Joseph was sold into Egypt when he was 17 (37:2, 28; 1898 BC). Isaac died at the age of 180 (35:28; 1886 BC). Jacob moved to Egypt at the age of 130 when Joseph was about 39 (47:9; 1876 BC). Jacob died at the age of 147, 17 years after moving to Egypt (47:28; 1859 BC). Joseph died at the age of 110 (50:26; 1805 BC). It was not long before a new king came to power who did not know Joseph, probably in the middle of the next century when the Hyksos took over in Egypt. The bondage would intensify, as Abraham's vision had prophesied, until Moses was born (ca. 1526 BC) to lead the nation of Israel out of bondage (1446 BC) and to the Promised Land (ca. 1405 BC).

46:34 *Goshen.* This area is not referred to in ancient Egyptian texts; the name it bore in later Egyptian writings was "the region of Rameses" (47:11; cf. Exod 1:11). This, plus the fact that the land was fertile and near to Joseph's court, suggests that it was located on the eastern side of the Nile Delta.

COMMENTARY

This section of the book (45:16-47:12) constitutes a transition wherein we see Jacob's family move from Canaan to Goshen, where they would live for the next four centuries. Goshen was in the northeast corner of the land of Egypt, only a few days' walk from Canaan. But the family of Jacob stayed there because there was food and water; later they were kept there by the Egyptians and were put to slave labor.

The brothers were given instructions about bringing Jacob and the entire family to Egypt (45:16-24). Pharaoh himself instructed them to return, offering them the best of the land, providing carts for transporting the family members back to the Delta (cf. 46:5), and promising them the best of the land of Egypt.

Joseph gave his brothers elaborate provisions for the journey—clothing, food, and for Jacob, the best things of Egypt. Joseph also gave them some advice as they left: "Don't quarrel about all this along the way" (45:24). There was the chance that on their journey home they might become anxious anticipating Jacob's reaction, or what Joseph might do later on, and in the process try to blame one another for the past. It was now time to put the past behind them and enjoy the reunion. The advice was timely because they would have to explain a lot to Jacob when they got home.

As might be expected, the old patriarch was completely stunned when he heard the news that his son Joseph was still alive and was ruling over Egypt. But then, as he listened to the details of his sons' story and saw all that Joseph had sent him, he was convinced it was true. He immediately began to prepare to move to Egypt and see his son Joseph, whom he had not seen for 22 years (45:26-27). This royal invitation to Jacob, an old man near the end of hope, and to the brothers, including the older 10, burdened with guilty fears, was a turning point in their lives and a fulfillment of God's prediction (15:13-16) that they would go into seclusion in a foreign country and there become a great nation without losing their identity. The joyful news about Joseph completely changed the lives of everyone in this family for the good.

Many years earlier Abraham had gone down into Egypt during a famine in Canaan (12:10; a little over 200 years earlier). Now Abraham's grandson Jacob and 11 great-grandsons (not counting Joseph who was already there) were moving there. God comforted Jacob about his move to Egypt. Leaving Hebron (cf. 37:14), Jacob's first stop was Beersheba, where he sacrificed to the Lord (46:1). This was where Isaac had lived and where Jacob had lived before he had to flee from Esau's anger (28:10). In the night, Jacob received a vision from the Lord, who repeated the promise that he would go with Jacob, make his family into a great nation there in Egypt, and bring them back again to this land (46:3-4). This revelation to Jacob would have been helpful for the Israelites in bondage to hear; it would have reminded them that God, the same God who led the family into Egypt promised to bring them out of Egypt to live in the land of Canaan.

After this the text lists the descendants of Jacob involved in the move to Egypt (46:8-27). In 46:26 the number of the descendants is said to be 66, whereas the number in 46:27 is 70. The first number represents those who traveled with Jacob to Egypt, and the second number includes the children and grandchildren already in

Egypt. Leah's children and grandchildren numbered 33 (46:15); Zilpah's children and grandchildren numbered 16 (46:18); there were 14 children and grandchildren of Rachel (46:22), and seven children and grandchildren of Bilhah (46:25)—totalling 66 people. Joseph, Ephraim, Manasseh, and Jacob make the total 70. This number does not cover the other members of the family, the wives, the servants, and others attached to them. But it is from these 70 that the nation of Israel would grow.

When Jacob saw his son Joseph, their reunion was overwhelmingly joyful (46:28-29). Once again Joseph wept (cf. 42:24; 43:30; 45:2, 14-15), and understandably so. The last time Joseph saw his father was when he was 17 (37:2). Jacob was satisfied just to see his son alive, his beloved son, the firstborn of his chosen wife, Rachel, and the one designated as the heir to the leadership of the family. So this was more than a family reunion; it was a confirmation that God's plan was intact—that they had not misread the signs so many years ago when Joseph first seemed to be God's choice.

When it came time for Joseph to present his family to Pharaoh, he encouraged them to stress that they were cattle raisers as opposed to sheepherders because Egyptians detested the latter (46:33-34). Joseph did not want to upset Egyptian custom and preference (cf. 41:14; 43:32), but when Joseph presented some of the brothers to Pharaoh, they did not respond with such diplomacy: They told Pharaoh outright that they were shepherds (47:3). Nonetheless, Pharaoh still gave Jacob's family the best part of the land, namely Goshen (cf. 45:10), even giving some of the brothers oversight of his own livestock (47:6).

When Jacob was presented before Pharaoh, the patriarch acknowledged his troubled life: "I have traveled this earth for 130 hard years" (47:9). It had been a long and difficult pilgrimage. When Jacob both entered and departed Pharaoh's courts, he blessed Pharaoh. God had promised that he would bless those who blessed the family of Abraham, and Pharaoh had certainly done that (cf. 12:1-3).

◆ **F. The Wisdom of Joseph's Rule (47:13-27)**

[13]Meanwhile, the famine became so severe that all the food was used up, and people were starving throughout the lands of Egypt and Canaan. [14]By selling grain to the people, Joseph eventually collected all the money in Egypt and Canaan, and he put the money in Pharaoh's treasury. [15]When the people of Egypt and Canaan ran out of money, all the Egyptians came to Joseph. "Our money is gone!" they cried. "But please give us food, or we will die before your very eyes!"

[16]Joseph replied, "Since your money is gone, bring me your livestock. I will give you food in exchange for your livestock." [17]So they brought their livestock to Joseph in exchange for food. In exchange for their horses, flocks of sheep and goats, herds of cattle, and donkeys, Joseph provided them with food for another year.

[18]But that year ended, and the next year they came again and said, "We cannot hide the truth from you, my lord. Our money is gone, and all our livestock and cattle are yours. We have nothing left to give but our bodies and our land. [19]Why should we die before your very eyes? Buy us and our land in exchange for food; we offer our land and ourselves as slaves for Pharaoh. Just give us grain so we may live and not die, and so the land does not become empty and desolate."

²⁰So Joseph bought all the land of Egypt for Pharaoh. All the Egyptians sold him their fields because the famine was so severe, and soon all the land belonged to Pharaoh. ²¹As for the people, he made them all slaves,* from one end of Egypt to the other. ²²The only land he did not buy was the land belonging to the priests. They received an allotment of food directly from Pharaoh, so they didn't need to sell their land.

²³Then Joseph said to the people, "Look, today I have bought you and your land for Pharaoh. I will provide you with seed so you can plant the fields. ²⁴Then when you harvest it, one-fifth of your crop will belong to Pharaoh. You may keep the remaining four-fifths as seed for your fields and as food for you, your households, and your little ones."

²⁵"You have saved our lives!" they exclaimed. "May it please you, my lord, to let us be Pharaoh's servants." ²⁶Joseph then issued a decree still in effect in the land of Egypt, that Pharaoh should receive one-fifth of all the crops grown on his land. Only the land belonging to the priests was not given to Pharaoh.

²⁷Meanwhile, the people of Israel settled in the region of Goshen in Egypt. There they acquired property, and they were fruitful, and their population grew rapidly.

47:21 As in Greek version and Samaritan Pentateuch; Hebrew reads *he moved them all into the towns.*

NOTES

47:21 he made them all slaves. The MT and the Syriac read, "he moved them all into the towns" (*he'ebir . . . le'arim* [TH5892, ZH6551]); but the ancient versions, notably the Samaritan, Greek, and Vulgate say that "he made them all slaves" (*he'ebid . . . le'abadim* [TH5650, ZH6269]). The difference involves a pair of similar looking letters (ר [*r*] and ד [*d*]) and one other letter (ב [*b*]), and either reading can be attributed to visual error by a scribe. Presumably the MT means that Joseph moved all the people to the places where there was food; but to reassign the population to towns would have served no purpose. The reading in the versions (which is followed here by the NLT) makes better sense in the light of the meaning of v. 20. Thus, the Egyptians worked for Pharaoh primarily and were not free to stop.

COMMENTARY

Joseph continued to be a wise administrator in the land of Egypt so that under his authority the people were saved from starvation and Pharaoh prospered (the ruler by now was Senusret III, 1878–1843 BC). In selling food to the people during the years of famine, Joseph collected money and livestock (horses, sheep, goats, cattle, and donkeys) as payment, and finally land, until all the land of Egypt belonged to the state, except for the land of the priests. Then, once the land belonged to Pharaoh, Joseph instructed the people to plant the seed that he provided. His requirement was that of whatever they grew, one fifth of it should go to Pharaoh. The people survived the years of famine, but they were in bondage to Pharaoh who owned the land.

In the land of Goshen, the Hebrews prospered and multiplied greatly (47:27). So God blessed his people according to the promise to Abraham that his descendants would be innumerable. And God blessed Pharaoh because he had blessed the seed of Abraham with the best of Egypt. (Later, in the days of Moses, when a different Pharaoh treated Israel harshly, God cursed him and his land.) Now in the land of Goshen, the descendants of Abraham could begin to look forward to the fulfillment of the second promise to Abraham—namely, receiving the land of Canaan.

◆ G. The Blessing of Joseph's Sons (47:28–48:22)

²⁸Jacob lived for seventeen years after his arrival in Egypt, so he lived 147 years in all.

²⁹As the time of his death drew near, Jacob* called for his son Joseph and said to him, "Please do me this favor. Put your hand under my thigh and swear that you will treat me with unfailing love by honoring this last request: Do not bury me in Egypt. ³⁰When I die, please take my body out of Egypt and bury me with my ancestors."

So Joseph promised, "I will do as you ask."

³¹"Swear that you will do it," Jacob insisted. So Joseph gave his oath, and Jacob bowed humbly at the head of his bed.*

CHAPTER 48

One day not long after this, word came to Joseph, "Your father is failing rapidly." So Joseph went to visit his father, and he took with him his two sons, Manasseh and Ephraim.

²When Joseph arrived, Jacob was told, "Your son Joseph has come to see you." So Jacob* gathered his strength and sat up in his bed.

³Jacob said to Joseph, "God Almighty* appeared to me at Luz in the land of Canaan and blessed me. ⁴He said to me, 'I will make you fruitful, and I will multiply your descendants. I will make you a multitude of nations. And I will give this land of Canaan to your descendants* after you as an everlasting possession.'

⁵"Now I am claiming as my own sons these two boys of yours, Ephraim and Manasseh, who were born here in the land of Egypt before I arrived. They will be my sons, just as Reuben and Simeon are. ⁶But any children born to you in the future will be your own, and they will inherit land within the territories of their brothers Ephraim and Manasseh.

⁷"Long ago, as I was returning from Paddan-aram, Rachel died in the land of Canaan. We were still on the way, some distance from Ephrath (that is, Bethlehem). So with great sorrow I buried her there beside the road to Ephrath."

⁸Then Jacob looked over at the two boys. "Are these your sons?" he asked.

⁹"Yes," Joseph told him, "these are the sons God has given me here in Egypt."

And Jacob said, "Bring them closer to me, so I can bless them."

¹⁰Jacob was half blind because of his age and could hardly see. So Joseph brought the boys close to him, and Jacob kissed and embraced them. ¹¹Then Jacob said to Joseph, "I never thought I would see your face again, but now God has let me see your children, too!"

¹²Joseph moved the boys, who were at their grandfather's knees, and he bowed with his face to the ground. ¹³Then he positioned the boys in front of Jacob. With his right hand he directed Ephraim toward Jacob's left hand, and with his left hand he put Manasseh at Jacob's right hand. ¹⁴But Jacob crossed his arms as he reached out to lay his hands on the boys' heads. He put his right hand on the head of Ephraim, though he was the younger boy, and his left hand on the head of Manasseh, though he was the firstborn. ¹⁵Then he blessed Joseph and said,

"May the God before whom my
　grandfather Abraham
and my father, Isaac, walked—
the God who has been my shepherd
all my life, to this very day,
¹⁶the Angel who has redeemed me from
　all harm—
may he bless these boys.
May they preserve my name
and the names of Abraham and
　Isaac.
And may their descendants multiply
　greatly
throughout the earth."

¹⁷But Joseph was upset when he saw that his father placed his right hand on Ephraim's head. So Joseph lifted it to move it from Ephraim's head to Manasseh's head. ¹⁸"No, my father," he said.

"This one is the firstborn. Put your right hand on his head."

¹⁹But his father refused. "I know, my son; I know," he replied. "Manasseh will also become a great people, but his younger brother will become even greater. And his descendants will become a multitude of nations."

²⁰So Jacob blessed the boys that day with this blessing: "The people of Israel will use your names when they give a blessing. They will say, 'May God make you as prosperous as Ephraim and Manasseh.'" In this way, Jacob put Ephraim ahead of Manasseh.

²¹Then Jacob said to Joseph, "Look, I am about to die, but God will be with you and will take you back to Canaan, the land of your ancestors. ²²And beyond what I have given your brothers, I am giving you an extra portion of the land* that I took from the Amorites with my sword and bow."

47:29 Hebrew *Israel;* also in 47:31b. See note on 35:21. 47:31 Greek version reads *and Israel bowed in worship as he leaned on his staff.* Compare Heb 11:21. 48:2 Hebrew *Israel;* also in 48:8, 10, 11, 13, 14, 21. See note on 35:21. 48:3 Hebrew *El-Shaddai.* 48:4 Hebrew *seed;* also in 48:19. 48:22 Or *an extra ridge of land.* The meaning of the Hebrew is uncertain.

NOTES

47:31 *Jacob bowed humbly at the head of his bed.* This is the reading of the MT; the Greek version reads, "Israel bowed in worship as he leaned on his staff." It may be that the Greek translator was thinking of some formality with a staff in sealing oaths, but all the other versions concur with the MT. The verb used in the MT is the primary word for worship in the OT; it means to bow oneself low to the ground. Probably Jacob turned over at the head of his bed to prostrate himself in silent gratitude to God for granting his last wish (cf. 1 Kgs 1:47).

48:16 *the Angel who has redeemed me from all harm.* The word for "redeemed" (*ga'al* [TH1350, ZH1457]) expresses the protection and reclamation from his troubles that Jacob experienced. It can also be rendered as "delivered." The "Angel" clearly refers to the Lord himself, for it is expressed in parallelism to "God" in this verse and along with "God" forms the subject of the verb "bless" in 48:16. Jacob probably had in mind the divine appearances and interventions of the Lord to protect him from his enemies (e.g., Hosea says he struggled with "the angel" and overcame him [Hos 12:4, referring to 32:22-32] so that he was blessed and delivered from Esau).

48:22 *I am giving you an extra portion of the land.* Convinced that God would take his family back to the land, Jacob said that a double portion belonged to Joseph (lit., "I give you one portion more than your brothers"). The word for "portion" is *shekem* [TH7926, ZH8900], a wordplay on the name of the town of Shechem (*shekem* [TH7927, ZH8901]; cf. 12:6; 33:18; 34:2). Later, Joseph was buried at Shechem (Josh 24:32) as a sign that he possessed this bequeathed land.

COMMENTARY

Out of Jacob's long life, the writer to the Hebrews selected the blessing of Joseph's sons as his great act of faith (Heb 11:21). This was an appropriate selection because in blessing Ephraim and Manasseh, Jacob was reaching out for the continuation of the promise in the face of death. Ironically, this is the very thing that he had tried to do by deception (ch 27). But this time Jacob was acting by faith—he now understood the plan of God and followed it fully. Once again the primary blessing would be given to the younger instead of the older son, but it would not be done with scheming.

Jacob lived for 17 years in Egypt, until he was 147 (47:28). Near the time of his death, he exhorted Joseph to swear that he would not bury him in Egypt but in Canaan where his fathers were buried (cf. 49:29-33). He was referring to the cave of Machpelah, which had been purchased by Abraham (ch 23). Jacob wanted Joseph to affirm that he would carry through on his promise, and so he asked his son to put his hand under his (Jacob's) thigh (47:29). This custom, seen earlier in the book (24:1-9), signaled a serious oath to carry on the covenant, which had as its main promise innumerable descendants in the Promised Land. When the oath was taken, Jacob worshiped (*wayyishtakhu* [TH7812A, ZH2556]) from the head of his bed (see note on 47:31).

Though Jacob was very frail, he sat up in his bed and rehearsed how Almighty God (*'el shadday* [TH410A/7706, ZH446/8724]; see note on 17:1) had appeared to him at Luz, which he had renamed Bethel, and had promised him the patriarchal blessing of innumerable descendants dwelling in the land as an everlasting possession (48:1-4; cf. 28:10-22). The words of this promise had provided the patriarch with hope throughout his life, just as they would bring hope to the people of Israel that sprang from him. They had the sure word from God.

When it came time to pass on the birthright, the double portion, Jacob gave it to Joseph by elevating his two sons (41:51-52) to the rank of firstborn sons. Later, these tribes of Ephraim and Manasseh would have equal shares with the other tribes that came from Jacob. In a way, these two tribes replaced Reuben and Simeon, Jacob's first two sons, born to Leah, because Ephraim and Manasseh became the prominent tribes of the north, and the tribes of Reuben and Simeon all but disappeared (1 Chr 5:1-2). In such passages where the tribes are listed, Ephraim and Manasseh inherit Joseph's double portion, and Levi, being the priestly tribe, receives no allotted inheritance. The blessing of Joseph's sons would have had an effect on the apportioning of the land of promise in the days of Joshua (Josh 16-17). Jacob's elevation of the sons of Joseph was prompted by the old man's fond recollection of Rachel, his beloved wife who died in the land of Canaan (35:16-20).

When Joseph presented his two sons to his father to receive a blessing, Jacob's eyesight was failing (as was the case earlier with his father, Isaac). And when Jacob blessed them, he crossed his hands (48:14) so that his right hand was on the head of Ephraim and his left on Manasseh—even though Manasseh was the oldest and would have been blessed with Jacob's right hand. This was clearly Jacob's decision in contrast to Joseph's instructions. Joseph, like so many others, expected that God should act in a certain way, according to convention, but found that he is often pleased to work unconventionally. Faith recognizes that God's ways are not man's ways and God's thoughts are not man's thoughts. It had taken Jacob a lifetime to learn this fact. But he did learn it, so now he deliberately blessed the younger over the elder. For four consecutive generations, that was the pattern that was followed: Isaac over Ishmael; Jacob over Esau; Joseph over Reuben; and Ephraim over Manasseh.

In his blessing on Joseph, Jacob used a threefold invocation (48:15-16): (1) the God who was in covenant with his fathers Abraham and Isaac (28:13; 31:5, 42;

32:9; 46:3); (2) the one who had been his shepherd (cf. 49:24; Exod 6:6; Ps 23:1; Isa 59:20); and (3) the Angel who delivered him from all harm (see note on 48:16). With these remarkable descriptions of God, Jacob prayed for God's gracious blessing on the boys. Here is another glimpse of Jacob's faith.

When Joseph saw what his father was doing, he was upset (48:17). But Jacob's words, "I know, my son; I know" (48:19), expressed the confidence of his faith—he was blessing according to the divine plan, not normal custom. He had learned that in spite of what man tried to do, God had blessed him, the younger brother. This he now carried forward to Joseph's sons. Years later, Ephraim became the leading tribe in the northern kingdom, superior to the tribe of Manasseh. In fact, the northern kingdom of Israel is occasionally called Ephraim (see, e.g., the NASB at Isa 7:2, 17; Hos 4:17; 5:3; 7:8; 9:3; 11:2-12:2).

◆ H. Jacob's Oracle for the Tribes (49:1-28)

Then Jacob called together all his sons and said, "Gather around me, and I will tell you what will happen to each of you in the days to come.

2 "Come and listen, you sons of Jacob;
 listen to Israel, your father.

3 "Reuben, you are my firstborn, my strength,
 the child of my vigorous youth.
 You are first in rank and first in power.
4 But you are as unruly as a flood,
 and you will be first no longer.
 For you went to bed with my wife;
 you defiled my marriage couch.

5 "Simeon and Levi are two of a kind;
 their weapons are instruments of violence.
6 May I never join in their meetings;
 may I never be a party to their plans.
 For in their anger they murdered men,
 and they crippled oxen just for sport.
7 A curse on their anger, for it is fierce;
 a curse on their wrath, for it is cruel.
 I will scatter them among the descendants of Jacob;
 I will disperse them throughout Israel.

8 "Judah, your brothers will praise you.
 You will grasp your enemies by the neck.
 All your relatives will bow before you.
9 Judah, my son, is a young lion
 that has finished eating its prey.
 Like a lion he crouches and lies down;
 like a lioness—who dares to rouse him?
10 The scepter will not depart from Judah,
 nor the ruler's staff from his descendants,*
 until the coming of the one to whom it belongs,*
 the one whom all nations will honor.
11 He ties his foal to a grapevine,
 the colt of his donkey to a choice vine.
 He washes his clothes in wine,
 his robes in the blood of grapes.
12 His eyes are darker than wine,
 and his teeth are whiter than milk.

13 "Zebulun will settle by the seashore
 and will be a harbor for ships;
 his borders will extend to Sidon.

14 "Issachar is a sturdy donkey,
 resting between two saddlepacks.*
15 When he sees how good the countryside is

and how pleasant the land,
he will bend his shoulder to the load
and submit himself to hard labor.

16 "Dan will govern his people,
like any other tribe in Israel.
17 Dan will be a snake beside the road,
a poisonous viper along the path
that bites the horse's hooves
so its rider is thrown off.
18 I trust in you for salvation, O LORD!

19 "Gad will be attacked by marauding bands,
but he will attack them when they retreat.

20 "Asher will dine on rich foods
and produce food fit for kings.

21 "Naphtali is a doe set free
that bears beautiful fawns.

22 "Joseph is the foal of a wild donkey,
the foal of a wild donkey at a spring—
one of the wild donkeys on the ridge.*
23 Archers attacked him savagely;
they shot at him and harassed him.
24 But his bow remained taut,
and his arms were strengthened
by the hands of the Mighty One of Jacob,
by the Shepherd, the Rock of Israel.
25 May the God of your father help you;
May the Almighty bless you
with the blessings of the heavens above,
and blessings of the watery depths below,
and blessings of the breasts and womb.
26 May the blessings of your father
surpass the blessings of the ancient mountains,*
reaching to the heights of the eternal hills.
May these blessings rest on the head of Joseph,
who is a prince among his brothers.

27 "Benjamin is a ravenous wolf,
devouring his enemies in the morning
and dividing his plunder in the evening."

28These are the twelve tribes of Israel, and this is what their father said as he told his sons good-bye. He blessed each one with an appropriate message.

49:10a Hebrew *from between his feet.* 49:10b Or *until tribute is brought to him and the peoples obey;* traditionally rendered *until Shiloh comes.* 49:14 Or *sheepfolds,* or *hearths.* 49:22 Or *Joseph is a fruitful tree, / a fruitful tree beside a spring. / His branches reach over the wall.* The meaning of the Hebrew is uncertain. 49:26 Or *of my ancestors.*

NOTES

49:1 *the days to come.* Lit., "the latter days" (*be'akharith* [TH8712/319, ZH928/344] *hayyomim* [TH18861/3117, ZH2021/3427]). The term referenced the distant future from Jacob's point of view.

49:8 *Judah, your brothers will praise you.* The name "Judah" is a related to the verb "to praise." Earlier Leah had said, "I will praise the Lord" (see note on 29:35). Here the sentiment is that his brothers will give him praise.

49:10 *scepter.* This is the symbol of kingship; it represents the authority of the government to rule over the affairs of the people (see Num 24:17; Ps 45:6; see also Isa 14:5; Amos 1:5, 8; Zech 10:11, NASB). The oracle declares that kingship will remain in the tribe of Judah until the one great king comes to whom it belongs forever.

from his descendants. Lit., "from between his feet." "Descendants" is a euphemistic translation that parallels the euphemism found in the Hebrew text, "from between his feet," which means "from his loins." The expression is parallel to Judah in the first half, so it refers to the descendants of Judah.

until the coming of the one to whom it belongs. As noted in the NLT mg this may be rendered "until tribute is brought to him and the peoples obey," and is traditionally rendered as "until Shiloh comes." The Hebrew word *shiloh* [TH7886/7887A, ZH8869/8870], often rendered as a name, "Shiloh," has been given a number of interpretations. It can be understood as meaning "who—to him" or "to whom it [the scepter] belongs" (in which case it is usually repointed as *shelloh* [TH7578.7/3807.1/2050.2, ZH8611/4200/2257]). Some versions, including the Aramaic Targums, see the word as a title of the Messiah. So the scepter would not depart from the line of Judah until the one to whom it was promised claimed it.

49:18 *I trust in you for salvation, O LORD!* The verb could be rendered as "hope." At this point in the oracle, Jacob interjected an expression of hope. He may have been indirectly reminding his sons of their need for dependence on the Lord (if he needed it, they certainly did too). Or he may have been expressing his desire to enjoy the messianic hope, when he would be delivered from all trouble and grief (cf. Anna's encouragement to those waiting for God to rescue them in Luke 2:38).

COMMENTARY

A fundamental principle in Genesis is that the characters and actions of the ancestors will affect the lives of their descendants, or, to put it another way, the sins of the fathers will be visited on subsequent generations. Both in Genesis 9 and 49, as well as in Genesis 3 (to some extent), God predicts the destinies and deeds of his people according to their inherited moral and spiritual distinctives. Genesis 49 gives the reader just such a plan; furthermore, it includes the last of the great sayings in the book—blessings, curses, judgments, prophecies, and promises. Jacob, as God's spokesman, looked forward to Israel's settlement in the land, and even beyond that to the glorious future age to come, and foretold what would happen to each tribe.

God gave the people this prophecy to see them through the long years of bondage outside the Promised Land and to show them that he had the future planned for them. For Jacob's family, the future was not in Egypt but in the Promised Land, where they would enjoy the manifold blessings of God. But the enjoyment of those promises would depend on the participants' faithfulness. So from the solemnity of his deathbed, Jacob evaluated his sons one by one, carrying his evaluation well into the future.

In calling his sons around his deathbed, Jacob announced that he was going to tell them what would become of them in the latter days (see note on 49:1). His words, then, were a deliberately chosen prophetic oracle, for the latter days would be in the future, extending to the conquest and settlement and beyond to the messianic age. They all would have a share in the blessing; all the tribes would enter the land with Joshua. But they would not all have equal participation in the many aspects of the blessing—and that is what this oracle announces.

The first oracle was for Reuben (49:3-4). At first Jacob heaped praise on Reuben, his firstborn, his strength. But the praise collapsed when he announced that Reuben had defiled his father's marriage bed, a clear reference to the son's adultery with Jacob's concubine Bilhah (35:22). As firstborn, Reuben would have been entitled to the leadership of the family and a double inheritance (1 Chr 5:1-2), but because he had ungoverned impulses, being like boiling or turbulent waters, he would fail in leadership. Jacob prophesied that Reuben would no longer excel. Reuben should have been a strong leader, the firstborn of Jacob's strength, but because of his internal weaknesses, he would never assume that role. In the time of the Judges, the tribe of Reuben was characterized by indecision (Judg 5:15-16), and afterward, Reuben played no major role in the history of Israel.

Simeon and Levi had proven to be men of anarchy and violence, not justice, men of uncontrolled anger and fury, with disregard for life, human or animal (49:5-7). This was God's oracle against their slaughter of the people of Shechem (34:24-29). God distinguishes holy war and justice from vengeance. Later, in the period of the settlement, both these tribes were scattered (49:7). Simeon was largely disintegrated with its land inside Judah's (Josh 19:1, 9), but Levi was given a more honorable settlement because it became the priestly tribe—and yet, this tribe had no land to possess (Josh 21).

The blessing on Judah commands the most attention (49:8-12). In this oracle Jacob predicted a fierce lionlike dominance of Judah over his enemies and over his brothers, who would praise him. A wordplay on the name of Judah (which means "praise") calls attention to the message (see note on 49:8). The scepter would not depart from Judah until the coming of the one to whom it belongs. The oracle pivots on the word "until" (49:10b). These verses anticipate the kingship in Judah culminating in the reign of the Messiah, when all the nations will obey him. There was going to be a long line of kings who would retain the scepter; the last one would be the one to whom it belonged. The Old Testament looked forward to the coming king who would take up the scepter of Judah (e.g., Pss 2, 45; Isa 9:6-7; Mic 5:2). The New Testament confirmed that the fulfillment of these promises would be in Jesus the Messiah (e.g., Luke 2:29-33), but that the universal reign of righteousness and peace awaits his second coming (see Heb 1:5 for his exaltation to the throne; Heb 1:6 [NLT mg] for the second coming, and Heb 1:8-9 for his righteous reign; see also 1 Cor 15:20-28).

When the Messiah comes there will be Paradise-like splendor on the earth. Kidner observes that every line in 49:11-12 "speaks of exuberant, intoxicating abundance: it is the golden age of the coming one, whose universal rule was glimpsed in v. 10c" (1967:219). According to this vision, grapevines will be so abundant that they will be used for hitching posts; wine will be as abundant as fresh water. In Judah, people's eyes will be red or bright from the wine, and their teeth will be white from the milk. These are picturesque ways of describing the suitability of Judah's territory for vineyards and abundant herds; they are also predictions of the paradisal abundance that will be evident in the Kingdom of God (Isa 61:6-7; 65:21-25; Zech 3:10). Jesus' miracle of changing water into wine, his first sign (John 2:1-12), was an announcement that Messiah had come, and a foretaste of things to come.

Zebulun was to be enriched by seaborne trade (49:13). The poetry of this oracle is difficult, but the description indicates that Zebulun would live near or in the direction of the seashore and be a haven for ships, its area extending as far north as Sidon. According to Joshua 19:10-15, the tribe was to be settled mainly inland.

Probably the exact borders of the settled tribes fluctuated somewhat through history (with Dan even moving from the south to the north).

Like a strong donkey, the tribe of Issachar would be forced to work for others (49:14-15). Issachar was located in the fertile, broad, pleasant plain of Esdraelon (identified with the Jezreel Valley). This is the valley that stretches from the Mediterranean Sea to the Jordan Valley; the major routes from the north and the south, east and west, passed through this valley. Because of its strategic location and its flat land, it formed a natural battlefield—as the history of Megiddo on its southern side attests (see 2 Kgs 23:29; see also Rev 16:16), or as the battle of Deborah and Barak on the northern side also shows (Judg 4:14-16; 5:19-21).

Dan was exposed for showing disparity between his calling and his achievements (49:16-17; cf. 49:3-4). Dan was to provide justice ("Dan" means "judge"), but the tribe chose treachery, like a snake by the roadside. In the time of the judges, the first major practice of idolatry appeared in the tribe of Dan (Judg 18:1-31).

The oracle concerning Gad focuses on attacking and being attacked (49:19). Three of the six words in verse 19 are a play on the name "Gad" using the verb *gud* [TH1464, ZH1574] (to break into, attack): Gad will be attacked by a raid of attackers, but he will attack. Border raids were often experienced by the tribes that settled east of the Jordan River (e.g., 1 Chr 5:18-19).

Asher would be fertile and productive, providing rich food (49:20). That tribe settled along the rich northern coast of Canaan. Naphtali, like a doe, would be free mountain people (49:21). Later, Deborah sang of the people of Naphtali risking their lives on the heights of the field (Judg 5:18). The tribe settled northwest of the Sea of Kinnereth (Galilee).

The oracle in 49:22-26 treats Joseph more lavishly than any of the others, for he received the greatest blessing (cf. 1 Chr 5:1-2). Jacob took up the promise of fruitfulness from the name of Joseph's son Ephraim (which means "fruitful") and lavished the promise of victory (49:23-24a) and prosperity (49:25b) on Joseph's two tribes. Victory in battle was experienced by Joshua, Deborah, and Samuel, all from the tribe of Ephraim, and by Gideon and Jephthah, both of Manasseh. In these verses, we have several marvelous titles for God: the Mighty One of Jacob, the Shepherd, the Rock of Israel, the God of your father, the Almighty, the one who ensures blessings from the heavens above (i.e., rain for crops), from the watery depths below (i.e., streams and wells of water), and from the breasts and womb (i.e., abundant offspring). Jacob bestowed on Joseph the greater blessings because he was the prince among his brothers (cf. 41:41).

The oracle about Benjamin describes a tribe violent in spirit (49:27)—a ravenous, devouring wolf. This spirit can be seen in the cruel behavior of the Benjamites (Judg 20), as well as in Saul, a Benjamite (1 Sam 9:1-2; 19:10; 22:17).

These prophecies are necessarily broad in their scope; thus they foretell the general circumstances of the different tribes. Individuals from any of the tribes could find, by faith and obedience, the great blessing of God no matter what might happen in general to their family and their clan.

◆ I. The Death and Burial of Jacob (49:29–50:14)

²⁹Then Jacob instructed them, "Soon I will die and join my ancestors. Bury me with my father and grandfather in the cave in the field of Ephron the Hittite. ³⁰This is the cave in the field of Machpelah, near Mamre in Canaan, that Abraham bought from Ephron the Hittite as a permanent burial site. ³¹There Abraham and his wife Sarah are buried. There Isaac and his wife, Rebekah, are buried. And there I buried Leah. ³²It is the plot of land and the cave that my grandfather Abraham bought from the Hittites."

³³When Jacob had finished this charge to his sons, he drew his feet into the bed, breathed his last, and joined his ancestors in death.

CHAPTER 50

Joseph threw himself on his father and wept over him and kissed him. ²Then Joseph told the physicians who served him to embalm his father's body; so Jacob* was embalmed. ³The embalming process took the usual forty days. And the Egyptians mourned his death for seventy days.

⁴When the period of mourning was over, Joseph approached Pharaoh's advisers and said, "Please do me this favor and speak to Pharaoh on my behalf. ⁵Tell him that my father made me swear an oath. He said to me, 'Listen, I am about to die. Take my body back to the land of Canaan, and bury me in the tomb I prepared for myself.' So please allow me to go and bury my father. After his burial, I will return without delay."

⁶Pharaoh agreed to Joseph's request. "Go and bury your father, as he made you promise," he said. ⁷So Joseph went up to bury his father. He was accompanied by all of Pharaoh's officials, all the senior members of Pharaoh's household, and all the senior officers of Egypt. ⁸Joseph also took his entire household and his brothers and their households. But they left their little children and flocks and herds in the land of Goshen. ⁹A great number of chariots and charioteers accompanied Joseph.

¹⁰When they arrived at the threshing floor of Atad, near the Jordan River, they held a very great and solemn memorial service, with a seven-day period of mourning for Joseph's father. ¹¹The local residents, the Canaanites, watched them mourning at the threshing floor of Atad. Then they renamed that place (which is near the Jordan) Abel-mizraim,* for they said, "This is a place of deep mourning for these Egyptians."

¹²So Jacob's sons did as he had commanded them. ¹³They carried his body to the land of Canaan and buried him in the cave in the field of Machpelah, near Mamre. This is the cave that Abraham had bought as a permanent burial site from Ephron the Hittite.

¹⁴After burying Jacob, Joseph returned to Egypt with his brothers and all who had accompanied him to his father's burial.

50:2 Hebrew *Israel*. See note on 35:21.   50:11 *Abel-mizraim* means "mourning of the Egyptians."

NOTES

50:11 *they renamed that place (which is near the Jordan) Abel-mizraim, for they said, "This is a place of deep mourning for these Egyptians."* The mourning for Jacob for seven days at a threshing floor near the Jordan River prompted some local Canaanites to name the place Abel-mizraim, meaning "meadow (*'abel* [TH67, ZH73]) of Egyptians," but by a wordplay it suggests "mourning (*'ebel* [TH60, ZH65]) of Egyptians."

COMMENTARY

Once more the death of a patriarch marks the end of an era; once more a grave in the land of Canaan becomes important as Jacob instructs Joseph to bury him with his fathers in the land of promise, not in Egypt (cf. 47:29-30). That is where the hope was; that is where the future lay. At the cave of Machpelah near Hebron were buried Sarah (23:19), Abraham (25:8-9), Isaac (35:27-29), Rebekah (49:31), and Leah, Jacob's first wife (49:31). And so Jacob died at the age of 147 (47:28), his life of struggling and sorrow coming to an end. Jacob always had an unquenchable desire for God's blessing. He had a deep piety that habitually relied on God in spite of all else. In the end, he died a man of genuine faith.

After weeping over his father's death (cf. Joseph's other occasions for weeping in 42:24; 43:30; 45:2, 14; 50:17), Joseph instructed that Jacob's body be embalmed for burial in typical Egyptian fashion (50:1-3). The embalming period was seldom less than a month, and usually took 40 days. The Egyptians mourned for Jacob for 70 days—two and a half months, just two days short of the time of mourning for a Pharaoh. This showed the great respect that the Egyptians had for Joseph. After the time of mourning had passed, Joseph asked Pharaoh for permission to go bury his father in the land of Canaan (50:4-6).

Joseph led a large procession, including Egyptian dignitaries, Joseph's family and brothers, and a number of charioteers, to Canaan to bury his father (50:7-9). This was Joseph's first time back in the homeland in 39 years. Centuries later, the family of Israel would again leave the land of Egypt, taking with them the bones of Joseph himself. But that would not be solely for a burial—it would begin a whole new life. Here, however, the trip was temporary; the grave was only a claim to the land of promise for the future. God had promised Jacob that he would bring him back to the land and that Joseph would bury him (46:4). The Canaanites observed that this was a significantly somber event for the Egyptians and appropriately gave the name of the place as "Abel-mizraim," perhaps meaning "mourning of the Egyptians" (see note on 50:11).

◆ J. Reassurance of the Blessing (50:15-26)

¹⁵But now that their father was dead, Joseph's brothers became fearful. "Now Joseph will show his anger and pay us back for all the wrong we did to him," they said.

¹⁶So they sent this message to Joseph: "Before your father died, he instructed us ¹⁷to say to you: 'Please forgive your brothers for the great wrong they did to you—for their sin in treating you so cruelly.' So we, the servants of the God of your father, beg you to forgive our sin." When Joseph received the message, he broke down and wept. ¹⁸Then his brothers came and threw themselves down before Joseph. "Look, we are your slaves!" they said.

¹⁹But Joseph replied, "Don't be afraid of me. Am I God, that I can punish you? ²⁰You intended to harm me, but God intended it all for good. He brought me to this position so I could save the lives of many people. ²¹No, don't be afraid. I will continue to take care of you and your children." So he reassured them by speaking kindly to them.

²²So Joseph and his brothers and their families continued to live in Egypt. Joseph lived to the age of 110. ²³He lived to see three generations of descendants of his son Ephraim, and he lived to see the birth of the children of Manasseh's son Makir, whom he claimed as his own.*

²⁴"Soon I will die," Joseph told his

brothers, "but God will surely come to help you and lead you out of this land of Egypt. He will bring you back to the land he solemnly promised to give to Abraham, to Isaac, and to Jacob."

25Then Joseph made the sons of Israel swear an oath, and he said, "When God comes to help you and lead you back, you must take my bones with you." 26So Joseph died at the age of 110. The Egyptians embalmed him, and his body was placed in a coffin in Egypt.

50:23 Hebrew *who were born on Joseph's knees.*

NOTES

50:25 When God comes to help you. The verb translated "help" here is *paqad* [TH6485, ZH7212], which is more often translated "visit." Neither translation fully captures the intensity of the word. It refers to divine intervention to bless or to curse; in this instance, it means "to bless." Such a visitation from on high always changed the destiny of those visited.

COMMENTARY

After Jacob died, the brothers began to fear that Joseph finally would deal harshly with them for the wrongs they had done to him (cf. 45:3; see also 27:41). They came and pleaded for forgiveness, claiming Jacob had instructed Joseph to grant it. Once again they referred to themselves as Joseph's slaves (cf. 44:16; see also 37:7). After weeping, Joseph reassured them by telling them twice: "Don't be afraid" (50:19, 21; cf. 43:23). And then he uttered the powerful words: "You intended to harm me, but God intended it all for good" (50:20). All that had happened to Joseph was part of God's plan to bring about the fulfillment of the promised blessing (cf. 45:5, 7-9).

Years later, Joseph also died in the land of Egypt. Like his father before him, he made his brothers promise that his bones would be taken out of the land of Egypt at the great deliverance (50:24-25; cf. Exod 13:19; Josh 24:32; Heb 11:22). This deliverance, he assured them, would take place when God would visit them to fulfill his promises to their fathers (see note on 50:24). Joseph lived to see his great-great-grandchildren by Ephraim and his great-grandchildren by Manasseh. Placing them on his knees at their birth was a symbolic act signifying that they came from him and belonged to him (cf. 30:3 [NLT mg]; Job 3:12). Then Joseph died at the age of 110 and, like Jacob, was embalmed. Embalming was an Egyptian custom; the Hebrews simply placed the bodies in the tombs and let them decompose for a year. Then they would return to the tomb and remove the bones to a recess in the tomb to make room for other burials. In New Testament times they collected the bones in a bone box known as an ossuary and put it on a shelf. Since Joseph was being embalmed, his use of the word "bones" would refer to all of his remains.

The book of Genesis closes with the promise of the land yet unfulfilled but with the promise of a future visitation from on high (50:24). The words of Joseph, given twice, amazingly summarize the hope expressed throughout the Old Testament as well as the New Testament: God will surely visit you (50:24-25). So the company of the faithful would wait in expectation for the visitation of the Seed, the Messiah, who would bring the Curse to an end and establish the long-awaited blessing of God in a new creation—an expectation that is also seen, for example, in Luke 1:68, where Zechariah anticipates the fulfillment of the promises: "Praise the Lord, the God of Israel, because he has visited and redeemed his people" (see also Heb 2:5-9; Rev 21:1-7).

BIBLIOGRAPHY

Albright, W. F.
1941 New Light on the Early History of Phoenician Colonization. *Bulletin of the American School of Oriental Research* 83:21.

Barr, James
1959 The Meaning of Mythology in Relation to the Old Testament. *Vetus Testamentum* 9:1-10.

Barton, J., and J. Muddiman, editors
2001 *The Oxford Bible Commentary.* New York: Oxford University Press.

Blenkinsopp, J.
1992 *The Pentateuch: An Introduction to the First Five Books of the Bible.* New York: Doubleday.

Blocher, H.
1984 *In the Beginning.* Leicester: InterVarsity.

Brichto, H. C.
1963 *The Problem of "Curse" in the Hebrew Bible.* Philadelphia: Society of Biblical Literature and Exegesis.

Bright, John
1956 *Early Israel in Recent History Writing.* London: Student Christian Movement.

Brueggemann, Walter
1982 *Genesis.* Interpretation: A Bible Commentary for Preaching and Teaching. Atlanta: John Knox.

Campbell, A. F., and M. A. O'Brien
1993 *Sources of the Pentateuch: Text, Introductions, Annotations.* Minneapolis: Fortress.

Carpenter, Eugene E.
1986 Recent Pentateuchal Studies. *Asbury Theological Journal* 41:19-30.

Carr, David M.
2005 *Writing on the Tablet of the Heart: Origins of Scripture and Literature.* Oxford: Oxford University Press.

Cassuto, Umberto
1961 *The Documentary Hypothesis and the Composition of the Pentateuch.* Jerusalem: Magnes.

1964 *A Commentary on the Book of Genesis.* 2 vols. Jerusalem: Magnes.

1973 The Episode of the Sons of God and the Daughters of Man, in *Biblical and Oriental Studies, Volume 1: Bible.* Jerusalem: Magnes.

Childs, Brevard S.
1960 *Myth and Reality in the Old Testament.* Naperville, IL: Alec R. Allenson.

1974 The Etiological Tale Re-examined. *Vetus Testamentum* 24:387-397.

Cohn, R. L.
1983 Narrative Structure and Canonical Perspective in Genesis. *Journal for the Study of the Old Testament* 25:3-16.

Coote, R. B. and D. R. Ord
1989 *The Bible's First History: From Eden to the Court of David with the Yahwist.* Philadelphia: Fortress.

Cryer, F. H.
1994 *Divination in Ancient Israel and Its Near Eastern Environment.* Journal for the Study of the Old Testament Supplement 142. Sheffield: JSOT Press.

Day, John
1985 *God's Conflict with the Dragon and the Sea: Echoes of a Canaanite Myth in the Old Testament.* Cambridge: Cambridge University Press.

Delitzsch, F.
1889 *A New Commentary on Genesis.* Edinburgh: T & T Clark.

Dods, Marcus
1893 *The Book of Genesis.* London: Hodder & Stoughton.

Doukhan, J. B.
1978 *The Genesis Creation Story: Its Literary Structure.* Berrien Springs, MI: Andrews University Press.

Driver, S. R.
1891 *An Introduction to the Literature of the Old Testament.* New York: Charles Scribner's Sons.
1904 *Genesis.* London: Methuen.

Emerton, J. A.
1987 An Examination of Some Attempts to Defend the Unity of the Flood Narrative in Genesis, Part I. *Vetus Testamentum* 37:401-420.
1988 An Examination of Some Attempts to Defend the Unity of the Flood Narrative in Genesis Part II. *Vetus Testamentum* 38:1-21.

Fields, W.
1997 *Sodom and Gomorrah: History and Motif in Biblical Narratives.* Journal for the Study of the Old Testament Supplement 231. Sheffield: Sheffield Academic.

Fokkelman, J. P.
1991 *Narrative Art in Genesis.* 2nd ed. Sheffield: Journal for the Study of the Old Testament Press.

Friedman, R. E.
1987 *Who Wrote the Bible?* New York: Harper & Row.

Garrett, D.
1991 *Rethinking Genesis: The Sources and Authority of the First Book of the Pentateuch.* Grand Rapids: Baker.

Grintz, J. M.
1945 The Immigration of the First Philistines in the Inscriptions. *Tarbiz* 17:32-42.

Gunkel, Hermann
1964 *The Legends of Genesis.* New York: Schocken. (Orig. Pub. 1901)

Gunn, D. M. and D. N. Fewell
1993 *Narrative in the Hebrew Bible.* Oxford: Oxford University Press.

Hals, R.
1969 *The Theology of the Book of Ruth.* Philadelphia: Fortress.

Harrison, R. K.
1969 *Introduction to the Old Testament.* Grand Rapids: Eerdmans.

Hasel, Gerhard
1974 The Polemic Nature of the Genesis Cosmology. *Evangelical Quarterly* 46:81-102.

Heidel, Alexander
1954 *The Gilgamesh Epic and Old Testament Parallels.* Chicago: University of Chicago Press.
1963 *The Babylonian Genesis.* Chicago: University of Chicago Press.

Hendel, R. S.
1987 Of Demi-gods and the Deluge: Toward an Interpretation of Genesis 6:1-4. *Journal of Biblical Literature.* 106:13-26.

Hestrin, Ruth
1970 *The Philistines and the Other Sea Peoples.* Jerusalem: The Israel Museum.

Holmes, Y. Lynn
1971 The Location of Alashiya. *Journal of the American Oriental Society* 91:426-429.

Jacob, Benno
1974 *The First Book of the Bible: Genesis.* Editors, E. J. Jacob and W. Jacob. New York: KTAV.

Kidner, Derek
1967 *Genesis.* Downers Grove: InterVarsity.

Kikawada, I. M.
1983 The Double Creation of Mankind in Enki and Ninmah, Atrahasis I, 1-351 and Genesis 1-2. *Iraq* 45:43-45.

Kikawada, I. M. and A. Quinn
1987 *Before Abraham Was: A Provocative Challenge to the Documentary Hypothesis.* Nashville: Abingdon.

Kitchen, Kenneth A.
1966 *Ancient Orient and Old Testament.* Chicago: InterVarsity.
1971 The Old Testament in Its Context 1: From the Origin to the Eve of the Exodus. *Theological Students Fellowship Bulletin* 59:1-10.
1973 *The Philistines in Peoples of Old Testament Times.* Editor, D. J. Wiseman. Oxford: Clarendon.

Knierim, Rolf
1985a The Composition of the Pentateuch. *Society of Biblical Literature Seminar Papers* 24:393-415.
1985b Criticism of Literary Features, Form, Tradition and Redaction. Pp. 123-165 in *The Hebrew Bible and Its Modern Interpreters*. Editors, D. A. Knight and G. M. Tucker. Philadelphia: Fortress.

Livingston, G. Herbert
1974 *The Pentateuch in Its Cultural Environment*. Grand Rapids: Baker.

Longman, Tremper III
1987 *Literary Approaches to Biblical Interpretation*. Grand Rapids: Zondervan.

Lurker, Manfred
1974 *The Gods and Symbols of Ancient Egypt*. London: Thames & Hudson.

Matthews, Kenneth A.
1996 *Genesis*. 2 vols. Nashville: Broadman & Holman.

McCarter, P. K.
1988 A New Challenge to the Documentary Hypothesis. Have Modern Scholars Failed to Appreciate the Overall Structure of Genesis 1-11? *Biblical Review* 4:34-39.

Mellinkoff, R.
1981 *The Mark of Cain*. Berkeley: University of California Press.

Merrill, Eugene
1987 *Kingdom of Priests: A History of Old Testament Israel*. Grand Rapids: Baker.

Moberly, R. W. L.
1992 *The Old Testament of the Old Testament: Patriarchal Narratives and Mosaic Yahwism*. Minneapolis: Fortress.

Neiman, David
1965 Phoenician Place-Names. *Journal of Near Eastern Studies* 24:113-115.

Nicholson, E. W.
1989 The Pentateuch in Recent Research: A Time for Caution. Pp. 10-21 in *Congress Volume, Leuven*. Editor, J. Emerton. Leiden: Brill.

Niditch, S.
1985 *Chaos to Cosmos: Studies in Biblical Patterns of Creation*. Chico, CA: Scholars Press.

Porteous, Norman
1972 The Old Testament and History. *Annual of the Swedish Theological Institute*, vol. 8. Leiden: E. J. Brill.

Rad, Gerhard von
1961 *Genesis*. Philadelphia: Westminster.
1962 *Old Testament Theology*. Translator, D. M. G. Stalker. New York: Harper & Row.

Rendsburg, G. A.
1986 *The Redaction of Genesis*. Winona Lake, IN: Eisenbrauns.

Rendtorff, R.
1992 The Paradigm Is Changing: Hopes—and Fears. *Biblical Interpretation* 1.34-54.
1993 *Canon and Theology*. Translator and editor, M. Kohl. Minneapolis: Fortress.

Rogerson, J. W.
1974 *Myth in Old Testament Interpretation*. New York: Walter de Gruyter.

Ross, Allen P.
1980 Studies in the Book of Genesis Part 1: The Curse of Canaan. *Bibliotheca Sacra* 137:223-240.
1981 The Dispersion of the Nations in Genesis 11:1-9. *Bibliotheca Sacra* 138:119-138.
1988 *Creation and Blessing: A Guide to the Study and Exposition of the Book of Genesis*. Grand Rapids: Baker.
2003 Did the Patriarchs Know the Name of the Lord? Pp. 323-339 in *Giving the Sense*. Editors, M. Grisanti and D. M. Howard, Jr. Grand Rapids: Kregel.

Sailhamer, John
1992 *The Pentateuch as Narrative*. Grand Rapids: Zondervan.

Sarna, Nahum M.
1966 *Understanding Genesis*. New York: McGraw-Hill.

Segal, Moses
1967 *The Pentateuch: Its Composition and Its Authorship and Other Biblical Studies*. Jerusalem: Magnes.

Skinner, J.
1930 *Genesis.* Edinburgh: T & T Clark.

Speiser, E. A.
1957 The Biblical Idea of History in the Common Near Eastern Setting. *Israel Exploration Journal* 7:201-216.
1964 *Genesis.* The Anchor Bible. New York: Doubleday.

Thompson, T. L.
1974 *The Historicity of the Patriarchal Narratives: The Quest for the Historical Abraham.* Berlin: Walter de Gruyter.

Tsumura, David
1994 The Earth in Genesis 1. Pp. 310-328 in *I Studied Inscriptions from Before the Flood: Ancient Near Eastern, Literary and Linguistic Approaches to Genesis 1-11.* Editors, Richard S. Hess and David Tsumura. Winona Lake, IN: Eisenbrauns.

Tucker, Gene
1971 *Form Criticism of the Old Testament.* Philadelphia: Fortress.

Unger, Merrill F.
1954 *Archaeology and the Old Testament.* Grand Rapids: Zondervan.

VanGemeren, W. A.
1981 The Sons of God in Genesis 6:1-4. *Westminster Theological Journal* 43:320-348.

Wainwright, G. A.
1959 Some Early Philistine History. *Vetus Testamentum* 9:73-84.

Waltke, Bruce K.
1975 The Creation Account in Genesis 1:1-3, Part 3: The Initial Chaos Theory and the Precreation Chaos Theory. *Bibliotheca Sacra* 132:216-228.

Walton, John H.
1989 *Ancient Israelite Literature in Its Cultural Context.* Grand Rapids: Zondervan.

Wenham, Gordon J.
1986 Sanctuary Symbolism in the Garden of Eden Story. *Proceedings of the World Congress of Jewish Studies* 9:19-25.
1987, 1994 *Genesis.* 2 vols. Word Biblical Commentary. Waco: Word.

Westermann, Claus
1978 *Blessing in the Bible and in the Life of the Church.* Philadelphia: Fortress.
1984-1986 *Genesis.* 3 vols. Minneapolis: Augsburg.

Wiseman, P. J.
1937 *New Discoveries in Babylonia about Genesis.* London: Marshall, Morgan & Scott.
1949 *Creation Revealed in Six Days.* London: Marshall, Morgan & Scott.

Woudstra, M. H.
1970 The *Toledot* of the Book of Genesis and Their Redemptive-Historical Significance. *Calvin Theological Journal* 5:184-189.

Wouk, H.
1959 *This Is My God.* Garden City: Doubleday.

Exodus

JOHN N. OSWALT

INTRODUCTION TO
Exodus

READERS OF THE NEW TESTAMENT need to understand the book of Exodus. In fact, it might be said that aside from the book of Genesis, Exodus is the most important Old Testament book for Christians to be familiar with. To be sure, the New Testament does not quote this second book of the Canon as frequently as it does such books as Isaiah, Deuteronomy, and Psalms, but knowledge of the events narrated in Exodus, such as the giving of the Torah and the construction of the Tabernacle, are everywhere assumed in the New Testament. That the people called Israel—the people of the Messiah—came into existence at all was only because God miraculously delivered them from Egypt. The parallels between the exodus from Egypt and the resurrection of Christ are too many to enumerate here. But let it be said that from the Lord's Supper (Passover) to Pentecost (the giving of the Torah), the book of Exodus provides the subtext of the Gospels and Acts. One other point that must not be overlooked is that the work of Christ in making a new covenant possible is only understandable against the backdrop of the old covenant, a proper understanding of which is impossible without a grasp of Exodus. In the end, it is the book of Exodus that shapes the biblical understanding of what a life-giving relationship with God looks like.

THE PLACE OF THE BOOK IN THE TORAH

The division of the biblical material into books is very old, but it is somewhat unfortunate because it tends to make modern readers approach each book as a separate entity. That may be the correct approach in some cases, as for instance, the book of Job, but in other cases it is quite incorrect. One of those cases is the first five books, called the Torah (Hebrew for "Instruction"), or the Pentateuch (Greek for the "Five Books"). These books are clearly intended to be read as a whole. And it is very possible that the fifth book, Deuteronomy, both ends the first five and also leads into the next four: Joshua, Judges, Samuel, and Kings, with all nine books giving a connected history of God's people from the creation until the return from Babylonian exile. The Torah, the first of these two divisions, takes the reader up to the point of entering the land that was first promised to Abraham in Genesis 12:7. It contains six great "scenes": (1) Creation and the Fallen World (Gen 1–11); (2) Canaan, Land of Promise (Gen 12–50); (3) Slaves in Egypt (Exod 1–15); (4) Sinai (Exod 16—Num 10); (5) In the Wilderness (Num 11–36); and (6) The Fields of Moab (Deut 1–34).

Within these different "scenes" there is a single line of thought, revolving around the question, "Who supplies my needs, and how are they to be supplied?"[1] If we conclude that *we* are the suppliers of our needs, then the answer to the second part of the question is, "by manipulating the forces in the world." A certain view of the world is inevitable. In the Pentateuch (as in the whole Bible), God is attempting to demonstrate that *he* is the only one who can supply our needs, and that the supply is fully available to those who are in a lovingly submissive relationship with him. Genesis shows how the belief that we must each supply our own needs has blighted the world. It then illustrates in three different individuals—Abraham, Jacob, and Joseph—that if God will be trusted and obeyed, he will supply our needs better than we ever could on our own.[2]

But God does not merely wish to care for a few scattered individuals. This is clear not only from the blessing given to Adam, and thus to all his descendants (Gen 1:28), but also from God's promise to bless the whole world through Abraham (Gen 12:3). The first move in this progression from Abraham to the world is a move from an individual scope to a national one. That is what takes place in the book of Exodus. One thing inherent in such a move was that the lovingly submissive relationship with God would be put into more formal and wide-ranging terms than it had been previously. The flexibility and simplicity of "one-on-one" relationships is not possible when an entire national group is involved.

The move from individual to national also provided the occasion whereby a much fuller revelation of the character of God and the character of humans could be revealed. That had not been necessary in the initial relationships with the patriarchs; God was simply establishing an open connection with human beings. Such revelation as the patriarchs received, however, was an absolute necessity if the relationship between God and humans was to rest on any kind of solid foundation. What we ultimately see in Exodus is the nature of the salvation God has planned. We see what the need, the cause, the purpose, and the goal of salvation are. In this way, the book of Exodus provides an irreplaceable foundation for understanding the rest of the Bible, both Old and New Testaments.

AUTHOR AND DATE

Author. The tradition that the church inherited from the Jews was that the human author of the Torah was Moses. Jesus clearly reflected this conviction when he quoted passages from the Torah and said, "Moses gave you this law from God," (Mark 7:10; cf. Mark 10:3), and when he said, "haven't you ever read about this in the writings of Moses" (Mark 12:26), and then recounted the story of the burning bush from Exodus 3. This position was largely unchallenged until the seventeenth century in Europe, when biblical scholars, imbued with the tenets of rationalism, became convinced that the kind of inspiration involved in Mosaic authorship was impossible. Over the next 100 years (1775–1875), a very complex theory of the authorship of the Pentateuch evolved. Eventually it came to be accepted that Moses was responsible for little, if any, of the Pentateuch. Instead, the Torah was the result of the combining of at least four different books, with the last source, the so-called "Priestly work," only being added after the Exile, around 400 BC. In the book of Exodus, all of the Tabernacle material after chapter 24 was thought to have been taken from this Priestly work (Friedman [1987:250-252] has a chart showing what parts of Exodus he believes came from each of the four different works).

This theory, known as the Documentary Hypothesis, came to rule the thinking of all but the most conservative biblical scholars after 1875. This was the situation until the middle 1930s when new ideas about the origins of literature began to make an impression on Old Testament scholarship. These new ideas, arising from research into European folk literature, asserted that folk literature was never authored by single individuals but grew up in oral forms among communities in which a given narrative or song served some particular purpose in the community. The effect of this new outlook was the proposition that although the written forms from which the present Pentateuch was constructed may have been later (between 1000 and 400 BC), the original oral forms may have appeared much earlier. This seemed to make a place for the original accounts relating to the Exodus having actually first emerged in the Israelite community sometime near to the event (c. 1440 BC). There was still no place for Mosaic authorship, but there did seem to be a place for a certain historical authenticity in the narratives.

But the problem with this new approach, often called Form Criticism, is that it placed a new theory on top of an old theory, neither of which had any objective evidence to support it. Supposedly, if one wished to determine the original form of any portion of the Pentateuch, one would first have to decide which document that portion had come from. Then it would be necessary to determine what the oral prehistory of that portion of that document had been. Of necessity, this process became highly subjective, with different scholars coming to widely differing conclusions about which parts of a passage were "original" and which were not.

As a result of this subjectivism, many scholars have given up on the whole process of trying to determine what was original, and now treat the Torah as a literary whole that must be interpreted as such. There is much about this development that is welcome. For instance, it is much less common today to find scholars interpreting one part of a verse in isolation from another part because it is supposed that the two parts originally came from two different documents. Neither is it so common to dismiss one part of a poem because it was "obviously" not part of the original oral form. But there is one great misfortune to this approach. That misfortune is the tacit, and sometimes not-so-tacit, assumption that the original historical setting is not only unrecoverable, but indeed, is of no necessary interest to the interpreter.

This assumption has tragic consequences because the entire claim of the Bible to authenticity and authority rests upon the fact that God has acted in observable history in the ways reported in the text. If God did not act in the ways recorded, then the unique theology of the Bible becomes both inexplicable and suspect. Why should we give allegiance to a faith whose evidence has been manufactured? The well-known statement of the apostle Paul that if Christ has not been raised from the dead, we Christians are the most pitiable people on earth (1 Cor 15:13-19) expresses the overall situation for the entire biblical revelation. While not every biblical book roots its theology in the specific activity of God in human history (e.g., Job), the revelation as a whole, culminating in Christ, does. Thus, those who believe in the God of the Bible have reason to expect that the book of Exodus reports accurately the historical events surrounding the exodus from Egypt and the establishment of the covenant at Mount Sinai. And this suggests that the accounts would have been written at or near the time of the events themselves.

All that having been said, is there any insuperable objection to Moses having been the author of the work? The simple answer is "no." Whereas seventeenth- and eighteenth-century scholars believed that writing did not exist before about 1000 BC, we now know that it has been in existence at least since about 3000 BC. Moreover, the great advance in writing that we call the alphabet (one written symbol for one sound—requiring only about 35 characters as opposed to hundreds or even thousands for earlier systems) was certainly developed by 1400 BC (as at Ugarit, see Hamilton 2006). While the ancient manuscripts we have do not use an alphabet from this period and do use a later form of the Hebrew language than what would have been spoken at Moses's time, this says nothing about the date of the book's original composition. (For example, the fact that an edition of *Pilgrim's Progress* appears in twenty-first century American English, printed in a newly created font, does not prove that *Pilgrim's Progress* was written in the twenty-first century.) Additionally, the theological sophistication that scholars of previous centuries insisted was unknown in the 1400s BC was, in fact, quite common (cf. Kitchen 1964; 2003). If we accept the biblical claim that Moses was reared in the Egyptian royal court, there is every reason to believe that he would have had both the technical and intellectual skills to create a work such as the Pentateuch.

But is there any reason to think that Moses would have felt a need to compose such a work? Indeed there is. It is apparent that the covenant between God and Israel follows a literary form that was well-known in the latter half of the second millennium BC. It was a form utilized by emperors when they entered into treaties with subject peoples (see the discussion below on ch 20). One of the features of this form is that the covenant was required to be written down and deposited in a safe place, often in the temple of the people's chief god. There it could be reread regularly (see Deut 31:10-13; 24-25) and appealed to in the case of any disagreement among the parties. It would be natural for Moses, having written the covenant according to the form required, to continue and supervise the composition of other related writings: the patriarchal history that explained the promises of the covenant; the Egyptian sojourn that led up to the reception of the Torah; and the people's subsequent acts of disobedience and experiences of God's discipline and grace as he continued to keep his side of the agreement.

One of the features of the Pentateuch that gave rise to the Documentary Hypothesis, however, was the presence of different styles, vocabularies, and approaches throughout the work. Since the European biblical scholars had been raised on the classical literary ideals of unity of place, plot, time, and style, it seemed impossible that one person could have been the author of the whole Torah. The first thing that needs to be said in response to this is that it is a mistake to apply modern literary standards to an ancient work. There is now clear evidence that ancient authors did not work with the same commitment to the literary unities that came to hold sway in Europe. The second thing is that different kinds of material often necessitate different styles, vocabulary, and so forth. The most gifted narrator in the world would have a hard time writing a compelling manual on sacrifices. The third point rests upon the recent recognition of biblical scholars that the most fruitful approach to biblical interpretation is to treat books as wholes. If that is true, and it certainly seems to be, it is a strong argument against those books being the product of a haphazard and often unconscious evolution. Finally, it should be noted that nowhere does the Bible say that Moses wrote every word of the Pentateuch. To be sure, we are told that he wrote major parts of it, such as the book of Deuteronomy (Deut 31:9, 24), but it is nowhere said that he is the sole author of the whole. Thus, it may be entirely consistent with the facts to say that Moses, under the inspiration of the Spirit, provided the guiding direction and focus for the writing of the Pentateuch, writing large parts of it himself, directing the transcribing of oral narratives such as those of the Creation, the Flood, and the patriarchs, and directing the compilation of the additional commandments revealed at various points along the way. He is the single figure that explains the thematic unity of the whole, but it is quite possible that other hands were involved in the work with him.[3]

Date. As already mentioned, it seems logical that Moses would have recorded the events of the Exodus and Sinai at a time close to their occurrences. But when was that time? The earliest biblical date that we can tie into our dating system with some sense of accuracy is the death of King Solomon. This is possible because the Egyptian king lists come all the way down into the Christian era, giving the number of years each king reigned, and we can, with correlations with Assyrian lists (e.g., the Assyrian Eponym Canon) work backward to assign dates to the various pharaohs. If the pharaoh of the Exodus were named in the Bible, we could establish the date of the event to within 10 or 15 years (see Gardiner 1966:64-66). Unfortunately, that is not the case. The first pharaoh named in the Bible is Shishak, who attacked Jerusalem five years after Solomon's death (1 Kgs 14:25). Since Shishak's dates are only accurate to plus or minus about 10 years, we can say that Solomon's death occurred between 931 and 922 BC. First Kings 6:1 tells us that the founding of the Temple, which occurred in Solomon's third year (967 BC?) took place 480 years after the departure from Egypt. That date would be about 1447 BC.

But several factors complicate the matter. Foremost among these has been the claim of archaeologists in the last century that there was no evidence of a conquest of the land of Canaan before about 1225 BC. The first extrabiblical mention of Israel occurs also at about this time. As a result, it became fairly common for biblical scholars of all theological persuasions to accept a date of about 1275 BC for the Exodus (taking the 480 years to be symbolic: 12 generations of 40 years each).

However, recent reviews of the archaeological data have argued that the evidence for a 1275 conquest is no more persuasive than that for one in 1400. The result is that many archaeologists now deny that there was a conquest (and consequently, an Exodus) at all (see Finkelstein and Silberman 2001).

But another possibility is that archaeologists are using a faulty dating system. It is known that many of the Canaanite cities experienced destruction in what is now taken to be about 1500, and there is no explanation for this in the records we now have. But that date of 1500 depends on the assumed dates of one type of pottery. If that pottery actually appeared some 100 years after the date now assumed (and there is reason to believe that is the case) then these destructions, the details of which accord well with the biblical claims, would have actually occurred about 1400 BC and would provide significant evidence of the dates of the Exodus and conquest (see Bimson 1978). If Bimson is correct, we may assume that the book of Exodus was first written down in the wilderness period between about 1445 and 1405 BC.

OCCASION OF WRITING

As noted above, the literary form of the covenant God entered into with his people at Mount Sinai required that the covenant be written down (see 24:4; 34:27-28) and kept in a place that was both prominent and secure (25:16). That being so, there is every reason to believe that Moses would have also felt inspired to write down an explanation of the setting for the covenant (Beckwith 1985:127-138). The form of the covenant (see the discussion below) began with a historical prologue, "I am the LORD your God, who rescued you from . . . slavery" (20:2). That bare statement begs for amplification: Who is the LORD? Why were the people in Egypt in the first place? How did they become slaves? Why did the LORD decide to rescue them? What purpose did the LORD have in rescuing them? And those are the questions the book answers for us.

AUDIENCE

If the positions taken above are correct, the projected audience for the book of Exodus was very large. The first audience was the Israelite people of that day, who seemed to suffer from a sort of spiritual amnesia. As soon as the going got difficult, they seemed to forget everything that they had seen and heard from God, what God had done for them, and what they had solemnly committed themselves to. Within days of the Exodus itself they were wishing that they were back in Egypt (16:3). Within weeks of taking an oath in blood to keep the covenant at all costs, they were dancing around a gold calf, praising it for having delivered them from Egypt. How desperately these people needed to be reminded of all that God had done for them and revealed to them in rescuing them from Egypt and in committing himself to them in the covenant. If God's saving purpose was ever to be realized in the world through these people, then the lessons of Egypt and Sinai had to be impressed upon them.

But there was an even larger audience: the ensuing generations. Exodus 13:14-15 makes it very plain that God had not simply performed a sideshow for one group of people because they were his special favorites or because he wanted to puff himself up. That was the way the surrounding nations viewed the actions of their gods in their national histories. But this God had larger purposes and goals than that. Thus, it was the responsibility of the elders to explain to the upcoming generation what God had done with them and what the significance of those events was for the life of the new generation. Deuteronomy 6:4-9, 20-25 expands yet further on this theme of remembering and recounting, adding the content of the covenant itself to the events surrounding the giving of the covenant. Thus, the Exodus narrative, the account of the covenant, and the report of the building of the Tabernacle were all vital information to be written down for succeeding generations. These succeeding generations were to understand themselves as standing in solidarity with their forebears as part of God's plan for all ages. They too were intended to have a part in the lovingly submissive relationship that God and Abraham had enjoyed, and they were to be a vital part of the process of making that relationship available to all people everywhere. And that indicates the still larger audience that Moses had in mind—people everywhere. The specific evidence for this is found in Exodus 18, where Jethro, Moses's father-in-law, comes to meet Moses and the people in the wilderness and hears the story of the deliverance. His response is a very telling one: "I know now that the LORD is greater than all other gods, because he rescued his people from the proud Egyptians" (18:11). Although Jethro was not physically present to receive the revelation of God's surpassing greatness, the narrative itself became that revelation, and he responded as though he had been there. Thus Moses's ultimate audience was the entire world—all those who would read his inspired record of what God had done and said and would enter into a lovingly submissive relationship because of that reading.

CANONICITY AND TEXTUAL HISTORY

As far back as one looks for testimony as to the authoritative sources for the Jewish and Christian faiths, one finds the Torah (which includes Exodus) at the top of the list. Ezra speaks of the Book of Moses as specifying the service of the Levites (Ezra 6:18). According to Beckwith (1985:71), Ben Sira, or Ecclesiasticus (c. 130 BC), virtually identifies the Pentateuch with the personified Wisdom of God. Likewise, Beckwith notes that Eusebius's *Preparation for the Gospel* 9.29 (4th century AD) records that the sympathetic pagan writer Alexander Polyhistor (c. 60 BC) referred to Exodus as "the holy book." In the Dead Sea Scrolls, whenever Exodus is quoted, the standard formula for Scripture, "it is written," is employed. It is quoted by Luke (Luke 2:23), by John (John 19:36), and by Paul (Rom 9:17) as authoritative Scripture. In Josephus, the five books of Moses are at the head of his list of the 22 books that the Jews have always accepted as inspired.

Unlike the New Testament, where multiple copies and editions make it possible to trace the development of the text in some detail, the Old Testament manuscripts and editions are fewer and date further from the time of original composition. Owing to the Jewish practice of burning worn-out or replaced biblical scrolls in the first millennium AD, the earliest complete manuscript of the Hebrew Bible we have is dated AD 1008. Before 1948 and the discovery of the Dead Sea Scrolls, the only other witnesses to the history of the Hebrew text were some fragments of scrolls from the fifth and sixth centuries AD that had been recovered from a forgotten storeroom in a Cairo synagogue in 1895. These facts explain some of the initial excitement over the discovery of the Dead Sea Scrolls in 1948. Overnight the history of the text was pushed back almost 1000 years. Unfortunately, most biblical texts among the Dead Sea Scrolls, apart from a few dramatic exceptions like the Isaiah scroll, are fragmentary, and their evidence is often more tantalizing than conclusive.

In general, the picture of textual development that the Dead Sea Scrolls have presented to us is a complicated one. On the one hand, they seem to show that the so-called Masoretic text (MT), the text used as the basis for virtually all translations since the Reformation, has a long and respectable history. Its overall claim to best represent the original seems to be confirmed by the Scrolls. However, it is also clear that there were many other versions existing alongside the MT. While these other versions do not differ from the MT in their broad outlines, they include many variations of wording, spelling, and expression. The scrolls confirm that many of the variations of the Septuagint (the Greek translation of the Old Testament) from the MT are not merely idiosyncratic or even sloppy translations. Rather, those variants seem to have been faithful translations of variants that already existed in the Hebrew texts being translated. It is significant for the textual history of the Pentateuch that the Septuagint varies from the MT least in these five books. This is often taken to be evidence that by 200–100 BC, when the Septuagint translation was made, the Pentateuch was already of such venerable authority that its text had become much more standardized and less open to variation than was the case with some later books.

LITERARY STYLE

In general, the literary style of the book of Exodus conforms to the type of literature (genre) involved. The narrative portions of the book (chs 1–19, 24, 32–34) are written in a free-flowing and engaging prose. In a few places variations appear, as with the genealogical list in chapter 6 and Moses's poetic "Song of the Sea" in 15:1-21. Whereas the Documentary Hypothesis would suggest that these are evidence of another author's material being inserted at these points, ancient literature commonly shows these kinds of variation with no indication that portions of several documents have been pasted together. Furthermore, if Moses was overseeing the process but not writing every piece, as suggested above, that too would allow for style variations.

As would be entirely expected, the style in the covenant (chs 20–23) and Tabernacle sections (chs 25–31, 35–40) is very much different from that appearing in the narrative. Again, this in no way necessitates a hypothesis of other documents. As already noted above, the covenant form used dictates a certain structure and style. This is particularly evident in the commandments section, with most of the commandments following the very widely documented "if . . . then" style of the ancient Near Eastern law codes, such as the one attributed to the Babylonian ruler Hammurabi.

A similar situation applies to the instructions for (chs 25–31) and the report of (chs 35–40) the building of the Tabernacle. There is no way in which a list of specifications and instructions can be other than dry and formal. The same sort of style appears in the book of Ezekiel, where the final chapters of the book (Ezek 40–48) are taken up with the instructions for a Temple and for the allotment of the land in the perfect kingdom. After some of the more colorful parts of the book, readers typically find the style of these chapters much less engaging. Unlike the situation with Exodus, however, the final chapters of Ezekiel are not attributed to another author. Thus, it stands to reason that Exodus's variation in style need not be attributed to multiple authorship rather than the nature of the content being recorded.

MAJOR THEOLOGICAL THEMES

The book of Genesis lays down the nature of the human problem and the basis upon which that problem can be solved. The book of Exodus explains how that problem can be solved. It does so in the very specific context of the promises to the family of Abraham. But in so doing it establishes the parameters for the way in which the race may be delivered back to its true identity.

The Need for Deliverance. The first and second chapters of the book show a parallel between the universal need for deliverance and the Hebrews' need for deliverance from slavery at that time. The Israelites were suffering oppression and a planned genocide. They were in a desperate condition that, in the end, could only be solved by a power outside themselves. Not only was their present condition intolerable because of slavery, their very existence was threatened because of the pharaoh's intent to destroy the male infants through whom the nation would have been perpetuated. When this is compared with the human problem, the analogy is very clear. Humans are clearly not free. We are bound by what theologians call depravity. There is a bent in us toward what is self-destructive. We think we are free to do what we want, never realizing that we are not free to do what is in our best interests: submit to God (cf. Rom 6:16-20). As a result we are alienated from God, the source of spiritual life, and after the end of this physical life are doomed to an existence where all the residual effects of God's grace that we now enjoy are forever removed. We are in bondage and our very existence is threatened.

Exodus also shows us that the problem was not only of interest to humans. The Israelite bondage also constituted a problem for God because he had committed himself to Abraham and his descendants. He had promised that Abraham would have more descendants than the stars of the heavens or the sand of the seashore, that those descendants would become a great nation in their own land, and that they would be a blessing to those who blessed them and a curse to those who cursed them (Gen 12:1-3). But all that began to seem highly questionable. Of what worth were those glowing promises to a nation of slaves on the brink of ethnic extinction? Thus the bondage of Israel called into question both God's power and his faithfulness. Did he want to keep his promises but was simply too weak to do so? Or was he strong enough but simply did not care about whatever he may have said in the past? Thus Israel's problem was not only their own; it was God's problem too.

In the same way, the human predicament is not only our problem, it is also God's. God clearly made humans to share the blessing of his life with them (cf. Gen 1:27 and the whole tenor of the Bible). He invites us both to live with him (Gen 17:1) and to live like him (Eph 5:2). Yet our fall into the bondage of sin and death has seemed to frustrate all those plans and to present him with an insoluble predicament. He made us to bless us, but his very presence is a source of terror to us. We know instinctively that his presence is deadly (Isa 6:1-3). The reason is that sin (that which is contrary to the terms of created existence) cannot exist in the presence of the Creator. Instead of being a source of life and blessing to us, our Father has become a source of death and curse. So, if God's creative purposes are to be realized, he must somehow deliver humans from bondage and death. If he cannot or will not, his own nature is called into question.

The Means of Deliverance. The manner in which God chose to implement the deliverance of his people is very significant. If his goal had been to simply get them out of Egypt, it seems that he could have done one climactic miracle and had them out and on their way. But that is most definitely not the case. One devastating plague after another fell on Egypt, until finally Pharaoh had no choice but to let his valuable slaves go. What is the point? Is it that God underestimated Pharaoh's stubbornness and had to keep trying in a process of trial and error to find the final, essential combination? Hardly! In fact, the Bible is quite clear that Pharaoh's stubbornness is the result of God's work. So what was the point? The point of the plagues was the self-revelation of God. Deliverance occurs when God steps into human experience and manifests himself. As already mentioned, the real human predicament is not physical bondage and oppression, as real as those are, and as much as God cares about them. The real problem is that we are alienated from God, the source of life. Thus, if God had simply supernaturally "airlifted" the Israelites out of Egypt, they would have missed the real point of the whole thing. That point is that the only real deliverance occurs when God himself, in his character as sovereign creator and faithful Savior, intervenes in our lives.

Of course, we as Christians are in a position to appreciate this truth in ways that Old Testament believers never could. We can appreciate it because we have seen its fulfillment. How could God deliver us from the bondage of sin and death? Only in one way: by revealing himself in the context of our life. It is as we see him and know him, being willing to become identified with him that genuine deliverance occurs. What Exodus tells us is that the incarnation of Christ was not some innovation in the plan and working of God. Incarnation was what God had been doing from the outset. It is not information that we need, neither is it merely the removal of certain consequences; it is the life of God in our life—that is the means of deliverance.

The Purpose of Deliverance. The point just made is further illuminated when we notice the recurrence of a particular phrase in the book of Exodus. That phrase is "know that I am the LORD." Some form of that phrase occurs no less than ten times between 6:7 and 31:13.[4] And the word "know" occurs in connection with the Lord another nine times in the book.[5] It seems unquestionable that Moses was trying to make a point. The issue is opened in 5:2 when Pharaoh baldly states, "I don't know the LORD." What does God want to come out of this experience of deliverance? He wants both the Egyptians and the Israelites to "know the LORD," whether negatively or positively. We must remember that "the LORD" occurs most commonly in the Old Testament as a replacement for God's personal name YHWH, probably pronounced "Yahweh." Furthermore, it is important to remember that "know" in Hebrew almost always assumes an experiential element. Thus, to "know the LORD" is not to have abstract knowledge about him, but it is to have experienced who he is as a result of personal acquaintance with him. Israel's deliverance is to be as a result of this personal acquaintance, and so also Egypt's condemnation (cf. Rom 1:21, "Yes, they knew God, but they wouldn't worship him as God or even give him thanks").

God did not merely want to get his people out of Egypt or merely to get them into the Promised Land. That is not deliverance, not in any final sense. The human condition can only be cured by an ongoing relationship with a source of life that is outside of ourselves. The meaning of "Yahweh," in the context of the burning bush experience of chapter 3, must be at least, "He is," or perhaps more likely, "He who causes to be." He alone is self-sufficient; he alone has the source of life in himself. Everything else in the universe is derivative, dependent on a source of life outside itself. Thus, the only hope of lasting deliverance is an ongoing relationship of loving submission to the One who is Life itself. Notice that this is exactly how John begins the letter of 1 John. John has known Life, and he wants his readers to have that same experience because the meaning of life is to have fellowship with the source of life (1 John 1:1-4).

The Goal of Deliverance. If the purpose of deliverance is to know Yahweh as a vital reality in our lives, then what must deliverance result in? The structure of the book of Exodus makes this point vitally clear. Most readers will instinctively assume that the point of the exodus experience is realized once the people are out of Egypt and well on their way to Canaan. But if that is so, what is the point of the immense digression between Exodus 19 and Numbers 10? In fact this material is no digression at all. The book of Exodus shows us that from God's point of view, the goal of the Exodus was his taking up residence in the midst of the camp. This can be seen in the clear climax of the book at 40:34, where the glory of the Lord fills the Tabernacle. The giving of the covenant and the building of the Tabernacle are not a sideshow to the main event. God will certainly keep his promise to take Abraham's descendants to the Promised Land. But, as much as the people might have believed it to be, the Promised Land was not an end. It was a means. The end was that all the world might be restored to the kind of lovingly submissive relationship with God that our first parents enjoyed and that God intended all humanity to have. Thus, the real goal of deliverance will have been achieved when people live in a covenant with God where they are living his life in loving obedience and are experiencing the joy of his presence in their midst. And until that is the case, deliverance has not truly occurred. To suggest that deliverance is only a changed position (in this case, geographical), which does not necessarily produce changed behavior and changed relationships, is to misrepresent not only what the book of Exodus is saying about deliverance but indeed what the entire Bible is saying. Likewise, to suggest that deliverance makes it possible for the delivered to have an unlimited draw on the treasuries of heaven without responsibility and in the absence of changed behavior is a misrepresentation. The goal of deliverance is for the delivered to share the character of God and to experience unbroken fellowship with God who is Father, Son, and Holy Spirit.

God versus the Gods. The self-revelation that is central to the book of Exodus is particularly aimed at correcting the false view of deity that is at the heart of every worldview except the biblical one and those worldviews directly influenced by it (the prime example being Islam). Briefly, that conception is this: All things in the universe—including humans, gods, and nature—are related continuously. Thus what is done in one of the three realms is automatically reproduced in the other two. Everywhere in the world, human speculation has led to the same view. There are superficial differences in the way this view is expressed in different cultures, but beneath the surface the conception is nearly the same. The classic expression of this is idolatry in which the idol is typically a god in human form expressing some psycho-socio-natural force in the universe. So the Egyptian god Amon-Re was the sun, and humans, by doing things to the idol, could do things to the sun. Understandably, magical ritual is central to this worship. It also means that humans understand invisible (divine) reality by analogy to visible reality. Thus, since there are many different elements in the visible world, there are many gods. Furthermore, since humans and animals have no ultimate purpose except survival with maximum pleasure, comfort, and security, neither do the gods. Ethics has no absolute basis since the many gods differ in their wishes and desires. This list could be continued at length, but these examples will serve to illustrate the basic concept.

This concept of reality, the one which all worldly wisdom arrives at sooner or later, dominated the ancient world from Sumer in the Tigris-Euphrates Valley in 3000 BC to Rome in Italy in AD 300. But because the fundamental premise of this view is wrong, every idea that flows from it is wrong. The divine world is *not* continuous with humanity and nature. It is radically *dis*continuous. Thus, God is not the world and cannot be represented by anything in it. There are not many gods, but only one, and he cannot be manipulated by doing magical things to this world. He is the sole creator and he created the universe with a specific plan. Humans are not an afterthought but are at the heart of the whole plan. The divine nature is completely consistent. Just as he is one in his essence, he is one in his character. He is absolutely faithful and dependable. More than that, he can always be depended upon to act for the benefit and well-being of his creation.

So what is God to do? The human race is in bondage to sin and death because it has rejected all the intimations of God in his creation and has created gods to its own liking. It has done so because a God who is discontinuous with his creation cannot be manipulated. His blessings can only be secured through surrender, trust, and obedience. That does not suit fearful human pride at all. We want to obtain the maximum benefits for ourselves with no cost to ourselves. More than that, we want to obtain those benefits while retaining control of ourselves and of the divine resources as well. By conceiving of the gods as continuous with this world, we are able to maintain the illusion that we can make the gods bless us by manipulating this world. At heart, modern secularists are no different from the ancients on this point; there is still the belief that we can make the creation bless us through physical manipulation of it. We have taken the faces off the gods, but we still see manipulation of the forces of the world as the key to fulfillment. Interestingly, in the last 50 years we have discovered that the attempt to leave the spiritual component out of reality leaves us with a strangely flat feeling in all our affluence. As a result, secular humanism is turning more and more rapidly to various forms of "spirituality" (e.g., New Age, the occult) to satisfy this emptiness. But it is a spirituality that assumes contiguity and is basically consistent with the spirituality of the ancient Egyptians.

Again, what is God to do? The humans he has created will never find fulfillment down the roads of their own devising. What they inevitably find is a worse end bondage than any they might have ever suffered in surrender to the transcendent God (see Rom 1:18-23). If they are to be delivered, they must be brought to an experiential knowledge of him who is Life and Truth. But how is that to happen? It would not be enough to drop a book of factual truth statements or logical arguments on them. They do not need knowledge; they need God in their lives. That is why the self-revelation of God is the only effective cause of deliverance. God must break the power of the false understanding of reality by confronting it with himself.

The plagues were the first step in God's personal confrontation of the false understanding. The plagues were an attack on the gods of Egypt. In that attack, God demonstrated the powerlessness—and in fact, deadly nature—of everything that humans try to put in his place. The Nile is not the source of Egypt's life but a river of bloody death. The amphibians do not know the secret of living in two worlds but are the harbingers of death. The flies, worshiped because they know how to turn rotting meat into squirming life, are only the source of pestilence. Although vegetation seems to have the key to life in itself because it returns from the dead each spring, it is helpless before the ravages of the world. The bull, the goat, and the ram do not embody the thrusting life-principle but die covered with boils. The sun, Amon-Re himself, is not self-sustaining but can be turned off at will by the Creator. And finally, life itself, the ultimate god not only of the Egyptians but of all lost and enslaved humanity, is shown to be only the forerunner of death in the death of Egypt's firstborn. Thus, the plagues demonstrate the sole Lordship of Yahweh, the God of Abraham, Isaac, and Jacob.

But the revelation of the truth about God is not completed at the Red Sea in chapter 14. In some ways it is only begun. Does this God of absolute power care about human needs? The deliverance from Egypt proves that he is able and willing to fulfill his ancient promises. But does he really care about our fragile condition as exemplified in our daily needs? Chapters 15–18 demonstrate that he does care. These chapters reveal the providence of God. Unlike the gods that humans create, who are arbitrary and heartless, mere forces wearing human-like masks, the God who is truly God is personally concerned about his creatures' needs. Thus, he provides food, water, protection, and even organizational order. He is a God who cares.

But what is his nature? The deepest questions about God remain unanswered at the end of chapter 18. We know that he is certainly superior to the Egyptian gods, both in power and providential care. But what sort of a being is he? What is he like? Is he reliable? Is he consistent? What does he want of humans? How does he want us to relate to to him? All these questions remain unanswered as the Hebrews reach the foot of the holy mountain. Once again, it is the resolution of these questions that is uppermost in God's mind. The blessings of the Promised Land are worthless unless the Israelites have some basis for knowing God and knowing what he wants. For as Abraham so beautifully demonstrated with Isaac on Mount Moriah (Gen 22), if we must choose between the gifts and the Giver, it is the Giver we must have. Moses recognized the same thing after the gold calf incident. God suggested to Moses that he and the people had better go on to the Promised Land without him since, given their persistent sinfulness, his presence would likely be destructive to them. But Moses steadfastly refused to even consider that suggestion. It was God's presence they must have. As far as Moses was concerned, if God would not go with them, then they would stay right there where God still was (33:15-16). Without God, the Promised Land would be no blessing.

The revelation of God's character and nature is made in the context of the covenant. Again, God's problem was a difficult one. These were people with little or no education who had lived for 400 years in the middle of one of the most thoroughly pagan cultures the world has known. God could not simply give them a course in theology, even if he were inclined to do so. Somehow he had to allow them to learn the fallacies of all they had been raised to believe about deity in a way that would connect with them in life. The covenant form which he used, sometimes called the Suzerainty treaty, was ideally suited to serve that purpose. The form seems to have originated among the Hittites in central Asia Minor (modern Turkey) at just about the time of the Exodus (c. 1500 BC). Emperors used it to formalize relationships with subject peoples. In the covenant the people swore absolute allegiance to one king, agreeing to conduct their lives in the ways that the king demanded. In return, the king promised to protect and care for the people.

The form consisted of several elements in a more-or-less fixed order. There was the introduction identifying the king who was offering the covenant. There was a historical prologue briefly describing the historical situation that had led up to the making of the treaty. After that, the stipulations followed, that is, the terms to which the parties agreed. Unlike the law codes of the ancient Near East, covenants often contained absolute prohibitions. It seems probable that this was the case because of the absolute allegiance the people were giving the king. He could demand absolute obedience because he was the only other party in the relationship. With the law codes, there were always a number of gods standing in the background, and what one god might prohibit another one might permit. Thus, the most that a given local ruler could do was to say that certain cases would be treated in certain ways. Polytheism prevents the formation of absolute ethical principles.

Following the stipulations were the two elements that varied the most from one covenant to the next. The first was the so-called "document clause" that told when the covenant was to be read first and at what intervals it was to be read in the future. The next clause told where the covenant document was to be kept safe, usually in the sanctuary of the chief god. If any element were to be left out of the treaty, or moved to another location in it, these two were the most likely candidates. Finally, there was a list of gods called to witness the treaty or covenant and a statement of the blessings that would come to those who kept the covenant and the curses that would come to those who broke it (for an expanded discussion see Kitchen 2003:283-304).

It is possible to recognize this covenant form in both Exodus and Deuteronomy. It provides the structure of the entire book of Deuteronomy (see the Introduction to that book in this series), and it shapes Exodus 20–24. Why did God use it? I believe there are three reasons. First, it was something that was a part of the people's general experience. They could relate to it easily. Second, it was not thoroughly contaminated with the pagan worldview. And those parts that did reflect pagan ideas could be replaced (e.g., the gods as witnesses; see 24:4 and comments). Third, and most important, it provided a way for the people to learn the truth about God in the context of life. It was as they fulfilled their covenant obligations that the Israelites learned who God was. This was the case because the stipulations of the various covenants always reflected the character and nature of the king involved. If he required the people to do certain things, it was because those were his own preferences. In the same way, if he prohibited certain things, he did so because he himself opposed them.

Thus, the first stipulation of God's covenant with his people was absolute allegiance to him alone. There is no complex philosophical discussion of monotheism, but long years of such absolute allegiance would prepare people to hear the words of Deuteronomy 32:39, "Look now; I myself am he! There is no other god but me!" The same thing was true for the concept of transcendence. How could slaves be taught such a difficult idea, especially when it was foreign to the most brilliant minds of their day? The second commandment prohibited the making of any idols. Again, there was no philosophical explanation; it was simply a condition for being in a covenant relationship with this God. But eventually, the Israelites were ready to understand that the reason why God cannot be represented by any created thing is that God is not in this world. They were learning in the context of life.

Even more significant than these elements is the profoundly ethical character of the covenant stipulations. How were the Hebrew people to express their total allegiance to God? One might think that the great majority of the stipulations would have to do with what we think of as "religious" behavior: when and where to pray, what kinds of offerings to bring, how to worship, specifications for rituals, and the like. In fact, that is not the case at all. The point is clearly made in the brief summary of the stipulations we know as the Ten Commandments. Only four of them have to do with activities directly related to God, while six of them have to do with how we treat other people. What does our treatment of other people have to do with our relationship to God? Elsewhere in the world, the answer was, "Precisely nothing." Law codes were the province of the civil administration of the country, and the temple had little or nothing to do with it. The reason for this situation is not hard to understand. In a world where the gods are personified psycho-socio-physical forces, ethics have nothing to do with religion. Does the thunder storm care how it treats people? Does passion? Does the moon? Does death? Of course not.

We have learned that, strangely enough, a society where everyone lies cannot survive, but we refuse to believe that has anything to do with ultimate reality. The reason we refuse to believe it is that it might restrict our freedom to lie when we think lying would be in our best interests. But since it is agreed that lying and similar activities on the part of others is detrimental, the civil administration can only seek to enforce those ethical norms by coercion.

But God says that those who wish to be in covenant with him must treat other people ethically. Why? The covenant form says it all; *it is because his ethic expresses the character of the covenant Lord, the sole creator of the universe.* He does not lie to protect himself; he does not appropriate our things when it serves his own interests; he does not break solemn oaths to play around with the pretty goddess next door; he does not lie in wait to murder us because he has taken a disliking to us. These are the astonishing kinds of things the covenant was designed to teach. The worldview of the continuity of all things, which teaches us that ethics are completely relative, that "truth" only applies to physics, is absolutely wrong. God is profoundly ethical and has made us, his children, to be so as well. It is not an accident that no society whose members habitually lie to one another and steal from one another can long survive. That is a reflection of the very nature of creation. Like the denial of the principles of gravity, denial of the ethical principles of reality has deadly consequences. The gods are human creations, created to justify human sin and arrogance. Thus they are all that we are, only more so. They are more benevolent than we are and more cruel; they are more dependable than we are and more fickle; they are more pure than we are and more degraded. The book of Exodus, however, tells us that they are just a fiction and cannot justify human sin. On the contrary, the true Creator is not cruel, fickle, or degraded—he is only benevolent, dependable, and pure—and humans are sinful because they have left him.

The Holiness of God. The Hebrew root denoting holiness (*qadash* [TH6942, ZH7727]) only occurs four times in the entire book of Genesis, and none of its uses refers to God's nature. Three of these occurrences are in the technical term for "shrine prostitute" (that is, a woman who has been dedicated to a goddess) in Genesis 38. The only other occurrence is in Genesis 2:3, where it is said that God declared the Sabbath day to be holy. But in Exodus the root occurs in all its forms more than 100 times. And in the rest of the Old Testament it occurs over 700 more times. What are we to make of this?

In the ancient Near East, the root *qadash* denoted that which was other than human. In particular it described the gods and that which belonged to them (such as a shrine prostitute). It had no moral connotation whatsoever. The reason for this becomes clear with a little thought. All the gods were holy by definition. The gods of life were holy, but so were the gods of death. The gods of fertility were holy, but so were the gods of war. The gods of purity were holy, but so were the gods of pestilence. "Holy" merely describes divine essence. As such, it is used relatively infrequently in extrabiblical literature.

This is not the case in the Old Testament. As we have seen, once we get beyond Genesis, the root is one of the most frequently used. Furthermore, the word has unmistakable moral connotations in the Bible. The basis of this transformation becomes clear in Exodus. I suggest that the reason the word is never applied to God in Genesis is precisely related to the problem mentioned above. The very concept of "god" had become so contaminated that God had to start over with the patriarchs by avoiding words that would give them the wrong impression about his character. At the outset he simply had to establish that he could be trusted, that he really had the best interests of humans at heart. To a large extent that is what all the patriarchal narratives are about: God can be trusted; what he says can be believed; and obeying what he says is the way to blessing. It is as though God was saying to these people, "Forget everything you have ever learned about deity, and just walk with me."

With those foundational elements laid down, it was possible to build on them, to take on some of the wrong concepts and begin to correct them. That is what begins to happen in Exodus. This is also why God continues to emphasize in the early chapters of Exodus that he *is* the God of their fathers, the God of Abraham, Isaac, and Jacob. It is as though he is asking the people to remember the essential goodness, trustworthiness, and approachability he has demonstrated with the patriarchs. But now he needs to show them what kinds of barriers have to be crossed if they are truly to experience this good, trustworthy, and approachable God. Thus, it cannot be an accident that after he called out "Moses!" the first words from within the burning bush were, "Do not come any closer. . . . Take off your sandals, for you are standing on holy ground" (3:5). If it is true that God is good, trustworthy, and approachable, it is *also* true that he is absolutely other than we are—in fact, far more other than a pagan could either understand or allow.

What begins to emerge in Exodus, and is further underscored in the succeeding Old Testament books, is that there is really only one being in the universe who is truly other than the universe, and that is Yahweh. The gods are not really other, as the practice of idolatry conclusively shows. Nowhere is this more bitingly portrayed than in Isaiah 44, where the prophet depicts the idolater taking a log, cutting up half of it to make a fire for himself, and using the other half to make an idol for himself. We can almost hear the ridicule in the prophet's voice, "And you call that holy!? Are you crazy?" A man-made religion does not create "otherness." In fact, its underlying purpose is to minimize the distance between deity and humanity. Exodus tells us that God is determined to minimize that distance too, but that it can only happen from his side and only if we understand what the distance really involves.

So the Bible declares that holiness, on its most basic level, denotes the absolute distance between human and divine. But what exactly is that distance? It is first of all a matter of incompatible essences. The common dirt on the bottom of Moses's sandals was of a different essence than the dirt around the bush where the transcendent God had chosen to manifest his presence. So the two kinds of dirt could not be mixed. By this statement God was alerting Moses at the very outset of the exodus and covenant experiences that this matter of fellowship with God was a good deal more complicated than might have been expected given his encounters with the patriarchs. (But the patriarchs were not completely oblivious to the critical differences. Notice Gen 32:30 where Jacob marvels that he has seen God and is still alive; cf. Exod 33:20. By the time of Isaiah it has been made abundantly clear; cf. Isa 6:5). But it is not so much God's essence as it is his character that separates him from us fallen humans. That is perhaps the most important point the covenant exists to teach. The matter is highlighted by God again before he presents the covenant to the people: In Exodus 19 he is preparing the people to receive the covenant. He first engages in cognitive preparation as he invites the people to reflect on the different fates of themselves and the Egyptians. The Egyptians have been humiliated and defeated as a result of their refusal to recognize God. But God has "carried [the Hebrews] on eagles' wings and brought" them to himself (19:4). Notice that it is not said they have been delivered from bondage. As has been said frequently above, neither release from bondage nor even the gift of the Promised Land was God's ultimate purpose in the Exodus. Rather, he intended to bring the Israelites to the place where it was safe for them to have a blessed relationship with their Father, to be his "own special treasure" (19:5).

In this cognitive preparation for the covenant, the emphasis shifts from an invitation to reflection to a promise. Not only did God mean to make the people his "special treasure," he also meant to make them a "kingdom of priests, my holy nation" (19:6). One might say that "holy" here is like the dirt around the burning bush: The people will come to share the otherness of God simply by proximity, by becoming his possession, just as the equipment of the Tabernacle became holy by being dedicated to God's service (see, e.g., 29:37). But unlike the equipment of the Tabernacle, there is no ceremony of dedication that makes the people holy. Here, as 19:5 shows, it is obedience to the covenant that will make the people holy. How can that be? What this means is that "holy" does not merely denote an essential difference between God and his creatures but, perhaps even more significantly, a behavioral difference.

This behavioral, or better, character difference is highlighted in the stipulations of the covenant. God is characterized by ethical behavior. In the deepest, truest sense, this is what defines his "holiness." And if his people will live and act like he does, by obeying him and keeping his covenant, they too will be holy. This point is not developed completely in Exodus, but it is in Leviticus in passages such as Leviticus 19. At the outset (Lev 19:2), the people are commanded to be holy as God is holy, and then are directed to engage in certain practices, from honoring their parents (Lev 19:3) to leaving some of the harvest behind for the poor (Lev 19:9-10) to keeping the Sabbath (Lev 9:30). And almost every injunction is ended with the words "I am the LORD." In other words, you must act in certain (holy) ways because this is the expression of the character of the holy Lord who delivered you from Egypt. Note that this behavior is not required to experience deliverance. Keeping the covenant is not the way to enter into a relationship with God. Rather, a life of covenant obedience to the holy God is the way in which the relationship is lived out.

But a problem would soon become evident in this relationship. Just as God's essence is foreign to created things, his character is foreign to fallen human beings. It is not quite so simple for humans to live with God as the Genesis narratives might suggest. In Exodus, this becomes very clear in chapter 32. As reported in chapter 24, the Israelites had sworn in blood to keep the covenant. They seem to have done so very blithely, without a second thought. They did not recognize the deep hostility we all harbor toward the idea of entrusting ourselves and our needs to God. Within only five weeks, that hostility manifested itself as they danced around a gold bull idol, praising it for having delivered them from Egypt. So the question emerges, how can a holy God live with fallen, sinful humans? Ironically, that was the very issue God was addressing with Moses when the people in the valley were succumbing more and more to their fears. We can only live with God on God's terms, by fully recognizing who we are in ourselves and who he is in himself and by employing the means he has made available. That alone makes it possible for us to live with him and not be destroyed by his holiness. But how will the expectation of the covenant be realized, that we shall be holy in our behavior as God is holy? God's people waited for the New Testament era and the provision of the Holy Spirit for that experience, when, in the words of Jeremiah, the covenant would be written on our hearts.

The Purpose of the Covenant. It is important to recognize where the covenant stands in the story of deliverance. Keeping the covenant does not effect deliverance for the Hebrew people. When they stood at the foot of Mount Sinai, they already stood before God as delivered. As 19:4 says, God had already brought them to himself. They had been delivered as a result of the gracious self-revelation of God in their experience. So if the covenant is not the way to God, what is it? The covenant is the blueprint for a living relationship with God. In this regard, it does four things: (1) It provides the means whereby the delivered relationship may be maintained (note that the covenant contains no provision whereby a person can continue to receive the blessings of God while willfully disobeying him); (2) it teaches the holy character of God through the medium of expected behavior; (3) it teaches the character that God desires in his people if they are to be his "holy nation"; (4) it teaches that there is a fundamental hostility in fallen human nature to the holy character of God (what the New Testament calls "the flesh"; NLT, "sinful nature," e.g., Rom 7:25).

As Paul says in several places, the covenant was never given to make us right with God (Rom 8:3; Gal 3:21). It could not do that because of our sin. The Pharisaic attempt to use law-keeping as a means of self-justification was a misappropriation of the covenant and a misreading of God's plan; it was to make the covenant a source of curse because by our own strength, we can never keep it. No, only grace can deliver us from our bondage and carry us to God "on eagles' wings." That was as true in the Old Testament as it is in the New. But was the covenant then abrogated with the coming of Christ? Has it taught us its lessons and can now thankfully be dispensed with? Jesus says that is not the case; he says that he has not come to do away with the covenant, but to fulfill it, that is, to bring it to its intended purpose (Matt 5:17). Why were the Israelites unable to keep the covenant? Because the covenant did not have in itself the dynamic to defeat our selfish will—the "flesh" or "the sinful nature" (Rom 8:3). Is there such a dynamic? There certainly is. Paul speaks of it in Romans 8. It is the Holy Spirit, who has been made available to us all through the death and resurrection of Christ. Paul says that if we will "walk" (i.e., "live") in the Spirit whom we have in Christ, we will not obey that sinful self-will but will fulfill the righteous requirements of the covenant (Rom 8:1-4). Just as it was grace alone that could provide deliverance, it is grace alone that can provide the means of realizing the goal of deliverance: behavior that is like God's. This is not to suggest that every aspect of the Torah is obligatory upon Christians. Clearly, the ceremonial laws, such as those requiring sacrifices, were designed as object lessons to teach spiritual truths. Likewise the civil laws teach eternal principles in time-bound forms. But it is to say that the *purpose* of the Torah—inculcating godly character—is hardly done away with by the grace of Christ.

The Significance of Revelation in History. I have already spoken of the importance of God's self-revelation as the cause of deliverance. But the implications of this fact for the nature of biblical revelation need to be explored more fully. The Bible claims that its understanding of reality, one that is radically different from that of all the peoples around Israel, is not the result of philosophical speculation but the result of a different experience than that of those other peoples. Israel claimed that God broke into her history in ways that he did not break into any other people's history and that he inspired certain persons to record what God had done and to give authoritative interpretations of his actions and words. Thus, the Israelites knew that God transcends nature because he demonstrated in history that he is able to make any aspect of nature do his bidding. Jethro knew that Yahweh was a different order of being from the gods of Egypt because of what he did in history to demonstrate that fact. Throughout all the rest of Israel's history, the people testified that God had chosen them in love because he delivered them from Egypt with signs and wonders.

But today there is great skepticism about whether God can or does ever break into human history. We do not see any cataclysmic actions like those recorded in Exodus taking place today. Or if we see any events approaching this magnitude, there seem to be as many interpretations of their causes and meaning as there are interpreters. As a result, many biblical scholars today suggest that the narratives of God's actions in history, up to and including the life of Jesus, are expressions of faith using the medium of fictional history. Such things are said in this regard as, "Fiction is often a more effective expression of truth than a mere recitation of historic facts" (see e.g., Alter 1981:37-45).

The problem with this view, as I see it, is two-fold. The first issue is that the Hebrews (and their spiritual descendants, the early Christians) alone present their theology in the garb of historical narrative, not only in the ancient world, but in the whole world. By this I mean to say that God is revealed almost entirely in the context of the connected accounts of a single people's human-historical experience. This is not to deny that the literatures of other peoples speak of their gods as acting in isolated events of human history. But nowhere else is contiguous human history made the sole vehicle for divine revelation. Why this difference? If the Hebrew writers arrived at their ideas of reality in the same way everybody else did—by speculative thought applied to the psycho-socio-physical cosmos—why is their view radically different from everybody else's, and why did they resort to a medium no one else has ever used? Why did the Israelites do everything in their power to convince us readers that these things did take place? One answer might be that the original storytellers and hearers knew it was just a good yarn, whereas later tellers and hearers did not know this and dressed it up to look as "real" as they supposed it was. That will not do because it does not answer the first question: Why did the Hebrews ever express their convictions about God in this bizarre way? But the most telling point of all is that, if we accept that any of these accounts are fictional, then there is no basis for believing their theology at all. In particular, the exclusivism of biblical faith condemns that faith to destruction if its historical claims are false. The Hebrews (and Christians) tell us that there is only one God and Savior of the world, the one who revealed himself, as no so-called god could, in the realm of verifiable time and space. If they are lying about this, or even deluded about this, then biblical faith is not one more of the great world religions. It is, in fact, a fraudulent understanding of reality that must be discarded. The Israelites told us they had this bizarre understanding of reality because God broke into their everyday experiences and would not let them believe anything else. We must decide whether they are right or wrong. There is no middle ground. If they are wrong, the Bible cannot be salvaged, and we are doomed to go back into the night of paganism, where there is neither right nor wrong, and where the only salvation is self-assertion. Fortunately, we need not go back. God *has* broken into our lost, broken world with the power of self-giving love, and we may find our truest selves in giving ourselves away to him and to others.

OUTLINE
I. Deliverance: A Revelation of Yahweh's Power (1:1–15:21)
   A. Preparation for Deliverance (1:1–7:7)
      1. The need for deliverance (1:1-22)
      2. The preparation of the deliverer (2:1-25)
      3. The call of the deliverer (3:1–4:28)
      4. The offer of deliverance (4:29–7:7)
   B. The Events of Deliverance (7:8–15:21)
      1. The plagues (7:8–12:30)
         a. Moses's staff and the first series of plagues (7:8–8:19)
         b. The second series of plagues (8:20–9:12)
         c. The third series of plagues (9:13–10:29)
         d. The death of the firstborn and the Passover (11:1–12:30)
      2. The Exodus (12:31–14:31)
         a. Journey into the wilderness (12:31–13:22)
         b. Crossing the sea (14:1-31)
      3. The song of the sea (15:1-21)
II. Wilderness: A Revelation of Yahweh's Providential Care (15:22–18:27)
   A. Water at Marah (15:22-27)
   B. Manna and Quail from Heaven (16:1-36)
   C. Water from the Rock (17:1-7)
   D. Protection from the Amalekites (17:8-16)
   E. Jethro's Visit to Moses (18:1-27)
      1. Jethro's faith in response to Moses's report (18:1-12)
      2. Jethro's advice for organizing the people (18:13-27)
III. Covenant: A Revelation of Yahweh's Character (19:1–24:18)
   A. Motivation to Accept the Covenant (19:1-25)
   B. Presentation of the Covenant (20:1–23:33)
      1. The Ten Commandments: a summary of the terms (20:1-17)
      2. The terms of the covenant for the people (20:18–23:19)
         a. Introduction (20:18-21)
         b. Proper use of altars (20:22-26)
         c. Fair treatment of slaves (21:1-11)
         d. Cases of personal injury (21:12-36)
         e. Protection of property (22:1-15)
         f. Social responsibility (22:16-31)
         g. A call for justice (23:1-13)
         h. Three annual festivals (23:14-19)
      3. Yahweh's covenant promises (23:20-33)
   C. Acceptance of the Covenant (24:1-18)

IV. The Tabernacle: A Revelation of Yahweh's Purpose (25:1–40:38)
   A. Instructions for the Tabernacle and Its Service: The Right Way to God's Presence (25:1–31:18)
      1. Instructions for building the structure and furnishings (25:1–27:19)
      2. Instructions relating to the priesthood (27:20–30:38)
      3. Craftsmen: Bezalel and Oholiab (31:1-11)
      4. Instructions for the Sabbath (31:12-18)
   B. The Gold Calf: The Wrong Way to Secure God's Presence (32:1–34:35)
      1. The making of the calf (32:1-6)
      2. The Lord's response and Moses's intercession (32:7-14)
      3. Moses's response and intercession (32:15-35)
      4. The Lord's presence will go with them (33:1-23)
      5. The renewal of the covenant (34:1-35)
   C. Report of Building the Tabernacle: Securing Yahweh's Presence in Yahweh's Way (35:1–40:38)
      1. Instructions for the Sabbath and a call for material and skills for the Tabernacle (35:1–36:7)
      2. Building the Tabernacle (36:8–39:43)
         a. Constructing the sanctuary (36:8-38)
         b. Constructing the furniture for the sanctuary (37:1-29)
         c. Constructing the courtyard and its equipment (38:1-20)
         d. Inventory of materials (38:21-31)
         e. Making the clothing for the priests (39:1-31)
         f. Moses inspects the work (39:32-43)
      3. The Tabernacle completed (40:1-38)
         a. Setting up the Tabernacle (40:1-33)
         b. The Lord's glory fills the Tabernacle (40:34-38)

ENDNOTES
1. For further discussion of the theme of the Pentateuch, see Clines 1978 and Alexander 1998.
2. It might be said that Isaac forms a fourth illustration of the truth, but the Isaac narrative is distinctly secondary (for whatever reason) to the other three.
3. See Harrison 1969:3-82, 566-575 for a penetrating discussion of Old Testament higher criticism in general and Exodus in particular.
4. 6:7; 7:5, 17; 8:22; 10:2; 14:4, 19; 16:12; 29:46; 31:13.
5. 5:2; 8:10; 9:14, 29; 11:7; 16:6, 12; 18:11; 33:13.

COMMENTARY ON
Exodus

◆ **I. Deliverance: A Revelation of Yahweh's Power (1:1–15:21)**
   A. Preparation for Deliverance (1:1–7:7)
      1. The need for deliverance (1:1-22)

These are the names of the sons of Israel (that is, Jacob) who moved to Egypt with their father, each with his family: ²Reuben, Simeon, Levi, Judah, ³Issachar, Zebulun, Benjamin, ⁴Dan, Naphtali, Gad, and Asher. ⁵In all, Jacob had seventy* descendants in Egypt, including Joseph, who was already there.

⁶In time, Joseph and all of his brothers died, ending that entire generation. ⁷But their descendants, the Israelites, had many children and grandchildren. In fact, they multiplied so greatly that they became extremely powerful and filled the land.

⁸Eventually, a new king came to power in Egypt who knew nothing about Joseph or what he had done. ⁹He said to his people, "Look, the people of Israel now outnumber us and are stronger than we are. ¹⁰We must make a plan to keep them from growing even more. If we don't, and if war breaks out, they will join our enemies and fight against us. Then they will escape from the country.*"

¹¹So the Egyptians made the Israelites their slaves. They appointed brutal slave drivers over them, hoping to wear them down with crushing labor. They forced them to build the cities of Pithom and Rameses as supply centers for the king. ¹²But the more the Egyptians oppressed them, the more the Israelites multiplied and spread, and the more alarmed the Egyptians became. ¹³So the Egyptians worked the people of Israel without mercy. ¹⁴They made their lives bitter, forcing them to mix mortar and make bricks and do all the work in the fields. They were ruthless in all their demands.

¹⁵Then Pharaoh, the king of Egypt, gave this order to the Hebrew midwives, Shiphrah and Puah: ¹⁶"When you help the Hebrew women as they give birth, watch as they deliver.* If the baby is a boy, kill him; if it is a girl, let her live." ¹⁷But because the midwives feared God, they refused to obey the king's orders. They allowed the boys to live, too.

¹⁸So the king of Egypt called for the midwives. "Why have you done this?" he demanded. "Why have you allowed the boys to live?"

¹⁹"The Hebrew women are not like the Egyptian women," the midwives replied. "They are more vigorous and have their babies so quickly that we cannot get there in time."

²⁰So God was good to the midwives, and the Israelites continued to multiply, growing more and more powerful. ²¹And because the midwives feared God, he gave them families of their own.

²²Then Pharaoh gave this order to all his people: "Throw every newborn Hebrew boy into the Nile River. But you may let the girls live."

1:5 Dead Sea Scrolls and Greek version read *seventy-five;* see notes on Gen 46:27. 1:10 Or *will take the country.* 1:16 Hebrew *look upon the two stones;* perhaps the reference is to a birthstool.

NOTES

1:1 *that is, Jacob.* An addition to the NLT to clarify the sense of "Israel." The Hebrew text tends to use "Israel" and "Jacob" somewhat interchangeably after Gen 32:25-31.

family. Lit., "house." Since extended families tended to live in the same building, or "house," the extended family is often referred to as a man's "house" (cf. 2 Sam 7:5, 11).

1:5 *Jacob had.* Lit., "those going out of the thigh of Jacob." "Thigh" here is euphemistic for genitalia; thus, it means those who were procreated by Jacob.

seventy. The LXX reads "75" instead of the MT's "70" both here and in Gen 46:27 (see NLT mg). It is difficult to judge between the two. There are numerous discrepancies between the LXX and the MT in numbers. The total of the actual names cited in Gen 46:18-27 is 66; 70 would then be a round number.

1:7 The Hebrew here has no less than three verbs to express the idea of multiplication. Clearly the point is being emphasized. So also the adverb "strongly" (*me'od* [TH3966, ZH4394]) is repeated twice in reference to "became . . . powerful."

1:10 *We must make a plan.* Lit., "come, let us be wise"; this suggests an element of shrewdness. They would not wait for events to overtake them.

1:11 *to wear them down.* The NLT captures the idea of *'anah* [TH6031, ZH6700], which has the connotation of bringing a person down either in spirit ("humiliate") or physically ("afflict").

1:12 *alarmed.* Heb. *quts* [TH6973, ZH7762], a rather strong term associated with dread and loathing. The Egyptians were not just worried, they were terrified. It denotes the same emotion that Ahaz felt when confronted with the Syro-Israelite attempt to depose him (Isa 7:6, 16).

1:15 *Shiphrah and Puah.* It seems likely that these two women are only named as representatives of a much larger group of midwives, since two women could not have served all the midwife needs of the entire people.

Hebrew. This word occurs 12 times in the first 10 chs of the book, and only 22 times elsewhere in the OT. Six occurrences are in Genesis in the Joseph story, and eight are in 1 Samuel in connection with the Philistines. Six others (21:2; Deut 15:12; Jer 34:9, 14) have to do with a "Hebrew" slave. The word is often used in a dismissive way by either Egyptians or Philistines. It seems to reflect not so much an ethnic group as it does a class, and a lower class, at that. Cf. Gen 14:13; Jonah 1:9.

1:16 *watch as they deliver.* Lit., "you look upon the two stones" (see NLT mg). Egyptian women squatted on two bricks to give birth.

1:21 *families.* Lit., "houses" (see note on 1:1).

COMMENTARY

It is immediately apparent from the opening verses of Exodus that the book does not stand alone. We are introduced to a family about whom the book gives no prior information. We are told that they "moved to Egypt," but not where they moved from. We also learn (1:5) that one member of the family, Joseph, was already in Egypt, but we are not told why. The narrator assumes that the reader has already read the "prequel," to use a neologism from the movie industry. But if the book of Exodus assumes the existence of the book of Genesis, the opposite is also true. Genesis assumes a sequel; it is not complete in itself. It has shown that the path to cursing is distrust, disbelief, and disobedience (Gen 3), and the path to blessing is trust, belief, and obedience (Gen 12, 15, 22, and likewise in the stories of Jacob and Joseph). But the basis of trust was a succession of divine promises that, if they convinced the patriarchs that God sincerely wanted to give them what they longed for, were still largely unfulfilled at the end of Genesis.

Furthermore, as discussed in the Introduction, it is evident in Genesis that God intends for his blessing to be experienced not just by a few patriarchs, or even their extended family, but indeed by the whole world. This is implied in Genesis 4-11 where the effects of the curse are seen as extending to the whole world (i.e., all the children of Adam and Eve). Thus, if God is the sole creator and if his intention was to bless the human race, then it would not do for only Jacob and his children to share that blessing. This intention is made explicit in Genesis 12:1-3 where God says that "all the families of the earth will be blessed through" Abraham. The book of Exodus is necessary, then, to continue the saga of God's promises: how they can be indeed fulfilled for Abraham's descendants and what may be necessary to extend them to the whole world.

It seems very probable that some portion of the Egyptian sojourn of the Israelites occurred during the time when Semitic peoples, whom the Egyptians called "rulers of foreign nations" (anglicized as Hyksos), had invaded and were ruling northern Egypt. This was a roughly 200-year period between 1750 and 1550 BC. (Shaw [2000] considers this period to have begun about 1665. The actual length of the Egyptian sojourn is open to some question. Note that Gal 3:17 [supporting the LXX reading of 12:40] reduces it from 430 years to about 220.) It is easy to imagine that a pharaoh who himself had Semitic antecedents would have been sympathetic to the Israelites, along the lines of the pharaoh depicted in Genesis 47. With that kind of patronage, the Israelites could have easily grown numerous and "powerful" (1:7).

But about 1550, a new Egyptian dynasty arose (the eighteenth) and evicted the Hyksos, reestablishing native Egyptian rule over the entire land. Again, it is easy to imagine that this new king, whose throne name was Ahmoses, was the one "who knew nothing about Joseph or what he had done" (1:8). If any residual knowledge of the great man had been preserved among later Hyksos pharaohs, it would have disappeared, or even been purged, when the new dynasty found itself in power. Anything reminiscent of the hated past would have been erased, as a later dynasty erased the memory of the heretical pharaoh Akhenaton. Sarna (1991:5) points out that the use of the verb *qum* [TH6965, ZH7756] ("arose," 1:8; NLT, "came to power"), instead of *malak* [TH4427, ZH4887] (reigned), signals the beginning of a new dynasty.

This Hyksos background also makes it easier to understand why the Egyptians were very uneasy about the Israelites. Jacob's family had settled in the northeast delta of Egypt just inside the border with the Sinai peninsula, near where the Suez Canal is today. The Bible calls this part of Egypt "the region of Goshen" (Gen 47:1). The Hyksos had been ejected back into the land of Canaan, but if they determined to try to come back, the only people standing between them and the heart of Egypt was a vast horde of their Semitic relatives! It is no wonder that the pharaoh was worried that "they will join our enemies" (1:10). At the same time, he was also worried that they might leave entirely, perhaps depopulating this rich region. Thus, it is easy to see why he thought they needed to make a plan. On the one hand, they had to make it so the Israelites were not in a position to help Egypt's enemies, but on the other hand, they had to make it so that Israel would not go off with the evicted Hyksos.

The plan was simple enough. They would enslave the Israelites, not merely limiting their freedom to develop military skills, but also limiting their power to pick up and move out. But there was a further intent, and that was to break their spirits, or "wear them down" (see note on 1:11). The verb *'anah* [TH6031, ZH6700] can be translated in several ways including "afflict" and "humble" (KBL 719), but the underlying sense is "to put down." God had dramatically exalted the people and now the Egyptians were setting out to reverse that. They believed that a thoroughly subjugated people would lose the will to resist.

But, in a situation similar to that which Jacob experienced in the house of his uncle Laban, the Egyptians discovered that their stratagems could not overthrow the intentions of God. Laban consistently tried to trick Jacob and misuse him, but God continued to counteract those efforts and to bless Jacob in spite of Laban (Gen 31:6-13). So here, it seemed that the Egyptian efforts to put the Israelites down were actually having the opposite effect, and the Egyptians grew "alarmed" (1:12; see note) over the apparent failure of their plan. They were faced with a situation that did not fit their paradigms and were filled with dread. As is often the case with dictatorial power, the Egyptians tried to quell their fear with the application of force. They were "without mercy" (1:13) and "ruthless" (*perek* [TH6531, ZH7266], 1:14), apparently forcing the Israelites to engage in the building work while also working the fields to provide their own food.

The pharaohs of the eighteenth dynasty were a new breed of Egyptian leader. They were military dictators who were intent on building an empire. The pharaohs of the Old Kingdom (3000–2400 BC) and the Middle Kingdom (1950–1750 BC) seem to have been more aloof from the people and the daily affairs of the realm. Not so with these New Kingdom (1550–1325 BC) pharaohs. They were much more men of the world, and they were determined to extend their imperial borders as far up the Canaanite coast and as far down the Nile valley as necessary to forestall the invaders they believed had been responsible for the fall of the first two kingdoms. No one could excel the building efforts of the Old Kingdom pharaohs (builders of the great pyramids), but every pharaoh had to at least make an effort to reach that standard. But not only were they expected to build temples and palaces, they also needed to build military garrisons and store cities for the dramatically enlarged armies. Those kinds of projects required vast labor forces. It appears the Egyptian people themselves provided the labor for the Old Kingdom's pyramids, laboring freely for the distant and unapproachable god-king. It may well be that for the much more human pharaohs of the New Kingdom, the Egyptians did not find themselves quite so ready to donate their labor for every edifice that the pharaoh decided to build, and that made the enslavement of an underclass like the Hebrews (see the note on 1:15) necessary. Part of this New Kingdom building frenzy was the construction of the cities of Pithom and Rameses (1:11), which are tentatively identified with Retebe and Qantir (Daba') in the northeast delta region. They would have been erected as supply bases for the troops campaigning in Canaan.

The emphasis on population growth, child-bearing, and fertility in this chapter reflects a common concern throughout the ancient world, one that is very foreign to us today. In that time—with little to mitigate the effects of natural disasters, warfare, and very high infant mortality—there was a very real danger of a people group simply disappearing off the face of the earth. The empty cities of Teotihuacán in Mexico and Angkor in Cambodia are only two examples. This fact helps to explain some of the fixation of pagan religion on matters of fertility and sexuality. Somehow power had to be gained over these natural forces to insure that "I and my family" would not be one of those that disappeared. Thus, it is hardly accidental that at the heart of God's promises to Abraham was the assurance that his family, far from disappearing, would cover the earth like sand on the shore or stars in heaven. Furthermore, it is not accidental that every one of the three primary matriarchs—Sarah, Rebecca, and Rachel—was unable to conceive in a natural way. God was making a point. Fertility and fecundity are not gods to be gained control of and manipulated for our own supposed benefit. Rather, they are gifts that fall upon those who are in a lovingly submissive relation with the Creator. So here, even though the Israelites are in a strange land, they were still experiencing the blessing of God, and they multiplied explosively (see the note on 1:7). And even when there was a concerted attempt to bring them down, God continued to multiply them.

This is why the pharaoh was finally driven to a desperate stratagem. If he let things continue as they were, the Hebrews would become more numerous than the Egyptians, at least in the northern part of the country. But if he simply turned his army loose on them, slaughtering them all, he would be depriving himself of his prime labor source. So he had to find a way to break the Israelite fertility cycle without simply erasing a large group of individual laborers. Clearly he had reason to congratulate himself on the plan he devised. He would kill all the Israelite boy babies but leave the girls alive (1:16). This would have the effect of bringing the Israelite nation to an end within not more than two generations. However, the girls, with their evidently high child-bearing potential, could be married into other lower-class groups, thus keeping the supply of slave labor constant for the foreseeable future. But the pharaoh failed to account for a group of women who feared God more than they feared the mightiest man on earth. He also failed to realize that he was arraying himself against one who was not a man nor a personified force of nature but the creator of the universe who had committed himself to make the descendants of Abraham into a great nation. It is hard to avoid the conclusion that when this pharaoh set himself to destroy the Israelite babies (in effect, God's firstborn; cf. Exod 4:22-23; 13:2), he was setting in motion a chain of events that could only end in the death of the Egyptian firstborn.

The challenge to God's power and veracity was now coming to a head. God had promised Abraham that his descendants would be a great and numerous people living in the land of Canaan. But these descendants were not living in the land of Canaan, and there seemed no prospect of that ever happening. Furthermore, the single most powerful man on earth had made up his mind to wipe out the Israelite people group. If the Israelites had a problem, God also had a problem. If the Israelites needed to be delivered, God had a reason to deliver them. If he could not or would not deliver them, then everything in the book of Genesis was a dead letter. On the other hand, if he could keep his promises against these impediments, then what would that say about his nature and character? What kind of a God would *that* be, who could triumph against these odds?

And what would it take for that process of deliverance to begin? What would it take for the will of earth's mightiest man to be frustrated? It would only take a few powerless women who would dare to take God seriously. The contrast between Pharaoh and the "midwives" (1:15) could hardly be more stark. He is the emperor, they are slaves; he is a male, they are females; he is rich, they are poor; he is all-powerful, they are powerless. If there was anyone in the universe they should fear, it would be he. He had the power to snuff out their lives as casually as snuffing out a candle. But these women, two of whom (see note on 1:15) are named for all eternity while the mighty pharaoh is left nameless, refused to obey him, regardless of whatever fear they may have had. Why? Because they had a greater fear. They were more worried about offending God than they were about offending the pharaoh. They had the right perspective, the same perspective Jesus spoke about when he said we should not fear those who can only kill the body (Matt 10:28). But the fear of God is not simply a dread of what he might do to us. Rather, it is a way of living that takes into account all that God is, not only his greatness, but also his faithfulness and kindness (cf. Gen 20:11 [KJV]; Deut 10:12-13; Pss 19:9; 25:12-14). It is to live with reality in view. Thus, to fear the Lord is to do what he says. The midwives were governed by this attitude.

The response of the midwives to the pharaoh's inquiry (1:19) continues to underscore the theme of fertility. Whether their statement was true or not, it served to reinforce the Egyptians' perceptions that the Israelites were for some reason enjoying the blessing of fertility while the Egyptians were not. As a result, the pharaoh was driven to a final, desperate ploy: The Egyptian people were given the duty to go among the Hebrew slaves, get their baby boys, and "throw [them] into the Nile River" (1:22). It is somewhat odd that this method of killing the babies is the only one mentioned, but it is not quite as odd as it first appears. In the Nile delta there are literally hundreds of branches of the river, so it would not have been necessary to go for miles to reach the river and throw the babies in. It may well be that other methods for killing the babies were used as well but that this method is highlighted because of what takes place in the next chapter in connection with the Nile. Just as the attempts to wear the people down by means of oppression failed (1:11ff), so the attempt to use the Nile as the means of their destruction was doomed to failure. In fact, God was going to turn the device directly on its head and use the Nile as a key element in the preparation of their deliverer. This was as Joseph said to his brothers, "You intended to harm me, but God intended it all for good" (Gen 50:20). At the same time, one wonders whether the turning of the Nile to blood in the first plague (7:14-25) was a judgment for this horrible crime.

The stage is now fully set. We, the readers, understand how desperate the need for deliverance was. The Hebrew people, the descendants of Abraham, were being ruthlessly oppressed. But more than that, there was a concerted effort afoot to destroy them as a people. Clearly, there was a great human need. But the situation also posed a problem for God. If the descendants of Abraham disappeared off the earth in the context of slavery in Egypt, then he would be seen as a fraud. He could not leave these people in this condition; he needed to deliver them if his promises to Abraham, Isaac, and Jacob were to have any meaning at all. Furthermore, if the world was to know him and experience his blessings, he could not leave the people in the clutches of a pagan human emperor. He would have to reveal who he is if the world was to be saved through a proper knowledge of him. The situation was very similar in the Babylonian exile hundreds of year later. Is Yahweh the only Holy One, or not? If other gods can take his people out of his hand and hold them captive, it would certainly appear he is not. At that time, God again said he would demonstrate his holiness to the world through his people. He would do so by delivering them from their captors, cleansing them from their idolatry, giving them a new spiritual sensitivity, and putting his Spirit within them (Ezek 36:19-28). Interestingly, in that passage, God says several times that Israel should not think they had deserved this deliverance but rather that God was doing it for his name's sake. That is, sin and its consequences pose a problem for God that is as serious as it is for the sinner. God needs to deliver his people to continue to demonstrate to the world who he really is and where the only hope of deliverance lies.

◆ ## 2. The preparation of the deliverer (2:1-25)

About this time, a man and woman from the tribe of Levi got married. ²The woman became pregnant and gave birth to a son. She saw that he was a special baby and kept him hidden for three months. ³But when she could no longer hide him, she got a basket made of papyrus reeds and waterproofed it with tar and pitch. She put the baby in the basket and laid it among the reeds along the bank of the Nile River. ⁴The baby's sister then stood at a distance, watching to see what would happen to him.

⁵Soon Pharaoh's daughter came down to bathe in the river, and her attendants walked along the riverbank. When the princess saw the basket among the reeds, she sent her maid to get it for her. ⁶When the princess opened it, she saw the baby. The little boy was crying, and she felt sorry for him. "This must be one of the Hebrew children," she said.

⁷Then the baby's sister approached the princess. "Should I go and find one of the Hebrew women to nurse the baby for you?" she asked.

⁸"Yes, do!" the princess replied. So the girl went and called the baby's mother.

⁹"Take this baby and nurse him for me," the princess told the baby's mother. "I will pay you for your help." So the woman took her baby home and nursed him.

¹⁰Later, when the boy was older, his mother brought him back to Pharaoh's daughter, who adopted him as her own son. The princess named him Moses,* for she explained, "I lifted him out of the water."

¹¹Many years later, when Moses had grown up, he went out to visit his own people, the Hebrews, and he saw how hard they were forced to work. During his visit, he saw an Egyptian beating one of his fellow Hebrews. ¹²After looking in all directions to make sure no one was watching, Moses killed the Egyptian and hid the body in the sand.

¹³The next day, when Moses went out to visit his people again, he saw two Hebrew men fighting. "Why are you beating up your friend?" Moses said to the one who had started the fight.

¹⁴The man replied, "Who appointed you to be our prince and judge? Are you going to kill me as you killed that Egyptian yesterday?"

Then Moses was afraid, thinking, "Everyone knows what I did." ¹⁵And sure enough, Pharaoh heard what had happened, and he tried to kill Moses. But Moses fled from Pharaoh and went to live in the land of Midian.

When Moses arrived in Midian, he sat down beside a well. ¹⁶Now the priest of Midian had seven daughters who came as usual to draw water and fill the water troughs for their father's flocks. ¹⁷But some other shepherds came and chased them away. So Moses jumped up and rescued the girls from the shepherds. Then he drew water for their flocks.

¹⁸When the girls returned to Reuel, their father, he asked, "Why are you back so soon today?"

¹⁹"An Egyptian rescued us from the shepherds," they answered. "And then he drew water for us and watered our flocks."

²⁰"Then where is he?" their father asked. "Why did you leave him there? Invite him to come and eat with us."

²¹Moses accepted the invitation, and he settled there with him. In time, Reuel gave Moses his daughter Zipporah to be his wife. ²²Later she gave birth to a son, and Moses named him Gershom,* for he explained, "I have been a foreigner in a foreign land."

²³Years passed, and the king of Egypt died. But the Israelites continued to groan under their burden of slavery. They cried out for help, and their cry rose up to God. ²⁴God heard their groaning, and he remembered his covenant promise to Abraham, Isaac, and Jacob. ²⁵He looked down on the people of Israel and knew it was time to act.*

2:10 *Moses* sounds like a Hebrew term that means "to lift out." 2:22 *Gershom* sounds like a Hebrew term that means "a foreigner there." 2:25 Or *and acknowledged his obligation to help them.*

NOTES

2:2 he was a special baby. Lit., "he was good." Commentators have debated the significance of this phrase at some length. Clearly the point is not that he was a well-behaved baby! The use of the word "special" reflects the connection that many make with the frequent refrain in Genesis 1 that the creation was "very good." Thus, this child was a key part of God's creative plan, and Jochebed, his mother (6:20), recognized this. For a more mundane possibility, see the commentary below.

2:3 basket. This word (*tebah* [TH8392, ZH9310]) is translated "ark" in the KJV, and it is the same word used of the boat that Noah built to save his family and the world's animals from the Flood (Gen 6:14). The fact that the Bible only uses the word here and in the flood narrative ("the ark of the covenant" uses a different Hebrew word) strongly suggests that there is an intentional connection being made between the two accounts. See the commentary below for further discussion.

among the reeds. The Hebrew word used for "reeds" here is the Egyptian loan word *sup* [TH5488, ZH6068], which is the same word used in 13:18 and elsewhere to identify the sea that God led his people across (28 occurences; see also Jonah 2:5). This creates a strong impression that the narrator wanted the reader to make a connection between the two events. These reeds, once common along all the Egyptian waterways, grew thickly and to a height of 10 feet or more.

2:5 her maid. This may refer to her personal attendant, but it may also refer to any of the multiple "attendants" mentioned in the verse whom she may have directed to pick up the basket.

2:9 Take. Sarna (1991:10) points out that the Hebrew word used here is an unusual word for this idea (lit., "you [fem.] cause him to walk"), and suggests that it may have been used because it sounds very much like a similar construction meaning "Here, he's yours."

2:10 brought him back . . . adopted him . . . named him. In the adoption documents of Mesopotamia, it is made clear that "foundling infants" were often farmed out to foster nursing mothers who contracted to care for the child for a minimum period of time, often until weaning, which seems to have occurred between the child's third and fifth year. It was only after this period of time, the child having survived the deadly first three to five years, that the formal adoption and naming of the child took place. What is being described here seems to fit that same pattern (Sarna 1991:10).

she explained. This is one way of mitigating a problem in the Hebrew text, which has the Egyptian princess giving a Hebrew quotation. Presumably these are not the princess's actual words but a Hebrew translation of what she said. The Egyptian word *msy* means "to bring forth, to give birth," and a number of well-known Egyptian names contain the element. Perhaps the best known is that of Pharaoh Thutmoses, who may have been the pharaoh of the Exodus; his name probably means something like "Born of [the god] Thoth." The princess may well have said something like, "I gave birth to him out of the water."

2:11 Hebrews. See note on 1:15.

beating. The same Hebrew root, *nkh* [TH5221, ZH5782] (to strike), appears in all three of the words translated "beating" (2:11), "killed" (2:12), and "beating up" (2:13). This may explain some of the Hebrew's insolence in 2:14. What right had Moses to judge him for doing the same thing Moses did? At least he had not yet beaten his opponent to death like Moses did! Interestingly, the attacker then accused Moses of murder (2:14; NLT "killed"; *harag* [TH2026, ZH2222], "to murder").

2:12 in all directions. Lit., "thus and thus," giving rise to the KJV "this way and that way."

2:13 who had started the fight. This is a good representation of the word *rasha'* [TH7563A, ZH8401], meaning "the wicked, the one in the wrong."

2:14 "Everyone knows what I did." This is perhaps a little strong for the literal, "Surely the thing is known." Moses had thought that no one knew what he had done. But at least one person did, and that meant that the most important person, the pharaoh, could very soon know about it, as he did.

2:15 Midian. This was the region inhabited by the Midianites on both sides of the Gulf of Aqaba, which separates the Sinai peninsula from the Arabian peninsula. While there continues to be debate about the actual location to which Moses fled, it seems unlikely that he traveled as far as the Arabian side of the Gulf.

2:17 jumped up. While this may be fairly taken as implicit, the verb is simply "he got up" (from where he was sitting, 2:15).

2:18 Reuel. This name means "friend of God"; he is elsewhere called "Jethro" (3:1; 18:1). Some commentators suggest that one of the names was a formal name relating to his role as "priest" (2:16), while the other was a personal name. There is disagreement about which was which. The LXX supplies the name "Jethro" in 2:16.

2:18 back so soon. This implies that the girls regularly had to wait until the male shepherds had watered their flocks and gone away before they were able to draw water. Bedouin today allow their daughters to mind their flocks only until the age of puberty, so these girls may have been quite young and easily intimidated.

2:19 An Egyptian. This was probably detectable both by his dress and his manner. The haughty Egyptian bearing toward those they contemptuously dismissed as "sand-dwellers" was probably not easily shed.

2:21 Moses accepted the invitation. This supplies an item of information that is surely correct, but it is only implied in the text. The text jumps straight from Reuel's command inviting Moses to a meal (2:20) to Moses's accepting of another much more far-reaching invitation, namely, one to take up residence with Reuel and his daughters. Thus, the text simply says, "Moses was willing to live with the man."

2:22 Gershom. It seems significant that the verbal root of this name (*garash* [TH1644, ZH1763]) is also that of the verb describing what the shepherds customarily did to Reuel's daughters: "chased them away" (2:17). Moses had been chased away from his homeland, and he had chased away those who chased away his future wife, so it is fitting that his first son's name should reflect these facts of his life. At the same time, as the NLT mg note explains, the name sounds like "a foreigner there"—a wordplay Moses clearly draws on in the verse. These fortuitous similarities in sounds and meanings were very important to the Hebrews and other ancient peoples. They did not believe anything was by accident.

2:23 the king of Egypt died. It was not uncommon for a new ruler at the beginning of his reign to give amnesty to prisoners and criminals and to lighten requirements for other of his subjects. We would call it a "morale-booster" today. That is what the Israelites asked Rehoboam for at the beginning of his reign (1 Kgs 12:4). But this new pharaoh, like Rehoboam 500 years later, had apparently not lightened the burdens at all. This probably made the Hebrews' distress over their situation that much more severe since their hopes of some reprieve had been shattered.

2:25 knew it was time to act. I think the NLT mg better expresses the text: "acknowledged his obligation to help." The Hebrew is very terse, merely saying, "And God knew." But in the larger context of the previous three verbs (see the commentary), it seems most likely that the assumed object of the verb is "them"—that is, God acknowledged his people. The verb regularly conveys experiential and relational knowledge. So God refused to sit back as though he had no responsibility for these people's welfare. He did not say, "Well, I don't know those people." Rather, he said, "Yes, those are my people by covenant, and I can't let this situation continue."

COMMENTARY

With the necessity of deliverance (from both human and divine perspectives) having been fully established in chapter 1, the story now turns to the means God used to accomplish that deliverance. Initially, that means is a human couple. And this is the way it always is in the Bible: God never starts with a program but always with a person. It is so with Noah (Gen 6:8), with Abraham (Gen 12:1), with Joseph (Gen 50:20), with the judges (e.g., Judg 3:9), with David (1 Sam 16:13), with Josiah (2 Kgs 22:1-2), and ultimately with Jesus Christ. (Notice how the prophecies of deliverance in Isaiah and elsewhere all focus on the person of the Messiah; Isa 9:1-7; 11:1-5.) God always uses human persons in his efforts to bring the world into conformity with the plan he has had for it since the beginning.

Just as the world's problems began with a single couple, a man and a woman

(Gen 1–3), and as world redemption began with a couple, a man and a woman (Gen 12), so here the specific deliverance of the people, and the continuation of world redemption, begins with a couple. It is no accident that it is primarily the West, as a result of the influence of the Bible, that values individual worth. God is interested in, and uses, specific individuals. Unlike paganism (both ancient and modern), he does not see our value as residing in how well we each reflect some ideal of humanity. It is also significant that couples are emphasized. It is evident that God sees humanity as a "binary" unit. That is, if you want to know what real humanity is, you must look at two of us, a male and a female together. If you study only one of us you will draw a faulty conclusion about what humanity is.

At the same time, it is interesting that the parents are not named here. The reader must wait until the genealogy of Moses and Aaron in chapter 6 for that information. It seems clear that Moses is here only giving us the information that is essential to the main point: the preparation of the deliverer. Thus, it is significant that we *are* told what Israelite tribe the parents, and thus the child, are from. Moses's Levitical lineage establishes his mediatorial role from the outset. The task of the priestly line that Moses and Aaron were later to inaugurate was to stand between the people and God, both to represent God to the people and to represent the people to God. Throughout all of his ministry, Moses would be doing those things, not so much in a ritual way, as Aaron and his descendants did, but in the actual events of life (32:7-14, 30-34). So we are told from the beginning that this deliverer will not merely produce some "rabbit out of a hat" kind of deliverance with no cost to himself or personal involvement. No, the deliverance will be the result of his revealing God to the people personally and bearing the people before God. The parallel with the ministry of Christ is very clear. And until Christ came, there was no other parallel to Moses's ministry (Deut 18:15; 34:10).

If God always uses persons to effect deliverance, another common feature of his working is that he uses unlikely persons. The apostle Paul sums this up when he says, "Few of you were wise in the world's eyes or powerful or wealthy when God called you" (1 Cor 1:26). He then explains the reason for this phenomenon:

> Instead, God chose things the world considers foolish in order to shame those who think they are wise. And he chose things that are powerless to shame those who are powerful. God chose things despised by the world, things counted as nothing at all, and used them to bring to nothing what the world considers important. As a result, no one can ever boast in the presence of God. (1 Cor 1:27-29)

In other words, God uses the weak and unlikely so that no one can say that they accomplished God's deliverance for him in their own strength. Human pride, power, and position do not accomplish real deliverance, only more bondage to human pride, power, and position!

It is certainly the case here that the deliverer is an unlikely one. Ranged against the Israelites and their God is the most powerful nation in the world—and God sends a baby? Not only that but a double death sentence hangs over this baby's head. In the unlikely event that he survives the diseases of infancy, the pharaoh will have him killed. But this is exactly what God delights to do. It is no accident that the three primary matriarchs, Sarah, Rebecca, and Rachel, were unable to conceive without the intervention of God. Neither is it an accident that God's entire redemptive plan was made to hang on the conception and birth of a baby from Sarah, a woman long past menopause. Neither is it an accident that the father of the nation of Israel is second-born, a child with almost no rights and fewer prospects in the normal course of human affairs at that time. Neither is it accidental that the deliverer of Jacob's family from a devastating famine is the eleventh-born son or that the prototypical king of Israel, David, is the eighth-born. In all these cases, God was demonstrating conclusively that deliverance is never the product of human fecundity and power. It is a gift of God made available to the world through unlikely people who made themselves available to God in loving submission and active cooperation.

While it is very possible that the literal "the child was good" (NLT, "a special baby") is intended to make the reader draw a connection with Genesis 1 and the creative purposes of God (see note on 2:2), it is also possible that something much more mundane is intended. "Good" (*tob* [TH2896, ZH3202]) in the Old Testament has a wide range of connotations, much as "good" does in English, ranging all the way from morally sound to generally acceptable. Here, it may be possible that the mother saw in the child just what people today see when they look at a baby and exclaim, "Oh, he's just perfect!" The child may actually be rather ugly, but we mean that he is whole and healthy, everything a baby should be, with all the potential of life beaming out of his little face. Perhaps that is the case here, making the thought of snuffing out that little life all the more heartbreaking.

Once again, it is the powerless (in this case, three women; see the discussion of the midwives above on 1:15-20) who frustrate the will of the pharaoh. It seems very likely that Jochebed, Moses's mother, planned very carefully what to do with her baby. She did not simply set the baby afloat on the broad Nile to see what "fate" might bring. Instead, she "laid [the basket] among the reeds along the bank" (2:3). As mentioned in the note above, these reeds grew thick and tall. The basket was not going to float away from that place.

"Pharaoh's daughter" (2:5) did not bathe just anywhere. She certainly did not bathe in view of the whole population, and she almost certainly did not bathe in a different place each day. It was not an accident that she happened to come to the place where the basket was on that particular day. It seems very likely that Jochebed carefully chose that place in the hopes that what did happen would happen. Thus, the Nile, whom the Egyptians considered to be their special goddess, along with the pharaoh's own daughter became the means of preserving the deliverer's life. The irony of the situation is very clear. To oppose oneself to God is to run the very clear chance that one's own resources will become the means of God's accomplishing his purposes. Along these lines, some (e.g., Rice 2007) have wondered if there would have ever been a state of Israel unless Hitler and his minions had set themselves to wipe the Jews off the face of the earth.

It is interesting that the pharaoh's daughter seems never to have entertained the idea of obeying her father's edict. While it is hard for a man to resist a baby's cries, it seems doubly difficult for a woman to do so. Thus, "she felt sorry for him" (2:6) even though she recognized at once (perhaps because the Egyptians practiced a different style of circumcision) that this was a "Hebrew" child. It is not impossible that Jochebed chose her woman carefully, knowing something about her, and knowing how she was likely to respond. But in any case, the pharaoh's daughter chose life over death, and the world has been different ever since.

Moses's "sister," and we are tempted to think it was Miriam (see 15:20), immediately approached her in case the Egyptian princess might be hesitating over logistics and offered to find a woman to nurse the child. If many babies had been killed, there would have been a number of women available for the task. But it is still hard to imagine that the princess was so naive as not to imagine that the nurse would be the child's mother. Yet she betrayed no hesitancy at all. She seemed quite willing to enter into a loving conspiracy to spare this little boy's life. It is a comment on the providence of God that not only did he spare the life of the baby, but he had the mother paid to nurse her own child.

While we have no idea what Moses's actual experiences were growing up as a grandson of the pharaoh (Josephus's report of him having been a general in Nubia has no support), it is very reasonable to suppose that he would have had a good education in order to train him for leadership in the kingdom (cf. Acts 7:22). A pharaoh was expected to engender as many children as possible, and the males were often placed in the army or the civil administration. Again it is interesting to see the deliverer receiving his training from the hands of the oppressors. God is very economical. Why construct some other training device when a very effective one was right at hand?

It is not clear whether Moses knew himself to be a Hebrew from the outset. As mentioned above, the differing styles of circumcision may have made the situation unmistakable. But by the time of the events described in 2:11-15 he knew that the Israelites were "his own people." His sense of attachment to them is suggested by the fact that they are twice in 2:11 referred to literally as "his brothers." What follows shows us two things about Moses that will be born out in the ensuing narrative. One is his hot temper. He could flare up very suddenly, as his smashing of the tablets containing the Ten Commandments illustrates (32:19). But we also see his deeply ingrained sense of justice, which would stand him well in the coming years as he was forced to adjudicate many a case for his people.

But there is something else that this account illustrates. That is a failure on the part of the deliverer to deliver his people. He failed for two reasons. One was that he thought he could bring about deliverance with no threat to his own position and security. That is never the case. But the second reason he failed is that he entered into the attempt with neither the guidance nor the strength of God. The result is abject failure and defeat. And this defeat may have been as important a part of his preparation as anything else that happened to him. Now when the call of God came to him, Moses would not believe that he could possibly enter into this arrangement without a cost to himself. Neither would he dare to make such an attempt again without absolute assurance that he was acting under the guidance and power of God. The first attempt was made in what the New Testament writers would call "the flesh" (*sarx* [TG4561, ZG4922]), that is, human ability and self-serving (NLT, "confidence in my own effort," e.g., Phil 3:4). Happy is the person who has learned that it is deadly to attempt to do God's work with that motivation and energy. The response of the Hebrew in 2:14 (see note) shows that the man could see no difference in the violence he was engaging in and that which Moses had engaged in the day before. Both actions had been carried out "in the flesh."

So Moses ran away. We know from Acts 7:30 that he was away from Egypt for a long period, although Stephen's report of 40 years there has the marks of a round figure. Moses may well have consoled himself that he had made an effort and that no one could be expected to do more than that. But it also seems probable that this was God's way of bringing Moses to the utter end of himself. Why did God make Abraham and Sarah wait so long after they had arrived in Canaan for the birth of Isaac? Surely it was so that no one could claim that this birth was the result of human effort. Why wait until Moses was an old man to call him to this task that would be impossible even for a man of 35? For the very same reason. It was not until the self-confident young Egyptian finally knew himself to be an old Midianite shepherd, past the days of further human accomplishment, that he was finally usable for God.

It is interesting that the same temper and hatred of injustice that had driven Moses from Egypt (2:11-15) were the means of finding him a home and eventually a wife in Midian (2:16-21). God uses our individual traits to accomplish different things in different settings. It is a fallacy to think that in order for God to use us, he must destroy our distinctive personalities. He does not want to destroy what he has crafted. What he does want to do is to cleanse those traits of whatever taint of arrogance and self-serving may cling to them. Sometimes that is the work of a moment, but then the working out of the implications of that moment may be a matter of years.

Moses's comment on the similarity of Gershom's name to the phrase "a foreigner there" (see note on 2:22) gives the reader a sense of the continuing feeling of alienation he had, even though he had found a home and a wife in his new land. This sense, too, was a part of what God could use in the deliverer. Had Moses completely forgotten his identity as an Israelite and had he been completely acculturated to his new setting, there would have been no spark of concern for God to ignite in him. In God's economy, nothing is lost.

From a human perspective we have come to a dead end in 2:22. The deliverer is simply an alien in a strange land. He had attempted to do some good for his people, but that attempt had resulted in nothing but contempt from his people and the hatred of a pharaoh who probably saw Moses as trampling on the generosity that his household had extended to this ungrateful Hebrew. But verse 22 is not the end of the story. The deliverer had been fully prepared, as much in the isolation of the desert (so also with Paul more than a millennium later, cf. Gal. 1:17-18) as in the training centers of Egypt. But as vital as all of that preparation was, it would be worthless apart from the motivation and empowerment of God, and it is on that note that the chapter ends.

The mention of the death of "the king of Egypt" suggests that the passage of time that God allowed before mobilizing Moses may have had something to do with a bringing together of all the right circumstances for the stupendous events that were to take place. The same thing occurred in connection with the revelation of his Son (Gal 4:4; see also 2 Pet 3:9). At any rate, the crowning of a new king did not bring the decrease of oppression that might have been hoped for (see note on 2:23), and the Hebrews' despair fell to a new low. In verses 24 and 25 there is a succession of verbs describing God's response to his people. Typically, one would expect the subject of the second, third, and fourth verbs in the series to be simply the pronominal element "he." But in all four cases, the subject "God" is explicitly written, indicating God's direct personal involvement in every aspect of the response. The first and third responses, "heard" and "saw," convey God's sensitivity to human need. He is not "the Force" who neither knows nor cares what we suffer. Rather, he is the Heavenly Father whose heart is attuned to the slightest whispers of his children.

The second and fourth verbs convey God's positive response to what he hears and sees. It is not enough that God is keenly aware of what his children are experiencing. He could know what we are going through but shun all personal involvement with it. Aristotle conceived that the First Cause *must* be unaffected by all that it set in motion because if it were affected it would no longer be only a First Cause. Fortunately for the world, the revelation given to the Hebrews rises above the limits of human reason. For the Bible tells us that God "remembered his covenant promise." God was willing to limit his freedom by committing himself to us in blessing, and he will not deny our claims upon him ("God knew [them]"; see note on 2:25), either for arbitrary reasons or for reasons of difficulty. When we suffer, we can know that it is not because God has forgotten his promises to us.

◆   3. The call of the deliverer (3:1–4:28)

One day Moses was tending the flock of his father-in-law, Jethro,* the priest of Midian. He led the flock far into the wilderness and came to Sinai,* the mountain of God. ²There the angel of the LORD appeared to him in a blazing fire from the middle of a bush. Moses stared in amazement. Though the bush was engulfed in flames, it didn't burn up. ³"This is amazing," Moses said to himself. "Why isn't that bush burning up? I must go see it."

⁴When the LORD saw Moses coming to take a closer look, God called to him from the middle of the bush, "Moses! Moses!"

"Here I am!" Moses replied.

⁵"Do not come any closer," the LORD warned. "Take off your sandals, for you are standing on holy ground. ⁶I am the God of your father*—the God of Abraham, the God of Isaac, and the God of Jacob." When Moses heard this, he covered his face because he was afraid to look at God.

⁷Then the LORD told him, "I have certainly seen the oppression of my people in Egypt. I have heard their cries of distress because of their harsh slave drivers. Yes, I am aware of their suffering. ⁸So I have come down to rescue them from the power of the Egyptians and lead them out of Egypt into their own fertile and spacious land. It is a land flowing with milk and honey—the land where the Canaanites, Hittites, Amorites, Perizzites, Hivites, and Jebusites now live. ⁹Look! The cry of the people of Israel has reached me, and I have seen how harshly the Egyptians abuse them. ¹⁰Now go, for I am sending you to Pharaoh. You must lead my people Israel out of Egypt."

¹¹But Moses protested to God, "Who am I to appear before Pharaoh? Who am I to lead the people of Israel out of Egypt?"

¹²God answered, "I will be with you. And this is your sign that I am the one who has sent you: When you have brought the people out of Egypt, you will worship God at this very mountain."

¹³But Moses protested, "If I go to the people of Israel and tell them, 'The God of your ancestors has sent me to you,' they will ask me, 'What is his name?' Then what should I tell them?"

¹⁴God replied to Moses, "I AM WHO I AM.* Say this to the people of Israel: I AM has sent me to you." ¹⁵God also said to Moses, "Say this to the people of Israel: Yahweh,* the God of your ancestors—the God of Abraham, the God of Isaac, and the God of Jacob—has sent me to you.

This is my eternal name,
 my name to remember for all
 generations.

¹⁶"Now go and call together all the elders of Israel. Tell them, 'The LORD, the God of your ancestors—the God of Abraham, Isaac, and Jacob—has appeared to me. He told me, "I have been watching closely, and I see how the Egyptians are treating you. ¹⁷I have promised to rescue you from your oppression in Egypt. I will lead you to a land flowing with milk and honey—the land where the Canaanites, Hittites, Amorites, Perizzites, Hivites, and Jebusites now live."'

¹⁸"The elders of Israel will accept your message. Then you and the elders must go to the king of Egypt and tell him, 'The LORD, the God of the Hebrews, has met with us. So please let us take a three-day journey into the wilderness to offer sacrifices to the LORD, our God.'

¹⁹"But I know that the king of Egypt will not let you go unless a mighty hand forces him.* ²⁰So I will raise my hand and strike the Egyptians, performing all kinds of miracles among them. Then at last he will let you go. ²¹And I will cause the Egyptians to look favorably on you. They will give you gifts when you go so you will not leave empty-handed. ²²Every Israelite woman will ask for articles of silver and gold and fine clothing from her Egyptian neighbors and from the foreign women in their houses. You will dress your sons and daughters with these, stripping the Egyptians of their wealth."

CHAPTER 4

But Moses protested again, "What if they won't believe me or listen to me? What if they say, 'The LORD never appeared to you'?"

²Then the LORD asked him, "What is that in your hand?"

"A shepherd's staff," Moses replied.

³"Throw it down on the ground," the LORD told him. So Moses threw down the staff, and it turned into a snake! Moses jumped back.

⁴Then the LORD told him, "Reach out and grab its tail." So Moses reached out and grabbed it, and it turned back into a shepherd's staff in his hand.

⁵"Perform this sign," the LORD told him. "Then they will believe that the LORD, the God of their ancestors—the God of Abraham, the God of Isaac, and the God of Jacob—really has appeared to you."

⁶Then the LORD said to Moses, "Now put

your hand inside your cloak." So Moses put his hand inside his cloak, and when he took it out again, his hand was white as snow with a severe skin disease.* ⁷"Now put your hand back into your cloak," the LORD said. So Moses put his hand back in, and when he took it out again, it was as healthy as the rest of his body.

⁸The LORD said to Moses, "If they do not believe you and are not convinced by the first miraculous sign, they will be convinced by the second sign. ⁹And if they don't believe you or listen to you even after these two signs, then take some water from the Nile River and pour it out on the dry ground. When you do, the water from the Nile will turn to blood on the ground."

¹⁰But Moses pleaded with the LORD, "O Lord, I'm not very good with words. I never have been, and I'm not now, even though you have spoken to me. I get tongue-tied, and my words get tangled."

¹¹Then the LORD asked Moses, "Who makes a person's mouth? Who decides whether people speak or do not speak, hear or do not hear, see or do not see? Is it not I, the LORD? ¹²Now go! I will be with you as you speak, and I will instruct you in what to say."

¹³But Moses again pleaded, "Lord, please! Send anyone else."

¹⁴Then the LORD became angry with Moses. "All right," he said. "What about your brother, Aaron the Levite? I know he speaks well. And look! He is on his way to meet you now. He will be delighted to see you. ¹⁵Talk to him, and put the words in his mouth. I will be with both of you as you speak, and I will instruct you both in what to do. ¹⁶Aaron will be your spokesman to the people. He will be your mouthpiece, and you will stand in the place of God for him, telling him what to say.

¹⁷And take your shepherd's staff with you, and use it to perform the miraculous signs I have shown you."

¹⁸So Moses went back home to Jethro, his father-in-law. "Please let me return to my relatives in Egypt," Moses said. "I don't even know if they are still alive."

"Go in peace," Jethro replied.

¹⁹Before Moses left Midian, the LORD said to him, "Return to Egypt, for all those who wanted to kill you have died."

²⁰So Moses took his wife and sons, put them on a donkey, and headed back to the land of Egypt. In his hand he carried the staff of God.

²¹And the LORD told Moses, "When you arrive back in Egypt, go to Pharaoh and perform all the miracles I have empowered you to do. But I will harden his heart so he will refuse to let the people go. ²²Then you will tell him, 'This is what the LORD says: Israel is my firstborn son. ²³I commanded you, "Let my son go, so he can worship me." But since you have refused, I will now kill your firstborn son!'"

²⁴On the way to Egypt, at a place where Moses and his family had stopped for the night, the LORD confronted him and was about to kill him. ²⁵But Moses' wife, Zipporah, took a flint knife and circumcised her son. She touched his feet* with the foreskin and said, "Now you are a bridegroom of blood to me." ²⁶(When she said "a bridegroom of blood," she was referring to the circumcision.) After that, the LORD left him alone.

²⁷Now the LORD had said to Aaron, "Go out into the wilderness to meet Moses." So Aaron went and met Moses at the mountain of God, and he embraced him. ²⁸Moses then told Aaron everything the LORD had commanded him to say. And he told him about the miraculous signs the LORD had commanded him to perform.

3:1a Moses' father-in-law went by two names, Jethro and Reuel.   3:1b Hebrew *Horeb,* another name for Sinai.
3:6 Greek version reads *your fathers.*   3:14 Or *I Will Be What I Will Be.*   3:15 *Yahweh* is a transliteration of the proper name YHWH that is sometimes rendered "Jehovah"; in this translation it is usually rendered "the LORD" (note the use of small capitals).   3:19 As in Greek and Latin versions; Hebrew reads *will not let you go, not by a mighty hand.*   4:6 Or *with leprosy.* The Hebrew word used here can describe various skin diseases.
4:25 The Hebrew word for "feet" may refer here to the male sex organ.

NOTES

3:1 far into the wilderness. This is a good representation of the Hebrew *'akhar hammidbar* [TH4057, ZH4497], traditionally rendered "the backside of the desert." While it is true that *'akhar* [TH310, ZH339] can mean "behind," it also means "west," since Hebrew geographic orientation considered east to be "forward" or "in front." Thus, west was behind one's back. So the idea may be that Moses had led the flocks to the far western side of the territory where the Midianites lived, that is, toward the middle of the Sinai peninsula.

Sinai, the mountain of God. As the NLT mg notes, the Hebrew here refers to Horeb. There is every reason to take this to be equal to Mount Sinai, especially since 3:12 says that the delivered Israelites would one day worship at that mountain. It is also probable that Horeb is here called "the mountain of God" not so much because of this blazing bush episode but because of the much more significant events that were to take place there in connection with the giving of the covenant. Exodus 17:6 suggests the name might have originally applied to the region where the mountain stood, but all the other occurrences of the word in the OT (33:6; 9 times in Deut; and 5 times elsewhere) directly associate the term with Mount Sinai.

3:2 the angel of the LORD. Throughout the OT, when God appears to someone, it is characteristic to first say that it is the angel of the LORD and then for any conversation to proceed with the Lord speaking directly as though there was no mediator (Gen 16:7-14; 22:11-19; Judg 2:1-4; 6:11-23, 36; 13:2-22). It seems likely that this expression is an attempt to say two things simultaneously: (1) that it is really God whom the person is seeing and talking with but (2) that it is impossible for the Transcendent One to be localized in a single place. This concept finds its ultimate expression in Jesus Christ, who was truly God on this earth but is also one of three persons of the Triune God. For further discussion, see ch 33.

3:6 the God of your father. Most commentators agree that the MT is correct with the singular "father" (as opposed to "fathers" in the LXX, see NLT mg). They believe that the point being made here is that God is not merely the God of the rather abstract "fathers" but that he is the personal God who was known from father to son.

he was afraid to look at God. In the future on this very mountain, Moses's sense of intimacy with God would make him request such an opportunity (33:18).

3:8 fertile and spacious land. The land of Canaan is not particularly fertile on an absolute scale, but compared to the Sinai desert, it was a veritable garden.

milk and honey. Normally this "milk" would have been the milk of goats; thus it was a land where herds of goats could be raised. The "honey" referred to is sweet syrup made from dates, and thus it is a land of date palms and other fruit trees.

Canaanites . . . Jebusites. The desirability of the land is indicated by the number of different people groups contending for it. But this number also reflects two other factors. One of these is the fact that Canaan was the bridge between Mesopotamia and Egypt. Thus, the great powers were always trying to control it and, in the process, to break up any unified indigenous political structure that might develop. The second factor was the great number of geographically distinct areas encompassed by Canaan, making it difficult for one group to maintain unified control over all of them.

3:9 The cry of the people. Sarna (1991:15) points out that the word used here (and also in 3:7), *tse'aqah* [TH6818, ZH7591], is the strongest Hebrew word for an outcry. It is close to the English "scream" in the intensity it connotes.

3:10 Now. Both 3:9 and 3:10 begin with the word *we'attah* [TH20501/6258, ZH2256/6964], meaning "and now." This repetition intensifies the comparison and contrast between the two verses. Verse 9 speaks of God's awareness of the plight of his people, while v. 10 specifies his response: Moses!

3:11 Moses protested. The verb here is merely "said" (*wayyo'mer* [TH559, ZH606]). However, that verb is used to express a great number of ideas that are expressed by different verbs in English. Thus, it is quite appropriate to render it with "protested" in this context. That is clearly what Moses was doing.

3:12 this is your sign. The syntax of this verse is very difficult, making it somewhat unclear what the referent of "sign" is. Some think it is the burning bush. Others believe it to be God's presence. However, the most obvious alternative is the one that virtually all modern translations take: The delivered Israelites "will worship God at this very mountain." The objection to this view, other than the difficult syntax, is that a sign that is not fulfilled until a somewhat distant future time is not likely to produce faith at the moment. But that objection is without merit. Many of the signs of the Bible are of just that sort. This is especially true in the book of Isaiah. Signs do not produce faith. Rather, at a later date they confirm that the faith position taken earlier was the correct one (cf. Isa 7:14; 16:13-14; 21:16). The fact that God is confident enough of the outcome to make such a prediction helps to encourage faith, but it does not create faith where none exists. The Pharisees asked for that kind of a sign and none was given them except the promise that in the future Jesus would rise from the dead after three days (Matt 12:38-40).

3:13 God of your ancestors. This rendering of "God of your fathers" has much to commend it. The phrase is clearly not saying that God was only the God of the patriarchs and not of the matriarchs as well. And it is to be presumed that those who would insist on a more literal or formal translation do not believe that either. If it be said that we lose the emphasis on fathers being the spiritual heads of their families, there are many other explicit passages of Scripture that make that point. What the passage *is* clearly saying is that this was not a new God about to reveal himself to the Israelite people. Rather, it was the God who had revealed himself to the past generations of ancestors through promises that obligated him to intervene in the lives of the descendants of those ancestors.

3:14 I AM WHO I AM. There are many interpretations of this enigmatic phrase, ranging from Enns's suggestion (2000:103) that it is a refusal to give an answer to what was in fact a request for a magic formula to Fretheim's opinion (1991:63) that it is a declaration of God's continuing faithfulness to his people. Sarna (1991:18) offers the intriguing suggestion that the phrase is in the first person because God is naming himself (since in the ancient Near East the person who names another has power over the person named). The suggestion has much to commend it because otherwise the connection between this phrase and the name itself, presumably "Yahweh," is unclear. On this understanding, God would be saying that he names himself Yahweh (3:15; see NLT mg), meaning "He is," or perhaps "He who causes to be," because he is the one who eternally *is* and upon whom all other things depend.

In this discussion, it is also worth noting that originally the Hebrew scriptures were written without vowels. Thus the name of God was written as the equivalent of YHWH and probably pronounced *Yahweh*. However, in the intertestamental period, Jewish piety came to dictate that the name of God should never be spoken. Instead, whenever they encountered the divine name, called the Tetragrammaton ("the four letters"), they trained themselves to say *'adonai*, "Lord." By the fifth century AD, the dispersion of the Jews had become so widespread that it became advisable to put vowels in the text to insure uniform pronunciation. Thus, when it came time to put vowels in the Tetragrammaton, the vowels inserted were those of *'adonai*, leading those who did not know about this process, like the Europeans of the Reformation, to say that God's name was "Yahowah" (or with German/English influence, "Jehovah"), a word that never existed before that time. Since we do not know for certain how the name was pronounced, modern translations usually translate the name with

"LORD" in small capitals to distinguish it from the use of the ordinary word "lord." For an example of the distinction see Isa 1:24a.

3:18 *a three-day journey*. This does not necessarily limit the journey to three days only. In Hebrew idiom, "the third day" may designate the indefinite future: There is "today," there is "tomorrow," and there is "the third day" (see 1 Sam 20:12; Hos 6:2, KJV). Thus, this is a long journey, one that will take the Israelites well beyond the borders of Egypt and beyond any likelihood that they would ever return to their slavery.

to offer sacrifices to the LORD. It would be necessary to leave Egypt to offer such sacrifices because they would be an abomination to the Egyptians (8:26). But there is another important issue here. This request is made numerous times by Moses. It is not merely a "smokescreen" to cover the real motive for the request, namely, escape. In fact, it expresses the real reason for the Exodus: that Israel might worship the Lord rightly. See the commentary for further discussion.

3:19 *unless a mighty hand forces him*. See the NLT mg, which indicates the source of this translation in the LXX and the Latin Vulgate. (Many other versions that also accept this variant do not list the source.) It is possible that the MT "not by a mighty hand" should be read this way, but if so, it is certainly not clear.

3:21 *give you gifts*. The Israelites will not creep out by night so that the Egyptians might say the escape was accidental. No, the Egyptians will be so glad to see them go that they will give the Israelites whatever they ask (v. 22).

3:22 *Every Israelite woman*. Perhaps the intent is here as it has been throughout these early chapters of the book to stress that the powerless (as represented by women in that culture) will be able to defeat the most powerful enemy—under the hand of God. Normally, the plunder belongs to the conquering warriors, but here it is the women who will plunder their Egyptian enemies.

ask. This is a more accurate rendering than the KJV "borrow." These "loans" were never coming back!

4:1 *But Moses protested again*. Cassuto (1967:45) says that the Hebrew phrase "answered and said" is often used to open a new phase in a discussion. Here he believes it signals a change from the more genuine concerns addressed in ch 3 to those borne simply from doubt.

4:2 *What is that*. Normally, the Hebrew for this phrase would be *mah zeh* [TH4100/2088, ZH4537/2296], but here the Kethiv of the MT has *mazzeh*. Cassuto (1967:45) suggests it is given this form here as a wordplay on Moses's response: *matteh* [TH4294, ZH4751]—"staff." The question seems designed to highlight the fact that the sign is going to be performed with a very ordinary object.

4:5 *"Perform this sign," the LORD told him*. This is an explanatory insertion in NLT. The Hebrew sentence structure in 4:4-5 makes a very odd sentence when translated literally in English (cf. NASB). The information that Moses grabbed the snake and that it turned back into a staff (4:4b) occurs in the middle of a quotation from God (4:4a, 5).

4:6 *inside your cloak*. The literal "into your bosom" gives a wrong impression. He was to put his hand on his chest under his outer robe.

severe skin disease. This is a more accurate rendering of the Hebrew than "leprosy" (cf. KJV, ESV, NASB, NIV). While it is possible that the disease now called "leprosy" (Hansen's disease) may have been included among the diseases denoted by *tsara'* [TH6879B, ZH7665], it is clear that many other skin diseases are also described by it. Thus, to limit the translation to "leprosy" is inadequate (see Houtman 1993:1.395-396 for a full discussion). In this case, Moses's affliction definitely was not Hansen's disease, since whiteness of the skin ("white as snow") is not a symptom of that disease. Nevertheless, it seems probable from the other two signs that it was a life-threatening disease of some sort.

4:10 Moses pleaded. This reflects the very polite form of address used here and again in 4:13.

O Lord. This translates the word *'adonay* [TH136, ZH151], but in this context it is preceded by the prepositional phrase *bi* [TH994, ZH1065] (in/upon me). Together, these two words yield something like "Excuse me, Sir, but . . ." It gives the impression that Moses knows he is grasping at straws.

I get tongue-tied, and my words get tangled. These expressions represent the literal, "I am heavy-mouthed and heavy-lipped" (cf. "uncircumcised lips," rendered in NLT as "clumsy speaker" in 6:12, 30). Many different interpretations of this idiom have been given, ranging from the idea that he was no longer fluent in Egyptian to the suggestion that he had the affliction of stuttering, but there is no way to give a definitive answer. At a minimum Moses was claiming that public speaking was hard for him.

4:13 Send anyone else. This is clearly what Moses meant to say, but his phrasing was more polite and more carefully ambiguous, "Excuse me, Sir, but please send whomever you would like to send." (And this, as Houtman [1993:1.413] points out, from a man who supposedly was not good with words!)

4:14 the Levite. It is not clear why Aaron is described in this way here before the Levites had been designated as the priestly class. Three major possibilities may be offered: (1) The Levites may have already been an educated elite (Sarna 1991:22); (2) the narrator is reminding the reader of the mediatorial role that the Levites were to fulfill (Enns 2000:112-113); (3) it is a wordplay on the idea of "joined to," which is what "levi" means in Hebrew (Cassuto 1967:50).

4:18 Jethro. The Hebrew form of the name here is *yether* [TH3500, ZH3858], an updated form of the older pronunciation of the name (*yithro* [TH3503, ZH3861]). Hebrew tended to drop final vowels, and when that dropping meant that a word would end in two consonants, a segol (short *e*) was inserted between them.

"I don't even know if they are still alive." This is taking the literal sense of the Hebrew "whether they are yet living." Houtman takes it this way (1993:1.419), but Cassuto (1967:52) and Sarna (1991:22) argue that the phrase is actually an idiom for "see what their condition is."

4:19 the Lord said to him. Since the information in this verse seems somewhat anticlimactic at this point, the NIV renders this as "had said," a legitimate possibility for the verb form used, but not strictly necessary (see the commentary).

4:20 sons. Many scholars (see the discussion in Houtman 1993:1.427) have proposed that the text should be emended to "son" since only Gershom has been mentioned to this point (2:22) and since only one son is mentioned in the circumcision incident in 4:24-26. However, the ancient versions support the MT, and reasonable solutions to the other problems can be offered (see the commentary).

put them on a donkey. Cassuto (1967:53-54) says this detail is typical of epic narrative and sees it as support for the antiquity of the material in its original form.

the staff of God. This seems to be the narrator's way of both showing Moses's obedience (cf. 4:17) and of showing that, ultimately, the authority in which Moses went was not his own, but God's.

4:21 the miracles I have empowered you to do. Moses was not endowed with magical abilities so that he could do whatever signs he wished. He was strictly an emissary of God, doing what he said and nothing else (Knight 1976:32-33).

4:22 This is what the LORD says. This is the so-called "messenger formula" that marks the opening of a prophetic speech (Westermann 1967). It would be the language of a royal herald as he presented a message from his king. Moses was an ambassador, nothing more.

4:23 I will now kill. This conveys some of the sense of immediacy that is implicit in the participial form of the verb used here.

4:24 confronted him. Sarna (1991:24) points out that this is the same verb used to express the meeting with Aaron in 4:27 ("met"). Likewise, he observes the recurrence here of the verb "seeking to" (NLT, "wanted to") from 4:19 ("was about to," 4:24, NLT). He argues that these connections point away from the accidental insertion of a "night-demon" story here, as a number of nineteenth and twentieth century scholars proposed.

4:25 flint knife. Although bronze had been in use for hundreds of years by this time, the innate conservatism of religion demanded that a ritual act be conducted with the older material.

touched. Given the range of meaning of *naga'* [TH5060, ZH5595], "touch" is much more likely than the KJV "cast." Fretheim (1991:79) observes that this is the same verb used for applying the blood of the lamb to the doorpost in 12:22.

feet. This may be a euphemism for the male sex organ (cf. NLT mg). Another place where "feet" might refer to genitalia is Isa 6:2. See also Isa 36:12 where urine is referred to as "water of the feet" (NIDOTTE 3.1048). The word for "foot" can refer to the entire appendage from the hip to the toes, just as the word for "hand" can refer to everything from the shoulder to the fingers. Thus, the genital region is "between the feet" (cf. Deut 28:57).

a bridegroom of blood. No one knows the precise significance of this phrase. It may be a ritual statement that was used at circumcision and had some special meaning for those who used it. Sarna (1991:26) points out that the consonants of the Hebrew for "bridegroom" (*khatan* [TH2860, ZH3163]) occur in Arabic words for circumcision. Thus, it is possible that "bridegroom" is a mistranslation of an older term referring to circumcision. Cassuto (1967:61) suggests that since Moses has been spared from death because of the blood, he is a new man and it is as though he is Zipporah's bridegroom for a second time.

4:27 met. See note on 4:24. Because Moses's life has been spared, this encounter, unlike the previous one, is a cause for joy and not for dread.

COMMENTARY

God's Call to Moses (3:1-10). The time had come for the deliverer, Moses, to be called by God. Several commentators (e.g., Fretheim 1991:51-53) have observed that there are similarities between this call and those of the prophets, notably Samuel's (1 Sam 3:1-14) and Jeremiah's (Jer 1:1-10). This underscores the point made in the Introduction that a primary purpose of the Exodus events was revelation. Thus, Moses was not appointed a "judge," "champion," or "deliverer" like Samson to deliver his people from oppression so much as he was appointed a prophet who would reveal God to them. He was to reveal a God who is a faithful deliverer, but he would reveal much more about him than just that.

But in comparison with the similar prophetic call narratives, this one is greatly extended. In fact, it is equal in length to everything that precedes it in the book. Why is this? It is because God is patiently answering every one of the objections that Moses raised against the call. Here again, revelation as God's fundamental purpose is made clear as God uses these objections as an occasion to unveil new depths of himself to Moses. And indeed, while Moses's objections seem focused on himself and his inadequacies, the answers God gave show that he understood that what Moses was really questioning was God himself. Fretheim (1991:54-55) makes a very valuable point in this regard. He observes that although God eventually became angry at Moses's foot-dragging (4:14), he showed great patience and care in dealing with the underlying issues being raised. The point is that the questions and the dialogue constituted an opportunity for God that would not have existed otherwise. God is not a tyrant who merely shouts, "Either do it or die!" Neither is he a dictator who says, "You don't need to know anything, just do what I say!" Instead, he invites his people into dialogue with him. Whereas pagan prophets are "possessed," becoming mere mouthpieces for a god, the Hebrew prophets are "filled." This means that God's message is shaped by the unique character and personality of the one being filled. God has no interest in destroying unique personality, as the personal address "Moses! Moses!" (3:4) demonstrates. He, who is Three Persons in One, loves distinctive personality and is glad to enter into communion with each one, especially when that results in dialogue between him and them. It is only in mutual dialogue that personalities are revealed to each other.

Thus, while the Bible is everywhere scornful of that kind of disbelief that declares it will not believe until overwhelming evidence is presented (so the narrative of Thomas found in John 20:24-29), it everywhere invites honest and sincere investigation of the bases for belief. So God invites, "Taste and see that the LORD is good" (Ps 34:8), or he cries, "Try it! Put me to the test!" (Mal 3:10). So the very length of this passage suggests that God welcomed the opportunity that Moses's questions gave to reveal himself more fully than he had yet been able to do. God does not invite a merely passive response to his appeal; he invites us into an active dialogue that will confront our fears with his faithfulness.

The opening scene of this drama is freighted with significance (3:1-6). Moses was gifted with a vision that was to provide the foundation of his thinking for the rest of his life. It seems to have been designed by God to touch Moses on every level. First, there was the affective level. Moses saw something that captured his whole attention. He also heard something that moved him. But there was also the cognitive aspect. The old shepherd was not simply transported into a mystical experience. He wanted to see why the fire did not consume the bush. That is, he had a reasonable question. Moreover, what he heard was entirely intelligible to his thinking, even if it was not entirely understandable. He did not hear some heavenly language that could never be repeated. Finally, there was the volitional element; he was given something to do. From the outset God was engaging Moses on every level of his selfhood.

The significance of the imagery used in this experience is not explained by the Bible, and that should promote caution in our giving a too-easy explanation. However, there are some clear probabilities. "Fire" is used not only elsewhere in Exodus (12:10; 13:21-22; 14:24; 19:18; 24:17; 40:38) but throughout the Bible as an expression of the character of God. He is energizing; he is awe-inspiring; he is a wonderful blessing; he is potentially destructive; he is never easily contained; he is light; he is purifying. He is all this and more. But there was something remarkable about the fire Moses saw. Everywhere else a fixed characteristic of fire is that it consumes its fuel as it turns mass into energy. That did not happen here, and it caught Moses's attention. This was not normal fire. Was it only an attention-getting device, or was more being symbolized by this phenomenon? One possibility is that it was intended to convey that the Israelite people would not be consumed in the fire of Egypt (Enns 2000:96, citing Philo; so also Sarna 1991:14). Another possibility is that it prefigures the plagues, demonstrating that God is not nature but can do with nature what he pleases (Enns 2000:97). But there is another possibility that I believe should not be dismissed (contra Ellison 1982:16): In this experience God was inviting Moses to become the bush inhabited by the divine fire. What would that mean? Surely it would mean destruction. Moses himself spoke of this when he called God "a devouring fire" (or "consuming fire," 24:17; Deut 4:24; 9:3; quoted in Heb 12:29). Likewise, Isaiah spoke of it when he asked, "Who can survive this all-consuming fire?" (Isa 33:14; see also Isa 29:6; 30:27, 30). This is what the enemy whispers to every person called of God: "He will destroy you." But here Moses is given a vision of a fire that enlightens and enlivens but does not destroy. I cannot help but feel that this is a visual statement of what God communicated to Moses verbally in the rest of this encounter.

As noted in the Introduction, except for the reference to making the Sabbath day holy in Genesis 2:3, this (3:5) is only the second reference to God's holiness in the Bible. Yet the concept appears more than 100 times in the remainder of the book of Exodus. That fact tells us that the occurrence here is not a matter of chance but a deliberate emphasis at the outset of the covenant experience: The God who wants to enter into a revelatory and saving dialogue, not only with Moses and not only with Israel but with the whole world, is of a dramatically different essence from his creatures. And if he is to have fellowship with us, that fact will have to be taken into account. It can be ignored only at our peril. It is important enough that it was repeated again with Joshua at the end of the wilderness wandering experience before Israel entered into a new phase of its experience (Josh 5:15). If humans are to live in close fellowship with God, the fact of God's absolute otherness from us can never be overlooked or ignored. Furthermore, it is God who will determine the terms of how we are to live in his holy presence, not us.

As with the unconsumed bush, the Bible does not explain the symbolism of taking off the "sandals." Two possibilities suggest themselves. One is that the sandals are a product of human making and that nothing we have created can come between ourselves and our Creator (Clements 1972:20). Another is that the dirt on the bottom of the sandals is common dirt that must not be mingled with that dirt that has come to share God's essence by proximity with him. But in either case, note that this was not an intrinsically holy place. It was not a sanctuary or a cult center. It was an ordinary place in this world, and it was an ordinary bush. Its acute holiness was due to one reason only: The holy God was there. Wherever he is, is a holy place, and we must live and act accordingly in all those places.

God's message to Moses (3:6-10) stresses the points that have been made in various ways in the first two chapters: (1) This God who is revealing himself to Moses and is calling him into service is not some new deity, or even some local deity. He is the God who called Abraham in Mesopotamia and Jacob in Syria. He is the God who has entered into and maintained a relationship with generations of that same family. (2) He is a God who is faithful to his promises. The fact that the family was in deep distress at that time was not an indication that God had forgotten them, that he was insensitive to their distress, or that he was powerless to do anything about that distress. Rather, he had "seen" and was "aware of their suffering" (3:7), he had "come down to rescue them," and he had come to "lead them" (3:8) into that land he promised to each of the patriarchs in turn.

Although the Bible never specifically tells us why God chose to locate his people in Canaan, there seem to be at least two characteristics of that land that offer themselves as possible reasons (see note on 3:8). The first is its strategic significance. As Dennis Baly, geographer of Palestine, shows, Canaan is the hinge between three continents: Europe, Asia, and Africa (1957:5). Trade between Europe and Africa passed along its coasts, while trade between Europe and the Far East and between Africa and Asia passed directly through it. Consequently, and in closer focus, virtually all trade between the two great centers of ancient Near Eastern culture, Egypt and Mesopotamia, had to pass through Canaan. Thus, the people were in a unique position to relay God's message to the world.

But along with this strategic position, the distinctive geography also meant that there were areas of the region that were very much isolated from contact with the world. The central ridge running north and south and the Jordan rift to the east of the ridge created places where the Israelite people could remain without being overwhelmed by the influences of surrounding cultures and could develop strong theological positions that would, in fact, deny the influence of those cultures. These two factors together made Canaan a good place for God's message to flower and from which to disseminate it. This came to be most especially true in New Testament times when the Mediterranean world was ruled by Rome.

As noted above on 3:10, there is a surprise element that comes at the end of God's declaration of his faithfulness to his people. God knew their distress and would deliver them—so he was "sending" Moses. Moses's surprise at this turn of events is *not* surprising. If God was the one who would deliver them, why wouldn't he just go ahead and do it? Why commit this precious enterprise to an old man who had already failed at the task once and may well still be under sentence of death? And beyond that, why commit it to any fallible human being? There are three points to be made here. Moses was being sent because he had been carefully prepared for the task, no less by the years in the desert than by the training in Egypt. The second point relates directly to God's purpose in creating humans in the first place. He created us for fellowship with himself. That implies both the dignity and the significance of our participation with God in the work of this world. In the garden, God invited Adam and Eve to share with him in the cultivation of the world of nature, bringing it to its full potential. Now in a fallen world, God invites his people to share with him in the work of redeeming the world. The third point relates to God's chosen means of revelation: incarnation. God does not shower us with balms of love from lofty and perfect isolation. He has chosen to put his truth into the common dust of earth. Whatever else the statement that Christ was slain from the foundation of the world means (Rev 13:8, KJV; cf. NLT mg), it means that the incarnation of Christ was not some spur-of-the-moment thing that occurred to God in 4 BC. No, it has been God's means of revelation from the very outset.

Moses's Objections to God's Plan (3:11-4:17). Moses's objections to God's plan all seem to focus on his own inadequacies: He had no status or power (3:11-12); he did not even know who God really was (3:13-22); he had no means of compelling belief (4:1-9); he was not a capable speaker (4:10-17). But, as God's responses show, these are really questions about God: Will you abandon me? What are you really like? Do you have the power to do this thing? Are you able to use human weakness? If this deliverance is really to be the work of God through a human agent, then who is this God anyway? As said at the outset of this section, God did not chide Moses for his questions but seemed to welcome the opportunity to begin that self-revelation that would eventually bring his people into his arms.

Moses's initial question about his fitness for the task (3:11) might have prompted God to a fulsome reply listing all of the man's gifts and skills. He had the Egyptian training and education; he was decisive, a man of action; he had instinctive compassion for the downtrodden; he had courage; and he was not full of himself. Yet, as valuable and as necessary as all those things were to be, they were not decisive. And ultimately, as the answer (3:12) shows, Moses's fitness was not his real question. The real question was *Would God leave Moses "hanging out to dry"?* Would Moses be expected to carry out this task with only his own abilities? The answer to that question was a profound "no." God would go with Moses. And that would make all the difference. With God's presence, all that Moses brought to his calling would be of great benefit. Without God's presence it would all be dust and ashes. Ultimately, this is the ground of all deliverance. God has found a way across the barriers of time and space to enter into our lives. Deliverance is not anything else but the presence of God.

Moses's second objection (3:13-22) seems to focus on the inadequacy of his knowledge. He did not know enough about this God who was offering deliverance to make a convincing presentation to the people. The differences between the English word "name" and its equivalent in Hebrew (*shem* [TH8034, ZH9005]; 3:13ff) immediately create an interpretive problem. We think of a name as a "label" and tend to restrict the meaning of the word to that narrow connotation. But in many ways "label" is the least significant of the connotations of the Hebrew word. Much more in focus are concepts like reputation and character, like the English "he has a good name in this community," which has very little to do with a label. As God's answer (3:14-22) shows, the matter of a label is only secondary here. It is involved, but only as a marker for the kind of God he is and one's knowledge of him. That is the issue.

"So the God of our ancestors has sent you here with this amazing story. Do you really know him? Who is he really? Are you on intimate terms with him?"—these were questions Moses would face. Consider the humorous story in the New Testament of people attempting to cast out demons on second-hand authority. The demons respond that they know Paul and they know Jesus, but they have no idea who these fellows are and promptly beat them up (Acts 19:13-16). There is no authority like the authority of personal acquaintance.

I tend to agree with Enns (see the note on 3:14) that the phrase "I AM WHO I AM" is not intended to be an answer to the question of God's label, but I have different reasons than Enns does. He thinks that God was offended that Moses should ask such a question when he knew perfectly well what God's name/label was and that God then responded with a refusal to answer the question. I think that the question, if somewhat self-serving, was more sincere than that, and that God responds in kind. The issue is not what God's *label* is but *who* he is, and God proceeded to answer that question. To be sure, his label, Yahweh ("the LORD," see note on 3:14) reflects his character, but his character itself is the issue.[1]

In God's response, he emphasized two things about his character. They are the two unchanging essentials, the two irreconcilable factors that have driven philosophers crazy for centuries (Isa 44:25): God's transcendence and his immanence. How can God be absolutely other-and-good and yet be fully, directly, and immediately participating in the life of this sinful world? While the Bible helps us to answer that question, most especially in the doctrine of the Incarnation, it never does so fully. It simply asserts that both are so, and we can either accept the facts and build our lives accordingly, or we can refuse to accept them until we can reconcile them.

God's response was that he is the I AM. That is, he is the one eternally self-existent being in the universe, the one upon which all other beings depend for their existence. He is the one being who is absolutely noncontingent. He is complete in himself and does not depend on any other thing for his being. He is utterly other than his creation. Furthermore, he is the one for whom all time is now. The book of Revelation signifies this truth by saying that he is "the one who is, who always was, and who is still to come" (Rev 1:4, 8). When Jesus applied the "I AM" to himself, the Jews knew exactly what he was saying and tried to stone him for blasphemy (John 8:58-59). So the one who offers deliverance to his people is also the one who is without any of the limitations of creation.

In contrast to Plotinus's "One" or Aristotle's "Unmoved Mover," he who is "I AM" is so much without limitation that he can intervene in his creation at any point without affecting or altering his eternal being in any way. His "eternal name" (3:15) is such that he can become intimately, personally involved with individual humans. He can stoop to become "the God of (i.e., "who belongs to") Abraham" (3:15) and, in fact, delights to do so. But God's immanence goes farther than that. He does not only involve himself in the "inner-personal" world of religious encounter. He acts in the outer, interpersonal world of history. That is what 3:16-22 establish in this "name" context. Is he really God, the one God, the saving God, great enough to be the Creator, near enough to be the Savior? Yes! But how do we know? We may say, "I have met him in the secret places of my heart, and I know." That is vitally important, but it is not enough. It is not enough because that is the same authority that the insane appeal to. "I am a tomato," says the poor wretch. We ask, "How do you know?" and he replies, "Why, I just know in my heart!" How do we verify truth? Truth is what conforms to the shared experience of many people in areas external to their own psyches, that is, in the realm of history. Is God immanent? Yes! How do we know? Because he has broken into history and "has met with us" (3:18). He has bent a pharaoh to his will and brought his people out of Egypt, not as slaves, but as conquerors. What is his name? He is the I AM who delights to be called the God of Abraham.

Moses's third objection (4:1) in effect says, "Well, that is all wonderful in theory. But it is useless because I won't be able to convince them that I have really seen you. I don't have the ability to compel belief." Again, God seems to say, "Remember, this is not about you," and gives Moses some very specific evidences to show that he had indeed seen Yahweh. Interestingly, he did not merely give Moses carte blanche magical powers. Instead, he gave him some very specific "signs" that would certify that Moses had indeed encountered God. Moses would not be able to convince the people by anything that was resident in him, but God could convince them if Moses would simply do what God had told him to do.

While the Bible does not tell us the precise significance of the three signs that are given, it is possible to see their general significance and to draw some likely inferences from that data. All three signs are about transformation (Houtman 1993:1.387). The Creator has the power to change elements in his creation from one thing to another. But more than that, it is about transformations that have to do with life and death. The deity who has power over both the lively and the deadly forces of the cosmos has unlimited power. Thus, he can turn an ordinary shepherd's staff into a deadly snake, but then he can turn it back again. Likewise, he can take a healthy hand and cover it with an unclean "skin disease," but then he can make it whole again. Finally, he can take the Nile, the source of Egypt's life and turn it to blood coagulating on "the dry ground" (4:9). It is important to note that in all three of these cases, Yahweh was not teaching Moses magical techniques so that he could perform all kinds of magic at will. Yahweh was telling Moses to do certain things and that certain other things would follow. It was God's power at work through Moses as an expression of God's will, not Moses learning how to tap into God's power at his own will. This method would be the case throughout the entire Exodus experience.

It is of interest that two of the symbols of pharaonic authority were the shepherd's crook and the cobra (i.e., a snake). Pharaohs were often represented with the crook in one hand and a winnowing flail in the other; and the cobra appeared on the front of the pharaoh's crown. Thus, it may be that those facts have something to do with the first sign. It has also been observed that snake charmers are reported to be able to make a snake go rigid and then hold it out by the tail before throwing it to the ground where the paralysis leaves it. In that case the reversal in Moses's hands may be of significance. To be able to change the lifeless to the living and back to the lifeless is no small feat (Cassuto 1967:46). But again, the primary point seems to be that God can take an ordinary object and do incredible things with it.

By the same token, when Yahweh moves from the staff for the first sign to the hand that holds the staff for the second, it may be that God was saying something about the hands themselves: The universal connection that the Bible makes between skin diseases and the defilement of sin suggests that part of the import of the sign was that unless God made Moses's "hands" clean, everything Moses tried to do for his people would be tainted by his own sinful self-serving.

The third sign (4:9), the changing of Nile water into blood, could not be done in the wilderness but could only be performed in Egypt. Since this became the first of the plagues, it may be that it was intended to be symbolic of all the plagues and that God was saying that his people would only finally be convinced by that whole series of signs. This seems to be supported when the statement "Then you will know that I am the LORD," which is usually addressed to the Egyptians throughout the plague sequence (7:5, 17; 8:10, 22; 9:14, 29), is also addressed to Israel in 6:7 and 10:2. Thus, Childs (1974:77-78) is correct when he says that the signs served to convince three different audiences that Yahweh really had appeared to Moses: Moses, the people, and the Egyptians.

By this point, Moses's material objections had been rather thoroughly demolished. His lack of status and standing was swallowed up by God's presence in and with him. God had removed Moses's lack of understanding by revealing himself as the self-existent Yahweh who had stepped into time and space to be the God of Abraham and his descendants. Moses's attempts to convince God of his incompetence had been obliterated by God's designation of him to be the agent of God's life-transforming and death-defying power. But there is not enough evidence in the world to overcome a stubborn will, and that is what Moses's deeper issue was revealed to be. It is clear by the self-effacing and polite language Moses uses in 4:10 and 4:13 (see the note on 4:10) that Moses realized his final objection was nearly worthless. But it is also clear that if there was any way he could avoid going back to Egypt on this obviously dangerous and possibly doomed mission, he was going to try it.

As mentioned in the note on 4:10, the text does not specify exactly what Moses's speech problem was. This suggests the real possibility that Moses himself could not identify it very clearly! Since he was grasping at straws, the problem may have been largely imaginary.[2] He may have seized on the fact that he was not as facile with words as some. His opening statement that he was not good with words seems to point in that direction. In fact, one wonders if he may have even had Aaron in mind as a comparison. And despite the polite language, Moses was desperate enough to suggest that since God had not corrected the problem since they started speaking, it must be really serious (4:10)! Throughout his statement, the Hebrew exhibits the recurring use of the independent first person pronoun *'anoki* [TH595, ZH644] (I).

The inference is clear: Since *I* have this problem and since *you* have not cleared it up, you need to send someone else who does not have such a problem. But Yahweh would have none of it. Throughout the entire dialogue, he had been trying to get Moses to see that the focus was not to be on Moses and his deficiencies but upon the I AM and his limitless power. In 4:11, God explodes with a series of questions having only one conceivable answer: "Who makes a person's mouth? Who decides whether people speak or do not speak, hear or do not hear, see or do not see? Is it not I (*'anoki* [TH595, ZH644]), the LORD?" Then in 4:12 he commands Moses to go with his own emphatic *'anoki:* "I will be with you as you speak, and I will instruct you in what to say." Everything comes down to this question: Who is God in my world? We did not make ourselves, and we did not choose the particular set of gifts or hindrances we have. But if we will be submissive, the one who did make us and did choose those gifts and hindrances can use them wonderfully to accomplish his purposes.

But one of Moses's gifts was the fact that he did not give up easily once he had settled on a course of action. An ordinary person would have surely been cowed into submission by now. But not Moses. Although he had no arguments left, he still had his stubborn will and, from the way God answered him, it appears that he was still attempting to cloak that in the rags of his last objection. So he said, as politely as possible, "Send anyone else you like [because I can't speak]." Nonetheless, God made it plain that Moses could not escape the summons. Not only is Yahweh the creator of the earth, but he is also the Lord of history who can act and react within its confines. The fact that God could and would accommodate his plans to the extent of using Aaron must have been the final proof to Moses that he really had no choice. God would send another, but *with* Moses and not *instead* of Moses. God is great enough and creative enough that nothing can foil his ultimate strategy. This seems to have convinced Moses that he might as well go and get it over with.

The relationship between Moses and Aaron is clearly supposed to be a model of the relationship between God and his prophets. This is underscored when it is said, "you will stand in the place of God for him" (4:16; lit., "you will be God to him"). The message comes from God, and the prophet is God's mouthpiece. But this does not mean that the Hebrew prophets were merely mindless conduits, mechanically repeating words that had no real meaning for them. This extended dialogue between Moses and God shows the extent of the interaction that God was willing to engage in to make his message clear. The prophets spoke as "stand-ins" for Yahweh himself.

It is interesting that Aaron was already on his way (4:14) when this encounter took place. This suggests some of the depths of Yahweh's "contingency planning." Aaron would be in place and ready if Moses should indeed balk at God's commands to him. If Moses had acquiesced at an earlier point in the proceedings, the meeting with Aaron would have been merely a brotherly engagement. This kind of thinking can quickly degenerate into an endless debate over foreknowledge, sovereignty, and predestination—endless because of human limitations (see below on 4:21)—but that is not my point. The Bible clearly says that God knows the future, *and* that we make responsible (or irresponsible) choices that change the future, *and* that God is great enough to accommodate his tactics to those changes so that his ultimate strategy is not changed in the least. By human reasoning, all of those things cannot be true at the same time. The Bible simply insists they are.

Final Preparations for Moses's Task (4:18-28). The final segment of the call of the deliverer (4:18-28) contains three episodes: the departure from Midian (4:18-23), the midnight encounter with God (4:24-26), and the meeting with Aaron (4:27-28). All three episodes are involved with the final preparation of Moses for his task.

Commentators have debated the reason why Moses did not disclose his full purpose for going to Egypt when he asked his father-in-law for permission to go (4:18). Most have concluded that it was out of fear that if Jethro knew the real reason, he would think it foolhardy and refuse permission (so Sarna 1991:22; Enns 2000:127). Houtman (1993:1.419) offers a more nuanced suggestion that it may betray some continuing uncertainty on Moses's part about his mission. Yes, he was going to go; it seemed he had no real choice, but he was still not entirely certain what he would do when he got there. In 4:19 Yahweh assures him that the death warrant hanging over him from the past is no longer in effect. Then in 4:21-23 Yahweh seems to repeat what he had already said about the real reason for Moses's going, although he gives further theological depth to it. Moses is to "perform all the miracles" before Pharaoh. But they will have no immediate effect upon him because God will "harden his heart." That will serve to highlight the real nature of what is taking place. It is a contest between Yahweh and Pharaoh to see who is God. Yahweh's "firstborn" must be allowed to go, "so he can worship me." Pharaoh's refusal to permit that is going to cost him his own "firstborn son." This trip is not about checking up on the Hebrew people; it is about nothing less than the nature of reality—the identity of the one true God, his relationship to his creation and to his people.

A great deal has been written about God's hardening of Pharaoh's heart. What must be clearly stated at the outset is that this is certainly not a case of God's forcing a person to do something that is against his own will and character. Pharaoh was not a gentle, kindly-inclined man whom God changed against his will into a tyrant. Of the 20 references to the hardness of Pharaoh's heart in the book, only half of them speak of this as Yahweh's work. The remaining references nuance the idea in some way, from saying that Pharaoh's heart became hard to saying that Pharaoh hardened his own heart. The fundamental point that is being made is that Pharaoh was not "I AM." He believed he was; he believed that he had absolute freedom to make whatever choices he wished. He believed he was the living image of Amon-Re and therefore was dependent on nothing and nobody. That was not true; he was a created being and was therefore subject to all the contingencies of creation. One of those contingencies is the law of cause and effect. If a creature chooses one course of action long enough, that creature soon discovers he or she no longer has a choice. Pharaoh had believed all his life that he was God and could do whatever he wished.

For him to now "knuckle under" to this "god" of the despicable Hebrews would be to deny all he had ever believed. He no longer had the freedom to do that.

Was Yahweh the ultimate cause of Pharaoh's inability to allow the people to go? Absolutely! He made a world in which a pattern of choices ultimately renders one unable to choose otherwise. But did he personally "decree" that Pharaoh would never have chosen to be other than a tyrant so that he could get glory out of his destruction? Never.

The second of the three episodes (4:24-26) is so mysterious and enigmatic that it has occasioned thousands of pages of discussion over the last two millennia. It takes Houtman eight pages of dense print (1993:1.439-447) just to summarize some of the things that have been said about this scene! The issue relates to circumcision, but circumcision of whom? And why would God seek to kill the man that he had just labored at such length to persuade to go? Without denying all the complexities here, let me offer a possible interpretation. For whatever reason, Moses and Zipporah had decided that it was not necessary to circumcise at least one of their sons, even though this was the sign of the covenant with God (Gen 17:13-14). The fact that Zipporah instantly took action when Moses fell ill seems to support this supposition. But what was the problem? The problem was this: Moses was going to go to Egypt as the representative of the God of the fathers and was going to call upon the people to reaffirm their ancient covenant with him. The sign of one's exclusive loyalty to God, as had been outlined to Abraham, was circumcision. Yet Moses apparently did not even think enough of this God to carry out his most basic directive. Under those circumstances, Moses's mission could not help but fail in its most essential purpose, bringing the people to a true understanding of who the covenant God is.

It is significant that God did not simply kill Moses for his considered failure to obey but "was about to [lit., 'was seeking to'] kill him" (4:24). This suggests that Yahweh was giving a warning and an opportunity to correct the situation, which Zipporah instantly did. Once again, as with the midwives, Jochebed, Miriam, and the pharaoh's daughter, it is a woman who took courageous action to further the cause of Yahweh's redemptive purposes.

All of this speaks to the deadly danger of attempting to serve the holy God in a half-hearted way. God wants a close relationship with us, and we were created for such a relationship. But in our sinfulness, we want God's way and our own ways at the same time. That can never be. Death may not come suddenly as it did with Nadab and Abihu (Lev 10:1-2) or Ananias and Sapphira (Acts 5:1-11), and as it almost did with Moses, but it is nonetheless sure. We cannot be instruments of God's life when our lives are contaminated with self-serving. We will only kill the work of God and ultimately ourselves. We must come to God on his terms or not at all.

One cannot help but feel that Moses came out of this encounter a deeply chastened man. Thus the encounter (see note on 4:24) with Aaron (4:27-28) was of a very different kind. It can hardly be an accident that their meeting was at "the mountain of God." This was another confirmation to Moses that this entire experience was from God. Not only did Aaron come, as Yahweh said he would, but they met at the very place where God had revealed himself to Moses. Then Moses told Aaron "everything the LORD had commanded him to say" and all about "the miraculous signs the LORD had commanded him to perform" (4:28). Here now, finally, Moses had fully embraced the call from God.

ENDNOTES
1. On the question of whether the label YHWH was known prior to this, see the notes and commentary on 6:3.
2. Note that by the fourth plague, Moses is speaking for himself (8:26), and that while Aaron continues to be present, he does not enter into the discussions again.

◆ 4. The offer of deliverance (4:29–7:7)

²⁹Then Moses and Aaron returned to Egypt and called all the elders of Israel together. ³⁰Aaron told them everything the LORD had told Moses, and Moses performed the miraculous signs as they watched. ³¹Then the people of Israel were convinced that the LORD had sent Moses and Aaron. When they heard that the LORD was concerned about them and had seen their misery, they bowed down and worshiped.

CHAPTER 5

After this presentation to Israel's leaders, Moses and Aaron went and spoke to Pharaoh. They told him, "This is what the LORD, the God of Israel, says: Let my people go so they may hold a festival in my honor in the wilderness."

²"Is that so?" retorted Pharaoh. "And who is the LORD? Why should I listen to him and let Israel go? I don't know the LORD, and I will not let Israel go."

³But Aaron and Moses persisted. "The God of the Hebrews has met with us," they declared. "So let us take a three-day journey into the wilderness so we can offer sacrifices to the LORD our God. If we don't, he will kill us with a plague or with the sword."

⁴Pharaoh replied, "Moses and Aaron, why are you distracting the people from their tasks? Get back to work! ⁵Look, there are many of your people in the land, and you are stopping them from their work."

⁶That same day Pharaoh sent this order to the Egyptian slave drivers and the Israelite foremen: ⁷"Do not supply any more straw for making bricks. Make the people get it themselves! ⁸But still require them to make the same number of bricks as before. Don't reduce the quota. They are lazy. That's why they are crying out, 'Let us go and offer sacrifices to our God.' ⁹Load them down with more work. Make them sweat! That will teach them to listen to lies!"

¹⁰So the slave drivers and foremen went out and told the people: "This is what Pharaoh says: I will not provide any more straw for you. ¹¹Go and get it yourselves. Find it wherever you can. But you must produce just as many bricks as before!" ¹²So the people scattered throughout the land of Egypt in search of stubble to use as straw.

¹³Meanwhile, the Egyptian slave drivers continued to push hard. "Meet your daily quota of bricks, just as you did when we provided you with straw!" they demanded. ¹⁴Then they whipped the Israelite foremen they had put in charge of the work crews. "Why haven't you met your quotas either yesterday or today?" they demanded.

¹⁵So the Israelite foremen went to Pharaoh and pleaded with him. "Please don't

treat your servants like this," they begged. ¹⁶"We are given no straw, but the slave drivers still demand, 'Make bricks!' We are being beaten, but it isn't our fault! Your own people are to blame!"

¹⁷But Pharaoh shouted, "You're just lazy! Lazy! That's why you're saying, 'Let us go and offer sacrifices to the LORD.' ¹⁸Now get back to work! No straw will be given to you, but you must still produce the full quota of bricks."

¹⁹The Israelite foremen could see that they were in serious trouble when they were told, "You must not reduce the number of bricks you make each day." ²⁰As they left Pharaoh's court, they confronted Moses and Aaron, who were waiting outside for them. ²¹The foremen said to them, "May the LORD judge and punish you for making us stink before Pharaoh and his officials. You have put a sword into their hands, an excuse to kill us!"

²²Then Moses went back to the LORD and protested, "Why have you brought all this trouble on your own people, Lord? Why did you send me? ²³Ever since I came to Pharaoh as your spokesman, he has been even more brutal to your people. And you have done nothing to rescue them!"

CHAPTER 6

Then the LORD told Moses, "Now you will see what I will do to Pharaoh. When he feels the force of my strong hand, he will let the people go. In fact, he will force them to leave his land!"

²And God said to Moses, "I am Yahweh—'the LORD.'* ³I appeared to Abraham, to Isaac, and to Jacob as El-Shaddai—'God Almighty'*—but I did not reveal my name, Yahweh, to them. ⁴And I reaffirmed my covenant with them. Under its terms, I promised to give them the land of Canaan, where they were living as foreigners. ⁵You can be sure that I have heard the groans of the people of Israel, who are now slaves to the Egyptians. And I am well aware of my covenant with them.

⁶"Therefore, say to the people of Israel: 'I am the LORD. I will free you from your oppression and will rescue you from your slavery in Egypt. I will redeem you with a powerful arm and great acts of judgment. ⁷I will claim you as my own people, and I will be your God. Then you will know that I am the LORD your God who has freed you from your oppression in Egypt. ⁸I will bring you into the land I swore to give to Abraham, Isaac, and Jacob. I will give it to you as your very own possession. I am the LORD!'"

⁹So Moses told the people of Israel what the LORD had said, but they refused to listen anymore. They had become too discouraged by the brutality of their slavery.

¹⁰Then the LORD said to Moses, ¹¹"Go back to Pharaoh, the king of Egypt, and tell him to let the people of Israel leave his country."

¹²"But LORD!" Moses objected. "My own people won't listen to me anymore. How can I expect Pharaoh to listen? I'm such a clumsy speaker!*"

¹³But the LORD spoke to Moses and Aaron and gave them orders for the Israelites and for Pharaoh, the king of Egypt. The LORD commanded Moses and Aaron to lead the people of Israel out of Egypt.

¹⁴These are the ancestors of some of the clans of Israel:

The sons of Reuben, Israel's oldest son, were Hanoch, Pallu, Hezron, and Carmi. Their descendants became the clans of Reuben.
¹⁵The sons of Simeon were Jemuel, Jamin, Ohad, Jakin, Zohar, and Shaul. (Shaul's mother was a Canaanite woman.) Their descendants became the clans of Simeon.
¹⁶These are the descendants of Levi, as listed in their family records: The sons of Levi were Gershon, Kohath, and Merari. (Levi lived to be 137 years old.)
¹⁷The descendants of Gershon included Libni and Shimei, each of whom became the ancestor of a clan.
¹⁸The descendants of Kohath

included Amram, Izhar, Hebron, and Uzziel. (Kohath lived to be 133 years old.)

¹⁹The descendants of Merari included Mahli and Mushi.

These are the clans of the Levites, as listed in their family records.

²⁰Amram married his father's sister Jochebed, and she gave birth to his sons, Aaron and Moses. (Amram lived to be 137 years old.) ²¹The sons of Izhar were Korah, Nepheg, and Zicri. ²²The sons of Uzziel were Mishael, Elzaphan, and Sithri. ²³Aaron married Elisheba, the daughter of Amminadab and sister of Nahshon, and she gave birth to his sons, Nadab, Abihu, Eleazar, and Ithamar. ²⁴The sons of Korah were Assir, Elkanah, and Abiasaph. Their descendants became the clans of Korah. ²⁵Eleazar son of Aaron married one of the daughters of Putiel, and she gave birth to his son, Phinehas.

These are the ancestors of the Levite families, listed according to their clans.

²⁶The Aaron and Moses named in this list are the same ones to whom the LORD said, "Lead the people of Israel out of the land of Egypt like an army." ²⁷It was Moses and Aaron who spoke to Pharaoh, the king of Egypt, about leading the people of Israel out of Egypt.

²⁸When the LORD spoke to Moses in the land of Egypt, ²⁹he said to him, "I am the LORD! Tell Pharaoh, the king of Egypt, everything I am telling you." ³⁰But Moses argued with the LORD, saying, "I can't do it! I'm such a clumsy speaker! Why should Pharaoh listen to me?"

CHAPTER 7

Then the LORD said to Moses, "Pay close attention to this. I will make you seem like God to Pharaoh, and your brother, Aaron, will be your prophet. ²Tell Aaron everything I command you, and Aaron must command Pharaoh to let the people of Israel leave his country. ³But I will make Pharaoh's heart stubborn so I can multiply my miraculous signs and wonders in the land of Egypt. ⁴Even then Pharaoh will refuse to listen to you. So I will bring down my fist on Egypt. Then I will rescue my forces—my people, the Israelites—from the land of Egypt with great acts of judgment. ⁵When I raise my powerful hand and bring out the Israelites, the Egyptians will know that I am the LORD."

⁶So Moses and Aaron did just as the LORD had commanded them. ⁷Moses was eighty years old, and Aaron was eighty-three when they made their demands to Pharaoh.

6:2 *Yahweh* is a transliteration of the proper name *YHWH* that is sometimes rendered "Jehovah"; in this translation it is usually rendered "the LORD" (note the use of small capitals). 6:3 *El-Shaddai*, which means "God Almighty," is the name for God used in Gen 17:1; 28:3; 35:11; 43:14; 48:3. 6:12 Hebrew *I have uncircumcised lips*; also in 6:30.

NOTES

4:30 *Moses performed.* The Hebrew text has simply "he performed," and since "Aaron" is the subject of sentence, some believe that Aaron may have actually performed the signs. However, "Moses" is the immediate antecedent of the pronoun, and since God had told Moses to perform the signs (4:17, 28), it seems most likely the NLT has made the correct choice.

4:31 *were convinced.* The verb here, *'aman* [TH539, ZH586], has the sense of "to be firm," or "to make firm." Other translations usually use forms of "believe" to translate it. Fretheim (1991:82) points out that the next time the word is used of the Israelites, they have just crossed the Reed Sea (14:31).

bowed down and worshiped. Two different Hebrew verbs are used here. The first, *qadad* [TH6915, ZH7702], is the less common of the two (15 occurrences), and when it does occur it is always in combination with the second, *khawah* [TH7812A, ZH2556] (172 occurrences), which only occurs in an odd grammatical form, apparently an old reflexive form. Both words mean approximately the same thing: to bow down to the ground, or to prostrate oneself (KBL 821, 959). The combination (occurring again in 12:27 and 34:8) seems to reinforce the idea that the only truly reverential position in which to worship the Creator is one of complete prostration.

5:1 hold a festival in my honor. The verb used here, *khagag* [TH2287, ZH2510], signifies making a sacrificial feast in connection with a pilgrimage. It is etymologically identical to the Arabic word for the pilgrimage all Muslims are to make to Mecca once in their lives, the hajj.

the wilderness. From Goshen in the northeast delta of Egypt, the wilderness would be Sinai, beyond the borders of Egypt. It was unthinkable that once out of the country, the slaves would be coming back. The implication was clear to Pharaoh.

5:2 I don't know the LORD. The verb translated "know" (*yada'* [TH3045, ZH3359]) always has the idea of experiential knowledge (see note on 2:25). Thus, while it is possible that Pharaoh was saying he had never heard of Yahweh before, it is more likely that he was saying he did not acknowledge or recognize this god as having any authority over him. Note the literal, "Who is the LORD that I should obey him?"

5:3 The God of the Hebrews. On "Hebrews" see note on 1:15. This might be an attempt to give Pharaoh more information about who this Yahweh is.

three-day journey. This makes it more explicit that this pilgrimage will take the slaves beyond Egypt's reach.

5:5 Look, there are many of your people in the land. This is one possible interpretation. The verse begins with a repetition of the verb "said," a syntax Cassuto (1967:67) says denotes speaking to oneself. The following quotation is literally, "behold, many now [are] the people of the land." "People of the land" is a fairly standard biblical phrase for "the inhabitants" of a place (cf. Gen 23:7, 12-13). Thus, it seems odd for Pharaoh to call the Hebrews by that name. The Samaritan Pentateuch adds the comparative "than," probably yielding "[They] are more than the people of the land." This is very attractive and Childs (1974:105) thinks it is the correct reading. However, since it is not supported by the other versions, it looks like an intentional correction of the difficult MT reading.

5:6 That same day Pharaoh sent this order. Cassuto (1967:69) says Pharaoh did so to make it clear that the increased oppression was Moses and Aaron's fault.

5:7 straw. Mud bricks usually need some substance (such as straw) added to the mud to improve its cohesiveness so the bricks will hold their shape after they have been removed from the mold and are set aside to dry in the sun or fired in a kiln.

5:9 Make them sweat! That will teach them to listen to lies! The two verbs used here (*'asah* [TH6213, ZH6913], "to do, make," and *sha'ah* [TH8159, ZH9120], "to pay attention to") would look almost identical in an unvocalized text. This explains the variation between the MT and the LXX. The LXX (followed by the Samaritan Pentateuch and Syriac) reads both as the same verb, "let them pay attention to these things, and not pay attention to lies." Obviously, one of these is an error of the eye, and it is difficult to determine which is the original. Most commentators prefer the MT. If so, the MT may have used *'asah*, somewhat unusual in this context, as an intentional wordplay.

5:12 in search of . . . straw. Lit., "searching for chaff for straw." This suggests that the straw had all been harvested and was in the barns so that the only thing left was the refuse in the fields and on the threshing floors.

5:13 just as you did when we provided you with straw. The NLT gives the correct sense, but it seems to adopt a textual variant without giving notice of that fact. A literal translation of the MT would say, "just as in being straw." A smoother translation would say, "just as when there was straw." But the LXX, Vulgate, Syriac, and Samaritan Pentateuch all add "given to you." Childs (1974:93) thinks this phrase is original, but Houtman (1993:1.475) says the addition has all the marks of an explanatory gloss. I agree with Houtman.

5:14 *yesterday or today?* Almost all translations follow this rendering. However, there is another possibility. The text is elliptical. Literally, it says, ". . . your quotas as you did formerly, even yesterday, even today." The elliptical ending suggests that "yesterday" may function as a repetition of "formerly." Thus the sentence would end with a clipped demand, "As yesterday; so today!" In other words, they're going to make just as many bricks today as they did "yesterday."

5:15 *pleaded.* The Hebrew is *tsa'aq* [TH6817, ZH7590], meaning "cry out, scream" (cf. 5:8).

5:16 *Your own people are to blame!* The Hebrew is problematic. The verb rendered "to blame" (also "commit sin"), is in the feminine gender, but "people" is a masculine noun. With different vocalization, "blame" could be a second masculine singular, yielding, "You have sinned [against] your people [the Hebrews]." This is the way the LXX translates the sentence, and Childs (1974:93) thinks this is the original. Cassuto (1967:71) thinks the foremen started out to say that, but thought it impolitic and changed in mid-sentence, resulting in the ungrammatical form. Yet another possibility was proposed by the medieval Jewish scholar Rashi and is put forward by Houtman (1993:1.477). This also involves a revocalization of the verb and would result in the idea that "this matter brings guilt upon your people." If the NLT (along with most other translations) is correct, the foremen are saying it was not their fault that the quotas were not being met; it was the Egyptians' fault.

5:18 *No straw will be given to you, but you must still produce.* "Produce" is the same verbal root as "given." They will be *given* no straw, but they must *give* the same number of bricks. The fact that it is unusual to use "give" in the second sense suggests that the narrator was representing Pharaoh as "rubbing in" the inequity of the situation he was imposing upon them.

5:19 *in serious trouble.* The Hebrew word used here (*ra'* [TH7451, ZH8273]) is often translated "evil" (cf. KJV). However, the word has a very wide range of meanings, rather similar to the English word "bad." Like "bad," *ra'* can range in meaning all the way from "misfortune" (its meaning here) to moral "evil."

5:20 *confronted.* This is the verb *paga'* [TH6293, ZH7003], which was used in 5:3 (NLT, "he will kill"). It expresses face-to-face contact, either intentional or unintentional, rather like the contemporary slang "run into." In the Hebrew, the atmosphere surrounding the sense may vary from neutral to hostile, depending on the context. Here the atmosphere was decidedly hostile.

were waiting. Houtman (1993:1.481) believes the "foremen" "were waiting" for Moses and Aaron, rather than the reverse. That is grammatically possible, but it would not be the normal function of the syntax here.

5:21 *making us stink before.* This correctly translates the sense of the mixed-metaphor idioms used by the Hebrew. Literally it says, "You have made us a stench in the nostrils in the eyes of Pharaoh." If we changed the imagery completely into abstractions, we would say, "You have made us hateful in Pharaoh's judgment."

6:1 *the force of my strong hand.* The Hebrew has "with/in a strong hand he will let them go; with/in a strong hand he will drive them out." The NLT (along with NIV, NASB, and REB) understands "the strong hand" as the Lord's, whereas the KJV, NRSV, and ESV at least imply that the hand is Pharaoh's. Cassuto (1967:74) supports the NLT interpretation when he says the repeated phrase denotes compulsion (i.e., he will be compelled to let them go).

6:2 And God said. Most of the ancient versions read "And the Lord said." But the MT (which the NLT is following) seems to be the harder reading, and is thus more preferable.

6:3 God Almighty. This translation of the name "El-Shaddai" is supplied by the NLT. It is not in the Hebrew. Sarna (1991:31) argues that there is no clear evidence for the meaning of the name. The LXX has at least two different translations of it. Cassuto (1967:78) says that it appears in contexts where fruitfulness is prominent (cf. Gen 28:3; 35:11; 48:3). While that may be true in Genesis, it is not apparent in its other occurrences, particularly not in Job, where the majority is found (31 out of 48). There the connotations of absolute lordship seem most obvious.

but I did not reveal my name, Yahweh, to them. A literal translation would be "but (in) my name Yahweh, I was not known to them." Cassuto (1967:78) argues that this language favors the idea that this is not a new revelation of an unknown name but introduces a further revelation of the character (name) of God. See the commentary on this verse.

6:4 And. Verses 4 and 5 both begin with the Hebrew particle *gam* [TH1571, ZH1685], which often means "moreover," or "also." Here, however, it seems to have an emphatic force (Williams 1976:63). Houtman (1993:1.500-501) renders them with "[v. 4] I not only . . . , [v. 5] but I have also. . . ."

reaffirmed. This translation rightly captures the idea that "to erect a covenant," as the literal meaning here and in Gen 17:2, is different from "to cut a covenant" (e.g., Gen 31:44). The emphasis is on the keeping of the covenant rather than the making of it. On when this reaffirmation occurred, see the commentary.

6:5 well aware of. Lit., "remembered." But "to remember" in Hebrew implies more than mere mental activity. It implies taking appropriate action on the basis of recalled facts. That is what this translation seeks to convey.

6:6 powerful arm. Lit., "outstretched arm." The image may well be drawn from a common Egyptian motif, showing the pharaoh with his arm raised, holding a mace to strike his enemies. See also Deut 4:34; 26:8; 1 Kgs 8:42; Ps 136:12; Jer 32:17.

6:8 swore to give. Lit., "lifted up my hand to give." This is the imagery of taking an oath. The self-identification at the end of the verse suggests that Yahweh had sworn by his own character.

6:9 too discouraged. Lit., "short of spirit." This translation is based on the LXX rendering, but Childs (1974:110) points out that the occurrences of the phrase in Job 21:4; Prov 14:29; and Mic 2:7 suggest another meaning could be "impatient." On this understanding, the people simply had no time for what they took to be Moses's empty words.

6:12 Moses objected. Lit., "Moses spoke in the presence of the Lord." Houtman (1993:1.506) says this phrasing suggests prayerful speaking and that Moses was more in awe of the Lord than when he voiced his previous objections.

clumsy speaker! Lit., "uncircumcised of lips." This phrase is parallel to Moses's earlier statement that he was "tongue-tied" (4:10). The precise significance of the imagery is not clear. It is used several times in the Bible, as in Jer 6:10, where the peoples' ears are said to be "uncircumcised" (NLT, "closed"). In all these cases, it means that the element so described is not functional. Sarna (1991:33) suggests it is as though the member was obstructed by the presence of a foreskin.

6:14 These are the ancestors of some of the clans of Israel. Lit., "These are the heads of the fathers' houses." Although "Israel" is helpful to the modern reader because it tells what historic line these families were in, it is not present in the text, and its appearance here is somewhat misleading. It is clear from the content of the genealogy that this is not about some of the clans of Israel but in particular about the family of Aaron in the

Kohathite clan in the tribe of Levi. Perhaps a better contemporary expression would be: "This is a family tree."

6:20 Amram married. The mention of only the wives of Amram, Aaron (6:23), and Eleazar (6:25) serves to highlight the particular emphasis that is being given to Aaron's descendants.

6:23 Elisheba, the daughter of Amminadab and sister of Nahshon. Sarna (1991:35) suggests that the reason for identifying Elisheba in this way is to connect Aaron's lineage with David's, since Nahshon was an ancestor of David (1 Chr 2:11-15).

6:26 Aaron and Moses. Aaron may be named first because the preceding genealogy focuses on him. But it may also reflect the fact that from a genealogical point of view he is the firstborn. Here is another biblical example (like Jacob and David) of a son who is not firstborn being used by God. God uses less likely persons in order to demonstrate his power.

like an army. Lit., "according to their troops." Commentators debate the precise meaning of this phrase (see also 7:4; Num 1:52). Cassuto (1967:88) is probably right when he says that the point is that the Israelites went out in orderly ranks and not like a mob of fleeing slaves. Houtman (1993:1.520) attempts to convey the same idea when he translates "arrayed by tribes."

6:27 who spoke. A participle is used here and could be translated, "they were the ones speaking to." The stress would be on their role rather than what they did at some time.

6:30 Moses argued. The same construction as in 6:12 (see note).

7:4 forces. See note on 6:26.

7:5 raise my powerful hand. Lit., "stretch out my hand" (see note on 6:6).

COMMENTARY

The declaration of God's deliverance is recorded in three parts: the Israelites' response (4:29-31), Pharaoh's response (5:1-23), and Yahweh's reassertion of his intent (6:1-7:7). The first two parts are notable for the stark differences in the amount of detail given. The part over which Moses had worried so much—how he would be received by the people—is dealt with in three verses. But the part that does not seem to have concerned him so much—his confrontation with Pharaoh—takes 23 verses (5:1-23). There is also a difference in the two responses. The people "were convinced" and "bowed down and worshiped" (4:31). But Pharaoh, far from being convinced, refused to acknowledge that Yahweh had any authority over him at all (5:2). Instead of letting the people go to "serve" ("worship," 3:12; 4:23, NLT) God at Mount Sinai, he made their "service" ("work," 5:9, NLT) for him even more onerous. As Fretheim (1991:83) observes, the function of this block of material is to set the real issue squarely before the reader. The issue is not merely oppression and suffering; the issue is *who is God?* Who is the one being in the universe who rightly deserves our glad service and our loving submission?

The third component of this section, 6:1-7:7, highlights this point. It begins with God's reiteration of all his promises to Moses and the people (6:1-8). "Now you will see what I will do to Pharaoh." The real conflict between worldviews is now set up. That was enough to re-energize Moses, who went back to the people with the promises. But they, having thought their problems were over when Moses arrived, only to find them greatly worsened, "refused to listen" (6:9). God told Moses to go back to Pharaoh, but Moses balked, noting that if the people wouldn't listen there was no chance Pharaoh would. Reverting to his earlier excuse, he claimed to be "a clumsy speaker" (6:10-12, 28-30). But God put his commands in the form of an order (6:13) and reiterated his provision of Aaron as a spokesman (7:1-5). This finally convinced the reluctant messenger, and along with Aaron, Moses went back into the battle (7:6-7). The stage was set for the events of deliverance, which would center on the revelation of God's superiority over the gods of Egypt.

The Offer of Deliverance to the Israelites (4:29-31). The people gladly received the good news of Yahweh's continuing love and care for them. And beyond that, they were deeply impressed with the evidence that Yahweh's love was backed up with miracle-working power. Why would they not receive such a demonstration with belief and worship? They had serious problems that they seemed unable to solve. Now God was going to solve all their problems. The analogy with modern approaches to evangelism is striking: Were we surprised when thousands of Russians and eastern Europeans surged forward to "accept Christ" after the Berlin Wall fell and international communism collapsed? We should not have been. Why would they not accept such a proposition? But did they know (in the Hebrew sense of the word) the Christ they were accepting? Hardly at all in most cases. Is "salvation" merely turning "the Great Problem Solver" loose on the conundrums of our lives? Never! It is to change kingdoms, to change citizenships, to change families; it is to change views of reality, and that is not going to happen merely because we accept an offer no sensible person could turn down.

In fact, to accept a transfer from the kingdom of darkness to the kingdom of light is very likely to be just the beginning of one's problems. And why not? Before, you were no problem to the powers of darkness. You quietly labored in their brick works while they attended to more pressing problems elsewhere. But change allegiance? Who do you think you are? Now *you* have become a pressing problem. Will that kingdom let its slaves go without a fight? Never. That is why the lands of Russia and eastern Europe are today figuratively littered with the corpses of dead and dying "evangelical" babies. They believed Christians when they told them that if they would just "accept Jesus" they would have no more problems, when in fact, their problems were just beginning. Many Christians in America are in no less spiritual danger due to such flawed evangelistic approaches.

Pharaoh's Reaction (5:1-23). The disproportionate attention given to the second event in the narration speaks directly to these issues. The real problem the Hebrews had was that they did not know God, and until they did, merely delivering them out of their problems was no salvation at all. For salvation is a living, ongoing relationship with God. To say a prayer, to bow a knee, is no guarantee of salvation. Initial acts of commitment are vital entry points into the relationship, but individuals cannot have a relationship with someone they do not know. Salvation is not a magical transaction that takes us from being damned one moment to blessed the next. We are saved through our attachment to the living God. That attachment begins in a moment of belief in his promises and is accompanied by prostrate worship before him, but it is not the belief and worship that saves us, it is our attachment to Life, to our Father.

This is why, from one perspective, Pharaoh's opposition was necessary and inescapable. Pharaoh had allied himself with that kingdom that is the enemy of the true God. He was the willing devotee of the idea that God can be manipulated to humans' advantage through the world. To that worldview, acquisition of power is the greatest and only good, and voluntary submission is the greatest evil. Thus, Pharaoh had no choice but to violently oppose anything that would require his submission. As the representative of that other worldview, he could not help but violently contend with anyone who challenged it. To do otherwise was to deny the very ground upon which he stood.

Furthermore, this confrontation was necessary if the Israelites were to have any true conception of who their deliverer was. Suppose that Pharaoh had mildly said, "Yes, I think it is a good idea for you to go and worship your Yahweh, whoever that is. And, of course, I don't expect you back." None of the revelation of God's power and love, of his absolute lordship over all that this world calls "god," would ever have happened. Neither the Egyptians nor, more importantly, the Israelites would have known that Yahweh is the only Lord of the universe. The Israelites would have been out of Egypt, but their real problem, their ignorance of the nature of reality, would have been just as severe at it ever was, preventing them from experiencing the only thing that could really "save" them, a living, ongoing relationship with the only source of life.

Several commentators note the apparently self-confident note of Moses and Aaron's first presentation to Pharaoh (5:1). The Israelite spokesmen use the so-called "messenger formula" by which the message of a superior is addressed to an inferior and demand that the people be allowed to go on a religious pilgrimage into "the wilderness." Perhaps the confident tone was the result of the satisfying response of the people. Perhaps the two ambassadors were seduced by this response into thinking, "This will be easy." Whatever their reasoning, they were soon to be disabused of their confidence.

The request to be permitted to go on a pilgrimage often seems deceptive to those who think that the purpose of the Exodus was political freedom. In honesty, should not Moses have said, "Let my people go free"? But that is to misunderstand the purpose of these events. In fact, the purpose of the Exodus was to bring the Israelites from an oppressive, deadly servitude to Pharaoh into a freeing, life-giving servitude to God. This point is very clear in Joshua's farewell address (Josh 24:1-28). The Israelites had been delivered from the "house of servitude" ("from slavery," Josh 24:17, NLT) and now they had to choose whom they would "serve" (Josh 24:14). Life is not a question of serving or not serving. It is only a question of whom we will serve. Thus, Moses and Aaron's request here and repeatedly throughout chapters 7-11 was not deceptive but squarely addressed the real nature of what was taking place.

Neither was the request misleading. Moses never implied they would go and then voluntarily come back. As noted above on 5:1, "the wilderness" would be the Sinai wilderness beyond Egypt's borders. If there were any question, the stipulation that it would be a "three-day journey" (5:3) made it clear. Once these slaves were beyond Egypt's reach, they would never be coming back. In part, that is the reason for Pharaoh's furious response. He was not simply refusing to grant his slaves a few days off work for religious purposes. He was doing everything in his power to keep them from escaping his oppressive grasp.

Pharaoh clearly understood the nature of the contest (5:2); it was one of ultimate authority. Was there someone superior to him who had the right to tell him what to do with his slaves? There could not be. He refused to acknowledge any such authority, and he would not bow to it. It was not a question of knowledge (see note on 5:2) but of recognition of authority.

Moses and Aaron were somewhat cowed by this response, but they did not lack courage (5:3). They rephrased their request in more polite terms and offered some more explanation of it. The way they stated the consequences of their not going went well beyond anything Yahweh had said, but they may have been trying to put the situation in terms a pharaoh would understand: "Obey or die!" But this was not a rational discussion of possible options; it was a power struggle, and Pharaoh knew it. If he was to deflect this challenge to his authority, he had to break his opponents' will. He sought to do that in two ways that were closely connected (5:6-19). He made the oppression worse, and he sought to undermine Moses's leadership. In both efforts he succeeded admirably. However, he badly underestimated exactly who was challenging his authority, and he also underestimated the level of commitment on the part of the leaders.

Presumably the people knew that Moses and Aaron were making their presentation on a certain day. Thus, when the oppressive orders came down on that same day (5:6), there was no doubt whose was at fault for the situation. By asserting that Moses and Aaron's claims about impending freedom were "lies," Pharaoh made his challenge of their leadership even clearer. The command that the Hebrews must now find their own "straw" (5:7-12; see note on 5:7) was ingenious. Not only did it make the workload much heavier, it also "scattered" (5:12) the people, keeping them from encouraging each other. The use of the "messenger formula" (5:10) for Pharaoh's command underscores the contest. Yahweh made one demand, and Pharaoh made another, as if to say, "Now we will see who is in charge here. Yahweh says, 'Go and worship'? I say, 'Go and work!'"

The system of "Egyptian slave drivers" (5:13) overseeing "Israelite foremen" (5:14) is a pattern that has worked in a variety of tyrannies across the centuries right up to the present. It is reminiscent of the system the Nazis used in the death camps between 1938 and 1945. The pressure flows inexorably down from the top, with the immediate enforcers of the oppression being members of the oppressed group itself. Houtman (1993:1.457) observes that the entire structure, from Pharaoh on down, was based on fear. Neither was Pharaoh himself exempt, for he was living in deadly fear of losing his power.

The picture of Pharaoh's recalcitrance is rounded out by his responses to the

"Israelite foremen" (5:15-18). Despite their reasonable request that they could not be expected to make the same number of bricks as they had previously when they now had to find their own straw, he merely insulted them, calling them "lazy," and reiterated his decree. It is immaterial whether he really thought they were lazy or not. The point was to break the Israelites' will to resist.

Clearly, if the situation of the ordinary Israelite was bad (see note on 5:19), that of the "foremen" was worse. They were caught between the pressure of the slave drivers from above and the resistance of the people beneath. The slave drivers could not very well whip a whole people, but they could certainly whip all the foremen. So it is not surprising that when the foremen came upon Moses and Aaron "waiting outside for them" (5:20), perhaps having accompanied them to the audience, they cursed them (5:21). Pharaoh's strategy had worked to perfection: He had broken the will to resist, and he had discredited the leadership.

Moses's reaction to all this (5:22-23) put the real problem in sharp relief. As terrible as the slavery was, that was not the deepest problem that the Exodus was to address. The real issue was the nature and identity of Yahweh. The pronouns in the two verses are instructive. Five times Moses says to God in one way or another, "*You* are the problem here. *You* sent me as *your* spokesman to *your* people, and instead of delivering them, *you* have brought disaster on *your* people! Why have *you* done this?!" The repetition of *ra'* [TH7451, ZH8273] (see note on 5:19) is also significant. Yes, Pharaoh "had been brutal" (*ra'a'* [TH7489, ZH8317], 5:23) to God's people, but in a wider sense, it seemed that God had "brought all this trouble" (*ra'a'*, 5:22). What kind of a God is Yahweh anyway? Is he good, or is he actually bad? Who is he? This was the real issue, and the offer of deliverance had served chiefly to highlight that issue.

Yahweh's Response (6:1-8). It is precisely this issue of the nature and identity of God that is addressed in Yahweh's response to all of this in 6:1-8 and 7:1-5. Yahweh did not upbraid Moses for a lack of faith or courage, or for his effrontery in accusing him of doing evil to his people; he simply told him that "now" Moses would "see what [Yahweh] will do to Pharaoh." It seems that Yahweh expected these reactions and that as a result the central issue could now be addressed. And that issue will be so clearly addressed that Pharaoh will not merely turn his head and allow the people to sneak out; he will actually "force them to leave" (6:1). As Enns (2000:172-173) says, we have seen what Moses can do, and what Pharaoh proposed to do. It is now Yahweh's turn.

If there remained any question that the issue at hand was who and what is deity, it is laid to rest by Yahweh's words in 6:2-8. He begins with the self-identification formula that is well-known from the openings of Moabite and Phoenician royal inscriptions: "I am Yahweh." That statement is repeated three more times in the course of the declaration (6:6, 7, 8). As both Cassuto (1967:76) and Sarna (1991:31) point out, such an identification would lose its force if in fact no one had heard of the name before. Rather, Yahweh was saying, "Make no mistake about who is speaking to you. This is the King. You have heard of me in the past, but now I am going to put the past, the present, and the future together for you in ways you have never imagined." There follow no less than 10 first-person verbs with Yahweh as the subject. Those verbs address the past (6:2-4), the present (6:5), and the future (6:6-8). Although it would take the Israelites most of the next millennium to actually assimilate what they were going to learn about God in the following months and years, the events that were about to transpire would be an inescapable revelation of the nature and purpose of reality. Fortunately, the revelation that was about to be given was faithfully recorded, and the record has remained for future generations to learn from.[1]

The statement that the patriarchs did not know God in his name Yahweh ("I did not reveal my name, Yahweh, to them," 6:3, NLT) has evoked endless discussion. Since the name appears in Genesis, what does that statement mean? Does it mean that here is the evidence of different documents, where one that originally used "God" (*'elohim* [TH430, ZH466]) exclusively has been merged with one that used "Yahweh" (*yhwh* [TH3068, ZH3378], see NLT mg and endnote 1 on 3:14) exclusively? Or does it mean that Moses, or someone working under his direction, has gone back and inserted "Yahweh" in places where it seemed appropriate in the light of the new revelation? The former suggestion is more and more admitted to be groundless, as more evidence comes to light regarding the ways in which ancient literature was created (see the discussion on authorship in the Introduction). The latter is possible, but is probably not necessary. As was pointed out in the commentary and notes on 3:13-15, "name" (*shem* [TH8034, ZH9005]) in Hebrew means much more than merely "label." Rather, it speaks of character, nature, and reputation. Thus, it seems very likely that while the patriarchs knew about a God with the label "Yahweh," and even knew him as the one speaking to them, they had no idea what his real nature was. They knew him as a somewhat distant God of blessing, *'el shadday* [TH410A/7706, ZH446/8724] (Gen 17:1; 28:3; 35:11; 43:14; 48:3; 49:25),[2] who preserved their lives and expanded their families, and they knew that he had made a lot of promises about land and future significance, but not much more. They did not really know his "name"—that is, they did not know his character and person extensively.

But now Yahweh was going to change all that. He was going to show them an independence of, and control over, nature that would leave no doubt in their minds that he was not just a deity, but The Deity. He was going to show them a level of constancy they never imagined to exist in deity. He was going to show them a level of caring and commitment to his people they had only dared to hope existed in deity. He was going to show them an intimacy of relating that had never occurred to them to think of as possible with deity. And who was going to show them these things? Yahweh! What does it mean that he is "Yahweh," the "I AM"? It means that all those other royal pretenders who arrogantly asserted "I am so-and-so, and you had better pay attention to me," are exposed for just what they are: pretenders. There is only one being in the universe who can rightly say, "I AM" and who deserves to be listened to with the greatest of care. He is the one from whom all that exists draws its being, and he is the one who never regrets the past nor is surprised by the future. He is the one who is not one thing in what he says today and another in what he says tomorrow. This was the God who had appeared to their ancestors and asked if they would let him give them the things they longed for. Did Abraham understand that this was the "name" of the Yahweh who came to him? Hardly. Did Jacob know that this was the "name" of the "man" who wrestled with him through the night? Not at all. But after the events that were to take place in their immediate future, the descendants of Abraham, Isaac, and Jacob would never be able to say again that they did not know Yahweh's "name." Their hymns would resound with phrases like "your name is great, holy, glorious, majestic,"[3] and the thought that his "name" might be profaned by the way his people lived was a source of horror to the prophets (Jer 34:16; Ezek 36:20; Mal 1:6).

As already noted, the 10 first-person verbs in 6:2-8 pertain to the past, the present, and the future. Yahweh asserts that he is the one who appeared to the ancestors (6:3), the one who bound himself to them in a covenant (6:4). He has not forgotten that covenant (6:5), nor its promises to give them the land of Canaan (6:4). Yahweh had entered into a committed relationship with some particular humans, and that he would not repudiate that commitment for any reason. Neither can any circumstance, no matter how difficult or unfortunate, prevent the realization of that commitment. The emphatic particle *gam* at the head of verses 4 and 5 underscores these points. "I *have* entered into a covenant, and I *have* heard my covenant people crying." Yahweh is profoundly good. If evil comes, it is not because he arbitrarily does it. If it comes, it is in service of a greater good. Nowhere can this be seen more clearly than in the cross of Christ.

As the Cross would show, Yahweh's commitment is not a theological abstraction; it is a commitment to real human persons. This is also made explicit in verses 5 and 6. He was very conscious of the suffering of his people and did not intend to let them languish in that "oppression" (6:6); he would intervene in history with "great acts of judgment." The Hebrew root underlying "judgment" is *shpt* [TH8199, ZH9149]. While this root has to do with establishing justice, the concept is larger than that. It has to do with bringing God's intended order into the world. Injustice occurs when the world is not ordered according to the Creator's plan. When a human pharaoh dominates a people because he believes himself to be divine, he has violated the divine order or *mishpat* [TH4941, ZH5477]. So God promised to come and impose his order on the situation, demonstrating the folly of Pharaoh's pretensions and delivering his people from that disordered view of reality.

But lest we should think of the Exodus as merely an act of impartial, divine justice, or of the fulfillment of covenant obligations by the King, two images are used here which call us back to the realm of personal relationship. The first is "redeem" in verse 6. This is the activity of a near relative on behalf of a family member who has come into straitened circumstances. The activity of Boaz on behalf of Ruth and Naomi as recorded in the book of Ruth is one of the clearest examples of this kind of activity. So God would come as the near relative to "redeem" his family members.

The second image is that of marriage. As Sarna (1991:32) points out, the language of verse 7 is that of matrimony. When Yahweh says that he will "take you to myself as my people," ("I will claim you as my own people," 6:7, NLT), he is speaking of making Israel his bride (cf. Gen 4:19; 6:2; 11:29; Lev 21:3; Deut 24:4; Judg 14:20; Hos 3:3). I think Fretheim (1991:93) is too literalistic in arguing that since Israel was already God's people (e.g., Exod 3:7), the language here merely refers to delivering the people from Egypt. While that is true to some degree, it seems to me to be too limited. Everything that God was doing in the Exodus and Sinai was moving his relationship with Israel to a new level of intimacy. The repeated use of "know," with its connotations of sexual intimacy, underscores this point. He wanted to know his people, and he wanted them to know him in ways they never had before. Giving the land to Israel (6:8) was not merely a matter of keeping a judicial promise or of legalistically fulfilling a covenant obligation. It was more in the nature of a wedding gift. "I AM" finally implies a personal immediacy, and for Israel to know Yahweh's name means they will know him as an intimate, personal presence in their lives. Canaan may be their "possession" (6:8), but Israel will be Yahweh's possession.

Moses Speaks to the People (6:9-13). However deep Moses's discouragement and despair may have been, this revelation of God was enough to send him back to the people with renewed vigor. But Pharaoh's stratagems had been too successful. He had thoroughly discredited Moses's (and Aaron's) leadership and broken the will of the Israelites to resist. Whatever the precise connotations of "short of spirit" (NLT, "discouraged") might be (see note on 6:9), the point is clear: They had neither the motivation nor the will to give any credence to what Moses was talking about. So when Yahweh told Moses to "go back to Pharaoh" (6:11), Moses was incredulous. The previous time Moses and Aaron had gone into the royal presence they were full of confidence because of the way the people had responded. Now, not even the people would listen (6:12). Interestingly, Moses had still not quite gotten the picture. This was not about whether he could muster the eloquence to convince the Egyptian king to do something he was not willing to do. It was about the nature and identity of God. So God reiterated to Moses the "orders for the Israelites and for Pharaoh" (6:13) that he wanted relayed. Moses and Aaron did not have to be successful. All they had to be was obedient. Yahweh would handle the success factor. That point is made very clear in the continuation of his instructions in 7:1-5, a fact that should not be obscured by the intervening genealogy.

The Genealogy (6:14-25). This genealogy starts out as though it is for the whole Israelite nation because it begins by naming the descendants of Reuben, Jacob's firstborn, and moves to those of Simeon, his second son, and to those of Levi, his third (6:14-16). But instead of moving to Jacob's fourth son, the genealogy moves to the descendants of Levi's descendants (6:17-19). The same pattern is followed through the next three generations (6:20-25) with one name being selected for tracing to the succeeding generation. The line of interest is Levi–Kohath–Amram–Aaron–Eleazar–Phinehas. The one exception to the pattern is that one of the descendants of Amram's brother Izhar (6:18) is traced to a second generation: Korah (6:24).[4]

This pattern makes it clear that the focus of the genealogy is on the Levitical family, in particular, Aaron's clan, and the reader's realization of this fact is not left to chance. The final sentence of 6:25 makes it explicit: "These are the ancestors of the Levite families, listed according to their clans." But the reason for placing this genealogy here is not so clear. Perhaps the most likely reason is to reassert the leadership credentials of Moses and Aaron. Verses 26 and 27 support this idea. The Moses and Aaron who were saying these fantastic things were not foreigners, hangers-on who had attached themselves to the Israelites. They were at the core of the nation's heritage and were a central part of that honored family that would play such a part in the nation's future.

But the very nature of the genealogy shows that it was not written at the time when Moses's and Aaron's reputations needed restoration. Eleazar was high priest during the conquest period (Josh 14:1; 17:4), and Phinehas served even later than that (Josh 24:33). So this genealogy, in its present form at least, was added to the book of Exodus long after the events described in the book.[5] When we consider this fact along with the fact that the focus of the genealogy is not really on Moses and Aaron but on Aaron alone, another possible purpose emerges. It may be that this form of the genealogy appears here to show later readers that God's choice of Aaron to serve as Moses's spokesman (a point that is reemphasized in 7:1-8) was neither a hastily-considered one, nor something that was only of short-term significance. Rather, it was in keeping with Yahweh's larger plans for Aaron's family.

The genealogy raises a chronological question. Exodus 12:40 explicitly states that Israel had lived in Egypt for 430 years. Yet this genealogy only gives four generations between Levi and Moses and Aaron. One alternative is to say that the number 430 is merely intended to express a long period of time and that there really were only four generations of Israelites who lived in Egypt. Cassuto (1967:86-87) seems to accept this view and points to Genesis 15:16, where God tells Abraham that his descendants will return in the fourth generation. But Cassuto's somewhat convoluted attempt to explain how the number 400 in Genesis 15:13 and 430 in Exodus 12:40 arose (as per Rashi), "leaves some doubt," as Childs (1974:117) says.

Another alternative is to say that the numbers are generally correct (see endnote 1 on 12:31–13:21), and that the genealogy is "gapped." That is, not every generation between Levi and Moses and Aaron is listed. Evidence that such an approach to genealogy was used in biblical times can be found in Matthew's genealogy of Jesus (Matt 1:1-16), where two generations between David and Jesus are clearly omitted (Matt 1:8, 11). The Hebrew word *ben* [TH1121, ZH1201], often translated "son," leaves open this possibility, because it is also used of "grandson" and "great-grandson." The NLT, with its translation "descendants," is following this line of thinking. This seems to me to be the more likely explanation.

Yahweh Affirms Moses and Aaron (6:28–7:7). Verses 28-30 resume and summarize 6:2-12 (as shown by the repetition of "I am the LORD," [6:2] in 6:29). This argues for the verses being composed in the light of the intervening genealogy, showing that it has not been merely interpolated into a preexisting text. The fact that the interchange between God and Moses ends in both places with Moses saying he is a "clumsy speaker," strongly suggests that in one way or another the Aaronide genealogy was included here in support of God's choice of Aaron to help Moses with his problem.

In response to Moses's objection, God reminded Moses that he had already made provision for Moses's speech problem. Just as Aaron had been Moses's "spokesman to the people" (4:16), so now he would be Moses's spokesman to Pharaoh (7:2). But the language used here is more direct. At Sinai, Moses was to be in the place of God to Aaron (4:16). Here Yahweh says he will make Moses God to Pharaoh ("make you seem like God," 7:1, NLT). This exile who had gone over to the Semites, the contemptible "sand-dwellers," would speak as God to this one who considered himself to be God incarnate.

But even with Aaron's fluency, Moses was not to expect that Pharaoh would simply accede to their requests. What lay ahead would be a long road of rejection and defiance. Pharaoh might have thought he had complete freedom, as a god, to act in any way he wished, but that was not so. He had chosen a way of life and of thinking that now left him no freedom at all. He *could not* permit the Hebrews to leave his realm now. To do so would be to admit that there was an authority superior to his own. That he could not do. God had "hardened his heart" in the same sense that it might be said that God makes it impossible for the person who has defied gravity and jumped off a tall building to decide not to hit the sidewalk. In this world of cause and effect, Pharaoh had set in motion a train of events long ago, the results of which had now become inexorable. (On this point see also the commentary and notes on 4:21).

The only way the Hebrews would be able to leave the servitude of Pharaoh in Egypt and enter into the servitude of Yahweh in Canaan was if Yahweh was powerful enough to force Pharaoh to let them go. That Yahweh had such power was exactly what he intended to demonstrate. He was going to do "signs and wonders" (7:3). That is, he was going to provide convincing evidence of his complete power over the entire world of nature and humanity. He was going to reveal himself. But even then Moses should not expect to be listened to. These events were not about Moses's and Aaron's fluency or persuasiveness. These events were about Yahweh, and the only issue was whether these men were willing to be used for the display of his character and nature. It was Yahweh who would "bring down his fist" (7:4); it was Yahweh who would "rescue [his] forces." It was Yahweh who would raise his powerful hand and bring out the Israelites. Then this pharaoh, who had so contemptuously said, "I don't know this Yahweh," (cf. 5:2), would know him very well indeed (7:5). As Fretheim comments (1991:94), this knowing involves both positive and negative aspects. From the Israelites' perspective, they came to know a God who was forever faithful, endlessly compassionate, and unlimited in power for those who would recognize his covenant lordship. But for Pharaoh, and for all those who refuse to recognize Yahweh's absolute right as creator to determine what is true and what is false, what is right and what is wrong, to know Yahweh was to discover pain, horror, and humiliation (cf. 1 Pet 5:5-7). How blessed are those who come to know him as Covenant Lord early in their days.

As with 4:18, the response of Moses and Aaron to all of this is almost anticlimactic. We look for words of adoration and praise or for a description of their abject surrender to this overwhelming announcement of divine glory, power, and grace. But all we have are the sparse words, "So Moses and Aaron did just as the Lord had commanded them" (7:6). In the end, this is all that matters. Yes, there may be great experiences like Isaiah's (Isa 6), where the human, emotional aspects of what takes place are important to revive and recall. But there is a terrible tendency on our part to try to enshrine those moments, as Peter wanted to do on the Mount of Transfiguration (Mark 9:5-6), as if recapturing the feelings were the most important thing. But whatever the experience, if it does not issue in obedience, the experience is not worth much. The reason we know about Isaiah's experience at all is that he willingly embraced the frightening commission given to him to speak a message that would actually drive his own generation farther from God. So here, what has made the difference for all eternity is that these two old men—men who could have justly expected to lay down their arms for younger men to take up—said "yes" to Yahweh's commands.

While no reason is given for the record of the ages of Moses and Aaron here (7:7), it seems likely that it is done to mark a turning point in their lives. What had taken place up to this point had all been preliminary, even when they were at a point where they could easily have thought their lives' work was over. Now the stage was fully set, and as Fretheim says (1991:96), "the drama is ready to unfold."

ENDNOTES

1. The so-called "Documentary Hypothesis," brought to its apex by the German scholar, Julius Wellhausen, in the 1870s, cited 6:2–7:7 as one of the strongest indicators that the Pentateuch had been put together from the parts of several preexisting documents. In this case, the hypothesis understands 3:1–6:1 as the report of Moses's call from the "J" (or "JE"?) document, while 6:2–7:7 is the report of the same events from the "P" document. As Knight (1976:43) sees it, the two passages are clearly doublets, each independent of the other. For some reason, the "P" (or priestly) editor—supposedly creating the final version of the Pentateuch around 400 BC—did not take the liberty to simply revise the "J" (or "JE") report to make it say what he wanted it to say (although he supposedly does make such revisions in other passages). So he simply added his version after the older one. Conservative scholars were quick to point out the difficulties of such a scheme, none doing it better than James Orr in his *The Problem of the Old Testament* (1909). Many modern scholars, while still holding to the outlines of the hypothesis, have admitted that many of the grounds on which it was constructed will not stand up. So in this case, Childs (1974:112) and Houtman (1993:1.496) both recognize that the two accounts are not fully independent here; they have been so "worked over" as to assume each other. But, if they do assume each other, what happens to the argument that they must have once existed independently in separate documents? In my opinion, the explanation given here—that 6:2–7:7 is a reiteration and amplification in the light of the clarified and intensified issue obviates any need to propose the existence of independent accounts.
2. Note that in Gen 17:1 and 35:11, "El-Shaddai" is used precisely as here, in a self-identification formula. Thus, a conscious contrast with those occurrences may be

intended here. Yahweh was moving the relationship to a new, expanded, and more personal level.
3. Yahweh's name is called great, Ps 76:1; exalted, Isa 12:4, KJV; holy, Isa 57:15, KJV; feared, Mal 1:14; powerful, Jer 10:6; a source of joy, Pss 89:16, KJV; 92:1, KJV; good, Pss 52:9; 54:6; enduring, Ps 135:13; praiseworthy, Pss 48:10; 66:4; 140:13; 145:1; glorious, Pss 79:9; 86:9, 12; 115:1; and the desire of the heart, Isa 26:8.
4. Perhaps the reason for this exception is that the Korahite clan was to be singled out for service in the Temple (1 Chr 9:19). Although Korah died in the rebellion in the wilderness, his descendants survived (Num 26:11).
5. It is possible that the original form of the book did have a genealogy of Aaron and Moses at this point but that it stopped with what is now 6:22. In that case the point would have been to reestablish the credibility of Moses and Aaron. This might explain why no children of Moses are listed. Later editors would have added the later data with the particular purpose of justifying the choice of Aaron.

◆ B. The Events of Deliverance (7:8–15:21)
　1. The plagues (7:8–12:30)
　　a. Moses's staff and the first series of plagues (7:8–8:19)

⁸Then the LORD said to Moses and Aaron, ⁹"Pharaoh will demand, 'Show me a miracle.' When he does this, say to Aaron, 'Take your staff and throw it down in front of Pharaoh, and it will become a serpent.*'"

¹⁰So Moses and Aaron went to Pharaoh and did what the LORD had commanded them. Aaron threw down his staff before Pharaoh and his officials, and it became a serpent! ¹¹Then Pharaoh called in his own wise men and sorcerers, and these Egyptian magicians did the same thing with their magic. ¹²They threw down their staffs, which also became serpents! But then Aaron's staff swallowed up their staffs. ¹³Pharaoh's heart, however, remained hard. He still refused to listen, just as the LORD had predicted.

¹⁴Then the LORD said to Moses, "Pharaoh's heart is stubborn,* and he still refuses to let the people go. ¹⁵So go to Pharaoh in the morning as he goes down to the river. Stand on the bank of the Nile and meet him there. Be sure to take along the staff that turned into a snake. ¹⁶Then announce to him, 'The LORD, the God of the Hebrews, has sent me to tell you, "Let my people go, so they can worship me in the wilderness." Until now, you have refused to listen to him. ¹⁷So this is what the LORD says: "I will show you that I am the LORD." Look! I will strike the water of the Nile with this staff in my hand, and the river will turn to blood. ¹⁸The fish in it will die, and the river will stink. The Egyptians will not be able to drink any water from the Nile.'"

¹⁹Then the LORD said to Moses: "Tell Aaron, 'Take your staff and raise your hand over the waters of Egypt—all its rivers, canals, ponds, and all the reservoirs. Turn all the water to blood. Everywhere in Egypt the water will turn to blood, even the water stored in wooden bowls and stone pots.'"

²⁰So Moses and Aaron did just as the LORD commanded them. As Pharaoh and all of his officials watched, Aaron raised his staff and struck the water of the Nile. Suddenly, the whole river turned to blood! ²¹The fish in the river died, and the water became so foul that the Egyptians couldn't drink it. There was blood everywhere throughout the land of Egypt. ²²But again the magicians of Egypt used their magic, and they, too, turned water into blood. So Pharaoh's heart remained hard.

He refused to listen to Moses and Aaron, just as the LORD had predicted. ²³Pharaoh returned to his palace and put the whole thing out of his mind. ²⁴Then all the Egyptians dug along the riverbank to find drinking water, for they couldn't drink the water from the Nile.

²⁵Seven days passed from the time the LORD struck the Nile.

CHAPTER 8

¹*Then the LORD said to Moses, "Go back to Pharaoh and announce to him, 'This is what the LORD says: Let my people go, so they can worship me. ²If you refuse to let them go, I will send a plague of frogs across your entire land. ³The Nile River will swarm with frogs. They will come up out of the river and into your palace, even into your bedroom and onto your bed! They will enter the houses of your officials and your people. They will even jump into your ovens and your kneading bowls. ⁴Frogs will jump on you, your people, and all your officials.'"

⁵*Then the LORD said to Moses, "Tell Aaron, 'Raise the staff in your hand over all the rivers, canals, and ponds of Egypt, and bring up frogs over all the land.'" ⁶So Aaron raised his hand over the waters of Egypt, and frogs came up and covered the whole land! ⁷But the magicians were able to do the same thing with their magic. They, too, caused frogs to come up on the land of Egypt.

⁸Then Pharaoh summoned Moses and Aaron and begged, "Plead with the LORD to take the frogs away from me and my people. I will let your people go, so they can offer sacrifices to the LORD."

⁹"You set the time!" Moses replied. "Tell me when you want me to pray for you, your officials, and your people. Then you and your houses will be rid of the frogs. They will remain only in the Nile River."

¹⁰"Do it tomorrow," Pharaoh said.

"All right," Moses replied, "it will be as you have said. Then you will know that there is no one like the LORD our God. ¹¹The frogs will leave you and your houses, your officials, and your people. They will remain only in the Nile River."

¹²So Moses and Aaron left Pharaoh's palace, and Moses cried out to the LORD about the frogs he had inflicted on Pharaoh. ¹³And the LORD did just what Moses had predicted. The frogs in the houses, the courtyards, and the fields all died. ¹⁴The Egyptians piled them into great heaps, and a terrible stench filled the land. ¹⁵But when Pharaoh saw that relief had come, he became stubborn.* He refused to listen to Moses and Aaron, just as the LORD had predicted.

¹⁶So the LORD said to Moses, "Tell Aaron, 'Raise your staff and strike the ground. The dust will turn into swarms of gnats throughout the land of Egypt.'" ¹⁷So Moses and Aaron did just as the LORD had commanded them. When Aaron raised his hand and struck the ground with his staff, gnats infested the entire land, covering the Egyptians and their animals. All the dust in the land of Egypt turned into gnats. ¹⁸Pharaoh's magicians tried to do the same thing with their secret arts, but this time they failed. And the gnats covered everyone, people and animals alike.

¹⁹"This is the finger of God!" the magicians exclaimed to Pharaoh. But Pharaoh's heart remained hard. He wouldn't listen to them, just as the LORD had predicted.

7:9 Hebrew *tannin*, which elsewhere refers to a sea monster. Greek version translates it "dragon." **7:14** Hebrew *heavy*. **8:1** Verses 8:1-4 are numbered 7:26-29 in Hebrew text. **8:5** Verses 8:5-32 are numbered 8:1-28 in Hebrew text. **8:15** Hebrew *made his heart heavy*; also in 8:32.

NOTES

7:9 *"Show me a miracle."* Lit., "Give for/to you [masc. pl.] a wonder." The LXX reads "to us" and Syriac has "to me." The MT is the harder reading, but the idea is "for yourselves," i.e., "show your credentials." Pharaoh asked for a "wonder," and he got many more than he bargained for (cf. 11:10).

a serpent. See NLT mg. Here, this is *tannin* [TH8577, ZH9490], meaning "dragon, monster" (also used in 7:10 and 12), not the same word translated "snake" in 4:3 and again in 7:15, which is *nakhash* [TH5175, ZH5729]. Cassuto (1967:94) argues that it refers to a crocodile, appropriate to Egypt. In Ezek 32:2 (also in Ezek 29:3), Pharaoh is described as a *tannin*, and the activities attributed to him in the succeeding verses are those of a crocodile. Freitheim (1991:114) and Enns (2000:196) suggest that the word was used for theological purposes since elsewhere *tannin* is used for the chaos monster that the gods in the various myths of the ancient Near East defeated in order to bring about the present cosmos (cf. Ps 74:13; Isa 27:1 for allusions to these tales). Thus, Yahweh would be saying by this sign that the whole created order is under his control.

7:11 *Then Pharaoh.* In Hebrew "Pharaoh" is preceded by the particle *gam-* [TH1571, ZH1685] which indicates parallel actions: On the one hand Moses and Aaron did this, on the other hand Pharaoh did that (Williams 1976:64).

magicians. The word *khartom* [TH2748, ZH3033] is apparently an Egyptian loan word denoting a class of priests who were especially associated with rituals and incantations, which probably defines the type of "magic" they employed.

magic. This is the only occurrence of the Hebrew word in this form (*lehatim* [TH3858A, ZH4268]). Elsewhere in the OT (8:7, 18; Ruth 3:7; 1 Sam 18:22; 24:4) the form is *lat* [TH3909, ZH4319], and the root seems to be *lut* [TH3874, ZH4286] which has the idea of secrecy. The insertion of the Hebrew letter *he* may be a dialectal variation.

7:15 *snake.* See the note on 7:9.

7:16 *sent me . . . Let my people go.* Cassuto (1967:97) observes the wordplay between two different verb forms from the same root, *shalakh* [TH7971, ZH8938] (to send). God has *sent* Moses to tell Pharaoh to *send* his people from the land.

7:17 *"I will show you that I am the LORD."* Lit., "You will know that I am Yahweh." This is another of the frequent recurrences of this idea throughout this section.

will strike. A participial form, probably expressing imminence: "I am about to strike."

in my hand. An example of what was meant when Yahweh said to Moses that he would be God to Pharaoh. In the sentence, the subject is Yahweh.

7:19 *wooden bowls and stone pots.* Lit., "wooden things and stone things." The interpretation of these as water vessels goes back to the LXX. But it is somewhat uncertain since wood was very rare in Egypt and there are no known examples of wooden water vessels there. This has prompted a great deal of scholarly inventiveness, ranging from Sarna's suggestion (1991:39) that the pair might be a figure of speech (known as a merism) representing all things in creation from Cassuto's stone and wooden idols that were washed daily (1967:99) to Houtman's buildings of wood and stone (1993:2.37). Given the antiquity of the LXX and its supposed Egyptian provenance, it seems best to remain with its understanding.

7:20 *Suddenly.* This is a logical inference, although not in the Hebrew.

7:22 *magicians.* See the note on 7:11.

7:23 *put the whole thing out of his mind.* Lit., "did not take it (*shith* [TH7896, ZH8883]) to heart." Cf. Hag 1:5, 7, which uses a parallel verb *sim* [TH7760, ZH8492]. He did not draw the appropriate conclusions.

7:25 *passed.* Most interpreters understand this sentence to mean that the plague of blood lasted "seven days."

8:2 [7:27] *I will send.* The Hebrew uses *nogep* [TH5062, ZH5597], a participle of imminence:

"I am about to strike [NLT, 'send']." A similar participial expression is used in 7:17 and in succeeding plagues. Pharaoh stands on the edge of another catastrophe unless he acts quickly.

8:3 [7:28] swarm. Cassuto (1967:101) sees a connection with Gen 1:20 and suggests this is a reaffirmation of Yahweh's creative power.

your ovens and your kneading bowls. The fact that the frogs would even be found in these places, among the last where a frog would be found, emphasizes the totality of the event and its miraculous nature.

8:7 [3] magicians . . . magic. See the notes on 7:11.

8:8 [4] I will let your people go. The form of the verb in Hebrew is cohortative, normally connoting "let me do such and such" or "that I may do such and such." Perhaps this was a bit of sophistry that later enabled Pharaoh to say that he had never actually promised that he would let the Israelites go.

8:9 [5] "You set the time!" Lit., "Glorify yourself over me." Commentators have offered a number of different translations to convey what is meant here: Sarna (1991:41) reads "I defer to you"; Cassuto (1967:103) reads "have glory over me"; Childs (1974:156) reads "I'll give you the advantage"; Houtman (1993:2.48) reads "the honor is yours." Moses, either ironically or sincerely, is inviting Pharaoh to take the upper hand in the contest by dictating when the plague of frogs is to stop.

8:13 [9] had predicted. Lit., "according to the word of Moses." Cassuto (1967:104) points out the repetition of *dabar* [TH1697, ZH1821] (word) in 8:10, 12, and 13 (8:6, 8, 9 in MT): the "word" of Pharaoh; the "word" (matter) of the frogs; and the "word" of Moses.

8:14 [10] great heaps. Lit., "heaps of heaps." This is a climactic expression, perhaps meaning "heaps upon heaps."

8:16 [12] strike the ground. The dust. Lit., "strike the dust of the earth" (also 8:17). Some commentators (e.g., Houtman) argue that the narrator wants us to believe that every mote of dust became a tiny, biting insect. But this phrase suggests a class of material rather than every single bit of that material (see commentary).

gnats. The word *kinnim* [TH3654, ZH4031] is very indefinite (the *-im* ending is collective). It comes close to the English word "bugs." Ellison (1982:47) translates "ticks," whereas Clements (1972:49), following the NEB, translates "maggots." Houtman (1993:2.55) prefers "lice" because that relieves the commentator of having to find an Egyptian setting (lice are not endemic to Egypt)—that is surely the weakest reason to choose a particular rendering!

8:18 [14] tried to do the same thing. The NLT has correctly captured the sense of a somewhat elliptical Hebrew statement, "the magicians did thus . . . and they were not able." Cassuto (1967:105-106) wrestled with this problem at some length, but his explanation seems forced.

COMMENTARY

We come now to that episode in the book known as "the plagues" (although they are only called such four times, via three different words (*deber* [TH1698, ZH1822], 9:3, 15; *maggepah* [TH4046, ZH4487], 9:14; *nega'* [TH5061, ZH5596], 11:1). As I said in the Introduction and in previous commentary sections, the purpose of the plagues was divine self-revelation. The people's response to the offer of deliverance (4:29–5:23) had highlighted the underlying issue: the nature and character of deity. It would not be enough for Yahweh to do one stupendous miracle and get his people out of

Egypt. Real deliverance from the bondage of the world must include deliverance from the world's wrong understanding of reality. Ultimately, that deliverance is the purpose the plagues served.

In this light, it seems to me that the biblical explanation of the plagues as being aimed against Egypt's gods (12:12; 18:11) is quite correct (as per Sarna [1991:38] and contra Houtman [1993:2.21]). It is not necessary to suggest that each plague is aimed at a specific Egyptian god. It is enough to observe that like all pagans, the Egyptians believed in the continuity of humans, nature, and deity (Kaufmann 1960:56). Thus, for Yahweh to demonstrate his absolute lordship over all the forces of nature, from the Nile to life itself, showing that apart from him these forces are not life-giving, but death-dealing, was to demonstrate that he *is not* one of the gods but is a different order of being altogether.[1]

Medieval Jewish exegetes pointed out that the literary structure of the plague account has the first nine plagues divided into three sets of three. The pattern is this: Plagues 1, 4, and 7 have Moses standing to meet Pharaoh in the morning out of doors; plagues 2, 5, and 8 have him appearing before Pharaoh apparently indoors at an indeterminate time; and plagues 3, 6, and 9 occur with no prior warning to Pharaoh. Furthermore, plagues 1-3 have Aaron as the effective agent, plagues 4-6 seem to have both Moses and Aaron acting, while in the final three, Moses is the effective agent. Sarna (1991:38) suggests the purpose of this patterning is to make it clear these are not randomly occurring natural disasters.

The cumulative effect of the plagues was to make Pharaoh willing to negotiate with Moses and Aaron. He tried to find a way to grant the letter of their request to go and worship Yahweh while making sure that they would return to their slavery. Thus, after the second plague he said he would let them go but then retracted the permission (8:8, 15). After the fourth plague, he offered to let them worship in Egypt (8:25). After the seventh plague, he again said he would let them go and then retracted the permission (9:28, 35). After the eighth, he offered to let the men go (10:11). Finally, after the ninth he said all the people could go, but they must leave their livestock behind (10:24). To each of the three attempts at negotiation, Moses had a deft answer (his self-description as "tongue-tied" [4:10; cf. 6:12] notwithstanding) that put the responsibility back upon Pharaoh. Pharaoh had acted as absolute master over these people; it was inconceivable for him to surrender unconditionally to their God.

Over the years commentators have spent a good deal of energy attempting to explain the nature of the plagues.[2] While some of the most critical scholars simply dismissed them as the product of fanciful imaginations, others have argued that there must have been some historical basis for them. Thus, it has been common in some quarters to argue that the bloody Nile was the result of an "algae bloom," which in turn deprived the fish of oxygen so that they died. The combination of the first two drove the frogs out of the river, and they died on land resulting in a great increase of flies and other insects. The growth in the insect population produced an upsurge in disease, both in animals and humans. Add to this a devastating hailstorm, a plague of locusts, and an eclipse of the sun, and you have a very bad few months in Egypt. But what one does with these "facts" is completely dependent on one's theology. If one believes that the Bible is merely the product of a people's attempt to create their own religion, then one concludes that the people creatively incorporated certain remembered events into their emerging theology. If one believes that the Holy Spirit was at work shaping the emerging Hebrew religion, then one may say that God is at work in all of nature and that these natural events were fortuitously arranged so that they helped to serve the people's religious speculation.

But none of these things is what the text says, as even Houtman points out (1993:2.29), who is not inclined to give the text much historical credibility. The narrator tells us that the water was turned to blood, not something that looked like blood. And it occurred at the very time when Aaron's rod was stretched over it. Furthermore, the phenomenon was gone within seven days, something that is not the case with an algae bloom. These are not "natural" occurrences. They are supernatural occurrences. To be sure, they are within the broadest scope of nature. With the exception of the water turning into blood, the other events are not a destruction of natural processes. But they are special, divinely caused events that would not have occurred without specific divine intervention. This is what the writer wants us, the readers, to believe. We may choose not to believe what the writer says. But we cannot "save" the situation by suggesting that really this was a natural sequence of events that has been adapted for theological purposes.

What evidence is there that we are dealing with "wonders" or miracles? The four critical elements are timing, intensity, extent, and selectivity. It is not a miracle if an earthquake occurs in western Kentucky—they have occurred there before. But it is a miracle if I announce that one will occur precisely at 2:15 p.m. tomorrow and that the last aftershock will be felt at 3:00 a.m. three days later and those things occur as predicted. Similarly, it is a miracle if I announce that this will be the worst earthquake ever experienced, affecting a 20-state area, and it comes to pass. Finally, it is a miracle if I announce that Cairo, Illinois, will feel nothing, and they do not. Someone may reply that such things are not reasonable. But that is precisely the Bible's point. Yahweh completely transcends our categories of rationality and possibility. The creation is his and he can do with it as he wishes. He is not bound by the cycles of nature as the gods are.

Prologue to the Plagues (7:8-13). This incident is a prologue to the plagues themselves. It opens the proceedings, as it were, and establishes the pattern for the first several plagues: a sign from the Lord (7:10), a duplication from the Egyptian magicians (7:11-12), Pharaoh's heart is hardened (7:13). Pharaoh is depicted in a more expansive mood. Since he had won the opening skirmishes of the war, he could afford to play with these Semitic adventurers a bit. So he demands that they give some evidence that they really were the ambassadors of this God who thinks he can command a pharaoh.

Four points should be made regarding this event. The first concerns the agency of

Aaron. Sarna (1991:37) points out that Aaron was active as long as the Egyptian magicians were on the scene and that this permitted Moses to remain on a par with Pharaoh. It was only after the magicians had been discredited (8:19) that Aaron began to recede into the background. In this regard, note that it is specifically said that it was Aaron's staff that was used in this sign and the subsequent three miracles (7:10, 20; 8:5, 17). After that, a staff only appears again in the seventh plague (hail), and it is in Moses's hand (9:23), where it also appears in the eighth (10:13), and possibly the ninth (10:22).

The second point is that Moses, the narrator, was making a clear contrast between the way in which Aaron worked and the way the magicians worked. Aaron did not produce a sign on demand by means of his manipulation of "secret arts" (8:18; cf. "magic," 7:11, 22; 8:2). Rather, he simply obeyed a command from God relayed through Moses and threw his "staff" on the ground. It is also significant that Aaron did nothing to cause his staff to swallow up the magicians' staffs (7:12). The point is that Aaron had not tapped into divine or cosmic power to use it on his own initiative. He had been delegated to demonstrate Yahweh's power under specific direction from Yahweh himself.

The third point is that the magicians were never able to deliver Egypt from the deadly signs or even to counter them. For instance, they were not able to turn Aaron's staff back from a snake to a staff. Neither were they able to make their snakes swallow up his. The most they could do was to appear to duplicate what Moses and Aaron had done. Although that would be enough to confirm Pharaoh in the course of disbelief he had already decided on, it would not be enough to wrench Egypt out of the terrible grasp into which Pharaoh's ego had placed them.

Finally, it appears that the magicians themselves understood that what they were doing was the result of human ingenuity and inventiveness. The evidence is found in their response when they were finally defeated (8:18-19). They said, "This is the finger of God!" an admission that what they had been doing was not from the divine realm at all. Since they could not reproduce this sign, it had to have come from God.

The First Plague (7:14-25). The first plague struck the Nile River. That can hardly be an accident. Historically, the Egyptians have called their land "the gift of the Nile," and indeed it is. If it were not for the waters of the Nile, the Sahara Desert would sweep in unbroken desolation right to the shores of the Red Sea. But the river brings life-giving water that unleashes the fertility of the land and makes abundant life possible in a 400-mile long swath through the desert. But the absolute dependency of the land upon the Nile water is demonstrated by the fact that only yards beyond the farthest irrigation ditch, the desert reigns supreme.

So it is hardly surprising that the Nile, particularly in the inundation phase, was considered to be a goddess and was worshipped as such—she was the giver of life. But that was not really the case. The only giver of life in the universe is "I AM." If we attribute to any of his creatures the power of life and especially if we arrogate that power to ourselves, we will have all unwittingly handed ourselves over to the power of death. From beginning to end, that is the message of the plagues. Whatever we worship in place of the one God cannot give us life; it can only give us death. This is the reason the Nile was turned to blood and not fruit juice. This was not just a carnival stunt in which Yahweh would perform amazing feats. Everything the Egyptians had worshiped as a source of life was really only death apart from the good hand of life's creator, and Yahweh was about to prove that in multiple ways.[3]

Again, it can hardly be an accident that Moses met Pharaoh on the bank of the Nile. That river bank was important here for two reasons. It was the place where this pharaoh's predecessor had commanded that all Israelite baby boys be drowned (1:22). But it was also the place (2:5) where God had frustrated all those evil designs by using an Egyptian princess, who was perhaps one of this pharaoh's own sisters, to spare the life of Israel's future deliverer. Pharaoh may have thought the Nile belonged to him (Ezek 29:3), but it really was Yahweh's, and his justice reigns supreme. It may also be that Pharaoh was at the riverbank to engage in some sort of worship; if so, that would make even more poignant Yahweh's repetition of his demand that his people be freed to "worship" him (lit., "serve," 7:16).

Houtman (1993.2:25-26) argues that the account is neither homogenous nor historically reliable because of what he sees as discrepancies in it. For instance, he says that the command in 7:19 is at odds with 7:17 and 20. Furthermore, he says that the idea that "all" the water in Egypt became blood is absurd. But it is one thing to say that an account reports a historic event accurately and another to say that an account seeks to report all aspects of an event as exactly as possible. It is probably fair to say that Exodus is not history in the latter sense, but that does not discredit it as a historical document. While it may not be precise to say that every bit of water in Egypt became blood (e.g., the magicians got water from somewhere, 7:22; and apparently Pharaoh had access to water so that the event did not greatly concern him, 7:23), the point is surely that this was not a 30-second phenomenon, nor was it a merely localized event. It took place over a lengthy time span (perhaps a week, cf. 7:25), and it affected people all over the land.[4] To demand that an account either conform to modern definitions of history-writing or be consigned to the level of folktale is to overlook other valid options between those extremes.

Once again, the "magicians" (7:22) were only able to duplicate the sign. They were not able to deliver Egypt from it; they were not able to turn the bloody Nile back to water. This fact should have given Pharaoh some pause: Why couldn't Egypt's wise men save Egypt from this attack? But apparently the magicians' ability to duplicate the sign in some manner just confirmed him in thinking that this event really did not provide any evidence that there was a God superior to him and his gods; it was only magical mumbo-jumbo that any reasonably skilled technician could perform.

The Plague of Frogs (8:1-15). One week later (7:25) Moses returned to Pharaoh with Yahweh's insistent demand that his people be allowed to go and "worship" (8:1; lit., "serve") him. As I have pointed out previously, this is not subterfuge on either Yahweh's or Moses's part. That was the real purpose of the Exodus. It was not merely political freedom; it was a dramatic change of masters. God was calling his people to himself, and no pharaoh in the world could prevent that.

Once again, Yahweh was demonstrating that whatever the Egyptians revered as a source of life apart from him was really a source of death. Frogs were sacred to the Egyptians because they knew how to live in two worlds at once. The Egyptians saw in this a parallel to their concern with finding the keys to living in the next world, the world beyond death. Thus, Heqet, the wife of the ram-headed god Khnum, was depicted as a woman with a frog's head, blowing life into the clay figures of humans her husband had formed on a potter's wheel. But frogs do not know the secret of life, and Yahweh was going to prove it. If the Egyptians wanted frogs, he would give them frogs, more than they ever imagined.

The repetition of "your" addressed to Pharaoh (10 times in 8:2-4) underscores two facts. First, this is a contest between Yahweh and Pharaoh, and second, Pharaoh could not evade it. He may have given little consideration to the bloody Nile (7:23) because it did not affect him directly. But that was not going to be the case in the future. He would not be able to ignore the frogs that were suddenly everywhere he turned—even where food was being prepared (8:3-4).

The threefold description of the event in the form of a warning (8:2-4), a command (8:5), and a carrying out of a command (8:6) has been regularly seen by critical scholars as evidence of different original documents that have been put together, in this case without much attention to harmonization and consistency (Hyatt 1971:48; see endnote 1 on 6:1-7:7). However, students of ancient literature have demonstrated that this kind of repetition is typical, especially if the text had any period of oral transmission. It is clear that ancient hearers and readers enjoyed a kind of repetition that modern readers, with their passion for action, find boring.

The fact that the magicians were able to do something similar to what Moses and Aaron had done is a good reminder of the dangers of an overly literal reading. If indeed there were frogs *everywhere*, then what was there left for the ritual priests to do? Surely the point is to say that this incredible swarm of frogs could not have been merely a natural event on an unusually large scale. It was the work of God. To then push the language to the point of absurdity is clearly to make it go beyond what was intended. As to what the magicians did, I suspect that they took some pails of water in which there were no frogs to be seen, and suddenly made frogs appear to come out of them. All that was necessary was to show that Moses and Aaron were not so special; other people could do the same kind of things they did, even if not on quite such a disgustingly gross scale as these Semites did.

But perhaps this time Pharaoh began to recognize the problem. It was not enough to duplicate the sign in some way. The question was: Could his ritual priests counteract Yahweh's stroke upon the land? The very absence of that discussion in the text is suggestive. Was there no point in even raising it since the answer was so obvious? At any rate, verse 8 signifies a new point in the proceedings: Pharaoh recognized Yahweh ("the LORD") as the only one who could remove the plague, and he seemed to offer a complete capitulation (although it may not have been as complete as the English makes it seem; see the note on this verse). Childs (1974:155) argues that Pharaoh was simply displaying the skills of a shrewd bargainer: raising the hopes of the opposing side with an apparent concession, which is never intended but which leads to whatever lesser concessions one is actually willing to make. The lesser offers he did make in future cases (e.g., 8:25) seem to offer support for this understanding of what was taking place.

But if Pharaoh was demonstrating his negotiating ability, Moses was as well. He very courteously invited Pharaoh to get glory for himself (see the note on 8:9) by dictating when the plague should be removed from "you, your officials, and your people" (note the contrast with "your people" in 8:8). If there should be any remaining question about the miraculous nature of the incident, it would surely be removed when the miracle happened on Pharaoh's own time schedule. Commentators are not agreed as to the significance of the time selected: "tomorrow" (8:10). Basically, there seem to be two alternative interpretations. The first is the thought that Moses would expect to do it immediately and that by deferring it for a day Pharaoh was hoping to throw Moses "off his stride" and have the thing go away on its own (Knight 1976:61-62), but the majority of commentators take it that "tomorrow" means "as soon as possible" with the hope that Moses cannot do the thing that quickly (Durham 1987:105).

If the latter was the case, it was a false hope, for Moses agreed to it instantly and made one of his earliest declarations of complete faith in God. He said that the frogs would disappear on the day Pharaoh asked so that he would know that the God whom he had said he would not recognize is absolutely incomparable (8:10). I label it as a declaration of faith because Moses could not know at that point that God would answer his prayer. Moses himself had no power to make his word come true. He had no technique that could make divine power accessible for him to use as he wished. Rather, he could only believe that God would keep faith with him. But real faith does not remove the uncertainty which accompanies the act of apparently stepping out onto thin air. Something of that tension can be seen in the verb "cried out" (8:12) that describes Moses's prayer. It is the same word used to describe the outcry of the Hebrews over their oppression (2:23). But God was quite happy to validate Moses's word and to do what Moses had said he would.[5]

The removal might not have been exactly as Pharaoh had envisioned it. And it is often true that our sins, even when forgiven, have long-lasting consequences. So in this case the frogs were indeed removed in one day. But their rotting carcasses and the accompanying "stench" remained. Still, as is also often the case today, as soon as the immediate discomfort was gone, Pharaoh saw no reason to carry through on his (at least) tacit promise (see the note on 8:8) to send the Israelites on their way to serve Yahweh. "Just as the LORD had predicted," he would never let the Israelites go of his own free will. It would only happen when he was forced to do so, and Yahweh had a great deal still to show Pharaoh, Israel, and the world before he was ready to apply that force. The repetition of "just as the LORD had predicted" at the end of several of the plagues (8:15, 19; 9:12, 35) probably indicates how much the memory of that prediction served to bolster Moses and Aaron's courage as they seemed to face an endless series of apparent victories and actual defeats. They knew they were serving God's larger purposes.

The Plague of Gnats (8:16–19). The third plague in each of the three series is unannounced, and that is the case here. Pharaoh had gone back on his promise, and the next plague simply dropped from the sky, as it were. Although most commentators translate the Hebrew *kinnim* as "gnats," there is no real assurance that this is what is intended. All that we can say with confidence is that some sort of small "vermin" is meant. Of all of the plagues, this is the one that is least obvious in its connection with a specific god of Egypt. However, the connection is still there, and in my opinion one does not have to strain to see it. Much like the Hindus, the Egyptians revered "life" of every sort, no matter how obscure. Thus, for instance, the Egyptians worshipped the dung-beetle, or scarab, which, because it laid its eggs in a ball of manure, seemed to have the ability to produce life from manure. This seemed like a very valuable skill to people who were so concerned that they might have to eat manure in the next world that they inscribed on the walls of their tombs rituals thought to prevent that sort of thing. It is the reason why mummies are often found with dozens of stone scarabs wrapped in the linen strips wound around them. But again, "I AM" says that however many vermin might squirm from earth's bosom, they are not a source of blessing apart from his ruling hand but a curse.

It is with this third plague that the Egyptian ritual priests, the "magicians," reached their Waterloo. Although they had been able to duplicate turning a staff into a serpent and turning Nile water into blood, and although they had been able to bring frogs from water, they could not turn the dust of the earth into swarms of vermin. As mentioned above, their response suggests very strongly that they had known all along that what they were doing was a work of their own ingenuity and technique, and not anything of a divine origin. For finally, with something that they could not reproduce, they announced that the miracle was clearly God's doing. Some commentators point out that they did not specifically recognize Yahweh, but perhaps not too much should be made of that. When Egyptians wanted to talk of deity in general, they spoke of "the god" (see Redford 2002:106-107, 225-226). Thus, this may simply be a way of saying, "This is a divine action."

But in spite of his magicians' admission of defeat, Pharaoh was unmoved. By this time he may have lost faith in them anyway. The fact that he had turned to Moses for relief from the plague of frogs seems to suggest this. It may also be that the swarms of vermin were not as unbearable as the crowds of frogs.[6] In any case, Yahweh's prediction came true once again.

ENDNOTES
1. This addresses Houtman's observation (1993:2.20) that the first nine plagues do not really seem to build on one another so that each succeeding one is more forceful to the end of forcing Pharaoh's hand. Their effect is not climactic but cumulative. When Yahweh is finished showing that there is *no* area of life outside of his capacity to intervene in and control, that will be time to bring Pharaoh to heel with a climactic show of power.

2. After a very lengthy review of critical views of the plague narrative, Houtman (1993:2.22) concludes that it is "a simple, small-scale scenario" that "is constructed as a folktale." I believe the atmosphere is markedly different from anything the Grimm brothers identified as folktales. Folktales make no effort to cause their hearers to consider the account to be factual. This narrative clearly does have that intent. What takes place is certainly supernatural and dramatic, but it is nothing like even the "Pied Piper of Hamlin," let alone "The Bremen Town Musicians."
3. It also cannot be an accident that Jesus' "first sign" (John 2:11) was to turn water into wine. Instead of turning life-giving water into death-dealing blood, he turns it into life-enhancing wine. Jesus was demonstrating that he is the new Moses (cf. John 1:17).
4. One possibility is that all *Nile water* became blood, whereas any other water did not. The fact that it was possible to dig shallow wells for drinking water along the banks of the Nile (7:24) supports this supposition.
5. Elijah's encounter with the prophets of Baal (1Kgs 18:20-40) is strongly reminiscent of this situation. To counter the plethora of ritual manipulation that the prophets engaged in, Elijah had only prayer. But that was enough.
6. Again, Houtman (1993:2.55) wishes to push the story to the point of absurdity by suggesting that since there is no word of the cessation of this plague, apparently there was no dust in Egypt thereafter. Fretheim (1991:119) does not go as far, but he suggests the text may want to convey that gnats were a part of Egyptian life thereafter. But neither is there any word of the Nile water's ceasing to be blood either (7:25), nor any report of the cessation of the boils (9:13). Such attempts to undermine the credibility of the story as a report of a historic event demand unrealistic completeness in what is obviously a highly condensed account.

◆ ### b. The second series of plagues (8:20-9:12)

20Then the LORD told Moses, "Get up early in the morning and stand in Pharaoh's way as he goes down to the river. Say to him, 'This is what the LORD says: Let my people go, so they can worship me. 21If you refuse, then I will send swarms of flies on you, your officials, your people, and all the houses. The Egyptian homes will be filled with flies, and the ground will be covered with them. 22But this time I will spare the region of Goshen, where my people live. No flies will be found there. Then you will know that I am the LORD and that I am present even in the heart of your land. 23I will make a clear distinction between* my people and your people. This miraculous sign will happen tomorrow.'"

24And the LORD did just as he had said. A thick swarm of flies filled Pharaoh's palace and the houses of his officials. The whole land of Egypt was thrown into chaos by the flies.

25Pharaoh called for Moses and Aaron. "All right! Go ahead and offer sacrifices to your God," he said. "But do it here in this land."

26But Moses replied, "That wouldn't be right. The Egyptians detest the sacrifices that we offer to the LORD our God. Look, if we offer our sacrifices here where the Egyptians can see us, they will stone us. 27We must take a three-day trip into the wilderness to offer sacrifices to the LORD our God, just as he has commanded us."

28"All right, go ahead," Pharaoh replied. "I will let you go into the wilderness to offer sacrifices to the LORD your God. But don't go too far away. Now hurry and pray for me."

29Moses answered, "As soon as I leave you, I will pray to the LORD, and tomorrow the swarms of flies will disappear from you and your officials and all your people. But I am warning you, Pharaoh, don't lie to us again and refuse to let the people go to sacrifice to the LORD."

30So Moses left Pharaoh's palace and pleaded with the LORD to remove all the flies. 31And the LORD did as Moses asked and caused the swarms of flies to disappear from Pharaoh, his officials, and his people. Not a single fly remained. 32But Pharaoh again became stubborn and refused to let the people go.

CHAPTER 9

"Go back to Pharaoh," the LORD commanded Moses. "Tell him, 'This is what the LORD, the God of the Hebrews, says: Let my people go, so they can worship me. 2If you continue to hold them and refuse to let them go, 3the hand of the LORD will strike all your livestock—your horses, donkeys, camels, cattle, sheep, and goats—with a deadly plague. 4But the LORD will again make a distinction between the livestock of the Israelites and that of the Egyptians. Not a single one of Israel's animals will die! 5The LORD has already set the time for the plague to begin. He has declared that he will strike the land tomorrow.'"

6And the LORD did just as he had said. The next morning all the livestock of the Egyptians died, but the Israelites didn't lose a single animal. 7Pharaoh sent his officials to investigate, and they discovered that the Israelites had not lost a single animal! But even so, Pharaoh's heart remained stubborn,* and he still refused to let the people go.

8Then the LORD said to Moses and Aaron, "Take handfuls of soot from a brick kiln, and have Moses toss it into the air while Pharaoh watches. 9The ashes will spread like fine dust over the whole land of Egypt, causing festering boils to break out on people and animals throughout the land."

10So they took soot from a brick kiln and went and stood before Pharaoh. As Pharaoh watched, Moses threw the soot into the air, and boils broke out on people and animals alike. 11Even the magicians were unable to stand before Moses, because the boils had broken out on them and all the Egyptians. 12But the LORD hardened Pharaoh's heart, and just as the LORD had predicted to Moses, Pharaoh refused to listen.

8:23 As in Greek and Latin versions; Hebrew reads *I will set redemption between.* 9:7 Hebrew *heavy.*

NOTES

8:20 [16] *Get up early in the morning.* See also 7:15.

stand in Pharaoh's way. Lit., "position yourself."

8:21 [17] *then I will send.* This is a wordplay with "send" (*shalakh* [TH7971, ZH8938]) in the previous verse. If Pharaoh will not send, then Yahweh will send. As in the previous plagues, the warning is expressed with a participle of imminence: "I am about to send."

flies. As with *kinnam* [TH3654A, ZH4038] (8:17, 18) or *kinnim* [TH3654, ZH4031] (8:16, 17, 18) in the previous plague, the word used here (*'arob* [TH6157, ZH6856]) is very indefinite, meaning simply "swarms." The LXX identifies it as a kind of biting insect known as the "dog fly." Egypt is known in the Bible as a place of flies (*zebub* [TH2070, ZH2279], Isa 7:18).

8:22 [18] *Goshen* was located in the northeastern area of Egypt, probably in the Wadi Tumeilat between the Nile delta and the Gulf of Suez (see the Introduction).

8:23 [19] *distinction.* This follows the Greek and Latin versions (so NLT mg). Although Houtman (1993:2.63) considers the LXX and Vulgate renderings (something like "distinction") to be just an interpretation of *peduth* [TH6304, ZH7014] (redemption), that seems to be too much of a stretch to me. Since the verb "to distinguish" is *palah* [TH6395, ZH7111], one of its noun forms (though not attested elsewhere) could be *peluth* [TH6431.1, ZH7151] (distinction), and Clements makes the plausible suggestion that the MT reading is an error for that original (1972:52).

8:24 [20] *thrown into chaos.* The Hebrew verb is in the imperfect, normally translated with the present or future tense in English. But it is clear that the past tense is intended here. There are a number of examples of this phenomenon in the Bible, and it has usually been explained as incomplete action occurring in the past (Gesenius §107b; thus here, "was being thrown into chaos," or "was being ruined"). However, it is possible that some prefixed forms, like this one, are simply to be understood as "preterites" (i.e., simple past tenses; Waltke and O'Connor 1990:496-501).

8:26 [22] *The Egyptians detest the sacrifices.* This is probably the correct interpretation of the genitive phrase "an abomination of the Egyptians," but it is also possible to take it as a subjective genitive: "We dare not sacrifice Egyptian abominations."

8:28 [24] *I will let you go.* The Hebrew has the first person independent pronoun with the first person verb to emphasize the "I" (see commentary).

Now hurry, and pray for me. This seeks to capture the atmosphere of the very terse two-word clause, "pray for me," that ends Pharaoh's somewhat rambling preceding statement.

8:29 [25] *from you.* Moses shifts to the third person to address Pharaoh in this verse ("from Pharaoh and from his servants, etc."). Perhaps this more formal and courteous style of address is because Moses was here speaking for himself and not for Yahweh.

lie. Perhaps better, "deceive" or "mock." The word *hathel* [TH2048A, ZH9438] is not typically used to mean "lie."

9:1 *Go back.* See also 8:1.

9:4 *Not a single one.* The word *dabar* [TH1697, ZH1821] (word, event, thing) is used here to express "one." It is unusual to use it with animate objects, and Cassuto (1967:111) is probably correct when he says it is used here as a wordplay with *deber* [TH1698, ZH1822], meaning "plague" or "pestilence." For other uses of *deber*, see Deut 28:21; 2 Sam 24:13; 1Kgs 8:35; Ps 91:3, 6; Jer 21:6.

9:7 *Pharaoh sent his officials.* This is the correct interpretation, but the Hebrew only reads, "Pharaoh sent," which seems to emphasize the verb *shalakh* [TH7971, ZH8938], which is the same one used repeatedly in God's demand that Pharaoh send the Israelites out of the land (7:14; 8:1, 20). Because the king would not send in one way, he was reduced to sending in another.

9:8 *brick kiln.* Lit., "furnace." The Hebrew does not specify what kind of furnace this was. While pottery was regularly fired in a furnace in Egypt at this time, there are not many examples of fired bricks. Nevertheless, there are some examples, so it is attractive to think that Yahweh was here using one of the products of the Israelites' slavery to bring retribution on the oppressors.

9:9 *festering boils.* This translation is the result of combining two words: "boils" and "swollen places."

COMMENTARY

The second series of plagues shows the same literary pattern as the first series: Moses and Aaron waylay Pharaoh on his way to the river; then they go to him, presumably in the palace; and the third plague occurs without a warning. But there is also an intensification of the pressure on Pharaoh in this series. For the first time, actual pain and injury, and not mere discomfort, is inflicted on the Egyptians and their livestock (9:6). Also for the first time, a distinction is made between the Israelites and the Egyptians (8:22-23). Tragically, because of Pharaoh's recalcitrance, these two themes would continue until they came together in the distinction between

Israel and Egypt at the death of the firstborn (11:6-7). Finally, the humiliation of the magicians is complete when they too experience the plague of boils and can do nothing about it (9:11). Thus, we see Pharaoh beginning to negotiate with a little more realism, as opposed to his response to the plague of frogs (8:8), which was probably duplicitous from the outset. He apparently recognized that he would have to make some concession in the end, and so he first offered to allow the Israelites to sacrifice in the land (8:25), or if not that, in a nearby wilderness area (8:28).

In this second series of plagues we also see Aaron beginning to fade from the picture as the active agent of Yahweh's word. As noted earlier (commentary on 7:9), Sarna (1991:37) suggests this is because the magicians were no longer a factor. Aaron was still with Moses and assisted him in gathering the "soot" (9:10), but Moses was the speaker (8:26, 29) as well as the actor (9:10). It is interesting that in this series, no staff appears. Yahweh simply announced that something was going to happen, and it did. Only in the case of the "boils" did the Hebrew spokesman carry out any activity, but that did not involve the staff.

A Plague of Flies (8:20-32). As was pointed out in the note on 8:21, we do not know for certain what kind of an insect is intended here. If it is some sort of fly, as the Septuagint indicates, the connection with Egyptian deity is demonstrated again because the Egyptians revered the fly in that it seemed to have the capacity to bring life out of death. As the maggots came crawling out of rotting flesh, only to fly away, they manifested a power over death that was very appealing to a people obsessed with surviving after death. While flies were not worshiped per se, they were nevertheless seen as having divine powers. To all of this, Yahweh says no. The flies have no blessing to offer. Life is the gift of the sole creator of the universe, and apart from him, all is death.

Once again, Yahweh specifically framed the plague as a contest between himself and Pharaoh. It would fall upon "you and your officials, and all your people" (8:29). And the only way Pharaoh could prevent Yahweh's sending the flies was if he sent Yahweh's people out of the land to worship him. Not only this, but here Pharaoh would see that he was not even the master of his own land. This was not merely a foreign god coming in with superior power and wresting his people from Pharaoh's hand. He was the Creator who can do with any land exactly as he pleases. Thus, the flies would be so abundant that they would cover the "ground" (8:21) where the Egyptians lived, but there would be none at all in Goshen, that part of Egypt where the Israelites lived. Yahweh was going to make a "distinction between my people and your people" (8:23). As a result, Pharaoh was going to know that Yahweh was "present even in the heart of your land" (8:22). The first and second of these "knowing" sentences (7:5, 17) said that Pharaoh and the Egyptians were going to learn the identity of this God: Yahweh. The third (8:10) said that they were going to learn that he is incomparable. Now they were about to learn that there is no place that is exempt from his power. His incomparable transcendence does not mean that he is unable to intersect his world and intervene in it at any point in time and space. In fact, the very opposite is true.

If there had still remained any question about Yahweh's freedom and power, the definition of the time and the manner in which the plague would occur (8:21-23) was designed to answer such a question. Then, when the event did occur in just that way (8:24), the point was fully made. This was not just an unusual "natural" event. The use of the Hebrew word *shakhath* [TH7843, ZH8845] ("in chaos" or "ruined") suggests that these were more than just houseflies but were rather some kind of a biting fly that caused serious distress. As a result, Pharaoh offered his first real concession: The Hebrews might "offer sacrifices to your God" (8:25). (Did he have difficulty uttering the name Yahweh?) But he wanted to keep them in bondage while they served their God. This is always the world's way. Pharaoh was in effect saying, "Yes, you can have your religion, so long as it does not conflict with your primary allegiance to me."

But if Pharaoh was attempting to be shrewd, Moses was equally shrewd. Enns (2000:214) suggests that Moses was saying in effect, "If you want to get into a sparring match, I can give back as good as I get." So he did not merely reject the meaningless concession. Instead, he deftly showed why it could not possibly work. (Again, this is interesting coming from the mouth of a man who was supposedly not good with words [4:10]!) Since the sacrifices that the Hebrews would offer would be outrageous (lit., "an abomination") to the Egyptian people, the Egyptians would kill the Hebrews.[1] It is not known exactly what Israelite sacrifices were so detestable to the Egyptians, but since the Egyptians considered cattle sacred (like modern Hindus), it may be that it was the sacrifice of cattle that would have been the problem. At any rate, Moses showed Pharaoh that his concession was not a workable alternative and reiterated the necessity of going outside Egypt's borders ("a three-day trip," 8:27).

Pharaoh conceded the point but tried to avoid total surrender. He asserted that this was a matter of his own choice, certainly not a matter of being forced to do so (see note on 8:28). He would let them go "into the wilderness," but not "too far away." We sense a certain feeling of desperation here. It is as though the king was saying, "Okay, okay, whatever. Just get these things off me!" As mentioned in the note on 8:28, the very terse conclusion to the sentence, "pray for me," supports this sense of what was taking place. Moses had turned Pharaoh's ploy back upon him. If the Egyptian wanted to get into a lengthy discussion laced with diplomatic niceties while swarms of stinging flies settled upon him, that was fine with Moses. It turned out not to be fine with Pharaoh.

Interestingly, Moses seems to have taken some pity on his adversary. He did not prolong the discussion over the precise meaning of "far away." Perhaps he thought that it was a flexible enough term that they could stretch it as they wished once they were out of the brick pits and on their way. At any rate, he promised that he would pray and that the plague would be removed "tomorrow" (8:23; see also commentary on this term in 8:10). It is important to point out that neither Pharaoh nor Moses made any pretense that Moses himself had the power to bring the plagues or take them away. It was only Yahweh who could do these things, and his power was only available through prayer. Even Pharaoh understood that. The performance of rituals that were seen as efficacious in themselves was not a part of the picture.

Perhaps the formal language (use of the third person) that Moses employed to admonish Pharaoh was a part of the whole facade of diplomacy that seems to go with this particular encounter. Perhaps Moses did not feel quite able to accuse this mighty man of duplicity to his face, as it were (cf. the note on 8:29 for another possible explanation).

But once the immediate pain was gone, Pharaoh reverted to his old ways and blithely reasserted his absolute authority. The loss of that authority would be a pain greater than all the plagues combined. (See the commentary on 9:7 for further discussion.)

A Plague against Livestock (9:1-7). In keeping with the literary pattern, Moses was told to "go back" to Pharaoh for the warning concerning the second plague in the series (9:1-3). The pressure was going to increase if Pharaoh still refused to obey Yahweh's command. Now the animals of the Egyptians would die of "a deadly plague." The Bible does not specify what kind of a disease it was. Sarna (1991:43) and others propose that it was anthrax, carried by the flies, and suggest that this explains why no Israelite cattle died—there had been no flies in Goshen. While this is plausible, there were many other such diseases known in Egypt, and the point is again that this event was specifically caused by Yahweh.

As noted above, many animals, and especially cattle, were understood by the Egyptians to be divine. The gods were all regularly represented as the bull, the ram, and the goat. Amon-Re, the high god of Egypt at this time, was particularly associated with these animals. They expressed fecundity and power. From their loins life burst forth to perpetuate itself on the earth. Such pulsing life was to be worshiped and tapped into. But again, both in this plague and also in the next, Yahweh shows that no creature has the power of life in itself. It does not matter how assiduously the Apis bulls may have been cared for in life and mummified in death, they were all in one of two classes, the dead or the dying. These plagues drive that point home. There is only one being in the universe worthy of true reverence: the sole creator, the "I AM," Yahweh. In him alone is life to be found.

"The hand of the LORD" is an image for the unconquerable power of God (see commentary on 3:19-20). Some commentators make a distinction between this phrase and "the finger of God," which is used by the magicians in 8:19, suggesting that this one conveys greater power, but I think that such a distinction is exaggerated.

Here, as in the first plague in this series, the refusal of Pharaoh is assumed. Although he could still avert the disaster, quick action would have to be taken because the time for the plague was already set: "tomorrow" (9:5). There was still today for repentance and change, but without those responses Yahweh would demonstrate conclusively that the animal kingdom does not possess life in itself.

Also, origin of the plagues in Yahweh alone was clarified by the survival of the Israelites' cattle. It was one thing for no swarms of flies to have appeared in Goshen;

it was another thing for disease to be ravaging every kind of Egyptian animal on every side,[2] while the Israelite animals were unaffected. Explanations for these events with no reference to Yahweh were fast disappearing. Pharaoh clearly understood the significance of the distinction in that he "*sent* his officials" (emphasis mine; see the note on 9:7) to verify that what Moses had predicted did indeed happen.

The statement that "all the livestock of the Egyptians died" (9:6) has provoked a good deal of discussion among commentators, especially since there were still animals alive to suffer the boils of the next plague (9:10), and the hail of the succeeding one (9:19). Basically, the suggestions that have been offered fall into three categories: (1) "All" is not intended literally, but hyperbolically, to make the point that the deaths were not simply here and there (Cassuto 1967:111). (2) "All" applies only to those animals which were not under cover (9:3; lit., "your animal property in the field"). (3) "All" is intended literally; this is a folktale, and the author or redactor was not concerned with consistency (Houtman 1993:2.70). I believe the first is the most likely and agree with Childs (1974:157) who says "the narrative style should not be overplayed."

Despite the accumulated evidence of the first five plagues, Pharaoh still refused to believe there could be some limit to his authority. And it is important to remember that this is what his "hard-heartedness" is all about. It is not a matter of being insensitive to the plight of his slaves. It is a resolute refusal to admit that he was not in sole charge of his own life. This is why the evidence continued to be insufficient. It was a matter of the will, and a matter that would involve an entire change of Pharaoh's perspective on the meaning of his life.

A Plague of Festering Boils (9:8-12). Again, as with the third plague, this sixth one comes without any prior warning or call to let the people go. It is as though Pharaoh's reneging on his offer (8:32), however it was conditioned, merited a double blow. And there is some sense in which this plague is an extension of the previous one. Now it was not merely the animals that suffered but the "people" as well (9:9). Again, Yahweh was demonstrating that just as life is not in the animals, neither is it in humans. I think this is the significance of the reference to the ritual priests, the "magicians," here as suffering from the boils. Amon-Re, the Great Bull, does not have the key to life, and neither do those humans who are magically identified with him and his power. Moses and Aaron, representatives of Yahweh, were able to stand "before Pharaoh" (9:10). But the priests "were unable to stand before Moses" (9:11), much less Yahweh. Magical ritual had never been able to remove the plague, only duplicate it. Now the futility of that exercise is clearly shown. For Yahweh not only has the power to turn into death and destruction whatever idol humans worship as a giver of life but even more to the point, he is able to take the death and destruction that we have brought into the world by our idolatry and restore his creation to life again. Nothing in creation can do that on its own.

If "brick kiln" is the correct interpretation of the Hebrew "furnace" (see the note on 9:8), then there is an irony in this sign. The "soot" (9:8) from the furnaces at which Hebrew slaves toiled became a source of "hot things" (the probable root of "boils," *shekhin* [TH7822, ZH8825], 9:9, is *shakhan*, which means "to become hot") breaking out on the bodies of the oppressors and their livestock.

Some commentators conclude that Pharaoh must have been outside for Moses to throw "the soot into the air" (9:10), but that does not seem necessary to me. Clearly, what Moses was doing was a symbolic sign that could have been done as well in the royal audience chamber as anywhere else. What was important was that Pharaoh should see the sign performed so that there was no possibility of his attributing the onset of the boils to chance. On a similar note, Cassuto (1967:113) thinks it necessary to explain that since the command to "take handfuls of soot" (9:8) was addressed to both Moses and Aaron, Aaron must have helped Moses collect the soot, although only Moses threw it in the air. Again, this seems to me to push the narrative too far.

Finally, we note that for the first time in the narrative of the plagues, it is said that Yahweh "hardened Pharaoh's heart" (9:12). In my opinion, the timing of this statement supports the view that what is being expressed is the inevitability that follows upon a determined and repeated set of choices. See the commentary on 4:21 for further discussion.

ENDNOTES

1. Houtman (1993:2.66) points out that Egypt did not have stones lying around on the ground, whereas Palestine did, and therefore argues that the reference to "stoning" here as a means of execution supports his contention that Exodus never did have an Egyptian milieu. While his geological observation is correct, his conclusion is unwarranted in view of the many evidences in the book in favor of such a milieu. The terminology may be explained as a result of later updating or as the use of a term for execution that had come into Moses's vocabulary from his years in the wilderness of Midian.
2. Sarna (1991:44) gives a concise, but thorough, discussion of camels in this list (9:3), showing that while they may not have been in Egypt in great numbers at this time, there is evidence supporting their existence. They may well have been included in the list precisely because they would have been considered luxury items. No animal, however rare and priceless, would escape.

◆ ### c. The third series of plagues (9:13–10:29)

¹³Then the LORD said to Moses, "Get up early in the morning and stand before Pharaoh. Tell him, 'This is what the LORD, the God of the Hebrews, says: Let my people go, so they can worship me. ¹⁴If you don't, I will send more plagues on you* and your officials and your people. Then you will know that there is no one like me in all the earth. ¹⁵By now I could have lifted my hand and struck you and your people with a plague to wipe you off the face of the earth. ¹⁶But I have spared you for a purpose—to show you my power* and to spread my fame throughout the earth. ¹⁷But you still lord it over my people and refuse to let them go. ¹⁸So tomorrow at this time I will send a hailstorm more devastating than any in all the history of Egypt. ¹⁹Quick! Order your livestock and servants to come in from the fields to find shelter. Any person or animal left outside will die when the hail falls.'"

²⁰Some of Pharaoh's officials were afraid because of what the LORD had said. They quickly brought their servants and livestock in from the fields. ²¹But those who paid no attention to the word of the LORD left theirs out in the open.

²²Then the LORD said to Moses, "Lift your hand toward the sky so hail may fall on the people, the livestock, and all the plants throughout the land of Egypt."

²³So Moses lifted his staff toward the sky, and the LORD sent thunder and hail, and lightning flashed toward the earth. The LORD sent a tremendous hailstorm against all the land of Egypt. ²⁴Never in all the history of Egypt had there been a storm like that, with such devastating hail and continuous lightning. ²⁵It left all of Egypt in ruins. The hail struck down everything in the open field—people, animals, and plants alike. Even the trees were destroyed. ²⁶The only place without hail was the region of Goshen, where the people of Israel lived.

²⁷Then Pharaoh quickly summoned Moses and Aaron. "This time I have sinned," he confessed. "The LORD is the righteous one, and my people and I are wrong. ²⁸Please beg the LORD to end this terrifying thunder and hail. We've had enough. I will let you go; you don't need to stay any longer."

²⁹"All right," Moses replied. "As soon as I leave the city, I will lift my hands and pray to the LORD. Then the thunder and hail will stop, and you will know that the earth belongs to the LORD. ³⁰But I know that you and your officials still do not fear the LORD God."

³¹(All the flax and barley were ruined by the hail, because the barley had formed heads and the flax was budding. ³²But the wheat and the emmer wheat were spared, because they had not yet sprouted from the ground.)

³³So Moses left Pharaoh's court and went out of the city. When he lifted his hands to the LORD, the thunder and hail stopped, and the downpour ceased. ³⁴But when Pharaoh saw that the rain, hail, and thunder had stopped, he and his officials sinned again, and Pharaoh again became stubborn.* ³⁵Because his heart was hard, Pharaoh refused to let the people leave, just as the LORD had predicted through Moses.

CHAPTER 10

Then the LORD said to Moses, "Return to Pharaoh and make your demands again. I have made him and his officials stubborn* so I can display my miraculous signs among them. ²I've also done it so you can tell your children and grandchildren about how I made a mockery of the Egyptians and about the signs I displayed among them—and so you will know that I am the LORD."

³So Moses and Aaron went to Pharaoh and said, "This is what the LORD, the God of the Hebrews, says: How long will you refuse to submit to me? Let my people go, so they can worship me. ⁴If you refuse, watch out! For tomorrow I will bring a swarm of locusts on your country. ⁵They will cover the land so that you won't be able to see the ground. They will devour what little is left of your crops after the hailstorm, including all the trees growing in the fields. ⁶They will overrun your palaces and the homes of your officials and all the houses in Egypt. Never in the history of Egypt have your ancestors seen a plague like this one!" And with that, Moses turned and left Pharaoh.

⁷Pharaoh's officials now came to Pharaoh and appealed to him. "How long will you let this man hold us hostage? Let the men go to worship the LORD their God! Don't you realize that Egypt lies in ruins?"

⁸So Moses and Aaron were brought back to Pharaoh. "All right," he told them, "go and worship the LORD your God. But who exactly will be going with you?"

⁹Moses replied, "We will all go—young and old, our sons and daughters, and our flocks and herds. We must all join together in celebrating a festival to the LORD."

¹⁰Pharaoh retorted, "The LORD will certainly need to be with you if I let you take your little ones! I can see through your evil plan. ¹¹Never! Only the men may go and worship the LORD, since that is what you requested." And Pharaoh threw them out of the palace.

¹²Then the LORD said to Moses, "Raise your hand over the land of Egypt to bring on the locusts. Let them cover the land and devour every plant that survived the hailstorm."

¹³So Moses raised his staff over Egypt, and the LORD caused an east wind to blow over the land all that day and through the night. When morning arrived, the east wind had brought the locusts. ¹⁴And the locusts swarmed over the whole land of Egypt, settling in dense swarms from one end of the country to the other. It was the worst locust plague in Egyptian history, and there has never been another one like it. ¹⁵For the locusts covered the whole country and darkened the land. They devoured every plant in the fields and all the fruit on the trees that had survived the hailstorm. Not a single leaf was left on the trees and plants throughout the land of Egypt.

¹⁶Pharaoh quickly summoned Moses and Aaron. "I have sinned against the LORD your God and against you," he confessed. ¹⁷"Forgive my sin, just this once, and plead with the LORD your God to take away this death from me."

¹⁸So Moses left Pharaoh's court and pleaded with the LORD. ¹⁹The LORD responded by shifting the wind, and the strong west wind blew the locusts into the Red Sea.* Not a single locust remained in all the land of Egypt. ²⁰But the LORD hardened Pharaoh's heart again, so he refused to let the people go.

²¹Then the LORD said to Moses, "Lift your hand toward heaven, and the land of Egypt will be covered with a darkness so thick you can feel it." ²²So Moses lifted his hand to the sky, and a deep darkness covered the entire land of Egypt for three days. ²³During all that time the people could not see each other, and no one moved. But there was light as usual where the people of Israel lived.

²⁴Finally, Pharaoh called for Moses. "Go and worship the LORD," he said. "But leave your flocks and herds here. You may even take your little ones with you."

²⁵"No," Moses said, "you must provide us with animals for sacrifices and burnt offerings to the LORD our God. ²⁶All our livestock must go with us, too; not a hoof can be left behind. We must choose our sacrifices for the LORD our God from among these animals. And we won't know how we are to worship the LORD until we get there."

²⁷But the LORD hardened Pharaoh's heart once more, and he would not let them go. ²⁸"Get out of here!" Pharaoh shouted at Moses. "I'm warning you. Never come back to see me again! The day you see my face, you will die!"

²⁹"Very well," Moses replied. "I will never see your face again."

9:14 Hebrew *on your heart.*   9:16 Greek version reads *to display my power in you;* compare Rom 9:17.
9:34 Hebrew *made his heart heavy.*   10:1 Hebrew *have made his heart and his officials' hearts heavy.*
10:19 Hebrew *sea of reeds.*

NOTES

9:14 more plagues. Lit., "all my plagues." The NLT is following the common interpretation that "all" refers to "all the rest of."

9:15 I could have lifted my hand. The Hebrew has the perfect conjugation here, which would usually be read "I sent my hand." But commentators agree that a conditional use is what is intended (Williams 1976:30). See the commentary on this verse for further discussion.

9:16 my fame. Lit., "my name." The NLT correctly understands that "name" refers to reputation and character. See the commentary on 3:13-17 and 6:2-5.

9:20 afraid because of what the LORD had said. The literal "those who feared the word of the Lord" might be understood in the more formal sense of "took seriously and acted upon." Such a translation is further supported by the antithesis, "paid no attention to" (lit., "did not put it on his heart,"), found in 9:21.

9:23 sent thunder. Lit., "gave voices." Thunder is regularly referred to in the Bible as the voice of God (19:16; 1 Sam 7:10; 12:17; Job 37:2).

9:24 continuous lightning. The Hebrew word rendered "continuous" is the reflexive form of the verb *laqakh* [TH3947, ZH4374], meaning something like "taking hold of oneself," perhaps reflecting the jagged appearance of lightning.

9:27 This time. The irony is that he did not consider the other expressions of his hard-heartedness as sins.

the righteous one. While *hatsaddiq* [TH6662, ZH7404] is frequently used in this way, I believe the translation is misleading here. It would be better to render this as "Yahweh is in the right." The point here is not so much on the rightness of Yahweh's character, as on the rightness of what he had been doing. Pharaoh is admitting that Yahweh had been right in what he had been doing, while Pharaoh and his people had been wrong to resist him.

10:2 made a mockery of. While the basic forms of this verb have a more neutral meaning, such as to "deal with severely," the hithpael forms (as here) have a more negative meaning, such as "to abuse a woman" or "to deal ruthlessly with." Thus Houtman suggests here "dealt gruesomely with" (1993:2.102), but that seems more specific than the context warrants.

10:5 cover the land. Lit., "cover the eye of the land," i.e., the surface of the land. So also 10:15.

10:7 How long. This is an exact duplication of the opening of Moses's question in 10:3.

hold us hostage. This effectively captures the sense of "be a snare to us."

10:9 The rhythm and cadences of the Hebrew suggest that this is a formal declaration.

10:10 The LORD will certainly need to be with you. The Hebrew (lit., "let the Lord thus be with you") is elliptical and several different translations are possible. See the commentary on this verse for some of the other possibilities.

I can see through your evil plan. Lit., "See, indeed evil is before your faces." Another possible translation is, "Watch out, you're headed for trouble." See the commentary on this verse for an evaluation of these alternatives.

10:13 an east wind. As Sarna (1991:50) points out, this is any hot, dry wind, and not strictly an east wind (cf. Job 27:21; Ps 48:7; Isa 27:8; Jer 18:17; Ezek 17:10; Hos 13:15). The appelation arose because in Palestine such a wind often comes from the east.

10:17 Forgive my sin, just this once. Perhaps, "Forgive my sin this time."

10:24-26 you may even take. "Even" here translates the Hebrew particle *gam-* [TH1571, ZH1685]. This same particle appears twice in Moses's response where he seems to be echoing Pharaoh intentionally. In 10:25 he says, "No, you must [even] provide us with animals . . ." And in 10:26 "[Even] all our livestock must go with us, too."

COMMENTARY

The third series of three plagues follows the literary pattern of the first and second series (see above on 7:8–8:19), but the discourse surrounding the first and second plagues in this series, the hail and the locusts, is much longer than in any of the other plagues. This probably reflects two factors: the increasing seriousness of the plagues, and Pharaoh's increasingly complicated negotiations as he attempted to avoid the inevitable—surrender to the authority of Yahweh.

These three plagues are directed at two more of the forces of nature that were deified in Egyptian thought: vegetation and the sun. The hail and the locusts devastated the vegetation, while Yahweh almost casually "turned off" the sun in the ninth plague. The vegetation was deified in the person of the god Osiris. In the myths surrounding him, it was believed that his evil half-brother Seth, a jackal from the desert, had killed him, dismembering his body and sending him into the underworld. But Osiris's sister, Isis, succeeded in finding all the parts of his body (except the genitalia). She placed these parts in a mummy case filled with sand, watered the sand, closed the case for three days, and opening it, found Osiris sprouting from the sand (it is evident that when this myth was acted out in ritual, grains of wheat had been put in the mummy case).[1] Thus, Osiris was considered to be the god who helped the dead through the underworld, and he was also the life of the sprouting grain.

But the seventh and eighth plagues show that there is no life innately resident in the vegetation. Exodus 9:31-32, seen by some critics as an unfortunate insertion that breaks the flow of the account, really serves to underscore the double devastation. Some grain had sprouted and budded and was destroyed by the hail. However, vegetation is not so easily subdued! Other grain was still growing, too small to be damaged by the hail. So Osiris does prevail! Not so. For what the hail left, the locusts devoured (note the specific attention given to that fact in 10:12). There is no life inherent in anything created. Life is a gift from the one Creator. If he withdraws his hand for a moment, all is death.

But beyond all the other gods whose power and popularity waxed and waned throughout Egyptian history, beyond the Nile and the amphibians and the insects and the animals and the plants, there stood one serene, unchanging deity: the Sun. Above all the others, the sun god Re, or Amon-Re, as he was known at the time of the Exodus, stood supreme. It is easy to see why this should be so. Because of the vast Sahara to the west, rain and clouds are very rare in Egypt. Day after day, with absolute inevitability, the sun rises from his couch on the eastern horizon, sails unchecked across the river of the sky, and gracefully sinks to his rest in the West. In one version of the myths surrounding the sun, he is swallowed up at sunset by a dragon of darkness, but the dragon cannot hold him. Every night Re defeats him and emerges triumphant in the morning. In various Egyptian art works, Re is depicted with hands at the ends of his rays. And in these hands is the hieroglyph for life. Surely the mighty sun, giver of life, is a match for this Yahweh of the Hebrew slaves. But it was not to be. Yahweh demonstrated that Amon-Re was powerless before him. For three days (10:22) the god was nowhere to be seen, and it was reinforced yet again that there is no God but Yahweh, no life but that which comes from the sun's creator.

Plague of Hail (9:13-35). As in plagues 1 and 4, Moses (Aaron is not mentioned until 9:27) was told to station himself "early in the morning" to meet Pharaoh, although in this case there is no mention of going to the river. Once again, he was told to speak for Yahweh and to command the release of the Israelites so they could worship Yahweh (9:13). The issue was becoming more and more focused on Pharaoh; thus 9:14 says that the coming plagues would fall first and foremost on the "heart" (see NLT mg) of Pharaoh himself, to the end that Pharaoh will recognize ("know") that Yahweh is absolutely incomparable on "the earth" (i.e., in creation). There is no other god who is even in the same league with Yahweh, including a supposedly divine pharaoh.

Verses 15 and 16 make the purpose of the plagues crystal clear for the first time. If Yahweh had simply wanted to get his people out of Egypt, if their deliverance had only consisted of freedom, he could have wiped Pharaoh and Egypt "off the face of the earth" with one terrible blow. But, as I have said repeatedly, mere political freedom is not what deliverance is about. The deepest human problem is that we do not know Yahweh, and until we do, freedom is very apt to become just another type of bondage. Thus, the most important thing Yahweh could do would be to demonstrate in unforgettable ways that he alone is the "I AM," the sole creator, the only source of life. This was why he "spared" Pharaoh and Egypt. That point needs to be underscored. He *did* spare them; he did not merely wipe them out. If he brought terrible judgments on them, those judgments came from the heart that was touched by the plight of 120,000 Assyrians living in spiritual darkness along with their many cattle (Jonah 4:11). And every one of those judgments was only temporary. Whatever is said about the hardening of Pharaoh's heart (see above on 4:21), this factor must also be taken into account.[2]

The purpose of the plagues was that Yahweh's power be seen and his "fame" (lit., "name") be spread over all "the earth" (9:16). This emphasis on the name of God once again focuses attention on the revelatory purpose of the Exodus events. It reminds the reader of Isaiah 12:4, where the redeemed are to "tell the nations what he has done" (see also Isa 43:21), or Ezekiel 36:23, where Yahweh says that the nations will know his name when he shows himself holy in his people. Of course, God does not intend to limit his revelation to a select, chosen people. Rather, he wants the entire world to know who he is. He wants this because to "know" him rightly is to be in an intimate relationship with him, and to be redeemed, reconciled, and restored (cf. 2 Cor 5:18-19).

One of the features of this series of plagues is the succession of comparisons. Just as there is no one like Yahweh in all the earth (9:14), so the hailstorm is like none other in all Egypt's history (9:18, 24), and the locust plague is likewise incomparable (10:6, 14). Only an incomparable God can produce incomparable plagues.

Commentators debate the reason for Yahweh's warning to bring the animals and servants under cover before the hailstorm began (9:19). Some would say it was an indication of his fundamental grace, that even in the midst of the plagues he was concerned to lessen their impact on the "bystanders" as much as possible. While that may well be true, it seems more likely in the larger context that this was an opportunity both to break the solidarity of Pharaoh's courtiers, and also to move Pharaoh to make some first move of obedience (note the use of the word "send"

[NLT, "order"], something Yahweh had been commanding Pharaoh to do to the Israelites for a long time). While there is no indication that Pharaoh made such a move, the solidarity of the courtiers was broken. Some of them were now ready to take seriously (see note on 9:20) anything Yahweh had said, and they reacted accordingly. Others reacted just as Pharaoh had to the first plague (7:23; lit., "did not set his heart upon"), dismissing what Yahweh had said.

Hail is often used in the Bible as an expression of divine judgment (Isa 28:2, 17; 30:30-31; Ezek 13:11-13; 38:22-23; Hag 2:17; Rev 8:7; 11:19; 16:21). The exception of "Goshen" emphasizes God's sovereignty in the act of judgment. It also emphasizes his complete power over the forces of nature. Sarna suggests (1991:47) that the reason Goshen was exempt was because it is in the eastern delta, while such storms, when they do occur, come up the valley proper. This seems to me to miss the point of what is being said.

For the first time, Pharaoh was moved to admit that the Lord had been right in what he had done (9:27; see note) and that he, Pharaoh, had been wrong, and he called his action a sin. This is a stunning turnaround. It is an admission that Yahweh has the right to determine what is right behavior and what is wrong behavior, and that it is a sin to oppose him. Yet, Pharaoh's admission did not change his behavior. When the immediate pain was removed, both he and "his officials" reverted immediately (9:34-35). What does this say about the nature of repentance? It says that mere cognitive awareness of sin accomplishes very little. Sin is not primarily a matter of knowledge; rather, it is a matter of the will. We think of King Saul's eventual admission of sin to Samuel in 1 Samuel 15:24-25 and compare it to the repentance attributed to King David in Psalm 51, and we see the difference. In Saul's and Pharaoh's cases, the admission was primarily motivated by a desire to escape punishment. In David's case, the admission was motivated by a passionate desire for reconciliation and restoration. Only the latter results in long-term behavioral change, and only such change is what is meant by the fear of the Lord (9:30).

Moses understood the shallowness of Pharaoh's repentance (9:30) and thus the worthlessness of his apparently complete surrender (9:28). That being so, we may wonder why Moses would pray for the man (9:29, 33). Why not let him suffer a little longer, or even a lot longer? Perhaps two reasons may be offered. The first is at least implied by the text. Moses was going to ask God to lift the plague for the same reason he sent it in the first place: to offer incontrovertible proof "that the earth belongs to the LORD" (9:29), not to Osiris and not to Pharaoh. The second reason is that God was not done revealing himself to the Egyptians, the Israelites, and the world. What it means for him to be Yahweh required further disclosure.

A Plague of Locusts (10:1-20). As is typical for the second plague in each series, Moses was told to go to Pharaoh, presumably in the palace, and warn Pharaoh that unless he obeyed Yahweh's "demands" (10:1), another blow was going to fall. Pharaoh may have thought he was free to do whatever he might wish, but it was far too late for that. We can think of certain dictators who, when faced with incontrovertible proof of their imminent destruction, had no choice but to pursue the course that they had become fixed upon to its end. So Pharaoh had become fixed in his need to rule his own life, and he could no more change the patterns of his life than he could fly. And so, nothing was left for God to do but to make a "mockery" (10:2) of all such attempts by humans to pretend that they are self-existent, self-sustaining, or self-fulfilling. We are reminded of Psalm 2, which portrays God laughing at the nations' attempts to break the limitations that he, the Creator, has placed upon them (Ps 2:3-5).

The knowledge of Yahweh that came to the Egyptians was primarily negative (7:17; 8:10, 22; 9:14), but there is another side to his character that these same events were revealing to the Israelites (10:2)—namely that he is the Savior, the Deliverer who is aware of his peoples' suffering, whose heart is moved by compassion, and whose actions are predicated upon his complete faithfulness, his "truth" (cf. 2:23-25; 3:7-9). Thus, the same events that revealed to the Egyptians that to defy Yahweh and to give his glory to any created thing is to court death were also those that revealed his love, his dependability, and his saving power to the Israelites. As is true in all of life, God does not change, but whether we experience him as Savior or Judge depends solely on our relationship to him and whether it is defiant or submissive.

One of the subtle shifts that takes place throughout the plague narratives is the change in control of the situation. If we compare the relationship between Moses and Pharaoh that we saw in chapter 5 with what we see here, the contrast is remarkable. Moses, speaking for Yahweh (10:3), put forth an ultimatum (10:3-6). Pharaoh could take it or leave it; the outcome was entirely up to him. And without waiting for an answer, Moses turned and left (10:6). Yahweh had brought his messenger into the ascendancy, and that fact could not have been lost on Pharaoh.

Then Pharaoh received another blow: The solid front of support for him among his courtiers had been breached by the previous plague, the hailstorm (9:20-21). Now that support apparently collapsed completely (10:7). Undoubtedly, the desperate state of affairs had "gotten to them." The animals were wounded and dying, the flax and barley were gone, and now if the locusts came, all the wheat and fruit would be gone too. They must have thought, "How much is one man's ego worth?"

The double blow of Moses gaining the ascendancy over Pharaoh and the courtiers' abandonment may explain what almost appears to be diffidence in Pharaoh's remarks to Moses (and Aaron with him) when the two Hebrews were brought back into the audience chamber. He agreed to let the Israelites go (with their animals, it was understood) but wondered what persons would go along with the "men" (10:7) who would be worshiping. Moses did not hesitate or equivocate. He even seemed to make a point of "all," specifying exactly what it meant. It included all ages and both genders and, unwilling to let Pharaoh simply slide over his capitulation on the previous point, Moses specified that all the "flocks and herds" would go too (10:9). It seems clear that Moses had finally believed what God had said all along: There was no persuasion, no diplomatic nicety that was going to bring Pharaoh around. He was only going to obey God when he was forced to. So Moses was finally finished with trying to make it easy. What he was asking for involved total surrender on Pharaoh's part, and so he gave the demand to the Egyptian monarch at full strength.

Some would suggest that Pharaoh's insulting and furious response to this demand (10:10-11) was because he had finally seen through the "worship ploy," realizing that all along it had really only been covering up a demand for political freedom (so Enns 2000:227). That is not the case. Pharaoh was not so naive as to have ever believed that slaves who went three days into the desert were ever coming back. That was why he had tried in his previous "concessions" to find a way to prevent that. His anger was over the worst of all outcomes for a proud man: complete humiliation. His courtiers had abandoned him, and these nobodies that he had once treated so cavalierly now were acting as if they owned the place. And he was not even being given some sop for his ego so that he could lie to himself and say he had not really given in. Moses was not asking for political freedom; he was insisting that his people, all of them, should change masters, should change whom they were serving. Thus worship was not merely about giving sacrifices, involving the men alone. It was about a "festival," a joyous celebration of fellowship with the good Creator. That kind of worship was for everyone. In Moses's rolling, inclusive phrases we hear overtones of Joel's words many centuries later (Joel 2:28-29). The Spirit of God would come on "all people"—young, old, rich, poor, men and women. Yahweh was not calling his people to a religious event, he was calling them to a way of life, a whole new set of allegiances, and that way of life had no place in it for an arrogant pharaoh who believed he and his world were God.

The exact sense of Pharaoh's curse in 10:10 is unclear (lit., "Let it be thus the Lord with you if I let . . ."). Probably the sarcastic tone in his voice carried the biting inference that the NLT has made explicit: "The LORD will certainly need to be with you!" An alternative is Houtman's rendering, "may Yahweh's help be as little as mine" (1993:2.107), but something like the NLT's rendering seems less expansive and more likely.[3] In any case, he spoke truer than he knew because Yahweh *was* indeed with them and Pharaoh *did* let their "little ones" go with them.

In the locust plague (10:13-19), there were some overtones of what was going to come in the future. Just as the stretching out of Moses's hand with his staff unleashed the hot, dry wind of the *qadim* [TH6921, ZH7708] (see note on 10:13) to bring the horde of locusts on the land (10:13), the same kind of signal would bring the same wind to pile up the waters of the Red Sea (14:21). And just as the entire swarm of locusts died in the *yam sup* [TH3220/5488A, ZH3542/6068] ("sea of reeds," 10:19; see the NLT mg), so the entire Egyptian army died (14:23, 27-28) in that same sea. Interestingly, the book of Joel compares locusts to a mighty army (Joel 2:2).

Both Pharaoh's response to the plague and Moses's response to Pharaoh are indicative of the hardening lines of the situation. Pharaoh now admitted that he had not only sinned against God but also against "Moses and Aaron." He had mistreated these two servants of Yahweh, and he knew it. But, he did not make any promises, and Moses did not demand any. Neither did Moses accuse the Egyptian of duplicity or deception. It is as though Moses was now fully aware that these events were going to have to run their allotted course—whatever it was—that God was going to have to be fully revealed before the final act in the drama, and that he should simply go ahead and play his part. He seems to have had no illusions about the likelihood of Pharaoh's changing his settled pattern of behavior, but neither did he display any vindictiveness about praying to God for the removal of the plague. He did not try to "twist Pharaoh's arm" or threaten him. He was content now to play his part, and if that looked to some like a continuing pattern of failure to reach the goal, he seems to have been willing for that inference to be drawn. This was now clearly Yahweh's affair altogether. But in some ways, as Sarna (1991:50) observes, the mere silent departure after Pharaoh's previous passionate curse, and now his equally passionate plea, must have been yet a further humiliation.

A Plague of Darkness (10:21-29). If Pharaoh was at all alert to the pattern of events in the past, he must have been prepared for something to now fall upon him without warning. That is exactly what happened, but we wonder if he could have possibly been prepared for the actuality. It would be terrible enough for us today if the sun were not to be seen some day, but how much more terrible for a people who were convinced that the sun is God? The failure of all the other gods, as difficult as those failures were, could all be explained away. Those were lesser gods, or at least lesser manifestations of the great gods, but the Sun himself?

It is common for commentators to explain this plague as the result of a sandstorm such as occasionally strikes Egypt (so Cassuto 1967:129, who explains that "three days" [10:22] would be consistent with such a phenomenon). While this is not impossible, it seems to me that the text takes us beyond that option. It makes no mention of the cause of the darkness, and the description of the darkness as being "so thick you can feel it" (10:21) describes a different darkness than the twilight, however deep it may be, that accompanies a sandstorm. The point is not that something obscured what light there was but rather that *there was no light* except "where the people of Israel lived" (10:23). That latter fact also argues against a sandstorm. Such storms do not admit of neat boundaries between dark and light. Surely the text wants us to believe that this was a different order of event from a worse hailstorm than had ever happened before or a worse plague of locusts than had ever happened before. It seems to me the text is saying that this final plague in the third series of plagues was unlike *anything* that had ever happened before.

Amazingly, Pharaoh still attempted to bargain (10:24). And what is more amazing is that the bargain he pursued seems so meaningless. Once again, Moses was in no mood to quibble. The hour for meeting this man partway, in the hopes that it would enable him to gracefully come all the way, was far gone. So Moses bore down on him. Pharaoh had made a point of saying that they could *even* take their children with them, while leaving the livestock. But Moses said, "You are *even* going to provide livestock for us . . . while we *even* take our own livestock as well" (10:25-26; translation mine). And the reason for all of that was that the Israelites were going to be in a position where they could gladly and fully comply with every request that their new, their true, overlord might make of them. They would fully obey Yahweh, and never obey Pharaoh again.

It seems Pharaoh's purpose in holding the "little ones" hostage (10:10) was to be sure that his slaves would come back under his authority and service after they had temporarily acknowledged the lordship of Yahweh. But now Pharaoh allowed his slaves to take their children even while demanding that they leave their "flocks and herds" behind (10:24). What possible leverage could the "flocks and herds" give him once he let the children go (10:24)? None! So why did he do it? He did it for one reason only: The human will *hates* absolute surrender. We will hang onto something that is really quite meaningless, refusing to give it to God, solely because it makes us believe that we have not given up complete control of our lives. So the apostle Paul begged his converts to come to the place of dying to their selves and their own rights (Col 3:1-12) because it was only on the other side of such a death that the evidence of the Spirit's life in transformed relationships could become possible. Pharaoh was being called upon to die to himself, and he resolutely refused to do that.

The result by now was perfectly predictable. This puts the Lord's hardening of Pharaoh's heart into its proper perspective. It is quite unthinkable that this man would now make an abrupt about-face and not merely admit wrongdoing but genuinely admit that he was not God and had no right to himself and then completely change his behavior. God has made the world and the human heart in such a way that our continued choices in one direction have a cumulative effect to the point that finally we really cannot choose anything else were it not for divine intervention. This is not because God in some coldly calculated way has determined that he will get the most glory from this creature of his by depriving it of ever having the possibility of repenting. Such a thought is not consistent with the plain statement that God does not wish anyone to die in their sin (2 Pet 3:9). At the same time, it must be equally clear that a person who continues in willful sin does not forever retain his or her ability to repent. They do not, and this account of Pharaoh should make that terribly obvious.

The issue had been made perfectly clear. Only Yahweh is God. There is no other in heaven or on earth. He alone holds life and death in his hand, and the only rational response to these facts is complete surrender and total trust. There was no rationalizing left to do. Pharaoh knew the truth; that could not be denied. The only issue was how he would act on the truth. Either he would surrender or not. Of course he would not, and that meant that he was in denial of the truth. The only recourse to that was rage, and that is what he succumbed to, driving Moses, the truth-teller, out of his presence, and determining never to confront the truth again. Of course that is never a real possibility, as Pharaoh's future was to make abundantly clear.

ENDNOTES

1. A similar kind of imagery appears in the Canaanite Baal and Anat myths, where, when Death has eaten Baal, Anat cuts down Death with a sword and sows him in the field, after which Baal is restored to life (see Arnold and Beyer 2002:61).
2. Fretheim (1991:124) argues that the conditional use of the verb in 9:15 (see note) does not speak so much of potentiality (I could have, if I wished) as of intentionality (I should have, but I have chosen to spare). It is hard to adjudicate between the two. The main thing that seems to me to favor the former is that there is really no word in the context about Pharaoh's deserving to be wiped off the earth. It is all about Yahweh's power (so also Houtman 1993:2.86).
3. Some other alternatives are "the LORD be with you if . . ." (NIV, REB); "the LORD indeed will be with you if . . ." (NRSV); "may the LORD be with you just as soon as I . . ." (*The Complete Bible: An American Translation*).

◆ ### d. The death of the firstborn and the Passover (11:1–12:30)

Then the LORD said to Moses, "I will strike Pharaoh and the land of Egypt with one more blow. After that, Pharaoh will let you leave this country. In fact, he will be so eager to get rid of you that he will force you all to leave. ²Tell all the Israelite men and women to ask their Egyptian neighbors for articles of silver and gold." ³(Now the LORD had caused the Egyptians to look favorably on the people of Israel. And Moses was considered a very great man in the land of Egypt, respected by Pharaoh's officials and the Egyptian people alike.)

⁴Moses had announced to Pharaoh, "This is what the LORD says: At midnight tonight I will pass through the heart of Egypt. ⁵All the firstborn sons will die in every family in Egypt, from the oldest son of Pharaoh, who sits on his throne, to the oldest son of his lowliest servant girl who grinds the flour. Even the firstborn of all the livestock will die. ⁶Then a loud wail will rise throughout the land of Egypt, a wail like no one has heard before or will ever hear again. ⁷But among the Israelites it will be so peaceful that not even a dog will bark. Then you will know that the LORD makes a distinction between the Egyptians and the Israelites. ⁸All the officials of Egypt will run to me and fall to the ground before me. 'Please leave!' they will beg. 'Hurry! And take all your followers with you.' Only then will I go!" Then, burning with anger, Moses left Pharaoh.

⁹Now the LORD had told Moses earlier, "Pharaoh will not listen to you, but then I will do even more mighty miracles in the land of Egypt." ¹⁰Moses and Aaron performed these miracles in Pharaoh's presence, but the LORD hardened Pharaoh's heart, and he wouldn't let the Israelites leave the country.

CHAPTER 12

While the Israelites were still in the land of Egypt, the LORD gave the following instructions to Moses and Aaron: ²"From now on, this month will be the first month of the year for you. ³Announce to the whole community of Israel that on the tenth day of this month each family must choose a lamb or a young goat for a sacrifice, one animal for each household. ⁴If a family is too small to eat a whole animal, let them share with another family in the neighborhood. Divide the animal according to the size of each family and how much they can eat. ⁵The animal you select must be a one-year-old male, either a sheep or a goat, with no defects.

⁶"Take special care of this chosen animal until the evening of the fourteenth day of this first month. Then the whole assembly of the community of Israel must

slaughter their lamb or young goat at twilight. ⁷They are to take some of the blood and smear it on the sides and top of the doorframes of the houses where they eat the animal. ⁸That same night they must roast the meat over a fire and eat it along with bitter salad greens and bread made without yeast. ⁹Do not eat any of the meat raw or boiled in water. The whole animal—including the head, legs, and internal organs—must be roasted over a fire. ¹⁰Do not leave any of it until the next morning. Burn whatever is not eaten before morning.

¹¹"These are your instructions for eating this meal: Be fully dressed,* wear your sandals, and carry your walking stick in your hand. Eat the meal with urgency, for this is the LORD's Passover. ¹²On that night I will pass through the land of Egypt and strike down every firstborn son and firstborn male animal in the land of Egypt. I will execute judgment against all the gods of Egypt, for I am the LORD! ¹³But the blood on your doorposts will serve as a sign, marking the houses where you are staying. When I see the blood, I will pass over you. This plague of death will not touch you when I strike the land of Egypt.

¹⁴"This is a day to remember. Each year, from generation to generation, you must celebrate it as a special festival to the LORD. This is a law for all time. ¹⁵For seven days the bread you eat must be made without yeast. On the first day of the festival, remove every trace of yeast from your homes. Anyone who eats bread made with yeast during the seven days of the festival will be cut off from the community of Israel. ¹⁶On the first day of the festival and again on the seventh day, all the people must observe an official day for holy assembly. No work of any kind may be done on these days except in the preparation of food.

¹⁷"Celebrate this Festival of Unleavened Bread, for it will remind you that I brought your forces out of the land of Egypt on this very day. This festival will be a permanent law for you; celebrate this day from generation to generation. ¹⁸The bread you eat must be made without yeast from the evening of the fourteenth day of the first month until the evening of the twenty-first day of that month. ¹⁹During those seven days, there must be no trace of yeast in your homes. Anyone who eats anything made with yeast during this week will be cut off from the community of Israel. These regulations apply both to the foreigners living among you and to the native-born Israelites. ²⁰During those days you must not eat anything made with yeast. Wherever you live, eat only bread made without yeast."

²¹Then Moses called all the elders of Israel together and said to them, "Go, pick out a lamb or young goat for each of your families, and slaughter the Passover animal. ²²Drain the blood into a basin. Then take a bundle of hyssop branches and dip it into the blood. Brush the hyssop across the top and sides of the doorframes of your houses. And no one may go out through the door until morning. ²³For the LORD will pass through the land to strike down the Egyptians. But when he sees the blood on the top and sides of the doorframe, the LORD will pass over your home. He will not permit his death angel to enter your house and strike you down.

²⁴"Remember, these instructions are a permanent law that you and your descendants must observe forever. ²⁵When you enter the land the LORD has promised to give you, you will continue to observe this ceremony. ²⁶Then your children will ask, 'What does this ceremony mean?' ²⁷And you will reply, 'It is the Passover sacrifice to the LORD, for he passed over the houses of the Israelites in Egypt. And though he struck the Egyptians, he spared our families.'" When Moses had finished speaking, all the people bowed down to the ground and worshiped.

²⁸So the people of Israel did just as the LORD had commanded through Moses and

Aaron. ²⁹And that night at midnight, the LORD struck down all the firstborn sons in the land of Egypt, from the firstborn son of Pharaoh, who sat on his throne, to the firstborn son of the prisoner in the dungeon. Even the firstborn of their livestock were killed. ³⁰Pharaoh and all his officials and all the people of Egypt woke up during the night, and loud wailing was heard throughout the land of Egypt. There was not a single house where someone had not died.

12:11 Hebrew *Bind up your loins.*

NOTES

11:1 *Then the LORD said.* The exact sequence of events from 10:29–11:3 is unclear. Some interpreters have concluded that Yahweh must have given the revelation contained in 11:1-2 at an earlier time. Thus they hold that the Hebrew perfect form (normally translated as a simple past tense) of the verb "said" should be translated as a pluperfect "had said" (so NIV). This is a legitimate translation of the Hebrew form, but there is no formal way to verify whether it is correct or not. See the commentary for further discussion; see also the note on 11:4.

blow. This is the word *nega'* [TH5061, ZH5596], often translated "plague" (cf. KJV, NIV, NASB). In popular usage, the English term has come to describe all 10 of the acts of Yahweh directed against the Egyptians. Elsewhere in the Bible the term is often used for disease (Gen 12:17; 1 Kgs 8:37; Ps 91:10).

11:3 *look favorably on.* Lit., "gave the people grace in the eyes of Egypt." See Gen 6:8 and the commentary on 33:12.

11:4 *Moses had announced.* See the note on 11:1; the NLT is attempting to solve the problem of the sequence of events by suggesting that this announcement had actually occurred before 10:29. The same comment concerning the pluperfect in 11:1 applies here—the translation is a possibility. See the commentary for a fuller discussion.

11:7 *not even a dog will bark.* Lit., "a dog will not sharpen its tongue against man or beast."

11:9 *Now the LORD had told Moses earlier.* Lit., "the Lord said to Moses." See the notes on 11:1 and 4 about the translation of the perfect verb form as a pluperfect. In this case, there is the supporting evidence of 4:21 and 10:1-2.

12:2 *From now on.* Even though this is an addition, the sense it conveys is very likely implicit in the text. The sentence is verbless, simply saying "This month [is] to you first of months; it [is] the first of the months of the year to you." Most commentators agree that a new calendar is being instituted, but Cassuto (1967:137) says the sentence only means that this event will make this month, the first of the year, the most important month to them.

12:3 *community.* The Hebrew is *'edah* [TH5712, ZH6337]. Sarna (1991:54) says this refers to a national assembly when used in the pre-monarchic era (see also 12:6 and note).

12:4 This sentence is complex in Hebrew and yields two different possible interpretations: The other family to share the meal shall be chosen for its proximity, or it shall be chosen for its size. The MT seems to favor the former, while the LXX favors the latter. Probably both factors are to be taken into account. Thus, it might be better to translate the last sentence in the verse as "choose this family on the basis of its size and how much they can eat." The goal was to have enough people present to eat all of the meat, leaving none to be burned (12:10).

12:6 *Take special care.* Lit., "it shall be a guarded thing for you" (*mishmereth* [TH4931, ZH5466]). This same word appears in 16:23 where it refers to the manna gathered for the Sabbath on the day before, and in 16:32-34, where it refers to the manna kept in the Ark of the Covenant.

assembly of the community. The Hebrew is *qahal 'edah* [TH6951/5712, ZH7736/6337] (see 12:3 and note). Houtman (1993:2.168) regards the two words as synonyms expressing the same idea. This seems probable.

at twilight. Lit., "between the two settings." It is not known precisely what this phrase means. The rabbinic commentators take it to mean between noon—the first setting—and sunset—the second setting (Sarna 1991:55). Others have taken it to mean between sunset on the fourteenth day of the month and sunset on the fifteenth day (Childs 1974:197). Still others take it as referring to the time between sunset (when the sun touches the horizon) and sundown (Houtman 1993:2.175).

12:11 ***Passover.*** The exact derivation of this term is questioned. BDB (820) suggests that there were two different roots having the same consonants, *pskh*, one meaning "to pass over" or "to spring over," and the other meaning "to limp." However, there really only seems to be one idea involved, but having both physical connotations ("to hop, limp," 1 Kgs 18:21) and metaphorical ones ("to skip over, to spare"; Isa 31:5; Amos 7:8; so KBL [769]). There is an Akkadian cognate which means "to appease," but there is no clear connection between the Hebrew and the Akkadian on this point.

12:17 ***your forces.*** Lit., "your hosts." At several points in this narrative, Israel is spoken of in this way (6:26; 7:4; 12:41, 51). Perhaps the point is to stress that they did not go out simply as a disorganized rabble but in an organized and disciplined way, like an army would march out.

12:22 ***a basin.*** The word *sap* [TH5592/A/B, ZH6195] can mean either a bowl or a threshold. The LXX takes it as "threshold." If that were correct, the animal would be slaughtered on the threshold, and a sprig of "hyssop" (marjoram) would be dipped into the blood that collected there to sprinkle it on the "top and sides of the doorframes." The strongest argument in favor of "basin" is that in 12:23 it is said that the Lord would see the blood on the top and sides of the door, and no mention is made of any blood on the threshold.

12:23 ***his death angel.*** Lit., "the destroyer." See 2 Sam 24:16 where "the destroyer" is identified as an angel.

12:27 ***When Moses had finished speaking.*** This wording is added by the NLT.

bowed down to the ground and worshiped. The final word is literally "prostrated themselves on the ground." Whether this prostration refers to an act of worship or not is determined by the context. Here the context is clearly one of worship (see also 4:31). In 11:8 ("fall to the ground before me"), it is apparently not so much worship as supplication.

COMMENTARY

There is considerable uncertainty among commentators about the literary structure of 11:1–15:21. Fretheim (1991:133) considers chapters 12–15 to be a single unit, with chapter 11 concluding the plague narrative. Childs (1974:184) agrees regarding chapter 11 but considers that the next unit is 12:1–13:16 (so also Cassuto 1967:136, but with 13:1-16 as appendices). Houtman (1993:2.141) agrees regarding 12:1–13:16 but regards chapter 11 as part of a single unit with 10:21-29 (1993:2.114). Enns (2000:244) thinks chapter 11 forms part of a unit with 12:1–13:16. I agree with Enns that chapter 11, with its announcement of the final act of the drama, is not part of the cycle of three threes that constitute the first nine plagues (7:8–10:29). This one stands apart from the others partly because it is the one that forces Pharaoh's hand but also because the actual event is not reported until 12:28-30, after the discussion of the Passover observance. It does not seem to me that the announcement of the plague and the report of its occurrence should be placed in two different literary units.

But if a new unit begins at 11:1, where does it end? The majority of commentators see the first major break occurring between 13:16 and 13:17, where the discussion of the Reed Sea crossing begins. They are influenced in this direction because 12:43–13:16 contains further discussion of ritual, like that found in 12:1-28, and they believe these should be kept together. I think this overlooks a continuity that begins at 12:31 and extends to 15:21. That continuity pertains to the discussion of the Exodus, which begins with Pharaoh's response to the death of the firstborn in 12:31 and continues until the end of the Song of the Sea in 15:21. The fact that there is discussion of worship both before and after the defining moment of 12:31 should not be allowed to camouflage that defining moment. Before the event of 12:31, Israel was still in slavery. After that point, they were slaves no more. For these reasons, I think 11:1–12:30 constitute a unit in which the final act of the drama of the plagues is played out.

As mentioned in the note on 11:1, it is not quite clear how or when the revelation contained in 11:1-2 came to Moses. The NLT translators seem to envision that God spoke to Moses in Pharaoh's presence after Moses's retort in 10:29. Cassuto (1967:132) argues that such revelation always came in solitude and that Moses must have been recalling things that God had said to him earlier (3:19-21; 4:22-23). As noted above (note on 11:1), the NIV translators support the idea of an earlier revelation. But it is also possible that both the revelation and the warning had been given earlier and that they are reported here in a kind of topical arrangement in order to set apart and highlight the final plague.

At this point no explanation is given for the request for "articles of silver and gold" from the Egyptians (see also 3:22; 12:35-36). Later commentators and authors offered a number of different justifications for the act (e.g., repayment for the years of slavery), but whatever the justification, it seems likely that this is where the large amounts of gold, silver, and other precious objects later used in the building of the Tabernacle came from (see 38:24-31). God made the Egyptians "look favorably on" (see the note on 11:3) the Israelites so that they would give gifts to them. What a change had occurred from the first visit to Pharaoh! God's promises had all come true: The slaves and their leader had become "great," and Pharaoh had become almost completely isolated from his people in his refusal to admit what was clearly demonstrated before his eyes.

The moment for the final stroke had come. Pharaoh had done everything he could to hold onto Jacob, Yahweh's "firstborn." There was nothing left for Pharaoh but to lose his firstborn in retribution (cf. 4:22-23). And none of us acts alone. We all have a circle of influence. In Pharaoh's case that circle of influence was "every family in Egypt" (11:5). Because of what Pharaoh had done, the suffering in the land would extend from his own throne to the "lowliest servant girl" kneeling on the ground to roll the grinding stone back and forth over grain to crush it into flour (see 12:29, where "prisoner in the dungeon" is used to express the same extreme of inclusiveness). Even the animals in Pharaoh's Egypt would suffer. The features that had been coming into prominence in the previous plagues are also highlighted here. One of these is incomparability. The "wail" (11:6) that would be heard in the land would be like none before or after. ("Wail" is the same word used of Israel's "cry" in 2:23 and 3:9.) Another is the distinction between the Israelites and the Egyptians. The distinction could hardly be greater: The death angel (12:23) would be stalking the Egyptians and their screams would be heard throughout the land, but "not even a dog" (11:7) would be barking at the Israelites and their animals. Under such circumstances there could be no question that Israel's Yahweh is God and that the things the Egyptians worshiped were powerless (cf. 12:12).

This plague was the final attack on all that Egypt worshiped. Apart from all the natural forces that the Egyptians attempted to propitiate, what they really worshiped in the end was life itself. This is the reason for all of their elaborate funerary preparations. Life in Egypt was very good, with a benign climate, a beneficent sun, a very predictable river, and fertile soil brought down by the floods. To them the greatest good was the continuation of such a life. And in the end it was for the perpetuation of that life that they worshiped their myriad gods. But Yahweh had shown them in case after case that these so-called gods did not have the secret of life and that in fact, they could only produce death. Thus, this final plague is an attack on life itself. Even life does not have life in itself. It is a gift from the sole creator of the earth, and that creator is Yahweh of Israel. How humiliating this must have been to intelligent, cultured, and sophisticated Egyptians, that the stupid Hebrew slaves had found God without looking for him, while they with all their careful searching had found nothing but death.

Although it might be true that Moses would never see Pharaoh's face again (10:29), that did not mean Pharaoh would never have anything more to say to Moses. The day would come when Pharaoh's "officials" (11:8) would "run" (lit., "come down" [from the palace to the slave quarters?]) and "fall to the ground" (the same word translated "worship" in 12:27; see note). Far from Moses and Aaron reverently asking Pharaoh to let the Israelites go, as in 5:3, it would be the Egyptian officials on Pharaoh's behalf worshipfully begging the Israelites to go. If Pharaoh was angry at the end of the interview (10:28), Moses's anger more than matched his (11:8).

Exodus 11:9-10 forms a summary bringing Moses and Aaron's interactions with Pharaoh to a close. Everything that could be said to that man was now at an end. As a result of his hardness of heart, one miracle after another had been done, revealing the completeness of Yahweh's control of all the earth and its powers. If Moses and Aaron seemed to have failed until this point, that was not the case. They had been faithful and God's purpose of self-revelation was about to be brought to a rousing climax. From this point on, all that Moses and Aaron would have to say would be to a people who were free to worship the true Lord of the universe, not a mere man parading as such.

The final act of distinction between Israel and the Egyptians, as reported in 12:1-30, is different from the others. In the previous plagues, the Israelites did not need to do anything to experience exemption from the plague. Not so with this final one. That is very important. What is the enemy? It is not the Egypts of this world. They are the enemy only to the extent that they have over us the power of the true enemy. The true enemy is death. Thus scholars who seek to discover the hypothetical original texts behind the present one are often wont to make a good deal of the fact that the Passover (originally) had nothing to do with the Exodus, whereas the Festival of Unleavened Bread did. I believe that is to miss the point. It is true that Passover does not so much celebrate physical freedom as it does spiritual freedom, the freedom from death. But that is the point running through the entire book. Yahweh is the Lord of life and death. Those who would be delivered need to recognize that the only true deliverance is that which is found in trusting and obeying this Yahweh. That is what the Passover celebration is about: a trusting and obedient relationship with him. Thus, Jesus' appropriation of Passover in the Lord's Supper does not change a celebration of physical liberation into one of spiritual liberation. The celebration had always been, when rightly understood, a celebration of deliverance from death (see 12:27). What Jesus did was to show much more specifically how it is that God conquered the power of death (both in Egypt and for all time), namely, through Jesus' own supreme trust and obedience.

This truth—that the Exodus is really about becoming rightly related to God—explains why some 50 verses (12:1-27, 43-50; 13:1-16) are given over to discussion of worship practices—just as the narrative reaches its most exciting point, just when what appears to be the goal of the whole operation is on the point of being achieved. Was this merely an editor's way of increasing the suspense? Or was it a later priest's way of intruding his special (and rather boring) interests into the text? It is neither.[1] This extended discussion is the means by which the author makes his point that even if these slaves manage to escape their oppressors, they will have missed the point of the event unless they surround their memories of it with appropriate acts of worship. The question for humans is not *whether* we will serve a master but only *what* master we will serve. If we live our lives in service to our Creator, we will be free to be all we were made to be. If we refuse that service, we are seeking to live in ways we were never made for, and the result will be a worse bondage than we ever dreamed, whether to our own self-will or to the will of another.

It is important to note that this worship was centered in the memory of something God had done in time and space (12:14, 24; 13:3, 8, 14, 16). Fretheim (1991:132), while correctly noting the interchange of narrative and worship throughout chapters 12-15, says that what we have is "a liturgical event." According to him, whatever may have happened originally is not of very much significance but rather that it is the "event" that occurs in worship that is significant. Unfortunately, this concept blurs the fundamental distinction between true biblical worship and pagan worship. Pagan worshippers seek to recreate some primordial activity in the present in order to actualize in their own lives what is considered to be constantly occurring outside of time and space. Their worship is "a liturgical event." That is not what the Bible is talking about. God did something in our time and space once for all. What he did changed everything thereafter. Worship (liturgy) does not involve the magical actualization of those events in the present. Worship is to accurately remember the wonderful things God has done on our behalf and to realign our beliefs and behaviors on the basis of what God did. Moses is here, under divine inspiration, seeking to lay the essential foundations for what Israelite, Jewish, and Christian worship should consist of. If God *did not* do the things the Bible reports, then liturgical activities are valueless. They do not constitute an "event" with meaning in itself. God's power is not ours to tap into through magical rituals.

So what is the point of these two discussions of worship on either side of the death of the firstborn (12:29-30)? And why not consider them part of one literary unit? Exodus 12:1-28 is rather clearly focused on what took place in Egypt in preparation for the death angel's visitation.[2] This is particularly true of the instructions for the Passover celebration as discussed in 12:1-14 and 12:21-23. It does not seem that the seven-day Festival of Unleavened Bread (12:15-20) was intended to be celebrated in Egypt since the Israelites were on the way into the wilderness on the day after the death of the firstborn (12:39, 51; note also that in Moses's instructions in 12:21-27, no mention is made of the Festival of Unleavened Bread). Nonetheless, the connection of unleavened bread with the act of leaving Egypt is clear enough (12:34, 39). Thus, it seems that although the instructions given in 12:15-20 are focused on the future, they were included here with the instructions for the first Passover to focus attention on the importance of what was to take place shortly.

The instructions that are given in 12:43-49 and 13:1-16 are entirely focused on the future. Now that the Egyptian firstborn had died, the Israelite firstborn had been spared, and the Israelites had been driven out and were on the way to the Promised Land loaded down with Egyptian wealth, there were some instructions for worship that needed to be reiterated, expanded, and adjusted for the future. So the two sets of instructions are differentiated by the event between them, an event that would change everything, including the way the Israelites marked time (12:1-2).[3]

That event was the death of the firstborn. As already noted above, the Israelites were required to do something in order to be exempt from this plague. Were the specific actions important or was it the faith, trust, and obedience that the actions represented that were important? I believe that the answer to both questions is "yes." In a pagan worldview, it is the actions that are important. If done correctly, they will achieve the desired results apart from any attitude of the worshipper. In the worldview that is reflected in the European Enlightenment, one that is often called "Greek," the action is merely symbolic of the attitude and has no real significance at all and could be changed at will. I believe the biblical worldview falls midway between these two. On the one hand, actions done merely because they will have some supposed effect on metaphysical realities are roundly condemned. Examples abound in the Hebrew prophets (e.g., Isa 1:10-15; Hos 5:6-7; Amos 5:18-24). On the other hand, certain attitudes can only be adequately symbolized by certain actions. The person who refused to sacrifice in the way God had directed could hardly say he or she truly was trusting in, believing, and obeying God (Mal 1:6-14). Thus, while it is true that it is the attitude with which the Israelites carried out the actions prescribed in 12:1-13 that was most important, the nature of the action prescribed was important too. Again, it is important to avoid two extremes. Sarna (1991:55) is certainly correct when he points out that nothing is said in the text about the blood's having any magical effect. It is merely a "sign" (12:13).[4] Very clearly, the author is seeking to deprive this event of any mythological connection. It may well be that other cultures practiced similar rituals in the springtime (although this is not quite so confidently asserted today as it was 75 years ago), but if they did, God was providing his people with an alternate understanding of the practice.

That having been said, why *these* requirements? Why a lamb or a kid "with no defects" (12:5)? Why the blood on the doorframes (12:7)? Why eat all the meat together as a family (12:3-4)? These are not insignificant details. The Bible does not answer these in any detail; however, there are enough implied answers to be found in the Bible's pages to enable us to draw some inferences. The family context is of crucial importance for the development and continuation of any religious faith. The Bible shows that faith is communicated in and through the family and that if it is not communicated there, it is likely that it will never be successfully communicated. Furthermore, there is something very significant about sharing a meal together that shapes the nature of the communication. Communication that takes place in the informal setting of a shared meal has a depth and an intimacy that is often not present in more formalized settings. The meal lends a certain enduring character to the sharing of values that are at the heart of the participants' lives. When all of this is taken into account, it is easy to see why, both in the Old Testament and in the New Testament, the final declaration of God's victory over death is made in the context of a meal (Isa 25:1-8; Rev 19:6-8).

The choice of a lamb or a kid without defects signifies a level of both innocence and perfection. This animal is the best of the oncoming generation. Something is conveyed here of the power of death. Death is not to be confronted with the leftovers or the castoffs of life. If it is to be defeated, it will take the best there is to offer. Moreover, the animal's life is given for this event alone. Its meat cannot be carried over for another, ordinary meal.[5] This event is too solemn and too serious to be treated in a light and casual way. Furthermore, if there is no magical power in the lamb's death and in its consumption by those who will be spared death's depredations, there is still the powerful symbolism that in the end death can only be defeated by death and in our partaking in the death of another. Ultimately, all this symbolism comes together in the death of Jesus Christ (Matt 26:26-29; John 1:29; Eph 1:7; Col 1:19-22; Heb 10:19-20; 1 Pet 1:18-19; Rev 5:6).

This explains the symbolic power of the blood. The Bible agrees with other ancient cultures that "the life of every creature is in its blood" (Lev 17:14). Placing the blood on the doorpost made it unmistakable that the lamb or kid did not die by accident, nor was it killed merely to be eaten. The animal had been slain and the death angel could not enter there because of that fact. The blood itself accomplished nothing, but it was a "sign" (12:13). A sign of what? Its presence was a sign that those within that house, unlike their first parents, Adam and Eve, trusted, believed, and obeyed God. They had selected the animal four days in advance (12:3) and then had slaughtered it in accord with God's command, making a public testimony of their faith with this very visible evidence. Thus, the death that Adam and Eve brought into the world is deprived of its power, at least on this one night. But it is also a sign in another sense. Everyone in those Israelite homes eventually succumbed to death. Was this event only to postpone the inevitable, or was it a sign of something else? The Bible tells us the latter is the case. In the end, Jesus Christ would defeat all death for all time, for those who would trust, believe, and obey him. That one night in Egypt was a foretaste of what God had in store for all humanity through his Son. The Lamb had been slain "before the world was made" (Rev 13:8), and his blood would be available to all who would choose to listen to the word of God (1 Pet 1:19).

Although the Passover celebration was particularly associated with deliverance from death, Yahweh wanted this "day to remember" (12:14) to be celebrated with an additional set of rituals that extended throughout the following week, those associated with the Feast of Unleavened Bread. While the instructions seem to be primarily focused on the way in which the celebration would be carried on in the future, when Israel was settled in the land ("no trace of yeast in your homes," 12:19), they were still relevant to the situation in Egypt, not only because the Israelites left in such haste that they had no time to put yeast in their bread (12:34, 39) but also because unleavened bread "travels" better.

Those issues are not addressed in 12:15-20, however. The use of leaven was not forbidden so as to remind the Israelites of their ancestors' situation. It was simply forbidden, and that in no uncertain terms (12:15, 18-20). While the language "cut off from the community" (12:15, 19) is somewhat ambiguous (Did it involve death or expulsion? Did the community do it? Did God do it?), it was clearly a very serious punishment (cf. Num 15:30-31). Why such a serious punishment for what appears to be a rather minor ceremonial violation? It looks as if yeast was not forbidden merely as a way of remembering what the ancestors experienced in the past. In 12:17 Yahweh says that they are to celebrate the festival to "remind you that I brought your forces out of the land of Egypt." Is it possible that there is a deeper symbolism at work here? In the New Testament Jesus warns his disciples to avoid "the yeast of the Pharisees" (Matt 16:6, 11). For them, that "yeast" was a reliance on one's own efforts to become acceptable to God. Perhaps that is the issue here. Perhaps yeast was forbidden as a way of underscoring that it was not through any human effort that the Israelites had been delivered from Egypt but purely by the grace of God. But if that application seems too specific, it would at least seem to me very defensible that yeast is representative of anything in one's life that is displeasing to God, and that if we are to have the benefits of his "Passover" we dare not hide such a thing in the tents of our lives (cf. Josh 7:1-2, 22-23).

When Moses relayed God's commands concerning Passover to the people

(12:21-27), he did not repeat several of the things God had said and he included several things that had not been mentioned previously (such as catching the blood in a "basin" and the use of "hyssop" to brush the blood on the doorframes). Cassuto (1967:143) makes the very plausible suggestion that the writer chose not to repeat the same details from God's address in Moses's but included a broad outline (12:21, 23-24) and those elements that were unique to Moses's statement (12:22, 25-27). The most significant thing not stated previously is the nature of the communication that was to take place around this meal in the future. It would provide an opportunity to explain to future generations the historic event that had marked them (cf. 13:16) for all future time. Again, I point out that there is nothing here of "making the past present" in some magical way. The death angel was not deflected anew in each Passover. The parents were simply to tell the children that they as a family were engaging in this act of worship (note that it is a "Passover sacrifice") because of what God did for them once and for all in the past. They would be reflecting a sense of solidarity with the ancestors and testifying that the past activity of God had implications for their attitudes and behaviors in the present, but there is no hint of using ritual to "lay hold of sacred reality"—that is the pagan attitude that the Bible is at such pains to reject.

The response of the people to all of this is reported first in 12:27. It is the same one that was given months earlier and reported in 4:31. A great deal had transpired between that response and this one. The first act of worship was given out of a very inadequate understanding of the Yahweh who promised to deliver them, and when it did not appear that he was going to keep his word immediately and without any difficulty on their part, they had turned their backs on him and his representatives (6:9). Now they had had a much fuller revelation of the one who had extended his promises to them. They had seen his incomparable power and the futility of all that the world is tempted to worship. They had also experienced his delivering power on several occasions while the Egyptians were suffering. This worship was still an act of faith, and there would be all too many occasions in the future when the shallowness of this worship would be revealed (32:1-2; Num 14:1-4). Nevertheless, if it was only a small step, it was a step, and one in the right direction.

Equally important was the fact that the worship was followed up by obedience, as reported in 12:28. Ultimately, these are the goals of deliverance: obedience and worship. The structure of the book demonstrates this fact. Deliverance issues in covenant and Tabernacle. Unless obedience and worship issue from God's revelation of himself to us, the revelation is abortive. It was because Pharaoh refused to give worship and obedience to God—in spite of his correct recognition of who God was (9:27; 10:16-17)—that all the disasters befell him and his people. It is not enough to recognize Yahweh, or even to accept his gifts. To truly *know* him is to gladly do what he asks and to revel in the wonder of his presence. Those who will not do this do not know him.

After all of this, the terse report of the occurrence of the plague in 12:29-30 seems almost anticlimactic, but in fact, nothing more remained to be said. The Israelites had believed what God had said, and they had obeyed him. Pharaoh had refused to do that. The outcome was a foregone conclusion. What the world needs to know is that if the shape of Yahweh's actions is not always predictable, those actions are always absolutely consistent with his word. If he says that the person who sins will die (Ezek. 18:4; John 8:21, 24), that is a fact. And if he says that whoever has his Son has eternal life (1 John 5:11-12), that is also a fact. Yahweh had said that a great cry would fill the land of Egypt (11:6), and that is what happened, even to the extent of waking the entire people from sleep. "It is a terrible thing to fall into the hands of the living God" (Heb 10:31).

ENDNOTES
1. On this point, it seems to me that Childs wants to hold two mutually exclusive positions simultaneously. On the one hand, he criticizes Cassuto for not taking adequate account of the tradition-historical problems in the Exodus text (1974:189), by which he means the scholarly opinion that several originally unrelated texts from very different settings and eras were combined. But then he shows that except for one or two passages, there is no consensus among scholars as to what the extent of the actual texts was or what their supposed origins actually were (1974:190-195). Similarly, while Childs's conclusion is that Passover, Unleavened Bread, and the Dedication of the Firstborn originally had nothing to do with each other or with the Exodus, whatever that may have been, he says that it *is* possible to read the present text in a way that makes coherent sense. If his conclusion is correct, it is impossible to read the present text as coherent—it is a collection of unrelated texts from unrelated events. If the text can be read as coherent, then much of the evidence used to support his conclusion is shown to be invalid (even as the lack of scholarly agreement about the proposed source texts suggests). Perhaps materials dating to the time of the Exodus and stemming from its events have been collected and reorganized to make a point in a clearer way, but that is far from saying that completely unrelated, and indeed, opposing accounts have now been welded into a unified whole to give witness to things that never happened.
2. On this point and in regard to earlier discussions about the composition of this material, note the very explicit statement of 12:1 that these instructions were given to Moses and Aaron "while the Israelites were still in the land of Egypt."
3. In some ways the two sets of instructions are analogous to the giving of the covenant in Exodus and its reiteration in Deuteronomy after the wilderness experience and prior to entering the land.
4. The prohibitions from drinking blood or from eating meat with the blood in it strike at this point (Lev 7:26-27; 19:26). Pagans often drank the blood of sacrificial victims because they believed it had a magical power. That is not true, and God will not allow his people to attempt to use blood in that way. Here, the requirement that the meat not be eaten raw (12:9) speaks to this point. The same strictures apply to fat (Lev 7:22-25), which probably explains the requirement to roast the flesh, thus melting away any fat.
5. This concern—that as much of the meat as possible be used for its intended purpose—explains the stipulation that if the family is not large enough to eat all the meat, a neighboring family of the right size should be invited to join them to eat the remainder (12:4).

2. The Exodus (12:31–14:31)
a. Journey into the wilderness (12:31–13:22)

³¹Pharaoh sent for Moses and Aaron during the night. "Get out!" he ordered. "Leave my people—and take the rest of the Israelites with you! Go and worship the LORD as you have requested. ³²Take your flocks and herds, as you said, and be gone. Go, but bless me as you leave." ³³All the Egyptians urged the people of Israel to get out of the land as quickly as possible, for they thought, "We will all die!"

³⁴The Israelites took their bread dough before yeast was added. They wrapped their kneading boards in their cloaks and carried them on their shoulders. ³⁵And the people of Israel did as Moses had instructed; they asked the Egyptians for clothing and articles of silver and gold. ³⁶The LORD caused the Egyptians to look favorably on the Israelites, and they gave the Israelites whatever they asked for. So they stripped the Egyptians of their wealth!

³⁷That night the people of Israel left Rameses and started for Succoth. There were about 600,000 men,* plus all the women and children. ³⁸A rabble of non-Israelites went with them, along with great flocks and herds of livestock. ³⁹For bread they baked flat cakes from the dough without yeast they had brought from Egypt. It was made without yeast because the people were driven out of Egypt in such a hurry that they had no time to prepare the bread or other food.

⁴⁰The people of Israel had lived in Egypt* for 430 years. ⁴¹In fact, it was on the last day of the 430th year that all the LORD's forces left the land. ⁴²On this night the LORD kept his promise to bring his people out of the land of Egypt. So this night belongs to him, and it must be commemorated every year by all the Israelites, from generation to generation.

⁴³Then the LORD said to Moses and Aaron, "These are the instructions for the festival of Passover. No outsiders are allowed to eat the Passover meal. ⁴⁴But any slave who has been purchased may eat it if he has been circumcised. ⁴⁵Temporary residents and hired servants may not eat it. ⁴⁶Each Passover lamb must be eaten in one house. Do not carry any of its meat outside, and do not break any of its bones. ⁴⁷The whole community of Israel must celebrate this Passover festival.

⁴⁸"If there are foreigners living among you who want to celebrate the LORD's Passover, let all their males be circumcised. Only then may they celebrate the Passover with you like any native-born Israelite. But no uncircumcised male may ever eat the Passover meal. ⁴⁹This instruction applies to everyone, whether a native-born Israelite or a foreigner living among you."

⁵⁰So all the people of Israel followed all the LORD's commands to Moses and Aaron. ⁵¹On that very day the LORD brought the people of Israel out of the land of Egypt like an army.

CHAPTER 13

Then the LORD said to Moses, ²"Dedicate to me every firstborn among the Israelites. The first offspring to be born, of both humans and animals, belongs to me."

³So Moses said to the people, "This is a day to remember forever—the day you left Egypt, the place of your slavery. Today the LORD has brought you out by the power of his mighty hand. (Remember, eat no food containing yeast.) ⁴On this day in early spring, in the month of Abib,* you have been set free. ⁵You must celebrate this event in this month each year after the LORD brings you into the land of the Canaanites, Hittites, Amorites, Hivites, and Jebusites. (He swore to your ancestors that he would give you this land—a land flowing with milk and honey.) ⁶For seven days the bread you eat must be made without yeast. Then on the seventh day,

celebrate a feast to the LORD. ⁷Eat bread without yeast during those seven days. In fact, there must be no yeast bread or any yeast at all found within the borders of your land during this time.

⁸"On the seventh day you must explain to your children, 'I am celebrating what the LORD did for me when I left Egypt.' ⁹This annual festival will be a visible sign to you, like a mark branded on your hand or your forehead. Let it remind you always to recite this teaching of the LORD: 'With a strong hand, the LORD rescued you from Egypt.'* ¹⁰So observe the decree of this festival at the appointed time each year.

¹¹"This is what you must do when the LORD fulfills the promise he swore to you and to your ancestors. When he gives you the land where the Canaanites now live, ¹²you must present all firstborn sons and firstborn male animals to the LORD, for they belong to him. ¹³A firstborn donkey may be bought back from the LORD by presenting a lamb or young goat in its place. But if you do not buy it back, you must break its neck. However, you must buy back every firstborn son.

¹⁴"And in the future, your children will ask you, 'What does all this mean?' Then you will tell them, 'With the power of his mighty hand, the LORD brought us out of Egypt, the place of our slavery. ¹⁵Pharaoh stubbornly refused to let us go, so the LORD killed all the firstborn males throughout the land of Egypt, both people and animals. That is why I now sacrifice all the firstborn males to the LORD—except that the firstborn sons are always bought back.' ¹⁶This ceremony will be like a mark branded on your hand or your forehead. It is a reminder that the power of the LORD's mighty hand brought us out of Egypt."

¹⁷When Pharaoh finally let the people go, God did not lead them along the main road that runs through Philistine territory, even though that was the shortest route to the Promised Land. God said, "If the people are faced with a battle, they might change their minds and return to Egypt." ¹⁸So God led them in a roundabout way through the wilderness toward the Red Sea.* Thus the Israelites left Egypt like an army ready for battle.*

¹⁹Moses took the bones of Joseph with him, for Joseph had made the sons of Israel swear to do this. He said, "God will certainly come to help you. When he does, you must take my bones with you from this place."

²⁰The Israelites left Succoth and camped at Etham on the edge of the wilderness. ²¹The LORD went ahead of them. He guided them during the day with a pillar of cloud, and he provided light at night with a pillar of fire. This allowed them to travel by day or by night. ²²And the LORD did not remove the pillar of cloud or pillar of fire from its place in front of the people.

12:37 Or *fighting men;* Hebrew reads *men on foot.* 12:40 Samaritan Pentateuch reads *in Canaan and Egypt;* Greek version reads *in Egypt and Canaan.* 13:4 Hebrew *On this day in the month of Abib.* This first month of the ancient Hebrew lunar calendar usually occurs within the months of March and April. 13:9 Or *Let it remind you always to keep the instructions of the Lord on the tip of your tongue, because with a strong hand, the Lord rescued you from Egypt.* 13:18a Hebrew *sea of reeds.* 13:18b Greek version reads *left Egypt in the fifth generation.*

NOTES

12:33 urged. Lit., "hardened to hasten" with the sense of "they pressed them to hurry."

"We will all die!" "Die" is in the participial form, which may here suggest imminence: "We are all about to die."

12:37 women and children. Lit., "besides children."

12:38 A rabble of non-Israelites. The Hebrew is *'ereb rab* [TH6154A/7227, ZH6850/8041], meaning "mixture" and "multitude," thus KJV's "a mixed multitude." But Cassuto (1967:147-148) suggests plausibly that the original was *'erebrab,* which would be a reduplicated form of "mixture," very much like the *ha'sapsup* [TH628, ZH671] in Num 11:4 referring to the same group. There the reduplicated root is *'asap* [TH622, ZH665] (to collect). For other examples of this phenomenon, see Isa 2:20; 51:1.

12:42 The Hebrew is unclear whether the Lord is the subject (NLT, NIV) or the object (NASB, Houtman [1993:2.204]) of the action of reserving (or keeping vigil). A literal reading would be, "It was a night of vigil to the Lord to bring them out." The parallel between the Lord's action and that expected of the people seems to slightly favor the former.

12:43 *outsiders.* The Hebrew is *ben-nekar* [TH1121/5236, ZH1201/5797], "son of a foreigner." Knight (1976:95) argues that this should be understood as the son of a foreign god (cf. Mal 2:11, *bat 'el nekar* [TH1323/410A/5236, ZH1426/446/5797], "daughter of a foreign god"), i.e., a pagan. However, that point is hard to maintain in the several usages of the phrase elsewhere in the Bible. But the term does have the flavor of alienation about it. Thus, these are people who were distinctly other than the Israelites and wanted to maintain that otherness. Such persons could not partake of the covenant meal.

12:45 *Temporary residents and hired servants.* Unlike the "outsiders" (12:44), these were living in the community on a semipermanent basis.

12:48 *foreigners.* The Hebrew is *ger* [TH1616, ZH1731], meaning someone who is a more-or-less permanent resident in a community although not of the same ethnic stock or nationality as the community. This was the term often used of proselytes from outside Israel.

12:51 The punctuation in the Hebrew text (MT) links this verse with the next chapter.

13:2 *first offspring to be born.* Lit., "the opener of the womb."

13:4 *Abib.* This is the name of the first month of the year in the Canaanite calendar. This month was called "Nisan" in Babylonian (Neh 2:1; Ezra 3:8).

13:5 *You must celebrate.* The term translated "celebrate" here is the same one translated "slavery" in 13:3. A literal translation might be, "you must serve this service." This is reminiscent of the people's response to Joshua in Josh 24:16-18, where they recognize that the Lord delivered them from the house of slavery (servitude) and then declare that they will serve the Lord. The wordplay underscores the truth that the issue is not *whether* we will serve but only *whom* we will serve.

13:9 *like a mark branded.* Lit., "like a sign on your hand, or a memorial on your forehead." See the commentary on this verse.

recite this teaching. Note the alternative reading in the NLT mg.

13:12 *you must present.* Lit., "you must cause to pass over" = "transfer to."

firstborn male animals. Lit., "every opener of the womb (*sheger*) of an animal." See Sarna (1991:67) for the possible connection of *sheger* [TH7698, ZH8715] with the name of a fertility deity.

13:13 *break its neck.* An unclean animal could not be offered as a sacrifice to God. By breaking its neck (thus leaving the blood inside the animal), the owner would be making it clear that he was not intending to use the animal as a sacrifice.

13:15 *stubbornly refused to let us go.* Lit., "he hardened to let us go."

13:16 *like a mark branded.* See the note on 13:9. Here a different word is used than "memorial." It suggests "headband." It might refer to a headband marking the devotee of a god or goddess (cf. Houtman 1993:2.218-219).

13:18 *Red Sea.* Lit., "sea of reeds." The Bible includes the entire region including the Red Sea proper, the Gulf of Suez, and the Bitter Lakes north of Suez under this heading (so the LXX regularly translates the phrase as "Red Sea"). While there is still no consensus as to the precise location being referred to here, it seems most likely that it is one of the Bitter Lakes (see the careful analysis by Hoffmeier 1996:199-222).

ready for battle. The Hebrew is *khamushim* [TH2567, ZH2821]. Scholars do not agree on the precise meaning of this term. Houtman (1993:2.252) argues persuasively that it is better translated "in an orderly fashion." But see Josh 1:14 and 4:12-13, where "ready for battle" might be more appropriate.

13:21 *the LORD went ahead.* The verb is a participle which emphasizes that the Lord continued to go before them. Sarna (1991:70) says this indicates the uninterrupted nature of the divine manifestation.

COMMENTARY

In Exodus 12:31-14:31 we come to the second set of events of deliverance. The first set was the plagues narrated in 7:8-12:30. There God demonstrated his climactic power over all the gods of Egypt, forcing Pharaoh to recognize the Lord's absolute supremacy. Those events then precipitated the events described here: the events of the Exodus. Here Pharaoh is decisively and disastrously defeated. Here is the final demonstration of God's power to deliver. He allowed his people to be maneuvered into a situation from which there was no possible human escape. But in that hour, God delivered them in a way that would not only shape Israelite faith but also Christian faith as well throughout all the centuries to come.

Although many commentators think the two discussions of the Passover and Unleavened Bread in 12:4-27 and 12:43-13:16 should be treated together, I do not, as I argued in the previous section. I think the author has placed the two discussions on either side of the departure narrative in 12:31-42 for a reason. The first discussion (12:4-27) was related to the particular celebration that occurred on the night of the last plague. The second discussion (12:43-13:16) has to do with the universalization of those celebrations for all the future generations. An event of earth-shaking proportions had taken place between the two: Israel had left her chains behind, and death had been defeated. Those events have implications for all of future history; the endless cycles of oppression and destruction had been broken, and that event had to be memorialized for all future generations.

The unit of Exodus 12:31-14:31 may be divided at 13:22. Exodus 12:31-13:22 deals with the wilderness journey (and the commands for commemorating what had taken place), while 14:1-31 deals with the actual crossing of the sea.

The Departure (12:31-42). Pharaoh had said that Moses and Aaron would never see his face again (10:28-29). Now Pharaoh had to retract that, and in a speech, which Cassuto (1967:145) describes as jerky and monosyllabic, he made a complete surrender. For the first time he called the people "Israelites," recognizing their ethic identity, he let them take the livestock which he had previously denied (10:24), and he told them to go and worship (serve) the Lord. And finally, incredibly, he was reduced to asking a blessing of God. In this hour of incredible loss, he finally realized that he did not have the ability to produce the blessings of life— that they came from a source other than himself or the gods of Egypt. Cassuto (1967:145-146) points out that the first encounter of Jacob with the pharaoh in

Genesis 47:10 issued in a blessing, and now this last encounter of his children with the pharaoh of their time does also. So Cassuto wonders if this is an expression of Genesis 12:3, in which God promised that Abraham's offspring would be a blessing to the world.

Houtman (1993:2.142) argues that the reference to worshiping the Lord assumes that Pharaoh was only giving the Israelites three days' leave and was continuing to assert some measure of authority over them. Therefore, he explains the Egyptian pursuit in chapter 14 as the result of the realization that the Hebrews had no intention of coming back. But that is to read too much into the text. As mentioned above on 5:3, the idea of slaves meekly coming back to their shackles after putting three days' distance between themselves and their oppressors is unthinkable. Both Moses and Pharaoh understood what was being said: When Pharaoh said that the Israelites should go and serve (worship) God, he was admitting that there was someone who had a greater claim upon their service than he did. That he later changed his mind and tried to get them back is simply one more example of the kind of reneging on his word that had been going on throughout the whole plague cycle.

The hastiness of the departure is emphasized in several ways. Verse 33 suggests that the Egyptians were all but pushing the Hebrews out the door in panic, for as long as these slaves were still in the land they were all in danger. In that context it is not hard to imagine them gladly acceding to any requests the Hebrews might make of them (12:35-36; cf. 3:21-22): "Silver? Of course, just go! Gold? Yes, just leave! Clothing? Yes, yes—just get away from here." The reference to the kneading boards on the shoulders (12:34) also points to great haste. The people were leaving in the middle of bread-making. Perhaps they expected to be able to leaven the bread the next day. But that was not to be (12:39). And as they went, others, "a rabble" (12:38), joined them. The Hebrew word, having to do with mixture (see note on 12:38), has been taken by some to suggest that many of this group might have been the product of mixed marriages, people who were part Egyptian and part Israelite. But in any case, the later behavior of this group suggests that they were those on the rootless fringes of society, people who were always ready to try some new thing, people who are always sure that good things can be achieved with no effort or commitment. But whatever the range of motives that might have been involved, here is another example of the truth that what God had done in delivering Israel across the centuries was not for Israel alone but for others as well.

The number "600,000 men" (12:37) is troublesome because of the logistical issues it raises. Estimates of the total number of the group, when "women and children" (12:37) are included, have been made, ranging from 2.5 to 3.5 million people. Apart from the fact that neither Canaan nor Egypt seem to have had that large a population in the Late Bronze Age, the very size of such a group, covering several square miles, would make the logistics of movement and organization completely unmanageable. Several solutions have been proposed. One of the following three seems most likely. (1) The Hebrew word *'elep* [TH505, ZH547], meaning "1,000," is a mistake for the original *'allup* [TH441A, ZH477] (chief over a clan or troop). Thus, the original would have said, "600 troops of men each under a captain." (2) The total number of those departing (including women and children) was 600,000. (3) The number was not intended to be understood literally.[1] In any case, it is clear that the text intends us to understand that this was not a handful of people who skulked out into the night with no one the wiser until considerably later. This was an unmistakably large group who, despite the suddenness of their actual departure, marched out in full array.

Instructions for the Future Passover (12:42-49). Verse 42 introduces verses 43-49, which speak of the future of the Passover celebration.[2] That event in Egypt was not a happenstance, something that God cobbled together in view of the developing situation. No, it had been in God's plan since before the time of Abraham. God had reserved (or "kept watch for") "this night" (12:42) with all its symbolism, pointing both backwards (God kept his promises to Abraham) and forward (on a night yet to come the death angel would be defeated forever in Jesus Christ). Thus, that night was to be literally *"reserved* by all the Israelites" (12:42) for all the years to come. It was a night when the past was remembered, but also a night when it was reaffirmed that that past would forever shape the future.

The fundamental point that is made about the Passover, as it was to be practiced in the future, was that no one could participate in it who was not a full participant in the covenant as indicated by circumcision (12:44, 48). Thus, the significance of Passover is not merely that it is an "Independence Day" celebration. It is something much deeper. Why is there an "Independence Day"? It is because of God's historic faithfulness. He is "true," true to his ancient covenant with Abraham. But it is also a testimony to the fact that God's goal is not merely deliverance; it is relationship. God was calling his people into a life-changing relationship with himself, and every spring the Israelites were called upon to remember that fact. God had called Abraham to "serve me faithfully and live a blameless life" (i.e., "all that a human was made to be") (Gen 17:1), and the acceptance of the mark of circumcision was Abraham's testimony to his willingness to live in a relationship like that (see above on 4:24-26). Persons unwilling to be part of such a relationship could not enter into the Passover celebration.

Verses 46 and 47 underscore four other features that were evidently important enough to be stressed for the future Passover celebrations. (1) While the Passover was to be celebrated by the whole community, (2) it was to be celebrated in individual "houses," that is, in the context of the extended family. Here is a statement of the importance of the family for theological education, as well as the Old Testament's remarkable blend of the communal and the individual. It was to be a national celebration, but provision was made so that everyone was a participant; there were no spectators. (3) Furthermore, the Passover lamb was not for mere eating, so that some could be saved for "leftovers" or could be sold or even given away to others; and (4) no bone of the lamb could be broken. Perhaps the prohibition of breaking the bones (see the application to Jesus in John 19:36) relates to this same point. One could not divide up the carcass, cutting some off for later.[3]

Verses 50 and 51 form both a summary and a bridge. Verse 50, looking both backward and forward, says that the people kept the Passover as God commanded it to be. Since the people had already departed, that statement is a retrospective speaking of the obedience given after these commands. Likewise, verse 51, looking in both directions, affirms the significance of the fifteenth day of Nisan as a day of significance for both "the LORD" and "the people."

Festival of Unleavened Bread and Dedication of the Firstborn (13:1-16). In this section, God commands the people to engage in two additional sets of symbolic activities designed to insure that they will never forget the events that confirmed to them the character and nature of God.[4] The first is the Festival of Unleavened Bread (13:3-10), and the second is the sacrifice or redemption of firstborn males (13:11-16). Verses 1 and 2, although they make specific reference to the firstborn, provide a superscription to the whole: These practices are at the command of God. Houtman (1993:2.144) says these customs will "make transparent . . . that the people of Israel belong to Yahweh and are to be a nation consecrated to Yahweh . . . which out of gratitude for Yahweh's mighty deeds is called to live according to his commandments." Thus, while Israel must never live in the past, the past is to shape every response of Israel to new situations and challenges.[5]

There is no specific explanation given in verses 3-10 why it was forbidden to eat yeast for the week following Passover. Eventually, yeast (leaven) was understood to represent sin (cf. Matt 16:6, 11-12), but no such indication is given here. In this context it seems obvious that the abstinence was required as a remembrance of the fact that the ancestors did not have yeast for their bread in the days immediately following their departure. The emphasis of verse 5 that this festival continue to be performed in Canaan underscores the concern that the new situation would not cause the Israelites to forget who they were as the chosen and delivered people of God. In fact, the book of Judges informs us that that is exactly what happened to the majority of the people, in spite of all of God's careful preparations.[6] One can only wonder what would have happened if these provisions had not been made.

The importance of memory is stressed at the beginning of the instructions in verse 3 ("remember") and at the end in verse 9 ("remind you"). Unlike pagan festivals in which the goal is to connect what is occurring in time (and therefore, insignificant) with what is recurring endlessly in the primeval realm (and therefore, significant), the Israelite festivals sought to connect present and future choices with past realities. In so doing, they laid the groundwork for historical thinking. The issue has nothing to do with the great cycles of nature that are called to our attention by the return of spring. Everything here has to do with the deliverance from the cycle of bondage and death which God effected once for all in the world of human events (13:3-4, 8-9).

As indicated in the notes above (13:9, 16), the reference in verse 9 (and again in 13:16) to "a mark branded on your hand or your forehead," when taken in conjunction with the command in Deuteronomy 6:8 (also Deut 11:18), gave rise in intertestamental Judaism to the practice of phylacteries (small boxes holding a portion of Scripture tied on the backs of the hands and foreheads). This seems like another example of giving prominence to the "letter" of the law, rather than the spirit (Rom 2:29). While the command in Deuteronomy can be interpreted as having a literal intent, the statements here are much more difficult to take in that way. Surely the point is that both our thinking (forehead) and our actions (hands) ought to be continually shaped by the realization that we are people whom God has redeemed to himself (cf. Isa 44:1-5).

The second set of symbolic actions designed not to let the Israelites forget who they were has to do with the sacrifice of the firstborn (13:11-16). Here the connection to the Exodus events is made explicit. It is because the Lord "killed all the firstborn males" in Egypt (13:15) that the Israelites were commanded to redeem their firstborn. Sarna (1991:65) suggests that there may also have been a desire to disassociate from the pagan idea of the intrinsic holiness of the firstborn, but the precise reasoning is not made clear. The expression "they belong to him" (13:12) might suggest that as the children were redeemed on that first Passover night, so firstborn children must forever after be redeemed. But the chief point is once again to provide a mechanism for the Israelites when they are in Canaan to remember how it was that they had gotten there (13:11, 14-15). The reference to "children" in 13:14 underscores this concern. Israel would have a future, and God was concerned about the shape of that future. Although the people might fall into the trap of thinking that the receipt of the Promised Land was the end of the story, it was not. God was concerned to establish his kingdom in the hearts of human beings, and that could only happen if Israel retained an accurate understanding of the revelation that had been given to them at the outset of their national existence.[7]

Israel's Wilderness Detour (13:17-22). In these verses we receive the final information to prepare us for the climactic Exodus event: the crossing of the sea. Here we see the final realization of what Moses had been asking of Pharaoh: "Let the people go" (13:17). This "sending out" (*shalakh* [TH7971, ZH8938]) was what God had promised to Moses in the beginning (3:20) and what Pharaoh had steadfastly refused to do (5:2; 8:32; 9:7), making it a clear contest between himself and God. But now the contest was over; God was right and Pharaoh was wrong.

Here we learn why the crossing of the sea was even necessitated. God did not take the Israelites on "the shortest route," which was along the Mediterranean coast, and eventually "through Philistine territory" (13:17).[8] This road was guarded by Egyptian fortresses and would have been easily accessible to the large forces of chariotry available to Pharaoh. Thus, the Israelites would have been put in a position of having to mount a military defense immediately, before they were in a position to do so (13:18). However, as valid as that reason for another road might be, there was clearly something else at work, for just as God later defeated the Amalekites at the hand of Israel (17:8-13), he certainly could have done the same to the Egyptians. But that later event was on the other side of the crossing of the sea. And however poorly the Hebrews sometimes seemed to draw the appropriate conclusions from the crossing, the experience of the crossing did make them able to receive God's miraculous defense against the Amalekites in ways that might not have been possible without such a faith-building event.

God maneuvered his people into a place where they could do nothing else but trust him. He led them on "a roundabout way" (13:18) to experience the most significant event in all of biblical faith next to the resurrection of Jesus Christ. This context of faith is referred to in an interesting way in 13:19. Many years earlier, Joseph had manifested the faith that we now think of as typical of him. As recorded in the last paragraph of the book of Genesis, Joseph had expressed the faith that God would keep his promises to the patriarchs and would not leave their descendants in Egypt (Gen 50:24-26). Further, in a statement quoted here, he had asked that the delivered people take his bones with them when God took them out to Canaan. In recounting this incident and his fulfillment of Joseph's request, Moses was making it absolutely explicit that upcoming events—the crossing of the sea and the departure from Egypt—were a fulfillment of historical prophecy and of God's historical plan. If all of this is an ingenious fiction created in postexilic Judah in the fifth century BC, as is said in some scholarly circles today, it is beyond remarkable. If God does not work in human history with a sustained purpose and a predictable goal, there is no satisfactory explanation for where the Jewish people got the idea that he does.

Finally, we learn how the people were led to the sea (13:20-22). The Egyptians might think the Hebrews were wandering around confused (see 14:3), but that was not the case; they were led by God. The verb "went ahead" (13:21) is a participle which suggests customary action. God was continually going before his people. There is God's immanence: He is continually present for us. But who is it that is present? As Sarna (1991:70) suggests, the miraculous imagery here is designed to make it clear that God transcends the limits of time and space and thus of human imagining. Attempts to give explanations that correspond to natural phenomena are unconvincing. The God who is beyond nature has broken into nature and has utilized some of its elements to make it plain that he can deliver people from all the bondages inherent in fallen nature. Fire is illustrative of God throughout Scripture.[9] Its mystery and yet its comfort, its power to devastate and yet to bless, to destroy and also to cleanse—all these qualities and more make it an apt symbol of him. So also throughout Scripture God is associated with clouds.[10] In their majesty and variety, in their revealing and concealing of the heavens, in the blessing of the rain that falls from them, they speak of the character of God. Thus, it is significant that Jesus was received into the clouds (Acts 1:9) and will come again in the clouds (Rev 1:7). He is the ultimate manifestation of the presence of the transcendent one among his people.

ENDNOTES
1. It is difficult for us in the West, where numbers are understood almost completely in a literal sense, to realize that in the ancient world, this was not the case. The qualitative sense of numbers was at least as important as their literal meaning (e.g., the idea of seven as the "perfect" number, etc.). The difficulty comes in trying to determine

when a number is used in one sense or the other. The interpreter has to keep both possibilities constantly in mind. Another example in this passage is the number "430" (12:40-41). The Septuagint, quoted in Gal 3:17, takes it that there were 430 years from the promise to Abraham until the Exodus. Ibn Ezra (Sarna 1991:62-63) says that there were 215 years from Haran to Egypt and then 215 years in Egypt. The same kind of patterning can be seen in the genealogy of Jesus in Matt 1, with 14 generations from Adam to David and 14 generations from David to Jesus. This is not to say that the numbers are merely fanciful or intended to mislead. It is only to say that we must not impose our system upon theirs as we seek to understand the truth being conveyed.
2. Cassuto (1967:149) considers 12:43-49 and 13:1-16 to be "appendices." But most other commentators, even those who do not consider these to have been part of the original narrative, agree that these segments are directly related to the theological purpose of the narrative as it now stands. Enns's comment is apropos: "The theology of this narrative will not allow us to separate the departure from Egypt from the rituals that remind the people of the lasting significance of that event" (2000:256).
3. The fact that some of the customs and practices associated with Passover show similarities with those practiced elsewhere in the ancient Near East, and the fact that the celebration occurred at the same time as some of the New Year's festivals celebrated in the surrounding cultures, has led some scholars to argue that the Bible is simply giving a fictitious explanation for a preexisting religious rite. Houtman (1993.2:157) is correct when he says that while the evidence does point to the adaptation of certain existing customs and symbols, the fundamentally different explanation of the practices argues against mere adoption of a pagan festival.
4. One cannot help but be grateful for Childs's insistence that this interpretive material is as significant as the reports of the events themselves. He says (1974:203-204) that event and interpretation cannot be separated. However, given his serious doubts about the validity of the historic reportage, the affirmation rings somewhat hollow. Can we have interpretation without event?
5. For other biblical discussions of the Hebrew festivals, see 23:10-19; 34:18-26; Lev 23:4-8; Num 28:16-25; Deut 16:1-8; Ezra 6:19-22; Ezek 45:21-24.
6. Many scholars, holding the view that Israel's religion simply emerged from paganism and that the patriarchal and Exodus narratives are fictional explanations, argue that Passover was a festival of herders while Unleavened Bread was a festival of farmers and that their conjunction was the result of the two groups merging. Apart from the fact that there is no evidence in support of such a merger in Israelite history, the thoroughgoing nature of the reinterpretation that supposedly took place strains credulity too far. So, for instance, there is no reference whatsoever here to any overtones of an agricultural festival.
7. For further discussion of the sacrifice of the firstborn, see Deut 15:19-23.
8. Since, according to extrabiblical evidence, the Philistines did not settle in their traditional territory on the coast southwest of Israel until the thirteenth century BC, this statement is usually said to be anachronistic, reflecting a later period. However, the references to Philistines in the Abraham and Isaac narratives (Gen 21, 26) might indicate that the ancestors of the later Philistines actually came from this area before a migration westward to Cyprus and Crete and an eventual return (see Gordon 1965:206). Cassuto (1967:155), reflecting on these same biblical data, suggests that "the way of the Philistines" was not the coast road but the way up the middle of the Sinai peninsula, through Beersheba, where the Philistines of Genesis were located.

God took the people on neither of those roads but on the southern one, he says, away from all population.
9. 24:17; Gen 15:17; Deut 4:24; 5:25-26; 9:3; 1 Kgs 18:24; 2 Kgs 1:10, 12; Job 1:16; Ps 50:3; Isa 33:14.
10. 40:34; Deut 33:26; Pss 18:11; 68:4, 33-34; 104:3.

◆ b. Crossing the sea (14:1-31)

Then the LORD gave these instructions to Moses: ²"Order the Israelites to turn back and camp by Pi-hahiroth between Migdol and the sea. Camp there along the shore, across from Baal-zephon. ³Then Pharaoh will think, 'The Israelites are confused. They are trapped in the wilderness!' ⁴And once again I will harden Pharaoh's heart, and he will chase after you.* I have planned this in order to display my glory through Pharaoh and his whole army. After this the Egyptians will know that I am the LORD!" So the Israelites camped there as they were told.

⁵When word reached the king of Egypt that the Israelites had fled, Pharaoh and his officials changed their minds. "What have we done, letting all those Israelite slaves get away?" they asked. ⁶So Pharaoh harnessed his chariot and called up his troops. ⁷He took with him 600 of Egypt's best chariots, along with the rest of the chariots of Egypt, each with its commander. ⁸The LORD hardened the heart of Pharaoh, the king of Egypt, so he chased after the people of Israel, who had left with fists raised in defiance. ⁹The Egyptians chased after them with all the forces in Pharaoh's army—all his horses and chariots, his charioteers, and his troops. The Egyptians caught up with the people of Israel as they were camped beside the shore near Pi-hahiroth, across from Baal-zephon.

¹⁰As Pharaoh approached, the people of Israel looked up and panicked when they saw the Egyptians overtaking them. They cried out to the LORD, ¹¹and they said to Moses, "Why did you bring us out here to die in the wilderness? Weren't there enough graves for us in Egypt? What have you done to us? Why did you make us leave Egypt? ¹²Didn't we tell you this would happen while we were still in Egypt? We said, 'Leave us alone! Let us be slaves to the Egyptians. It's better to be a slave in Egypt than a corpse in the wilderness!'"

¹³But Moses told the people, "Don't be afraid. Just stand still and watch the LORD rescue you today. The Egyptians you see today will never be seen again. ¹⁴The LORD himself will fight for you. Just stay calm."

¹⁵Then the LORD said to Moses, "Why are you crying out to me? Tell the people to get moving! ¹⁶Pick up your staff and raise your hand over the sea. Divide the water so the Israelites can walk through the middle of the sea on dry ground. ¹⁷And I will harden the hearts of the Egyptians, and they will charge in after the Israelites. My great glory will be displayed through Pharaoh and his troops, his chariots, and his charioteers. ¹⁸When my glory is displayed through them, all Egypt will see my glory and know that I am the LORD!"

¹⁹Then the angel of God, who had been leading the people of Israel, moved to the rear of the camp. The pillar of cloud also moved from the front and stood behind them. ²⁰The cloud settled between the Egyptian and Israelite camps. As darkness fell, the cloud turned to fire, lighting up the night. But the Egyptians and Israelites did not approach each other all night.

²¹Then Moses raised his hand over the sea, and the LORD opened up a path through the water with a strong east wind. The wind blew all that night, turning the seabed into dry land. ²²So the people

of Israel walked through the middle of the sea on dry ground, with walls of water on each side!

²³Then the Egyptians—all of Pharaoh's horses, chariots, and charioteers—chased them into the middle of the sea. ²⁴But just before dawn the LORD looked down on the Egyptian army from the pillar of fire and cloud, and he threw their forces into total confusion. ²⁵He twisted* their chariot wheels, making their chariots difficult to drive. "Let's get out of here—away from these Israelites!" the Egyptians shouted. "The LORD is fighting for them against Egypt!"

²⁶When all the Israelites had reached the other side, the LORD said to Moses, "Raise your hand over the sea again. Then the waters will rush back and cover the Egyptians and their chariots and charioteers." ²⁷So as the sun began to rise, Moses raised his hand over the sea, and the water rushed back into its usual place. The Egyptians tried to escape, but the LORD swept them into the sea. ²⁸Then the waters returned and covered all the chariots and charioteers—the entire army of Pharaoh. Of all the Egyptians who had chased the Israelites into the sea, not a single one survived.

²⁹But the people of Israel had walked through the middle of the sea on dry ground, as the water stood up like a wall on both sides. ³⁰That is how the LORD rescued Israel from the hand of the Egyptians that day. And the Israelites saw the bodies of the Egyptians washed up on the seashore. ³¹When the people of Israel saw the mighty power that the LORD had unleashed against the Egyptians, they were filled with awe before him. They put their faith in the LORD and in his servant Moses.

14:4 Hebrew *after them.* 14:25 As in Greek version, Samaritan Pentateuch, and Syriac version; Hebrew reads *He removed.*

NOTES

14:2 Pi-hahiroth . . . Migdol . . . Baal-zephon. Despite extensive study, the location of these places remains unknown. It now seems clear that Eissfeldt's location of Baal-zephon near Lake Sirbonis on the Mediterranean coast is untenable. For careful analysis of all the data, see Hoffmeier 1996:182-191.

the sea. This is the "Sea of Reeds" referred to in 13:18 (see note).

14:4 *harden Pharaoh's heart.* See the discussion on 4:21.

14:7 *600 of Egypt's best chariots.* Sarna (1991:71) says that this was evidently a standard military unit, but Cassuto (1967:162) argues plausibly that this was a round number based on a sexagesimal arithmetic system.

commander. The Hebrew is *shalish* [TH7991B, ZH8957] (third). This term is a technical one that perhaps may have originally referred to the "third" man of a three-man chariot crew in northern Mesopotamia where the chariot probably originated. Egyptian chariots seem to have had only a two-man crew, but the term had moved beyond its original, literal connotation.

14:8 *fists raised in defiance.* The NLT correctly interprets the Hebrew figure of speech "with a high hand" (see also Num 15:30). The Israelites had not left the land as escaping fugitives but had gone out confidently.

14:9 *his charioteers.* In later portions of Scripture, this term, *parash* [TH6571A, ZH7305], refers to cavalrymen, but since cavalry was unknown in the Late Bronze period, the term is more correctly translated "charioteers" here.

14:12 *Didn't we tell you this would happen.* It is not clear whether such an incident actually had taken place but was not reported in the text, or whether, as seems more likely, this is something the people could have said and, now in the crisis, think of themselves as actually having said it.

14:13 see. The verb "see" is repeated three times in this verse, emphasizing the firsthand experience of the deliverance.

14:14 Just stay calm. This may not be strong enough for what is being said here. Numbers 30:4 and 2 Kgs 18:36, among other references, suggest that "keep quiet!" is the sense.

14:20 As darkness fell, the cloud turned to fire, lighting up the night. This is a possible interpretation of the difficult Hebrew, which says literally, "There was the cloud and the darkness and it lighted (?) the night." Sarna (1991:73) takes the verb "lighted" (*'or* [TH215, ZH239]) to be an error for the verb *'arar* [TH779, ZH826] "to curse" and reads "it cast a spell on the night." But there is no support for this reading in other mss or versions. The LXX reads "and there was darkness and blackness and the night passed." The KJV reading (followed by NIV) "it was darkness (to them), but it gave light (to these)" does not seem warranted.

14:24 just before dawn. This is an apt translation of *'ashmoreth haboqer* [TH821/1242A, ZH874/1332] (the early morning watch)—i.e., from about 2:00 a.m. to 6:00 a.m.

the pillar. Cassuto (1967:169) notes correctly that there is no definite article in the Hebrew and concludes that the author was differentiating this pillar from the one referred to in 13:21 and 14:19 and speaking of a thunderstorm. However, the fact that the text calls this (lit.) "a pillar of fire and cloud," using the same terms used for "*the* pillar," seems to argue against him.

14:25 he twisted their chariot wheels. As NLT mg notes, the Hebrew verb here is *sur* [TH5493, ZH6073] ("he removed" or "he turned aside"), which is very difficult to make sense of. The Samaritan Pentateuch has *'asar* [TH631, ZH673], meaning "he bound up, tied up," and this is supported by LXX and Syriac. This seems to be the more probable reading. Perhaps a better contemporary rendering would be "he clogged up [or locked up] their chariot wheels."

14:27 swept them. Cassuto (1967:171) points out that the literal sense of the verb is "to shake off" (used again of this incident in Ps 136:15, and only nine times elsewhere). See the commentary below on this verse.

14:31 They put their faith in the LORD and in his servant Moses. Fretheim (1991:160-161) comments that this speaks of the fearful responsibility to mirror God correctly that any agent of God has.

COMMENTARY

In this chapter we come to the climactic event of deliverance: the crossing of the sea. Here the contest for supremacy between Pharaoh and Yahweh reaches its climax with Pharaoh suffering a crushing defeat. Interestingly, there is not another mention of an Egyptian pharaoh in the Bible until the report in 1 Kings 9:16 that the Israelite king Solomon married the daughter of a pharaoh! But more than a revelation of Pharaoh's fallibility, this event was an unmistakable revelation of the character and nature of Yahweh: "After this the Egyptians will know that I am the LORD" (14:4).[1] But it was not only the Egyptians who recognized the power and faithfulness of God, it was also the Israelites (14:31). The poetic reflection on this event recorded in 15:1-21 is a powerful expression of the truth that the means of deliverance was a self-revelation of God. In delivering his people God displayed not merely his power but his very nature. Here is the culmination of "the mighty acts of God" that would shape the Hebrews' understanding of him and of themselves through all the years to come. They and their descendents forever after would be the people God led through the sea (Pss 78:13; 136:10-15; Isa 51:10; 63:12-14).

The Setting for the Crossing (14:1-20). The first part of the chapter describes the setting for the crossing. Since we do not know the precise location of the sites mentioned (see the notes above), it is not easy to determine precisely what took place. However, the general point is quite clear. After the people were on the way toward the Sinai wilderness, God had them make a "turn" toward "the sea" (14:2). As noted above, this "sea" was probably one of the Bitter Lakes in the southern Isthmus of Suez. These lakes have this name because they were produced by an upwelling of salty water from the Gulf of Suez. Because of this fact, the level of the water in the lakes is influenced by the level of water in the Gulf. The reason for God's action is clear: He was setting up a situation in which Pharaoh would be tempted to think he could recoup his loss. In this way the confrontation between Pharaoh and Yahweh would be brought to a head: Either the Egyptian tyrant would be able to snatch the Israelites out of God's hand, or God would break the power of Pharaoh's hand. The Hebrew word for "hand" is repeated nine times in this chapter (14:8, 16, 21, 22, 26, 27, 29 [RSV], 30, 31) with the climactic occurrences in the last two verses, where it is said that God "rescued Israel from the hand of the Egyptians" with a display of "mighty power" (lit., "the great hand"). In this way Yahweh's true "glory" (14:4) would be demonstrated. In Hebrew, the word "glory" has connotations of weightiness, heaviness, or significance. Thus, in the final destruction of Pharaoh's power the world would get some glimpse of just how significant the God of Israel is. He is not some small tribal deity but the God who triumphs over the greatest of earth's deified monarchs and uses even the mighty sea, the symbol of the powers of chaos to the pagans, to do it. Nor was this merely a power struggle. Pharaoh had imprisoned these people against their will and had attempted to use genocide to keep them imprisoned. Now, having apparently lost them, he intended to use military might to re-imprison them. Thus, this is a conflict between human wickedness and the divinely-ordained moral order. The destruction of wickedness demonstrates the triumph of that moral order to the glory of the Creator (see also 14:17-18.)

The vignette in 14:5 illustrates again the subtleties in human motivation. Why did Pharaoh pursue the Israelites? If verses 4 and 8 are taken by themselves, the answer to that question is very simple: God made Pharaoh do it by hardening his heart. But when 14:5 is taken into account, we see that the matter is not so simple. We are treated to a "morning-after" experience. Here the decision made "the night before" looks very different in the cold light of day. Several commentators, among them Enns (2000:271), suggest that this conversation took place after three days when it dawned on Pharaoh and his officials that the Hebrew slaves were not coming back. As I have said above, the text does not say that, and I see no reason to surmise it. It is merely that what seemed best to do as a frantic reaction to the death of the firstborn did not seem nearly as wise when some of the terror had worn off and the real results of losing a large part of the country's labor force began to become clear. In that situation, it was not God who made these people say to one another, "What have we done?" Rather it was their own lust for comfort, power, and dominance (How could the "defiance" [14:8] of these slaves be allowed to go unpunished?) that made them regret the earlier decision. To be sure, this pattern of behavior came out at this point because they had ingrained it into themselves earlier. Thus, although they might think themselves to be free, they were not; so in that sense it is true that God had hardened their hearts. But he did not make them do something that they themselves did not want to do or that was contrary to their normal behavior. What he did was to make it appear to them that they could get what they wanted for themselves, and given that appearance, the ingrained results of years of selfish living could not but express themselves in one more foolish attempt to defeat God.

Just as direct speech was used to express the change of heart on the part of the Egyptians, the narrator also used it to express the Israelites' change of heart (14:10-12). They too had a "morning-after" experience (the Egyptians: "What have we done?"; the Israelites: "What have you (Moses) done?"). They had been living in the euphoria of their new-found freedom and had obviously not considered the possible dangers and complications of this new life. Now in the cold light of day, they discovered that this new life was not going to be an easy one, and they were unprepared to face that fact. When we recognize that the verb "cried out" (14:10) is precisely the same one used at the beginning of this story in 2:23, we are tempted to think that nothing has changed at all. The sarcastic tone of the language underscores the level of their panic. Whatever else Egypt is known for, it is known for its graves (14:11), so if they had just come out to the desert to die anyway, why not stay there? Fretheim (1991:156) observes that this is a typical reaction to be expected from a recently liberated people who have had no opportunity to take responsibility for their own actions or learn to apply initiative in difficulties, and that is probably a fair point. At the same time, Enns (2000:273) also seems correct when he says that surely we can expect these people to have learned something from the plagues.[2] But the missing element was trust. And that issue will resurface again and again throughout the remainder of the wilderness journey. Are God's intentions toward us really good? Or, as the snake said in the garden, is God (like everyone else) looking out for his own interests and quite willing to use or abuse his creatures for those interests? What would happen in the next hours would go far toward demonstrating that at least God *can* be trusted (whether we will trust or not).

Verses 13 and 14 represent a shining hour for Moses. If no one else among the Israelites had learned the lessons of the first set of the events of deliverance, at least he had. We have no reason to think that he knew what God was going to do, but he had no fear that God was going to break his promise at this moment. Neither did he think for one moment, apparently, that God could be defeated. To a panicked people, rushing about aimlessly, gabbling like chickens, he shouted, "Don't be afraid. Stand still. Be calm." The issue was not in their hands or his but in God's, and Moses, for one, was quite content to leave it there. As Christ must have been so proud of Peter when he stepped out of the boat (Matt 14:29), so Yahweh must have been proud of Moses at this moment. But this makes verse 15 the more surprising. Why does God accuse Moses of *crying out* to him? Enns (2000:274) is almost certainly right when he says that Moses was the representative of the people. He did not exist in some individual bubble apart from them. If they were crying out, then in a real sense Moses was crying out too. But the other side of the coin also applies, and this is good news: If Moses was daring to believe, so were they, and they were shortly to enjoy the benefits of his faith.

As with Passover night a few days earlier, the Israelites were called upon to endure another portentous night (14:19-20). The mightiest army of that day was arrayed against them, armed with what was the ultimate weapon of the day, the light two-horsed chariot, carrying an archer armed with a powerful compound bow. Surely the morning would bring their destruction. Yet the word of God came to the Israelites: "Don't be afraid. Stand still. Stay calm." The symbolism seems obvious: Faith forever calls us to live through the nights of uncertainty and fear, with no assurance of a good outcome apart from the word of God and the signs of his presence. Now the cloud that had led them moved around to stand between them and the enemy. The text says that this was "the angel of God." Throughout the Bible this description expresses the reality of God as he is present in his world. As in Malachi 3:1-2, it is not clear where this "messenger" of God ends and God himself begins.[3] But the point here is that as God called his people to wait for the morning of deliverance, he did not leave them without protection and the evidence of his care.

Crossing the Sea (14:21-31). The stage has now been fully set, the players are at hand, and the action is ready to begin. Critics who have attempted to define the extent of the sources that supposedly lie behind the present text have emphasized the idea that one source had Moses as the central figure in what was essentially a fortuitous natural event (whose actual details were not clear), while the other source had God dividing the sea in two in a clear demonstration of supernatural power.[4] But that is not the case at all. What the text does, as Childs (1974:227-229) recognizes, is make quite clear that God regularly works through human agency. Moses raised his hand (14:21) and the sea parted. Moses raised his hand and the water rushed back (14:27). But Moses acted on the command of God (14:16, 26); it was God who did the work (14:21, 27; cf. Isa 63:12). The agent does not perform the work without the power and direction of God, but God does not accomplish his purposes except through the human agent. That has been at the heart of this book's theology from the beginning. God was the deliverer of his people, but he would not act except through a human agent. If we ask why this is so, perhaps we find one more clue to God's ultimate purpose in creation and redemption: to share with his creatures that self-giving, self-denying love he knows in his triune nature. Mere deliverance that did not involve human fellowship would hardly contribute to or exemplify that purpose.

Fretheim (1991:158) attempts to avoid discussion of the event by saying that it is "an impressionistic picture." But that will not do, and his metaphor makes that very point. There is no question that Monet, even in his most impressionistic works, was seeking to convey to his viewers his sense of an actual place. To be sure, Monet was not concerned to give us every detail, but it is unquestionable that his impressions are based on a reality external to himself. The same is true here. Although two readers may differ in their conclusions about the precise details of the events being narrated, the text clearly intends for us to believe that actual events did occur and that what is being said here is not a misrepresentation either of what took place or of the significance we are to draw from the events. Unlike myths, this narration is clearly concerned to root these events in one place on this planet and at one time in its history.

In fact, as Cassuto (1967:167-168) shows, it is possible, using the details given here, to arrive at a very comprehensive explanation of what took place.[5] Still, we do not need to agree that his is the only possible explanation of the details of the narrative, and indeed other plausible readings have been put forward. My point is to say that what is described here is not some fanciful tale taking place in "Never-Never-Land," from which we are expected to draw great theological truth. Moses was, either truthfully or fallaciously, encouraging us to draw certain theological conclusions from a series of events that he experienced—events that he neither imagined nor created. And the fact that the details he gives us can be understood easily enough as historic events is strong confirmation of his claims.

This insistence on the way in which the text intends for us to understand it is in no way to agree with the motive of "natural" explanations that are often put forward to explain away the direct involvement of God in these events. The extent, the timing, and the duration of what took place make it very clear that we are being told that the event was a miracle. God was intervening in the course of nature at a time and in a manner of his choosing. We are not talking about a handful of escaped slaves whose pursuers were frustrated when the dry ground across which the slaves had run was turned into a swamp by a fortuitous cloud-burst. We are being told of actual events in which the finest troops of ancient Egypt were destroyed when they tried to follow the Israelites through a sea that was divided and then rejoined by the power of God, an event that occurred when Moses, at the command of God, directed it to.

Verses 30 and 31 form a bridge between the prose account of the event of the crossing in 14:1-29 and the poetic reflection in 15:1-21. The recurrence of the verb "saw" in both verses is both a confirmation of Moses's prediction regarding the experience (14:13) and a further affirmation of the reality of the historical experience. They "saw" some things that proved God's dependability to them. The event did not create their "faith" (14:31), but neither was their faith merely a matter of wishful thinking for which they created the "metaphor" of a fictional experience. The event gave them good and sufficient reasons to believe the trustworthiness and the goodness of God, something they would not have believed without that experience.

ENDNOTES

1. See also 6:7; 7:5, 17; 8:10, 22; 9:14, 29; 10:2; 11:7; 14:18.
2. Enns goes on to say that the people had not learned that God's "purpose was not merely to save them, but to maintain his covenant tie to all people, past, present, and future." If, in saying that, he means that they did not realize God's covenant-making and covenant-keeping nature (and thus his innate trustworthiness), I agree.
3. See such other references as Gen 16:7-14; Num 22:22-36; Judg 6:11-24; 13:3-22.
4. Childs (1974:227-229), as is typical of his particular commentary, gives a lengthy discussion of the extent and character of the supposed sources here. But then he says that the final form has woven the two together in a skillful way that makes a wonderful theological point that neither can make alone, thereby demonstrating that event and interpretation cannot be separated. He makes this point to say that those who think the event was revelatory while the interpretation was not (such as G. E. Wright) were wrong. But surely when Childs is done, we are left with an inspiring interpretation that is based on a complete fictionalizing of an unrecoverable historical event.
5. In brief, Cassuto argues that the largest of the Bitter Lakes is divided into two deeper areas by a strip of land running between them underwater. The waters of the Reed Sea subsided, drawing the water down in the lake and leaving this strip of land exposed. A strong wind dried out the strip making it easily passable. After the Israelites had passed over it, the waters of the Reed Sea returned, with subsequent upwelling in the lake. The first evidence of this was when the strip of land became boggy, clogging the wheels of the chariots. Then as the waters returned more rapidly a storm arose ("a pillar of cloud and fire"; see the note on 14:24), and in the ensuing maelstrom, the Egyptians were "shaken off" (see the note on 14:27) the now submerged land bridge into the deeper waters. Again, the point is not to say that this is the only way in which the details can be explained but that since the details are susceptible to such a literal explanation they are not merely the product of fanciful imagination.

◆   ### 3. The song of the sea (15:1-21)

Then Moses and the people of Israel sang this song to the LORD:

"I will sing to the LORD,
  for he has triumphed gloriously;
he has hurled both horse and rider
  into the sea.
² The LORD is my strength and my song;
  he has given me victory.
This is my God, and I will praise him—
  my father's God, and I will exalt
  him!
³ The LORD is a warrior;
  Yahweh* is his name!
⁴ Pharaoh's chariots and army
  he has hurled into the sea.
The finest of Pharaoh's officers
  are drowned in the Red Sea.*
⁵ The deep waters gushed over them;
  they sank to the bottom like a stone.

⁶ "Your right hand, O LORD,
  is glorious in power.
Your right hand, O LORD,
  smashes the enemy.
⁷ In the greatness of your majesty,
  you overthrow those who rise
  against you.
You unleash your blazing fury;
  it consumes them like straw.
⁸ At the blast of your breath,
  the waters piled up!
The surging waters stood straight like
  a wall;

in the heart of the sea the deep
    waters became hard.
9 "The enemy boasted, 'I will chase them
    and catch up with them.
I will plunder them
    and consume them.
I will flash my sword;
    my powerful hand will destroy them!'
10 But you blew with your breath,
    and the sea covered them.
They sank like lead
    in the mighty waters.
11 "Who is like you among the gods,
    O LORD—
glorious in holiness,
awesome in splendor,
    performing great wonders?
12 You raised your right hand,
    and the earth swallowed our enemies.

13 "With your unfailing love you lead
    the people you have redeemed.
In your might, you guide them
    to your sacred home.
14 The peoples hear and tremble;
    anguish grips those who live in
      Philistia.
15 The leaders of Edom are terrified;
    the nobles of Moab tremble.
All who live in Canaan melt away;
16   terror and dread fall upon them.
The power of your arm
    makes them lifeless as stone
until your people pass by, O LORD,
    until the people you purchased pass
      by.
17 You will bring them in and plant them
    on your own mountain—
the place, O LORD, reserved for your
    own dwelling,
the sanctuary, O Lord, that your
    hands have established.
18 The LORD will reign forever and ever!"

19 When Pharaoh's horses, chariots, and charioteers rushed into the sea, the LORD brought the water crashing down on them. But the people of Israel had walked through the middle of the sea on dry ground! 20 Then Miriam the prophet, Aaron's sister, took a tambourine and led all the women as they played their tambourines and danced. 21 And Miriam sang this song:

"Sing to the LORD,
    for he has triumphed gloriously;
he has hurled both horse and rider
    into the sea."

15:3 *Yahweh* is a transliteration of the proper name *YHWH* that is sometimes rendered "Jehovah"; in this translation it is usually rendered "the LORD" (note the use of small capitals).   15:4 Hebrew *sea of reeds*; also in 15:22.

NOTES

15:1 rider. While this translation is literally correct, Sarna (1991:77) suggests the Hebrew word *rokeb* should be translated "driver" since the "rider" is not on horseback but in a chariot.

15:2 The LORD. In Hebrew, this is the abbreviated name *yah* [TH3050, ZH3363], which is used elsewhere in poetry (e.g., Ps 68:18[19]; Isa 12:2). It occurs most frequently in the call to praise: *halelu-yah* [TH1984A/3050, ZH2146/3363] (Praise the LORD).

song. There is considerable disagreement over the correct translation of this word (*zimrath* [TH2172/6, ZH2379]). A number of recent commentators (Cassuto and Childs, but not Houtman) have suggested that a homonym meaning "help, strength, defense" is intended (see Childs 1974:242 for the sources of the discussion). The versions are divided, with LXX and Syriac supporting "defense" (or something like it) and Vulgate supporting "song." Without compelling evidence to the contrary, it seems best to remain with "song."

15:3 Yahweh. Although the NLT does not use the personal name of God everywhere it occurs and most often substitutes "the LORD" where the name appears in the text (a reflection of a convention used in traditional Judaism), in this instance and a few others where the name itself is emphasized, the translators have broken with custom and used it (see note on 3:14).

15:6 The Hebrew exhibits a feature of early Canaanite poetry here, so-called "incremental parallelism," in which the second line of the parallel structure completes the thought of the first. Thus, a literal translation would be "Your right hand, O LORD, glorious in strength, your right hand, O LORD, smashes the enemy."

glorious. The Hebrew word has the connotations of "majestic, mighty, awe-inspiring."

15:8 *became hard.* The sense of the word is "to thicken," or "condense."

15:9-10 The Hebrew contains no conjunctions in these two verses. Thus, a staccato effect is produced as the enemy (15:9) boastfully declares what he will do, and the Lord (15:10) instantly negates his declarations.

destroy. The most common meaning of the word *yarash* [TH3423, ZH3769] is "to possess, dispossess." In fact, of all the occurrences of the word (232), only here and possibly in Num 14:12 does BDB translate it with "destroy." Thus, the point may be that Pharaoh thinks he is going to regain possession of his former slaves. (The LXX reads "gain control over them.")

15:11 *glorious in holiness.* Houtman (1993:2.286) believes that this line should be read "glorious among the holy ones"—i.e., the gods—and he cites Ps 89:6-7 [7-8]. However, the parallel here "awesome in splendor" argues that the Hebrew text is correct as is, and the ancient versions support the MT.

15:12 *earth.* This seems strange when it was drowning that claimed the Egyptian hosts. However, in the OT "earth" can sometimes refer to the underworld or the grave (Jonah 2:6), and that is probably the sense here.

15:13 *unfailing love.* This term (*khesed* [TH2617, ZH2876]), occurring about 250 times in the OT, and so far not attested in any other Semitic language, is one of the premier expressions of the nature and character of Yahweh. There is no single English word that encompasses all the connotations of *khesed*. Thus, it is translated with words like "mercy," "grace," "love," "goodness," "kindness," "loving-kindness," "steadfast love," "unfailing love," and several more. The basic idea is the passionate loyalty of a superior to an inferior, especially when it is undeserved.

15:16 *purchased.* This is a fine translation of the verb *qanah* [TH7069/B, ZH7864], but this verb also has the connotation "to create for oneself," very similar to the modern English expression "to create wealth." As it is used in Deut 32:6, the word means that God brought this people into existence.

15:17 *O LORD . . . O Lord.* The first of these is the divine name *yhwh* [TH3068, ZH3378] (represented in NLT by "LORD" in small capitals; see the notes above on 15:2 and 15:3), but the second, in what seems like a completely synonymous usage, is the word *'adonay* [TH136, ZH151] (Lord). Sarna (1991:82) suggests this may be so that *yhwh* occurs exactly 10 times in the poem. But it is also possible that this is simply a poetic variation between the two lines.

COMMENTARY

This poem, in every sense a psalm,[1] has become one of the centerpieces of Jewish worship.[2] It was influential in early Israelite religion, with verse 2 being quoted verbatim in Psalm 118:14 and Isaiah 12:2. As a poetic reflection on what Yahweh had done at the sea and upon the implications of those acts, it is without peer as a lyrical expression of his love, his power, and his ultimate purposes for his people.[3] As such, it is easy to understand why it became the core of Israel's expressions of faith. In the same way, the hymnody of the Christian church is an ongoing testimony to the power that theological truth gains when it is linked to rhythm and melody. The music of the book of Revelation suggests that this is because in some sense our earthly music reflects a musical reality that transcends time and space, a reality that will be expressed eternally in heaven.

There is no agreement about the specific structure of the psalm beyond the general acceptance that verses 1-12 look backward, while 13-18 look forward. However, I believe that careful examination of verses 1-12 reveals two stanzas, the first being verses 1-5, "My Saving God," and the second being verses 6-12, "You and Them." The opening five verses are an affirmation of personal faith in God (cf. 14:31), centering on the first-person pronouns in verse 2. In verses 6-12 Yahweh is no longer addressed in the third person (as in verses 1-5) but in the second person with continuing contrast between him and his enemies. This second-person address continues through the remainder of the poem until the climactic declaration in verse 18, but the focus has shifted after verse 12 from the enemies of the past to the enemies of the future and their inability to frustrate God's ultimate purpose in the Exodus for his people.[4]

The First Stanza (15:1-5). As noted above, these opening verses of the poem constitute a statement of personal testimony. Moses and the people[5] sing about their realized faith. The first-person language of verse 2 is telling. Yahweh is no longer an abstraction, and neither is he merely the god of their ancestors, nor is he the god of their collected clans. Now he is "my God" (15:2). Each of the Israelites has seen the Lord act on his or her behalf and claims him as his or her own. This is not the almost-pathological individualism of early twenty-first century American evangelicalism, but neither is God merely a vaguely conceived "force for good" as seems true for many "mainline" Protestants. The Lord is the God of Israel. Each Israelite knows the personal reality of a God who is the source of "strength," "song," and "victory" (15:2). If God cannot be known personally, if he does not take a personal interest in each of our lives, then the world is a dark place. But in fact, he does take such an interest, and that means that in the end there is nothing in the world that can finally conquer us.

This is what is meant when Moses calls God a "warrior" in 15:3. There is nothing in Scripture, when it is taken as a whole in both its testaments, to suggest that God is warlike by nature, that he is fierce and aggressive, finding his identity in military destruction. In fact, the promises of his final kingdom are marked by promises of the end of warfare (Ps 46:9; Isa 9:4-5; 11:6-9; 65:25; Rev 21:24–22:5). No, God is a "warrior" only in defense of his people (cf. Isa 63:1-6) because of the evil in the world. He is implacably opposed to that which defies his created order, as Pharaoh did, and which would destroy his creatures, as Pharaoh intended to do. Thus, across the ages, believers have taken great comfort in the belief that God was fighting on their behalf.

Fretheim (1991:168) makes a great deal of the song's supposed use of "creation theology." The general point is well-taken: God is the creator, this is his world, and he rules it for the sake of his people. This emphasis is in reaction to a theology that suggests that the world is an evil place, under the dominion of the evil one, that to be "saved" is simply to be delivered from this evil world, and that the believer has no obligation to work for justice and righteousness in this world. Surely this song will have none of that. While there are things in the world that stand in defiance to God, they cannot defeat him. He will overcome them with ease, and in love he will establish his people in the world as the very stones of his sanctuary (1 Pet 2:5).

While Fretheim rightly sees overtones of ancient Near East myth in this psalm, he goes too far when he says that the Bible utilizes not merely the language but the outlook of myth: Yahweh, like Marduk or Baal, has defeated the sea monster of chaos in the primeval realm and has established his creation order upon the body of the monster. So Fretheim says the Hebrews, like the Babylonians or the Canaanites, in telling this story of dubious historical worth, sought to bring the primeval reality into their national existence so as to give that existence some enduring meaning. He says, "It is precisely because what happens here is cosmic that it has universal effect" (1991:168). Again he says, "The historical victory is real because it participates in the cosmic victory" (1991:169). In fact, the very opposite is the case. There is no cosmic victory apart from the historical one. It is true that there are places in the Old Testament where God's victory at the sea is described in the language of the myths (though as Cassuto [1967:179] points out, never in the Torah). A classic example is found in Isa 51:9-10:

> Awake, awake, put on strength,
>   O arm of the LORD!
> Awake, as in days of old,
>   the generations of long ago!
> Was it not you who cut Rahab in pieces,
>   who pierced the dragon?
> Was it not you who dried up the sea,
>   the waters of the great deep;
> who made the depths of the sea a way
>   for the redeemed to cross over? (NRSV)

Rahab was a name given to the mythical sea monster that represented chaos, but the name is used here poetically to refer to Egypt, as can be seen from the lines following it, which refer to the Exodus event (See also Ps 87:4 and Isa 30:7). Thus, the NLT rendering of the fifth and sixth lines with the idea "you slew Egypt, the dragon of the Nile" is accurate. Note that there is no appeal to some "cosmic" victory in the passage at all. Rather, the hope of a new exodus from Babylon rests solely upon the *historical* event that happened in time and space. The *language* of myth is used, just as we might call some strong man of our acquaintance "a real Hercules," or say that someone "moved heaven and earth," but it is used without any appeal to the worldview of myth whatsoever. When the Hebrews allude to myth, what they are actually saying is, "Do you want to know when chaos was really conquered? It was conquered in time and space at the Reed Sea! And do you want to know what chaos is? It is human oppression and evil, not some cosmic entity inherent in the stuff of matter!"[6] The Bible is saying the very opposite of what Fretheim wants it to say. *It is saying that because God really intervened in human history the cosmos is different!* And that is climactically true in the historical events to which the Passover and the Exodus pointed: the crucifixion and the resurrection of Jesus Christ.

The Second Stanza (15:6-12). The note of personal testimony continues in this second stanza, as God is addressed throughout in the second person. The people feel an intimacy with God that they had not felt previously. Now, having been put into a situation where they could not help but trust him, they have a sense of his personal reality that they did not have before. The same sense appears in Isaiah 12, as well as in Ezra 9:6-15. It also appears in passages from the New Testament such as Acts 4:24-30. The people recount their experience: Pharaoh refused to "unleash" (*shalakh* [TH7971, ZH8938], "let go, send") us, so you unleashed your "blazing fury" on him (15:7). You gave a "blast" from your nostrils, and the sea stood up like whipped cream![7]

The artistry of the powerful contrast in verses 9 and 10 is impressive. The enemy boasts in a staccato succession of first-person verbs about what he will do. God had merely to do one thing, blow with his breath, and it was all over. All Pharaoh's vain claims were rendered as inert as "lead" sinking to the bottom of the sea. The conclusion is inescapable: There is none like Yahweh. He is another order of being from anything this world might bring forth. That is the point of the phrase "glorious in holiness." The "holy" is that which is other. Thus the pagans called their gods "holy" because the gods expressed what was outside ordinary human experience. But what the Old Testament writers say to us is that those things—deified and anthropomorphized natural and social forces—are not other at all! They are a part of the cosmos just as we are. Israel, however, had been confronted by one who is *truly* other! He is not this world and is no part of it. He cannot be manipulated through it and cannot be represented by anything in it. He alone is exalted ("triumphed gloriously," 15:1), and anyone or anything that exalts itself against him ("rise against you," 15:7) is doomed to failure. Thus, I think both Sarna (1991:79) and Enns (2000:299-300) are both correct when they assert seemingly contradictory ideas: Sarna says that the expression "Who is like you among the gods" does not imply recognition of other divine beings, and he cites the explicit denial in Deuteronomy 4:39 as support. Enns, on the other hand, says that the phrase can only imply such a recognition. I think Enns is correct that the Hebrews recognized other divine beings as objects of belief for the people around them. But I believe Sarna is correct that Moses and later Israelite leaders recognized that those things were not in the same category as Yahweh. He was another kind of being altogether. This is what Hezekiah says in his prayer in Isaiah 37:19: "[The Assyrians] have thrown the gods of these nations into the fire. . . . They were not gods at all." Do things that people call "gods" exist? Yes. Are they in any way comparable to Yahweh? Not in the least. And in fact, if Yahweh defines the category "god," then there are no others. He alone is holy.

The Third Stanza (15:13-18). In the world of paganism, there is nothing new. Everything that will happen has happened, and everything that has happened will happen. Life here and now is simply a dim reflection of the endless circle of cosmic reality. To all of that, the Bible replies with a profound "no." God has broken into time and space and has done something that has never happened before and will never happen again. The implications of this earth-shaking event will shape the future. Will these events, partaking of some endless cosmic cycle, precondition the future so that things will have to happen in a recurrence of this event? Never. Yahweh is the creator, and his human creatures are in his image. Thus, just as he responds to events in responsible and creative ways, so may we. But it is God's intention that the revelation of himself that was accomplished in the events of deliverance from Egypt will forever shape the responses of his people. Thus, it seems to me that to say that this discussion of the future implications of the Exodus event could only have been written after those implications had been realized is to miss the thrust of all of biblical thinking. Humans have real choices to make, and those choices have consequences. God has broken into our experience in order to redeem those choices and to change the consequences. In this stanza, through Moses his prophet, on the bank of the sea, God explores what the continuing choice of faith over disbelief would mean in terms of future consequences.

There are two consequences and one conclusion outlined here. The first consequence is the leadership of God and its ultimate goal (15:13, 17). God has displayed his *khesed* [TH2617, ZH2876] (NLT, "unfailing love") in this great deliverance (see note on 15:13). He has displayed a passionate, undeserved loyalty to his people. Why has he done this? Merely because he had compassion on their suffering? No, rather because he understood their problem was not merely bondage. Their problem was that they did not know him and, as sinful humans, were alienated from him. That realization is apparent in his promises to Abraham, Isaac, and Jacob. So God's *khesed* must issue in a shepherd's care ("lead," "guide," 15:13) that will bring the people to the ultimate solution to their (and our) problem. He must bring them to his own "sacred home" (15:13), his "own mountain," his "own dwelling," his "sanctuary" (15:17).

Commentators disagree over whether Sinai, Canaan, or the Jerusalem temple is intended by these terms. I believe the answer to all of them is "yes" (so also Enns 2000:300). Many years later it would be made clear that God's purpose in delivering his people from Babylon was that all the world might one day, like the Israelites, know the joy of living in intimate fellowship with God (Isa 66:18-23). The same point (deliverance as a means to intimate fellowship with God) found here is seen in the very structure of the book of Exodus (see the Introduction). What is the climax of the book? It is the glory of the Lord filling the Tabernacle in the center of the Israelite camp at Sinai (40:34-35). But the Tabernacle was not to be the only symbol of the reality. In a real sense, the Promised Land itself was to be the symbol, with Jerusalem and the Temple in the center of it all. This fellowship with God is a consequence of the deliverance at the sea.

A second consequence is the inescapable defeat of any people who would stand in opposition to God's plans for his people. If the might of Egypt was not able to stand against Yahweh's power, how could such peoples as the Philistines (15:14), the Moabites, the Edomites, or the Canaanites stand (15:15)? Just as the Egyptians had sunk in the waters "like a stone" (15:5), so also any future enemies would be as "lifeless as stone" (15:16). Again, it is unnecessary to think that the reference to these nations necessarily locates the writing of this part of the poem after the conquest. The entire experience of deliverance had been predicated upon God's promise to return his people to the Promised Land of Canaan. It would take only the most rudimentary knowledge of geography to know which peoples would likely oppose such a return. But what God had done at the sea showed that whoever might oppose his plan was in a hopeless situation (Josh 2:10).[8]

The conclusion to be drawn from what God had done in bringing his people through the sea is found in verse 18: "The LORD will reign forever and ever!" There is only one King in the universe, and that is Yahweh. Pharaoh had pretended he was the King, but that pretense had been revealed for what it was again and again through the plagues: Pharaoh had no more control over the cosmos than did the lowest of his peasants. His pretense had been dealt a death blow at the Sea of Reeds. Pharaoh had dared to challenge Yahweh in a head-to-head duel for control of God's people, and the result was not merely that Yahweh kept his people out of Pharaoh's hand (15:9); he had only to raise his own "right hand" (15:12) and all the power of Pharaoh was gone. Could any question remain as to who was king of the universe? Could any conceivable force rise in the future to contest his rule? Of course not. The hands that had defeated Pharaoh would create a "sanctuary" for Yahweh's people, and none of the petty kings of earth had a hope of frustrating that intention.

Conclusion of the Poem (15:19-21). After the prose coda of 15:19, these two verses give a bit of further information about the singing. There are basically two opinions about what is being said here. One opinion is that the women repeated the entire song, as indicated by the repetition of the first verse (cf. 15:1). Another opinion is that they repeated that first verse antiphonally after each succeeding verse (cf. Ps 136 for a possible example of such practice). In either case, two important points are made. This song of praise was for *all* the people, including both genders, and it was praise that was expressed by the *whole* person—the body as well as the spirit.

ENDNOTES
1. The song has defied all attempts by form critics to classify its form. It has characteristics of the "Song of Thanksgiving" and of the "Hymn of Praise" as well as two or three others, but it does not conform to any one. Clearly the theme is too all-inclusive and the joy too lyrical to be straitjacketed by formal considerations. On these forms, see Westermann 1981.
2. Sarna (1991:76) notes that during the intertestamental period, Levitical choirs sang it on Sabbath afternoons and that the practice was continued among Palestinian communities after the destruction of the Temple in AD 70. Eventually, the song came to be included in the daily morning service of Jews around the world.

3. The conjoining of prose and poetic accounts of the same event is known from Egyptian literature. But there the accounts are used to laud a human pharaoh. Here it is Yahweh alone who is praised. In the Bible, the other well-known conjunction of prose and poetic accounts of the same events is found in Judges 4–5.
4. Critical scholars, unable to accept the possibility of predictive prophecy, have long argued that the references to the future mean that all or part of the poem cannot be contemporary with the Exodus events. Enns (2000:301-305), conservative in many respects, has come to the same conclusion. Central to his argument is the odd variety in the verb tenses in the psalm. He believes that if verses 13-18 were written at the time of the Exodus all the verbs should be in the imperfect tense (incomplete action, thus usually treated as future tense in English translations). In fact, they are not. Some are imperfect and some are perfect (complete action, thus usually treated as past tense). But this is a deeply flawed argument. The verb tenses are mixed in the first part as well, and he has no problem construing all of those as past tense. In fact, there is good reason to believe that in the older forms of the Canaanite (Hebrew) dialect there was a past action form that was identical to what is now called the imperfect (the so-called *yqtl* preterite), and it is very possible that it is what is being utilized here. In fact, *all* the verbs refer to action that is complete (from God's point of view), including things that have not happened yet. Referring to future events as already complete is quite typical in Hebrew prophecy. Thus, it is still only on the basis of presuppositions about predictive prophecy that this poem can be taken out of the context of the Exodus events.
5. There is ongoing discussion as to the nature of the singing. It is generally thought that some sort of antiphony took place, perhaps with the women in one choir (thus explaining verses 20 and 21) and the men in another. However, there is simply not enough evidence to arrive at conclusions that convince everyone.
6. So Sarna (1991:82) says that the standard ancient Near Eastern expressions have been emptied of any mythic content.
7. Questions as to whether it was an "east wind" that blew or a "blast of your breath" are surely beside the point. This is poetry. What is to the point is that both the prose and poetic accounts insist on the same thing. Whatever happens in nature results from God's will and purpose. Matters of first, second, or third causes may be of concern to philosophers, but they are of little moment for the OT writers who are at pains to assert that nothing happens outside of the will and purposes of God.
8. Sarna (1991:81), believing the account was written after the conquest, is surprised no mention is made of Ammon, especially since the defeat of the Ammonite king Sihon, always figures prominently in accounts of the conquest. This omission is no surprise at all if the account was written before the conquest.

◆ II. Wilderness: A Revelation of Yahweh's Providential Care (15:22–18:27)
   A. Water at Marah (15:22-27)

²²Then Moses led the people of Israel away from the Red Sea, and they moved out into the desert of Shur. They traveled in this desert for three days without finding any water. ²³When they came to the oasis of Marah, the water was too bitter to drink. So they called the place Marah (which means "bitter").

²⁴Then the people complained and turned against Moses. "What are we going to drink?" they demanded. ²⁵So Moses cried out to the LORD for help, and

the LORD showed him a piece of wood. Moses threw it into the water, and this made the water good to drink.

It was there at Marah that the LORD set before them the following decree as a standard to test their faithfulness to him. ²⁶He said, "If you will listen carefully to the voice of the LORD your God and do what is right in his sight, obeying his commands and keeping all his decrees, then I will not make you suffer any of the diseases I sent on the Egyptians; for I am the LORD who heals you."

²⁷After leaving Marah, the Israelites traveled on to the oasis of Elim, where they found twelve springs and seventy palm trees. They camped there beside the water.

NOTES

15:22 led. Lit., "he made them journey." "Made them journey" is not a common expression in this context, and it has led some commentators, including early Jewish ones, to speculate that the Israelites were not eager to set off into the desert, perhaps because they were too busy gathering spoil from the bodies of the drowned Egyptians.

the desert of Shur. One meaning for the name is "wall," and this has led some commentators to suggest that the region was named for a defensive wall erected by the Egyptians at one point on the border between Egypt and the Sinai Peninsula (see Sarna 1991:84).

three days. Perhaps literal, but also a literary convention for any journey of more than two days but less than a week (see commentary).

15:25 a piece of wood. The Hebrew word can mean "branch," "stick," or even "tree." The LXX supports the NLT rendering.

the following decree. Lit., "a statute and a regulation." The NLT does two things: It takes the two terms as a hendiadys, as do about half the commentators, and it assumes that the following sentence is what is being referred to. The first decision is supportable, but the second is, in my judgment, more questionable. It is possible that some commandments we are not told about were given to them. Sarna (1991:85) notes that the rabbis thought it might have been the Sabbath laws, since the next chapter seems to presuppose some knowledge in that regard, but it is equally possible that a more general statement is being made (see commentary).

COMMENTARY

A new major section of the book starts at 15:22. The deliverance at the sea is over, and the people start off on the journey for the Promised Land. As I said in the Introduction, in one sense, this should be the end of the book, given its Greek name: "Exodus"—"the way out." The people were now out of Egypt, so the Exodus was over. But in fact, the story is far from ended and that leads us to question, "The way out of what? If they are out of Egypt, but not yet 'out,' what more is there to get out of?" The answer to that question explains not only the rest of the book, but the whole book. The problem Israel needed to get out of was not merely Egyptian bondage: They did not know God, and beyond that, they were not ready to experience his presence among them. This deeper problem explains why God did not take them directly to Canaan. Unless those problems were solved, entry into the land of Canaan would accomplish nothing toward God's ultimate purpose for Israel: to bless the world through the arrival of the Messiah and the offer of salvation to all. Exodus 15:22–18:27 is an integral step in the solution to those problems in that they draw the Hebrew people out of their theological darkness and begin to remove that which alienated them from the presence of God.

The plagues and the crossing of the sea had demonstrated the incomparable power of God and his unassailable sovereignty. On that basis, the people had faith in him and in Moses (14:31). Thus they knew that God *could* care for them. But *did* God care for them? They did not know. Maybe they had been merely a useful tool chosen to humiliate an arrogant human. If they were to go to another level of intimacy with God, they needed to know that he cared for them and could be depended upon to supply their needs. This is another of the reasons God led them as he did. Going this way, they would quickly come up against their own inability to care for themselves and supply their needs. And they would be in a position to learn of the depths of God's providential care. If they had come to Canaan never having learned these things, they would have been in no position to survive all the threats that that good land would present them with. One could wish that these lessons would have only had to be learned once, but that was not the case then, as it is not now. Here the lessons are taught, even if not learned, before Sinai; and in the book of Numbers (Num 11–17), they will be taught again, in part to a new generation.

There are really five incidents dealt with in this segment (15:22-27, bitter water; 16:1-36, no food; 17:1-7, no water; 17:8-16, enemies; 18:1-27, organization), and commentators differ on how to group them. Most do not include the final one (18:27) with the first four because there is no explicit statement about divine intervention. Others separate 17:8-16 because it does not include an occurrence of complaining by the people. However, it seems to me that all five belong together as examples of the various ways God provides. If he sometimes provides in miraculous ways in response to our pleadings (15:22–17:7), he also sometimes supplies through leadership (17:8-16), and he sometimes supplies through wise advice (18:13-27). But all are evidence of the providential care of God.

The Miracle at Marah (15:22-27). From the verb used in 15:22 (see note), it appears likely that the people were not eager to start into the wilderness. They had just experienced a moment of spiritual ecstasy, and like Peter many years later on the Mount of Transfiguration (Mark 9:5), it seems likely that they were inclined to camp there and to enshrine the great moment. They did not understand that the purpose of great moments is to prosper in and survive the succession of not-so-great moments that make up life. And one of those no-so-great moments was just before them. After several days of journeying (see note on 15:22 on "three days") "without finding any water," they finally came upon an oasis (15:23). After finally having found what they so desperately needed, their joy was dashed all the more when they discovered that the inviting water was impossible to drink. One also wonders if there were those among them who were remembering that after "three days," Moses had promised them a festival (5:1-3). Instead of a festival, there was this threat of imminent death.

The result of this fear and disappointment is the first example of a verb (translated in the NLT as "complained," 15:24) that is rather common in this section (chs 15–17) and also in Numbers 14–17 but hardly anywhere else in the Old Testament. Commentators differ over how best to translate it. Suggestions range from "grumble" to "complain" to "rage" largely depending on how serious the reaction is taken to be. In any case, the euphoria by the sea had now fully dissipated. As Houtman (1993:2.302) says, "At the Water of Death . . . the hymn of praise is silenced." While it is possible to understand the situation and the reaction of despair, the reader still wonders what happened to the faith that had so recently characterized the people. After all, they had seen the plagues; they had seen their own miraculous escape and the destruction of Pharaoh's army. Would it have taken so much to ask God to undertake this? And why turn *against Moses*? Perhaps one answer is the euphoria itself. The aphorism says, "The higher it rises, the farther it falls," and that seems to be true of the human spirit. The more elated we are, the more prone we are to become depressed when the elation wears off. As for turning against Moses, this is the first of many events in which the people seem unwilling to look beyond the human representative to the God who stands behind him. Moses did not lead them to this place, God did; Moses did not "create" them to be his people, God did. Confusing the reality and the representation makes life very difficult for the representative, but it also makes abiding faith in God more difficult.

Interestingly, God did not condemn the people for this behavior, which makes me less inclined to think "rage" (Houtman 1993:2.306) is the correct translation for the people's reaction. Instead, in response to Moses's cry "for help," God gave Moses instructions. The verb here is *yarah* [TH3384, ZH3723] (to cast, throw, instruct), which is the base for *torah* [TH8451, ZH9368] (instruction, Torah). Especially in view of what is said in 15:25b and 26 about the call for obedience, it seems likely that the verb is used intentionally here. God was going to instruct Moses and the people in the ways of life and health, spiritually, physically, and socially, and he was beginning at once. God instructed Moses, Moses obeyed, and the result was survival and health.[1]

This is the explanation for 15:25b-26. If Israel was ever to know God, it would only be through trust and obedience. In bringing Israel to this situation, God was beginning a series of critical tests: Would they, in "faithfulness" to him, learn to follow his instructions? Everything hung on this.[2] Note the succession of verbs in verse 26: "Listen carefully . . . do what is right . . . obeying . . . keeping." In Hebrew "to listen" (to instructions) is synonymous with "to do." One cannot truly "hear" and not "do." Thus, every one of these verbs has to do with performance growing out of trust. If Israel would not "hear" God, then God could not heal them. Here, at this stage in their development, God did not make far-flung promises about the outcome of their trust and obedience. Rather, he gave them a very concrete and immediately verifiable promise: If they would do what he commanded, they would experience a kind of physical health they had never known in Egypt (see v. 26). Is physical provision all God has in mind for his people, and is it an iron-clad promise, contingent on human faith? We must answer no to both. Just as the physical sacrifices were intended to represent a change in personal relations between God and humans, so this physical health, as real as it was, was intended to point to spiritual health. And just as Job, whose faith was superlative, experienced complete loss of health, so may we. We cannot "twist God's arm," as it were, and demand that physical symbols of spiritual reality always apply directly to ourselves. God intends to heal the human race, but that will not be finally accomplished in this physical world.

In the Masoretic Text, verse 27 is set off from verses 22-26 as part of the next section. However, in the chapter divisions created sometime in the early Christian centuries, it was included in chapter 15. Perhaps Enns (2000:324) is right when he says that "Elim" is presented here as a foretaste of Canaan. Yes, the desert would present many challenges to faith and obedience, but there was a blessed end to look forward to for those who would persevere.

ENDNOTES

1. Again it seems bootless to ask whether this "healing" of the water was "natural" or "supernatural." The point is that if God had not intervened with instruction, the people would have died of thirst. Since the Bible does not explain how the "stick of wood" functioned in the miracle, that question too is beside the point.
2. Note that 15:25 says, literally, "The Lord set a statute and a regulation before *him* to test *him*." Who is "him"? The NLT assumes Israel, but I suspect the object is Moses. Will Moses as the representative of the people receive instruction and faithfully obey? That would be a first step toward the goal.

◆ B. Manna and Quail from Heaven (16:1-36)

Then the whole community of Israel set out from Elim and journeyed into the wilderness of Sin,* between Elim and Mount Sinai. They arrived there on the fifteenth day of the second month, one month after leaving the land of Egypt.* ²There, too, the whole community of Israel complained about Moses and Aaron.

³"If only the LORD had killed us back in Egypt," they moaned. "There we sat around pots filled with meat and ate all the bread we wanted. But now you have brought us into this wilderness to starve us all to death."

⁴Then the LORD said to Moses, "Look, I'm going to rain down food from heaven for you. Each day the people can go out and pick up as much food as they need for that day. I will test them in this to see whether or not they will follow my instructions. ⁵On the sixth day they will gather food, and when they prepare it, there will be twice as much as usual."

⁶So Moses and Aaron said to all the people of Israel, "By evening you will realize it was the LORD who brought you out of the land of Egypt. ⁷In the morning you will see the glory of the LORD, because he has heard your complaints, which are against him, not against us. What have we done that you should complain about us?" ⁸Then Moses added, "The LORD will give you meat to eat in the evening and bread to satisfy you in the morning, for he has heard all your complaints against him. What have we done? Yes, your complaints are against the LORD, not against us."

⁹Then Moses said to Aaron, "Announce this to the entire community of Israel: 'Present yourselves before the LORD, for he has heard your complaining.'" ¹⁰And as Aaron spoke to the whole community of Israel, they looked out toward the wilderness. There they could see the awesome glory of the LORD in the cloud.

¹¹Then the LORD said to Moses, ¹²"I have heard the Israelites' complaints. Now tell them, 'In the evening you will have meat to eat, and in the morning you will have all the bread you want. Then you will know that I am the LORD your God.'"

¹³That evening vast numbers of quail

flew in and covered the camp. And the next morning the area around the camp was wet with dew. ¹⁴When the dew evaporated, a flaky substance as fine as frost blanketed the ground. ¹⁵The Israelites were puzzled when they saw it. "What is it?" they asked each other. They had no idea what it was.

And Moses told them, "It is the food the LORD has given you to eat. ¹⁶These are the LORD's instructions: Each household should gather as much as it needs. Pick up two quarts* for each person in your tent."

¹⁷So the people of Israel did as they were told. Some gathered a lot, some only a little. ¹⁸But when they measured it out,* everyone had just enough. Those who gathered a lot had nothing left over, and those who gathered only a little had enough. Each family had just what it needed.

¹⁹Then Moses told them, "Do not keep any of it until morning." ²⁰But some of them didn't listen and kept some of it until morning. But by then it was full of maggots and had a terrible smell. Moses was very angry with them.

²¹After this the people gathered the food morning by morning, each family according to its need. And as the sun became hot, the flakes they had not picked up melted and disappeared. ²²On the sixth day, they gathered twice as much as usual—four quarts* for each person instead of two. Then all the leaders of the community came and asked Moses for an explanation. ²³He told them, "This is what the LORD commanded: Tomorrow will be a day of complete rest, a holy Sabbath day set apart for the LORD. So bake or boil as much as you want today, and set aside what is left for tomorrow."

²⁴So they put some aside until morning, just as Moses had commanded. And in the morning the leftover food was wholesome and good, without maggots or odor.

²⁵Moses said, "Eat this food today, for today is a Sabbath day dedicated to the LORD. There will be no food on the ground today. ²⁶You may gather the food for six days, but the seventh day is the Sabbath. There will be no food on the ground that day."

²⁷Some of the people went out anyway on the seventh day, but they found no food. ²⁸The LORD asked Moses, "How long will these people refuse to obey my commands and instructions? ²⁹They must realize that the Sabbath is the LORD's gift to you. That is why he gives you a two-day supply on the sixth day, so there will be enough for two days. On the Sabbath day you must each stay in your place. Do not go out to pick up food on the seventh day." ³⁰So the people did not gather any food on the seventh day.

³¹The Israelites called the food manna.* It was white like coriander seed, and it tasted like honey wafers.

³²Then Moses said, "This is what the LORD has commanded: Fill a two-quart container with manna to preserve it for your descendants. Then later generations will be able to see the food I gave you in the wilderness when I set you free from Egypt."

³³Moses said to Aaron, "Get a jar and fill it with two quarts of manna. Then put it in a sacred place before the LORD to preserve it for all future generations." ³⁴Aaron did just as the LORD had commanded Moses. He eventually placed it in the Ark of the Covenant—in front of the stone tablets inscribed with the terms of the covenant.* ³⁵So the people of Israel ate manna for forty years until they arrived at the land where they would settle. They ate manna until they came to the border of the land of Canaan.

³⁶The container used to measure the manna was an omer, which was one tenth of an ephah; it held about two quarts.*

16:1a The geographical name *Sin* is related to *Sinai* and should not be confused with the English word *sin*. **16:1b** The Exodus had occurred on the fifteenth day of the first month (see Num 33:3). **16:16** Hebrew *1 omer* [2 liters]; also in 16:32, 33. **16:18** Hebrew *measured it with an omer*. **16:22** Hebrew *2 omers* [4 liters]. **16:31** *Manna* means "What is it?" See 16:15. **16:34** Hebrew *He placed it in front of the Testimony;* see note on 25:16. **16:36** Hebrew *An omer is one tenth of an ephah.*

NOTES

16:1 community. This term (*'edah* [TH5712, ZH6337]) is frequent in Exodus (15 times)—especially after this point (previously only in ch 12, 4 times)—Leviticus (12 times), and especially in Numbers (83 times). It has the general meaning of "assembly" and is normally translated in the LXX with *sunagōgē* [TG4864, ZG5252]. Commentators have pointed out the several verbal agreements between the Passover passages (ch 12) and this one. Perhaps the point as far as this term goes is to stress that these memorable events affected the entire "community" of Israel, both at that time and throughout all the future (note the importance of the memorial of the manna in 16:34-35).

16:3 us all. This is one of only two occurrences of *qahal* [TH6951, ZH7736] (congregation) in the book. The term has the idea of "assembled for a purpose." Perhaps the reason it is used here is to make an ironic point: We have been assembled together to die!

16:4 instructions. This is the Hebrew *torah* [TH8451, ZH9368]. God was seeking to prepare his people in small ways for the much fuller "instructions" they were to receive at Mount Sinai (see also 16:28).

16:7 glory. It appears that this term is used differently here from 16:10. It is the word *kebod* [TH3519, ZH3883], which denotes "heaviness, weightiness, significance." Thus, whatever expresses the wonderful reality of God is his "glory." Here it seems to speak of his gracious, providential nature revealed in his provision of food. In 16:10, the revelation is apparently visual, perhaps of fire within *the cloud*. Enns (2000:326) suggests that 16:10 is a foretaste of the goal of the book when the cloud of God's glory fills the Tabernacle, symbolizing God's presence with his people.

heard your complaints. Cassuto (1967:192) thinks this is positive in the sense of "responded favorably to your concerns" (cf. 2:24). But Houtman (1993:2.232) seems more correct to the context when he reads "has taken notice of."

16:8 What have we done? Lit., "What are we?" The question word "what," normally applied only to inanimate objects, seems to be employed to further the contrast between God and Moses (together with Aaron).

16:14 flakey substance as fine as frost. The word for "flakes" (*mekhuspas* [TH2636, ZH2892]) only occurs here. The idea of "flakes" comes from an Arabic root meaning "flake-like." Houtman (1993:2.337) thinks the idea is "a fine layer like frost."

16:15 "What is it?" The Hebrew is *man hu'* [TH4478A/1931, ZH4943/2085], and this gives rise to the ironic name "manna" for the substance. For 40 years the Hebrews would eat "what is it?" *Man* is unknown as an interrogative particle in classical Hebrew, but the claim has been made (though contested) that it appears in Ugaritic (see Cassuto 1967:196).

16:20 some of them didn't listen. The NRSV reads, "but they did not listen . . . some [of them] left part of [the manna] until morning . . ." Houtman (1993:2.343) argues that the understanding of the Hebrew represented by the NLT is more correct.

16:23 a holy Sabbath. Sarna (1991:90) says that "holy" is used here to say that the idea of Sabbath lies in the cosmic order and not simply in an arbitrary divine choice.

16:30 did not gather any food. Lit., "rested," which seems more all-inclusive.

16:31 wafers. This word (*tsapikhith* [TH6838, ZH7613]) occurs only here; the LXX has *enkris* (cake), which supports the English translation.

16:33 jar. This is the third unique Hebrew word in this passage. The LXX has *stamnos* [TG4713, ZG5085] (jar). However, as Childs (1974:274) points out, the Hebrew word (*tsintseneth* [TH6803, ZH7573]) is cognate with Aramaic *nitsa'*(basket).

16:34 in front . . . covenant. The phrase explains what is meant by the Hebrew term traditionally translated "the Testimony" (see NLT mg). NJPS translates it as "the Pact."

COMMENTARY

The provision of manna is the second of the five evidences of God's providential care related in 15:22–18:27. Like the first, this one also relates to a basic human need, that of food. Again, when it appears this need is not going to be met, or at least not met in a timely fashion, the response of the people is not faith and prayer, but complaint, and interestingly enough, complaint against their leaders, Moses and Aaron. As Fretheim (1991:187) says, "a crisis of need creates a crisis of faith." God did not condemn the people for their lack of faith, but eventually he did condemn them for their slowness to obey his instructions (16:28). This relates to the second purpose of God revealed in these incidents: to test the people to bring them to the point where they would obey his commands. Clearly, the critical upcoming moment when the people would be called upon to accept the terms of the covenant was in view here. If they could learn to obey in smaller things, they would be able to do so in the larger ones.

The apparent disjointedness of this account has given rise to a great deal of discussion about its origins. The best brief review of this discussion is found in Childs (1974:274-283). But even with all the discussion there is no consensus. Childs believes he has explained the phenomena by finding what he believes to be a recurring form in the hypothetical P document, but to make his system work he must excise verse 8, a verse the authenticity of which is fully supported by the ancient versions. Briefly, the problem is that Moses gave commands to the people (16:6-8) that go beyond what God was reported to have said to him (16:4-5). Then God is reported to say what Moses had already said (16:11-12). The problem is further compounded when Moses does not tell the people the reason for only picking up manna on six days until 16:23-26 but treats this as a command that God had already given.

In my view, all of this is to strain the data too far, to seek to impose upon it the kind of linear plot development that we expect in modern narrative writing. Clearly, that was not a concern of the ancient writers. Childs (1974:275-276) is right when he says that some of Cassuto's attempts (1967:109-191) to explain what the ancient writers were doing are strained. However, Cassuto is right when he says that the Torah's first concerns are not narrative consistency but instruction. Thus, the point here is to show how the people obeyed or disobeyed the instructions of God, regardless of the order in which they may or may not have been given. The present order highlights the issues of obedience and disobedience, even when all the data is not necessarily given or understood.

God Is the Supplier of Their Needs (16:1-12). It is surely significant that these events are reported to have occurred exactly one month after the Passover ("fifteenth day of the second month," 16:1; see 12:6). Once again, Israel was faced with death, and once again, Yahweh delivered them. Here, however, it was not an extraordinary plague that threatened them, but the ordinary issue of need and supply. Can God help in this matter? Does he want to? And can he be depended upon to help even if our attitudes and performance are not the best? The answer to all these questions is "yes." And just as Passover was to be a memorial for all future generations of God's power to defeat death, so the "jar" of manna (16:32-34) was to be a reminder of God's providential care.

The response of the people in this crisis was more hysterical and sarcastic than in the previous one (15:24). "If God was going to kill us anyway, why not do it in Egypt when we had full stomachs?" they asked. Another new feature is the idealizing of the memory of Egypt. This is certainly a common human trait. Memory has a way of diminishing the troubles of the past and magnifying the good things. But in this case, it was a hindrance to the Israelites, making them ungrateful for the deliverance they had experienced and thus unable to apply the lessons of that deliverance to the subsequent crises of their lives. Another unfortunate trait manifested here—one that would continue to dog Moses and the people through the coming years—was their failure to remind themselves that God, not Moses, had brought them into the wilderness. If they had kept that fact in view, they would have been in a position to remember that the same person who got them into the difficulties could certainly get them out. This is what Isaiah sought to get the exiles to realize: It was not the Babylonians who had made them captives; it was God. And thus, God could deliver them from the Babylonians (Isa 41:21-29). Moses recognized this problem and called on them to realize that their complaints were against God, not against himself and Aaron (16:7-8). It was not Moses who would supply their needs, it was God alone (16:6-8).[1]

As noted above, these incidents in the wilderness not only demonstrate the reality of God's providential care, they are also designed as preparation for the giving of God's instructions (*torah* [TH8451, ZH9368]; 16:4) in the context of the covenant. The only appropriate response to the grace the Israelites had received was obedience; thus God offered his provisions here in a context that required believing what he said was true and then doing it. Verses 4 and 5 are an expression of this: The food needed to be gathered according to the one overriding reality of life with God—trust. In the first place, there could be no hoarding so that they did not need to trust God for the next day,[2] and second, every seventh day they had to remind themselves that it was not their work that supplied their needs but God's abundant grace.[3] Obviously, God could have simply dropped excesses of food on them without any restrictions whatsoever. But if he had, they would have come to believe the big lie: Humans are self-sufficient and don't need to live in a relationship with God shaped by his character (see Phil 3:2-8).

While it appears that God may have used occurrences that happen in limited ways in nature on the Sinai Peninsula,[4] there can be no question of the miraculous nature of the provisions. The timing of the quails' arrival and the 40-year duration of the manna make it quite clear that God is able to intervene in his creation and cause it to bless his people in extraordinary ways. But God does not intervene so miraculously every day—why did he do so there? He was revealing his caring nature in ways that were meant to be unforgettable. This is why the manna was to be saved. When I am feeling deprived and vulnerable, when I am tempted to take matters into my own hands and supply my needs in illegitimate ways, I can remember the behavior of God in the past (which was a revelation of his "glory," 16:7, 10; see the note on 16:7) and build my life on the truths taught in those unique incidents. That is to know that he is the Lord my God (16:12).

Manna and Quail (16:13-30). This segment of the chapter deals with the ways in which the people did or did not comply with God's instructions. In that context, it supplies further instruction about the observance of the Sabbath. One of the features of the manna was that there was enough for everyone, but not too much (16:16-18). The lesson is clear: God cares for the needs of every person, and he is opposed to greed. The fallen human spirit is certain that if some is good, more is better. Furthermore, we have an innate fear of not having enough. Thus, we amass for ourselves mounds of stuff we do not need and will never use, but what we do not realize is the corrosive effects of abundance. It leads to pride, oppression, and the myth of self-sufficiency. God was trying to teach this in the corruption of the unneeded manna (16:20). Karl Marx recognized these truths, but his error was thinking that human fallenness could be corrected through economic coercion. History has proven how wrong he was. It is significant that after the lesson of verse 20, the people did learn and began to follow the divine instructions (16:21). That response offers hope for the future.

When the people realized on Friday that they had twice as much manna as they needed for that day, they were perplexed (16:22). Evidently, although God had told Moses to expect this (16:5), Moses had not told the people. Sarna (1991:90) speculates that this was a pedagogic device on Moses's part; sometimes the most effective instruction is an answer to a question growing out of the student's experience. At any rate, Moses used the opportunity to convey some instructions about Sabbath observance. Most commentators argue that there must have been Sabbath regulations before this because, they say, such regulations are assumed here. Without denying that there was a pattern of seven-day weeks elsewhere in ancient Near Eastern culture and that the Israelites could well have had some sort of recognition of that, I would still argue that there is nothing here that assumes some prior religious understanding of the day. In fact, the people's surprise over the extra provision on Friday would seem to argue that they were not prepared to view Saturday as fundamentally different from the other six days. But Moses used the experience as a means to educate the people about the Sabbath: It is a "day of complete rest" (16:23); it is a holy day "set apart for the LORD" (16:23, 25); it "is the LORD's gift to you" (16:29). In other words, God had given one day in seven when humans don't have to work (what a blessing that must have been to former slaves), when they can rest. However, it is a rest that focuses on the Lord. It is not intended merely as a day of diversion, as it has become in the world today, even among believers. It is the Lord who gives work, and it is the Lord who gives rest. Rest that promotes a feeling of self-sufficiency is no more a blessing than is work that promotes such (see further below on 20:8-11).

Verse 24 is again hopeful: "So they put some aside . . . just as Moses had commanded." At least some were beginning to pass the test of obedience (cf. 16:4). But others were not (16:27). And here, unlike verse 20, where we are told Moses became "angry with them," it is God who for the first time in this division becomes angry. His words, "How long will these people refuse to obey my commands?" (16:28), have an ominous ring because they are the same words that he spoke to Pharaoh in 10:3. God is incredibly patient, as the whole Bible amply attests, but his patience has limits, and our obstinate human insistence on "doing it my way" pushes those limits to the end. Houtman (1993:2.350) is also almost certainly correct when he says that this anger is also because transgression of the Sabbath commandment is a terrible sin (cf. Num 15:32-36). It is interesting that throughout the Old Testament, people were condemned *for* giving merely ritualistic sacrifices and *for not* keeping the Sabbath. Does this suggest that Sabbath-keeping is less prone to being reduced to mere ritual than is sacrifice, or that Sabbath-keeping is more costly (and thus more valuable) than mere sacrifice? These are questions worth pondering (see below on 20:8-11 for further discussion).

An Appendix (16:31-36). The importance of the previous segment concerning God's faithful provision of food is attested to by this appendix (so Sarna 1991:91), containing reflections (some from later times) upon the segment. Five elements are contained in it: identification and description of manna (16:31);[5] provisions for maintaining a memorial of it (16:32-33); what was eventually done with the memorial (16:34); how long the manna lasted (16:35); and explanation of the obsolete term (*omer*) used originally for measuring manna (16:36).

The last three items obviously come from a time later than the events described in 16:1-30: (1) The Ark of the Covenant had not been constructed yet, (2) the manna had only begun, not ceased, and (3) the omer was the normal unit of measure. However, as Enns (2000:328) aptly observes, the very fact that the term "omer" has to be explained to a later generation is a testimony to the antiquity of the story upon which this comment is made. On this basis, it seems quite likely to me that Moses's direction to Aaron to preserve a sample of the manna as a memorial (16:32-33) was contemporary with the story. Moses understood how important it was to preserve a memory of the miracle for the days when miracles would no longer be the norm and people would be expected to live in the light of the truths that the miracles had taught. "Eventually" (as NLT happily has it), the Ark of the Covenant came to be that sacred place before the Lord.

ENDNOTES
1. Tragically, with the passing of the years Moses forgot this truth (Num 20:10).
2. Note Jesus' poignant expression of this truth in his words, "Give us *today* our *daily* bread" (Matt 6:11, NIV, italics mine; cf. Luke 11:3).
3. It is not clear whether there would be twice the manna available for them to gather on Friday (so Houtman 1993:2.230-231) or whether, as the NLT suggests, they would only discover they had twice as much when they prepared it. Verse 22, "they gathered twice as much as usual," seems to support Houtman's view.

4. Quail migrate in great numbers between Europe and Africa across this region, and they frequently arrive exhausted so that they can be caught easily. Likewise, aphids sucking the sap of certain plants in the spring of the year secrete a white flaky substance that has a sweet taste. Sarna (1991:88) observes that the terse discussion of the quail versus the more expansive treatment of the manna is because the request for meat was unreasonable while that for bread was not. But it seems more likely to me that the difference is because the appearance of the quail was only twice (cf. Num 11:31-35), while the manna was daily (except on Saturdays) for 40 years.

5. It is maintained in some commentaries (e.g., Childs 1974:291) that there is a discrepancy between the description here, "honey wafers," and that in Num 11:8, "pastries baked with olive oil," but that is to push the two brief descriptions much too far.

◆ C. Water from the Rock (17:1-7)

At the LORD's command, the whole community of Israel left the wilderness of Sin* and moved from place to place. Eventually they camped at Rephidim, but there was no water there for the people to drink. ²So once more the people complained against Moses. "Give us water to drink!" they demanded.

"Quiet!" Moses replied. "Why are you complaining against me? And why are you testing the LORD?"

³But tormented by thirst, they continued to argue with Moses. "Why did you bring us out of Egypt? Are you trying to kill us, our children, and our livestock with thirst?"

⁴Then Moses cried out to the LORD, "What should I do with these people? They are ready to stone me!"

⁵The LORD said to Moses, "Walk out in front of the people. Take your staff, the one you used when you struck the water of the Nile, and call some of the elders of Israel to join you. ⁶I will stand before you on the rock at Mount Sinai.* Strike the rock, and water will come gushing out. Then the people will be able to drink." So Moses struck the rock as he was told, and water gushed out as the elders looked on.

⁷Moses named the place Massah (which means "test") and Meribah (which means "arguing") because the people of Israel argued with Moses and tested the LORD by saying, "Is the LORD here with us or not?"

17:1 The geographical name *Sin* is related to *Sinai* and should not be confused with the English word *sin*.
17:6 Hebrew *Horeb*, another name for Sinai.

NOTES

17:1 the whole community. See note on 16:1.

17:2 complained. A different word (*rib* [TH7378, ZH8189]) than that which was translated "complain" in chs 15 and 16. That word (*lun* [TH3885, ZH4296]) does not occur again until 17:3 where it is translated "argue with." *Rib* is a stronger word with the connotations of "present charges against."

Give us. This is a plural imperative in Hebrew, perhaps indicating that the demand is addressed to both Moses and Aaron. The Samaritan Pentateuch, the LXX, and the Syriac, however, all have a singular imperative.

17:3 After "bring us" the pronouns shift to singular: "kill me, my children, and my livestock." Perhaps the reason for this is to emphasize the intensely personal nature of the situation and the demand.

17:4 What. This represents the interrogative particle *mah* [TH4100, ZH4537], which Cassuto (1967:203) suggests may underscore the tone of grievance.

17:5 Walk out in front of. This represents the Hebrew *'abor lipne* [TH5674/3807.1/6440, ZH6296/4200/7156] ("pass over before"). It might have the sense of "go on ahead of" (cf. Houtman 1993:2.365).

17:6 stand before. The sense is not entirely clear. Is it "appear before," or as Houtman (1993:2.364) thinks, is it to "wait on" in the sense of "to serve"? Houtman translates it "be available to."

and water gushed out. This is a justifiable inference, but it is not actually reported in the text.

COMMENTARY

In this, the third incident dealing with God's provision and his testing of the people, the situation was even more desperate than in the first two. In the first incident there was water—it was just not potable. In the second, there was no food, but it is possible to survive for some time without food. Now, there was no water, and there was no possibility of prolonged survival without water. The reaction of the people is commensurate with the gravity of the situation. They attacked Moses much more viciously than before, to the extent that Moses, rightly or wrongly, feared for his life (17:4). But again, God responds without rancor and provides for the people, and in so doing, once again vindicates Moses's leadership.

This incident—perhaps because of Moses's recognition that it involved the attempt to make God prove his love and care (17:2, 7)—is widely referred to in the Bible (Deut 6:16; 8:2, 15-16; 9:22; Pss 78:15-16, 20, 56; 95:8-9; and also probably Ps 114:8; Isa 48:21). These references highlight the issue between appropriate and inappropriate testing. It is appropriate to demonstrate faith and obedience, so God tests his people to see if they will do what they should when faith and obedience are required. But it is *not* appropriate to *require* that faithfulness or patience be demonstrated, which is what the Israelites were doing to God. In effect, they were saying that they would not trust God unless he proved his trustworthiness over and over again.

The incident started off well, with the people following "the LORD's command" and moving "from place to place" (17:1). It appears that they were beginning to learn the lessons of obedience. They were being led by God and they were on the way (Fretheim 1991:187-188). But eventually they came to "Rephidim" (17:1), which was apparently in vicinity of Mount Sinai (or Horeb, 17:6; cf. also 19:2). Presumably they came to this place expecting to find water, but they were not able to obtain any. Sarna (1991:93) suggests that the Amalekites may have prevented them from reaching it. In any case, the people reacted violently. They did not merely complain about the situation, but they accused Moses of outright malfeasance and more (see note on 17:2): He had intentionally brought them into this terrible place to destroy them. It appears that their repeated experiences of being forced to depend on God's provision, instead of making them more trustful and dependent, were making them more fearful and prone to hysteria. While it seems they were becoming more willing to obey God when his instructions were relayed to them, they were not developing a spirit of faith when faced with adversity. Instead, they were inclined to look for a scapegoat for the adversity, and Moses (and perhaps Aaron, see note on 17:2) was an easy target.

In his initial response (17:2), Moses attempted to get the people to recognize that he was not to blame for the situation. They should be taking the matter up with God. He was the one who had brought them to this place. Furthermore, he recognized, as verse 7 makes clear, what their real underlying attitude was. Though they were not saying it, they really wanted Yahweh to prove that he was there and was for them, and they wanted it proved their way and now. But they would not actually voice those feelings (perhaps because they were afraid of the result?) and instead assaulted Moses violently.

In his anxiety, Moses did what the people should have done: He turned to God in prayer (17:4). But from what he says, it appears that he still believed the problem was his to solve because he asked Yahweh what he, Moses, should do. Later on, during the crisis of the golden calf, he would fully realize that the people were God's problem, but here he seemed to feel they were his. God's response is very interesting. He neither corrected nor encouraged Moses, and he did not upbraid the people. He simply pointed the way to the supply of their need. His direction that Moses should take the staff with which Moses had "struck the water of the Nile" and should "strike the rock" is very significant (17:5-6). There the action deprived the unbelievers of water, and here the same action would give water to the believers. The point is that both life and death are in the hands of Yahweh alone and that the issue revolves around one thing: one's relationship with him. The apostle Paul recognized the pure grace involved in this act when he identified the rock as Jesus (1 Cor 10:4). Just as God gave the water to his people without condition, so he has given Christ to the world. But as Paul went on to point out, it is possible to taste that grace, as the Israelites did, and still not persevere in faith ultimately. That is the tragedy of tragedies that Paul was concerned to prevent (1 Cor 10:5-11).

The passage is unclear as to the precise location of the miracle. It appears that Moses and the elders of Israel left the camp and walked to Mount Horeb, where the elders saw what Moses did, thus being able to testify to the miraculous nature of the event. Perhaps the water then rushed down a wadi and back to the camp. If this is a correct reconstruction, it means that Mount Sinai (Horeb) is the site of both grace and law, underscoring the truth that the Sinai covenant is badly maligned when it is taken out of the context of grace. It is not the antithesis of grace but a further expression of grace. It was the Pharisaic attempt to make obedience to the law a means of self-justification that made it a curse. See the commentary on chapter 20 below for further discussion. Fretheim (1991:190) draws another valid inference when he says that the site's being Horeb shows that the moral order and the cosmic order are inextricably connected. There is no bifurcation between natural law and moral law. Both express the will and nature of the one Creator.

Once more, Yahweh vindicated his chosen servant Moses. Yahweh did not merely produce a miracle out of his "bag of tricks," as it were. Instead, he utilized Moses as his effective agent. Furthermore, if Houtman's understanding of the wording "stand before" is correct (see note on 17:6), then God was demonstrating to the elders and thus to the people that he was graciously putting his power into the hands of this man, Moses.[1] This is illustrative of the truth that God will not save the world merely as a *deus ex machina*, a god who breaks into the plot of the play to extricate people in spite of themselves. No, he values humans too highly for that. He will find persons whom he can use, even persons who seem to us very unworthy, like Samson for example, in order to bring his people to a position of freely chosen faith and obedience.

The final verse, as noted above (17:7), records the establishment of this event in memory. The place was made to carry a double name, Massah/Meribah, because of the events that took place there. It was a place where they charged their human leader with evil motives, "Meribah," and a place where they demanded that God prove his care for them, "Massah." Unlike pagan thinkers who think that a place only has significance as it corresponds to a similar element in the unchanging world of myth, Moses understood that places are unique because of what takes place there in history and that if the lessons of that history are learned, the future need not be a repetition of the past but can actually be different. By giving this place this descriptive name, he was trying to root it and its lessons in his people's minds in an unforgettable way and thus to change their behavior.

ENDNOTES

1. But such power can only be used safely by one who will use it without self-interest. The similar incident recounted in Num 20 demonstrates this truth. Moses felt confident that he had done all this before and knew how it should be done. His sin there was not in striking the rock rather than speaking to it. His sin was to make it appear that God's power was his to dispense as he chose. This is the curse of the professional ministry.

◆ D. Protection from the Amalekites (17:8-16)

⁸While the people of Israel were still at Rephidim, the warriors of Amalek attacked them. ⁹Moses commanded Joshua, "Choose some men to go out and fight the army of Amalek for us. Tomorrow, I will stand at the top of the hill, holding the staff of God in my hand."

¹⁰So Joshua did what Moses had commanded and fought the army of Amalek. Meanwhile, Moses, Aaron, and Hur climbed to the top of a nearby hill. ¹¹As long as Moses held up the staff in his hand, the Israelites had the advantage. But whenever he dropped his hand, the Amalekites gained the advantage. ¹²Moses' arms soon became so tired he could no longer hold them up. So Aaron and Hur found a stone for him to sit on. Then they stood on each side of Moses, holding up his hands. So his hands held steady until sunset. ¹³As a result, Joshua overwhelmed the army of Amalek in battle.

¹⁴After the victory, the LORD instructed Moses, "Write this down on a scroll as a permanent reminder, and read it aloud to Joshua: I will erase the memory of Amalek from under heaven." ¹⁵Moses built an altar there and named it Yahweh-nissi (which means "the LORD is my banner"). ¹⁶He said, "They have raised their fist against the LORD's throne, so now* the LORD will be at war with Amalek generation after generation."

17:16 Or *Hands have been lifted up to the Lord's throne, and now.*

NOTES

17:9 *Tomorrow.* The Hebrew placement of this word does not make it clear whether this refers to Joshua's actions (taking the men out to fight) or to Moses's (standing on the hilltop), both of which would occur the next day. I agree with Houtman (1993:2.380-381) that it probably refers to both. The NLT reading follows the understanding implicit in the MT punctuation.

17:12 *hands.* The reference to Moses's hands has puzzled some commentators since only one hand would be necessary to hold the staff. Perhaps he moved it from hand to hand as he grew tired, or perhaps he held it over his head with both hands.

held steady. This is the only place in the OT where the Hebrew *'emunah* [TH530, ZH575] is used in a physical sense. Normally it refers to the trait of faithfulness or dependability.

17:13 *overwhelmed.* This is a good representation of the Hebrew *khalash* [TH2522A, ZH2765] which could be translated "weakened, disabled, prostrated." The point is that they were soundly defeated, though not utterly destroyed.

in battle. Lit., "with the sword."

17:14 *I will erase.* This is emphatic in the Hebrew: "I will surely erase."

17:16 *They have raised their fist against the LORD's throne.* This is one possible understanding of a very obscure Hebrew phrase, *ki yad 'al kes yah*, meaning something like "because/surely a hand (is) upon/against/unto the [?] of Yahweh." Historically, the otherwise-unknown *kes* has been taken as a short poetic form of *kisse'* [TH3678, ZH4058] "throne." However, given the reference to "banner," which is *nes* [TH5251, ZH5812], in the previous sentence, it has been proposed that *kes* is a copyist's error for *nes*. Thus, the NRSV reads, "A hand upon the banner of the LORD." Unfortunately, there is no evidence from the mss or versions to support this attractive conjecture. If "throne" is correct, an alternative understanding is that this is an expression of oath-taking, with the hand raised to testify, hence NASB's "the Lord has sworn" or REB's "my oath upon it." In this context, this seems most likely to me.

COMMENTARY

The first three incidents reported concerning the journey to Sinai all relate to God's ability and desire to supply for his people's physical needs. This incident relates to another need, the need for protection. The terse report gives no explanation of where the Amalekites came from or why they chose to attack Israel. In other parts of Scripture we learn that they were from the family of Esau (Gen 36:16) and that they were a nomadic people who lived in the northern Sinai area (Gen 14:7; Num 13:29; 14:25, 43) in the vicinity of Kadesh. Deuteronomy 25:18 suggests that the attack was something of an ambush, falling first on the stragglers at the rear of the procession. It may well be that this was a preemptive strike aimed at destroying a potential enemy before it could gain further strength and cohesiveness (as in ch 18).

In any case, the existence of the people of God and the potential for the fulfillment of God's promises was threatened once again. If the people could survive the physical hardships of the desert under God's care, could they survive the threat of these desert-dwellers? Did God's providence extend to that? Once again, the answer was "yes." Since God did care, the Amalekites posed no serious threat to those who were under his blessing. This latter point is indeed the focus of the account. It is not about the Israelites' emerging military prowess. Neither is it about the emergence of the young general, Joshua. The point of the story is simple: As long as the Lord's blessing was extended to them, the Israelites and Joshua prevailed, and when it was not they did not prevail. The lesson they were intended to learn was "this is the LORD's battle " (1 Sam 17:47).

Moses appears here as a man of confidence and decisiveness. Houtman (1993:2.370) suggests that he had been rejuvenated by Yahweh's effective use of him in the previous account. At any rate, Moses gave terse, decisive orders to Joshua and declared confidently what his own role would be. Commentators vary widely on the significance of "the staff of God" in Moses's "hand." Some, like Fretheim (1991:193-194) make it simply a symbol of confidence in God. But this does not explain why Moses's lowering it in fatigue would have such a drastic effect on the effectiveness of the Israelite fighters. At the other extreme, Houtman (1993:2.370) compares it to a conjurer's rod. Hyatt (1971:184) notes that some commentators even doubt whether the staff is original to the story at all because its function is not spelled out. But I agree with Enns (2000:348) that the connection with the plagues is normative. (Note the importance of "tomorrow" in the plagues: 8:23, 29; 9:5, 18; 10:4.) From the very first (7:9-10; 8:5, 16) through to the end (14:16), the staff had been the symbol, but more than just a symbol, of God's power to intervene in human affairs and to accomplish his redemptive purposes. When God's power is at work and his blessing is in play, God's agents succeed in his purposes. The use of the staff in the previous miracle must have also been a factor. Yes, God's power ruled the realm of nature, but it was in no way limited to that realm. It was just as dominating in the realm of human affairs. But why was it necessary to hold up the staff throughout the entire day? Perhaps it is because this time the involvement of the people and their continuing faith was a much more essential factor in the accomplishment of God's plan than it had been previously.

I mentioned this factor of human agency in the comments on 17:5-6, but here it comes to the fore even more. There were God's agents in the valley, the Israelite warriors. If they had been unwilling to hurl themselves into the battle, and then to persevere in it, the battle would not have been won. Then there was God's agent on the hill. The fact that it was "the staff of God" that was held aloft made it perfectly clear that it was not some intrinsic power Moses possessed that was winning the battle, as was also shown by his fatigue. Nonetheless, it was Moses's responsibility to hold the staff aloft. If he failed in that responsibility the battle would be lost. But the significance of human agency here is not yet exhausted. When Moses, possessed of no superhuman strength, proved unable to hold the staff up all day, Aaron and Hur (17:12)[1] came alongside of him and held up his hands. Thus, the human agency extended beyond Moses. God desires to meet our needs in a dynamic partnership with us. We are neither the effective agents, nor are we spectators; we are called into the fellowship of partnership, and it seems that he was underlining that point by the ways in which he manifested himself at the battle with Amalek.

But why the remarkable closing to the account? The Amalekites had been decisively defeated. Yet God took an oath (see note on 17:16) that they would be so completely exterminated that even their "memory" (17:14) would be erased. This point is underscored in the dramatic contrast drawn from the idea of remembering: "Write this down on a scroll as a permanent reminder" versus "I will erase the memory" (17:14). Not only was the oath written down[2] but Moses built a memorial altar to commemorate the event (and the oath) for future generations.[3] What had Amalek done to deserve such perpetual animosity from the Lord? First of all, it must be said that since the Bible does not give an explicit reason, any suggestions we make must be tentative. However, it seems likely to me that there are two factors. The first is the level of hostility displayed in an unprovoked attack that was made at some distance from the Amalekite home territory. There was no reason for what was done; the Amalekites had no reason to believe they were threatened or would be threatened. This was war for sport and spoil, and God would have none of that, then or ever. But there is a second reason for God's continuing opposition to the Amalekites. In their attempt to exterminate the people of God, they were seeking to destroy God's attempt to save the world. Though they were part of his creation, they were determined to receive nothing from God and, indeed, to kill him if he insisted on opening his arms to them.[4] To attempt to thwart the love of God is as deadly as cutting through a high-voltage electric wire.

ENDNOTES
1. Many commentators observe that there is no introduction of either Joshua or Hur here. Clearly, the point is not to give a full history of the events or the personages involved in the events. Rather, the focus is on the revelation of the character and work of God. But if we say that the intent is not to give a history, we are in no way suggesting that this makes the work less historically reliable. The writer was simply selective in what historical data he chose to report.
2. This is the first reference to writing in the OT. Again, it seems that there may be a preparatory element at work. Shortly, Moses was to write another memorial document: the Sinai covenant. It seems very probable that these events then inspired Moses to oversee the recording of the Israelite family's earlier history (in oral form to this point?) and then the record of the subsequent journeys.
3. The fact that there is no mention of sacrifices offered seems to confirm that this was another of the memorial altars that are mentioned several times in the OT (Gen 12:7-8; 13:18; 33:20; 35:7; Josh 22:26-34).
4. It is instructive that Haman, the Persian prime minister who attempted to wipe out the captive Judeans, is called "an Agagite" (Esth 3:1), and the only reference in the Bible to Agag is that he was the Amalekite king killed by Samuel after Saul had brought Agag back as a captive (1 Sam 15:32-33). The Amalekites were not finally destroyed until during the reign of Hezekiah (1 Chr 4:43). Until that time they were a constant threat to God's people. In Judaism "Amalekite" has come to be a term used for any people out to destroy the Jews.

E. Jethro's Visit to Moses (18:1-27)
1. Jethro's faith in response to Moses's report (18:1-12)

Moses' father-in-law, Jethro, the priest of Midian, heard about everything God had done for Moses and his people, the Israelites. He heard especially about how the LORD had rescued them from Egypt.

²Earlier, Moses had sent his wife, Zipporah, and his two sons back to Jethro, who had taken them in. ³(Moses' first son was named Gershom,* for Moses had said when the boy was born, "I have been a foreigner in a foreign land." ⁴His second son was named Eliezer,* for Moses had said, "The God of my ancestors was my helper; he rescued me from the sword of Pharaoh.") ⁵Jethro, Moses' father-in-law, now came to visit Moses in the wilderness. He brought Moses' wife and two sons with him, and they arrived while Moses and the people were camped near the mountain of God. ⁶Jethro had sent a message to Moses, saying, "I, Jethro, your father-in-law, am coming to see you with your wife and your two sons."

⁷So Moses went out to meet his father-in-law. He bowed low and kissed him. They asked about each other's welfare and then went into Moses' tent. ⁸Moses told his father-in-law everything the LORD had done to Pharaoh and Egypt on behalf of Israel. He also told about all the hardships they had experienced along the way and how the LORD had rescued his people from all their troubles. ⁹Jethro was delighted when he heard about all the good things the LORD had done for Israel as he rescued them from the hand of the Egyptians.

¹⁰"Praise the LORD," Jethro said, "for he has rescued you from the Egyptians and from Pharaoh. Yes, he has rescued Israel from the powerful hand of Egypt! ¹¹I know now that the LORD is greater than all other gods, because he rescued his people from the oppression of the proud Egyptians."

¹²Then Jethro, Moses' father-in-law, brought a burnt offering and sacrifices to God. Aaron and all the elders of Israel came out and joined him in a sacrificial meal in God's presence.

18:3 *Gershom* sounds like a Hebrew term that means "a foreigner there." 18:4 *Eliezer* means "God is my helper."

NOTES

18:1 *He heard especially about how.* This captures the emphasis in the Hebrew clause structure.

18:2 *Earlier.* This is not in the text but is the correct inference.

sent. The verb *shilukheha* [TH7964, ZH8933] can refer to divorce (and some use Num 12:1 to suggest that this is the case here), but it seems highly unlikely that this was the case in view of the cordial relations with Jethro here.

18:5 *near the mountain of God.* This statement has troubled some commentators because 19:1 says the people arrived at Sinai then. As a result, early Jewish commentators (see Sarna and Cassuto for discussions) argued that this chapter is out of chronological sequence. However, it is not necessary to resort to that interpretation. As 17:6 indicates, Rephidim was relatively close to Mount Sinai.

18:6 *I, Jethro.* The Samaritan Pentateuch, the LXX, and the Syriac do not have "I" (*'ani* [TH589, ZH638]) but rather an introductory particle (Heb. *hinneh* [TH2009, ZH2180], "behold, now"). Thus, they treat the statement as indirect address and as what the messenger would have said (cf. Gen 48:2).

18:7 *bowed low.* Lit., "prostrated himself on the ground." This is a gesture of extreme respect.

welfare. This translation of the word *shalom* [TH7965, ZH8934] recognizes that much more than the usual translation "peace" is connoted by the word. It connotes "wholeness, completeness, health." Thus, when God offers *shalom* to his people, he is offering much more than the mere absence of conflict, more than is commonly meant by the English word "peace."

18:8 *told*. Lit., "recounted, declared, proclaimed." The same word appears in 9:16 (see the commentary below).

18:11 *because he rescued . . . Egyptians*. There is little agreement how the elliptical Hebrew phrase should be translated. Some have suggested that something has fallen out of the text. As it stands, the phrase literally says, "because/indeed/precisely in the matter which they boasted over them." The subject of "boasted" has been taken to be either the Egyptian gods or the Egyptians themselves, and the object of "over" has been taken as the matters over which boasts were made or as the Hebrew people. The NLT has chosen the latter option in each case. The problem with this reading is that the natural subject should be "gods," as per the preceding clause. In order to solve that discrepancy, the NRSV resorts to the draconian measure of transposing "because he delivered the people from the Egyptians" from 18:10 to precede this final clause. To my mind, Cassuto (1967:216) offers the best understanding when he reads "precisely in the matter of which [the gods] boasted, [the LORD] is over them." That is, in those very areas where the Egyptian gods were claimed to be all-powerful, such as the Nile, the weather, the sun, and even life itself, God had defeated them.

18:12 *sacrificial meal*. Lit., "bread" (see the commentary below and endnote 7).

COMMENTARY

This chapter is clearly transitional. Yet, I understand it to include the final demonstration of God's providential care exercised on behalf of his people within the larger section. The first 12 verses look back, recapping the wonderful things God had done for his people since last Moses had talked with his father-in-law, Jethro (4:18). The final 15 verses, presenting Jethro's solution to the social chaos Moses was trying to cope with, look forward to Moses's position as mediator and lawgiver. They prepare the reader for the shift in Moses's role that will take place in chapters 19–40.

As Childs (1974:326-327) notes, the author signals this transitional function with a much more expansive style than had been the case in the immediately preceding chapters. There is more personal information and considerably more dialogue. Childs believes the 12 occurrences of "father-in-law" in 27 verses establish a tone of "polite formality" that furthers the expansive style.

The contrast with chapter 17 could hardly be more striking. In place of the hatred of the Amalekites, we have the affection and support of another Sinai group, the Midianites. Here, the word of Yahweh's actions on Israel's behalf (18:1) does not provoke fear and jealousy but interest and even friendly curiosity. Had God really done all those things they had heard about? Taking the opportunity afforded by the presence with him of his daughter and grandsons, Jethro chose to find out for himself.

Again, as with the mention of Joshua and Hur in the previous chapter, we are left without background information as to how Zipporah, Gershom, and Eliezer ended up back with Jethro. We know that they at least started out for Egypt with Moses (4:20).[1] But we do not know how or why or when they returned. Cassuto (1967:213) argues very plausibly that this kind of information was contained in an earlier collection of traditions,[2] which was familiar to the first readers of the book of Exodus and thus did not need to be repeated for them. We might imagine that Moses "had sent" (18:2) them back when the fury of Pharaoh had reached threatening heights, but we do not know.

The emphasis on the names of Moses's two sons (18:3-4) contributes to the transitional function of the chapter. Gershom reminds the reader of Moses's situation not so long before. He had been "a foreigner in a foreign land" with his life essentially behind him. But then came that encounter with God on this nearby mountain, and everything changed forever. It was changed because of one thing only: The God who had appeared in the bush and had identified himself as Yahweh, the God of Abraham, Isaac, and Jacob (3:6, 14-15), had proven himself absolutely faithful. He had shown himself a "helper" (18:4) in every sense of the word.[3]

The detailed little scene presented to us in 18:5-7 is an example of the expansive style mentioned above. We see the arrival of the caravan in verse 5, then the dispatching of a messenger in verse 6, since it would be unseemly for an important guest to simply burst in upon someone unprepared. In verse 7, the message is received and appropriately acted upon. The leader of several hundreds of thousands of people prostrated himself on the ground (see the note on 18:7) before his elder, the priest (18:1), his father-in-law. According to ancient custom in the area, his father-in-law would have protested that such obeisance was really not necessary (although of course it was) and lifted him up. Then they kissed each other's cheeks and asked about each other's *shalom*—"How are you?—Well, I hope" (see note on 18:7). Finally they "went into Moses's tent."[4] All of this is in stark contrast to what the Israelites had experienced from the Amalekites.

It is interesting to speculate on whether what is reported next is a breach of ordinary custom or whether custom was observed and simply left unreported. Normally, one would never get right to the matter at hand with such a guest. Every possible topic of interest to either party would be touched upon, at length, as if by chance, before the topic both parties knew to be the purpose for meeting would come up. I suspect that in this case, Jethro was so interested and Moses so full of his subject that, in the privacy of the tent, by mutual consent, they dispensed with preliminaries and got right to the matter at hand. Moses recounted (see note on 18:8) "everything the LORD had done." This was more than mere telling; it was a declaration, a pronouncement, a rehearsing. It was what God told Pharaoh that he had been put on earth for (9:16): "to spread my fame throughout the earth" (the same verb as in 18:8: *sapar* [TH5608, ZH6218]). Not only did Moses tell of the evidence of God's power revealed in the deliverance from Egypt; he also told of the revelation of God's providential care in his rescuing them "from all their troubles" (18:8). Childs (1974:328) correctly points out that this is not the recital of a creed but simply the outpouring of an unforgettable set of experiences and of what they meant.

Jethro's response (18:9-12) was all that Moses could have hoped for. It is a testimony to the power of historical witness. Theological disputation did not evoke his response; as important as theological disputation is, theology is always secondary. It is a conclusion, a conclusion drawn from something else. It cannot stand on its own, for it is not self-authenticating. What the Bible tells us is that theology must be drawn from experience—not inner experience, but experience external to any human psyche. That is what happened here: Because of the effectiveness of Moses's witness to what had taken place in time and space, Jethro was able to draw for himself the appropriate theological conclusions. Thus, he became the first of multiplied millions who have and who will believe the historical witness of the Bible and will draw the appropriate conclusions from that history. It is these to whom Jesus referred when he said, "Blessed are those who believe without seeing me" (John 20:29).

Jethro's responses to Moses's witness and the inescapable conclusions of that witness are paradigmatic. They included joy (18:9), worship (18:10, 12), and theological conviction (18:11). The realization that human evil, including oppression and brutality, will not triumph and that those things are not expressions of the character of the Creator is a cause for joy. Likewise, the discovery that the most powerful being in the universe cares for the ordinary needs of human beings is cause for joy. And above all, the intimation that God has broken the power of death is a cause for joy. Out of joy springs worship. Who can encounter evidence that there is one supreme God who has limitless power at his disposal and yet is supremely good, filled with *khesed* [TH2617, ZH2876] (unfailing love), and not be moved to worship? If the presence of one's father-in-law would prompt one to throw oneself at his feet, how much more one's Father! An experience of God that is cold, bloodless, and cerebral is not an experience of Yahweh.[5] This is why all along Yahweh called upon Pharaoh to let his people go so that they could worship him. That would be the appropriate response to what Yahweh would do for his people. How fitting that it should be a non-Israelite who led "Aaron and all the elders of Israel" (18:12) in this worship. God had promised Abraham that all the world would be blessed because of him, and here that promise began to be fulfilled in an explicit way.

But the experience of the Yahweh of the Exodus can never be merely affective. There are intellectual conclusions to be drawn from a rehearsal of what God did in Egypt 3,400 years ago. Over and over again God had informed Moses, the Israelites, and Pharaoh and the Egyptians of what this whole experience was about. It was about knowing who is God: "Then you will know that I am the LORD."[6] As Elijah said 600 years later in his confrontation with the prophets of Baal, we must decide who is God. This is the fundamental question of existence. Is the world God, or does God stand outside the world? The Egyptians and every other brilliant people before or since have concluded that the first is true. So for them the Nile is god, and the stars are god, and the wind is god, and love is god, and hate is god, and most of all, I am god.

What God demonstrated in an unforgettable way along the banks of the Nile is that such propositions, with all their ramifications, are not so. And Jethro understood. "I know now that the LORD is greater than all other gods" (18:11). As I have said at various points in this study, the deepest problem of the Israelites was not bondage. If that had been the case, one stupendous miracle would have solved that problem. No, their deeper problems were theological: They did not know God, and they did not have a vital experience of his presence. In the Exodus and on the way to Sinai, God was addressing those deeper problems with revelations of himself that forever showed that this world is not God. Thus, the only hope in this world is in the God who stands outside of it and can break into it at any point. Jethro drew the right conclusions.

But did Jethro really become an exclusive worshiper of Yahweh? Commentators have long been divided over this. After all, Jethro did not deny that there were other gods, as Naaman, the Syrian general would do (2 Kgs 5:15). Furthermore, it has been pointed out that Jethro's sacrifices were made to Elohim ("God," 18:12) rather than to Yahweh. But I think these objections are beside the point. If the statement of incomparability here is not a sign of full commitment, then neither is the one made by Moses in his Song of the Sea (15:11). What both of these statements are saying is that Yahweh has shown himself to be a completely different category than the things called "gods" (see the comment on 15:11). As for the usage of the divine name, these 12 verses provide an interesting study. When referring to God as a divine reality, Elohim is used. But, when referring to the revelation of that divine reality given exclusively to the Israelites, Yahweh is used (18:1). Thus, in context with verse 11, verse 12 is clearly stating that the nature of the divine reality, Elohim, has been climactically revealed in Yahweh. To worship God is to worship Yahweh and vice versa. The fact that the elders of Israel joined with Jethro in the sacrificial meal[7] is clear evidence of their acceptance of his confession.[8]

ENDNOTES
1. Eliezer was not named prior to this, but the fact that 4:20 has "sons" in the plural indicates his presence.
2. Cf. the references to "The Book of the Wars of the Lord" (Num 21:14) or "The Book of Jashar" (Josh 10:13; 2 Sam 1:18).
3. I think Enns (2000:368) is correct when he says that the reference to "the sword of Pharaoh" refers not to a particular incident such as the one reported in 2:15 but to the entire experience of deliverance.
4. Some commentators (e.g., Fretheim 1991:196) point out that the text says "the tent" and believe that it was the temporary sanctuary that Moses had set up (cf. 33:7-11). However, that seems unlikely given the customs of hospitality that would require taking the guest into one's personal quarters.
5. It is not necessary to suppose that the references to "burnt offerings and sacrifices" here presuppose that the event must have happened after the giving of the Sinai covenant. Note that Moses referred to these in 10:25. Clearly there were such offerings made by people prior to Sinai. The Israelites' offerings and sacrifices were simply regularized in specific ways by that Covenant legislation.
6. See 5:2; 6:7; 7:17; 8:10, 22; 9:14, 30; 11:7; 14:18; 16:12.

7. The Hebrew word for "bread" is used here; Enns (2000:370) wonders where it came from. However, the term "bread" can be used as a figure of speech for "food" (cf. Gen 3:19; Lev 21:6), and that is probably the case here.
8. Since ceremonial meals of this sort are used elsewhere in the OT to solemnize covenants (cf. 24:5, 11; Gen 26:30; 31:54), Sarna (1991:99) and others suggest that that was what was taking place here. If so, it would further the contrast with the Amalekites. However, the absence of any actual reference to covenant-making or a covenant makes this suggestion unlikely in my judgment.

◆ ## 2. Jethro's advice for organizing the people (18:13-27)

¹³The next day, Moses took his seat to hear the people's disputes against each other. They waited before him from morning till evening.

¹⁴When Moses' father-in-law saw all that Moses was doing for the people, he asked, "What are you really accomplishing here? Why are you trying to do all this alone while everyone stands around you from morning till evening?"

¹⁵Moses replied, "Because the people come to me to get a ruling from God. ¹⁶When a dispute arises, they come to me, and I am the one who settles the case between the quarreling parties. I inform the people of God's decrees and give them his instructions."

¹⁷"This is not good!" Moses' father-in-law exclaimed. ¹⁸"You're going to wear yourself out—and the people, too. This job is too heavy a burden for you to handle all by yourself. ¹⁹Now listen to me, and let me give you a word of advice, and may God be with you. You should continue to be the people's representative before God, bringing their disputes to him. ²⁰Teach them God's decrees, and give them his instructions. Show them how to conduct their lives. ²¹But select from all the people some capable, honest men who fear God and hate bribes. Appoint them as leaders over groups of one thousand, one hundred, fifty, and ten. ²²They should always be available to solve the people's common disputes, but have them bring the major cases to you. Let the leaders decide the smaller matters themselves. They will help you carry the load, making the task easier for you. ²³If you follow this advice, and if God commands you to do so, then you will be able to endure the pressures, and all these people will go home in peace."

²⁴Moses listened to his father-in-law's advice and followed his suggestions. ²⁵He chose capable men from all over Israel and appointed them as leaders over the people. He put them in charge of groups of one thousand, one hundred, fifty, and ten. ²⁶These men were always available to solve the people's common disputes. They brought the major cases to Moses, but they took care of the smaller matters themselves.

²⁷Soon after this, Moses said good-bye to his father-in-law, who returned to his own land.

NOTES

18:13 *hear the people's disputes.* Lit., "to judge the people," which has a broader sense, something like "to bring order to the people." More seems to have been involved than merely the hearing of disputes (so 18:16).

18:14 *really accomplishing here.* This may go a bit farther than necessary. "What are you doing?" is probably the sense. The word *dabar* [TH1697, ZH1821] (word, event, thing) appears here for the first of 10 times in these 14 verses (also 18:16, 17, 18, 19, 22 [twice], 23, 26 [twice]). It is used in two ways: as here, the "activity" in which Moses is engaged (also

18:23); and the "matters" the people have to bring up for a decision of some sort.

18:18 *going to wear yourself out.* This is emphatic in Hebrew: "You will surely wear yourself out."

18:19 *and may God be with you.* Perhaps better understood as "and God will be with you."

18:20 *Teach.* A rather strong term having overtones of warning and admonition.

18:21 *capable.* This is a reasonable translation of *'anshe khayil* [TH376/2428, ZH408/2657] (men of force, or substance). The phrase may well speak of people in the noble class, and some would say the idea is of those who have wealth and thus are theoretically less open to bribery. However, while Ruth (*'esheth khayil* [TH802/2428, ZH851/2657]; Ruth 3:11) may have been of noble birth (in Moab), she definitely was not wealthy. Here I think the point is that these are men of noble character (so NIV in Ruth 3:11) or of excellence (so NASB in Ruth 3:11) or of virtue (so NLT in Ruth 3:11).

honest. Lit., "men of truth." The sense here is that these are men who will be true to their word, to their people, to their calling, and above all, to God. These are people who are reliable and trustworthy.

18:23 *and if God commands.* Although this rendering is traditional (see KJV, NIV, NASB), the conditional element is not specifically stated. Several recent commentators take the statement to be declarative: "and God is commanding it."

18:27 *Soon after this.* This is an inference, but it may not be correct. Numbers 10:29 suggests that Jethro's departure may not have occurred until the tribes were ready to leave Sinai.

COMMENTARY

If the first part of this chapter (18:1-12) looked back, recapping the significance of what had taken place previously, this second part looks forward, not only to the new administrative situation that would exist after Jethro's suggestions had been put in place, but also to the formalization of God's laws and instructions (18:20) in the Sinai covenant and to Moses's significant place in that process. The revelation of Yahweh's power and providence had taken place; now would come the revelation of those principles of life that express the character of this mighty God. In particular, as both Childs (1974:332, 335) and Fretheim (1991:197-198) observe, the report of this incident at this place makes it clear that there is no conflict between special revelation and wisdom, or between creation and redemption. In advising Moses how to organize the people, Jethro made no claim to special revelation, although he did clearly believe that he was speaking for God (see notes on 18:19, 23). This presentation of godly wisdom through Jethro emphasizes that what God gave from Mt. Sinai was not some arbitrary set of demands from a heavenly tyrant. Rather, he was codifying and regularizing the principles which he had built into his universe, many of which had been discovered by thoughtful people before this but apart from the realization that there was a transcendent creator—thus they had not realized that these principles were an expression of his very nature. Accordingly, while the instructions of the Sinai covenant did indeed reveal the sinful nature of humanity (Rom 7:7, 9), that is not the explanation of their purpose. As Moses would say later, they were given for our good (Deut 10:13), to help us know who our creator is and how he intends us to live.

But, as Houtman (1993:2.396) observes, Jethro's advice also prepared for the events of Sinai in another way. Because Moses was freed from the mass of administrative trivia that was engulfing him, he was able to focus on the main thing, communicating the covenant to the people. Furthermore, just as the system of delegation made it possible for the "major cases" (18:22, 26) to work their way up to Moses, so also there was an effective means for passing the words of God from Moses down to the smallest group of people, the "ten" (18:25). So here, as the old era is closed, the foundations for the new one are laid.

Moses was apparently functioning like a pharaoh. To date, no written law codes have been unearthed in Egypt. The pharaoh was the fount of wisdom, and apparently his judgments were *ad hoc*. Of course, there would have been precedents from previous rulings, and of course, there was a chain of administration. But still, everything revolved around the pharaoh and his judgments. Jethro could see that this would not work in the situation there in the desert. Not only was Moses being worn out but the people were too (18:18). Perhaps Jethro's "This is not good!" (18:17) goes even further than mere pragmatism: The language is reminiscent of Genesis 1 and 2 where "good" expresses agreement with God's creative purposes. And to be sure, it is not within God's creative plan for everything to revolve around one person. As the Tabernacle account shows most beautifully, God's plan is for every person to have something of value and significance to contribute to any process (35:20-29). Thus, I wonder if Jethro's comment does not go well beneath the surface of this scene. Certainly his comments in verses 19 and 23 point in this way. In verse 19 (see note) he says that if Moses follows his advice God will "be with" Moses. And in verse 23 (see note) it seems most likely that he actually says in a flat assertion, "God commands you to do it." It is possible that he softened the demand by suggesting that Moses should inquire of God for himself on the issue (as NLT has it in v. 23), but the fact that Moses immediately put the suggestion into force seems to argue for the first alternative.[1]

It is to Moses's credit that he did not hesitate to take the recommended action. To be sure, he may have seen it as a welcome relief. At the same time, normal human nature does not give up its prerogatives easily, and the fact that he did so at once says that he experienced a remarkable freedom from ego-centeredness, as is confirmed throughout the succeeding books. Instead, he chose the kind of men Jethro had indicated (18:21, 25).[2] They were marked by four characteristics: "capable" (see note on 18:21), "honest" (see note on 18:21), fearers of God, haters of bribes. Other descriptions of judges appear in Deuteronomy 1:16-17; 16:18-19; 1 Samuel 12:3-4; and 2 Chronicles 19:6. All of them have in common the prohibition of taking bribes. In God's world, fairness, equity, and justice cannot exist alongside self-interest. But the other qualities listed here are also significant. These must not be small, petty people. They need to be absolutely reliable. And above all, they must be people who know that a supreme God exists and that he will hold them accountable for their behavior (the "fear of God"). Such persons will handle the affairs of others without reference to themselves, or to their own personal standards of justice. They will do the right thing regardless of appearances.

Jethro did not suggest that Moses should simply quit doing all that he had been doing previously. Rather, he proposed a division of labor. Moses should continue to deal with the revelation and the promulgation of the divine principles (18:20). He should "teach them" (in the sense of warning and admonishing them; see note on 18:20) the laws and instructions of God. But except for major cases (18:22), he should leave the day-to-day administration of these to the chosen officials, who were again prevented from arrogating too much to themselves by the division into thousands, hundreds, fifties, and tens.[3] This division of Moses's roles prevented either principles or practice from becoming absolute. Too often the exigencies of practice can subtly change the principles, and we fall into the bottomless pit of "what works." Conversely, principles can become so sacrosanct that they become more important than people. This is what had happened in Jesus' day, and he had to remind people that the reason the Sabbath laws had been stated so prescriptively was for people's sake and not the other way around (Mark 2:27). When preservation of the principle (interpreted in certain ways) becomes the most important thing, we have missed the point of the principle. Moses was prevented from becoming immersed in practice, but still a way was preserved so that principles and practices were connected.

ENDNOTES
1. So both Houtman (1993:2.420) and Childs (1974:331).
2. Sarna (1991:100) points out the surprising fact that this selection completely bypassed the normal persons one might expect: elders, tribal leaders, priests and Levites. He sees this as evidence of the account's antiquity and authenticity, since it is hard to imagine a later, fictional account doing this. The choice is based on fitness for office and nothing else.
3. These divisions seem to correspond to military divisions, again cutting across exclusively tribal lines.

◆ III. Covenant: A Revelation of Yahweh's Character (19:1–24:18)
A. Motivation to Accept the Covenant (19:1-25)

Exactly two months after the Israelites left Egypt,* they arrived in the wilderness of Sinai. ²After breaking camp at Rephidim, they came to the wilderness of Sinai and set up camp there at the base of Mount Sinai.

³Then Moses climbed the mountain to appear before God. The LORD called to him from the mountain and said, "Give these instructions to the family of Jacob; announce it to the descendants of Israel: ⁴'You have seen what I did to the Egyptians. You know how I carried you on eagles' wings and brought you to myself. ⁵Now if you will obey me and keep my covenant, you will be my own special treasure from among all the peoples on earth; for all the earth belongs to me. ⁶And you will be my kingdom of priests, my holy nation.' This is the message you must give to the people of Israel."

⁷So Moses returned from the mountain and called together the elders of the people and told them everything the LORD had commanded him. ⁸And all the people responded together, "We will do everything

the LORD has commanded." So Moses brought the people's answer back to the LORD.

⁹Then the LORD said to Moses, "I will come to you in a thick cloud, Moses, so the people themselves can hear me when I speak with you. Then they will always trust you."

Moses told the LORD what the people had said. ¹⁰Then the LORD told Moses, "Go down and prepare the people for my arrival. Consecrate them today and tomorrow, and have them wash their clothing. ¹¹Be sure they are ready on the third day, for on that day the LORD will come down on Mount Sinai as all the people watch. ¹²Mark off a boundary all around the mountain. Warn the people, 'Be careful! Do not go up on the mountain or even touch its boundaries. Anyone who touches the mountain will certainly be put to death. ¹³No hand may touch the person or animal that crosses the boundary; instead, stone them or shoot them with arrows. They must be put to death.' However, when the ram's horn sounds a long blast, then the people may go up on the mountain.*"

¹⁴So Moses went down to the people. He consecrated them for worship, and they washed their clothes. ¹⁵He told them, "Get ready for the third day, and until then abstain from having sexual intercourse."

¹⁶On the morning of the third day, thunder roared and lightning flashed, and a dense cloud came down on the mountain. There was a long, loud blast from a ram's horn, and all the people trembled. ¹⁷Moses led them out from the camp to meet with God, and they stood at the foot of the mountain. ¹⁸All of Mount Sinai was covered with smoke because the LORD had descended on it in the form of fire. The smoke billowed into the sky like smoke from a brick kiln, and the whole mountain shook violently. ¹⁹As the blast of the ram's horn grew louder and louder, Moses spoke, and God thundered his reply. ²⁰The LORD came down on the top of Mount Sinai and called Moses to the top of the mountain. So Moses climbed the mountain.

²¹Then the LORD told Moses, "Go back down and warn the people not to break through the boundaries to see the LORD, or they will die. ²²Even the priests who regularly come near to the LORD must purify themselves so that the LORD does not break out and destroy them."

²³"But LORD," Moses protested, "the people cannot come up to Mount Sinai. You already warned us. You told me, 'Mark off a boundary all around the mountain to set it apart as holy.'"

²⁴But the LORD said, "Go down and bring Aaron back up with you. In the meantime, do not let the priests or the people break through to approach the LORD, or he will break out and destroy them."

²⁵So Moses went down to the people and told them what the LORD had said.

19:1 Hebrew *In the third month after the Israelites left Egypt, on the very day,* i.e., two lunar months to the day after leaving Egypt. Compare Num 33:3. 19:13 Or *up to the mountain.*

NOTES

19:1 *Exactly two months.* Lit., "in the third month, on this day." The NLT's interpretation is one possibility. Another is that the Israelites arrived at Sinai on the first day of the third month, which would have been approximately six weeks after the Exodus (which occurred sometime after the fifteenth day of the first month; see 12:6, 37). For a fuller discussion, see Cassuto 1967:223.

19:3 *Moses.* Since this stands in an emphatic position in the clause, Cassuto (1967:226) argues that it indicates a contrast between the people setting up camp and Moses immediately going up the mountain (see commentary).

19:5 *obey me.* Lit., "if you will surely hear my voice." The NLT is not incorrect, but it fails to convey the emphatic, personal nature of what is being said. To obey is to carry out the expressed wishes of not only the King but also the Father. This is the first of four significant occurrences of *qol* [TH6963, ZH7754] (voice, sound) in this chapter (cf. 19:16, 19).

special treasure. This term (*segullah* [TH5459, ZH6035]) is known from Akkadian (and as a loan word in Hittite) to indicate a personal possession to which the owner has exclusive rights. In those languages, as well as Hebrew, it can be applied to both things (1 Chr 29:3; Eccl 2:8) and to persons (cf. Ps 135:4; Mal 3:17). In the Torah its use is reserved for Israel's relation to God. (See commentary for further discussion.)

19:6 This is the message. Lit., "these are the words." The Hebrew idea for "word" is connected to the root *dabar* [TH1696, ZH1819]. Words having the consonants *d-b-r*, including two occurrences of the word *midbar* [TH4057, ZH4497] (wilderness), occur nine times in this chapter. Cassuto (1967:235) observes that if the occurrence of "words" (NLT, "instructions") in 20:1 is included, there are ten occurrences of *d-b-r* here, just as there were in ch 18. He concludes this is not accidental in view of the "ten words" of the Decalogue (see note on 20:1).

19:9 I will come. This is a participle in Hebrew, probably with the sense of imminence: "I am just about to come."

19:13 ram's horn. Not the same term as in 19:16 and 19. There it is *shopar* [TH7782, ZH8795]; here it is *yobel* [TH3104, ZH3413]. Perhaps the intent is to speak of two different events: a natural one in the first case, and a supernatural in the second. However, the text does not specify that the events are different. Houtman (1993:2.453) says that the difference is the result of combining originally separate accounts.

19:16 thunder. Heb. *qoloth* [TH6963, ZH7754] (sounds, voices); cf. 19:5.

19:18 the whole mountain shook violently. The LXX has "the people were amazed"; Vulgate and Syriac support MT. Other biblical examples of mountains shaking at God's presence (several of them reflective of this account) are Pss 18:7; 68:8; Isa 5:25; Nah 1:5; Hab 3:10.

19:19 thundered his reply. Lit., "answered him with a voice" (*beqol*). I agree with several commentators (Cassuto 1967:232; Houtman 1993:2.457; Childs 1974:369) who argue that the singular of *qol* [TH6963, ZH7754] here is intended to be a pun on and a contrast with the plural *qoloth* in 19:16 (see note). There it was thunder, here it is a voice (cf. Deut 4:12).

19:21 see. Sarna (1991:107) plausibly suggests that this is to cease to be a worshiper and to succumb to curiosity, i.e., to become a spectator.

19:24 priests. The fact that they were excluded from the mountain along with the people suggests a solution to the problem about what kind of "priests" these were. If priests had not yet been appointed (28:1; 32:26-29), how could there be priests? Unquestionably, the Hebrews had people who functioned as priests for them in the years prior to Sinai. What this is saying is that these functionaries had no special standing with God and were thus no different from *the people* in his mind.

COMMENTARY

With chapter 19 we come to the third main division of the book of Exodus, chapters 19–24, which contains the revelation of God's character by means of the giving of the covenant. The descendants of Abraham in Egypt had lived there for 400 years with only the oral reminiscences of their ancestors' encounter with a particular God. Now they had been given a new revelation of that God's identity (Yahweh) and a new firsthand experience of his power, culminating in the events of the Exodus. They had been given a revelation of his providential care during the journey through the wilderness. But who is this God, this Yahweh? What is his character? Is he consistent? Is he ethical? Does he have integrity? In fact, most of what the Israelites had learned about deity in their 400-year sojourn in Egypt had been diametrically opposite to the truth. They had learned that God is the world. That means he is many and that he is capable of being manipulated through the world. They had learned that God is profoundly sexual and that sexual behavior of all sorts is a participation in the divine. And since the gods are coterminous with this world, their character is precisely like that of humans, only more so. Thus, while the gods can be more trustworthy than humans, they can also be more fickle. While they can tell the truth more penetratingly than humans, they can also lie more cunningly. Thus, humans are an afterthought in the grand scheme of things, a distant reflection of the divine—so the Israelites had learned in Egypt.

But all of these ideas are untrue. God is not the world; he transcends it. God is not many; he is One. God cannot be manipulated through the world; he can only be trusted and surrendered to. God is not sexual and may not be approached through human sexual behavior. God is absolutely trustworthy; he never lies. In creation, humans are of ultimate worth, the very image of God. But how was God to teach his people these complex truths, so contrary to what the Egyptians and every other brilliant people in the world believed? They were former slaves, so no complex intellectual or philosophical educational scheme was feasible. The answer was the covenant. God would call his people to act in certain ways that would be expressive of their relationship with him.

God's goals in giving the covenant were not only educational. It is evident in the total context of Scripture that God does not merely intend for people to *know* his character, he also intends his people to *share* his character. God gave the people his covenant as a means to that end. As the people did what the covenant required, they would in fact be acting in conformity with God's character. As they learned to value their neighbor's property, life, spouse, and name, they would be treating people as being worthy of respect, just as God does. They would in fact be becoming "holy because I, the LORD your God, am holy" (Lev 19:2). This truth becomes even more apparent when we realize that Exodus 19 opens a block of material that extends through Numbers 10:10.[1] When that entire block of material is studied as a unit, God's goal of transforming his people into his own ethical likeness so that he can take up residence not merely among them but in them is unmistakable.

There is yet a third purpose of the covenant that is more implicit but also, in the total context of Scripture, unmistakable. If the people who crossed the sea did not know God, neither did they know themselves. They did not realize that ever since the events recorded in Genesis 3, there has been resident in us a settled hostility to God's will and way in our lives. They believed that to serve God only required an act of decision (evident in 19:8; 24:3, 7). They were not insincere in their declaration of their intention to obey God in everything. They simply did not know the problem. Their repeated failure to fulfill their sworn obligations, beginning as early as the event reported in Exodus 32, only a few weeks from the giving of the covenant, left them frustrated and defeated. There is no clearer expression of this frustration and defeat than that which the apostle Paul declares in Romans 7, where he recounts his experience as a faithful Jew. The thing which the Israelite, and then Jewish, people loved most, the Torah, condemned them at every turn for their inability to conform to it.

This raises one more issue we must discuss before we leave this introduction to the covenant. The covenant does not stand as the antithesis to grace. It *could* become that and did so in the emergence of Pharisaism during the intertestamental period (largely equivalent to the Second Temple period). But the context of Exodus makes it very clear that that such an understanding misses the point (as both Jesus and Paul said in a variety of ways). Conformity to God's character through obedience to his expressed will is a *response* to the prior grace of Passover and Exodus. Obedience does not earn admission into the saving presence of God. It never did and it never will, as Paul so eloquently expressed it in the first three chapters of Romans, as well as in the first four chapters of Galatians. Rather, it is the way in which delivered people express their undying gratitude to their deliverer (as 19:4-6 so clearly shows). It is one thing if a person does not want to emulate the life and behavior of another human who has delivered him or her from a terrible fate, but it is quite another if the Deliverer is both the beginning and the end of one's created life! Refusal to give one's life in conformity to the Deliverer is not merely gross ingratitude, it is also the height of stupidity. So the covenant was given to give direction to that grateful response. It was never intended to be the *way* to God; it was always intended shape one's *walk* with God.[2]

Chapters 19 and 24 provide "bookends" for the giving of the covenant.[3] Chapter 19 provides preparation for the giving, while chapter 24 tells the story of the consummation. This enclosure of the covenant stipulations in these narrative portions is very significant.[4] Above all, this structure roots obedience in life and in the context of a relationship with God. Too often, we view the Old Testament "law" as simply arbitrary demands dropped from heaven by an immutable divine tyrant, with a kind of "do or die" mentality. That is not the case, as the immediate structure, as well as the larger book structure, shows. God gave his people his covenant in the midst of their saving experience with him. Thus, the "Torah" ("Instruction") is not merely the 613 commandments that can be extracted from Exodus 19 through Deuteronomy 33. Rather, it is the entire story, from Genesis 1 to Deuteronomy 34. God's "instruction" for life is to be found in the *context* of life, and we are intended to live out God's will for us in the context of life.

Yahweh Talks to Moses (19:1-9). The giving of the covenant was the critical moment in God's plan for his people. If they refused to make a life commitment to him, then his plans for them would be effectively thwarted. As I have said before in several places, in God's mind, the giving of the land of Canaan was quite secondary. What God wanted to give the people was himself. This is ultimately why he led them through Sinai rather than taking them straight to the land. If they got the land but did not get him, they were forever lost. Their problem, and ours, is not a matter of landlessness but of Godlessness. Thus, it was critical that the people be properly prepared to make the right decision. The considerable lengths to which God went to prepare them, as reported in chapter 19, underscore that fact. God's preparation fully recognized the complexity of human personality in that it took place on the cognitive level (19:3-9), the volitional level (19:10-15), and the affective level (19:16-25).[5] When this preparation was completed, the response in chapter 24 was not quite a foregone conclusion, but it certainly meant that a refusal was very unlikely.

Attempts to locate Mount Sinai (19:2) have been frustrated from the beginning. Everything points to its having been an actual mountain on the Sinai peninsula, yet it seems impossible to go beyond that. Its identification with Jebel Musa ("Mount Moses") is of relatively recent date. Beyond the obvious connection of the name and the general possibility that that location could fit into one understanding of the wilderness itinerary (Num 33:5-49) there is no other reason to make a connection. There is a similar ambiguity in the case of Jesus: There can be no reasonable doubt of his historical existence, yet we lack even one description of his physical appearance. God clearly was seeking to prevent us from equating specific physical features with incarnation. So here, it seems God was guarding against any possibility of equating one place with his sole appearance. Cassuto (1967:225) says it is fitting that "the happening should be shrouded in the mists of sanctity."

Cassuto's understanding of verse 3 (see note) seems very likely to me. Once the people were settled at the base of Mount Sinai, Moses was on his way to the top. It is easy to understand why this might have been the case. This is where the whole experience had started, perhaps as much as a year earlier. And now the sign that God had promised (3:12) had been fulfilled in ways Moses could never have imagined. How eager he must have been. And he was not disappointed. God met him and, as before, spoke with him. What Yahweh said in those moments (as recorded in 19:4-6) could almost be taken as a summary of his whole plan for the human race. These three sentences are pregnant with meaning. Taken together they provide a theological (thus, cognitive) underpinning for everything the covenant was going to be about. They encompass references to the past, the present, and the future. They call the people to remember what had happened in the past and to draw sensible conclusions regarding appropriate responses to those happenings. They are pregnant with wonderful promises for the future and call upon the people to take present actions that will make the fulfillment of those promises a possibility.

Specifically, Yahweh called upon the people to remember what had happened in Egypt (19:4). He pointed out two diametrically opposite results. The Egyptians had sought to thwart God's will and Israel had "seen" (19:4) what had happened. By contrast, the Israelites had believed God and, however fearfully, had done what he told them to do. The result? God had carried them "on eagles' wings and brought" them to himself (19:4).[6] As opposed to the frightful cataclysms of nature that may well have destroyed nearly a whole Egyptian generation, Yahweh had made nature care for his people as he brought them through the wilderness. What kind of conclusion should one draw from these facts? Only fools refuse to trust, believe, and obey Yahweh! So the people were called on to reflect on the lessons of history.

We dare not leave this verse without noting what the purpose of the Exodus was: It was that God might bring the Israelites to himself. This is profoundly significant if we are to understand the biblical theology of salvation correctly. We tend to focus our understanding of salvation upon what God can do for us; thus, it can become a thoroughly self-centered kind of thing. Or, alternatively, we focus on what we, as disciples who have been saved, must do for him. But both these perspectives miss the central point. God delivers us from sin, sorrow, and shame in order *that he might have a vital relationship with us*. This will only become clearer as the book proceeds to its close. God delivers us from the bondage of sin because he wants fellowship with us and because we die without fellowship with him. Any understanding of salvation that misses this point is to that extent a deficient one.

Verse 5 continues the cognitive preparation for receiving the covenant with a conditional promise for the future: If the people will enter into a covenant relationship with Yahweh, they will become his "special treasure" (see note). Here is the other side of the previous verse: God delivered the people from Egypt in order to bring them to himself. But the fellowship he desires depends on a reciprocal response from the people! They will become his "special treasure" only if they agree to become so. Upon a moment's reflection, this is completely understandable. There is no true fellowship between persons without a reciprocal agreement that it shall be so. A bride may purchase her wedding jewelry (cf. *segullah* [TH5459, ZH6035] "jewels," Mal 3:17, KJV) and the jewelry has nothing to say about it, but a groom does not secure the love of his bride without her consent.[7]

But if Israel will say yes to a covenant relationship with God, there is nothing that can prevent God from making them his "special treasure from among all the peoples on earth" (19:5). The reason why is that "all the earth belongs" to him (19:5). This, of course, is an astounding statement. The other religions knew nothing so exclusive as this. Not even the high god of a given culture possessed all the earth. There were other cultures and other peoples, and one's own local god might or might not have the power to outface one of their gods for regional dominance, but even then that would not mean universal dominance. But Yahweh promised his people that if they would choose him in an exclusive way, he would be able to give them a unique place in all the world because as sole owner of the earth he could do whatever he chose in the earth.

Verse 6 spells out further what that unique relationship would mean for Israel. Two profound phrases are used to describe it: "my kingdom of priests" and "my holy nation." Note that both phrases are modified by the first-person possessive pronoun. Israel would be these things in relation to Yahweh: They would be a kingdom, a nation, for him and to him. Take that away and they would be nothing. The second thing to note is that the two phrases are probably roughly synonymous. If the Israelites accepted God's covenant and became his special treasure, they would become a particular kind of "kingdom," a particular kind of "nation." And once again, the qualifiers are distinctly relational. They would become a nation reflective of a unique relationship to God. That relationship would involve both special function and special character. Just as the priesthood was separated from the laity by virtue of a life given to the service of God and the revelation of his ways to the people, so Israel would be set apart from the rest of the kingdoms of the earth for service and revelation.[8] But that which belongs to a god exclusively (and is thus holy) must share the character of the god (*be* holy). Sarna (1991:104) makes the observation that wherever Israel is said to be the "special treasure" of God (Deut 7:6; 14:2; 26:18-19), there is emphasized "the inextricable association between being God's *segullah* [TH5459, ZH6035] and the pursuit of holiness." He goes on to say (citing Ps 114:1-2) that "holiness is to be achieved by human imitation of God's attributes." Peter shares this understanding when he makes it clear that to "be holy" is to live lives that reflect the character of God (1 Pet 1:13–2:3).

So Yahweh had given two powerful reasons why the Israelites should choose to enter a covenant with God in the present—namely, the past and the future. On the evidence of what God had done *to* their enemies and *for* them in the past, refusing his offer now would be foolish indeed. But beyond that were wonderful promises for the future. Israel could share a unique relationship with him that would involve both a special function and a special character in the world. The result was that the people were convinced. When they heard what God had said (19:7), they responded with alacrity that they would "do everything the LORD has commanded" (19:8). Commentators have been somewhat bemused by this response. How could Israel have "signed on the dotted line" without knowing what they were committing to do? Some have wondered whether in fact this was actually a response to the Abrahamic covenant.[9] Others cite this as evidence that the text is chronologically "disarranged" (Fretheim 1991:211-212). Still others think this points to the "laws and instructions" already given in the desert on the way to Sinai (cf. Houtman 1993:2.435-436). I don't think any of these options are correct. The fact is that Israel had not entered into the covenant at all at this stage. No ceremony had taken place; no oath had been sworn. The people had simply given a verbal agreement to what clearly lay ahead.[10] In the language of negotiation, they had agreed to continue the process, and that agreement would be part of the motivation for them to go ahead with the final agreement once they knew the precise terms of the commitment.

As it stands in the text now, verse 9 seems to be parenthetical. This is something that God had said in the course of the prior conversation as an aside. As such it relates to the question of whether Moses would be able to convince the people to actually accept the terms of the covenant when he came to give them. It is one thing for the people to say a quick (though sincere) yes while contemplating the glorious past and the promised future. It might be much more difficult for them to say a similar yes when faced with all the specific expectations that the covenant would actually place upon them. But God had assured Moses that he would provide additional evidences for the people that he was indeed speaking the very words of God. The result would be that the *trust* in Moses that had been given at the sea (14:31) and sorely tried in the desert would be reaffirmed powerfully at Sinai, with a result of complete acceptance of the covenant.[11]

Preparation of the People (19:10-15). In these verses, Yahweh continues to prepare his people, focusing especially on the volitional. Now he gives them specific tasks which they could choose to perform or not to perform. This is similar to what took place in the desert, where the people were called upon to follow certain directions with regard to the manna (see above on ch 16). God was training them for obedience to his word in small ways. Because the preparations are grouped together, it is difficult to determine how many times Moses went up and down the mountain. We note that in verse 7 Moses is reported to have gone down the mountain, and then in verse 10 Moses is told by the Lord to go down the mountain (and did so as reported in 19:14), and we conclude that he must have ascended again after the response in verse 8. That is not impossible. However, I suspect that there was one ascent and descent between 19:3 and 19:19, with one set of instructions, which have been divided in this report into the cognitive and the volitional areas.

God directed Moses to have the people engage in three kinds of activities. These included washing their clothing (19:10), marking "off a boundary all around the mountain" (19:12), and abstaining from sexual intercourse (19:15). As I have suggested above, all of these have their significance in the fact that they required the people to do something in response to God's directions, exactly what they would have to do in accepting the covenant. Thus, exactly what they did was not as important as that they did it. All three of these actions have symbolic significance for what was going to take place.

Ever since God first began to speak to Abraham, he had been revealing more and more about himself. There at the outset, he had to convince him that he could be trusted. Thus, there was not a special emphasis on the holiness of his character in those early encounters.[12] He needed to show that he is approachable. But he was now moving beyond that in these encounters at Sinai. He had proven himself incomparable both in power and providence. But who is this one whose power and providence are incomparable, who can be trusted to the farthest limits? Is he "first among equals" of the gods? Is he the most holy of the holy ones? No, he is the *only* holy one, absolutely transcendent over his creation, absolutely unapproachable by human initiative, absolutely incapable of being manipulated through this world. To be sure, if *this* one is trustworthy, if this one's power and providence are available for his children's good, that is great news. But it was now time for the people to come to realize just who it was who was inviting them into his embrace.

He is to us as a roaring blast furnace is to a bale of hay, and that point must never be forgotten. This, then is the significance of these required preparatory actions: God is clean and there is no defilement in him whatsoever, so those who come into his presence must wear clean clothes. God is unapproachable by human initiative and is never to be explained as some extension of human nature. There is an absolute boundary between him and his creation. So, there must be a "boundary all around the mountain," and whoever or whatever crossed that boundary except at his express invitation had to be put to death (19:12). Furthermore, holiness is so contagious and so deadly apart from God's grace that no one could touch whatever had crossed the barrier. They had to be shot with arrows or stoned to death (19:13).[13] Finally, it is not possible to participate in the mysterious power of God through sexual behavior—an idea they might have otherwise assumed based on practices in surrounding cultures. Sexuality is a great and good gift that God has given to his creatures, especially his human creatures, but he himself is "suprasexual." Thus, sex was not to be abstained from here as from something bad, it was to be abstained from as a witness that God is holy, utterly transcendent.[14]

The Final Preparations (19:16-25). These verses report the final phase of God's preparation of the people. Nowhere else in Scripture is a theophany (an appearance of God) accompanied by these kinds of visual, tactile, and aural manifestations. Again, this is a testimony to the incredible importance of what was about to take place, not only for Israel, but for the whole human race. If Israel, now having some glimpse of just who it was who was inviting them into covenant, would accept his offer and bind themselves exclusively to him, then it would be possible for God to reveal himself to them and to the world in ways that would mean God's creation purposes could be truly realized. If they would not, then perhaps God would have to begin all over again with a new Abraham. This was indeed a critical moment and anything consistent with God's integrity would be justified to bring the people to the place of response.

The period of preparatory activity leading up to this great experience was three days in length (19:11). Sarna (1991:105) suggests this was to allow ample time for sober reflection upon what they were going to be asked to do. I suspect it was also designed to heighten anticipation. At any rate, "on the morning of the third day" (19:16), the Israelites' nerves must have been on end. Thus, when the unseen ram's horn began to blow they rose to the doors of their tents as if on wires. And when they looked through the tent flaps and saw the mountain wrapped in "smoke" and "fire" (19:18), they needed no one to tell them what was happening. As he had said he would (19:11), God had "come down" on the mountain. How gingerly they must have stepped up to the boundary line all around the mountain,[15] and as they felt the ground shaking under their feet, saw the lightning and the billowing smoke, and listened to the "thunder" and the "blast" (19:16) of the ram's horn rising to a scream, one would think that they were as prepared as humanly possible to receive all that God wanted to give them.[16]

But the final verses of the chapter (19:21-25) tell us that with all the cognitive, volitional, and affective preparation that had taken place, Yahweh was still not satisfied that everyone had gotten the picture.[17] This is entirely understandable. These people had demonstrated an incredible obtuseness in a variety of ways. It was worth one more effort (despite Moses's rejoinder, 19:23) to drive the point home again: Yahweh is not this world; he is terrifyingly and awe-fully other. And if he gives himself in a binding commitment to humans, no one must ever think even once that this means that he has become a rabbit's foot or a four-leafed clover that humans can control or manipulate for their own selfish purposes. If Moses would drive that point home once more, then perhaps the people would be truly prepared to receive God's offer of such momentous dimensions.

ENDNOTES

1. So e.g., Houtman (1993.2:425) who cites Baentsch as saying that this block of material is "the heart and core of the Hexateuch" [i.e., the Pentateuch plus Joshua].
2. For a discussion of the relationship between the OT covenant and the ancient Near East treaty form and the implications of that relationship to an understanding of the biblical material, see the commentary on ch 20.
3. Cassuto (1967:223) observes that ch 19 begins abruptly and has an elevated, almost poetic, style that sets it off from the preceding chapters.
4. Fretheim (1991:201-207) takes this too far by including the rest of the book in an alternating structure of law and narrative. I do not think it is correct to include the Tabernacle instructions in the law. However, his reflections on the significance of the connection between law and narrative are helpful.
5. Critical commentators are agreed that this chapter is a compendium of pieces from several different original sources. But there is no agreement as to which materials go together and from which sources they came. Recent commentators like Fretheim, Childs, and Houtman, who are concerned to interpret the final form of the text, admit with a degree of surprise that the chapter does hold together rather well. But if anyone such as Cassuto attempts to explain how the chapter is genuinely unified, Childs will dismiss his efforts as "midrashic." In fact, when we recognize how the chapter as a whole prepares for the giving of the covenant, it is hard to believe that a redactor could have succeeded so well, while still leaving so much evidence (as the critics claim) of his inability to integrate elements of his sources successfully and coherently.
6. For a fuller description of the eagle's care, see Deut 32:11. On the idea of God carrying his people (as opposed to the gods who had to be carried by their worshipers), see Isa 45:20-46:7.
7. Christian theologians of both the Calvinist and the Arminian persuasions are agreed that human depravity is so complete that persons are unable to decide for God apart from his prior grace enabling the response. What they disagree upon is whether that grace is resistible or not.
8. Note that this understanding helps to further explain the final statement of 19:5. God did not choose Israel out of all the nations because he considered the other nations worthless. Rather he chose Israel precisely because those other nations belong to him and he cares about them. Israel is chosen so that they may be his vehicle for reaching them (cf. Isa 60:1-3; 66:18-24; Matt 12:18; Luke 2:32; Acts 15:15-18; Eph 3:1-13).
9. So Enns (2000:387), citing W. Dumbrell 1984:80-90.
10. As attractive as it is from the point of view of biblical theology to take Dumbrell's (and Enns's) position, there is nothing in the context pointing backward to Abraham and everything in the context pointing forward to the Sinai covenant.
11. Childs (1974:368, 374-375) mounts a full-scale form-critical analysis of ch 19 (including 20:18-21 in the analysis, although the canonical form of the text separates it from 19) and concludes that its purpose is to establish Moses's central role in the giving of the covenant. Thus v. 9 is a misplaced gloss on 8b designed to emphasize Moses's office. As I have argued above, the transparent purpose of ch 19 is to show how God prepared his people to accept a covenant with him.
12. It is not accidental that God is never referred to as "holy" in Genesis. The first intimation of this great truth is in this book (3:5). See the commentary on 3:1-10.
13. Sarna (1991:105) reports that Jewish exegetes saw the mountain as being equivalent to the sanctuary, with its three areas of increasing exclusivity. Thus, the area outside the boundary was for the people, the area inside the boundary but below the peak

was for the priests (symbolized by Aaron), and the peak was the Holy of Holies, where only Moses (representing the High Priest) could enter. That understanding may be correct, although it is not explicitly said that Aaron was excluded from the peak.

14. It is the Western canons of literature that demand absolute consistency. Thus, we note that while God is reported to have told Moses to tell the people to wash their clothes and set up a boundary around the mountain, Moses is not reported to have said anything about those but to have told them to abstain from sexual intercourse, which the text does not say God said! These kinds of things prompt Western literary critics to suggest that the text is composed of pieces from "heterogeneous origins" (cf. Houtman 1993:2.453). But note that the people are said to have washed their clothes (19:14) although there is no report of Moses having told them to. Clearly neither report is absolutely complete according to our standards, but each assumes all the information that is in the other.
15. Verse 17 shows that there is no conflict between vv. 12 and 13. When the trumpet sounded, it would be all right to come up to the foot of the mountain. Crossing the boundary was never in view under any circumstances.
16. Sarna (1991:106) aptly observes that there is no question that any of these "atmospherics" are to be identified with God. It is abundantly clear that while the thunder, lightning, smoke, fire, and shaking earth represent the presence of God, they are not that presence, as a pagan would assume, not recognizing a distinction between creator and creation.
17. Houtman (1993:2.460-461), reflecting the conclusions of several other commentators, concludes that the way in which these verses appear (with Moses having thus to run up and down the mountain) suggests an inept redactor who was merely combining all the pieces at hand to emphasize Yahweh's fearful holiness. The ease with which critical scholars can on the one hand commend the redactor(s) for great facility in combining disparate materials and on the other hand condemn him (them) for redactional failures is quite amazing.

◆ B. Presentation of the Covenant (20:1–23:33)
   1. The Ten Commandments: a summary of the terms (20:1-17)

Then God gave the people all these instructions*:

²"I am the LORD your God, who rescued you from the land of Egypt, the place of your slavery.
³"You must not have any other god but me.
⁴"You must not make for yourself an idol of any kind or an image of anything in the heavens or on the earth or in the sea. ⁵You must not bow down to them or worship them, for I, the LORD your God, am a jealous God who will not tolerate your affection for any other gods. I lay the sins of the parents upon their children; the entire family is affected—even children in the third and fourth generations of those who reject me. ⁶But I lavish unfailing love for a thousand generations on those* who love me and obey my commands.
⁷"You must not misuse the name of the LORD your God. The LORD will not let you go unpunished if you misuse his name.
⁸"Remember to observe the Sabbath day by keeping it holy. ⁹You have six days each week for your ordinary work, ¹⁰but the seventh day is a Sabbath day of rest dedicated to the LORD your God. On that day no one in your household may do any work. This includes you,

your sons and daughters, your male and female servants, your livestock, and any foreigners living among you. ¹¹For in six days the LORD made the heavens, the earth, the sea, and everything in them; but on the seventh day he rested. That is why the LORD blessed the Sabbath day and set it apart as holy.
¹²"Honor your father and mother. Then you will live a long, full life in the land the LORD your God is giving you.
¹³"You must not murder.
¹⁴"You must not commit adultery.
¹⁵"You must not steal.
¹⁶"You must not testify falsely against your neighbor.
¹⁷"You must not covet your neighbor's house. You must not covet your neighbor's wife, male or female servant, ox or donkey, or anything else that belongs to your neighbor."

20:1 Hebrew *all these words*. 20:6 Hebrew *for thousands of those*.

NOTES

20:1 *instructions.* Lit., "words," as per NLT mg. What Christians call "the Ten Commandments" are known in Judaism as "the Ten Words" (cf. 34:28; Deut 4:13; 10:4). In Hebrew, *dabar* [TH1696, ZH1819], often translated "word," has a much larger pool of connotations than the English term does. It can also refer to a "thing" or an "event." Thus, "the word of God" can refer to all the ways God communicated himself to humans, culminating in Jesus Christ (John 1:1-4; Heb 1:1-2).

20:3 *You must not have.* Lit., "there shall not be to you." The expression "not be" is singular; Cassuto (1967:241) argues that the sense is, "You shall not have even one other god." "You" here and throughout is in the singular, probably denoting the nation as a whole, but also facilitating application to each individual in the nation.

but me. Lit., "unto/upon/against my face." Because of the wide range of possible meanings of the preposition, it is difficult to gain agreement for a very precise translation. The traditional "before me" could mean "in my presence." The idea of "prior to me" is probably not a possibility. The NLT has opted for the sense "against (in opposition to) me," a very likely option. See the commentary for further discussion.

20:5 *jealous.* The Hebrew is *qanna'* [TH7067, ZH7862] (passionate concern, zeal). The particular form of the word found here is only used with God, probably to differentiate the form of the emotion in him from that of humans.

who will not tolerate your affection for any other gods. This is an addition to help explain the sense of "a jealous God."

20:6 *a thousand generations.* Although "generations" is not in the text, it is the correct inference as demonstrated by Deut 7:9.

20:7 *You must not misuse.* Lit., "you must not take up . . . in an empty way." Sarna (1991:111) says "take up" is an ellipsis for "take on your lips" (see commentary).

20:8 *by keeping it holy.* The Hebrew could also be taken as a purpose clause: "in order to keep it holy."

20:9 *your ordinary work.* "Ordinary" is an explanatory addition to help readers understand that not every burdensome activity is excluded.

20:10 *living among you.* Lit., "in your gates," i.e., "within your city, a part of your civic life."

20:13 *murder.* The Hebrew is *ratsakh* [TH7523, ZH8357]. Although the term can include manslaughter as well as intentional killing with malice, it does not refer to other kinds of killing, such as killing animals for food or carrying out executions.

COMMENTARY

In Exodus 20:1-23:33, God presents to his people the terms of the covenant, which he was inviting them to enter. The form that it takes is very close to that of the Hittite suzerainty covenants of the late-second millennium BC.[1] Thus, it begins with an introduction identifying the speaker (20:1). This is followed by a historical prologue telling what the occasion is that prompted the giving of the covenant (20:2). Then follow the stipulations, or terms, of the agreement (20:3-23:33). Many of the covenants also make provision for witnesses, a public reading, and safekeeping. These matters are addressed in chapters 23 and 24.

Why would God have made use of such a form to reveal his character and his will? Two interrelated reasons suggest themselves. First of all, in this instance God had to go outside any of the religious forms of the day. As I mentioned in the introduction to chapter 19, the truths he was revealing to his people about himself and the world were diametrically opposite to anything that the religions of Israel's neighbors held true. Thus, the religious literature was worse than useless, being permeated with an understanding of reality that was inimical to what God was revealing. A political form like the suzerainty covenant, while reflecting some of those understandings (see below on 24:4), was not necessarily saturated with them. The second reason why such a form was used was that God wanted his people to learn who he was in the context of relationship. He was not merely after education or obedience to some norms. The people needed to know *God*. And that knowing was only, *is* only, possible in the context of mutual, exclusive commitment. For this, a formalized covenant was ideal.

There were several features of the covenant form that made it highly appropriate for what God wanted to accomplish: (1) It called for exclusive commitment of the people to the great king. (2) It included absolute prohibitions. (3) It was rooted in history. (4) It reflected the personal wishes and behavior of the king. At the same time, the biblical adaptation produced something unlike anything that had existed before. As Sarna (1991:102-103) points out, nowhere else in the ancient world is there to be found this kind of committed relationship between God and an entire people. Furthermore, the location of the covenant within a broader narrative context is unique. The required responses were to be understood and worked out in the context of life.

In addition, the Bible offers a combination of covenant and law codes that is not found elsewhere. Law codes that predate Moses are known all over the ancient world. But apart from the opening lines where it is usually claimed these requirements were gotten from a god, there is no more religious grounding or motivation in the codes. They are, in fact, compilations of the pragmatic necessities for the functioning of earthly society. And the fulfillment of these requirements has nothing to do with any relationship. They are fulfilled as a result of civil and royal coercion. Thus ethics and religion were unrelated, and they were that way out of necessity since, on the whole, the gods were anything but ethical. But the Hebrew law code is markedly different, and it is so because of its location in the context of a covenant with God. To be sure, many of its requirements can be found in the other law codes of the ancient world, sometimes in almost the same words. That should not surprise us if there is one self-consistent creator of the world; thoughtful people around the world should be able to discover some of the principles by which human society functions best. And to the extent that those observations are correct, God, who is very economical, will confirm them and utilize them. What makes the biblical material radically different is that it presents ethical behavior as a profoundly religious response. It is an expression of love and gratitude to the covenant Lord. And while there are penalties for noncompliance, it is still true that the primary motivation for compliance is not coercion but religious affiliation.

But it was not only the understanding of law code that was profoundly altered by including it as the stipulations of the covenant. The idea that this covenant was with God altered the covenant form as well. Thus, there is a much greater concern for the interior life of the vassal than is found in any of the other covenants of the ancient world. That is as it should be, for this covenant lord is not a suzerain who has conquered his vassals by aggression and now demands their external obedience. This is the loving Creator who has delivered his people from oppression so that they can share a life with him in which they will be transformed into his own likeness. Thus, these stipulations touch on every area of life: religious, social, and personal. No longer is it necessary, or even possible, to separate these realms. This is a covenant with the Creator.

One of the features of the law codes of the ancient Near East is that the laws are always stated in the form of "case law." That is, each one is stated in terms of a hypothetical case and what the appropriate response is. Thus, for example, "if a man breaks through the wall of a house [to steal its contents] and he is caught, then he shall be walled up in the hole he made" (Code of Hammurabi 21, ANET 167). There are no absolute principles stated, simply a particular response to a particular situation. While there may be several reasons for this phenomenon, surely one of them is the polytheistic worldview. In a world of many competing gods where recurring chaos is the one certainty, there are no fixed principles, only recurring events. By contrast, in the suzerainty covenants there are some absolute requirements. Again the reason seems clear. For those covenant vassals, there *was* no other king; thus, he was in a position to make absolute demands upon them. This feature was made-to-order for what God wanted to accomplish through the covenant. For these people, there *is* no other God, and he is able to reveal to them the absolute principles upon which the ethical cases of life rest. No longer are ethics merely pragmatic discoveries. Now we discover *why* these behaviors are necessary for societies anywhere in the world to survive and prosper: They are rooted in the ethical nature of our covenant Lord, the Creator, the covenant-maker, Yahweh. Thus, the stipulations of the covenant are prefaced by 10 absolute principles of life with God. By and large, they are given without rationale and without result. They are stated, as Cassuto says (1967:238), with "lapidary" clarity and precision.[2]

The introduction to the covenant occurs in verse 1. It identifies the source as

"God"[3] and states that the following "words" (NLT, "instructions"; see the note on 20:1) are from him. The name used stresses the universal divinity of the one speaking.[4] Immediately following in verse 2, this universal divinity identifies himself as the very one who had revealed himself to Moses and who had "rescued" them from "slavery," namely Yahweh, "the LORD." As noted above, this verse is the historical prologue to the covenant. Something had happened in time and space that explains why this covenant was being offered. Faith that is not rooted in God's incarnation in history is worth no more than a mentally ill person's delusion that she is Dwight Eisenhower. But yes, God had intervened in the history of the Hebrew people, and that gave good reason why they should indeed enter into a binding covenant with their deliverer. Here the divine suzerain was not some brutal conqueror but a loving savior. Why would they not bind themselves to him?

As noted above, the stipulations of the covenant are here divided into two parts: the ten principles that "govern" the rest (20:3-17; so Houtman 1993:3.9), and the examples that explain the application of the principles (20:22-23:33).[5] These ten principles are stated largely (except for principles four and five) in the negative. As such, they set the outer limits of acceptable behavior in these areas and leave a maximum of freedom within those limits. For instance, while adultery is forbidden (20:14), no limitations are placed on the way fidelity is expressed within marriage. This means that there must be a good deal of extrapolation and interpretation as we seek to determine how to apply the principles to given situations. But that seems to be entirely in keeping with God's design for human dignity and responsibility in relationship with him.

One of the common features of the suzerainty covenant was the demand that the vassal recognize no other king than the one making the covenant. That feature was a nice match for what God was seeking to convey about himself to the Israelite people. Here (20:3) is no abstruse philosophical argument for monotheism. Such a thing would have been largely useless in ancient Israel's setting. Instead, God merely requested something entirely expected in that literary context: absolute, exclusive loyalty to himself. Did other beings called gods exist? It is assumed they did, just as there were other kings in the world of the vassals of the suzerainty covenant. But could Israel give any functional reality to those gods if Israel was going to be in covenant with Yahweh? No. In fact, monotheism is assumed here and everywhere in the covenant (see the note above on this verse; see also Deut 4:35, 39, and the comments on 15:9-10 above).[6] But the point was not to try to teach monotheism by argument. Instead, God wished the Israelites to learn it in practice. They could not "have any other god but me" (20:3). The issue was not intellectual but behavioral. And in fact, Israel's confession of one God was often betrayed by their behavior, as they tried to "have" Yahweh and the gods of this world at the same time. There is no more tragic example of this than Solomon, of whom it is said that his heart was no longer completely God's as he came to the end of his life (1 Kgs 11:4-6). Unless Israel's behavior was an expression of absolute loyalty to God, no matter what it might look like superficially, it was not a fulfillment of the covenant.

The second commandment (20:4-6) addresses a second key principle in God's educational and revelatory program.[7] Not only is he one without any rival but he transcends the world. It is almost impossible to overstate the importance of this insight. There are ultimately only two ways of understanding reality: the biblical one and the other one. The other one says that the physical-social-psychological cosmos is all there is to reality and that it is self-explanatory. If you want to know reality, all you have to do is study the world around you. That is the view of both the aboriginal shaman and the most sophisticated thinker in the world today. They both share this same central element in their worldview. In contrast, there is the view that the world is neither self-originating nor self-explanatory. Its reality can only be properly understood by reference to someone outside of it. There are three variations of that view: Judaism, Christianity, and Islam. And there is only a single fountainhead of all three: the Hebrew Scriptures. In other words, this alternate worldview, known as transcendence, has only one point of origin. Greek thinkers reasoned themselves to something close to it but were ultimately unable to sustain it, and Greek thought slipped back into the common view. The fact that the Hebrew Scriptures stood alone for so long in positing this truth from beginning to end argues strongly for the insight having been revealed and not discovered, just as those Scriptures claim.

So if transcendence is fact, how was God to teach it to these former Egyptian slaves? He did so by the simple expedient of requiring that his covenant partners never represent the divine in the form of anything created. There is an absolute gap from our side between the creation and the creator. We cannot make him in our image. Whenever we do so, we almost always condemn ourselves to that other worldview that can offer no true salvation. The reflection on the commandment in verses 5 and 6 is profoundly relational. The making of gods reflects a certain mindset and worldview, but more profoundly it reflects a certain set of the affections. To make God in the form of the world is to commit adultery with another lover (cf. 1 John 2:15-17). It is to place the secondary and derived in the place of the primary and original. To this corruption God responds with passionate heartbreak. Unfortunately, "jealousy" has come to connote a petty, self-serving emotion in modern English. That is not the sense here (see note on 20:5). God made humans to find their truest selves in loving him. When we love the creation more than we love him (and demonstrate that love by depending on it to supply our deepest needs), he is hurt and angered, not only for what it does to him, but even more for what it does to us.

Replacing God with the world has far-reaching implications. The children and grandchildren of world-worshipers will have a very hard time accepting the alternate (and true) understanding of reality. This is the way in which the statement "I lay the sins of the parents upon their children" (20:5) must be understood. That this is so is demonstrated by those statements in the Bible which make it clear that no one is condemned for any guilt but his or her own (Deut 24:16; Jer 31:29-30; Ezek 18:1-32). We are not punished for the guilt of our parents. In the world of cause and effect that God has made, where actions here have observable consequences here, the choices of the parents precondition the choices of the children. This has become clear in recent years in studies of the children of alcoholic parents (Quick 1990). The ways those children react to life have been shaped by their parents, and they do not have the same freedoms that children of nonalcoholic parents have. Is God holding those children guilty for their parents' sins? No. Is God applying the consequences of their parents' sins to them? Yes. We could wish that the Hebrew would have conveyed this nuance with some other word than "punish" here, but again it is clear that fine distinctions between primary, secondary, and tertiary causes would have had little meaning for former Egyptian slaves (for further discussion, see the commentary on 34:6-7).

However, if God limits the consequences of the parents' sins to three or four generations, there is literally no limit to his application of the consequences of faithfulness: "I lavish unfailing love" (see the commentary above on 15:13) "for a thousand generations" (20:6). Oddly enough, we do not think it unfair that children should experience the consequences of their parents' righteous choices. This is perhaps a witness to our warped sense of justice. But there are two other aspects of this thought in 20:6 that need to be explored. First is the nature of obedience. It is not an expression of a narrow-eyed wish to avoid punishment. Those who *obey* God's commandments are those who love him. This is not so much a covenant between king and vassal as it is between bride and groom. We do what God wants because he is our lover. And when we don't do what he wants, it is probably because we are in fact consorting with other lovers. And are we surprised if God is heartbroken and angry (20:5)?

The second point to be considered in 20:6 is the statement that Yahweh's love extends to "a thousand generations on those who love me and obey my commands." In other words, God's love is extended to those children who emulate the good choices of their parents. It is understood that the parents' choices have preconditioned the children to make the right choices, but the children are not blessed in spite of their own flagrant sinning simply because their first parents loved and obeyed God. This sheds further light on the probable interpretation of verse 5. The "punishment" falls on children who emulate the sins of their parents.[8]

Verse 7 presents the third principle of life with God. His *name* must not be misused (see note on 20:7). If we are to understand the intent of this command, we must understand the significance of "name" in the biblical world. Unlike modern English, "name" there is not restricted to "label." Rather, it refers to one's reputation or character (see note and commentary on 9:16). One's name is a reflection of oneself. So to use someone's name is the equivalent of having their power of attorney. This explains the New Testament injunction to pray in Jesus' name (John 14:13-14). This has nothing to do with a quasimagical appending of the label "Jesus" to a prayer. Rather, we are saying to the Father, "Your Son wants me to ask this of you." So how do we take God's name on our lips in an empty way (see note on 20:7)? There are several possibilities. God may be invoked as guarantee of an oath we do not intend to fulfill. God may be referred to in trivial or profane ways. We may ask for illegitimate or trivial things in his name. We may say things in God's name that are not true (e.g., false prophecy). All of these make God appear insignificant or faithless, that is, not holy. Thus, they defame his character (so NLT, "bring shame on"). But deeper than any of these is the effect on God's name that our lives may have. So Ezekiel says that when the Israelites had to go into captivity, making the Babylonians believe that their gods were mightier than Yahweh, the Israelites had "brought shame on [God's] holy name" (Ezek 36:19-21). Thus, at the heart of this commandment is the call for the covenant partner to do nothing that would portray God as anything less than absolutely holy, to do nothing that would seek to use him for our own ends, to do nothing that would cause the world to see him as less than he is.[9]

The fourth principle (20:8-11) gives a concrete way of bringing honor to the name of God by the way we understand time. Although the idea of grouping time into sevens is known elsewhere in the ancient Near East (dividing the 28-day lunar month into quarters), nowhere else is there the idea of having one complete day of rest in every seven. Furthermore, it is the seventh day that is made primary here, and it is disconnected from the lunar cycle. Every seventh day is a day of rest regardless of the moon's phases (see Cassuto 1967:244 for a discussion). Thus, as Sarna (1991:111) says, this command is a testimony to the fact that God is entirely outside of and sovereign over nature. What this command is saying is that time does not belong to us but to the creator of time. We cannot use our time to work constantly, as though our efforts were what supplied our needs. Neither can we force those in our households or our employ to submit all their time to us as though our goals were superior to theirs and our time more important than theirs (20:10). One day in every seven we are called upon to cease our labors to supply our own needs. One day in every seven, we are called upon to *remember* that each person, and indeed each animal, is special to God and that they have each been given the gift of time by him. One day in seven is to be "dedicated to the LORD" (20:10), a day when we remind ourselves (20:8) that we are not self-originating, self-sustaining, or self-authenticating. Everything we are is a gift from the Creator.[11] This means that if we do not avail ourselves of the gift of the Sabbath, we will be condemning ourselves to be less than what the Creator intends us to be, for creativity is not merely the production of goods and services. In the cycle of rest and work we are enabled to share in the true creativity of God. But this also means that if we merely use the Sabbath to rest from the "ordinary work" (20:9) of life without also using this time to "reorient our compass," as it were, in worshiping the Creator and Redeemer to whom we belong, we will have missed the point of this principle of life. We will have missed the point of why we rest. The Sabbath is a "holy-day," different from all the rest, but sanctifying all the rest.

The remaining six principles of covenant life with God are, at least on the surface, surprising. This is a covenant with God, so what do these wholly human-oriented principles have to do with that? They precisely confirm the covenant's function as a teaching device to reveal the character of God. God is profoundly ethical, and his ethics are grounded in self-giving, other-oriented love. As the Israelites realized that their covenant with God required them to honor those who had given them life and to cherish the life, the sexuality, the property, and the reputation of their neighbor, they were learning those precise points about God. And for the first time in the history of the world it became clear why human society cannot survive without ethical integrity: It is rooted in the character of the one who made human society. But beyond that, these principles are teaching that ethics, as productive as they are for human life, cannot be rooted in pragmatism. Ethical integrity is to be an expression of a covenantal love relationship with the Creator and Savior of the world. If ethical behavior is made dependent upon self-interest, such behavior cannot be sustained. This is so because while it is evident that ethical behavior is necessary for the survival of society, it is not self-evident that such behavior is in the immediate best interests of every individual in a society. The revolutionary significance of rooting ethics in the covenant context is that the whole "why" of ethics is changed. We are not ethical because a human society coerces us to it, and we are not ethical insofar as we think such behavior will "pay off" for us. We are ethical for the love of God and as a replication of his character.[12] It is as a direct result of this understanding that the civilization that has characterized the Western world for over a thousand years was made possible. Now that the desire to please God is disappearing before our eyes, ethical behavior is disappearing, and with it a whole way of life.

The fifth principle (20:12) can be seen as somewhat transitional from the first four that were focused on our relationship with God to the final six that focus on our relationship with our neighbor. The first four principles call upon us to recognize our complete dependence upon God and to place his honor above our own, giving up our right to manipulate him in the achievement of our own goals. This fifth "word" requires us to express that same approach toward those upon whom we are dependent for our earthly life: our "father and mother." To "honor" (20:12) these two is to be constantly reminded that we are not self-originating, that without them we would not even have survived. Thus, this command is a guard against a wholly self-focused life. It may be especially valuable for us in cases where we judge that our parents are not deserving of such treatment. This command is not about deserving; it is about a realization that our life is not our own, but is a gift. Surely this is the significance of the promise attached to this commandment. Societies made up of radically self-centered persons will not survive, nor will such persons survive. These "tribes" lack the permanent relations that exist where the blood ties and the freely given honor of families bind persons together regardless of shifting whims and feelings. Radical self-centeredness cuts us off from other people, and we cannot live without relationships. Nor can we live without the form created by committed family relationships.

The sixth through the ninth principles speak of the sanctity of the neighbor. They constitute a recognition of the fact that the world does not exist for us, that all persons have value in the sight of Yahweh, and that he will not allow us to trample upon the personhood of another for our own self-aggrandizement. It is no accident that the first consequence of sin after the Fall (Gen 3) was murder (20:13; Gen 4). When we become the sole suppliers of our needs, as Adam and Eve reckoned they were, any means of achieving that supply, including violence, is justifiable. And if we find others in competition for limited supplies, elimination of the competition is the obvious course of action. What is the antidote? John tells us (1 John 3:4-12) that it is love. Cain's problem was precisely that he did not see Abel as his brother. Instead, he saw him as a rival. If we have come into a covenant relationship with God in which we have committed our needs to his loving care, others are no longer rivals preventing us from having what we want, and we no longer need to "get them out of the way." Instead, we can see them as brothers and sisters and delight in the ways in which God is supplying their needs, sometimes even through us.

In the seventh principle (20:14), we are valuing our neighbor's marriage. In the world of the Old Testament, this is addressed to men because to a large extent they were the only ones with the degree of social freedom to initiate adulterous liaisons. But the issues are much the same for both genders. As with the previous commandment, there are two issues at stake. The first is the surrender of one's own needs and desires into God's hands. Given the nature and the complexity of sexual desire, encompassing so much of body, mind, and spirit, it has great power over us. We have the feeling that if this desire could be fully satisfied we would not only be fulfilled but in some sense we would have our hands on the mystery of the universe. This is not surprising because it is through sex that we are permitted to share some of God's own creative prerogative: Bringing life into existence that did not exist before. But this means that sexuality makes promises on which it can never deliver. Why do we fall prey, men and women alike, to impossible sexual or romantic fantasies? Because we have deep needs, and we have been duped into believing that sex can supply those needs, when in fact it is only God. Once again, this command calls us to surrender our needs to our covenant Lord and to find deep satisfaction in his all-encompassing provisions that mere sex could never provide. Having surrendered our needs to God, we should be able to value what our neighbor has for his or her sake, in this case a desirable spouse. But the "neighbor" to be valued here is not only the other married couple; it is also our own spouse. By what right do we break faith with them (which Mal 2:16 characterizes as "violence," NLT mg), breaking promises explicit and implicit because they are not meeting some supposed need of ours? Those who are in covenant with the God of truth, that is, the God of faithfulness, show it by the way they keep covenant with their "neighbors," especially in their sexuality.[13]

Given the "lapidary" quality of these principles, and given that they provide the foundation for the entire range of behavior that is expressive of God's nature and the nature of reality, these "words" obviously stand for much more than the bare details they explicitly touch upon. So it is significant that the activity chosen to represent the whole area of sexual ethics is adultery. I think the reason for this becomes clear upon reflection. The Bible declares that any sexual activity outside exclusive, committed heterosexual marriage is contrary to God's plan. By choosing adultery to represent all the rest, God is underscoring that point. Sexual behavior that destroys marriage is the antithesis of what sexuality was designed for. Furthermore, sexual behavior that undermines and denies covenant faithfulness flies squarely in the face of what sexual behavior was designed to do.

Principle eight (20:15) speaks of the sanctity of each person's own possessions. Perhaps no other sentence in human literature so clearly defines the principle of individual worth as this two-word (in Hebrew) statement. It says that people have a right to hold property that is distinctively theirs and that other persons have no right to take that property by force or stealth.[14] This property is typically gained through the expenditure of a person's foresight, energy, and diligence. Thus, to appropriate another's property is to steal those personal qualities. We may debate endlessly what actually constitutes stealing. Is it theft to get a huge judgment against a plaintiff when the insurance company will have to pay it anyway? After all, the insurance company got the money through crooked dealing anyway, didn't they? This kind of casuistic reasoning betrays a failure to understand the two principles that underlie all ten of these commandments: (1) Because I have entrusted my needs to my covenant Lord, (2) I do not have to manipulate others to get my needs supplied; in fact, I can value and honor others. The Bible says that those who live by these principles not only will not need to steal, they will have abundance to give away (Deut 15:6-8; 28:10-12).

Not only are the neighbor's life, sexuality, and property to be honored but so is his reputation (20:16). The form here ("you must not testify falsely") is helpful for keeping all of these principles in their proper perspective. They are not a checklist for demonstrating one's private rectitude. Thus the command is not, "You shall not tell a lie." It would be too easy for that command to be understood in a merely self-serving way. No, all ten of these principles are about relationships. The first four are about a relationship to God which then transforms our relationships to others, detailed in the final six. So the question is not whether I tell lies but whether I tell lies about *others!*[15] That is, am I "true"? The reason the Christian world came to believe that there are things that are "true" despite personal interest or desire is that it encountered a God who is absolutely true, that is, absolutely dependable. God calls his people to mimic that same behavior in their treatment of one another: They are to be true to one another, even at cost to themselves. Thus, the person who is in covenant with God does not need to destroy another person's reputation in order to make himself or herself look better or to gain some advantage over that other person. Knowing that God is the supplier of their needs, covenant people can afford to treat the reputation of the other with the same kindness with which they would like their own reputations to be treated. Fundamentally then, this principle is talking about the well-being of others, and this has something to say about some of the hypothetical questions that are sometimes raised (e.g., is it right to lie to save a life, etc.). But as real as those questions are, they must not be used to undermine the simple absolutism of the principle: You shall not give a false witness. The point is clear: Any variation from it will have to be in a very abnormal circumstance.

It may be that in the final principle (20:17) we have circled back to the first, circumscribing all of the others within the circle. But like the previous five, it is still about the neighbor and the neighbor's possessions. Yet whereas those clearly had actions in view, that is not so clear here.[16] Here, the focus is on a way of thinking, a way of thinking that could well produce the prohibited actions if it is not cut off at the source. In fact, it is a way of thinking about oneself and one's needs, and about how those needs are supplied and who supplies them. Moses is here speaking to that insidious conviction that "if a little is good, more will be better." In other words, we are again confronted with the question, who will define what my needs are and how they will be met? Will it be me? And will I define them and seek to meet them simply on the basis of those around me? Then the plain lesson of history is that there will never be enough. There will always be someone with more. Even if I stuffed myself to satiation and beyond with every good I could think of, it would not be enough. To paraphrase Pascal, such a person is trying to fill a God-shaped void with what is not God. Thus, in prescient words, Paul can say that covetousness is idolatry (Eph 5:3; Col 3:5). To be ruled by the desire to possess and to direct one's life toward that desire is to make this world the ultimate end, and to have other gods instead of Yahweh. It is to put me and my supposed needs at the center of the universe with all else circling around me. Anyone who has the misfortune to fall into that person's gravitational pull can only expect to be swallowed up.

Here then is the core of what God asks of people who are in covenant with himself. Here, in these 10 "words" is a revelation of his nature and, indeed, of reality as he made it to be. He asks his people to commit themselves and their needs to him and in so doing become free to value others for themselves just as he does. The person who will treat God and others in these ways will truly be part of a kingdom of priests, a holy nation (19:6).

ENDNOTES

1. For a handy discussion, see McCarthy 1972. For a more recent review of the data, see Walton 1989:95-107. See also Kitchen 2003:283-294.
2. Cassuto (1967:237) points out that the first four commandments are unique to Israel and thus require the explanations that are given, while the last five were known (in case form, at least) in the Ancient Near East and therefore did not need explanation.
3. Ever since the middle of the 1700s, OT scholars have attempted to isolate the hypothetical sources of the OT according to the different divine names used. Thus, v. 1, using the name 'elohim ("God"), would have come from one source, while v. 2, using the name "Yahweh," would have come from another.
4. Sarna (1991:109) believes that no addressee is named in order to include both the nation and individuals in the nation.
5. In general, Deuteronomy follows this same pattern with the exception that a theology of law stands between the principles in ch 5 and the applications in chs 12-26.
6. Childs says, "Israel did not gradually progress to a belief in one God, but this confession was constitutive to the covenant faith from the outset" (1974:403). Although many OT scholars have moved sharply away from this position in the 30 years since Childs's work was first published, it is still a true insight.
7. The Roman Catholic tradition takes 20:3-6 as one commandment and finds two in 20:17. While the commandment not to have any other gods is closely related to the

one not to make idols, it is hard to understand why the single command not to covet should be subdivided simply on the basis of the repeated verb.
8. Although the NLT words vv. 5 and 6 differently: "generations *of* those who reject" versus "generations *on* those who love," the Hebrew is the same in both cases: "to my haters" and "to my lovers." Both could be translated with "of" and both could be translated with "on."
9. There may also be an implicit condemnation of the sympathetic magic that is at the heart of nonbiblical religion. God's name may not be used as a magic talisman to produce certain results.
10. Interestingly, the parallel in Deut 5:15 amplifies the thought here by basing the rest upon God's deliverance of the Hebrews from the Egyptians' forced labor. Rest is thus rooted in creation, but it is also rooted in redemption. This is the basis, then, of the Christian church's celebration of the Sabbath on the first day of the week, the day of Resurrection and Pentecost.
11. Note Paul's remark that the whole law can be summed up in one word: love (Gal 5:14). This reflects the same understanding revealed in the interchange between Jesus and the authority on biblical law—the entire law can be summarized in two requirements: Love God, and love your neighbor (Matt 22:35-40).
12. Sarna (1991:114) observes that elsewhere in the ancient Near East adultery was purely a private sin, a matter of property rights. But in the OT, he says, marriage "had a sacral dimension."
13. It has been argued by some that the Hebrew word here (*ganab* [TH1589, ZH1704]) only refers to kidnapping and the taking of chattel possessions. However, a review of all uses of the root, including noun forms, shows that this interpretation is too narrow. See Houtman 1993:3.63-64 for a review of the argument.
14. This is not to suggest that telling lies to enhance oneself is permissible. It cannot be, if we have entrusted our needs to the God who is utterly true. It is only to say that those who are living the life and character of God through covenant obedience are what they are for the sake of others and not for themselves. To be a truth-teller for my own sake is no more to be living in covenant than is telling lies for my own sake. For the biblical attitude about lying, see Josh 7:11; Hos 4:2.
15. There has been an attempt to say that *khamad* [TH2530, ZH2773] (to desire) always includes the action of taking what is desired. However, if that were the case this command would be merely a duplication of those against stealing and adultery. Rather, as Houtman says, what is prohibited here is "a morally totally reprehensible mindset" (1993:3.69).

◆ **2. The terms of the covenant for the people (20:18–23:19)**
  a. Introduction (20:18-21)

¹⁸When the people heard the thunder and the loud blast of the ram's horn, and when they saw the flashes of lightning and the smoke billowing from the mountain, they stood at a distance, trembling with fear.

¹⁹And they said to Moses, "You speak to us, and we will listen. But don't let God speak directly to us, or we will die!"

²⁰"Don't be afraid," Moses answered them, "for God has come in this way to test you, and so that your fear of him will keep you from sinning!"

²¹As the people stood in the distance, Moses approached the dark cloud where God was.

NOTES

20:18 *heard . . . saw.* The Hebrew text begins the statement with a participle of "see" and does not include a verb for "heard": "Now all the people were seeing the thunder, the flames, the sound of the horn, and the mountain smoking." The sense of the participle is clearly something like "experiencing." The NASB uses "perceived" to convey the idea with limited success.

flashes of lightning. Heb. *lapidim* [TH3940, ZH4365] normally means "torches." Houtman (1993:3.75) thinks the idea is of the heavenly host carrying torches in procession. In view of 19:16, the NLT is almost certainly correct.

20:19 *speak directly.* The word "directly" is not in the Hebrew text. The NLT is attempting to make it clear that God did indeed continue to speak to the people, but by means of Moses.

20:20 *your fear of him.* Lit., "his fear may be on your faces." This is a graphic way of expressing the reality of this experience.

COMMENTARY

After the statement of the abiding principles upon which the terms of the covenant rested, God presented the people with the details of the terms. As noted above, these terms, as was the custom of the day, are largely stated as "if-then" cases. But by prefacing them with the "10 Words," God had made it clear that these examples were not merely the result of pragmatism but the outworking of principles rooted in the character and nature of the Creator and his creation.

After the opening prologue (20:18-21), there are regulations about worship (20:22-26). It is significant that the final group of terms relating to the people also has to do with worship (23:14-19). The enclosure of the rest of the terms between these two segments is certainly significant. Once again it tells us that all of one's behavior is to be an expression of worship to God and is to be shaped by that realization. There is no "secular" behavior for the people of God. Between these two segments are five other groupings. These can be grouped together in two larger collections primarily on the basis of form. The first extends from 21:1 to 22:15 (many scholars extend it to 22:16). These are all composed of case laws. The second collection (22:16-23:13) contains no case laws and is characterized by a somewhat more miscellaneous character.

Cassuto (1967:262) observes correctly that we do not have a full legal code here. There are numerous areas (such as inheritance) which are not addressed at all. Rather, he suggests, the covenant terms here presented are intended to show with selected examples how this new understanding of reality will affect all areas of life. Thus, it assumes an existing legal tradition which it either (1) amends, (2) opposes or invalidates, or (3) confirms specific aspects of.

It is not clear whether this introductory prologue (20:18-21) is intended to be understood chronologically or not. Houtman (1993:3.73) suggests that it is: The people heard God's voice speaking the Decalogue and could not stand it any longer. But the text says that it was the "atmospherics" that terrified them, as reported in 19:16. Thus, I think it is possible that the text is not in chronological order. Rather, this paragraph is given here in order to explain again why God speaks to the people through Moses (20:22). It is possible that 20:1-17 and 20:22–23:33 were given to Moses by God at the same time prior to Moses reporting any of what God had said to the people (19:25). To be sure, 20:1 says that God gave his instruction to the people. But I think the point there is not to give the details of delivery but to identify who was offering the covenant—God—and to whom it was offered—the people. Thus, even before Moses went up the mountain on the third morning, the people had told Moses not to "let God speak directly to" them (20:19). When Deuteronomy 4:33 says that Israel "heard the voice of God speaking from fire," I think it refers to 19:19 ("As the blast of the ram's horn grew louder and louder, Moses spoke, and God thundered his reply") and not to God's audibly speaking the Ten Commandments to them.

Why did God choose to represent himself to his people in such a terrifying way? As I discussed above on 19:16-20, one part of the reason was the crucial importance of the moment. If the people rejected the covenant, then all of human history would have been affected. But here Moses takes the matter one step further. He said they were not to be afraid because God had not come to destroy them but to refine them (which is the sense of "test" [20:20] in this context). He wanted them to base their behavior on a realistic assessment of who God is. An awareness of the incredible power, glory, and majesty of God ought to make them think twice before choosing to sin against him. The sum total of this awareness and its appropriate response is what is meant by "the fear of God" in the Bible. In other words, Moses was saying this experience should *not* make them afraid that God wanted to destroy them but that it *should* make them afraid of doing anything that is contrary to who he is and what he wants!

◆ b. Proper use of altars (20:22-26)

²²And the LORD said to Moses, "Say this to the people of Israel: You saw for yourselves that I spoke to you from heaven. ²³Remember, you must not make any idols of silver or gold to rival me.

²⁴"Build for me an altar made of earth, and offer your sacrifices to me—your burnt offerings and peace offerings, your sheep and goats, and your cattle. Build my altar wherever I cause my name to be remembered, and I will come to you and bless you. ²⁵If you use stones to build my altar, use only natural, uncut stones. Do not shape the stones with a tool, for that would make the altar unfit for holy use. ²⁶And do not approach my altar by going up steps. If you do, someone might look up under your clothing and see your nakedness.

NOTES

20:23 *you must not make.* The text contains this imperative twice and the second time adds "for yourselves."

to rival me. Lit., "with me." Perhaps the sense is "alongside of me." The NLT has captured the thought.

20:24 *Build.* The Hebrew here does not give an imperative form but an imperfect, which can have an imperative force but could also be permissive (see commentary).

EXODUS 20:22-26

COMMENTARY

Just as the statement of principles began with the priority of loyalty to God alone, so does the expanded statement of examples. Here the issue of the visual representation of God in worship (expressed in 20:23 using the plural "idols" for universality, so Sarna 1991:115) is expanded to address the matter of altars (expressed in the singular for particularity in 20:24-26). The prohibition of idols in 20:23 is, as in 20:4, not given a philosophical explanation but a practical one, just as in Deuteronomy 4:33-36: The Israelites saw no form but only heard the sound of a voice speaking. So there was no reason for them to try to represent God in a form, no matter how costly that form might be from an earthly point of view. We cannot make God accessible to ourselves by our efforts. He "spoke ... from heaven" (20:22) without any manipulation on the part of Israel.

But humans do need visual expressions of our inner spiritual life. If we cannot capture God in an earthly form, we do need ways to concretize our worship. Verses 24-26 graciously address that fact. Scholars have long debated exactly what the purpose of this passage is in light of the instructions for the Tabernacle and its altar that will shortly follow (27:1-8) and in the light of the commands in Deuteronomy that no sacrifices were to be offered except at the central sanctuary. Even if space permitted, those debates could not be resolved here. But surely it must be granted that those who put the text together in its present form, showing a great concern elsewhere to harmonize apparently conflicting matters, must have had a satisfactory explanation, or they would not have left them intact here.

I think that commentators like Sarna and Cassuto are correct when they see these stipulations as being provisional until the implications of the Deuteronomic legislation were finally put in force in Jerusalem with the Solomonic Temple. Thus, these terms speak of the situation in the wilderness and in the early history of Israel in Canaan. As such, they do not require the building of altars, but they permit the building of such in places that God might specify ("wherever I cause my name to be remembered"). Clearly, these were to be of simple, unpretentious construction ("earth" or "uncut stones," 20:24-25) with no air of permanence about them. Thus, they would not rival the Tabernacle, either in the wilderness or when it was located at Shiloh. But God was making provision for the needs of his people in interim times and places so that they could express their worship and so that they could experience the blessing of the sense of his presence (20:24).

Verse 26 ("going up steps") perhaps also addresses the issue of the permanence of the altar, but its main point has to do with the prohibition of even the appearance of utilizing sexuality in worship. Pagan worship, as mentioned above in several places, emphasized participation in divine life through sexual activity. In some cultures, priests served their gods in the nude. The Old Testament, insisting on an absolute distinction between creator and creature, is at pains to deny any magical means of blurring that distinction, especially through sexual activity. This prohibition was not necessary in regard to the altar of sacrifice in the Taber-

◆ c. Fair treatment of slaves (21:1-11)

"These are the regulations you must present to Israel.

²"If you buy a Hebrew slave, he may serve for no more than six years. Set him free in the seventh year, and he will owe you nothing for his freedom. ³If he was single when he became your slave, he shall leave single. But if he was married before he became a slave, then his wife must be freed with him.

⁴"If his master gave him a wife while he was a slave and they had sons or daughters, then only the man will be free in the seventh year, but his wife and children will still belong to his master. ⁵But the slave may declare, 'I love my master, my wife, and my children. I don't want to go free.' ⁶If he does this, his master must present him before God.* Then his master must take him to the door or doorpost and publicly pierce his ear with an awl. After that, the slave will serve his master for life.

⁷"When a man sells his daughter as a slave, she will not be freed at the end of six years as the men are. ⁸If she does not satisfy her owner, he must allow her to be bought back again. But he is not allowed to sell her to foreigners, since he is the one who broke the contract with her. ⁹But if the slave's owner arranges for her to marry his son, he may no longer treat her as a slave but as a daughter.

¹⁰"If a man who has married a slave wife takes another wife for himself, he must not neglect the rights of the first wife to food, clothing, and sexual intimacy. ¹¹If he fails in any of these three obligations, she may leave as a free woman without making any payment.

21:6 Or *before the judges.*

NOTES

21:2 *buy.* Lit., "acquire," which might include other means than outright purchase.

21:5 *may declare.* Lit., "surely say." The NLT is seeking to capture some of the emphasis with "declare."

21:6 *God.* The early versions translated this word (*'elohim* [TH430, ZH466]) with "judges" (see NLT mg; cf. KJV), probably on the basis of such passages as Ps 82. Exodus 22:7-8 seems to lend some support when it uses this same term with plural verbs.

publicly. This may be implied, but it is not explicitly stated (see commentary).

21:8-9 *must allow . . . . arranges for.* These are translations of the same Hebrew verb, which has the meaning of "designate, stipulate."

21:10 *sexual intimacy.* The Hebrew word occurs only here in the OT. The Semitic root consonants seem to have the idea of "dwell (together)." The concept of sexual intimacy appears in the early versions such as LXX, Vulgate, and Syriac. Some suggest "dwelling place," but as Houtman (2000:3.130) points out, the woman's right to motherhood, which the Bible strongly protects, seems to support the connotation of intimacy.

COMMENTARY

It is somewhat surprising that regulations concerning slaves come first in this listing of covenant terms. If such laws show up at all in law codes elsewhere in the ancient

Near East, they are far down in the list. Perhaps they show up first here because slavery had been such a recent Israelite experience (so Sarna 1991:118; Enns 2000:443). Thus, God was seeking to use the freshness of that experience to remind the newly freed Israelites not to fall into old patterns of oppression (cf. Deut 15:15). While these laws assume the existence of slavery, they seek to ensure that persons in this sad condition were not thereby reduced to mere possessions to be used as such. As I noted above regarding the introduction to this section (20:18-21), the stipulations of the covenant assume a certain existing legal tradition and make modifications to it. Thus, given that slavery was everywhere practiced in the ancient world, there is no wholesale condemnation of slavery here. Instead, there are changes made in the practice of slavery that reflect the character of the covenant Lord. At the same time, when that legal tradition was reinterpreted in the light of the universality of the God of *khesed* [TH2617, ZH2876] (see note on 15:13) and in the light of the death of Christ for the whole world, the resulting implications would finally require the destruction of the institution of slavery itself.

In the meantime, these stipulations place two very significant limitations on slavery. First, no "Hebrew" male could be forced into perpetual slavery against his will (21:2-6). Men could enslave themselves to another when they saw no way to survive a condition of grinding poverty (Lev 25:39), or they could be forced into slavery to pay off indebtedness. But if they did end up in this condition, they could not be kept in it for more than six years (21:2).[1]

At the end of that period, they were to go out as "free" men with no further obligation (20:2). In addition, if the man was married when he became a slave, his wife had to be freed with him (21:3). Deuteronomy 15:13-14, in revising this regulation for the new situation in Canaan, further provided that the master must provide for the slave so that his former poverty would not be a foregone conclusion.

The slave could voluntarily choose to remain in slavery, however. A factor in favor of such a choice was the regulation that if the slave chose to marry one of the master's female slaves and had children by her, she and her children would remain the master's when the husband went free (21:4). This was partly a result of a woman's different status, as dealt with in verses 7-11. If the slave chose not to leave his wife and children behind, he could choose to remain a slave. As Childs says (1974:468), we should not "romanticize" the occurrence of "love" here. As elsewhere in the Old Testament, the word has more to do with volition than with affection. Thus, it is an expression of choice. Of course affection is not excluded, but primarily the term is used to say that the slave has chosen his master and his family (21:5). This choice was symbolized in a physical and visual way, with a pierced ear (21:6).[2] The person who had made such a choice was thus easily identifiable.

The second set of limitations on slavery addressed the situation of a female slave (21:7-11), which was different from that of the male. The female had not entered slavery by her choice but rather at the choice of her father. Freeing her and sending her out of the household at the end of six years would very likely force her to enter a life of prostitution: She could not go back to her father's house, and she would not be attractive as a marriage partner. Thus, while her continued slavery was not a good thing, it was better than the alternative. What these regulations were all aimed at was being certain that a woman who found herself in these circumstances was cared for and continued to be treated as a person. Three specific matters are addressed here, all of them assuming that the slave had been purchased as a concubine either for her master or for her master's son. First, the master could not simply dispose of her if he determined he did not want her any more. He must continue to provide food and clothing for her, and he may not deny her sexual intimacy (21:10; but see note). He may not sell her outside of her family,[3] but he may allow her family to buy her back again (21:8). Finally, if a man buys a girl to be his son's concubine, "he may no longer treat her as [his] slave" (21:9). Now he must treat her as (lit., "in the manner of") a daughter. In other words, he may not have sex with her, which would be incest. That would be to no longer treat her as a person but as a toy.

ENDNOTES
1. It is not clear whether the *seventh year* referred to here is the sabbatical year (cf. Lev 25:5), in which case the enslavement might be for considerably less than six years, or whether the years were counted strictly from the date of enslavement.
2. Because the description of the ceremony is so terse, there is considerable disagreement over exactly what took place. Much of the disagreement centers around the connotation of *'elohim* [TH430, ZH466] (NLT, "God"; see the note on 21:6). If "judges" is correct, the *door* or *doorpost* would be in the gatehouse of the city where the judges sat. If "God" is correct, then it would be at the sanctuary. See Houtman 2000:116-121 for a long discussion of the alternatives in which he concludes that "household gods" is meant and that the event took place at the master's house. I cannot see how this alternative could be accepted unless one assumes a redactor who ignorantly forgets or negligently dismisses the prohibition of idols a few verses prior.
3. The Hebrew *'am nokri* [TH5971A/5237A, ZH6639/5799] (21:8) does not connote another people group (as "to foreigners," 21:8, NLT) but another family.

◆ d. Cases of personal injury (21:12-36)

[12]"Anyone who assaults and kills another person must be put to death. [13]But if it was simply an accident permitted by God, I will appoint a place of refuge where the slayer can run for safety. [14]However, if someone deliberately kills another person, then the slayer must be dragged even from my altar and be put to death.

[15]"Anyone who strikes father or mother must be put to death.

[16]"Kidnappers must be put to death, whether they are caught in possession of their victims or have already sold them as slaves.

[17]"Anyone who dishonors* father or mother must be put to death.

[18]"Now suppose two men quarrel, and one hits the other with a stone or fist, and the injured person does not die but is confined to bed. [19]If he is later able to walk outside again, even with a crutch, the assailant will not be punished but must compensate his victim for lost wages and provide for his full recovery.

[20]"If a man beats his male or female slave with a club and the slave dies as a result, the owner must be punished. [21]But if the slave recovers within a day or two,

then the owner shall not be punished, since the slave is his property.

²²"Now suppose two men are fighting, and in the process they accidentally strike a pregnant woman so she gives birth prematurely.* If no further injury results, the man who struck the woman must pay the amount of compensation the woman's husband demands and the judges approve. ²³But if there is further injury, the punishment must match the injury: a life for a life, ²⁴an eye for an eye, a tooth for a tooth, a hand for a hand, a foot for a foot, ²⁵a burn for a burn, a wound for a wound, a bruise for a bruise.

²⁶"If a man hits his male or female slave in the eye and the eye is blinded, he must let the slave go free to compensate for the eye. ²⁷And if a man knocks out the tooth of his male or female slave, he must let the slave go free to compensate for the tooth.

²⁸"If an ox* gores a man or woman to death, the ox must be stoned, and its flesh may not be eaten. In such a case, however, the owner will not be held liable. ²⁹But suppose the ox had a reputation for goring, and the owner had been informed but failed to keep it under control. If the ox then kills someone, it must be stoned, and the owner must also be put to death. ³⁰However, the dead person's relatives may accept payment to compensate for the loss of life. The owner of the ox may redeem his life by paying whatever is demanded.

³¹"The same regulation applies if the ox gores a boy or a girl. ³²But if the ox gores a slave, either male or female, the animal's owner must pay the slave's owner thirty silver coins,* and the ox must be stoned.

³³"Suppose someone digs or uncovers a pit and fails to cover it, and then an ox or a donkey falls into it. ³⁴The owner of the pit must pay full compensation to the owner of the animal, but then he gets to keep the dead animal.

³⁵"If someone's ox injures a neighbor's ox and the injured ox dies, then the two owners must sell the live ox and divide the price equally between them. They must also divide the dead animal. ³⁶But if the ox had a reputation for goring, yet its owner failed to keep it under control, he must pay full compensation—a live ox for the dead one—but he may keep the dead ox.

21:17 Greek version reads *Anyone who speaks disrespectfully of.* Compare Matt 15:4; Mark 7:10. 21:22 Or *so she has a miscarriage;* Hebrew reads *so her children come out.* 21:28 Or *bull,* or *cow;* also in 21:29-36. 21:32 Hebrew *30 shekels of silver,* about 12 ounces or 342 grams in weight.

NOTES

21:12 *must be put to death.* Lit., "shall surely die." The NLT conveys the emphasis with "must be."

21:13 *simply an accident permitted by God.* Lit., "did not lie in wait, but God caused him to happen into his hand." Both verbs ("lie in wait" and "caused him to happen into") are uncommon, the first occurring three times in the OT and the second only four times. This suggests that the phrase might be almost aphoristic, much as we speak of an unfortunate natural event that was not caused by human action, as an "act of God." Thus, we might translate "an accident that happened by chance."

21:17 *dishonors.* The root of this word is *qalal* [TH7043, ZH7837] (to belittle, make light of, profane). The NLT captures the broader meaning better than the narrower word, "curses" (as in KJV, NIV).

21:22 *gives birth prematurely.* While this interpretation is probably correct, the Hebrew is very general. Sarna (1991:123) says it is impossible to determine whether stillbirth, premature, or full-term birth is intended (see NLT mg).

further injury. Again, the Hebrew is very general. Houtman (2000:3.160, 163-164) argues that "fatal injury" (to the mother) is intended, but this seems very difficult to prove from the passage itself.

21:23-25 Sarna (1991:126) and Cassuto (1967:276-277) make a persuasive case that the so-called *lex talionis* here was not meant to be applied literally (nor in the other occurrences in Lev 24:17-22 and Deut 19:18-19, 21). They point out that the injury incurred is very unlikely to have been the loss of a hand or a foot. Furthermore, the opening phrase "you shall give" (omitted from NLT) sounds very stereotypical in the context. Finally Cassuto points out that "life for life" in this instance would be a violation of the principle enunciated in 21:13 that the death penalty should not be applied to instances of unintentional manslaughter. In the end the two commentators agree that the writer was quoting an ancient concrete statement of the general principle that the punishment must suit the crime. Houtman (2000:3.166) disagrees, insisting it is intended to be literally applied (although he does not address the above objections); he thinks it is an example of vicarious punishment, that is, the wife of the guilty party must be maimed in the same ways as the injured woman. Sarna (1991:127) says that this feature of ancient Near East law codes is specifically guarded against in the OT. I think Sarna and Cassuto have the better argument.

21:28-31 The regulations having to do with the "goring ox" are notable for appearing in several of the ancient Near East law codes in almost exactly the same words. Cassuto (1967:279) points out that the idea of stoning the ox to death and the prohibition of eating the meat are innovations which he considers connected to the sanctity accorded to human life in the OT.

COMMENTARY

This group of regulations has to do with personal injury. The regulations fall into three subdivisions: (1) injuries resulting in capital punishment (21:12-17), (2) injuries not resulting in capital punishment (21:18-27), and (3) injuries caused by or to an animal (21:28-36). In the way they are formulated and expressed, either by amending, correcting, or affirming the legal traditions of the day, these covenant terms continue to reveal the character of God. As such, they teach that Yahweh places very high value on human life; that he values humans as persons not objects; that physical injury ought to be compensated, but not with physical retaliation; that intention and knowledge must be considered in applying justice; that justice is so important that it is not a matter for personal or family application; and that punishment must rest on the guilty, not on others.

Cassuto (1967:271) points out that five issues relating to the death penalty are dealt with here in order of gravity (21:12-17). The first, and the gravest, is intentional murder (21:12). The contrast with verse 13 suggests that this is a premeditated and planned activity. An example is found in 1 Samuel 24:11 where David says that Saul had "been hunting for me to kill me." Human life is so valuable to God that wanton destruction of it for one's own advantage can only result in forfeiture of the murderer's life. This means that not even the sanctity of the sanctuary can supersede the sanctity of human life. Thus, even if the murderer were to try to wrap himself in the holiness of the altar (21:14), he could be taken from it.[1]

However, some deaths are not the result of malicious intent, and among tight-knit clans, even accidental death can create a demand for vengeance. Almost inevitably, these vengeful killings escalate into a "blood-feud" that is all but uncontrollable. This is why God insists that vengeance must be left in his hands (Deut 32:35;

Ps 94:1; Rom 12:19). However, human life is so precious that even accidental death cannot be simply dismissed. So God provided "a place of refuge" (21:13) where the killer could be protected while the case could be investigated and passions cooled. The fact that the precise nature of this refuge is not spelled out here is one more piece of evidence that these are covenant stipulations and not a full-blown law code. (For the further defining of these places of refuge and their administration, see Num 35:6-28 and Deut 19:1-13.)

The third stipulation concerning capital punishment related to the striking of "father or mother" (21:15). If the sanctity of human life was primary, the sanctity of the family was close behind. Sarna addresses this eloquently when he says, "The dissolution of the family unit must inevitably rend to shreds the entire social fabric" (1991:122). If the fundamental ties of family, expressed in courtesy, respect, and obedience are allowed to dissolve, then there is no foundation for these in society, and society will descend to the law of the jungle. As elsewhere in this section, the terseness of the statement begs for interpretation. The rabbis ruled that this referred to an adult child who struck an aged parent with intent to injure.

The fourth occasion for capital punishment was kidnapping (21:16). Once again, the issue revolves around contempt for human life and personhood. A kidnapped person is treated as an object to be used for one's own gain, and this can never be. The point is underscored when this command is compared with that regarding stealing an animal in 22:1, 4. There, if the animal is not recoverable, fivefold compensation to the owner is required. But if the animal is recovered, only twofold compensation must be given. However, in the case of kidnapping, death is the result whether the victim is restored or not. Persons are not objects to be used.

Finally, capital punishment was occasioned by dishonoring one's parents (21:17).[2] What is at stake here is almost certainly public humiliation, in which the worth of the parents is destroyed. Again, the rabbis took this to be the act of adult children with malicious intent. It is the negative side of the fifth commandment. Instead of presenting one's parents to the world as people of worth and dignity, persons from whom one's own identity is to be defined, the parents are exposed to ridicule by the very ones who ought to be protecting them. As said above, human society made up of such people cannot survive. To destroy the family unit is to murder society.

The stipulations in 21:18-27 deal with cases of bodily injury that do not result in death so that the death penalty is not entailed. There are four cases discussed: (1) injury to a free person (21:18-19); (2) injury to a slave (21:20-21); (3) injury resulting in miscarriage (21:22-25); and (4) disfigurement of a slave (21:26-27).[3] In these cases, compensation of some sort is required. Sarna and Cassuto attempt to maintain that slaves are given equal treatment with free persons, but Houtman and Childs seem more correct in maintaining that although the differences are not as great as those found in the other ancient Near East law codes, there is still a distinction.[4] Part of the issue relates to 21:20 in which it is said that if an owner beats a male or female slave to death, the owner must be punished. Does this mean he is executed? It is impossible to give a dogmatic answer. The rubric "he shall surely die" that was repeated in each of the previous five cases does not appear here. However, the failure to define the punishment could certainly suggest that the normal punishment for murder is assumed. That is as much as can be said. At the same time, as Sarna (1991:124) points out, the very appearance of these stipulations is unique in that nowhere else in the ancient Near East is injury to a slave even addressed. Likewise, while the loss of a slave's eye does not entail the loss of the master's eye (21:26), the idea that the master loses the slave for this action is unheard of elsewhere.

There are a couple of principles assumed in these cases. The first is compensation, which can include monetary payment (21:19, 22) or the release of the maimed slave (21:26). That is, a person has been deprived of some benefit by the action of another, whether intentional or not. That other person is therefore responsible to give some compensating benefit in place of what was taken. The principle is one of responsibility for one's actions in spite of the motivation for the action. But the second common principle takes this matter of intention a step farther. Anger, resulting in a desire to hurt, is assumed in all these cases. If death results, the striker cannot claim the circumstances of 21:14—that this was merely an accident. There will be punishment meted out—and punishment beyond compensation, perhaps even the death penalty. Allowing anger to play itself out in violence is a choice, and no one can say, "Well, I couldn't help it." Clearly, these cases say we *can* help it and we are responsible for the results.

As the notes above indicate, verses 22-25 are fraught with a number of uncertainties that exegetical skill cannot resolve. The uncertainties are complicated by the addition of the aphorism contained in 21:23-25 (see note). In brief, the situation is this: A woman gives birth as a result of being accidentally struck in someone else's quarrel. The one landing the blow must pay damages. Precisely what the damages are for is not specified. But that compensation does not compensate for "further injury" (21:23) that may result from the event. Those injuries must be compensated for on the basis of strict equivalence. Possibly what is intended is that because the birth is premature, the child dies. The father must be compensated for the economic value of the child. But perhaps it later appears that the woman is unable to have another child. There will then have to be compensation for the loss of her childbearing ability. This is but one of several possible scenarios. The point is to use an extreme example to illustrate the twin principles of responsibility for one's action and the right of compensation. This verse is sometimes used to show that intentional abortion is forbidden. Part of the difficulty of that position is that it cannot be shown that intentional abortion was ever a practice in the ancient Near East. A woman's ability to bear children was far too important to risk damaging. So, outside of Israel, if a baby was unwanted it was simply thrown out after birth (Ezekiel seems to be referring to this practice in Ezek 16:4-6). It is only in the modern West, that, in order to circumvent the biblical reverence for life for the sake of our own convenience, we have created the wholly artificial distinction between the life of a born child and the life of an unborn child.

The final group of covenant stipulations pertains to injury done by or to an animal (21:28-36). Here there are three principles being illustrated. The first is the sanctity of human life. So if an "ox" killed a man or woman, the ox had to be killed (21:28, 29, 32).[5] This is in keeping with Genesis 9:5-6, where God said that he would require the blood of either human or animal that killed a human, who bears the image of God. This case is found in almost the same words in virtually every law code in the ancient Near East, but the idea of the absolute value of human life apart from economic considerations is unique to the Hebrew version of the case. The point is further underscored by verse 35 which says that the ox which kills another ox is not required to be killed.

The second principle is that the degree of responsibility is mitigated by prior knowledge. If a person did not know that his ox posed a danger to others and thus did not take precautions, that person is absolved of responsibility for the ensuing death (21:28). The owner was doing everything that could be expected of him. However, failure to take precautions when the danger was known is not mere negligence; in the case of humans it is murder, and is to be treated as such (21:29),[6] with the one provision that since no malicious intent was involved, the owner can negotiate with the family for his life by paying whatever compensation they demand (21:30). This principle of knowledge as responsibility is further expressed in verses 33 and 34, where it is said that if an animal falls into an uncovered pit, the one who left the pit uncovered is held responsible.

The third principle is the right of compensation for the loss of benefits through the action of another. The negligent owner, if the family of the victim permits it, can pay compensation for the lost life, and he must pay compensation to the owner for the life of a slave. Likewise, he must give the owner of a dead animal the full price of the animal (21:34, 36). Only in the case of an unanticipated killing of one animal by another do the two owners share the loss equally (21:35).

ENDNOTES
1. Examples of this are found in 1 Kgs 1:50-53; 2:28-34.
2. The LXX places vv. 15 and 17 together, as logic would seem to dictate. Cassuto's suggestion that the crimes are discussed in order of gravity seems the only explanation for why they are separated. Houtman (1993:3.147) says this reasoning "is not convincing," but he offers no other explanation.
3. Cassuto (1967:278) wishes to see another group of five here (as in vv. 12-17), but to do so he has to divide vv. 26 and 27, which manifestly go together.
4. For instance, the owner of an injured slave is not required to compensate the slave in any way. However, it may be said that the point of "he is his property" is not to demean the slave but simply to contrast this situation with the former one. The slave cannot recover lost wages since it is the owner who has lost the slave's labor, and similarly, it is the owner who will have to pay the physician to get the slave well enough to work again.
5. Note that even though the liable owner is not to be killed for the death of a slave but to pay compensation, the ox is still to be killed (21:32). A slave is as valuable to God as a free person.

6. Cassuto (1967:286) says the statement that the same provisions apply to the death of *a boy or a girl* in 21:31 is meant to make it clear that vicarious punishment (the death of the owner's son for the dead son, etc.), something widely practiced in the ancient Near East, is not to be carried out here.

◆ ### e. Protection of property (22:1-15)

¹*"If someone steals an ox* or sheep and then kills or sells it, the thief must pay back five oxen for each ox stolen, and four sheep for each sheep stolen.

²*"If a thief is caught in the act of breaking into a house and is struck and killed in the process, the person who killed the thief is not guilty of murder. ³But if it happens in daylight, the one who killed the thief is guilty of murder.

"A thief who is caught must pay in full for everything he stole. If he cannot pay, he must be sold as a slave to pay for his theft. ⁴If someone steals an ox or a donkey or a sheep and it is found in the thief's possession, then the thief must pay double the value of the stolen animal.

⁵"If an animal is grazing in a field or vineyard and the owner lets it stray into someone else's field to graze, then the animal's owner must pay compensation from the best of his own grain or grapes.

⁶"If you are burning thornbushes and the fire gets out of control and spreads into another person's field, destroying the sheaves or the uncut grain or the whole crop, the one who started the fire must pay for the lost crop.

⁷"Suppose someone leaves money or goods with a neighbor for safekeeping, and they are stolen from the neighbor's house. If the thief is caught, the compensation is double the value of what was stolen. ⁸But if the thief is not caught, the neighbor must appear before God,* who will determine if he stole the property.

⁹"Suppose there is a dispute between two people who both claim to own a particular ox, donkey, sheep, article of clothing, or any lost property. Both parties must come before God, and the person whom God declares* guilty must pay double compensation to the other.

¹⁰"Now suppose someone leaves a donkey, ox, sheep, or any other animal with a neighbor for safekeeping, but it dies or is injured or gets away, and no one sees what happened. ¹¹The neighbor must then take an oath in the presence of the LORD. If the LORD confirms that the neighbor did not steal the property, the owner must accept the verdict, and no payment will be required. ¹²But if the animal was indeed stolen, the guilty person must pay compensation to the owner. ¹³If it was torn to pieces by a wild animal, the remains of the carcass must be shown as evidence, and no compensation will be required.

¹⁴"If someone borrows an animal from a neighbor and it is injured or dies when the owner is absent, the person who borrowed it must pay full compensation. ¹⁵But if the owner was present, no compensation is required. And no compensation is required if the animal was rented, for this loss is covered by the rental fee.

22:1a Verse 22:1 is numbered 21:37 in Hebrew text. 22:1b Or *bull*, or *cow*; also in 22:4, 9, 10. 22:2 Verses 22:2-31 are numbered 22:1-30 in Hebrew text. 22:8 Or *before the judges*. 22:9 Or *before the judges, and the person whom the judges declare*.

NOTES

22:3 [2] *if it happens in daylight.* Lit., "if the sun has risen on him." The NLT may have the correct interpretation, but another possibility is that the victim recognizes the thief in the daylight and kills him then.

22:4 [3] *must pay double.* It is nowhere specified whether this is the original value plus one or the original value plus two. In any case Zacchaeus doubled this (Luke 19:8).

22:5 [4] *grazing.* In this verse and the next, the Hebrew exhibits wordplay. The root consonants for "graze," "animal" (22:5), and "burn" (22:6) are all the same: *b'r* [TH1197/A, ZH1277/8].

22:8 [7] *who will determine.* This is not in the text. It may be that all that was required was simply swearing in the presence of "God" (or "judges," see the NLT mg and the comment above on 21:6) that no theft was done (see 22:11).

22:11 [10] *If the LORD . . . property.* This is not in the text. See note on 22:8 and the comments below.

22:12 [11] *the guilty person.* This is probably reading too much into the text's "he." A straightforward reading of the text would indicate that someone who allowed an animal to be stolen from him in the field was held responsible for the theft (see commentary).

COMMENTARY

This group of covenant terms gives examples relating to the prohibition of theft. Many commentators also include verses 16-17 in this section primarily for formal reasons. After verse 18, the great majority of the terms are stated as absolute prohibitions, whereas prior to that, as we have seen, most are in case form. Verses 16-17 are in case form; however, the Masoretic punctuation, which represents a very early understanding, places these verses in the following section, which is a rather miscellaneous one. It could be said that they coincide with verses 1-15 because they have to do with compensation for depriving someone of benefit, but beyond that they have little in common with those previous verses. See below on 22:16-31 for further discussion.

This collection has to do with outright theft (22:1-4), loss through negligence by another (22:5-6), loss of something left in safekeeping (22:7-13), and loss of something borrowed (22:14-15). The principles illustrated are similar to or identical with those already encountered above. They include: Human life is more valuable than property; failure to exercise due care brings liability; situations beyond one's control usually absolve one of responsibility; accepting things for safekeeping involves a lower level of responsibility than does borrowing them. Central are the matters of intentionality and diligence. God's world is one of cause and effect in which humans have freedom, worth, dignity, and accountability, and in which they are expected to exercise due care on behalf of their neighbors' possessions.

The shape of the first four verses (22:1-4) has troubled many students of the book because verses 2-3 seem to be inserted between verses 1 and 4. Cassuto (1967:281-283) says this was done intentionally to add specific Torah directives to a widely held general approach (see also Childs 1974:474). In many of the other ancient Near Eastern law codes theft was punishable by death. That is not the case in the Bible. The punishment for theft was restitution, and if the thief was unable to pay, he was enslaved, not executed. As already noted above, the amount of the restitution depended on whether the thief had already converted the property to his benefit when he was caught. Verses 2-3b present one caveat on the matter of death for the thief, but in so doing they actually protect the thief's life. If a thief breaks into a house at night, the homeowner will be held innocent if he kills the thief in the melee, but if the thief comes in the daytime his life is protected and the homeowner is held guilty if he kills the thief (see note on 22:3). Presumably, in the daylight the homeowner can see well enough to defend his property without having to resort to lethal force. This kind of protection for the life of a thief is unknown elsewhere.

Verses 5-6 deal with a situation where crops are destroyed through a neighbor's negligence. They are quite straightforward. If a person does not control his grazing animals or a fire that he has kindled on his land and the neighbor's crops are destroyed, the negligent person must replace the lost crop. Furthermore, in the case of the grazing, where presumably there was more possibility of control, the replacement had to be "from the best of" what the negligent person had.[1]

In 22:7-13 the issue is the loss of property that had been left in safekeeping with another person. Four possibilities are addressed: (1) money or goods stolen from a house (22:7-8); (2) animals lost by accident (22:10-11); (3) theft of animals from the field (22:12); and (4) attack by wild animals (22:13). In the first three cases, the person keeping the property must take an oath that he or she has not misappropriated the property for himself or herself (22:8-9, 11). As far as the text is concerned (see note on 22:8), the simple taking of the oath (calling a curse down on oneself if lying) was enough. There is no indication that any attempt was to be made to determine whether the person was actually lying or not. The owner had to accept that the speaker was telling the truth, and the owner had to bear the loss. Three qualifications are placed upon this disposition of the affairs. First, if the property was really stolen and the thief could be apprehended, the owner was entitled to the normal double compensation (22:7, 9; see 22:4). Second, if the owner accused the holder of stealing his property and it was determined that this was not the case, then the false accuser was required to compensate the one to whom the property was entrusted (22:9). Finally, if it could be shown that the trustee had allowed an animal to be stolen from his care in the field, negligence was assumed and he was required to compensate the owner (22:12).[2]

In the case of the fourth instance, destruction by wild animals, the trustee was required to present pieces of the animal's body as evidence in support of his testimony. David refers to such a circumstance in 1 Samuel 17:34-35, as does Amos in Amos 3:12.

The owner bore the major risk in the previous commands, whereas when the property was borrowed, the risk was the borrower's (22:14-15). As previously (22:10-13), it was the person initiating an action who was considered to bear the major responsibility. The borrower bears all the responsibility to return the animal to its owner in its original condition, and if he does not, he must compensate the owner for whatever loss occurred, whether the result of intention or accident. The only qualification is that if the owner was present when the injury or death occurred, the borrower is not responsible. Presumably, the owner could have prevented any intentional abuse, and if the loss was the result of an accident, he would have been there to witness the fact.

ENDNOTES

1. The LXX reads that if part of the neighbor's crop was destroyed, the compensation could be from normal crops, but that if the whole field was ruined, then the best had to be given. But it is hard to understand why this material would have come to be omitted from the MT if it was original.
2. Presumably, the reason such compensation was not required from the trustee when something was stolen from a house (22:7) was that negligence was unlikely in that circumstance (Houtman 1993:3.304).

◆ ### f. Social responsibility (22:16-31)

16"If a man seduces a virgin who is not engaged to anyone and has sex with her, he must pay the customary bride price and marry her. 17But if her father refuses to let him marry her, the man must still pay him an amount equal to the bride price of a virgin.

18"You must not allow a sorceress to live.

19"Anyone who has sexual relations with an animal must certainly be put to death.

20"Anyone who sacrifices to any god other than the LORD must be destroyed.*

21"You must not mistreat or oppress foreigners in any way. Remember, you yourselves were once foreigners in the land of Egypt.

22"You must not exploit a widow or an orphan. 23If you exploit them in any way and they cry out to me, then I will certainly hear their cry. 24My anger will blaze against you, and I will kill you with the sword. Then your wives will be widows and your children fatherless.

25"If you lend money to any of my people who are in need, do not charge interest as a money lender would. 26If you take your neighbor's cloak as security for a loan, you must return it before sunset. 27This coat may be the only blanket your neighbor has. How can a person sleep without it? If you do not return it and your neighbor cries out to me for help, then I will hear, for I am merciful.

28"You must not dishonor God or curse any of your rulers.

29"You must not hold anything back when you give me offerings from your crops and your wine.

"You must give me your firstborn sons. 30"You must also give me the firstborn of your cattle, sheep, and goats. But leave the newborn animal with its mother for seven days; then give it to me on the eighth day.

31"You must be my holy people. Therefore, do not eat any animal that has been torn up and killed by wild animals. Throw it to the dogs.

22:20 The Hebrew term used here refers to the complete consecration of things or people to the LORD, either by destroying them or by giving them as an offering.

NOTES

22:16 [15] *bride price*. In most traditional societies, the groom has to give the father of the bride an amount of money for the bride. At the same time, the father has to give his daughter a dowry when she marries. Typically, while the husband has the use of the money, he is expected to keep it intact so that upon his death or if he divorces her, she will have that money to use for her support. As noted before, the fact that only certain aspects of these kinds of arrangements are discussed here shows that the purpose is not to be a full-blown law code.

22:17 [16] *refuses.* This is emphatic in the Hebrew. A possible translation might be "absolutely refuses."

22:18 [17] *not allow . . . to live.* Elsewhere this phraseology is associated with the law of *kherem* [TH2764, ZH3051] (Num 31:15; Deut 20:16; 1 Sam 27:9-11). See the note on 22:20.

22:20 [19] *other than the LORD.* Lit., "except to the LORD alone." The emphatic nature of the wording, as well as its unusual placement in Hebrew at the end of the sentence, underscores the force of the exclusion. Childs (1974:479) rightly says that it is as forceful as anything found in Isaiah (e.g., Isa 46:9).

destroyed. See NLT mg. Here the word *kherem* [TH2764, ZH3051](see note on 22:18) is used. This is a much stronger term than merely putting to death. Not only the individual but his entire family and all their possessions were destroyed (see Josh 7:24-26). The person (or people, in the case of the Canaanites) was deemed to have transgressed onto what belonged to God alone and thus to have forfeited his family member's lives into God's hands. In a real sense they became a whole burnt offering.

22:21 [20] *foreigners.* Heb. *ger* [TH1616, ZH1731]. These were non-Israelite permanent residents who had no clan structure to protect them. They were to be distinguished from the *nokri* [TH5237A, ZH5799], who were temporary residents (cf. Deut 15:3), who did not need the same protections.

22:23 [22] All three of the verbs in this sentence are emphasized in the Hebrew.

22:25 [24] The assumed background to the prohibition of charging interest is an agrarian economy. It does not address borrowing capital for business purposes where a significant return on the investment could be expected. Rather, this is the person who is destitute and needs help just to survive. The level of destitution is hinted at here in that the only "security" (22:26) the person can offer is his cloak. This loan is not an investment. If it had to be repaid with interest, the result would probably be slavery. To approach this arrangement as a money lender would be markedly unlike the compassionate covenant Lord.

22:29 [28] The first sentence in this verse has only three words in Hebrew, and the translation of two of them is very uncertain. Apparently it is something like, "Your fullness (of crops) and your overflow (of wine) you shall not delay." In view of the second sentence, it has been taken to apply to the offerings of firstfruits (see commentary).

COMMENTARY

This section, as it is subdivided in the NLT (on the placement of verses 16-17, see the introductory comments on the previous section), contains four groups of laws: 22:16-17, 18-20, 21-27, and 28-31. On the surface, at least, they are somewhat miscellaneous in nature, and the heading "Social Responsibility" is a little misleading. In fact, these covenant stipulations combine religious, social, and ethical materials in a way that is typical of the entire "Book of the Covenant" (20:1–23:33).[1] In this covenant, every aspect of one's life is lived unto God without exception.

Although the main argument against including 22:16-17 with 22:18-31 is formal (see previous commentary section), there is also discussion about the intent of the command. Some suggest that the primary concern of verses 16-17 is the property rights of the girl's father. She is now "damaged goods," as it were, and the father must be compensated for his loss (Houtman 2000:3.207). In contrast, Childs (1974:476-477), even though he also places these verses in the previous section, still argues that there is an ethical factor involved that lifts the issue beyond merely financial concerns. Thus, the seducer is not able to use the girl and then toss her aside for a sum of money (see the similar incident with Amnon and Tamar related in 2 Sam 13:1-19). He must take her as his wife with all the normal procedures that involves. If the girl's father decides this would be an unsuitable marriage, he may prevent it, but the seducer does not have that option. And in any case, the seducer must pay the "bride price" (22:16). So I agree with Childs that the issue here is not compensation (a term that is not mentioned) but the treatment of another person as an object.

The three remaining paragraphs in the chapter (22:18-31) exhibit more unity of thought than many commentators have realized. They are addressing practices expressive of a pagan worldview (22:18-20), treatment of persons in ways that grow out of a pagan worldview (22:21-27), and practices expressive of the biblical worldview (22:28-31).[2]

The three stipulations in 22:18-20 involve the death penalty, probably because all of them involve behavior that grows out of the pagan understanding of reality and are thus in defiance of the true order of reality that God was trying to teach through the covenant (see above on 20:3, 4). As later Israelite history would show all too amply, to lose the battle on these points would, without divine intervention, be to lose the entire war. God is not the world; there is a boundary between him and it which creatures cannot cross. Furthermore, there is a boundary between humans and the rest of creation. Paganism, insisting that humans, the natural world, and the divine are continuous with one another, denies these boundaries in every way it can. Activities such as sorcery, bestiality, and polytheistic idolatry were central expressions of this worldview of continuity. If the actual nature of God's transcendence was to be learned and accepted, these activities and all that they represented could never be granted acceptable status in Israel.[3]

Somewhat unaccountably, Houtman (1993:3.210-212) makes the person referred to in verse 18 a "seductress." But study of the term elsewhere in the Old Testament makes the connection with magical activity unmistakable.[4] Undoubtedly there was a seductive aspect involved in magical activity and what it promised (note Isa 47:9, 12), and that may be the reason the command related to seduction is placed immediately prior to this one. But the reason these persons were not to be allowed "to live" (22:18) is that they were saying by their actions that humans can manipulate divine powers through rituals. The fact that sometimes these actions seem to get results makes them all the more dangerous as teachers of a deadly false worldview. It is for this reason that the Old Testament is univocal in forbidding magic of all sorts.

This same matter of worldview is almost certainly the reason that bestiality is forbidden here. In order to affirm the fundamental unity of all that exists, the pagan cults, as evidenced by the cult of Baal at Ugarit, not only had the gods and goddesses having sex with humans but also with animals (See ANET 139). Thus, what is forbidden here is not merely a behavior that some people find disgusting. Neither is it forbidden merely because the Canaanites, whom the Israelites were trying to dispossess, practiced it (Lev 18:23; 20:16). It is forbidden because it was a way of expressing (along with several other aberrant sexual behaviors) a false view of reality that must, because of its falseness, eventually enslave and destroy human beings.

The ultimate expression of this other worldview is polytheism, usually accompanied by the view that everything in the world is divine, and as such, is inhabited by a divine spirit. But this is absolutely wrong, and thus any attempt to propitiate these spirits by means of ritualistic sacrifice was to be treated with utmost seriousness. But why is *kherem* [TH2764, ZH3051] invoked (see notes on 22:18 and 20)? Why is it not only the one offering the "sacrifices" but also everything and everyone pertaining to him that is to be utterly "destroyed" (22:20)? The sense is very similar to what was being described in Exodus 19: There was nothing else to do with the person who had transgressed on the holy mountain but to destroy them. We might think of the person who has accidentally or willfully gone into an area contaminated with anthrax. He or she has become a deadly danger to all those around. So here, the person who has tried to manipulate God through sacrifices has become contaminated, and in this case, the only thing to do with them is to make them a sacrifice. In this way God was trying to communicate the ultimate seriousness of the matter.

Several commentators suggest that the reason for placing 22:21-27 in this section is to distinguish between foreign practices and "foreigners" (22:21) themselves. This may be the case, but the section as a whole is discussing the ways in which the disadvantaged must be treated. That being so, I suspect there is a deeper connection between this section and the previous one. If a person adopts the pagan worldview, a number of things follow. First, one comes to believe that it is possible to manipulate the cosmos to satisfy one's needs and desires. That leads almost inevitably to the idea that one can (and must) manipulate humans for those same ends. When this idea is coupled with the fundamentally low view of humanity that paganism produces, the end result is that the poor, the helpless, and the disadvantaged are where they are because they deserve to be. They are a second (or third) class of humanity who have no right to be treated with respect or care.

But if there is one God, who is not the world and cannot be manipulated through the world, and if he has made all humans in his own image and, as such, values them too much to manipulate them for his own ends, then everything is different. That is what we see in this section. Three specific classes of people are mentioned to represent all the rest. They are the non-Israelite permanent resident (22:21; see note), the widow and orphan (22:22-24), and the poor (22:25-27). All of these people are vulnerable in one way or another, either because they have no clan, no husband or father, or no economic means with which to protect themselves. So God establishes himself as their protector (22:24, 27). Anyone who tries to abuse them for his or her own ends will have God to contend with, and they may well find themselves in the condition of those they are trying to exploit (22:24). In all, God provides three reasons why the people should give up any attempt to manipulate those who are weaker than they. First, they should remember that they are finally no different than those they are tempted to oppress. They were once resident aliens in Egypt, and that they are no longer so is through no merit of their own (cf. Deut 10:18-19). Second, such manipulation is contrary to the character of the God with whom they are in covenant (22:27). Third, these are God's covenant people ("my people," 22:25), and it would be dangerous to tamper with his partners.

If I have understood the relationship between 22:18-20 and 22:21-27 correctly, it makes the content of the third section (22:28-31) more understandable. If it is necessary to counteract the wrong view of humanity that a wrong view of reality produces, what practices (and attitudes) will be characteristic of a right view of reality? That is the question I believe this group of stipulations is addressing. Verse 28 is then somewhat transitional. It would dishonor God to treat the poor as mere stepping stones to one's own wealth. He does not treat them as objects and neither may those who name themselves by his name. But they would also dishonor God when they gave him less than their best. If they gave him only what they did not have a better use for, they were suggesting that he is not the one, the ultimate creator, outside of time and space, beyond the grasp of their magical offerings. So verses 29 and 30 call for the giving of one's best, one's first, to God. By giving the first of crops, children, and animals, they were testifying that all they had was a gift from him. Thus, the offerings of the first and the firstborn were not an attempt to magically manipulate God into giving more, but rather a way of expressing thanks for what he had given and faith that as he had given so he would continue. The final verse, 22:31, wraps up this point first in a very holistic way and then in a very specific way. First, it sums up what has been said: "You must be my holy people." Why was God calling them to abandon the pagan way of understanding reality? Why was he calling them not to treat people as though they could be manipulated for one's own benefit? Because he wanted them to belong exclusively to him and to share his character—to be holy (cf. 19:6). That is God's goal for the entire human race, and he began with Israel. But then from the completely global he honed in to the narrowly specific. He gave Israel a glimpse of the broad picture, but knowing that they were hardly ready to grasp even the edges of that picture, he focused them on something practical that they could grasp in its entirety: Blood contains the mystery of life; that mystery is entirely in God's hands; people who belong completely to God leave that mystery in his hands, so they don't eat meat with blood in it.

ENDNOTES
1. Cassuto (1967:293) suggests that vv. 16-17, 18-20, and 21-27 are associated with one another because each passage contains some form of the root *shakab* [TH7901, ZH8886] (to lie down, lie with). The argument seems forced to me.
2. Beginning with 22:18, the stipulations continuing on through 23:13 have a very different form from those in 21:1-22:17, which take the "if-then" case approach. From 22:18 onwards, most of the stipulations take the form of absolute prohibitions or commands, with no statement of the consequences of conforming or not conforming to them. Sarna says that this is so because most of them are of a nature that "can only be enforced by human conscience quickened by the knowledge that they are expressions of the divine will" (1991:135).
3. Sarna (1991:136) says that these three are grouped together here because all are the activities of foreigners, citing Deut 18:9-14. While that is undoubtedly a correct

derivation for the actions, I think it is more the worldview they represent than their derivation that is the reason they are together.
4. 7:11; Deut 18:10, 12; 2 Kgs 9:22; 2 Chr 33:6; Isa 8:18-20; 47:9, 12; Jer 27:9; Dan 2:2; Mic 5:12; Nah 3:4; Mal 3:5.

◆ ### g. A call for justice (23:1-13)

"You must not pass along false rumors. You must not cooperate with evil people by lying on the witness stand.

²"You must not follow the crowd in doing wrong. When you are called to testify in a dispute, do not be swayed by the crowd to twist justice. ³And do not slant your testimony in favor of a person just because that person is poor.

⁴"If you come upon your enemy's ox or donkey that has strayed away, take it back to its owner. ⁵If you see that the donkey of someone who hates you has collapsed under its load, do not walk by. Instead, stop and help.

⁶"In a lawsuit, you must not deny justice to the poor.

⁷"Be sure never to charge anyone falsely with evil. Never sentence an innocent or blameless person to death, for I never declare a guilty person to be innocent.

⁸"Take no bribes, for a bribe makes you ignore something that you clearly see. A bribe makes even a righteous person twist the truth.

⁹"You must not oppress foreigners. You know what it's like to be a foreigner, for you yourselves were once foreigners in the land of Egypt.

¹⁰"Plant and harvest your crops for six years, ¹¹but let the land be renewed and lie uncultivated during the seventh year. Then let the poor among you harvest whatever grows on its own. Leave the rest for wild animals to eat. The same applies to your vineyards and olive groves.

¹²"You have six days each week for your ordinary work, but on the seventh day you must stop working. This gives your ox and your donkey a chance to rest. It also allows your slaves and the foreigners living among you to be refreshed.

¹³"Pay close attention to all my instructions. You must not call on the name of any other gods. Do not even speak their names.

NOTES

23:1 *false rumors.* I think Houtman (2000:3.238) is correct when he says that the context of the remainder of the verse suggests that slander leading to legal charges is what is in view here.

lying on the witness stand. Lit., "by being a violent witness"; thus a good rendering is "malicious witness" (NASB, NIV). More than mere "lying" is intended; it is lying with a violent result in mind. Houtman (2000:3.239) goes farther and translates it as "don't testify on behalf of a villain" (i.e., a witness on behalf of the violent).

23:3 *slant your testimony in favor of.* This is a good rendering of the literal "do honor to," or "give favor to." In Lev 19:15 the same word, *hadar* [TH1921, ZH2075], is used in a prohibition from favoring the rich.

23:4 *take it back.* This is emphatic in Hebrew.

23:5 The second part of the verse is difficult. Taken literally it would seem to say, "You will cease to forsake to him, you shall surely forsake with him," which makes no sense at all. Among many proposals, two stand out. One is that besides "forsake," another meaning of the verb *'azab* (which occurs 3 times in the verse) is "to release [the donkey]," which in the second half of the verse would imply the idea "to help" (so NLT). The problem is that "release" is very infrequent and usually has the idea of letting something go rather than to cause something to be released (as here). A second proposal is that there were two different words which came to have the same consonants (see KBL 694). This is possible because of a feature of the earlier Semitic language that produced Hebrew. It had a consonant that sounded like the voiced *th* (as in "these"). But as the various dialects developed, this sound tended to blend in with other sounds, with *d* in some dialects and *z* in others. Here the original of the word meaning "forsake" would have been *'azab* [TH5800, ZH6440] while the original root of the other word, meaning "make, arrange, set, restore," would have been *'adab*, appearing in biblical Hebrew as *'azab* [TH5800A, ZH6441]. (The second word appears in Ugaritic as *'db*.) This offers a good explanation of the occurrence of the word in Neh 3:8; 4:2 where "forsake" does not work but "arrange" or "set in order" or "restore" does. Thus, the translation here would be "you will refrain from abandoning him—you must surely restore it with him."

23:6 *the poor*. Lit., "your poor."

23:7 *Never sentence . . . to death*. This translation assumes that judges are being addressed. The text merely says, "You shall not murder an innocent or blameless person." It may be saying that a false witness who causes the death of an innocent person is in effect a murderer.

23:8 *makes even a righteous person twist the truth*. This is a very possible translation (supported by the LXX), especially in the way that it parallels the first sentence in the verse. Another possibility, however, is "it twists the words of the righteous," understanding "the righteous" to be the defendants. So Houtman (2000:3.246) translates "makes the causes of people who are in the right to have a bad outcome."

23:11 *the poor among you*. Lit., "the poor of your people."

23:12 *be refreshed*. Heb. *yinnapesh*. This root, *napash* [TH5314, ZH5882], which normally appears in a noun form and is usually translated with "soul, self, being" and the like, only appears as a verb two other times (31:17; 2 Sam 16:14). This kind of rarity is typical of this passage, in which a significant number of words occur that only appear infrequently elsewhere in the OT.

23:13 *call on the name of*. Lit., "cause the name to be remembered."

COMMENTARY

In this part of the covenant stipulations, we return to the kinds of treatment of other persons that are implications of the character of Yahweh, the covenant Lord. Sarna (1991:141) points out that in the Mekilta (a rabbinic midrash on Exodus), this section is headed by 22:31 with its call for Israel to be God's holy people. Thus, just as in Leviticus 19, no question is left that the holiness that God wants to impart to his people is of an ethical and moral nature and not merely of a cultic sort. To belong exclusively to this God meant giving other humans a different standing and acting toward them in different ways than a person would if he accepted the worldview of the gods. For this reason, I am confident that verses 1-13 are intended as a unit (as NLT has it) and that just as 22:31 was transitional between 22:16-30 and 23:1-12, so 23:13 is intended to be transitional into the closing section 23:14-19, even while closing the entire section encompassed in 22:16–23:12 with a call to absolute loyalty to Yahweh. It wraps up one thought and prepares for the next.

Many commentators include verses 10-13 with verses 14-19, labeling the section "ceremonial requirements" or the like (so Sarna, Cassuto, Childs, Enns, et al.). However, apart from missing the important concluding and introductory functions of verse 13 just mentioned, this view also misses the key fact that the commands to observe the sabbatical year (23:10-11) and the Sabbath (23:12) are not viewed at all here in relation to worship, ceremony, or cult but are entirely from the point of view of their social function. For this reason, I feel sure that they are intended to be read with the stipulations that precede them rather than with those that follow.[1]

If one takes verses 1-3 and 6-9 as being addressed to judges, as Childs (and others) does, it becomes difficult to explain what verses 4 and 5, which have nothing to do with the court, are doing in the middle. However, if one takes it, as Houtman does, that all nine verses are addressed to Israelites in general, the presence of verses 4 and 5 is more easily explained. All nine verses address doing wrong to others on account of social considerations. So, in verse 1 it is wrong to slander someone at the behest of an evil person (who perhaps has some hold over you?). Verse 2 commands resistance of the crowd's desire for evil. Verse 3 says you must not compromise the truth simply because you feel badly that a person is poor. In verses 4 and 5, the command is that you must not refuse to help those who are your enemies (23:4) or hate you (23:5).[2] According to verse 6, the opposite side of the coin to verse 3 is addressed: "You must not deny justice" to someone simply because he is poor.[3] Verses 7 and 8 expand on that thought: You must not deny justice to any innocent person. If you do and it results in that person's execution, you are a murderer (23:7). But even beyond the issue of perpetrating an injustice is the thought of doing it for the sake of a bribe (23:8).[4] Finally, "you must not oppress" (23:9) someone because he is a foreigner, a resident alien who has no tribe or clan to protect him (see note on 22:21). Again (as in 22:21 and elsewhere), the appeal is that the Israelites know what it is like to be in that situation.

Thus, these commands do not all assume a common setting, nor do they necessarily share the same origin. As I said in the introduction to the covenant stipulations, we can imagine that God directed Moses to use a good deal of material that was already in existence, amending, correcting, or supplementing it as necessary to achieve his theological and educational purposes. But what all of these do have in common is the idea that behind all the circumstances of life stands the inviolable truth. That truth stands regardless of a person's station in life, and regardless of the number or type of people who are for it or against it. Just as there are inviolate boundaries between creator and creation, and between human and nature, so there are inviolate boundaries between what is so and what is not so. And what is so—the truth—may not be corrupted for self-serving or self-protecting reasons. It supersedes the circumstances of a person's situation. If the truth is in a person's favor, then so be it. But if it is not in a person's favor, so be it as well. Thus, these deceptively simple requirements are a powerful attack on the relativity of truth. But at the same time, they are also an attack on truth as mere abstraction. Precisely because the truth about truth is presented in the context of the life and behavior of persons, it is made profoundly clear that God is not first of all concerned about truth for its own sake. Rather, just as he is "true" in all his dealings with his creation, he expects his people to be true in all their dealings with one another and with their world. It is in *being* true to others whether they are rich or poor, powerful or helpless, friends or enemies, innocent or guilty, that we show whether we know the truth.

These thoughts are extended in verses 10-12. God is who he is not for his own sake but for the sake of others. Thus, what he requires in service of himself is necessarily going to have a beneficial impact on his people and his world.[5] To be truly for God will necessarily mean that we are for people. When worship is a self-centered experience benefiting only ourselves, we are being true to no one, not God, not others, and not even ourselves (see Isa 58:1-14). So Moses says that the two reasons for the sabbatical year are that the land can be renewed (lit., "rest") and so that the poor[6] and the wild animals may freely eat whatever the fields, vineyards, and olive groves produce. Here there is nothing said of the religious aspects of this behavior. The focus is on what it does for others.

The same is true of the command to rest on the seventh day (23:12). Elsewhere, the reasons given for this required behavior have to do with creation (20:8-11) and redemption (Deut 5:12-15). But here the one reason given is that the ox and donkey will have a chance to rest and slaves and resident aliens will be refreshed, that is, they will experience, literally, "restoration of their being" (see note on 23:12). That is, when we obey God, living and worshiping as he wishes, those whose lives and well-being are dependent on us, far from being harmed, will, in fact, be helped. If we are true to God, we are necessarily true to those around us.

This leads directly into verse 13. Earlier we noted how commandments about worship (20:22-26) introduce the specific stipulations of the covenant for the people. We are about to see how commandments about worship also conclude those stipulations (23:14-19). Thus, it seems likely to me that verse 13 is intended to sum up everything between those opening and closing segments (21:1–23:13). If this is correct it makes what this verse has to say all the more important. In any case, whether the instructions under consideration are all of those from 21:1 onward or are only 23:1-9, the point is the same. It is the same one made by the first of the Ten Commandments: All these instructions express the will of the one God of the universe. To recognize any other gods is not merely to violate the central term of the covenant, it is to miss the whole point of the covenant which is to reveal the nature of reality as it really is, and not as paganism mistakenly thinks it to be. Persons who will give themselves unreservedly to the one God will discover that reality as they experience it. But that discovery and that experience will not be possible for people who affirm that opposing view of reality. If people who supposedly belong to Yahweh "bring to remembrance" (NLT, "call upon the name of") any other gods, they are attempting to hold contradictory ideas at once. It is like saying that the temperature of a room is "boiling hot" and "freezing cold" at the same time. One cannot say that the world *is* God and is *not* God at the same time.[7] Thus Joshua was to say to the descendants of these people 80 years later that they had to choose *either* the "gods of the Amorites" *or* Yahweh (Josh 24:14-15). That kind of exclusivity was scandalous then, and it still is today. Yet it was the only way the Israelites could learn the truth that God is not the world and at the same time bring the fruits of that knowledge into the world, fruits such as the worth of all people in spite of class and background.

ENDNOTES
1. So Houtman (2000:3.236), although he believes 23:13 should be read with verses 14-19. Hyatt (1971:247) treats vv. 10-12 as a separate paragraph and sees 23:13 as a "concluding admonition," although he is not certain where it originally stood.
2. Enns (2000:455) is right when he says that the primary focus here is not on animal welfare. An *ox* or *a donkey* was among a person's most valuable possessions, the loss of which could be very grievous. Note that this verse proves that when Jesus said, "You have heard the law that says, 'Love your neighbor' and hate your enemy. But I say, love your enemies! Pray for those who persecute you" (Matt 5:43-44) it was not a new teaching but a reinforcement and application of OT passages like these.
3. Cassuto (1967:298), noting the suffix "your" and the similar consonants between "poor" and "enemy" (see note on 23:6), takes it that 23:6 is a continuation of 23:4-5. There is no support in the versions for such a reading. Houtman (1993:3.246-247) suggests that the pronoun indicates that this is a reference to poor persons who are somehow dependent on the one being called on to give testimony, thus "a needy person who is dependent on you."
4. The OT is quite consistent in condemning the giving of a bribe to someone in order to persuade them to do wrong (Deut 10:17; 16:19; 1 Sam 8:3; 2 Chr 19:7; Prov 17:23; Isa 1:23; 5:23; 33:15; Ezek 22:12; Amos 5:12; Mic 7:3). However, this does not mean that *every* sort of bribe is condemned. The book of Proverbs says that giving someone a bribe in order to get them to do the right thing for you may be the essence of wisdom (Prov 17:8; 21:14).
5. Sarna (1991:143) says that vv. 10-11 are a bridge between 6-9 and 12-13. I believe vv. 10-12, speaking as they do about the social benefit of expressions of worship, are a bridge between 1-9—truth in social relationships—and 14-19—the great festivals of worship—with v. 13 being the hinge point.
6. The phrase "the poor of your people" suggests a sense of solidarity between the landowner and the landless poor. They may be poor, but they are as much a part of the people as the landowner is, and the landowner must not forget that.
7. This is almost certainly what Aaron and the people of Israel were attempting to do in identifying Yahweh with the golden calf (see below on ch 32).

◆ ### h. Three annual festivals (23:14-19)

¹⁴"Each year you must celebrate three festivals in my honor. ¹⁵First, celebrate the Festival of Unleavened Bread. For seven days the bread you eat must be made without yeast, just as I commanded you. Celebrate this festival annually at the appointed time in early spring, in the month of Abib,* for that is the anniversary of your departure from Egypt. No one may appear before me without an offering.

¹⁶"Second, celebrate the Festival of Harvest,* when you bring me the first crops of your harvest.

"Finally, celebrate the Festival of the Final Harvest* at the end of the harvest season, when you have harvested all the crops from your fields. ¹⁷At these three times each year, every man in Israel must appear before the Sovereign, the LORD.

18"You must not offer the blood of my sacrificial offerings together with any baked goods containing yeast. And do not leave the fat from the festival offerings until the next morning.

19"As you harvest your crops, bring the very best of the first harvest to the house of the LORD your God.

"You must not cook a young goat in its mother's milk.

23:15 Hebrew *appointed time in the month of Abib*. This first month of the ancient Hebrew lunar calendar usually occurs within the months of March and April.   **23:16a** Or *Festival of Weeks*. This was later called the Festival of Pentecost (see Acts 2:1). It is celebrated today as Shavuat (or Shabuoth).   **23:16b** Or *Festival of Ingathering*. This was later called the Festival of Shelters or Festival of Tabernacles (see Lev 23:33-36). It is celebrated today as Sukkot (or Succoth).

NOTES

23:14 *Each year you must celebrate three festivals in my honor.* Lit., "three times you must feast to me in the year." The Hebrew translated "times" is literally "feet" and is paralleled with a synonym in 23:17 which often has the idea of "footbeat." So a series of events is likened to a series of taps of the foot. Originally, the verb "to feast" (*khagag* [TH2287, ZH2510]) referred to any kind of feast, as in 32:5 where the Israelites held a feast for the golden calf. Eventually, as with the Arabic word *hajj* ("pilgrimage"), the term came to have a narrowed meaning—it referred especially to the three pilgrimage festivals mentioned in this paragraph.

23:15 *appear before me without an offering.* Lit., "my face shall not be seen emptily." The Hebrew makes the experience very graphic. These festivals are about experiencing the very presence of God.

23:17 *the Sovereign, the LORD.* Lit., "the Lord Yahweh." Cassuto (1967:303) says that *'adon* [TH113, ZH123] (Lord) is used here to make a clear distinction from the Canaanite god *ba'al* [TH1167/8, ZH1251], whose name meant "lord." Alongside that is the point that the one who is calling for this activity to be performed is the covenant Lord, the God who is making this covenant with them.

COMMENTARY

Just as the covenant terms for the people began with a section on the prescribed worship of Yahweh, so also they end. These six verses give, in broad outline, the method by which the people would be constantly reminded of their special relations to each other as a covenant people and to Yahweh, their covenant Lord.[1] The details of exactly how and when these festivals were to be celebrated would come later (Lev 23; Num 28-29; Deut 16-17), but here it was sufficient to paint the broad outlines of what would be expected of the people. The three festivals generally coincided with the agricultural calendar in Canaan, and although we do not have a great deal of evidence, there is reason to believe that the Canaanites had religious celebrations at these same times. It seems likely that God directed his people to celebrate at these times precisely to provide an alternative to the Canaanite festivals. The Canaanite festivals were magical rituals to guarantee the fertility of the earth (see Cassuto 1967:302) and were thus completely at odds with the biblical view of reality (see 34:18, 22-26).

The Festival of Unleavened Bread (23:15) immediately followed the Passover celebration (see commentary on 13:3-10) and occurred at the beginning of the harvest season, at the time of the cutting of barley (about the first of April). But, as was true of all of the festivals, this feast had nothing to do with any attempt to promote or guarantee a good harvest. Rather, it was a time to remember what God had done for them in the past in delivering them from Egypt. God could not be manipulated, but on the basis of what he had done in time and space, he could be trusted to care for his people in the future. There is some speculation that yeast was forbidden because of some unknown association with Canaanite ritual, but the biblical explanation is a strictly historical one relating to the hasty departure (see commentary on 12:14-15). Perhaps the command not to come into God's presence "without an offering" related to the time of year. No harvest had been received yet, so it would have been tempting to say that one would wait to see how things would turn out before making an offering. But that is not living in faith in the promised provision of the covenant Lord.

The second festival, the Festival of Harvest, occurred 50 days later[2] (near the end of May; see Lev 23:15-16), when the wheat harvest was at or near completion. This was a festival of thanks when the first crops (i.e., the best of the crop) were presented to the Lord (see also 23:19a). Again, this was an expression of faith. Perhaps the harvest had been small and it would be best to see what would be left over after a period of time. But that was not to be the case. Trust in God meant that his portion came off the top. The fact that the terms of the covenant may well have been given on the fiftieth day after that first Passover led later Jewish writers to say that the giving of the Torah was the historical event being celebrated by this festival, but the Old Testament makes no mention of this.

The third festival, the Festival of the Final Harvest (23:16; 34:22), elsewhere called "the Festival of Shelters" (Lev 23:34), occurred as the harvest season was ending with the gathering of the olives and the grapes (about the beginning of October). The second name was probably drawn from the fact that the harvesters, needing to save time from walking back to the village at the end of the day, and also to guard the harvest, would spend the nights in the field, sleeping in hastily-built shelters. Among Israel's neighbors this festival tended to be a time of sexual orgies aimed at ensuring that the god of vegetation would return from the dead in the spring. But for Israel it was once more a festival of thanks for God's immediate past provision and for his care in the more distant past when the people had lived in temporary shelters in the wilderness (cf. Lev 23:39-44).

The provision that every man had to "appear before . . . the LORD" (23:17) each year on these occasions required a very serious time commitment at key points during harvest: when harvest was just beginning, when one phase of it was just ending, and when the final phase was ending. Like the Sabbath, this was a way of saying that one's true life did not depend on one's own labor but on the gracious favor of God. Thus, the most important thing one could do for oneself and one's family was to seek his face (see Pss 27:8; 105:4).[3]

Verses 18 and 19 present four specific requirements relating to sacrificial worship. It is not clear how closely they were intended to relate to the festivals. Clearly the third of the four does relate closely (23:19a), and that leads to a presumption that the others do as well. Cassuto (1967:304) believes that they are mentioned here because each of them contradicted some specific Canaanite practice. That certainly seems possible, but it is hard to imagine what verse 19a would contradict. The first requirement underscores the prohibition from using "yeast" (23:18) in conjunction with any blood offering (cf. Lev 2:11). It may be the association of yeast with decay and corruption that is in focus (see the commentary on 12:15-20). The second requirement, to not leave the fat until morning, may have been designed to prevent the feast from turning into an all-night soiree (34:25 may support this idea when it says that none of the sacrifice is to be left over; cf. 12:10). The fourth requirement, prohibiting the cooking of a goat in its mother's milk, was clearly important, being repeated twice elsewhere in the Torah (34:26; Deut 14:21), but its importance is no longer understood. The most likely explanation is that such a practice was a significant part of Canaanite fertility rituals. That seemed to be supported when a damaged Ugaritic tablet was found that appeared to speak of such a custom, but recent studies of that tablet have contested the reading (ISBE 355). Nevertheless, this remains the most likely explanation.

ENDNOTES
1. This purpose of covenant reaffirmation probably explains why Passover and the Day of Atonement are not mentioned. This is not intended to be a full delineation of the religious calendar.
2. "Pentecost" (*pentēkostos* [TG4005, ZG4300]) is the Greek word for "fiftieth."
3. Deuteronomy 16:11-14 makes it clear that although the males were required to present themselves, these festivals were also intended to involve the whole family. That this was the custom is shown by the account in Luke 2:41-51 of the boy Jesus in the Temple.

◆   3. Yahweh's covenant promises (23:20-33)

[20]"See, I am sending an angel before you to protect you on your journey and lead you safely to the place I have prepared for you. [21]Pay close attention to him, and obey his instructions. Do not rebel against him, for he is my representative, and he will not forgive your rebellion. [22]But if you are careful to obey him, following all my instructions, then I will be an enemy to your enemies, and I will oppose those who oppose you. [23]For my angel will go before you and bring you into the land of the Amorites, Hittites, Perizzites, Canaanites, Hivites, and Jebusites, so you may live there. And I will destroy them completely. [24]You must not worship the gods of these nations or serve them in any way or imitate their evil practices. Instead, you must utterly destroy them and smash their sacred pillars.
[25]"You must serve only the LORD your God. If you do, I* will bless you with food and water, and I will protect you from illness. [26]There will be no miscarriages or infertility in your land, and I will give you long, full lives.
[27]"I will send my terror ahead of you and create panic among all the people whose lands you invade. I will make all your enemies turn and run. [28]I will send terror* ahead of you to drive out the Hivites, Canaanites, and Hittites. [29]But I will not drive them out in a single year, because the land would become desolate and the wild animals would multiply and

threaten you. ³⁰I will drive them out a little at a time until your population has increased enough to take possession of the land. ³¹And I will fix your boundaries from the Red Sea to the Mediterranean Sea,* and from the eastern wilderness to the Euphrates River.* I will hand over to you the people now living in the land, and you will drive them out ahead of you.

³²"Make no treaties with them or their gods. ³³They must not live in your land, or they will cause you to sin against me. If you serve their gods, you will be caught in the trap of idolatry."

23:25 As in Greek and Latin versions; Hebrew reads *he*. 23:28 Often rendered *the hornet*. The meaning of the Hebrew is uncertain. 23:31a Hebrew *from the sea of reeds to the sea of the Philistines*. 23:31b Hebrew *from the wilderness to the river*.

NOTES

23:20 *place.* Sarna (1991:148) notes that "place" frequently refers to the sanctuary. This would then be similar to 15:17 which speaks about God taking the people to Canaan, his holy place.

23:21 *he is my representative.* Lit., "my name is in him" (see commentary; see also 20:7).

23:24 *smash.* The verb is emphasized in Hebrew; perhaps it should be rendered "smash to bits."

23:25 *protect you from.* Lit., "take away, turn aside." This verb (*sur* [TH5493, ZH6073]) is used in a variety of circumstances where baneful influence is involved (such as the removal of idol altars).

23:28 *terror.* Or, "the hornet" (see NLT mg). The word only occurs two other times in the OT (Deut 7:20; Josh 24:12), and the precise connotation is not made clear in either of them. The abstract usage seems best.

23:31 *eastern wilderness.* "Eastern" is not in the text. It is a possible inference, but another is "southern," with the intent to talk about the extent of the territory from the north to the south.

I will hand over. In Hebrew this phrase is preceded by the particle *ki* [TH3588, ZH3954], which here could be either causal ("because I will hand over") or asseverative ("I will certainly hand over").

23:33 *in the trap of idolatry.* The words "of idolatry" are not in the Hebrew. The NLT is attempting to give the reader with little background some understanding of what the trap might involve. However, the trap being referred to connotes a good deal more than that (see commentary).

COMMENTARY

This final part of the "Book of the Covenant" (20:1–23:33) expresses the commitments of Yahweh, the covenant Lord, to his people. There is nothing quite like this in the suzerainty covenants upon which Exodus 20–24 is modeled. There are expressions of commitment by the suzerain, but nowhere else are they expressed in the mix of conditional and unconditional promises and warnings as they are here. The result is a heightened sense that this is not merely a legal proceeding but the expression of a much more personal, and thus more binding, relationship. This sense is increased when the content of the warnings is investigated. They all have to do with the recognition and worship of other gods. Thus, the covenant stipulations end precisely where they began—with the first commandment

(20:3). Why is this so? It is because of the purpose of the covenant: God was seeking to reveal who he is and what the nature of reality is. It was only through absolute, undying loyalty to him that the Israelites would be able to learn these truths. If they tried to hold both worldviews simultaneously, they could only come to erroneous and ultimately deadly conclusions. But in exclusive commitment to the one true God, there would be hope and along with that, all the benefits that the gods offered but could not provide.[1]

Yahweh committed himself to provide four things for his people. First, he promised his immediate presence, guiding and protecting them on their journey (23:22). Second, he promised to destroy all their enemies (23:22-23, 27-28). Third, he promised health, fertility, and long life (23:25-26). Fourth, he promised to establish them in the land (23:29-31). While some of these promises are stated in unconditional terms—"My angel will go before you and bring you into the land . . . I will destroy them completely" (23:23); "I will send my terror . . . I will make all your enemies turn and run" (23:27-28); "I will fix your boundaries . . . I will hand over to you" (23:31)—there is still a necessary condition that runs throughout. Sometimes it is stated explicitly—"if you are careful to obey" (23:22); if "you . . . serve only the LORD" (23:25); "if you serve their gods" (23:33)—and it is always at least implicit. If Israel broke its covenant with Yahweh on this most crucial of points, the worship of other gods, the covenant would be effectively nullified. To do such a thing is to rebel (23:21). As demonstrated by such passages as 1 Kings 12:19; 2 Kings 1:1; 3:5, 7; 8:20, 22 this term had a technical connotation of covenant-breaking. If the people broke the covenant with this behavior, Yahweh would have no more obligations to them.

This pervasive air of conditionality, however, cannot wipe out the unconditional thread that runs throughout these promises. God *will* give them the land; he *will* destroy their enemies; he *will* give them posterity in the land. This issue of God's faithfulness against all the odds will be one of the great themes of the Old Testament. For the people would break all their promises; they would rebel against him and his covenant again and again. Yet his determination to save them and the world by bringing as many as possible into a life-giving relationship with himself has won out again and again. The key to understanding this point is to recognize the intermingling of individual and community in the Old Testament. The fact that God *will* be faithful to his covenant to create a people for himself is not a guarantee to every individual under the covenant. Individuals who rebelled would experience the results of that rebellion, as that generation was to learn to its sorrow. But not every individual would rebel, and out of that remnant, God would forge a people again and again. The same is true of the church today. The church of Jesus Christ will survive and triumph because God keeps his word. But that does not mean that every individual who was ever once a faithful member of Christ's church will enter into the Kingdom of Heaven.

There is no easy explanation as to the identity of the angel (lit., "messenger") in 23:20-23. Many suggestions have been offered, including figurative speech for divine activity, Moses, Gabriel, and God himself. While the "messenger of the Lord" does not have to be a synonym for Yahweh (as it is not in 33:2-5), it frequently is (see the commentary on 14:19). Isaiah 63 makes the connection clear when it says that "the angel of his presence" (Isa 63:9, ESV) was the "Holy Spirit," who led the people through the sea and the wilderness (Isa 63:9-14). The "angel" language is a way of speaking about God when he is immediately (and sometimes visibly) present. In the light of the Christian understanding of the Trinity, this way of speaking about him becomes understandable. The "angel" *is* God, yet God is not limited to that manifestation of himself. This understanding is furthered by the statement in verse 21 that the "name" of God is "in" the angel (see note on 23:21). At the least, that statement means "he is my representative," but I suspect the intent is to make the connection even stronger: This being functions as God in immediate relation to Israel.[2]

Why would the Israelites be tempted to worship Baal and the other gods of the Canaanite pantheon? Apart from the larger issues of control and surrender (see endnote 1), there would have been the sense for people raised in a polytheistic milieu that these were the gods of that region who knew and controlled that region. Furthermore, there was an undeniable sophistication and culture possessed by the Canaanites. Former slaves coming in out of the desert would have felt themselves very backward and deprived and would want to emulate such gifted and talented people. But underneath it all would have been the basic issues of life: health, fertility, and longevity. The Canaanite religion (like the rest of the ancient Near Eastern religions) focused on the acquisition and the maintenance of these factors. Thus, it would be very tempting to think that while Yahweh had been all right for the austerities of the desert, they were now coming into a new area with special needs, which this opulent and complex Canaanite religion was set up to meet.

Yahweh met this challenge in two ways. First of all, he promised the very same things that Baal promised (23:25-26). He was not merely the god of the desert; he was the God of the whole world, and he could provide in fact what the gods only pretended to. But second, he demanded that no quarter be given to that religion. The gods and everything pertaining to them must be absolutely destroyed (23:24), and there must be no alliances made with their worshippers (23:32-33). If this seems unusually harsh, it must be remembered that the fate of the world hung on the survival of the Israelite faith as revealed to them by Yahweh.[3] An analogy would be the treatment of cancer. Shall we be gracious to the cancer cells since they are living things too and have a right to exist as much as any other cells do? Of course not! Cancer cells and other cells cannot coexist with each other. They are diametrically opposed to each other. And if the cancer is not absolutely destroyed, it will pose a threat to the rest of the body for as long as it exists. Paganism and Yahwism cannot exist together. It is interesting to think how history might have been different if the Israelites had obeyed God carefully in this matter. That they did not do so meant that Israel's history would be one of pain and tragedy, much of it undeserved to be sure, but too much of it as a result of not giving Yahweh that wholehearted devotion that results in gladly doing his will. This is the trap that is spoken of in 23:33. It is the trap of believing they could have God and the gods, the trap of trying to have their way and God's way, the trap of thinking they could trust God and themselves.

The explanation that God would not destroy the inhabitants of Canaan "in a single year" (23:29-31) suggests that he wanted to wean Israel from a dependence on instant results and to return them to a more normal experience of life. Surely, the God who had devastated Egypt and her chariot forces with a few stunning strokes could have so intervened in the normal course of affairs that the Canaanites would have simply ceased to exist while the land remained cultivated and wild animals were kept in check. But that is not the usual way in which God manages his affairs on earth. Usually, he allows matters to develop in slower and more involved ways, incorporating the full participation of human agency. He had used the more direct and immediate means in connection with the Exodus and Sinai because of the critical importance of those events. But he values human involvement too much to make that his normal mode of operation. So he told the people in this context to prepare for that new state of affairs. He would be no less involved in the events, and ultimately the Canaanites would only be defeated because of his involvement, but there would be a much greater proportion of human causality engaged in the future.[4]

ENDNOTES
1. We might ask why polytheism and its accompanying idolatry were such a temptation to Israel (and the rest of the world) if they do not supply what they promise. The answer is in the illusion of control. We think that we can manipulate forces that are part of the cosmos (and us). That thrill of power is satisfying even when it fails to produce. By contrast, the thought of having to relinquish control in surrender to a God we cannot manipulate is too horrific to contemplate, even if the results would be better than we imagined.
2. As Enns (2000:471) points out, listening to the angel means obeying God.
3. In this regard, Enns (2000:473) makes the important point that the precise limits of the land (23:31, probably from the Gulf of Aqaba to the Mediterranean [east to west], and from the Sinai wilderness to the Euphrates [south to north]) are not as important as the fact that God's ultimate sphere of dominion is the world (cf. Isa 51:5; 66:23).
4. Sarna (1991:143) says that this is one of four (rather contradictory) explanations for the fact that the Canaanites remained in the land. That is not strictly correct. There are three explanations that are mutually compatible, and one that stands in contrast. Judges 2:22-23 says that the Canaanites were left to try Israel's faith, while Judges 3:2 says they were left to train Israel in warfare. Both of those are compatible with the one given here. That is, God did not destroy the Canaanites *instantly* for these three reasons. But he did intend that they be destroyed. The reason they were not finally destroyed is that the Israelites were disobedient. They, in fact, consorted with the Canaanites, and as a result God did not carry out his final purpose.

◆ C. Acceptance of the Covenant (24:1-18)

Then the LORD instructed Moses: "Come up here to me, and bring along Aaron, Nadab, Abihu, and seventy of Israel's elders. All of you must worship from a distance. ²Only Moses is allowed to come near to the LORD. The others must not come near, and none of the other people are allowed to climb up the mountain with him."

³Then Moses went down to the people and repeated all the instructions and regulations the LORD had given him. All the people answered with one voice, "We will do everything the LORD has commanded."

⁴Then Moses carefully wrote down all the LORD's instructions. Early the next morning Moses got up and built an altar at the foot of the mountain. He also set up twelve pillars, one for each of the twelve tribes of Israel. ⁵Then he sent some of the young Israelite men to present burnt offerings and to sacrifice bulls as peace offerings to the LORD. ⁶Moses drained half the blood from these animals into basins. The other half he splattered against the altar.

⁷Then he took the Book of the Covenant and read it aloud to the people. Again they all responded, "We will do everything the LORD has commanded. We will obey."

⁸Then Moses took the blood from the basins and splattered it over the people, declaring, "Look, this blood confirms the covenant the LORD has made with you in giving you these instructions."

⁹Then Moses, Aaron, Nadab, Abihu, and the seventy elders of Israel climbed up the mountain. ¹⁰There they saw the God of Israel. Under his feet there seemed to be a surface of brilliant blue lapis lazuli, as clear as the sky itself. ¹¹And though these nobles of Israel gazed upon God, he did not destroy them. In fact, they ate a covenant meal, eating and drinking in his presence!

¹²Then the LORD said to Moses, "Come up to me on the mountain. Stay there, and I will give you the tablets of stone on which I have inscribed the instructions and commands so you can teach the people." ¹³So Moses and his assistant Joshua set out, and Moses climbed up the mountain of God.

¹⁴Moses told the elders, "Stay here and wait for us until we come back. Aaron and Hur are here with you. If anyone has a dispute while I am gone, consult with them."

¹⁵Then Moses climbed up the mountain, and the cloud covered it. ¹⁶And the glory of the LORD settled down on Mount Sinai, and the cloud covered it for six days. On the seventh day the LORD called to Moses from inside the cloud. ¹⁷To the Israelites at the foot of the mountain, the glory of the LORD appeared at the summit like a consuming fire. ¹⁸Then Moses disappeared into the cloud as he climbed higher up the mountain. He remained on the mountain forty days and forty nights.

NOTES

24:1 *the LORD instructed Moses: "Come up here to me."* Lit., "To Moses he said, 'Come up to the LORD.'" This abrupt syntax perhaps signals that in contrast to the previous words, which had been addressed to the people, these instructions are for Moses alone.

24:3 *instructions.* Lit., "words" (so also in 24:8). Terms using the root letters *dbr* [TH1696, ZH1819] and having to do with speech, occur seven times in this chapter. They also occur seven times in ch 19.

regulations. Commentators differ as to precisely what is intended by "instructions and regulations." Since "words" was used to identify the Decalogue (20:1), it seems likely that what is referred to here is the summary of the terms in the Decalogue ("the instructions") and the expansion of them in 20:22-23:33 ("the regulations").

24:7 We will obey. Lit., "We will hear." These words are added to the words that are reported in 24:3, which are themselves a duplicate of what was said in 19:8. The additional promise here makes the commitment even more firm.

24:11 nobles. There is considerable uncertainty about the precise derivation of the Hebrew word. But despite the uncertainty, there is general agreement that the connotation is "distinguished." See Houtman (2000:3.294-295) for a full discussion.

gazed. The Hebrew is *khazah* [TH2372, ZH2600] (to stare at, to peer at). This verb is often used of the prophetic vision. It involves seeing beyond the surface. See the note on 19:21, where the verb is "to look at."

24:12 the instructions and commands. The Hebrew is *hattorah wehammitswah* [TH8451/4687, ZH9368/5184]. These are two different terms than those used previously in ch 24 and earlier in this division. Perhaps they are intended to say that what is written is a digest and not the entirety of the "instructions and regulations" (24:3) comprising "the Book of the Covenant" (24:7).

so you can teach. The Hebrew does not specify a subject but simply has "in order to teach." Thus, the subject could well be Yahweh, which would be in keeping with the rule of the nearer antecedent.

24:14 anyone has a dispute. Lit., "whoever is a lord of matters" (*debarim* [TH1697, ZH1821]). To be the "lord of something" was often figurative for having or possessing it. See 18:16ff where *dabar* is also used for a legal contention.

COMMENTARY

This chapter and chapter 19 form literary bookends enclosing the "Book of the Covenant." Chapter 19 formed the introduction, setting the stage for the critical moment of presenting the terms of the covenant to the people. In this chapter we have the conclusion and the even more critical moment of the sealing of the covenant, the formal acceptance of the terms. The formalities are presented in three aspects: a ceremonial meal between the covenant parties (introduced in 24:1-2 and described in 24:9-11), the taking of the oath before witnesses (24:3-8), and the provision for receiving the official text of the covenant (24:12-18).

But chapter 24 not only signals the conclusion of the revelation of the covenant, the third major part of God's "way out" for his people, it also introduces the fourth major part of that "way out": the provision for the building of the Tabernacle. This final section of the book contains the revelation of God's purpose: residing among his people. Just as Sinai seems to have three successively more exclusive areas (see comments on 24:12-18), so does the Tabernacle. Thus, the Tabernacle may be presented as a way of making Sinai "portable" (Enns 2000:493). There are several features in verses 12-18 that signal this transition from the covenant to the Tabernacle. Sarna (1991:153) points out that the mention of the "tablets of stone" (24:12) prepares both for the Tabernacle (including the Ark of the Covenant, chs 25-31; 35-40) and for the golden calf incident (chs 32-34). Furthermore, the use of the verb *shakan* [TH7931, ZH8905] ("to dwell"; "settled down," 24:16, NLT) is picked up again in 25:8 and provides the basis of the noun form *mishkan* [TH4908, ZH5438] ("Tabernacle" or "residence") in 25:9 and 40:34. Likewise, the "glory of the LORD" and "the cloud" that appear on the mountain here (24:16) appear again in and on the Tabernacle

(40:34-35). So this chapter closes the section on the covenant and opens the one on the Tabernacle.

By starting with the reference to worship and the covenant meal in 24:1-2, 9-11, Moses was underscoring the ultimate goal of covenant obedience: personal relationship with God.[1] Although the actual meal would follow the sealing of the covenant, the notice of it at the beginning of the discussion prepares the reader not to see the sealing as an end in itself. As elsewhere in the Old Testament, the word translated "worship" actually refers to prostrating oneself on the ground. "Worship from a distance" may refer to the custom of approaching a great person with a series of prostrations, the first one being at some distance (cf. Jacob approaching Esau, Gen 33:3). There can be no question about the greatness and majesty of God. Manifesting himself to people in an expression of his desire for fellowship with humanity does not signal even the tiniest diminution in his terrifying holiness (see 24:15-18). Prostration in awe, gratitude, and praise is the only way to approach him.[2]

The sealing ceremony began with Moses reporting to the people what the terms of the covenant would be and securing from them another agreement (after 19:8) that they would do "everything the LORD has commanded" (24:3). With that agreement in hand, Moses then "carefully wrote" out the terms (24:4). The idea that there should be written copies of the covenant was a prominent feature of the covenant form.[3] The next day was the great day (24:4).[4] The verbal agreements to this point had certainly set the stage, but the covenant was not truly in force until an oath had been taken before witnesses. However, this matter of witnesses constituted a problem, given the normal covenant form. Normally, the witnesses to the sealing of the covenant were the gods of both the conqueror and the conquered. Obviously, that could not be the case with this covenant, which had as a central feature the denial of other gods and the undercutting of the whole worldview upon which polytheism depended. Almost certainly that is the significance of the pillars here. They were a historical witness to what had taken place at this particular time and in this particular space (see Josh 24:26-28, where this function is explicitly stated).[5] Nothing was taking place in some invisible parallel to the visible world that somehow gave meaning to the visible actions. It was the decisions that free and responsible humans made in response to the evidence of God's character, nature, and will revealed in this real world that were reality. As with Passover, worship is not the reactualization of some timeless reality. Rather, it is a reaffirmation of the truths revealed in past experiences in time and space as recalled in memory.

In verses 5-8 the actual oath ceremony is described.[6] The fact that there are no detailed explanations of the significance of the various actions suggests that all of this was familiar enough to the first readers that no explanations were needed. But the evidence is plain: Those entering into a covenant took an oath upon themselves. That oath involved blessings on those who complied with the terms and curses on those who failed to comply (see Deut 28–33; Josh 8:34; see also 23:20-33). This was much more than mere verbal agreement. If that had been enough, then surely the restatement of 19:8 in 24:3 would have been sufficient.

Rather, the participants were called upon to swear under the most solemn curses to keep the covenant, calling destruction on their heads if they did not. We can recreate something of the ritual by combining what is said in Genesis 15:9-21, Jeremiah 34:18, and Hebrews 6:13-18. A sacrificial animal was split in two, and the parties to the covenant stood between them and swore a blood-oath to God that they would keep the covenant. So what was happening here? Several commentators suggest that the blood was thrown on the altar (24:6) to make atonement for the people, while the blood thrown on the people affirmed a bond with God, to whom blood belongs.[7] But that does not fit the context at all. This is very clearly a covenant ceremony, and covenant ceremonies close with a blood oath. What else could be happening here? When the blood is divided into halves, with one half being thrown on God (the altar) and the other half being thrown on the people, the two parties to the covenant are swearing in blood that they will keep the covenant and are calling down death on themselves if they default. That, in my judgment, is the obvious significance of the statement, "this blood confirms the covenant the LORD has made with you in giving you [lit., "according to"] these instructions" (24:8). This was the moment that God had been preparing for in the near term ever since the people arrived at the foot of the mountain (19:1), and more distantly ever since his first unconditional promises to Abraham (Gen 12:1-3). In the context of this mutually binding commitment, God would be able to reveal his own nature, the character he wanted in his people, and the fundamental problem that prevented that character from being realized in them.

But, as mentioned above, the covenant and obedience to it was not an end in itself. God wants us to know about him in order that we may know him. Thus, the covenant sealing ceremony here ended with a covenant meal in God's presence (24:9-11). That such a thing would even be possible was clearly shocking to the author, who emphasized that even though these representatives of the people "gazed upon God, he did not destroy them" (24:11). When we remember that this was the very thing the people were prohibited from doing on pain of death in 19:21 (see the commentary), the reason for this shock is even more apparent. The point is that God *does* want to be "seen," to be personally experienced, but that such experience can only be had on his terms, terms that are in keeping with his own holy character. This kind of intimacy was the goal of the covenant, something that would finally be possible for all persons when the new covenant was written on our hearts by the blood of Christ (Jer 31:31-33) and the veil in the Temple torn from top to bottom (Matt 27:51). But this event was a great step on the road to that destination.

Commentators since the earliest days have attempted to determine what Moses and the others actually *saw*, especially since Exodus 33:20 says that no one can see God and live.[8] Most conclude that what took place was a visionary experience like that of Isaiah (Isa 6) or Ezekiel (Ezek 1). These people were gifted with a visual experience of God. But like Isaiah, the report of what was actually seen is decidedly limited. Just as Isaiah could only report that the hem of God's royal robe filled the Temple (Isa 6:1), so here the elders have left only a description of the gorgeous blue pavement under his feet (24:10). It is also interesting that like the descriptions found in Ezekiel, the one here is qualified. "There seemed to be a surface," we are told (24:10), just as Ezekiel said he saw "something that looked like a throne" (Ezek 1:26). Clearly, words could only approximate what was seen, and even those approximations can only reach the very outer edges of the experience itself.

Although the actual term "covenant meal" does not appear in the Hebrew of verse 11, there can be little doubt that this is intended.[9] As in Genesis 31:54, where Jacob and Laban sealed their covenant with a shared meal in conjunction with a sacrifice on a mountain, so here God and his people, represented by the elders, demonstrate their new relation of loyalty and alliance in the gesture of a shared meal, the most common symbol of a good relationship.[10]

Although it is not stated, it may be presumed that Moses, Aaron, Nadab, Abihu, and the 70 elders returned down the mountain and that it was from there that Yahweh called Moses to return (24:12-17). The stated purpose of this ascent was to receive stone tablets on which God had "inscribed the instructions and commands" (see note on 24:12). Houtman (2000:3.297-298) points out the absence of any mention of the instructions for the Tabernacle and thinks that is evidence of different (contradictory) sources having been combined (rather clumsily). But Sarna (1991:153) is surely correct in saying that for readers who were already familiar with the story, the reference to the tablets was all that was needed to bring up the picture of the Ark and the Tabernacle and the golden calf. But along with that is the fact that, transitional though it may be, this segment is still looking back, relating to the covenant and its sealing. The covenant form required that there be an official copy of the text of the covenant and that that text be kept in safekeeping in a prominent place, often a temple. That is precisely what was taking place here. Moses was to receive that official text, and instructions on where it was to be kept. The primary focus from this perspective was on receiving the text.

The reference to teaching in verse 12 is an important final witness to the function of the covenant. It was never intended to be a means whereby an alienated people could make themselves acceptable to God, a kind of ladder to heaven. Rather, these were people to whom God had already come in grace, taking them to himself (19:4-5). The covenant was intended to teach the people how to "walk" with the holy God (i.e., how to share his gracious life). It continues to function in that way today, amended, developed, and relocated through the incarnation of Christ.

The abrupt reference to "Joshua" in verse 13 is but another indication that this book is not intended to give a complete history. It assumes knowledge of that larger history and builds upon that knowledge. The statement that Joshua went with Moses, but then that Moses "disappeared into the cloud" (24:18), when taken together with the statements in verses 1 and 2, clearly suggests the idea of three areas on the mountain. There is the foot of the mountain, where Aaron and Hur (24:14) remained with the people (available to adjudicate their disputes in Moses's place, cf. 18:26). This would be analogous to the courtyard of the Tabernacle (27:9-18).

Then there was an intermediate place partway up the mountain, which is evidently where the covenant meal took place and where Joshua remained, unable to see the camp (cf. 32:17). This area would be analogous to the Holy Place, the outer room of the Tabernacle in which the priests alone served (26:33; 29:30). Finally, there was the pinnacle, where only Moses was allowed to go (24:2, 18). This would compare to the Most Holy Place, which only the high priest could enter (26:34; Lev 16:17).

Verses 15-16 remind us that the terrifying "glory" of Yahweh revealed in chapter 19 had not been diminished by his condescension to appear to Moses, the Aaronic men, and the elders. Here, just as previously, the "cloud" (24:15-18) and the "consuming fire" (24:17) were symbols of the transcendent holiness of God that creatures can never cross over. But the remarkable thing about the biblical understanding of transcendence is that while it forever limits creaturely initiative to participate in God, it places no conditions whatsoever upon God. He is able to come across the boundaries and to take creatures into his presence. And in doing so, he in no way compromises his transcendence. At this point, merely human understandings of logic give out, but there it is. God does not change himself to come to us, but he does intend to change us so that we can live in the midst of the fire as Moses did. In fact, that is the direction of the entire book of Exodus: While the goal of the people might be the Promised Land, God's goal is that he may dwell in their midst, in effect bringing the "mountain of God" (24:13; cf. 3:1; 19:1) into the center of the camp (40:34).

ENDNOTES
1. So Childs (1974:504) and Fretheim (1991:255). Houtman (2000:3.281) sees the verses as the conclusion to the previous section.
2. The mention of Nadab and Abihu and the 70 elders without any introduction is another indication that the readers were already familiar with the larger details of the story from other sources (Sarna 1991:150; Enns 2000:488).
3. It seems likely that this requirement provided the impetus for writing down the history of what had led up to this moment (Gen 1—Exod 19) and all that proceeded from it (Exod 24—Deut 34).
4. Specifying that something was done *early the next morning* is a way of saying that an act, whether of obedience or deliberation, was so important that no time could be wasted (see 8:20; 32:6; 34:4; Gen 19:27; 22:3; Josh 6:15; 7:16).
5. This historical incident may explain the large number of such pillars that are found in Israel today. Israelites may have gotten into the habit of commemorating important moments in their lives by erecting such stones of witness. Deuteronomy 16:22 prohibits the erection of pillars as idols; given Israel's idolatrous tendencies, there may have been a good deal of crossover from historical marker to idol.
6. Few modern commentators are willing to take a firm stand here (Fretheim 1991:256, 258, denies that it is a covenant ceremony at all, likening it to an ordination ceremony instead). In part this is because recent studies on covenant have pointed out the obvious truth that there is not a "one-for-one" correspondence between the biblical covenant and the ancient Near Eastern suzerainty covenants. But that is hardly surprising. This is an adaptation, taking over a form and an idea and applying them in ways that are quite different from their original usage. However, as I have shown

above (see the commentary on 20:1-17), the points of contact are far too many to be accidental. See Walton (1989:95-109) for a judicious review of the data and issues.
7. So Sarna (1991:152), Cassuto (1967:312), Childs (1974:506), and Fretheim (1991:258).
8. The LXX translates "they saw the place where God stood." Cassuto (1967:314) points out that it does not say they saw Yahweh but rather *'elohim* [TH430, ZH466] (God).
9. Houtman (2000:3.296) stands alone in arguing that "eating and drinking" is to be taken metaphorically, being simply a figurative way of saying that they were still alive.
10. Childs (1974:507) also cites Ugaritic text 51 as evidence that a ceremonial meal was part of a covenant sealing ceremony.

◆ **IV. The Tabernacle: A Revelation of Yahweh's Purpose (25:1–40:38)**
   A. Instructions for the Tabernacle and Its Service: The Right Way to God's Presence (25:1–31:18)
      1. Instructions for building the structure and furnishings (25:1–27:19)

The LORD said to Moses, ²"Tell the people of Israel to bring me their sacred offerings. Accept the contributions from all whose hearts are moved to offer them. ³Here is a list of sacred offerings you may accept from them:

   gold, silver, and bronze;
  ⁴blue, purple, and scarlet thread;
   fine linen and goat hair for cloth;
  ⁵tanned ram skins and fine goatskin leather;
   acacia wood;
  ⁶olive oil for the lamps;
   spices for the anointing oil and the fragrant incense;
  ⁷onyx stones, and other gemstones to be set in the ephod and the priest's chestpiece.

⁸"Have the people of Israel build me a holy sanctuary so I can live among them. ⁹You must build this Tabernacle and its furnishings exactly according to the pattern I will show you.

¹⁰"Have the people make an Ark of acacia wood—a sacred chest 45 inches long, 27 inches wide, and 27 inches high.* ¹¹Overlay it inside and outside with pure gold, and run a molding of gold all around it. ¹²Cast four gold rings and attach them to its four feet, two rings on each side. ¹³Make poles from acacia wood, and overlay them with gold. ¹⁴Insert the poles into the rings at the sides of the Ark to carry it. ¹⁵These carrying poles must stay inside the rings; never remove them. ¹⁶When the Ark is finished, place inside it the stone tablets inscribed with the terms of the covenant,* which I will give to you.

¹⁷"Then make the Ark's cover—the place of atonement—from pure gold. It must be 45 inches long and 27 inches wide.* ¹⁸Then make two cherubim from hammered gold, and place them on the two ends of the atonement cover. ¹⁹Mold the cherubim on each end of the atonement cover, making it all of one piece of gold. ²⁰The cherubim will face each other and look down on the atonement cover. With their wings spread above it, they will protect it. ²¹Place inside the Ark the stone tablets inscribed with the terms of the covenant, which I will give to you. Then put the atonement cover on top of the Ark. ²²I will meet with you there and talk to you from above the atonement cover between the gold cherubim that hover over the Ark of the Covenant.* From there I will give you my commands for the people of Israel.

²³"Then make a table of acacia wood, 36 inches long, 18 inches wide, and 27 inches high.* ²⁴Overlay it with pure gold and run a gold molding around the

edge. ²⁵Decorate it with a 3-inch border* all around, and run a gold molding along the border. ²⁶Make four gold rings for the table and attach them at the four corners next to the four legs. ²⁷Attach the rings near the border to hold the poles that are used to carry the table. ²⁸Make these poles from acacia wood, and overlay them with gold. ²⁹Make special containers of pure gold for the table—bowls, pans, pitchers, and jars—to be used in pouring out liquid offerings. ³⁰Place the Bread of the Presence on the table to remain before me at all times.

³¹"Make a lampstand of pure, hammered gold. Make the entire lampstand and its decorations of one piece—the base, center stem, lamp cups, buds, and petals. ³²Make it with six branches going out from the center stem, three on each side. ³³Each of the six branches will have three lamp cups shaped like almond blossoms, complete with buds and petals. ³⁴Craft the center stem of the lampstand with four lamp cups shaped like almond blossoms, complete with buds and petals. ³⁵There will also be an almond bud beneath each pair of branches where the six branches extend from the center stem. ³⁶The almond buds and branches must all be of one piece with the center stem, and they must be hammered from pure gold. ³⁷Then make the seven lamps for the lampstand, and set them so they reflect their light forward. ³⁸The lamp snuffers and trays must also be made of pure gold. ³⁹You will need seventy-five pounds* of pure gold for the lampstand and its accessories.

⁴⁰"Be sure that you make everything according to the pattern I have shown you here on the mountain.

CHAPTER 26

"Make the Tabernacle from ten curtains of finely woven linen. Decorate the curtains with blue, purple, and scarlet thread and with skillfully embroidered cherubim. ²These ten curtains must all be exactly the same size—42 feet long and 6 feet wide.* ³Join five of these curtains together to make one long curtain, then join the other five into a second long curtain. ⁴Put loops of blue yarn along the edge of the last curtain in each set. ⁵The fifty loops along the edge of one curtain are to match the fifty loops along the edge of the other curtain. ⁶Then make fifty gold clasps and fasten the long curtains together with the clasps. In this way, the Tabernacle will be made of one continuous piece.

⁷"Make eleven curtains of goat-hair cloth to serve as a tent covering for the Tabernacle. ⁸These eleven curtains must all be exactly the same size—45 feet long and 6 feet wide.* ⁹Join five of these curtains together to make one long curtain, and join the other six into a second long curtain. Allow 3 feet of material from the second set of curtains to hang over the front* of the sacred tent. ¹⁰Make fifty loops for one edge of each large curtain. ¹¹Then make fifty bronze clasps, and fasten the loops of the long curtains with the clasps. In this way, the tent covering will be made of one continuous piece. ¹²The remaining 3 feet* of this tent covering will be left to hang over the back of the Tabernacle. ¹³Allow 18 inches* of remaining material to hang down over each side, so the Tabernacle is completely covered. ¹⁴Complete the tent covering with a protective layer of tanned ram skins and a layer of fine goatskin leather.

¹⁵"For the framework of the Tabernacle, construct frames of acacia wood. ¹⁶Each frame must be 15 feet high and 27 inches wide,* ¹⁷with two pegs under each frame. Make all the frames identical. ¹⁸Make twenty of these frames to support the curtains on the south side of the Tabernacle. ¹⁹Also make forty silver bases—two bases under each frame, with the pegs fitting securely into the bases. ²⁰For the north side of the Tabernacle, make another twenty frames, ²¹with their forty silver bases, two bases under each frame. ²²Make six frames for the rear—the west

side of the Tabernacle—²³along with two additional frames to reinforce the rear corners of the Tabernacle. ²⁴These corner frames will be matched at the bottom and firmly attached at the top with a single ring, forming a single corner unit. Make both of these corner units the same way. ²⁵So there will be eight frames at the rear of the Tabernacle, set in sixteen silver bases—two bases under each frame.

²⁶"Make crossbars of acacia wood to link the frames, five crossbars for the north side of the Tabernacle ²⁷and five for the south side. Also make five crossbars for the rear of the Tabernacle, which will face west. ²⁸The middle crossbar, attached halfway up the frames, will run all the way from one end of the Tabernacle to the other. ²⁹Overlay the frames with gold, and make gold rings to hold the crossbars. Overlay the crossbars with gold as well.

³⁰"Set up this Tabernacle according to the pattern you were shown on the mountain.

³¹"For the inside of the Tabernacle, make a special curtain of finely woven linen. Decorate it with blue, purple, and scarlet thread and with skillfully embroidered cherubim. ³²Hang this curtain on gold hooks attached to four posts of acacia wood. Overlay the posts with gold, and set them in four silver bases. ³³Hang the inner curtain from clasps, and put the Ark of the Covenant* in the room behind it. This curtain will separate the Holy Place from the Most Holy Place.

³⁴"Then put the Ark's cover—the place of atonement—on top of the Ark of the Covenant inside the Most Holy Place. ³⁵Place the table outside the inner curtain on the north side of the Tabernacle, and place the lampstand across the room on the south side.

³⁶"Make another curtain for the entrance to the sacred tent. Make it of finely woven linen and embroider it with exquisite designs, using blue, purple, and scarlet thread. ³⁷Craft five posts from acacia wood. Overlay them with gold, and hang the curtain from them with gold hooks. Cast five bronze bases for the posts.

CHAPTER 27

"Using acacia wood, construct a square altar 7½ feet wide, 7½ feet long, and 4½ feet high.* ²Make horns for each of its four corners so that the horns and altar are all one piece. Overlay the altar with bronze. ³Make ash buckets, shovels, basins, meat forks, and firepans, all of bronze. ⁴Make a bronze grating for it, and attach four bronze rings at its four corners. ⁵Install the grating halfway down the side of the altar, under the ledge. ⁶For carrying the altar, make poles from acacia wood, and overlay them with bronze. ⁷Insert the poles through the rings on the two sides of the altar. ⁸The altar must be hollow, made from planks. Build it just as you were shown on the mountain.

⁹"Then make the courtyard for the Tabernacle, enclosed with curtains made of finely woven linen. On the south side, make the curtains 150 feet long.* ¹⁰They will be held up by twenty posts set securely in twenty bronze bases. Hang the curtains with silver hooks and rings. ¹¹Make the curtains the same on the north side—150 feet of curtains held up by twenty posts set securely in bronze bases. Hang the curtains with silver hooks and rings. ¹²The curtains on the west end of the courtyard will be 75 feet long,* supported by ten posts set into ten bases. ¹³The east end of the courtyard, the front, will also be 75 feet long. ¹⁴The courtyard entrance will be on the east end, flanked by two curtains. The curtain on the right side will be 22½ feet long,* supported by three posts set into three bases. ¹⁵The curtain on the left side will also be 22½ feet long, supported by three posts set into three bases.

¹⁶"For the entrance to the courtyard, make a curtain that is 30 feet long.* Make it from finely woven linen, and decorate it with beautiful embroidery in blue, purple,

and scarlet thread. Support it with four posts, each securely set in its own base. ¹⁷All the posts around the courtyard must have silver rings and hooks and bronze bases. ¹⁸So the entire courtyard will be 150 feet long and 75 feet wide, with curtain walls 7½ feet high,* made from finely woven linen. The bases for the posts will be made of bronze.

¹⁹"All the articles used in the rituals of the Tabernacle, including all the tent pegs used to support the Tabernacle and the courtyard curtains, must be made of bronze.

25:10 Hebrew *2.5 cubits* [115 centimeters] *long, 1.5 cubits* [69 centimeters] *wide, and 1.5 cubits high.* **25:16** Hebrew *Place inside the Ark the Testimony;* similarly in 25:21. The Hebrew word for "testimony" refers to the terms of the LORD's covenant with Israel as written on stone tablets, and also to the covenant itself. **25:17** Hebrew *2.5 cubits* [115 centimeters] *long and 1.5 cubits* [69 centimeters] *wide.* **25:22** Or *Ark of the Testimony.* **25:23** Hebrew *2 cubits* [92 centimeters] *long, 1 cubit* [46 centimeters] *wide, and 1.5 cubits* [69 centimeters] *high.* **25:25** Hebrew *a border of a handbreadth* [8 centimeters]. **25:39** Hebrew *1 talent* [34 kilograms]. **26:2** Hebrew *28 cubits* [12.9 meters] *long and 4 cubits* [1.8 meters] *wide.* **26:8** Hebrew *30 cubits* [13.8 meters] *long and 4 cubits* [1.8 meters] *wide.* **26:9** Hebrew *Double over the sixth sheet at the front.* **26:12** Hebrew *The half sheet that is left over.* **26:13** Hebrew *1 cubit* [46 centimeters]. **26:16** Hebrew *10 cubits* [4.6 meters] *high and 1.5 cubits* [69 centimeters] *wide.* **26:33** Or *Ark of the Testimony;* also in 26:34. **27:1** Hebrew *5 cubits* [2.3 meters] *wide, 5 cubits long, a square, and 3 cubits* [1.4 meters] *high.* **27:9** Hebrew *100 cubits* [46 meters]; also in 27:11. **27:12** Hebrew *50 cubits* [23 meters]; also in 27:13. **27:14** Hebrew *15 cubits* [6.9 meters]; also in 27:15. **27:16** Hebrew *20 cubits* [9.2 meters]. **27:18** Hebrew *100 cubits* [46 meters] *long and 50 by 50* [23 meters] *wide and 5 cubits* [2.3 meters] *high.*

NOTES

25:2 *sacred offerings.* Heb. *terumah* [TH8641, ZH9556]. This is a voluntary gift chosen by the owner and dedicated to God's use (see 29:27; 30:13; Num 15:19).

25:3 The precious metals are listed in order of value. Iron is conspicuously absent. If this account was first written down at a time well into the Iron Age (1200–550 BC), as many contemporary scholars maintain, it seems highly likely that iron would have been included in the list. Its absence seems to support a Late Bronze Age (1550–1200 BC) date for the writing of this material.

25:5 *goatskin.* This is almost certainly correct as opposed to the older interpretation of dugong or dolphin. An Akkadian root with these consonants is used to refer to goatskin dyed a tan color (so Sarna 1991:157-158).

25:6 Cassuto (1967:326) points out that it was necessary to identify the purpose for the "oil" and the "spices" to distinguish them from those used for human consumption.

25:8 *live.* Heb. *shakan* [TH7931, ZH8905]. This is not the normal word for "reside" or "dwell," which is *yashab* [TH3427, ZH3782]. This word has something of the idea of "to tent among, inhabit." Sarna (1991:158) makes the important point that it is not said that God would dwell "in it," as though the Tabernacle were God's residence but rather that God might dwell "among" the people.

25:10 *Ark.* This word was a regular term in Elizabethan English for "box" or "chest," which is what the Hebrew means. Though now archaic, the word has a powerful force of tradition behind it.

25:11 *Overlay it.* Despite all the detail in the Tabernacle instructions, there is still a good deal of information that we do not have. It is clear that people at the time of the writing understood what was being talked about and did not need further directions. We lack that understanding and so do not know exactly what was meant here. On the basis of Egyptian archaeology, this is understood to probably refer to thin sheets of hammered gold held in place with small nails (so Cassuto 1967:329), but Sarna (1991:159) suggests the possibility, on the basis of other Egyptian evidence, that there were three nested boxes, an outer one of gold, an inner one of wood, and the most inner one of gold.

molding. See also 25:25. These objects were not merely utilitarian. God is a God of beauty, so there was an aesthetic aspect to them as well.

25:12 feet. Although there is no description of these feet, it seems clear that this is what is intended instead of "corners" as per KJV (probably following the LXX, "sides").

25:17 cover—the place of atonement. Heb. *kapporeth* [TH3727, ZH4114]. The NLT is pointing out the probable double entendre in the Hebrew term. The root *kpr* [TH3722, ZH4105] has to do with covering, but terms for this root have both a literal and a symbolic use, the symbolic use having to do with covering over or blotting out sin (see commentary).

25:18 two cherubim. Note that "cherubim" is the Hebrew plural form of the singular "cherub." The correct English plural would be "cherubs." However, given the popular conception of "cherub" as a fat baby, the NLT has chosen to retain the Hebrew form. As per the note on 25:11, since no description of the cherubim is given, it is apparent that there must have been a widespread agreement at that time what cherubim looked like. A similar term in Akkadian refers to guardian deities who stood at the doors of palaces and temples. These were composite human/animal figures, and one can look to the descriptions in Ezekiel (Ezek 1:5-11) for a possible visualization. Given the limited space on the "cover," the figures were probably standing rather than crouching (as Egyptian sphinxes did, a suggested comparison.)

25:25 border. The root meaning is "to shut" or "close." Thus the idea is of an enclosure. However, whether that was a rim (NIV) around the top or a band farther down holding the pieces of the table together is not clear.

25:29 bowls . . . jars. These may have been merely ceremonial and never actually used (Cassuto 1967:337), or it may be that the priests used them when they ate the bread. In any case, 30:9 makes it clear that no liquid offerings were actually made in the Holy Place itself.

25:31 pure, hammered gold. Perhaps this was not gold-plated wood (like the Ark and the table) because of the presence of fire.

26:1 Tabernacle. The *mishkan* [TH4908, ZH5438] was a place for temporary residence.

finely woven linen. The word translated "finely" only occurs in the Tabernacle instructions in Exodus. The root meaning has to do with twisting and this may suggest the yarn had several strands.

skillfully embroidered. This translates the phrase *ma'aseh khosheb* [TH4639/2803A, ZH5126/3110] (work of a designer), which refers to the level of craftsmanship involved.

26:9 hang over. If the entire six-foot strip was doubled over (see NLT mg) and allowed to hang over, as per NLT, there is a problem because v. 12 says that there was three feet of excess at the back on the west end. Cassuto (1967:352) visualizes the first three feet of the goat-hair cloth on the east end doubling back under the linen cloth to protect the linen from the elements. This would solve the discrepancy.

26:14 goatskin. See note on 25:5.

26:17 pegs. This seems a likely possibility, corresponding to the two bases. However, the word is literally "hand" (*yad* [TH3027, ZH3338]), which NJPS takes to mean "tenon," another possibility.

27:2 horns. These were neither animal "horns" nor musical instruments. In the Hebrew vocabulary, any projection from another surface is described with this term. Thus the Hebrew says that Moses's face was "horned" with light (presumably "projecting rays of light") after he had seen God (34:30). It is unknown whether these vertical projections at the four corners of the altar were functional or ceremonial. It has been proposed that they served to keep the materials being offered in place, but examples of "horned" altars that have been found do not suggest that they would work very well for that purpose. The fact that atonement was to be made on the horns (30:10) and that a person seeking sanctuary could cling to the horns of the altar (cf. 1 Kgs 1:50) suggests they had some ceremonial value.

bronze. Gold and silver, the more precious metals, were reserved for the Tabernacle itself. Also, the harder bronze would be more functional around fire (see also 27:19).

27:4 ***at its four corners.*** The antecedent of "it" here is the "bronze grating" and not the altar itself.

COMMENTARY

We come now to the final section of the book, one that is often seen as somewhat secondary. The narrative disappears, with the exception of the rather exciting events surrounding the tragedy of the golden calf (chs 32–34). In its place we find not one but two highly detailed descriptions of the features and dimensions of the Tabernacle, primarily distinguished from each other only by different verb forms: imperatives in the first section and indicatives in the second.[1] Apart from this variation the two descriptions frequently have almost identical wording. But far from being a sort of priestly appendix to an otherwise-interesting book, this final section is indeed the climax of the book. Here we find the fullest revelation of God's "way out" (*exodus*) of the Israelite people's problem in Egypt. By the same token, we are enabled to understand what their deepest problem was, and indeed what all humanity's problem is. Their immediate problem was bondage and oppression in Egypt, and their compassionate God had provided deliverance as recorded in chapters 1–15 (and 16–18). But they had a deeper problem: They did not know who God, the God of their fathers, was. Thus, the deliverance and the subsequent journey through the wilderness was a revelation of Yahweh's power and providential care, not a mere catalog of the events of deliverance. But even so, the people did not really understand the character of this God or his will for human life. In chapters 19–24, Yahweh provided a much fuller solution to that problem in the revelation of his character through the covenant. Deeper than the problem of bondage and oppression was the problem of spiritual darkness, and God's way out was to give his people the covenant.

But there was an even deeper problem than spiritual darkness, which relates to Yahweh's ultimate purpose for human beings. It is not enough for him, or for us, that we should know *about* him. As the book of Genesis makes perfectly clear in its first 11 chapters, the human problem is alienation from God. We do not *know* God. We are derivative creatures, meant to draw our true humanity from a dependent relationship with God. We are meant to share his character, which is only possible if we are in such a relationship with him.[2] Thus, these final chapters of the book provide a picture of God's ultimate solution to the human problem: the sharing of his life with us in intimate union. This is why there are two descriptions of the Tabernacle, and this is why the incident of the golden calf is sandwiched between them. Even before the people knew they had a problem, God was giving Moses instructions on how to meet it (chs 25–31). But instead of waiting for God's way, the people insisted on solving their problem their way (chs 32–34). The result, far from bringing God near, was further alienation from him. The solution to the problem was to go back and do it God's way (chs 35–40). When that happened, using their hands and their gifts for God instead of for Pharaoh or for themselves, the glory of God came to reside in the very center of the camp and, symbolically, in the very center of their lives. This is the climax of the book.[3]

The plans for the structure and the service of the Tabernacle reveal that God understood the needs of the people. They needed some visual representation of the presence and power of God; they needed concrete ways to express their relationship to him; they needed to worship him in a setting of beauty and mystery; they needed an opportunity to feel they each had significant contributions to make. Understanding all this, God made plans to meet those needs in ways that far exceeded human imaginative powers. The tragedy of the story is that the Israelites, like all humans, were not of a mind to wait for God to act. They were not at all sure that God knew their problems, and if he did, they were not at all sure they could trust him to care. They were certain that only they could meet their needs, which is the same certainty that their first mother and father, Adam and Eve, had come to. That this occurred after the events of deliverance that the Israelites had experienced and after their solemn oath promising to keep the covenant on pain of death is witness both to the depth of our human insecurities and to the depth of our fears of unconditional trust.

The subdivision relating to the Tabernacle and its service (25:1–31:18) contains five different elements. After first discussing the materials needed for the project (25:1-9), it describes the furniture of the tent, the tent itself, the furniture of the courtyard, and the courtyard itself (25:10-27:19). Then comes a group of instructions relating to the priests, including their clothing, their ordination, and their activities (27:20-30:38). This is followed by the identification of God's chosen craftsmen (31:1-11) and finally, instructions relating to the Sabbath (31:12-18).[4]

Materials Offered for the Tabernacle (25:1-9). The instructions for the Tabernacle begin with a list of a wide variety of materials that the people could contribute to the construction. Two points are very important here by contrast with the construction of the golden calf. There, only one kind of material could be given: golden earrings. And they were not given as the people's hearts were "moved to offer them" (25:2). Rather, they were coerced; Aaron commanded that it be done, and there was no recourse (32:2). Here there was the likelihood that everyone would have some of these materials that they could contribute if they wished to. God did not need the gifts; he desired the willing hearts. The variety of materials also signals something of the intricacy and interest of the plan that God had to meet his people's need. There is a variety of color, of texture, and of material. Although not all the senses are specifically mentioned here, the fact that sight, touch, smell, and taste are intimated testifies to God's plan to engage the whole person in his worship. Already, even before the ways had been specified in which these materials would be used, the dramatic contrast with the rather boring simplicity of the calf is clear. Finally, this opening paragraph specifies the purpose of all of the following instructions. The people are to build a "holy sanctuary so I can live among them" (25:8). From here to the end of the book, words involving the root idea of "holy" occur more than 80 times. In the Tabernacle, God was attempting to convey his essential holiness to his people. He *is* the transcendent Creator, whose being, now that we are fallen, is absolutely other than ours, and therefore absolutely deadly to ours. That point had to be communicated, and God sought to communicate it in a variety of ways. Yet humans are made for God, made to find their truest life in intimate communion with him. We need God to "dwell in our midst," and he longs to do that very thing. So how are those two contradicting elements to be brought together? Only if we strictly follow the *pattern* God has shown us. We must do it his way, and not ours. Ultimately, of course, all of this points to the incarnation of Christ, when he comes to "tabernacle" among us (John 1:14; the Greek equivalent of the Hebrew in 25:8) so that through his ministry we may actually dwell in God and God in us (John 15:5-7; 17:22-23). But that wonderful goal will not be achieved by God's becoming less holy. It will be achieved only when we have, by his grace, been taken up into his holiness.

Plans for Structure and Furniture of the Tabernacle (25:10–27:19). The next section gives the plans for the structure and its furniture (25:10–27:19). Unlike Exodus 35:1ff, where the structures are described first, here the author begins by giving the plans for the three key pieces of furniture in the tent: the Ark, the table, and the lampstand (25:10-40). Only then does he give the plans for the tent itself (26:1-37). In the same fashion, the plans are first given for the altar for burnt offering, which stood in the court (27:1-8) and then the plans for the courtyard itself (27:9-19). There are two exceptions to this pattern. The plans for the incense altar that stood in the tent in front of the veil and the plans for the basin that stood in the court between the altar and the tent are not included in what we would think of as their proper sections. Instead, they are included with the instructions for priestly activities (29:38–30:38). For suggestions as to why this may be the case, see the commentary on that section below.

A possible reason for the order here is theological: Ultimately, the Ark of the Covenant was the single most important item in the entire complex, so it was appropriate to begin the discussion with it. Likewise, in the courtyard, the most critical element is the altar of burnt offering. The enclosure itself was distinctly secondary to that object which symbolized the deadliness of sin and the cost to bridge the gap between God and humans.[5]

The Ark (25:10–22). The Ark was the most important object in the Tabernacle. It was so for two reasons. The first had to do with the covenant. Here was the *testimony*, the written record of the covenantal relationship between Yahweh and Israel. Here were the terms to which each had agreed in blood. It stood in the part of the Tabernacle, the Most Holy Place, where the idol stood in pagan temples. For Israel there was no idol to be manipulated. Rather, there was a box, a beautiful box to be sure, but still just a box. Its significance: God had intersected Israel's life in some non-repeatable events in time and space, and artifacts from these events were kept for their memory in this beautiful box. This memory should motivate Israel in maintaining the love and obedience to the transcendent God that had grown out of those experiences and was crucial to the relationship itself.

It is significant that the cover (25:17) is mentioned separately. This suggests that it was more than just a cover. Its construction furthers that impression. It was a solid slab of gold, roughly two feet by four feet, with the two cherubim (25:18-20) at its ends molded into one piece with it (25:19). We are not told here about this cover's special function, but Leviticus 16:12-16 gives that information. On the Day of Atonement, the High Priest would enter the Most Holy Place alone and sprinkle atoning ("covering") blood on the "cover," thereby making atonement for "the defiling sin and rebellion of the Israelites" (Lev 16:16). The precise significance of these acts is never spelled out in Scripture, but it has been widely suggested that the blood was understood to intervene between the broken covenant beneath it and the Holy God who was present above the cherubim (cf. Heb 9:11-22).

Because the Old Testament several times refers to Yahweh as seated (enthroned) "with respect to" the cherubim (e.g., 2 Sam 6:2),[6] and since there are three places where the Ark might be called the "footstool" of God (1 Chr 28:2; Pss 99:5 [cf. KJV]; 132:7-8), many commentators think of the entire complex as being the throne of God upon which he sits invisibly. While I do not wish to deny that idea completely, I think it is wrong to say that is *the* correct understanding. The Hebrew does not say God is seated "on" (*'al* [TH5921, ZH6584]) the cherubim. The expression "the one who sits the cherubim" (without preposition; e.g., 2 Sam 6:2) makes the relationship much less concrete and considerably more metaphoric. Furthermore, the three references to the Lord's footstool are not as explicit as commentators might suggest. My point is not to deny that this visualization may be implied but to say that the Old Testament (and the Bible as a whole) is very careful to avoid even the appearance of a mythological understanding of God, and we should likewise deflect from concreteness here.[7] To be sure, at this stage in revelation, it was particularly in the Most Holy Place that God's presence would be manifested to Moses (note the singular "you"), and it was there that he would give further "commands" (25:22) about the service of the Tabernacle (cf. Lev 1:1). But the very absence of concrete language here ("I will meet with you there and talk to you from above," 25:22) is an important indicator that we should not overlook.

The Table for the Bread of the Presence (25:23-30). Outside the Most Holy Place there were two items of major importance in the Holy Place. The first of these was the "table" on which was placed "the Bread of the Presence" (25:30). In pagan temples, the food for the god would be placed on such a table. Here, the 12 loaves, one for each tribe, suggest that the process was reversed (cf. Lev 24:5-9). It was not Israel that fed God; rather, God was the One who invited his people into his "presence" (lit., "face") and there feasted with them, providing sustenance for each of the tribes of his people. This idea is further supported by the fact that Aaron and his sons, representing the 12 tribes (see 28:6-21 and commentary), were the ones who ate the bread (Lev 24:9; see Kiene 1977:103-108).

The Lampstand (25:31-40). The second major item in the Holy Place was the lampstand. Once again, not enough information is given for us to say exactly what this looked like. The varying depictions in different books and Bible dictionaries are testimony to that fact.[8] It may well be that the reference to a "pattern" (25:40; or "model,") indicates that God actually gave Moses a vision of what these objects and structures were to look like and that Moses was able to give Bezalel and Oholiab drawings (31:2, 6; see also Num 8:4). In any case, it is important to remember that these lamps were very different from modern Western ideas. They were flat bowls holding olive oil. On one side of the rim was a depression where a wick could hang down. When this wick was saturated with oil and was lit, it would burn so long as olive oil remained in the bowl. Thus, the lampstand had to have arms (or, since it was made to look like an almond tree, limbs) ending in these lamp cups which could support the specified seven lamps (25:37). This also meant that the lamps had to be positioned on the lamp cups so that the wicks were all toward the inside of the Holy Place (25:37). The almond tree is the first of the flowering trees to bud in the spring (late February/early March). With its abundant white flowers it is a symbol of renewed life. Thus, the lampstand may well have been a symbol of the life-giving light of God. Some commentators believe it represented the tree of life in the garden of Eden, but without any indication in the text, it is impossible to say whether that might have been so or not.[9] It is tempting to think that Jesus had the table and the lampstand in mind when he said that he was "the bread of life" (John 6:35) and "the light of the world" (John 8:12).

The Design of the Tabernacle (26:1-37). The design of the Tabernacle was perfectly suited to its purpose: a portable structure that when erected would be remarkably stable.[10] It was composed of uprights (NLT, "frames") "15 feet high and 27 inches wide" (26:15-16) each of which stood in two "silver bases" (26:19). At the corners at least, the two right-angled uprights were fastened together with a ring at the top (26:24), and that may have been true of the others as well, but we are not given that information. But all of the uprights were locked together with "crossbars" (26:26-29). The uprights were overlaid with gold, and there were "gold rings" attached to the overlay. The crossbars went through these rings, locking the uprights together. How the "middle crossbar" was constructed to go "from one end . . . to the other" (45 feet, 26:28) is not explained. But the end result would be a very solid three-sided structure 45 feet long and 15 feet wide open at one end.

Over the top of these walls were placed two layers of fabric (26:1-13) and two layers of leather (26:14). The inner layer of fabric was linen embroidered with figures of cherubim using blue, purple, and scarlet yarn (26:1). The second layer was of "goat-hair cloth" (26:7). Both of these coverings were to be made in the same way. They were first woven in six-foot strips (26:2), probably the widest strip that a loom of that day could produce. For the linen layer there were 10 strips produced, each 42 feet long (26:2). Then five of these strips were sewn together creating a sheet of fabric 42 feet long and 30 feet wide, and the same thing was done with the other five strips (26:3). In the case of the second layer made of goat-hair cloth, there were 11 strips 45 feet long (26:8). Five of these were sewn together in one sheet and six in the other (26:9). In each case, the two large sheets were joined together with fabric loops and gold clasps (26:4-6, 10-11). The linen layer was laid over the frames with no overhang at the front. This would mean that it would touch the ground on the west side and hang a foot and a half off the ground on the north and south sides. In the case of the goat-hair cloth, there was an extra six-foot strip which was to be doubled over so that there was a three-foot overhang at the open east end (see note on 26:9). Also, since it was three feet wider than the linen, it would have touched the ground on all sides (26:13). We are not told anything about the construction of the leather coverings.

Inside, the Tabernacle was divided into two spaces by a linen curtain, embroidered just like the inner covering (26:31), hanging from hooks on four posts overlaid with gold and standing in silver bases (26:32). We are not told here the size of these two spaces, but on the basis of the proportions given for the Temple (1 Kgs 6:16-18), it is virtually certain that the area of the Most Holy Place (15 by 15 feet) was half that of the Holy Place (30 by 15 feet). At the front of the structure, there was another curtain made in the same way as the inner one (26:36), but in this case, it was supported by five posts standing in bronze bases (26:37).

The expensive materials, the rich colors, the density of the layerings, whether of fabric and leather, or wood and metal, all contributed to a sense of wonder, mystery, and glory surrounding this structure. All in all, it was a fitting expression of the wonder, mystery, and glory that surrounded Yahweh, the God who transcended the gods as much as he did the rest of his creation, but who had nevertheless entered into a covenant with this very people.

The Altar for Burnt Offerings (27:1-8). The primary piece of furniture in the courtyard was the altar used for the burnt offerings. It had a wood frame (27:1), perhaps for reasons of weight, and was overlaid, presumably inside and out, with bronze (27:2). As with the other items of furniture, there are unanswered questions about the altar's design. The major issue here has to do with the "grating" (27:5-6). Some commentators envision this as a network of openings around the sides of the structure. This would fit well with the idea of the four rings being attached to the "grating," as the Hebrew has it (see the note on 27:4). But that understanding then leaves the functionality of the altar in doubt.[11] Cassuto (1967:362-364) imagines it being filled with rocks (in keeping with the instructions in 20:25) at each site and then being emptied and refilled when the Tabernacle was moved to a new location. The fact that neither the text here nor at 38:1-7 make any reference to such an arrangement makes this solution questionable. The presence of a solid metal grating stretching across the inside of the structure at about its midpoint would mean that sacrifices and wood could be placed upon it with the ashes falling through to a pit beneath.

These sacrifices on the altar of burnt offering covered the sinner who approached God. As we are told elsewhere in the Bible, no one can come to God on his or her own merits. Everyone of us has sinned, and the cost of sin is death. This is not some arbitrary choice on God's part. Just as the result of one pinhole in a spacesuit is death, so also the presence of one scrap of unholiness is deadly in the presence of the Holy One. What to do then? If we are to enjoy the presence of God, which the

Tabernacle symbolized, there must be a substitute. Someone must die in my place. That is what God provided in the altar of burnt offering, which stood inside the court before the Tabernacle. It represented the means of access to God. However, this should never be thought of as a means whereby crafty sinners who expected to continue to sin could force an unwilling God to forgive them. All the prophets spoke against such an idea in unequivocal terms (Isa 1:10-15; Jer 6:19-20; Amos 5:21-24). We come into God's presence solely on the basis of his gracious provision. If he chose not to forgive human sinners, there is nothing in the world that could make him do so. What the altar does is to represent the means that God has provided so that his grace might be available to us. That means is not the blood of bulls and goats, as Micah realized (Mic 6:6-7). It is the blood of God's Son, Jesus Christ (1 Pet 1:18-21). We ultimately show by the character of our lives whether we have accepted that means or not.

Plans for the Courtyard (27:9-19). The plans for the tent and the altar having been described, the plans are given for the enclosure, the courtyard (27:9), in which they were to stand. This enclosure was constructed of white linen curtains 7.5 feet high (27:18) hanging on wooden posts standing in bronze bases (27:10). The posts were spaced 7.5 feet apart. The courtyard was 150 by 75 feet, oriented on an east–west axis with a 30-foot opening on the east side (27:14-16). This opening was filled by a curtain of fine linen, embroidered like the inner covering of the Tabernacle and its veils.

Some commentators make a good deal of the symmetry and order of the total design,[12] asserting that this shows that the Tabernacle was intended to depict the creation as it was meant to be, as opposed to the chaos that has come to be as a result of sin. While this *might* be the case, the fact that absolutely nothing is said about such a thing in the text means that we should be very cautious about adopting this or any other interpretation. Furthermore, this interpretation depends heavily on the symmetrical placement of the items of furniture in the total design, when no figures at all are given for these placements. In the larger context, we are speaking of the character and nature of God, and it seems to me that if we are to read anything out of the design of the structure, it ought to relate to that subject: a God of order and balance, a God of beauty and serenity, a God who wishes to be present with his people, but who knows that without proper procedures and safeguards that presence would be positively destructive. The tripartite division of the Tabernacle corresponds to that which is known from contemporary Canaanite sanctuaries: an outer court; an inner room; and an inmost room. This is one more example, like the cherubim in all probability, of God using cultural elements with which the people were familiar but then transforming them. Thus, instead of an idol in the inner room, testifying to the fundamental unity of the human, the divine, and all nature, there was the Ark of the Covenant, testifying to the fact that the transcendent God, who is utterly other than his creation, has broken into it and called his creatures into a relationship with him.

ENDNOTES
1. The second account is also in a somewhat different, perhaps more logical, order. See the commentary on ch 35. See Houtman 2000:3.313-331 and Childs 1974:529-537 for lengthy discussions of the supposed origins of the text.
2. This is the point that Paul was making in Philippians 3. It was only when he had lost all the achievements of his supposed self-sufficiency in total dependence on Christ that he found his true self.
3. As noted above in the commentary on ch 19, the materials between that chapter and Numbers 10 form a unit. In that regard, it should be noted that the construction of the Tabernacle was not completed until the people had been at the mountain for nine months (40:17), with some of the content of Leviticus and Numbers 1-10 actually having occurred before the completion date. Thus, the placing of that event as the climax of the book of Exodus highlights its importance in God's revelatory program. The goal of everything in Exodus, Leviticus, and Numbers 1-10 is that God might take up residence among his people. For further discussion, see the commentary on 35:1.
4. Sarna (1991:156), along with Fretheim (1991:270) and Enns (2000:509), endorses the idea that there are seven sections (as marked by the repetition of "the LORD spoke/said to Moses") and that this signals an intention to connect these instructions with creation. However, when these supposed divisions (25:1; 30:11, 17, 22, 34; 31:1, 12) are examined, it is very difficult to see any connection beyond the mere number.
5. For one visualization of the Tabernacle, along with an extensive treatment of its supposed typological significance, see Paul F. Kiene, *The Tabernacle of God in the Wilderness of Sinai* (translator, John S. Crandall, Grand Rapids: Zondervan, 1977). The color photographs of the modeled structure and appurtenances are very effective.
6. See also 2 Kgs 19:15; 1 Chr 13:6; Pss 80:1; 99:1; Isa 37:16.
7. Fifty years ago it was common for OT scholars to recognize how carefully and thoroughly the OT distanced itself from anything mythological. Today such views are highly unpopular, with scholars sifting the text for any scraps that might testify to the accepted "truth" that OT religion is simply a natural evolution from mythological thinking. If that is so, it is remarkable that it is the only religion in the world that ever succeeded in arriving at thoroughgoing, nonmythological monotheism (Judaism, Christianity, and Islam are all derivative from it). It is equally remarkable that the OT has gone to such great pains to clearly show that it never evolved from such a source.
8. The traditional "menorah" is one of these possibilities, but that came from the Herodian temple, which was far removed in time and culture from the Tabernacle. Moreover, the depiction of the menorah on the Arch of Titus in Rome may show Roman artistic influence and thus not be entirely accurate.
9. Enns (2000:516, citing Levenson 1988:95) observes that the paucity of explanations may well be related to the intent to demythologize creation. Creation has no intrinsic meaning. Everything about it is derivative.
10. One must say that if this entire part of the book is an imaginary creation dating from the postexilic period, as many scholars assert, someone went to remarkably great lengths to imagine a design that would indeed be portable and beautifully functional. The fact that it also incorporates features from the known portable buildings of the late second millennium (Sarna 1991:156) makes such a feat all the more remarkable.
11. The sacrifices would be lying on the ground *4.5 feet below* (27:1) the top of the hollow structure. On the other hand, if the grating extended from side to side inside the altar, the sacrifices could rest upon it and air rising through it would hasten the

burning. But beyond this question is the larger one of the durability of the structure as a whole. If it was made of wood overlaid with bronze (which does not have a very high melting point) how was the altar able to withstand the heat of the burning sacrifices? One explanation is that since the whole complex was imaginary, the creator(s) just didn't think this aspect through far enough. That is hard to believe when such careful thought had clearly gone into the workability of other aspects of the structure (see footnote 10 above and the related comments). If the understanding of the grating presented here (and assumed in NLT) is correct, perhaps the burning material was kept away from the sides of the altar and lay on the solid metal of the grating.

12. E.g., Sarna (1991:155-156), Freitheim (1991:268-272), Enns (2000:521-522).

◆ ## 2. Instructions relating to the priesthood (27:20-30:38)

[20]"Command the people of Israel to bring you pure oil of pressed olives for the light, to keep the lamps burning continually. [21]The lampstand will stand in the Tabernacle, in front of the inner curtain that shields the Ark of the Covenant.* Aaron and his sons must keep the lamps burning in the LORD's presence all night. This is a permanent law for the people of Israel, and it must be observed from generation to generation.

CHAPTER 28

"Call for your brother, Aaron, and his sons, Nadab, Abihu, Eleazar, and Ithamar. Set them apart from the rest of the people of Israel so they may minister to me and be my priests. [2]Make sacred garments for Aaron that are glorious and beautiful. [3]Instruct all the skilled craftsmen whom I have filled with the spirit of wisdom. Have them make garments for Aaron that will distinguish him as a priest set apart for my service. [4]These are the garments they are to make: a chestpiece, an ephod, a robe, a patterned tunic, a turban, and a sash. They are to make these sacred garments for your brother, Aaron, and his sons to wear when they serve me as priests. [5]So give them fine linen cloth, gold thread, and blue, purple, and scarlet thread.

[6]"The craftsmen must make the ephod of finely woven linen and skillfully embroider it with gold and with blue, purple, and scarlet thread. [7]It will consist of two pieces, front and back, joined at the shoulders with two shoulder-pieces. [8]The decorative sash will be made of the same materials: finely woven linen embroidered with gold and with blue, purple, and scarlet thread.

[9]"Take two onyx stones, and engrave on them the names of the tribes of Israel. [10]Six names will be on each stone, arranged in the order of the births of the original sons of Israel. [11]Engrave these names on the two stones in the same way a jeweler engraves a seal. Then mount the stones in settings of gold filigree. [12]Fasten the two stones on the shoulder-pieces of the ephod as a reminder that Aaron represents the people of Israel. Aaron will carry these names on his shoulders as a constant reminder whenever he goes before the LORD. [13]Make the settings of gold filigree, [14]then braid two cords of pure gold and attach them to the filigree settings on the shoulders of the ephod.

[15]"Then, with great skill and care, make a chestpiece to be worn for seeking a decision from God.* Make it to match the ephod, using finely woven linen embroidered with gold and with blue, purple, and scarlet thread. [16]Make the chestpiece of a single piece of cloth folded to form a pouch nine inches* square. [17]Mount four rows of gemstones* on it. The first row will contain a red carnelian, a pale-green

peridot, and an emerald. ¹⁸The second row will contain a turquoise, a blue lapis lazuli, and a white moonstone. ¹⁹The third row will contain an orange jacinth, an agate, and a purple amethyst. ²⁰The fourth row will contain a blue-green beryl, an onyx, and a green jasper. All these stones will be set in gold filigree. ²¹Each stone will represent one of the twelve sons of Israel, and the name of that tribe will be engraved on it like a seal.

²²"To attach the chestpiece to the ephod, make braided cords of pure gold thread. ²³Then make two gold rings and attach them to the top corners of the chestpiece. ²⁴Tie the two gold cords to the two rings on the chestpiece. ²⁵Tie the other ends of the cords to the gold settings on the shoulder-pieces of the ephod. ²⁶Then make two more gold rings and attach them to the inside edges of the chestpiece next to the ephod. ²⁷And make two more gold rings and attach them to the front of the ephod, below the shoulder-pieces, just above the knot where the decorative sash is fastened to the ephod. ²⁸Then attach the bottom rings of the chestpiece to the rings on the ephod with blue cords. This will hold the chestpiece securely to the ephod above the decorative sash.

²⁹"In this way, Aaron will carry the names of the tribes of Israel on the sacred chestpiece* over his heart when he goes into the Holy Place. This will be a continual reminder that he represents the people when he comes before the LORD. ³⁰Insert the Urim and Thummim into the sacred chestpiece so they will be carried over Aaron's heart when he goes into the LORD's presence. In this way, Aaron will always carry over his heart the objects used to determine the LORD's will for his people whenever he goes in before the LORD.

³¹"Make the robe that is worn with the ephod from a single piece of blue cloth, ³²with an opening for Aaron's head in the middle of it. Reinforce the opening with a woven collar* so it will not tear. ³³Make pomegranates out of blue, purple, and scarlet yarn, and attach them to the hem of the robe, with gold bells between them. ³⁴The gold bells and pomegranates are to alternate all around the hem. ³⁵Aaron will wear this robe whenever he ministers before the LORD, and the bells will tinkle as he goes in and out of the LORD's presence in the Holy Place. If he wears it, he will not die.

³⁶"Next make a medallion of pure gold, and engrave it like a seal with these words: HOLY TO THE LORD. ³⁷Attach the medallion with a blue cord to the front of Aaron's turban, where it must remain. ³⁸Aaron must wear it on his forehead so he may take on himself any guilt of the people of Israel when they consecrate their sacred offerings. He must always wear it on his forehead so the LORD will accept the people.

³⁹"Weave Aaron's patterned tunic from fine linen cloth. Fashion the turban from this linen as well. Also make a sash, and decorate it with colorful embroidery.

⁴⁰"For Aaron's sons, make tunics, sashes, and special head coverings that are glorious and beautiful. ⁴¹Clothe your brother, Aaron, and his sons with these garments, and then anoint and ordain them. Consecrate them so they can serve as my priests. ⁴²Also make linen undergarments for them, to be worn next to their bodies, reaching from their hips to their thighs. ⁴³These must be worn whenever Aaron and his sons enter the Tabernacle* or approach the altar in the Holy Place to perform their priestly duties. Then they will not incur guilt and die. This is a permanent law for Aaron and all his descendants after him.

CHAPTER 29

"This is the ceremony you must follow when you consecrate Aaron and his sons to serve me as priests: Take a young bull and two rams with no defects. ²Then, using choice wheat flour and no yeast, make loaves of bread, thin cakes mixed with olive oil, and wafers spread with oil.

³Place them all in a single basket, and present them at the entrance of the Tabernacle, along with the young bull and the two rams.

⁴"Present Aaron and his sons at the entrance of the Tabernacle,* and wash them with water. ⁵Dress Aaron in his priestly garments—the tunic, the robe worn with the ephod, the ephod itself, and the chestpiece. Then wrap the decorative sash of the ephod around him. ⁶Place the turban on his head, and fasten the sacred medallion to the turban. ⁷Then anoint him by pouring the anointing oil over his head. ⁸Next present his sons, and dress them in their tunics. ⁹Wrap the sashes around the waists of Aaron and his sons, and put their special head coverings on them. Then the right to the priesthood will be theirs by law forever. In this way, you will ordain Aaron and his sons.

¹⁰"Bring the young bull to the entrance of the Tabernacle, where Aaron and his sons will lay their hands on its head. ¹¹Then slaughter the bull in the LORD's presence at the entrance of the Tabernacle. ¹²Put some of its blood on the horns of the altar with your finger, and pour out the rest at the base of the altar. ¹³Take all the fat around the internal organs, the long lobe of the liver, and the two kidneys and the fat around them, and burn it all on the altar. ¹⁴Then take the rest of the bull, including its hide, meat, and dung, and burn it outside the camp as a sin offering.

¹⁵"Next Aaron and his sons must lay their hands on the head of one of the rams. ¹⁶Then slaughter the ram, and splatter its blood against all sides of the altar. ¹⁷Cut the ram into pieces, and wash off the internal organs and the legs. Set them alongside the head and the other pieces of the body, ¹⁸then burn the entire animal on the altar. This is a burnt offering to the LORD; it is a pleasing aroma, a special gift presented to the LORD.

¹⁹"Now take the other ram, and have Aaron and his sons lay their hands on its head. ²⁰Then slaughter it, and apply some of its blood to the right earlobes of Aaron and his sons. Also put it on the thumbs of their right hands and the big toes of their right feet. Splatter the rest of the blood against all sides of the altar. ²¹Then take some of the blood from the altar and some of the anointing oil, and sprinkle it on Aaron and his sons and on their garments. In this way, they and their garments will be set apart as holy.

²²"Since this is the ram for the ordination of Aaron and his sons, take the fat of the ram, including the fat of the broad tail, the fat around the internal organs, the long lobe of the liver, and the two kidneys and the fat around them, along with the right thigh. ²³Then take one round loaf of bread, one thin cake mixed with olive oil, and one wafer from the basket of bread without yeast that was placed in the LORD's presence. ²⁴Put all these in the hands of Aaron and his sons to be lifted up as a special offering to the LORD. ²⁵Afterward take the various breads from their hands, and burn them on the altar along with the burnt offering. It is a pleasing aroma to the LORD, a special gift for him. ²⁶Then take the breast of Aaron's ordination ram, and lift it up in the LORD's presence as a special offering to him. Then keep it as your own portion.

²⁷"Set aside the portions of the ordination ram that belong to Aaron and his sons. This includes the breast and the thigh that were lifted up before the LORD as a special offering. ²⁸In the future, whenever the people of Israel lift up a peace offering, a portion of it must be set aside for Aaron and his descendants. This is their permanent right, and it is a sacred offering from the Israelites to the LORD.

²⁹"Aaron's sacred garments must be preserved for his descendants who succeed him, and they will wear them when they are anointed and ordained. ³⁰The descendant who succeeds him as high priest will wear these clothes for seven days as he ministers in the Tabernacle and the Holy Place.

31"Take the ram used in the ordination ceremony, and boil its meat in a sacred place. 32Then Aaron and his sons will eat this meat, along with the bread in the basket, at the Tabernacle entrance. 33They alone may eat the meat and bread used for their purification* in the ordination ceremony. No one else may eat them, for these things are set apart and holy. 34If any of the ordination meat or bread remains until the morning, it must be burned. It may not be eaten, for it is holy.

35"This is how you will ordain Aaron and his sons to their offices, just as I have commanded you. The ordination ceremony will go on for seven days. 36Each day you must sacrifice a young bull as a sin offering to purify them, making them right with the LORD.* Afterward, cleanse the altar by purifying it*; make it holy by anointing it with oil. 37Purify the altar, and consecrate it every day for seven days. After that, the altar will be absolutely holy, and whatever touches it will become holy.

38"These are the sacrifices you are to offer regularly on the altar. Each day, offer two lambs that are a year old, 39one in the morning and the other in the evening. 40With one of them, offer two quarts of choice flour mixed with one quart of pure oil of pressed olives; also, offer one quart of wine* as a liquid offering. 41Offer the other lamb in the evening, along with the same offerings of flour and wine as in the morning. It will be a pleasing aroma, a special gift presented to the LORD.

42"These burnt offerings are to be made each day from generation to generation. Offer them in the LORD's presence at the Tabernacle entrance; there I will meet with you and speak with you. 43I will meet the people of Israel there, in the place made holy by my glorious presence. 44Yes, I will consecrate the Tabernacle and the altar, and I will consecrate Aaron and his sons to serve me as priests. 45Then I will live among the people of Israel and be their God, 46and they will know that I am the LORD their God. I am the one who brought them out of the land of Egypt so that I could live among them. I am the LORD their God.

CHAPTER 30

"Then make another altar of acacia wood for burning incense. 2Make it 18 inches square and 36 inches high,* with horns at the corners carved from the same piece of wood as the altar itself. 3Overlay the top, sides, and horns of the altar with pure gold, and run a gold molding around the entire altar. 4Make two gold rings, and attach them on opposite sides of the altar below the gold molding to hold the carrying poles. 5Make the poles of acacia wood and overlay them with gold. 6Place the incense altar just outside the inner curtain that shields the Ark of the Covenant,* in front of the Ark's cover—the place of atonement—that covers the tablets inscribed with the terms of the covenant.* I will meet with you there.

7"Every morning when Aaron maintains the lamps, he must burn fragrant incense on the altar. 8And each evening when he lights the lamps, he must again burn incense in the LORD's presence. This must be done from generation to generation. 9Do not offer any unholy incense on this altar, or any burnt offerings, grain offerings, or liquid offerings.

10"Once a year Aaron must purify* the altar by smearing its horns with blood from the offering made to purify the people from their sin. This will be a regular, annual event from generation to generation, for this is the LORD's most holy altar."

11Then the LORD said to Moses, 12"Whenever you take a census of the people of Israel, each man who is counted must pay a ransom for himself to the LORD. Then no plague will strike the people as you count them. 13Each person who is counted must give a small piece of silver as a sacred offering to the LORD. (This payment is half a shekel,* based on the sanctuary shekel, which equals twenty gerahs.) 14All who have reached their twentieth birthday must give this sacred offering to the LORD. ¹⁵When this offering is given to the LORD to purify your lives, making you right with him,* the rich must not give more than the specified amount, and the poor must not give less. ¹⁶Receive this ransom money from the Israelites, and use it for the care of the Tabernacle.* It will bring the Israelites to the LORD's attention, and it will purify your lives."

¹⁷Then the LORD said to Moses, ¹⁸"Make a bronze washbasin with a bronze stand. Place it between the Tabernacle and the altar, and fill it with water. ¹⁹Aaron and his sons will wash their hands and feet there. ²⁰They must wash with water whenever they go into the Tabernacle to appear before the LORD and when they approach the altar to burn up their special gifts to the LORD—or they will die! ²¹They must always wash their hands and feet, or they will die. This is a permanent law for Aaron and his descendants, to be observed from generation to generation."

²²Then the LORD said to Moses, ²³"Collect choice spices—12½ pounds of pure myrrh, 6¼ pounds of fragrant cinnamon, 6¼ pounds of fragrant calamus,* ²⁴and 12½ pounds of cassia*—as measured by the weight of the sanctuary shekel. Also get one gallon of olive oil.* ²⁵Like a skilled incense maker, blend these ingredients to make a holy anointing oil. ²⁶Use this sacred oil to anoint the Tabernacle, the Ark of the Covenant, ²⁷the table and all its utensils, the lampstand and all its accessories, the incense altar, ²⁸the altar of burnt offering and all its utensils, and the washbasin with its stand. ²⁹Consecrate them to make them absolutely holy. After this, whatever touches them will also become holy.

³⁰"Anoint Aaron and his sons also, consecrating them to serve me as priests. ³¹And say to the people of Israel, 'This holy anointing oil is reserved for me from generation to generation. ³²It must never be used to anoint anyone else, and you must never make any blend like it for yourselves. It is holy, and you must treat it as holy. ³³Anyone who makes a blend like it or anoints someone other than a priest will be cut off from the community.'"

³⁴Then the LORD said to Moses, "Gather fragrant spices—resin droplets, mollusk shell, and galbanum—and mix these fragrant spices with pure frankincense, weighed out in equal amounts. ³⁵Using the usual techniques of the incense maker, blend the spices together and sprinkle them with salt to produce a pure and holy incense. ³⁶Grind some of the mixture into a very fine powder and put it in front of the Ark of the Covenant,* where I will meet with you in the Tabernacle. You must treat this incense as most holy. ³⁷Never use this formula to make this incense for yourselves. It is reserved for the LORD, and you must treat it as holy. ³⁸Anyone who makes incense like this for personal use will be cut off from the community."

27:21 Hebrew *in the Tent of Meeting, outside the inner curtain that is in front of the Testimony.* See note on 25:16. 28:15 Hebrew *a chestpiece for decision.* 28:16 Hebrew *1 span* [23 centimeters]. 28:17 The identification of some of these gemstones is uncertain. 28:29 Hebrew *the chestpiece for decision;* also in 28:30. See 28:15. 28:32 The meaning of the Hebrew is uncertain. 28:43 Hebrew *Tent of Meeting.* 29:4 Hebrew *Tent of Meeting;* also in 29:10, 11, 30, 32, 42, 44. 29:33 Or *their atonement.* 29:36a Or *to make atonement.* 29:36b Or *by making atonement for it;* similarly in 29:37. 29:40 Hebrew *1/10 of an ephah* [2.2 liters] *of choice flour . . . ¼ of a hin* [1 liter] *of pure oil . . . ¼ of a hin of wine.* 30:2 Hebrew *1 cubit* [46 centimeters] *long and 1 cubit wide, a square, and 2 cubits* [92 centimeters] *high.* 30:6a Or *Ark of the Testimony;* also in 30:26. 30:6b Hebrew *that covers the Testimony;* see note on 25:16. 30:10 Or *make atonement for;* also in 30:10b. 30:13 Or *0.2 ounces or 6 grams.* 30:15 Or *to make atonement for your lives;* similarly in 30:16. 30:16 Hebrew *Tent of Meeting;* also in 30:18, 20, 26, 36. 30:23 Hebrew *500 shekels* [5.7 kilograms] *of pure myrrh, 250 shekels* [2.9 kilograms] *of fragrant cinnamon, 250 shekels of fragrant calamus.* 30:24a Hebrew *500 shekels* [5.7 kilograms] *of cassia.* 30:24b Hebrew *1 hin* [3.8 liters] *of olive oil.* 30:36 Hebrew *in front of the Testimony;* see note on 25:16.

NOTES

27:20 pressed olives. Sarna (1991:175-176) says the point is that the olives were not ground up to produce the oil, and the lack of pulp in the oil meant that it gave a brighter and cleaner light.

27:21 Tabernacle. Lit., "tent of meeting." This term is used interchangeably with *mishkan* [TH4908, ZH5438] (Tabernacle) throughout the remainder of the book. It seems to refer to the Tabernacle as the place of revelation. In 33:7 the term is also applied to an interim tent that Moses set up outside the camp before the Tabernacle was completed.

that shields. Lit., "which is over." Friedman (1980:244) suggests that there was actually a separate canopy over the Ark. However, in the absence of other evidence, it seems better to take *'al* [TH5921, ZH6584] (on) here as being equivalent to *'el* [TH413, ZH448] (to) and read "before."

28:1 Set them apart. Lit., "bring them in front of you to serve me." Sarna (1991:177) suggests the point is that Moses should do this because up to this point he had been the chief officiator.

28:3 skilled craftsmen. Lit., "wise-hearted."

distinguish him as a priest set apart for my service. The NLT might be read to suggest that it is the clothes that will "set apart" (lit., "to make holy") the priests. This interpretation would not be correct. The Hebrew makes it clear that they are to be given the clothes *so that* they may be "set apart" or "sanctified." The clothes do nothing except to identify the person who has been taken into God's service and is thus expected to share his character.

28:5 So give them. Lit., "they shall take."

28:15 chestpiece . . . for seeking a decision. Lit., "a chestpiece for decision" (see NLT mg and also 28:29, 30). The NLT's rendering of the elliptical phrase *khoshen mishpat* [TH2833/4941, ZH3136/5477] is almost certainly correct. *Mishpat* has a very wide range of possible meanings. When the term is used in the context of the covenant, the NLT normally translates it with "regulation(s)." But it can mean "practice," "custom," "pattern," "judgment," "justice," and "order" (see KBL). Perhaps in the context here it has something of the idea of "direction(s)" in the sense that God would give his "direction(s)" for the people's behavior through the Urim and Thummim. See note on 28:30 and the commentary below.

28:30 Urim and Thummim. It is not clear exactly what these objects looked like or how they were used. They are referred to six other times in the OT (Lev 8:8; Num 27:21; Deut 33:8; 1 Sam 28:6; Ezra 2:63; Neh 7:65), but without further description or explanation. One suggestion, based on parallels in neighboring cultures, is that they were objects of stone or wood, each having some combination of white surfaces and black surfaces. A question was posed and the objects were thrown on the ground. If two white surfaces came out on top, the answer to the question was "yes." If two black surfaces were uppermost, the answer was "no." If both black and white were displayed, the objects either had to be thrown again at once or the question was deferred until a later time. An alternative is that one object was considered "yes" and the other "no." Whichever one the priest pulled out of the chestpiece gave the answer to the question.

28:36 medallion. Heb. *tsits* [TH6731, ZH7488]. Apart from the two other references to this same object (39:30; Lev 8:9), all but one of the other references (e.g., 1 Kgs 6:18; Ps 103:15; Isa 28:1) are to flowers or blossoms. Perhaps the sense is "a glittering thing."

28:38 take on himself any guilt. Lit., "carry the iniquity/guilt." In this context (cf. Lev 10:17), this phrase means "to forgive" (NIDOTTE 3.162-163). For other instances of the phrase being used in this way, see 10:17; Gen 50:17; 1 Sam 15:25.

29:1 with no defects. Heb. *tamim* [TH8549, ZH9459]. This does not imply that the animal was a "show" animal with perfect configuration, coat, etc. It merely means that the animal met expectations for a quality animal of its type. The same term is also applied to human behavior, as e.g., Noah and Abraham (Gen 6:9; 17:1).

29:13 the long lobe of the liver. Sarna (1991:188) suggests that the lobe of the liver was singled out to be burned because it figured strongly in pagan divination rites.

29:26 lift it up in the LORD's presence as a special offering. The lifting up may be a way of recognizing a change of ownership from the human to Yahweh.

30:7 burn fragrant incense. Cassuto (1967:391) suggests that one reason for burning incense when the lamps were lighted and extinguished is that the smell of the incense covered the unpleasant smell of smoldering wicks.

30:13 sanctuary shekel. Cassuto (1967:394) says this was double the weight of the standard shekel. But Powell (ABD 6.907) cites Josephus to the effect that it was only about two grams heavier (13.6 g as opposed to 11.4 g).

30:14 twentieth birthday. This was the age when a man was eligible for military service (cf. Num 1:3).

30:34 resin droplets, mollusk shell, and galbanum. The exact identity of these spices is still not known.

COMMENTARY

This second major block of material relating to the representation and experience of God's presence in the midst of the people relates to the service in the Tabernacle as conducted by the priests. The first subset of instructions has to do with the lamp (27:20-21). The second subset relates to the clothing worn by the priests (28:1-43). The third gives instructions for the ordination of the priests (29:1-46). The fourth subset (30:1-38) includes instruction for some miscellaneous priestly activities: the plan and service of the incense altar (30:1-10); the collection of ransom money (30:11-16); the plan and service of the washbasin (30:17-21); how to make and use the anointing oil (30:22-33); and how to make and use incense (30:34-38).

God truly wanted to live in the midst of his people. That was his goal, as this entire section makes clear. But how could he do that given the apparently uncrossable gulf between his holiness and their sinfulness? Perhaps one way of achieving that goal would have been to make himself less holy. But that would have defeated the still larger purpose he had in mind. God was coming down from the mountain of his holy transcendence in order to elevate humans to the level of his holy character (Lev 22:31-33). So if his holiness were somehow diminished, there would be no point in his coming. No, his holiness would have to remain in all its frightful purity. Thus, until the process of revelation was complete in Christ, making it possible for humans to share that holiness, there would have to be those who could stand between God and humans, mediating him to us and us to him. This is the profound significance of the priestly role and why so much space is given to it here. The priests were the chosen mediators between humans and God.

Ultimately, as the book of Hebrews makes plain, the Aaronic priesthood was symbolic of the one true mediator, the God-man, Jesus Christ (Heb 9:6-15), who forever defeated sin. The veil that divided the Most Holy Place from the Holy Place has been torn in two (Luke 23:45), and we have the privilege of being clothed in righteousness and entering the very presence of God because of the blood of the Lamb. That much seems clear from the way in which Scripture interprets itself. However, commentators have often been unwilling to stop here and have sought to find much more detailed correspondence between the details given here and scriptural truth. Perhaps some of those suggestions clarify the truth, but most of them seem to be merely an exercise in ingenuity.

The Lampstand (27:20-21). In the previous plans there were no instructions given as to how the objects were to be used. That seems to be the reason why the lampstand is mentioned again here. The plans had already been given (25:31-40), but here the priests were given instructions regarding what to burn in the lamps ("pure oil of pressed olives," 27:20) and how long they were to burn ("continually . . . all night," 27:20-21; cf. 1 Sam 3:3). The continual light would be a reminder that God's light shines no matter how dark it is (cf. Ps 139:11-12).

Clothing of the Priests (28:1-5). These first five verses of the chapter on the clothing of the priests spell out what clothing is to be made (28:4), who is to make it ("skilled craftsmen whom I have filled with the spirit of wisdom," 28:3), what materials they are to use (28:5), who is to wear it (28:2, 4), and above all, *why* the clothing is to be made and worn. Three times in five verses, the word "holy" occurs. The clothing is "holy" ("sacred," 28:2, 4, NLT), and it is to show that Aaron is "holy" ("set apart for my service," 28:3, NLT). As mentioned above, the priests were to stand between a holy God and a sinful people. As humans, the priests were sinful and needed continual atonement (Lev 16:17). But they were also the representatives of God and thus they had to mediate his holiness to the people. These "glorious and beautiful" (28:2) garments expressed something of the "beauty of holiness" (Pss 29:2; 96:9, NKJV), helping the people to picture something of the wonder of what God had in mind for them as they experienced his presence in their lives.

By way of preview, let it be said that the high priest wore several layers of clothing. On top of the linen undergarments (28:42) was a patterned tunic fastened at the waist with an embroidered sash (28:39). On top of that was a one-piece blue robe (28:31). On top of the robe was the embroidered linen ephod (28:6), which was evidently a kind of apron. On top of the ephod was the linen chestpiece (28:15), a remarkable embroidered and jewel-encrusted object, folded so as to make a small pouch (28:16). In addition, there was a turban (28:39). From the amount of space given the ephod and the chestpiece (25 verses), it is evident that special importance was attached to them.

The Ephod and Chestpiece (28:6-30). The ephod (28:6-14) was constructed from two pieces of linen embroidered with the same colors ("gold . . . blue, purple, and scarlet," 28:6) as the inner covering of the Tabernacle. The two pieces of cloth hung down the priest's front and back and were joined together at the top by shoulder straps (28:7).[1] On each of these shoulder straps was an onyx with the names of six of the twelve tribes engraved on it (28:9-10). The stones were set in gold filigree settings, and there were gold cords attached to the settings (28:13-14). The ephod was held at the waist by a sash of the same material as the ephod itself (28:8). It is unclear whether this ephod is the same kind of object as that mentioned in the book of Judges or not. There Gideon is said to have made himself a golden "ephod" and that Israel prostituted itself to the object (Judg 8:26-27). It is hard to imagine worshiping a priest's apron, no matter how beautiful it was! Perhaps the association of the ephod with the chestpiece, the Urim and Thummim, and divining God's will was involved, but we are left to speculate.

The chestpiece (28:15-30) was of the same kind of embroidered linen as the ephod (28:15) and was attached to the ephod by two sets of gold cords (28:22-28). The first set ran from gold rings on the top corners of the chestpiece to the gold settings on the shoulder straps of the ephod. The second set ran from rings on inside edges to rings attached to the ephod just above the sash. There were two special features about this object. The first was that it had 12 precious jewels fastened to it in gold settings (28:17-21). They were arranged in four rows of three, with the name of a different tribe engraved on each.[2] The second special feature was the fact that the cloth was folded so as to make it into a pouch (28:16), and in the pouch were kept the Urim and Thummim "used to determine the LORD's will" (28:30).

The significance of the ephod and the chestpiece is explained in 28:12, 15, 29-30. These two pieces of clothing embodied the twofold role of the priest. On the one hand, he was to represent the people "before the LORD" (28:12). This was made clear by the onyxes on his shoulders and the gems "over his heart" (28:29-30, three times). On these were engraved the names of the 12 tribes. Thus, it was in the priest that the people of the 12 tribes came before God, and the priest was to carry them on his shoulders and in his heart. On the other hand, he was to represent God to the people. This is expressed in the phrase "the chestpiece for decision" (see the note on 28:15). The priest was to give the people God's directions for their lives. One of the chief characteristics of the biblical God is that he cares deeply about his people's choices. This is why he had given them the covenant—so they could know his will for human behavior. Thus, it was the task of the priest to teach the people God's "instructions" (his *torah* [TH8451, ZH9368]; Mal 2:6-7). But not every choice could be addressed by the Torah. So God also gave the priest the tools (the Urim and Thummim) with which to determine his more specific will for a given situation and to declare that to the people as well. The reference to Urim and the Thummim represents the priest's larger task of teaching the people God's divine order for life (his *mishpat* [TH4941, ZH5477]; see note on 28:15).

Additional Clothing for the Priests (28:31-43). Although the additional clothing for the high priest and for his sons is not treated in as much detail as the ephod and the chestpiece, there are still some significant issues raised. The robe that was worn under those two items was to be of one piece (28:31) and to have alternating "bells and pomegranates . . . around the hem" (28:33-34). No explanation is given for the bells. The reference to their tinkling has suggested to some that they served to let those outside know that the priest inside the Holy Place was still alive and moving. Pomegranates are often taken to be symbols of life in the ancient Near East. But there was no special magic about the robe that bequeathed life on its wearer ("If he wears it, he will not die," 28:35). Rather, a spiritual lesson was being taught in physical terms. That lesson was that if humans are going to survive in the presence of the holy God, they will do it only on his terms and with his provision. We do not approach God on our terms and on our own merits. Approached in that way, God's holiness can only destroy us. Tragically, that was the lesson that Nadab and Abihu, Aaron's elder sons, did not learn except in their deaths (Lev 10:1-3). By contrast, if we approach God according to the means he has provided, we will find life (see also 28:43).

All this is captured in the medallion that the priest wore on his forehead, suspended from the front of his turban (28:36-38). The priest is to be the mediator between the holiness of the Lord and the sinfulness of the people. He himself is "HOLY TO THE LORD" (28:36; completely dedicated to and sharing the character of Yahweh) with the result that when sinful people consecrate ("make holy") their sacrifices, the priest can "carry away their guilt" in the name of God (see note on 28:38). God wants to forgive the sin of his people and to make them all a holy priesthood (19:6) for his service and the benefit of the world.

Aaron's sons (28:40) had clothing that was similar to Aaron's with the exception of the robe, the ephod, and the chestpiece. (Concerning the "linen undergarments," see the commentary on 20:26.)

Dedication of Priests (29:1-46). Chapter 29 addresses the installation of the priests, amplifying in detail the brief comments about this that were made in 28:41. The rituals described in these verses are designed to solemnize two matters: the consecration (29:1, 44) of the priests and the "filling of their hands," (cf. 29:9, Hebrew) or ordination (29:22, 27, 29, 31). The first speaks of the priests being removed from the ordinary order of life to belong exclusively to God for his service. They were rendered "holy" in this sense, just as the objects in the Tabernacle were (29:37). Neither the objects nor the priests could ever be used again for any function except God's functions (so 29:9). Again and again, the point is made that what belongs to God is holy, and what is holy is radically different from everything else. The whole point of this seven-day ceremony (29:35) was to drive home to the people that God is radically different from them and their fallen world and that unless God makes special provision for them, there is no way that the stated purpose of the Exodus, God dwelling in their midst (29:46), could occur.

The second matter being dealt with here is the ordination, or "the filling of the hands" (29:9, Hebrew) of the priests. The significance of that figurative language is that they were being given a task to fulfill. That task is largely assumed throughout the chapter, but it is spoken of more explicitly in verses 38-45. Once again, the two-fold nature of the priestly function is emphasized. First, they were to oversee and administer the sacrificial system, the means by which men and women could experience the life of God in their midst (29:38-41). Most people are surprised to discover that the goal of the sacrificial system, sketched here and filled out in much more detail in Leviticus 1-6, was not so that people who sinned intentionally could circumvent God's wrath.[3] Rather, this system was made available so that people who had been brought into the covenant by God's grace and who were determined to fulfill that covenant would not be prevented from experiencing the holy presence of their God by their unintentional sins. And that speaks to the second function of the priests: mediating the word of the holy God to the people (29:42-46). Through the ministry of the priests, God would "meet the people . . . there, in the place made holy by [his] glorious presence" (29:43). And, in fact, it was for the possibility of this fellowship that God had delivered his people from Egypt (29:46).

The rituals of ordination stressed three things: holy anointing, removal of the taint of sin, and enjoying God's provision in fellowship with him. In these respects, they correspond to the aspects of the priestly ministry. These rituals focused on death, blood, and total destruction. After Aaron and his sons had lain their hands on them, the three animals, a bull and two rams (29:1), were to be killed (29:11, 16, 20), and the first two were to be completely burned (29:13-14, 17-18). Some of the blood of all three was to be smeared, poured out, or splattered on the horns, base, and sides of the altar (29:12, 16, 20). These actions left no question as to the sinfulness of sin, or its deadly consequences. The Scriptures say that the soul that sins shall die (Ezek 18:20), and that the only forgiveness for sin is in the shedding of blood (Heb 9:22; cf. Lev 17:11). These rituals would make these truths unforgettable.

God provides a covering ("sin offering to purify" or "atonement"; 29:36-37 and mg) of life, as represented by the blood, so that what is other than God can live in his presence and function for him. This truth was further emphasized when some of the blood of the third animal was smeared on the right earlobes, thumbs, and big toes of Aaron and his sons (29:20). Unless one had been touched from head to foot with the life of an innocent victim, whom the holy God had recognized and provided, it would be impossible to survive an encounter with him.

These offerings were given in place of Aaron and his sons, as is indicated by their placing their hands upon the heads of the sacrifices before the animals were killed. It is also evident in the ritual of verses 22-26, where the parts of the ordination ram, along with the bread, were placed in the priests' hands "to be lifted up as a special offering to the LORD." These were lifted up to God in lieu of their own lives. They were lifted up as gifts, but also as a substitution, an atonement or covering (29:33) for themselves.

The expected outcome of this God-provided deliverance from death through participation in the death of another was fellowship with God. Certain portions of the ordination ram were to be eaten at the door of the Tabernacle (29:31-34). This was not the same as the meat that was regularly to be taken from the peace offering for the feeding of the priests and their families (29:28; cf. Lev 7:31-34). This was a meal in the presence of God, much like the meal the elders ate in his presence upon the sealing of the covenant (24:11). They would see God, yet they would not die. He had provided life for them so that they might enjoy life with him. That is always the goal of deliverance.

The third element of the ordination ceremonies, along with the offering of bloody sacrifices and the ceremonial meal, was anointing with the holy oil (29:7,

21, 29, 36). And just as atonement had to be made, not only for the priests, but also for the altar (29:36-37), so the altar too had to be anointed along with the priests (29:36). In a sense, the sacrificial rituals dealt with the negative side, the removal of sin, whereas the anointing dealt with the positive, the impartation of holiness (NIDOTTE 2.1123-1127). Persons who had been so anointed could not be associated with anything profane (cf. Lev 10:1-7). The association of the Holy Spirit with anointing (Isa 61:1; Acts 10:38) suggests strongly that the imagery here, insofar as it relates to humans, points to more than a mere state of holiness; it points to a positive spiritual endowment.

Plans for the Incense Altar (30:1-10). Chapter 30 contains a collection of instructions that do not appear to have much in common with each other, but what does unite them is that they all focus on activities of the priesthood. So there are instructions for the construction and use of the incense altar (30:1-10) and the washbasin (30:17-21). There are also instructions for how to make and use anointing oil (30:22-33) and incense (30:34-38). And there are also instructions about the collection and use of ransom money (30:11-16).

The incense altar is described in terms consistent with the table and the Ark: It was made of acacia wood overlaid with gold and decorated with a molding around the sides. It was to be placed before the veil dividing the Tabernacle into its two interior spaces, and incense was to be burned on it both in the morning and in the evening. Incense was a common feature of worship all across the ancient Near East, but nowhere is its function described with any detail. Undoubtedly, its expense, its heavy odor, and its musky smoke all spoke of the importance and the mystery of the divine and the service of the divine. The book of Revelation speaks of incense as the prayers of the saints (Rev 8:4); it is possible that this is the significance here, as a symbol of the people's supplications to God and his receiving them.

Ransom Money (30:11-16). As with many other parts of this section of the book, it is clear from the lacunae in this subsection concerning ransom money that the first readers had an understanding of the context that modern readers do not. Clearly there are a number of things assumed that would make what is being said more intelligible. For instance, it is not explained why taking a census might make the people liable to a plague (30:12; cf. 2 Sam 24:10, 15). As reported in Numbers 1, a census was taken and there was no mention of any such danger. Perhaps the answer is that the census in Numbers was commanded by God and that this situation only applies to humanly directed censuses, but we do not know.[4] In any case, we are brought once more to the realization that unless atonement (30:15-16) is continually made for God's people, they cannot survive in his presence. Whether it is an animal (ch 29) or money, as here, something must stand in our place, "covering" our fundamental unholiness in the sight of God. The fact that all persons had to pay the same amount underscores the fundamental value of persons before God. The ability to pay more did not make a person more valuable in God's sight, nor did poverty make him less valuable. One life is one life.

The Washbasin (30:17-21). The washbasin stood in the courtyard "between the Tabernacle and the altar" (30:18). Its purpose is fully spelled out. The priests had to wash whether they were going to enter the Tabernacle or serve at the altar (cf. 29:4). But we are left to speculate as to why this washing was required. It seems most likely that this is yet another set of images relating to the holiness of God. Just as Moses was required to take off his sandals and not mix common soil with holy soil, so here it appears that the priests were being reminded that there is a qualitative difference between the creator and all that is created. To be physically unclean in the presence of the absolutely clean one would have suggested that it is possible to mix the holy with the unholy. But this is not possible, and to do so, either intentionally or unintentionally, was to court death. Nadab and Abihu did not learn this (Lev 10:1-3), and it seems much of modern Christendom has not either.

The Anointing Oil and the Incense (30:22-38). Since the materials that made up the anointing oil were reasonably well known (30:23-24), we are not given an explicit recipe for the creation of the oil. This was clearly a part of the perfumer's art that did not have to be included here. Rather, these instructions were making a theological point. The point is that the oil was to be made to God's requirements, not just anyone's, and the finished product could not be used for any purpose but God's purposes. This is entirely consistent with the points that are made throughout these instructions from chapter 25 onward. If we are to come to God, it will be on his terms not ours. And there is a radical difference between all that pertains to God and all that does not, and that distinction is only blurred to our terrible loss.[5] This is the other side of a point that is often made regarding the biblical worldview: There is no distinction between the sacred and the secular in biblical thinking. There is no part of life that is cut off from God. Everything we do, think, or say is related to him. However, that is *not* to say that everything is therefore sacred, as is often said. Although everything in the cosmos relates to God, everything in the cosmos is *not* God. God's holy glory is his own, and it is only to be shared with those whom he specifically chooses and to whom he specifically endows it. These Tabernacle instructions are clearly designed to make this point.

The same points regarding the anointing oil also apply to the incense. This is not a recipe but a statement about the nature of God's holiness and how the Israelite believers could experience his presence without dying.

ENDNOTES
1. Cassuto (1967:373) considers the ephod to have hung below the sash at the waist. In that case it is difficult to imagine the purpose of the shoulder straps. Furthermore, 28:26 makes it seem that the ephod was under the chestpiece.
2. The stones named here are the same as those listed in Ezek 28:13 as being found on "the King of Tyre" (taken by some as representative of Satan) in Eden, where he is called blameless (Ezek 28:15). It is difficult to know how much to make of the correspondence.
3. The attempt to use the system in that way incurred nothing but scorn from the prophets.

4. Sarna (1991:201) says that it was because most censuses commanded by humans were in service of the king's ego, either for the purpose of collecting more taxes or for planning some military adventure. Cassuto (1967:393) says it showed a lack of faith in God. In the absence of a biblical explanation, both are speculative.
5. Note that "holy" appears seven times in relation to the anointing oil. God was making a point.

◆ ### 3. Craftsmen: Bezalel and Oholiab (31:1-11)

Then the LORD said to Moses, ²"Look, I have specifically chosen Bezalel son of Uri, grandson of Hur, of the tribe of Judah. ³I have filled him with the Spirit of God, giving him great wisdom, ability, and expertise in all kinds of crafts. ⁴He is a master craftsman, expert in working with gold, silver, and bronze. ⁵He is skilled in engraving and mounting gemstones and in carving wood. He is a master at every craft!

⁶"And I have personally appointed Oholiab son of Ahisamach, of the tribe of Dan, to be his assistant. Moreover, I have given special skill to all the gifted craftsmen so they can make all the things I have commanded you to make:

⁷the Tabernacle;*
the Ark of the Covenant;*
the Ark's cover—the place of atonement;
all the furnishings of the Tabernacle;
⁸the table and its utensils;
the pure gold lampstand with all its accessories;
the incense altar;
⁹the altar of burnt offering with all its utensils;
the washbasin with its stand;
¹⁰the beautifully stitched garments—the sacred garments for Aaron the priest, and the garments for his sons to wear as they minister as priests;
¹¹the anointing oil;
the fragrant incense for the Holy Place.

The craftsmen must make everything as I have commanded you."

1:7a Hebrew *the Tent of Meeting.* 31:7b Hebrew *the Ark of the Testimony.*

COMMENTARY

These verses identify the leading craftsmen ("Bezalel," 31:2, and "Oholiab," 31:6), tell what skills they would have (31:4-5), and summarize (from the previous chapters) all that they were to make, beginning with the Tabernacle (31:7) and concluding with the incense (31:11). Arguably, the most important thing said is in verse 3 about Bezalel. Only once previously in the Old Testament was someone reputed to be filled with "the Holy Spirit" and that was Joseph (Gen 41:38-39). We may debate whether the pharaoh there really understood what he was saying, but his point was a valid one nonetheless. Joseph was speaking beyond mere human wisdom. He had been endowed with superhuman abilities. The same thing, now spoken by God himself, is being said about Bezalel. He was going to demonstrate abilities in craftsmanship that would be beyond anything a mere human with a given skill could do, even understanding that all skills are ultimately a gift from God. This point is especially significant in this covenant context. Ultimately, the only way the holy God was going to be able to reach his ultimate goal of taking up residence in the human heart was by the work of the Holy Spirit.¹ It is as the Holy Spirit cleanses the heart and makes it a holy place that God can come home. The Master Craftsman himself will produce a temple in which God can dwell in all his holiness.²

ENDNOTES
1. Isa 32:15-16; Ezek 36:24-27; Eph 2:20-22.
2. Eph 2:19-22; 3:14-19; see also Rom 5:5; 1 Cor 6:19; 2 Tim 1:14; and Heb 6:4.

◆ 4. Instructions for the Sabbath (31:12-18)

¹²The LORD then gave these instructions to Moses: ¹³"Tell the people of Israel: 'Be careful to keep my Sabbath day, for the Sabbath is a sign of the covenant between me and you from generation to generation. It is given so you may know that I am the LORD, who makes you holy. ¹⁴You must keep the Sabbath day, for it is a holy day for you. Anyone who desecrates it must be put to death; anyone who works on that day will be cut off from the community. ¹⁵You have six days each week for your ordinary work, but the seventh day must be a Sabbath day of complete rest, a holy day dedicated to the LORD. Anyone who works on the Sabbath must be put to death. ¹⁶The people of Israel must keep the Sabbath day by observing it from generation to generation. This is a covenant obligation for all time. ¹⁷It is a permanent sign of my covenant with the people of Israel. For in six days the LORD made heaven and earth, but on the seventh day he stopped working and was refreshed.'"

¹⁸When the LORD finished speaking with Moses on Mount Sinai, he gave him the two stone tablets inscribed with the terms of the covenant,* written by the finger of God.

31:18 Hebrew *the two tablets of the Testimony;* see note on 25:16.

NOTES
31:13 *Be careful to.* The Hebrew begins with the particle *'ak* [TH389, ZH421], which could be translated "nevertheless." Sarna (1991:201) says it shows that the Sabbath ordinances take precedence even over the Tabernacle service.

31:17 *refreshed.* The same term was used regarding servants in 23:12.

COMMENTARY
To most modern ways of thinking it seems odd that these instructions for the Tabernacle and its service should conclude with instructions about the keeping of the Sabbath. On the surface, at least, it seems as though the two sets of instructions are unrelated. But if there were any question, it is laid to rest by the fact that the report of the implementation of the Tabernacle instructions *begins* with instructions about the Sabbath (35:1-3). Clearly, God and Moses saw a direct relationship between the two. What is that relationship? Sarna (1991:201) argues cogently that just as the Tabernacle demonstrates the holiness of God in space, so the Sabbath demonstrates it in time. In the opposing worldview it is necessary to escape these two dimensions in order to find the divine in realms of timeless continuity. But that is finally impossible and therefore wrong. Rather, the Divine One has come to find us, breaking

into time and space and sanctifying them with his own holy reality. Thus, the special designation of one day of the week for reflection on him and his character when coupled with the Tabernacle service becomes a way of refocusing one's life upon the purpose of one's living—sharing the character of the Holy One.

That this is indeed the point is underscored in verse 13: Keeping "the Sabbath is a sign of the covenant between me and you." The various activities and attitudes associated with Sabbath-keeping would assist in achieving the purpose of the Exodus—"so you will know that I am the LORD" (10:2)—and they would also facilitate the fulfillment of the purpose of the covenant—making them *holy*. Twice more, in verses 16 and 17, it is reiterated that Sabbath-keeping is *the* sign of acceptance of the covenant and of continuation in that covenant. Thus, "it is a permanent sign" (31:17). This connection to the covenant is the reason why Isaiah 58 puts condemnations of social injustice and of Sabbath-breaking side by side. Both are signs of refusal to keep the terms of the covenant. Persons who live in this way love neither their neighbor nor God.

Although the Sabbath is a sign of the covenant, it is not the aspect of redemption that is highlighted here (unlike Deut 5:15). Here, as in Exodus 20:11, the focus is upon Yahweh as creator (31:17). By refraining from work on the Sabbath day, I remind myself again that I did not create the earth, my Creator did; I am not the self-sufficient one, my Creator is; I do not determine the basis of my life, my Creator does—my Creator, who rested "and was refreshed" (31:17). If he rested, how dare I work, claiming to have given my whole life into his hands? Here, then, is a very concrete, identifiable sign of whether one is in covenant with Yahweh the Creator or not. The person who has left off his or her "ordinary work" (31:15) in order to reflect on the Lord and to rest in him does indeed know that he is Lord.

The final verse of this section (31:18) reminds us that the purpose of Moses's time on the mountain included more than merely the receipt of the Tabernacle instructions. His reception of the tablets (cf. 24:12) symbolized all of the additional materials he had received in support of and definition of the covenant (cf. Lev 25:1; 27:34). The reason the Tabernacle instructions are given so much space is to drive home Exodus's larger point about God's living among his people and their knowing him (see the comments at 25:1). Exodus 31:18 also sets the stage for the immediately following events: Moses's smashing of the tablets (32:15-19) and the provisions of the second set of commandments (34:1, 28).

◆ **B. The Gold Calf: The Wrong Way to Secure God's Presence (32:1–34:35)**

1. The making of the calf (32:1-6)

When the people saw how long it was taking Moses to come back down the mountain, they gathered around Aaron. "Come on," they said, "make us some gods who can lead us. We don't know what happened to this fellow Moses, who brought us here from the land of Egypt." ²So Aaron said, "Take the gold rings from the ears of your wives and sons and daughters, and bring them to me." ³All the people took the gold rings from their ears and brought them to Aaron. ⁴Then Aaron took the gold, melted it down, and molded it into the shape of a calf. When the people saw it, they exclaimed, "O Israel, these are the gods who brought you out of the land of Egypt!"

⁵Aaron saw how excited the people were, so he built an altar in front of the calf. Then he announced, "Tomorrow will be a festival to the LORD!"

⁶The people got up early the next morning to sacrifice burnt offerings and peace offerings. After this, they celebrated with feasting and drinking, and they indulged in pagan revelry.

NOTES

32:1 *gathered around.* Sarna (1991:203; also Childs 1974:564) points out that the verb used here always connotes hostility (cf. Num 16:3).

gods. The noun *'elohim* [TH430, ZH466] is usually taken as singular when it refers to God, but here it is understood as plural because it refers to pagan gods. Here, the verbs and pronouns associated with the noun are in the plural (as in 32:4, even though there was only one idol). Interestingly, when Nehemiah 9:18 quotes v. 4, it uses singular forms. It is possible that the plural is used here to emphasize the pagan nature of what was taking place.

32:2 *Take.* The word *paraq* [TH6561, ZH7293] means "tear off, break off." The verb is a graphic one that seems to have been chosen to express the violence of the action involved. Presumably these were solid rings through the earlobes that had to be broken to get them off. The same verb is used again in 32:3 ("took," NLT).

32:4 *took the gold, melted it down, and molded it into the shape of a calf.* The NLT is expansive, for the text literally reads, "He shaped it with a tool and made of it a calf, a molded image." It seems likely that "calf" here is not intended to connote an infant animal but a young bull which is, as Cassuto (1967:412) says, "full of vigor." But it is also possible that the text is mocking the supposedly all-powerful image by speaking of it in diminutive terms.

32:5 *Aaron saw how excited the people were.* This is an inference; the text says only "Aaron saw."

32:6 *got up early.* The parallel with 24:4, where it is said that "early the next morning Moses got up" on the day of the sealing of the covenant, is almost certainly an intentional contrast. See also 34:4 and the commentary there.

pagan revelry. This is a probable interpretation. The text says lit., "they rose up to play." Very possibly sexual activity was involved (cf. Gen 26:8, where the same word is used).

COMMENTARY

As I noted above in the comments at the beginning of chapter 25, chapters 32–34 are recorded between chapters 25–31 and 35–40 for a very specific purpose. The climax of the book is the coming of God to live among his people. This is why God led his people out of Egypt: so that he could take up residence among them (cf. 15:17; 19:4), so that the alienation between creator and creatures could begin to be solved. But that wonderful possibility can only take place on God's terms. Every human effort to solve the divine-human problem is doomed to failure. That truth is illustrated in the structure of chapters 25–40. It begins with the wonderful plans of God for meeting the need (chs 25–31). Then, in this section (chs 32–34), ironically, we see what happens when humans set out to meet their needs for themselves, believing that God does not know their needs, or if he does, does not care about them. The result is all but fatal disaster. It is only when the people, still alive as a result of God's gracious forgiveness, follow his instructions precisely (chs 35–40) that their needs can be truly supplied.

Chapters 32–34 fall into six sections. The first, and one of the shortest, details the actual sin, the making of the calf (32:1-6). The remaining five sections are the aftermath of the tragic event: (1) Exodus 32:7-14 covers the conversation of Yahweh and Moses; (2) Exodus 32:15-29 reports Moses's response to the people; (3) Exodus 32:30-35 contains Moses's intercession on behalf of the people; (4) then Exodus 33 reports the interchange between Moses and Yahweh as to whether Yahweh would go with them to Canaan; and (5) finally, Exodus 34 announces Yahweh's unilateral reaffirmation of the covenant.[1]

Humanly speaking, it is easy to see why the people would be apprehensive. Moses had been on the mountain for 40 days without food or water. That deprivation alone would have been enough to raise serious doubts about his return; in addition, the top of the mountain seemed to be clothed in "consuming fire" (24:17). Thus, they had reason to be anxious. But anxiety need not lead to sin unless it is allowed to overwhelm faith. And that is what happened here. Verse 1 highlights the problem: They had not drawn the appropriate inferences from all the experiences they had had. It was not "Moses, who brought [them] here from the land of Egypt" (32:1). It was Yahweh. And if Moses should not return, the power, the providence, and the character that Yahweh had revealed to them would still be theirs. Moses was not the one they needed but Yahweh.

Failing to realize that fundamental truth, the people made a fatal decision. Since they had need of protection and guidance and since it was highly unlikely that Moses could provide that for them, they would have to devise a way to provide for themselves. This is the heart of all idolatry; we seek out a way to manipulate the power of the world to provide for our needs. As I said in the comments at the beginning of this section (ch 25), the terrible irony is that God knew their needs better than they did themselves and that he had been taking steps to meet those needs before the people even knew they had them. But if that is true, why did God make the people wait in uncertainty for 40 days? There is a profound truth here. Throughout the Old Testament, one of the common synonyms for "trust" is "wait" (Isa 30:18; 40:31). It is only when we lay aside our timetables and plans, refusing to run ahead of God that we have really learned to trust him. When we define the need, the means to meet it, and the time when it shall be met, this is not trust at all but merely manipulation.

And what happens when we seek to meet our needs for ourselves? This passage answers that question very clearly: Our gifts are misused; giving is coerced; professionals are exalted; ordinary people are reduced to spectators; creation is worshiped; power and productivity are made ultimate; God is misperceived; and far from bringing him near, we further alienate ourselves from him. God had provided the people with the wealth of Egypt (12:36), not only for the building of the Tabernacle, but also for their own enjoyment. Now it was poured into a thing that would only take and give nothing back. Unlike the joyous freedom in giving that was specified in the instructions for the Tabernacle (25:2) and was demonstrated in the fulfillment of the instructions (35:20-29), this giving was specific and demanded (32:2). There was no freedom either in what was given or how much. Instead of a variety of skills in a variety of persons, all led by Spirit-filled persons, Aaron, the religious professional, took it upon himself to do all the work (32:4), and the people were merely allowed to be spectators ("When the people saw," 32:4). The choice of a bull for the object of worship reflects not only Egyptian religion, where the high god, Amon-Re, was represented by a bull, but also the other religions of the ancient Near East. The bull represented the power, domination, and fecundity that were believed to reside in nature and that the worshipers hoped to capture for themselves. But these qualities are not inherent in creation; they are gifts given by the Creator. To confuse gift and Giver is to make ultimate what is derivative and to make a person dependent on what is strictly limited and cannot reproduce itself.[2]

We may ask how a people who had only a few weeks earlier committed themselves in a blood oath not to recognize any other gods or to make any idols could have so soon, and apparently so lightly, dismissed all that. One possible answer is that they were insincere in accepting the covenant. But there is no evidence at all in support of such a position. Rather, the truth is that they did not understand the depth of the human problem. They were encountering for the first time the problem that the apostle Paul detailed so eloquently in Romans 7. That problem is twofold. First is the power of human desire; we want things, and not merely, or even chiefly, material things. We want security, pleasure, comfort, and power.[3] And these desires are so powerful that we are willing to do almost anything to get them, including things that are ultimately self-destructive and forbidden by God. The second aspect of the problem is that while the Torah points out why we should not live as slaves of desire, it cannot itself defeat desire. In fact, Paul says that by forbidding such a life, the Torah actually heightens our desires for it because the ultimate desire is the desire for our own ways, and we will allow nothing to contradict that desire. Ultimately, it is only when God, through Christ, resides in the human heart by the power of the Spirit that we are enabled to live by the covenant.[4] This is, of course, the truth that the Tabernacle was designed to point to, whereas the golden calf points to the exact opposite.

ENDNOTES

1. Source critics have divided and redivided this material on the basis of its supposed origins. For reviews of the various opinions, see Childs (1974:558-562; 584-586, 604-610). In the end, he thinks a redactor has done a "superb" job of bringing about an "*apparent* unity" (emphasis mine).
2. As early as the 1920s, scholars pointed out instances in the ancient Near East in which a god is depicted as standing on the back of a bull and suggested that the bull here was originally understood to be the pedestal of the invisible Yahweh, who was

thought of as standing on the bull's back. There is no evidence in the text to support this position. On the contrary, the regular representation of various gods as bulls argues that Yahweh was understood here (and later, see 1 Kgs 12:28) as a bull. Egyptian theology, based on the worldview of continuity in which human, nature, and divine are all one, saw no contradiction in saying that "God" was the world and was not the world or was visible and was not visible. So Aaron, when he said the calf was Yahweh, may have not believed that he was doing anything wrong. But God was revealing to Moses on the mountain that this worldview was completely wrong. God is *not* the world, and any attempt to capture him within the world is not merely wrong but deadly. See Cassuto 1967:407-409 for an attempt to exonerate Aaron of blame using the "pedestal" theory. Houtman (2000:3.611) doubts that theory but does see Aaron as attempting to keep the people from worshiping other gods by associating the calf with Yahweh. I think the confusion in worldviews is a more likely explanation. See my article, "The Golden Calves and the Egyptian Concept of Deity," *Evangelical Quarterly* 45 (1973): 13-20.
3. In 1 John 2:16 these are summed up in the memorable words "the lust of the flesh, the lust of the eyes, and the pride of life" (KJV; NLT, "a craving for physical pleasure, a craving for everything we see, and pride in our achievements and possessions").
4. See Isa 32:15-16; Ezek 36:24-27; Rom 8:4-5, 12-13; Gal 5:24-25; Eph 2:19-22; 3:14-19.

◆ ## 2. The Lord's response and Moses's intercession (32:7-14)

⁷The LORD told Moses, "Quick! Go down the mountain! Your people whom you brought from the land of Egypt have corrupted themselves. ⁸How quickly they have turned away from the way I commanded them to live! They have melted down gold and made a calf, and they have bowed down and sacrificed to it. They are saying, 'These are your gods, O Israel, who brought you out of the land of Egypt.'"

⁹Then the LORD said, "I have seen how stubborn and rebellious these people are. ¹⁰Now leave me alone so my fierce anger can blaze against them, and I will destroy them. Then I will make you, Moses, into a great nation."

¹¹But Moses tried to pacify the LORD his God. "O LORD!" he said. "Why are you so angry with your own people whom you brought from the land of Egypt with such great power and such a strong hand? ¹²Why let the Egyptians say, 'Their God rescued them with the evil intention of slaughtering them in the mountains and wiping them from the face of the earth'? Turn away from your fierce anger. Change your mind about this terrible disaster you have threatened against your people! ¹³Remember your servants Abraham, Isaac, and Jacob.* You bound yourself with an oath to them, saying, 'I will make your descendants as numerous as the stars of heaven. And I will give them all of this land that I have promised to your descendants, and they will possess it forever.'"

¹⁴So the LORD changed his mind about the terrible disaster he had threatened to bring on his people.

32:13 Hebrew *Israel*. The names "Jacob" and "Israel" are often interchanged throughout the Old Testament, referring sometimes to the individual patriarch and sometimes to the nation.

NOTES

32:9 stubborn and rebellious. Lit., "stiff-necked." The image is of an animal that refuses to be led. This image of the people as "stiff-necked" recurs again in 33:3, 5, and 34:9 (see also Deut 9:6; 10:16).

32:10 *so my fierce anger can blaze against.* This translates a graphic image: "so my nose can get hot against." Similar English imagery would say "to get red in the face at."

32:11 *tried to pacify.* Lit., "softened the face of." This is a graphic image reflecting the idea of changing an intractable expression into one of tenderness. The Hebrew does not include the idea of "trying." It simply says Moses did it.

32:12 *Change your mind.* The Hebrew is *nakham* [TH5162, ZH5714], meaning "to comfort" or "to comfort oneself concerning," thus "to relent" (so also in 32:14; see commentary).

32:14 *the terrible disaster.* The KJV renders this as "evil." When God was said (in the KJV) to "repent of evil" it led to serious misperceptions, suggesting that God was capable of moral evil that had to be repented of. But this is not the case. Had God punished the people, as he did in fact punish some of them (32:35), he would not have been committing moral evil. In fact, he would have been upholding justice. The word *ra'ah* [TH7451B, ZH8288], which KJV translates "evil," is a larger term than any one English term, but its connotations are rather close to the English word "bad," with its range from "misfortune" to "immoral." From the perspective of the Israelites, what God was threatening would be "bad" indeed, but if God had done it, it would not have been a "bad" act.

COMMENTARY

This passage is often cited as evidence in support of the contention that the God of the Old Testament is both short-tempered and arbitrary. In fact, that is not the case at all. If anything, the passage leads to the opposite conclusions when correctly understood. Two things must be borne in mind. The first is that the Israelites had taken a solemn blood oath calling death upon themselves if they failed to keep the covenant (24:7-8). Now they had broken it most flagrantly. Simple justice demanded that they be destroyed. If Yahweh had fulfilled his words to Moses in verse 10 and wiped them out, he would not have been exhibiting a short temper but merely justice. The second thing is that when God "changed his mind" (32:14) and did not bring their just desserts upon the people, he was not being arbitrary. In fact, he was demonstrating that fundamental consistency that Moses had come to recognize and to depend upon.[1] God is determined to bless anyone who will meet the barest minimum of terms consonant with that blessing. That is what Jonah knew, and that is why he determined to give the Assyrians no opportunity to meet those terms. Jonah knew that God is so ready to forgive ("change his mind about") people that he would even forgive the terrible Assyrians (Jonah 4:2). The wonder here is not that God became angry; the wonder is that he was so easily and quickly pacified. He was so gracious because of his own fundamental nature, the revelation of which was further confirmed in the word given to Moses in 34:6-7. He is slow to become angry and swift to forgive. We do not have here a picture of an implacable monster who is only barely and grudgingly placated by a terrified and cowering intercessor. Instead, we find God saying that all it will take for justice not to be carried out is for one person, Moses, to remain before God, interceding (32:9-10).[2] Thus, we have a picture of the justice of the universe being set aside in a moment merely on the basis of one person's calm demonstration to God that he understands who God really is.

In fact, this incident looks rather like a test of Moses. In verses 7 and 10 Yahweh seems to invite Moses to feel sorry for himself and to turn the experience to his own advantage. How could they have done this to Moses after all he had done for them? So why not just wipe them out and start over with a new people called "the children of Moses"? But if it was a test, Moses passed it with flying colors. These were not his people but Yahweh's (32:11). Moses did not bring them out, Yahweh did. This experience was not about Moses's reputation but about God's (32:12-13). It little matters what the Egyptians would think about Moses, but it matters to all eternity what people think about Yahweh. If he is a God who keeps his promises (32:13), even when there is no reason to, there is hope for the world. If he is not that kind of a God, and if, in fact, there is no such God, then all is lost.

ENDNOTES
1. It is unfortunate that "openness theology" has fastened on terms like this to suggest that God does not know the future. It is argued that if God knew in advance that he was going to change his mind, then he would not have started out to do the contrary. This is to apply limited human logic to divine reality in an attempt to say definitively what God must be up to. It is the same sort of limited logic that says that since God is sovereign, then everything that happens must be an expression of his will. The Scripture is quite clear when it says that God knows everything (Isa 46:8-10). If we cannot square these kinds of statements with the one here, that is indicative of our limitations, not God's.
2. Most commentators, for example, Fretheim (1991:284) and Childs (1974:568), see this statement as a veiled invitation by God to Moses to intercede.

◆ ### 3. Moses's response and intercession (32:15-35)

15Then Moses turned and went down the mountain. He held in his hands the two stone tablets inscribed with the terms of the covenant.* They were inscribed on both sides, front and back. 16These tablets were God's work; the words on them were written by God himself.

17When Joshua heard the boisterous noise of the people shouting below them, he exclaimed to Moses, "It sounds like war in the camp!"

18But Moses replied, "No, it's not a shout of victory nor the wailing of defeat. I hear the sound of a celebration."

19When they came near the camp, Moses saw the calf and the dancing, and he burned with anger. He threw the stone tablets to the ground, smashing them at the foot of the mountain. 20He took the calf they had made and burned it. Then he ground it into powder, threw it into the water, and forced the people to drink it.

21Finally, he turned to Aaron and demanded, "What did these people do to you to make you bring such terrible sin upon them?"

22"Don't get so upset, my lord," Aaron replied. "You yourself know how evil these people are. 23They said to me, 'Make us gods who will lead us. We don't know what happened to this fellow Moses, who brought us here from the land of Egypt.' 24So I told them, 'Whoever has gold jewelry, take it off.' When they brought it to me, I simply threw it into the fire—and out came this calf!"

25Moses saw that Aaron had let the people get completely out of control, much to the amusement of their enemies.* 26So he stood at the entrance to the camp and shouted, "All of you who are on the LORD's side, come here and join me." And all the Levites gathered around him.

27Moses told them, "This is what the

LORD, the God of Israel, says: Each of you, take your swords and go back and forth from one end of the camp to the other. Kill everyone—even your brothers, friends, and neighbors." ²⁸The Levites obeyed Moses' command, and about 3,000 people died that day.

²⁹Then Moses told the Levites, "Today you have ordained yourselves* for the service of the LORD, for you obeyed him even though it meant killing your own sons and brothers. Today you have earned a blessing."

³⁰The next day Moses said to the people, "You have committed a terrible sin, but I will go back up to the LORD on the mountain. Perhaps I will be able to obtain forgiveness* for your sin."

³¹So Moses returned to the LORD and said, "Oh, what a terrible sin these people have committed. They have made gods of gold for themselves. ³²But now, if you will only forgive their sin—but if not, erase my name from the record you have written!"

³³But the LORD replied to Moses, "No, I will erase the name of everyone who has sinned against me. ³⁴Now go, lead the people to the place I told you about. Look! My angel will lead the way before you. And when I come to call the people to account, I will certainly hold them responsible for their sins."

³⁵Then the LORD sent a great plague upon the people because they had worshiped the calf Aaron had made.

32:15 Hebrew *the two tablets of the Testimony*; see note on 25:16.   32:25 Or *out of control, and they mocked anyone who opposed them.* The meaning of the Hebrew is unclear.   32:29 As in Greek and Latin versions; Hebrew reads *Today ordain yourselves.*   32:30 Or *to make atonement.*

NOTES

32:16 *written by God himself.* It is not certain whether this is to be taken literally or not. It is possible that this is a hyperbolic way of saying that the terms of the covenant were directly from God (see Sarna 1991:206 for such an understanding). At the same time, given all the other miracles associated with the Exodus and the giving of the covenant, if literal writing is the intent of the statement, there is no reason to quibble over it.

32:17 *boisterous.* This is an inference from what was said in 32:6.

32:18 *I hear.* This is a participle in Hebrew, stressing the immediacy and the continuing nature of the experience: "I am hearing."

sound of a celebration. The phrase *qol 'anoth* [TH6030A, ZH6702] (typically translated in NLT by "sound of"; lit., "voice of answering") is used three times in this verse. The first two times it is modified by another word: "victory" and "defeat" respectively. But the third time there is no following word, so the last phrase is commonly translated "the sound of singing." In addition to the Hebrew root *'anah* meaning "to answer," there is a homograph, *'anah*, meaning "to sing" [see 15:21]. The MT pointing of the third occurrence as a Piel form, unlike the first two occurrences, is probably intended to point to that root). Houtman (1993:3.655-656) suggests the same root was actually repeated all three times and that the modifying term has fallen out from the third occurrence. He suggests the missing word was something like "partying," which is quite close to NLT. LXX has "the voice of the beginning of wine," which might lend support to Houtman's view. If that is correct, perhaps the MT pointing represents an attempt to make sense of the passage after the third element was accidentally lost.

32:20 *burned.* The word *sarap* [TH8313, ZH8596] is one of about 15 Hebrew words for burning. It is "used for destructive burning not usually for the ordinary kindling of a fire" (TWOT 2.884).

32:21 *terrible sin.* Sarna (1991:208) points out that this phrase is elsewhere used for adultery (Gen 20:9; 39:9) and idolatry (2 Kgs 17:21).

32:25 amusement. This word occurs only here. There is a noun with the same consonants that occurs in Job 4:12, where the context suggests it means "a whisper." That connection has suggested that the term here refers to "derision"—the picture being of something that is said behind one's hand. But Houtman (2000:3.663-664) argues that this does not fit the context and suggests "had become easy prey for their enemies." The versions vary enough from one another that it appears they are all trying to make some sense out of a term they do not know.

32:29 ordained yourselves. This is an apt translation for the image "you have filled your hands." This is the same language used for the service of ordination that was to be conducted for the priesthood upon the completion of the Tabernacle (29:9, 35).

32:30 You have. "You" is emphatic in the Hebrew.

obtain forgiveness. Lit., "make atonement for," which is a stronger statement. Literally, it means to "cover over" or even "blot out." So Moses proposed to cover over the people's sin. See commentary and note on 25:17.

32:34 My angel. This seems to connote something different from the Angel of the Lord, which often seems to be the visible representation of Yahweh himself. Here the point is that Yahweh will not go with them in a personal way but only his representative will accompany them. See endnote 1 on 33:1-11 for an alternative understanding.

when I come to call . . . I will certainly hold them responsible. This is a helpful attempt to represent a Hebrew word with very complex connotations. The term is *paqad* [TH6485, ZH7212], which is conventionally rendered "to visit" or "to visit upon" (cf. KJV). Here the word is used twice with the two different senses. But the term is also used to express the ideas of "numbering off" and "appointing." Apparently the idea is of an official inspection by a commanding general, in the course of which he passes out both commendations and condemnations, and makes other decisions, such as troop assignments (NIDOTTE 3.657-663). So here God says that at the time he makes his official visit, there will be retribution on those who have sinned.

COMMENTARY

Moses's Response (32:15-29). In a powerful narrative filled with vivid details (such as the conversation between him and Joshua on the way down the mountain, 32:17-18), Moses conveys his responses to the reality of what had taken place. His hot-blooded reactions in the valley are in rather clear contrast to his somewhat cool and objective discussion with God on the mountain about the theological ramifications of God's fulfilling the curses of the covenant (32:7-14). This contrast is highlighted when Moses is said to have experienced the same blazing anger ("a hot nose," 32:19; see note on 32:10) against that for which he had politely chided God on the mountain. Clearly the situation was no longer a hypothetical one for him but had become passionately real.

While we are not told the reason for Moses's smashing of the tablets with the terms of the covenant on them (32:19), it seems very probable, especially given the detailed description of the tablets in 32:15-16, that this was not merely the expression of a fit of fury. Rather, it expressed Moses's recognition of the fact that the covenant itself had been irrevocably broken. Once again, what he could consider dispassionately on the mountain had become vividly, terribly real. He knew the grace and the faithfulness of God—he had himself appealed to it—but he now realized the true implications of what had taken place and that there was no obvious way back.

Moses's actions with regard to the calf (32:20) were both literally and symbolically effective. His rage is apparent in the violence of the actions, as is effectively conveyed by the NLT. Clearly the sense of "burn" here is not to consume but to destroy.[1] It is probably significant that this term is used, rather than one having to do with "melt," although that was probably the effect of the burning. It is not merely that Moses melted the idol down but that he effectively "destroyed" it. He further desecrated it by smashing the shapeless mass into powder, putting it into water, and making the people drink the water. Whatever gold finally emerged from the people's urinary tracts would never be used again for the making of something supposedly holy![2]

The next segment of the narrative (32:21-24) is laced with humor. In his classic attempt to deny responsibility, Aaron tried first to placate Moses with deference ("my lord," 32:22). Then he said that it was the people's fault, as though he had tried to restrain them but failed, which was manifestly not the case (32:22-23). Finally, he had the effrontery to suggest that all he had done was to put the gold in the furnace and that the calf had emerged on its own (32:24)! Precisely because what he says is so ridiculous, its impact is the stronger. Saving face and avoiding punishment is so important to us that anything, even the ridiculous, seems justified in pursuing those ends. It is interesting that although Moses saw through Aaron's efforts at obfuscation (32:25), he did not openly condemn him. Equally, it is fascinating that Aaron was not among those killed by his brother Levites (32:27-29). No explanation is given for these facts. One can only assume that Aaron was spared because of his relationship to Moses and because of the place God had already chosen for him in the Tabernacle service. But all of this, coupled with the fact that nothing truly commendatory of Aaron is said in the Bible, makes it very plain that this high priest could never forgive sins on his own account. He could only represent the true High Priest who was to come (Heb 9:11-14).[3]

If Exodus 32:21-24 strikes a humorous note, there is no humor in the final segment (32:25-29). Here the Moses who had "tried to pacify" God (32:11) grimly called for a division of the people. The issue at stake was loyalty; who would be wholeheartedly for Yahweh (32:26)? This was, of course, the central question of the covenant, one that was applied to the kings of Israel again and again. Were their hearts "perfect" toward God (see 1 Kgs 15:3, 14; 2 Chr 25:2)? Or were they guilty of the kind of divided loyalties that eventually brought Solomon to ruin (1 Kgs 11:4-6; cf. 1 Chr 29:19)? Moses, like Joshua many years later (Josh 24:15), left no doubt as to his own position. He did not call people to an idea. Rather, he called them to himself, unashamed to represent himself as the embodiment of the idea of absolute loyalty. Here, it was the "Levites" (32:26) who instantly responded, gathering around Moses. And we may suppose that the 3,000 (32:28) who were killed by the Levites were those who were unashamedly and adamantly for the other side, leaving the great mass of people where the great mass usually is: neither hot nor cold.[4]

The mass slaughter described here cannot help but offend modern sensibilities with our sometimes inconsistent reverence for life.[5] But the fact is that the entire enterprise of divine revelation hung by a thread that day. If the ringleaders in the apostasy were allowed to continue to wield their influence, it was very unlikely that the worldview of transcendence would survive against the worldview of continuity, given its total dominance of the thought life of the ancient world. Just as Moses had to utterly destroy the calf, leaving no possibility of its being remade, so those who led its worship had to be removed from the scene. This is not to say that similar actions toward sinners would be justified today. That was a unique situation in history upon which all the rest of history hung. God's revelation is now complete and can stand before the world as a full participant. But this incident does call upon the modern believer to be equally ruthless toward sin in his or her life. Just as a surgeon will remove every cancerous cell if it is physically possible, so we must excise every sinful attitude and action, leaving no room for the enemy to retain a foothold (cf. 1 John 2:1-6; 3:6-10).

Moses's Intercession (32:30-35). Moses, having come to realize the terrible seriousness of the situation and perhaps recognizing that the mass of the people had not chosen their apostasy in a defiant way, decided that he needed to make intentional intercession for them. To be sure, he had interceded for them on the mountaintop the day before, but now, clearly, he felt much more deeply the validity of God's case for justice. It was not merely a question of how the surrounding nations would perceive God, but of how the cause-and-effect relationship between sin and its consequences would be dealt with. It was not merely divine restraint that was needed but "forgiveness for" sin (32:30).

It is hard to escape the feeling that Moses was here beginning to suffer from delusions of grandeur. If so, that was certainly understandable. What other mere human in the history of the world has been permitted that kind of prolonged access into the transcendent glory of God? But still, how did Moses think that he could "make atonement for" (see note on 32:30) the sins of his people? Was he a sinless being who could die in the place of the sinners, like the lambs that Yahweh had instructed Moses to use in the whole burnt offerings (29:38-46)? If that was his thought, he quickly abandoned it in God's presence and instead, tried to resort to a bit of pompous, emotional blackmail. He called upon God simply to forgive the people out of hand, and if God was not inclined to do that, he could just go ahead and kill Moses along with everybody else (32:32). Moses did not want to be included in the "book" (32:32; cf. "record," NLT) of a God who wouldn't forgive! So, if God valued Moses's life, he was going to have to forgive the rest of the people. It may be objected that this is to be too hard on a great man, and it is certainly possible that Moses was simply expressing his deep sense of solidarity with his people.[6] But the dryness of God's response (32:33) seems to point in the other direction. In essence God said, "Get off your high horse, Moses. I will punish the people who deserve it, and that doesn't include you." God does not have to have his arm twisted to engage in forgiveness.

Verses 33 and 34 make it plain that God had indeed forgiven the people. In spite of their having destroyed the covenant, they were not going to be wiped out at the foot of the mount of the covenant. God was going to permit them to survive and to experience the fulfillment of his covenant promises to Abraham. Furthermore, he was going to be present with them in the person of his "angel" (32:34). And still further, he was not going to let Moses escape his responsibilities by some dramatic gesture. Moses was going to lead the people to the fulfillment of the promises.

But forgiveness does not deliver us from the consequences of our actions, a point that we too easily overlook. If after engaging in promiscuous sex, a person genuinely repents, God will forgive him or her and allow them complete spiritual restoration. But that does not mean that he will prevent them from getting gonorrhea. In many cases, we are actually less concerned about being restored to fellowship with God than we are about escaping the consequences of our sins. So verses 34b and 35 are not inconsistent with 33 and 34a. God did indeed forgive the people; otherwise, his very presence would have destroyed them all. But that did not mean they could escape the immediate consequences of their actions (see note on 32:34). In this case, it is tempting to think that the "plague" (lit., "blow") that fell upon the people (32:35) was a direct consequence of their uncontrolled activities (see 32:25) in the worship of the bull-idol. The Bible has little interest in the fine points of secondary and tertiary causation. If something happened, it was because God did it (Isa 45:7; Amos 3:6). Ultimately that is certainly true, and it remains true today. However, it is also true that the normal way in which God's purposes are achieved is through the regular operation of the cause-and-effect relationships he has built into his creation, and that may be what took place here.

ENDNOTES
1. Cassuto (1967:419) argues that this reference to fire must mean the idol consisted of a wooden frame plated with gold. While this is certainly possible, other biblical references to "cast images" do not support this view.
2. Since the Bible does not specify why Moses made the people drink the gold-laden water, other suggestions have been offered. The most common one is that it was a similar "ordeal" to that described in Num 5:12-31, where a woman's reaction to drinking tainted water demonstrated her guilt or innocence (so Sarna 207). But, as Childs (1974:569) points out, the point here was not to indicate guilt but to eradicate it!
3. Sarna (1991:208) says Moses's silence in response to Aaron's self-justification is an indication that Moses considered Aaron's answer as beneath contempt. Cassuto (1967:420), however, says that Moses demonstrated that he accepted Aaron's limited responsibility! Childs (1974:570) says that the redactor is painting a clear contrast between Moses and Aaron. Sarna and Childs have the better part of the argument.
4. The specification of "brothers, friends, and neighbors" (32:27) has suggested to some that the real ringleaders of the apostasy may have been among the Levites themselves. If so, this would not be the last time the priesthood would be those leading Israel in idolatry (cf. Judg 17:7-13).
5. For example, the unborn can be condemned to death, but serial killers are excused from the death penalty.
6. In any case, contrary to the suggestions of some commentators, Moses was not offering his life as a substitute for the people. He was merely saying that if God was going to kill them, he should kill Moses too.

◆ 4. The Lord's presence will go with them (33:1-23)

The LORD said to Moses, "Get going, you and the people you brought up from the land of Egypt. Go up to the land I swore to give to Abraham, Isaac, and Jacob. I told them, 'I will give this land to your descendants.' 2And I will send an angel before you to drive out the Canaanites, Amorites, Hittites, Perizzites, Hivites, and Jebusites. 3Go up to this land that flows with milk and honey. But I will not travel among you, for you are a stubborn and rebellious people. If I did, I would surely destroy you along the way."

4When the people heard these stern words, they went into mourning and stopped wearing their jewelry and fine clothes. 5For the LORD had told Moses to tell them, "You are a stubborn and rebellious people. If I were to travel with you for even a moment, I would destroy you. Remove your jewelry and fine clothes while I decide what to do with you." 6So from the time they left Mount Sinai,* the Israelites wore no more jewelry or fine clothes.

7It was Moses' practice to take the Tent of Meeting* and set it up some distance from the camp. Everyone who wanted to make a request of the LORD would go to the Tent of Meeting outside the camp.

8Whenever Moses went out to the Tent of Meeting, all the people would get up and stand in the entrances of their own tents. They would all watch Moses until he disappeared inside. 9As he went into the tent, the pillar of cloud would come down and hover at its entrance while the LORD spoke with Moses. 10When the people saw the cloud standing at the entrance of the tent, they would stand and bow down in front of their own tents. 11Inside the Tent of Meeting, the LORD would speak to Moses face to face, as one speaks to a friend. Afterward Moses would return to the camp, but the young man who assisted him, Joshua son of Nun, would remain behind in the Tent of Meeting.

12One day Moses said to the LORD, "You have been telling me, 'Take these people up to the Promised Land.' But you haven't told me whom you will send with me. You have told me, 'I know you by name, and I look favorably on you.' 13If it is true that you look favorably on me, let me know your ways so I may understand you more fully and continue to enjoy your favor. And remember that this nation is your very own people."

14The LORD replied, "I will personally go with you, Moses, and I will give you rest—everything will be fine for you."

15Then Moses said, "If you don't personally go with us, don't make us leave this place. 16How will anyone know that you look favorably on me—on me and on your people—if you don't go with us? For your presence among us sets your people and me apart from all other people on the earth."

17The LORD replied to Moses, "I will indeed do what you have asked, for I look favorably on you, and I know you by name."

18Moses responded, "Then show me your glorious presence."

19The LORD replied, "I will make all my goodness pass before you, and I will call out my name, Yahweh,* before you. For I will show mercy to anyone I choose, and I will show compassion to anyone I choose. 20But you may not look directly at my face, for no one may see me and live." 21The LORD continued, "Look, stand near me on this rock. 22As my glorious presence passes by, I will hide you in the crevice of the rock and cover you with my hand until I have passed by. 23Then I will remove my hand and let you see me from behind. But my face will not be seen."

33:6 Hebrew *Horeb,* another name for Sinai. 33:7 This "Tent of Meeting" is different from the Tabernacle described in chapters 26 and 36. 33:19 *Yahweh* is a transliteration of the proper name YHWH that is sometimes rendered "Jehovah"; in this translation it is usually rendered "the LORD" (note the use of small capitals).

NOTES

33:3 Go up. These words are not in the text. The opening thought of the verse is almost parenthetical, describing the land from which the inhabitants will be driven out, while the rest of the verse continues the thought of 33:2 by saying that although the angel would lead and defend the people, Yahweh himself would not go with them.

33:4 stern. This word, *ra'* [TH7451, ZH8273], is conventionally translated "evil." See the commentary on 32:13 for a discussion of this term, noting that its connotation is very similar to the English word "bad." A good colloquial translation would be, "when they heard this bad news."

jewelry and fine clothes. While the precise meaning of the term is not clear, it does not seem likely to me that it includes the idea of clothing (so also Houtman 2000:2.690, contra Cassuto 1967:426). Examination of the other occurrences does not show any inclusion of clothing, and two of the references speak of these items as being of gold (2 Sam 1:24; Jer 4:30); thus "jewelry" alone seems best. Houtman (ibid.) wonders whether "taking off ornaments" was designated as a sign of mourning because of the use of earrings for the making of the idol.

33:7 The NLT mg makes it clear that although the Tabernacle also came to be called "the Tent of Meeting," it is not the Tabernacle that is being referred to here. The Hebrew text itself makes that point fairly clearly, but the NLT translation, unfortunately, does not convey it very effectively. A literal translation would be, "Moses used to take the tent and set it up outside the camp at some distance, and he used to call it 'The Tent of Meeting.'" "The tent" is obviously a specific tent that the people knew about. And apparently Moses's name for that tent was transferred to the Tabernacle when it was completed some months later.

33:9 LORD. Interestingly, there is no specification of the speaker in the Hebrew of this verse. It only says "he [or 'it' = the cloud] stood at the door of the tent, and he spoke to Moses." Virtually all English translations supply "the LORD."

33:10 bow down. Lit., "prostrate themselves," an expression used regularly to denote the act of worship.

33:12 I look favorably on you. This is an apt translation of the clause that is more literally translated "you have found grace in my eyes." An even more colloquial translation might be "you look beautiful to me."

33:13 understand you more fully. Lit., "that I may know you." While the experience of knowing God certainly includes a large element of intellectual understanding, it goes far beyond that into intimate personal relationship, in some ways only beginning where finite understanding leaves off.

33:14 I will personally go. Lit., "my face will go." Hebrew has no word expressing the abstract idea of "presence." So when it wishes to speak of someone being immediately present in a situation, it says their "face" is there. The NLT captures the idea well.

everything will be fine for you. This is an expansion of a legitimate inference drawn from the text.

33:18 your glorious presence. Lit., "your glory" (*kabod* [TH3519, ZH3883]; see note and commentary on 16:7). The Hebrew term conveys the idea of "heaviness, significance, importance." Thus it speaks of God's glorious reality, his essential being.

33:20 no one. The Hebrew has the term *ha'adam* [TH1886.1/0120, ZH2021/0132] here, specifying that no "human being" can see God and live.

COMMENTARY

This chapter is centered on the implications of the fact that the people's attempt to bring God near to them on their own terms and by their own effort had the opposite effect. It had, in fact, further alienated them from God, making it more difficult for his face to shine upon them (cf. Num 6:25; see note on 33:14). Verses 1-11 contain the announcement of that effect (33:1-3), the grief of the people over it (33:4-6), and the distance from the camp at which Moses met with God (33:7-11). Verses 12-23 contain Moses's petition that God might relent and agree to go with them to Canaan (33:12-13, 15-16), God's agreement to go (33:14, 17), and God's response to Moses's request for a renewed vision of God's glory (33:18-23).

The Lord Will Not Go with the People (33:1-11). The most profound effect of the golden calf incident was the very opposite of the effect that it was designed to produce. The people needed some tangible evidence that the Divine was in their midst and that his power was available to them to lead and guide them. But they sought to achieve these ends through their own means and efforts. The result was disaster. Whenever we suggest by our actions that the presence and power of God can be pressed into our service for the fulfillment of what we determine to be our needs and for the accomplishment of our goals, we drive a wedge of major proportions between ourselves and God. God does not exist for us to fulfill our needs and accomplish our goals. That is not the way the universe functions, and to attempt to use it in that way is spiritually deadly, just as for a human to attempt to breathe water would be physically deadly.

God declared to Moses that while he would indeed keep his ancient promises to the patriarchs (33:1) and would see that the people were successfully settled in the good land of Canaan (33:2-3), he himself could not be personally present with them, lest his holy presence "destroy [them] along the way" (33:3).[1] As I have said in previous comments, this kind of statement must not be taken to suggest that Yahweh was an arbitrary or vicious god, who might suddenly kill people without notice and for no apparent reason. That is not the case at all. In fact, it is because he does *not* want to destroy the people that he proposes not going with them. This is the same reasoning that Joshua was to use with these people's descendants some 80 years thereafter (Josh 24:12-24). He told them that it would be better if they did not choose Yahweh to be their God because to try to serve him halfheartedly (as they would certainly do) would be to court destruction. To try to use Yahweh in that way is as dangerous as trying to use electricity in ways that are not in keeping with its character. The point is not that Yahweh is so unpredictable but that he *is* so predictable. Considering who God is and how "stubborn and rebellious" (33:5) the people had just shown themselves to be, the danger level for them was very high.

The people's response to this "bad news" (see note on 33:4) is very significant. They were grieved and showed that grief by taking off their jewelry in response to God's command (33:5). It is a good sign that they were grieved. After all, they were going to get the blessing that they had been hoping for. If they could get to the land

and dispossess the people who were already there, what more did they need? But even among these people, whose level of spiritual sensitivity was not very high, there was the awareness that if you get the gifts but lose the Giver, you have not made a good deal. The fact that this was an act of obedience is hopeful. It was a small act, but even small acts are a move in the right direction. At the same time, the lack of any statement that there was a general repentance is ominous. To be remorseful over the impact of one's sins is not the same thing as rejecting those sins, admitting responsibility for them, and determining to leave them behind.

The ideal that had now become so much more distant from them was still set before them day after day, as verses 7-11 make clear.[2] One of their number, Moses, actually met with Yahweh "face to face" (33:11), and not on the high mountain, but in an ordinary "tent," even though it was distant from the camp. The three-fold repetition of tent "entrance(s)" (33:8, 9, 10) highlights both the awe of that experience for the people and the sense of longing that it engendered. Whenever Moses went out away from the camp, the people stood at the entrance of their tents, watching wonderingly. We can hear them whispering to one another, "He is actually going to talk to God!" And when the "pillar of cloud" came and stood at the entrance of the tent of meeting, the people fell down in worship in the entrances of their tents (33:9-10). They were overcome with the incredible nature of what was taking place at that moment, trying to imagine what it must be like to talk with God, and also wondering if that could ever, ever be their experience, especially now with the broken covenant staring them in the face.[3]

Moses Sees the Lord's Glory (33:12-23). In these verses we move from the people's response at the bad news of Yahweh's not going to Canaan with them to Moses's response. We also see here the expression of that face-to-face, friend-to-friend style of conversation that was mentioned in verse 11. There is nothing of restraint between the two conversationalists here, although there is no question of the relative positions of the speakers. The conversation is direct, straightforward, and personal. Here we sense the ideal having become real. We also see here how theologically acute Moses had become. He realized that without Yahweh, the Promised Land was worthless. In fact, the Sinai desert *with* the face of Yahweh was infinitely more desirable than Canaan *without* his face (33:15-16). He had also come to realize that beyond God's various actions, as wonderful as those might be, were God's "ways" (33:13; cf. Ps 103:7-8). Whether anyone else had, Moses had recognized what the covenant was all about: It was a revelation of the character and nature of God in the context of what he does and what he wants. Moses wanted above all else to "know" God (see note on 33:13), and he recognized that the way into that intimate knowledge led through a detailed study of God's ways. Much as a boy or a girl in love cannot find out enough about the beloved, so Moses wanted to know more and more about God.

Despite the unstrained nature of the relationship, Moses still approached his concern discretely. He did not simply blurt out, "You have to come with us!" That is not the way of traditional Near Eastern conversation, even among friends. Courtesy always leaves the other a way out. So Moses simply asked who it was who would be going with them, if God was not (33:12). But then he pressed a little more closely and displayed his understanding of the issues. It was not merely a matter of Yahweh's physical presence but of the necessity of the ongoing personal revelation of him. Moses and Israel did not need what God could do for them nearly as much as they needed God himself. Furthermore, Moses again deflected God's invitation for Moses to make too much of himself. God had suggested again that it was Moses who had brought the people thus far (and had done pretty well; 33:1). But here Moses reminded God once again that that was not true. These were not Moses's people; they were God's. They did not need Moses; they needed God, who alone could meet their real needs.[4]

The immediacy of Yahweh's response both in its first occurrence (33:14) and in its recurrence (33:17) argues once again that a test was taking place (see the comments on 32:7-14 above). God did not need to be argued down from a position to which he was holding fast. Rather, like any good teacher, he did not so much tell the student what he or she should think but elicited the appropriate response from the student. God intensely wanted to accompany his people to Canaan, and his refusal to do so was neither a way of "holding out" on them nor a way of getting them to beg him to change his mind. The question was whether anyone understood what the whole enterprise was about: the desperate need of humans to have God living within them in a love relationship. If just one person understood that fact, then there was hope. But if even Moses missed the point and thought that getting to the land was the point, then the cause truly was hopeless. So God probed the understanding of both Moses and the people, and if the people dimly glimpsed the issue, Moses completely recognized that it was God's personal presence, his "face" (see note on 33:14), that defined Israel's whole experience. Without it, they would be just one more lost, ancient people group, making up life as they went (33:16). God was overjoyed with his student's response.

The recurring phrase, "look favorably on" (33:12, 13, 16, 17) is very significant here, especially when it is twice coupled with "I know you by name" (33:12, 17). The phrase does not say that God had "grace" upon Moses, as we might expect (or upon Noah of whom this phrase is first used; Gen 6:8). Rather, it says that Moses (and Noah) "found grace in God's eyes" (see note on 33:12). What this is saying is that God looked at these men, and they appeared lovely to him. This is not speaking of performance as much as it is desirability. These men, compared to the masses around them, had seriously set their sights on what is right and good and true, and it was a beautiful thing in God's eyes. Thus, this is the language of a lover, someone who cannot get enough of the sight of his beloved. Others, looking on, might wonder what she sees in him, or he in her, but love can see things that others cannot. Moses, as a lover, longed to know God better and better; Yahweh, as a lover, found his beloved delightful. This, of course, speaks to the grace of God, the one who can see incredible and beautiful potential in the feeblest of sincere efforts, where others see only ridiculous failure. And that speaks to the importance of "name" (33:12, 17). There is no such thing as generic love. We love unique, irreplaceable individuals; those in love can spend long hours writing and ornamenting their beloved's name. God loves us by name.

Clearly God's enthusiastic, delighted response spurred a deeper response in Moses, as reported in 33:18-23. His longing for God expressed itself in a desire for a more tangible experience of God—to see his "glory" ("glorious presence," 33:18, NLT). In some manner, Moses had "seen" God with the elders when they celebrated the covenant meal in God's presence (24:10-11). And surely it must have been an incredible experience to be "in" Yahweh's glory on the mountaintop for 40 days (24:15-18). So we may wonder what accounts for this new desire. It may well be that Moses needed some reassurance after the shattering experience of the golden calf. Was the covenant Lord really committed to going ahead with some sort of a relationship after this devastating repudiation of the covenant? Would he reveal himself to Moses again as proof of that intention? But it may also be that Moses had become thirsty for new experiences. We humans are so made that we can never get the same stimulation again from the same experience. This is, of course, what leads to addiction. And that may be the case here. There are a couple of possible signals that this may be the case. The first is Yahweh's response. He says he will show Moses his "goodness" (33:19). When he says a few verses later that his "glory" ("glorious presence," 33:22, NLT) will indeed pass by, we are given a hint that Moses may need to understand better what God's true glory consists of. "Glory" might refer to God's transcendent essence, and that may be what Moses was thinking of. But God may be suggesting that his true glory is found in his character. In the context of creation (see Gen 1), that which is "good" is in keeping with the true nature and order of creation. Theoretically, the creator does not have to be "good." That being might find pleasure in frustrating and contravening the things he has made. Many of the pagan gods were like this, but Yahweh is not so. His desires for his creation are for its fulfillment, not its frustration, for the realization of all its potential, not for the contravention of that potential. He is good (cf. Ps 136:1)! But his essential goodness goes even farther than that. He is not merely a gardener calmly helping his plants come to their full flower. He is the Shepherd who carries the lambs in his bosom and tenderly leads the pregnant ewes (Isa 40:11). He has compassion on people not because they deserve it but simply because he chooses to (33:19).[5] It was more important for Moses to have this understanding of the nature of God driven deep within him than that he have another experience of God's awesome transcendence.

The second possible signal that Moses was in danger of developing a thirst for new religious sensations is the limited nature of the physical experience that was actually given to him. He who had been speaking to God face to face was not to be allowed to see the face of God (33:20). No matter how close a human (see note on 33:20) can come to God in personal experience, there is still an uncrossable barrier between the essence of the Transcendent One and that of his creatures, a barrier not even a Moses could cross.[6]

ENDNOTES
1. Several commentators, among them Sarna, Cassuto, Childs, and Fretheim, take it that this is a statement that the Tabernacle, the place of God's intimate presence in their midst, would not now be built. That may be the case, especially in the light of the reference to the distant Tent of Meeting in 33:7-11. God would be distantly present with them, as he had been thus far, in the Angel of the Lord. But the intimate presence he had planned for from this point on, now seemed impossible.
2. Source critical theory has determined that verses 7-11 have been inserted into the narrative here. Supposedly, there were originally two different versions of the tent shrine in the wilderness, and this version of the distant "Tent of Meeting" is the more original of the two. But a redactor has skillfully incorporated a piece of that original tradition into the later (more contrived) one for his own theological purposes. For a statement of this position, see Hyatt 1971:314-315. For reviews of the position in detail, demonstrating the lack of scholarly agreement in the details, see Houtman 2000:3.685 and Childs 1974:590-593. There is no external evidence in support of this position.
3. The significance of the comment in 33:11 about Joshua's remaining behind in the tent when Moses left is not clear. At the least, it suggests that this is intended to be taken as a real event and not merely some later theological homily dressed in the form of a story. If that were the case, this detail would be entirely superfluous. Perhaps it speaks to the issue of how the tent was taken care of when Moses was away from it.
4. Enns (2000:580-581) suggests that when Moses asks in 33:12 *whom you will send with me* he is asking whether God is going to send all the people with him or whether some more are going to be excluded. He further argues that much of what the ensuing conversation is about is whether God is only going to be personally present with Moses, or with everyone. Although he is not quite so explicit, Childs (1974:594-595) seems to agree on the second point. I do not see this, especially not Enns's first point. On the second, I do not see any clear distinction being made between God's being with Moses and his being with the people.
5. Houtman (2000:3.701-702) agrees with this interpretation, but Cassuto (1967:436) disagrees, saying that the point of this statement in v. 19 is that God retains for himself the right to decide when to be gracious. But the larger context, including 34:6-7, argues for my interpretation.
6. Sarna (1991:214) makes the excellent point that when God revealed his glory it was (1) a mass experience, (2) at a distance, and (3) at God's initiative. What Moses was asking for was the opposite.

◆ ## 5. The renewal of the covenant (34:1-35)

Then the LORD told Moses, "Chisel out two stone tablets like the first ones. I will write on them the same words that were on the tablets you smashed. ²Be ready in the morning to climb up Mount Sinai and present yourself to me on the top of the mountain. ³No one else may come with you. In fact, no one is to appear anywhere on the mountain. Do not even let the flocks or herds graze near the mountain."

⁴So Moses chiseled out two tablets of stone like the first ones. Early in the morning he climbed Mount Sinai as the LORD had commanded him, and he carried the two stone tablets in his hands.

⁵Then the LORD came down in a cloud

and stood there with him; and he called out his own name, Yahweh.* ⁶The LORD passed in front of Moses, calling out,

"Yahweh!* The LORD!
The God of compassion and mercy!
I am slow to anger
   and filled with unfailing love and faithfulness.
⁷I lavish unfailing love to a thousand generations.*
I forgive iniquity, rebellion, and sin.
But I do not excuse the guilty.
I lay the sins of the parents upon
   their children and grandchildren;
the entire family is affected—
   even children in the third and fourth generations."

⁸Moses immediately threw himself to the ground and worshiped. ⁹And he said, "O Lord, if it is true that I have found favor with you, then please travel with us. Yes, this is a stubborn and rebellious people, but please forgive our iniquity and our sins. Claim us as your own special possession."

¹⁰The LORD replied, "Listen, I am making a covenant with you in the presence of all your people. I will perform miracles that have never been performed anywhere in all the earth or in any nation. And all the people around you will see the power of the LORD—the awesome power I will display for you. ¹¹But listen carefully to everything I command you today. Then I will go ahead of you and drive out the Amorites, Canaanites, Hittites, Perizzites, Hivites, and Jebusites.

¹²"Be very careful never to make a treaty with the people who live in the land where you are going. If you do, you will follow their evil ways and be trapped. ¹³Instead, you must break down their pagan altars, smash their sacred pillars, and cut down their Asherah poles. ¹⁴You must worship no other gods, for the LORD, whose very name is Jealous, is a God who is jealous about his relationship with you.

¹⁵"You must not make a treaty of any kind with the people living in the land. They lust after their gods, offering sacrifices to them. They will invite you to join them in their sacrificial meals, and you will go with them. ¹⁶Then you will accept their daughters, who sacrifice to other gods, as wives for your sons. And they will seduce your sons to commit adultery against me by worshiping other gods.
¹⁷You must not make any gods of molten metal for yourselves.

¹⁸"You must celebrate the Festival of Unleavened Bread. For seven days the bread you eat must be made without yeast, just as I commanded you. Celebrate this festival annually at the appointed time in early spring, in the month of Abib,* for that is the anniversary of your departure from Egypt.

¹⁹"The firstborn of every animal belongs to me, including the firstborn males from your herds of cattle and your flocks of sheep and goats. ²⁰A firstborn donkey may be bought back from the LORD by presenting a lamb or young goat in its place. But if you do not buy it back, you must break its neck. However, you must buy back every firstborn son.

"No one may appear before me without an offering.

²¹"You have six days each week for your ordinary work, but on the seventh day you must stop working, even during the seasons of plowing and harvest.

²²"You must celebrate the Festival of Harvest* with the first crop of the wheat harvest, and celebrate the Festival of the Final Harvest* at the end of the harvest season. ²³Three times each year every man in Israel must appear before the Sovereign, the LORD, the God of Israel. ²⁴I will drive out the other nations ahead of you and expand your territory, so no one will covet and conquer your land while you appear before the LORD your God three times each year.

²⁵"You must not offer the blood of my sacrificial offerings together with any baked goods containing yeast. And none

of the meat of the Passover sacrifice may be kept over until the next morning.

²⁶"As you harvest your crops, bring the very best of the first harvest to the house of the LORD your God.

"You must not cook a young goat in its mother's milk."

²⁷Then the LORD said to Moses, "Write down all these instructions, for they represent the terms of the covenant I am making with you and with Israel."

²⁸Moses remained there on the mountain with the LORD forty days and forty nights. In all that time he ate no bread and drank no water. And the LORD* wrote the terms of the covenant—the Ten Commandments*—on the stone tablets.

²⁹When Moses came down Mount Sinai carrying the two stone tablets inscribed with the terms of the covenant,* he wasn't aware that his face had become radiant because he had spoken to the LORD. ³⁰So when Aaron and the people of Israel saw the radiance of Moses' face, they were afraid to come near him.

³¹But Moses called out to them and asked Aaron and all the leaders of the community to come over, and he talked with them. ³²Then all the people of Israel approached him, and Moses gave them all the instructions the LORD had given him on Mount Sinai. ³³When Moses finished speaking with them, he covered his face with a veil. ³⁴But whenever he went into the Tent of Meeting to speak with the LORD, he would remove the veil until he came out again. Then he would give the people whatever instructions the LORD had given him, ³⁵and the people of Israel would see the radiant glow of his face. So he would put the veil over his face until he returned to speak with the LORD.

34:5 *Yahweh* is a transliteration of the proper name *YHWH* that is sometimes rendered "Jehovah"; in this translation it is usually rendered "the LORD" (note the use of small capitals). 34:6 See note on 34:5. 34:7 Hebrew *for thousands.* 34:18 Hebrew *appointed time in the month of Abib.* This first month of the ancient Hebrew lunar calendar usually occurs within the months of March and April. 34:22a Hebrew *Festival of Weeks;* compare 23:16. This was later called the Festival of Pentecost. It is celebrated today as Shavuat (or Shabuoth). 34:22b Or *Festival of Ingathering.* This was later called the Festival of Shelters or Festival of Tabernacles (see Lev 23:33-36). It is celebrated today as Sukkot (or Succoth). 34:28a Hebrew *he.* 34:28b Hebrew *the ten words.* 34:29 Hebrew *the two tablets of the Testimony;* see note on 25:16.

NOTES

34:2 ***morning.*** It is stressed twice in the Hebrew of this verse that Moses was to go up the mountain in the morning. Perhaps the emphasis is made in view of the morning times of both the original giving of the covenant (24:4) and of the worship of the golden calf (32:6). See footnote 4 to the commentary on 24:1-18.

34:5 ***he called out his own name.*** Recent commentators agree that Yahweh is most likely the subject of "called" here, but the subject is not specified, so the alternative that Moses "called upon the name" is possible (so NASB).

34:6 ***calling out, "Yahweh, the LORD!*** By translating in this way, the NLT is conforming to the punctuation in the MT. However, another possibility is "The LORD was calling out, 'Yahweh'" (cf. Houtman 2000:3.706).

unfailing love. See note on 15:13 and the commentary on that verse.

faithfulness. Lit., "truth." The reason paganism cannot believe in objective truth is that its worldview has no place for it. Since the invisible world is constructed on the model of the visible human world, the spirit world and the natural world that embodies it are as fickle, as changeable, and as untrustworthy as we are. Thus, it does not occur to the pagan to think that the world of nature might exhibit patterns that are absolutely reliable apart from magical manipulation. The Israelites, however, were met by a God who is absolutely reliable and true. If that is so, and if he is the sole creator of the universe, then we ought to expect to find "truth" written into his universe. And so it is. But "truth" must first of all be found in relationships before it can be admitted as a principle in the world. Sarna (1991:216) and Cassuto (1967:439) take the two words as a hendiadys, thus, "faithful love," or "loving faithfulness." Most other commentators treat them as related but distinct attributes.

34:7 *a thousand generations.* Lit., "for thousands" (so NLT mg; see also the commentary on 20:6). This understanding of the intent of the text here is supported by Deut 7:9 which makes "generations" explicit.

iniquity, rebellion, and sin. These are the three most common terms used by the Hebrew OT to describe deviation from God's will and ways. They occur together several times elsewhere (e.g., 1 Sam 15:23; Pss 32:5; 51:2-3). "Iniquity" describes the deviation from a more subjective viewpoint, speaking both of the inner twistedness that causes the deviation and the twisted feeling (guilt) that results from it. "Rebellion" speaks of the broken relationship, especially from the point of view of covenant. A person has refused to abide by the will of another to whom they have committed themselves. "Sin" is the broadest of the three terms, speaking of any falling short of God's will and way.

lay the sins . . . upon. Heb. *paqad* [TH6485, ZH7212]. See note and commentary on 32:34.

34:9 *claim us as . . . special possession.* Heb. *nakhal* [TH5157, ZH5706]. This term is often translated "inherit" and is the term used to speak of Israel's ownership of the land of Canaan. Canaan is Israel's "special possession"; Israel is Yahweh's "special possession."

34:10 *people around you.* The word translated "people" here is *'am* [TH5971A, ZH6639], which normally refers to the Israelites. Thus, the rendering should perhaps be "the people you [Moses] live among" (cf. NCV, NASB).

I will display. This represents a Hebrew participle, which probably conveys the idea of imminence here. Thus, perhaps "I am about to display."

34:12 *If you do . . . evil ways.* These words are an expansion explaining how the people will be trapped.

34:13 *Asherah poles.* Asherah was the Canaanite mother goddess, consort of the high god El. As such, she represented fertility and fecundity. It is not clear why "poles" were associated with her worship. It has often been said that these were phallic symbols, but I am not aware of incontrovertible evidence to support that conclusion.

34:14 *whose very name is Jealous.* It is important that we not allow the modern English connotations of "jealousy" to overly color the interpretation of this statement. Those connotations often have to do with a petty possessiveness that is really unwarranted. The English word "passionate," while having its own difficulties, comes closer to the connotations of the Hebrew word. The point is that God cares passionately about what becomes of his people. As pointed out in the commentary on 34:6-7, this faculty of caring is indeed one of the defining characteristics of Yahweh. Like a father who cares deeply about his daughter's choice of boyfriends or a husband who would care deeply if his wife were carousing with a low class of people, Yahweh cares for his people.

about his relationship with you. This is an expansion defining the nature of the divine jealousy.

34:15 *lust after.* This explains the literal, "prostitute themselves with."

34:27-28 *Write down.* This commandment underscores the importance of not being too dogmatic about the origin of the writing on the tablets (see note and commentary on 32:16). Unquestionably the words originated with God, not Moses. But this is not to say that Moses did not write them. In this regard, note that the "he" which the NLT takes to refer to the Lord (see NLT mg) could just as well refer to Moses. And probably on the basis of being the nearest antecedent, Moses is the more likely referent.

34:29 had become radiant. Lit., "the skin of his face sent out horns" (cf. 34:30, 35). In the Hebrew language, a "ray" or "beam" is designated by the same word used for "horn" (so also in Hab 3:4). The literal rendering explains Michelangelo's sculpture of Moses with horns on his head. Sarna (1991:221) suggests that the root *qaran* [TH7160, ZH7966], with its connotation of horns, may have been chosen specifically to contrast this experience with the golden calf episode, which began this segment of the book.

COMMENTARY

This chapter contains the immediate resolution of the golden calf episode. As such, the concept of the presence of God undergirds its three parts. The first part relates to Moses's experience of "seeing" God (34:1-9). The second part contains God's unilateral reaffirmation of the covenant, which the Israelites had broken in their illegitimate attempt to gain God's presence (34:10-28). The third part recounts the impact to Moses's face from his intense experience of the presence of God (34:29-35).

Moses's Experience of Seeing God (34:1-9). Yahweh clearly signaled his intent when he told Moses to "chisel out two stone tablets like the first ones" (34:1). Despite the breach of covenant the people had committed, God was willing to continue on in a covenant relationship with them. The first tablets might have been smashed by Moses, but God was willing to continue a relationship on the basis of what had been written on those "first" tablets. At this point, we cannot understand how God could apparently suspend justice and act as if nothing had happened. Ultimately, we understand that it is on the basis of the blood of the Lamb slain from the foundation of the earth (1 Pet 1:19-20). But here, in an act of surprising grace, God was ready to go right on. This is why there is no covenant sealing included here and why a full statement of the terms is not given.[1]

But even if God was willing to continue in a covenant relationship, that did not mean that he was thereby signaling a diminishing of his own holiness or a lowering of the bar for fellowship with him. If anything, the representation of the incredible distance between God and creatures was heightened (34:3). Not only may no other person come up onto the mountain with Moses[2] but no one could even be seen in its vicinity. Not even animals were permitted in the holy precincts. No one should misunderstand the nature of what was taking place. This relationship would continue to be one with terms that were of God's making and that were indicative of the incredible gulf God was spanning to make it possible.

As mentioned above in the commentary on 33:18-23, whatever Moses may have expected from this experience, there was very little of the merely sensuous. In fact, we are told nothing of what Moses saw. What we are told is what he heard. This is exactly in keeping with the character of biblical revelation from start to finish. Knowing God is not first of all about mystical experience; it is first of all about the "word," the communication of one Person to other persons. The mystical idea of "participation" in the life of God is an amazingly small part of biblical revelation. God is not interested in absorbing us into his life. Rather, he wants a relationship with persons who are distinct from himself and from each other. And the only way such relationships are possible is through language. There is no place where this is more clearly seen than in marriage. Again and again, marriage counselors tell us that the one necessity for a successful marriage relationship is communication.

So what is it that God wished to communicate to Moses in this culmination of the golden calf crisis? The first thing was his name (34:5). There is no serious relationship possible between persons who do not know each other's names. So just as God knew Moses by name (33:12, 17), God here invited Moses, and through Moses, the people, to know him by name. Modern film has given us a good illustration here: Does anyone in the *Star Wars* movies have a relationship with The Force? Of course not. It would be impossible, because The Force is impersonal and thus unnameable. How very different is the case here. Yahweh is intensely personal and his name could not be applied to any other being in the universe. He is the one truly unique person in all of existence, and he invites his creatures to relate to him on a first-name basis.

The second thing Yahweh wanted to communicate in that moment was the most fundamental truth about his character. Far from being an "unmoved Mover" who merely sets all things into motion but is untouched and unaffected by any of those motions, the fundamental truth about Yahweh is that he *is* touched by what happens in his creation, and he *is* personally affected by what his creatures do, both to him and to each other. The significance of this statement about God can't be overstated. As the Greek philosopher Aristotle recognized, it has mind-boggling implications. If the First Cause can be acted upon (affected) by other causes, then it is no longer the First Cause! But the biblical God is untroubled by the limitations of human logic. He *is* the First Cause, the only sufficient cause of all that exists, and at the same time, he *is* deeply affected by all that takes place in his creation. Let us never say that what we cannot conceive of is impossible; on the contrary, accepting its possibility, let us never minimize the wonder of what it portends.

At the center of reality is Yahweh, whose name, if we understand correctly, means "He causes to be" (see note on 3:14). And the one who causes to be is deeply, passionately loyal to his creatures (*khesed* [TH2617, ZH2876], "unfailing love"; see note on 34:6) whom he has given the freedom to deviate from him and from the principles that he has built into creation. They can rebel against him, miss his targets, and twist his purposes, and his first response will be "compassion and mercy" (34:6). When they have been untrue to him, he will remain true (be faithful) to them. It takes him a long time to become truly angry, and when he is, it is quickly abated. The Israelites were not surprised when Yahweh became angry with them. They knew better than anyone else how richly that anger was deserved. No, the anger was not surprising; what was surprising was his compassion and mercy, his unfailing love and faithfulness, and in the end, his forgiveness. This was so surprising that these sentiments about God are quoted more than any others elsewhere in Scripture (Num 14:18; Deut 4:31; Neh 9:17; Ps 86:5, 15; Joel 2:13; Jonah 4:2).[3] They are his defining characteristics. And it was on this basis alone that this covenant relationship could continue to exist. Were God characterized merely by implacable righteousness and justice, the people of Israel would have ceased to exist the morning they danced around their golden bull. That this did not happen was a testimony to the truth about God, which he was putting into words for Moses two mornings later.

The third thing that Yahweh wanted to communicate to Moses was that no one should imagine that because God is fundamentally characterized by a forgiving heart, sin does not have consequences. It is sometimes easy to delude ourselves by saying, "Well, if God will always say, 'I forgive,' I will just go ahead and sin, knowing that I can obtain forgiveness and it will be as if I never did anything." On the contrary, sin sets into motion a whole series of effects that ripple out like a rock thrown into the water. God's punishment (*paqad* [TH6485, ZH7212]; see note on 34:7) is not the arbitrary act of someone who has been offended (see commentary on 32:34). He is not a monster who says, "If you cross me, I'll get your kids!" Rather, he is a Maker who does not prevent natural consequences from playing themselves out. The man who chooses to become a drunkard may be forgiven and even delivered from his addiction, but his children's ways of relating will have been deeply affected. And research has shown that those patterns are very likely to be played out in the next generation, as well. A woman who abuses her children will almost certainly produce a new generation of child abusers. But why doesn't a gracious and compassionate God just wipe out those longer-term effects of sinful choices? Because to do away with the law of cause and effect would be to tear the world apart: We could wake up some morning to find the sun rising in the West. We could step out our front door and be on the Matterhorn.

But what a gracious and compassionate God does do is to limit the effects of sin to three or four generations. Instead of the ripples of sin going on forever, God will slow them down and eventually stop them. By contrast, he is pleased to magnify covenant love to "a thousand generations" (34:7). Who can measure the effects of the smallest choice for God and against the rampant self? Who can trace the ultimate impact of the self-denying father and the faithful mother? It is our fallenness that makes us so quickly gloss over the undeserved *khesed* [TH2617, ZH2876] of God to a thousand generations and instead fixate on three or four generations of the effects of sin. The idea to take away from this third communication is that before we decide to take advantage of God's mercy, we ought to take a long look at the negative effects upon the generations that come after us.

Moses's response to all of this was distinctly different from the response recorded in chapter 32. There he quietly chided God for his anger at the people. There is none of that here! He fell on his face immediately (34:8), and recognizing again the people's true character ("stubborn and rebellious," words Yahweh had spoken in 32:9), meekly begging for the forgiveness that God had revealed was in his character to give. But beyond that, he showed again his grasp of the essentials. If the purposes of the Exodus were to be realized, then Yahweh would have to go with his people to the land, where they would be his "special possession" (34:9). Israel might get the land, but Yahweh had to get the people. If the first was accomplished without the second, then everything that had happened to this point would have been for nothing.

Yahweh's Reaffirmation of the Covenant (34:10-28). Yahweh's response to Moses's request was oblique, but clear. He did not respond directly to Moses's request that he make them his special possession or specifically say that he would accompany Israel to Canaan. But he did say that he would renew the covenant with Moses as the representative of the people. That was enough because those other effects could be understood to "come with the package" of the renewed covenant. Yahweh would continue to accept the obligations of covenant Lord, displaying his awesome power on his people's behalf (34:10). But the people were also going to continue to be held to the original terms of the covenant as represented by the selection that was reiterated here (34:11).

The representative covenant stipulations selected reflect both the situations the people would encounter in the pagan land and also those relating to the sin they had committed. If idolatry was a temptation in the desert, how much more would it be a temptation in the land of Canaan (34:12-17)? For that reason, special precautions were going to have to be taken. The Israelites could not enter into any covenant with the Canaanites ("treaty"; 34:12, 15) because that would necessarily involve tacit recognition of the Canaanite gods whom the Canaanites would call on as witnesses to such a covenant. Instead of that, the Israelites were explicitly told to destroy all traces of the worship of those gods (34:13).

Why this violent reaction? Is it merely a kind of petty possessiveness on the part of Yahweh (see note on 34:14)? Or worse, is it a cover for ethnic hatred? Was Canaanite religion to be destroyed simply because it was not Israelite religion? The answer to both these questions is *no*. What was at stake was the future of the world. The understanding of reality that is inherent in all the pagan religions is fundamentally wrong, perhaps best represented in Canaanite religion. It is built on the premise that this world is ultimate, and that everything in this world—spirit, human, and nature—is continuous with everything else (see the commentary on 19:1 and 20:1 for further discussion). That premise is attractive because it appears to make the world amenable to control by humans through sympathetic magic.[4] But the real result is a world that came from nowhere and is going nowhere, a world without purpose or meaning. It is a world of ethical relativism in which individual humans are of no ultimate significance. It is a world where all historical choices correspond to unseen realities. As I have said, this view is deeply and terribly wrong. It contradicts reality as Yahweh was revealing it to the Israelites at every point. Thus, there was no possibility of the two points of view existing side by side. Either reality must destroy falsity, or falsity must destroy reality. The issue was, and is, that stark.

But God's revelation, as full of philosophical content as it is, is much more than a worldview. It is a passionate love relationship, and that is why the language of religion here and elsewhere in the Bible is the language of marriage. To choose paganism is not merely to make a bad rational choice; it is to leave your true Lover and sell yourself for cash (blessings?) to someone who does not care for you at all ("prostitute yourself"; see note on 34:15). Worse than that, it is to break your covenant with your loving spouse and try to find stolen pleasure with another (34:16). Paganism is deadly not merely because it is the expression of a false understanding of reality but even more because it pretends to satisfy the deepest longings of the human heart and does so with poison.

Instead of that false worship, Israel was to worship in different ways that would unmistakably show that they held to a different understanding of reality and even participated in a relationship with Reality himself (34:18-28). Thus, we can understand the particular selection of covenant stipulations that Yahweh chose to reiterate here. The primary focus is on the three festivals which, occurring at roughly the same times as important festivals in the ancient Near East, but with very different rationales, would clearly differentiate the Israelites from their neighbors (see the commentary on 23:14-19; see also the article "Religion of Canaan," ABD 1:831-836). Two additional matters are brought into the discussion. The first is the sacrifice or redemption of the firstborn (34:19-20; see commentary on 13:11-13; 22:29-30). Perhaps the reason it is selected here is to emphasize that, unlike pagan worship, children (especially firstborn sons) could not be sacrificed (cf. 1 Kgs 16:34; 2 Kgs 3:27). The second matter is the Sabbath (34:21). Again, there is every reason to believe that this practice sharply differentiated the Israelites from the Canaanites.

Moses's Radiant Face (34:29-35). There is something fitting about this entire section regarding the golden calf ending with this passage about Moses's radiant face. What is it that God wants for his creatures? He wants us to be able to know him intimately. He wants us to reflect his character. He wants to transform our lives by the immediacy of his presence. The Israelites only knew that they needed the presence of the divine in a way that would meet their needs. And when they tried to cast the divine in a form that would be amenable to those purposes, they fell into that way of thinking described by the apostle Paul in Romans 1, which can only further alienate us from God and will ultimately destroy us. But God does not give up. And in Moses's experience we get a glimpse of the reason why he does not give up. Moses talked with Yahweh "face to face" (33:11; cf. 34:29). Moses had not "seen" Yahweh face-to-face (cf. 33:20) but something better than that had happened: He had spoken with Yahweh. And that experience was reflected in Moses's face (34:29-30), although he himself was completely unconscious of it. That is as it should be. Moses did not seek God so that his face would be "radiant" (see note on 34:29). He sought God because he wanted to know him and his ways (cf. 33:13). But if we have experienced the "face" of God, it must surely transform our "faces"—the expression of our lives—so that other people cannot avoid the reality, even if it might frighten them and make them uncomfortable at times. At the same time, the radiance is wholly derivative. It was when Moses had been with God again and came to share his word that the radiance was to be seen (34:34-35). The radiance did not become some permanent possession of Moses's. Yahweh alone is self-sufficient; we are but the filaments in a light bulb through which his glory flows. Cut the filament off from the source of electrical supply and it will be as lightless as a stone. The apostle Paul got it right when reflecting on this incident. If a covenant that could only show us that we are sinners produced a glory like that, what ought to be the effect of a covenant that can reproduce the very character of Christ in us (2 Cor 3:18)? The old covenant could not produce the character it called for because it could not overcome our disposition to sin (Rom 8:3), but now the Spirit of Christ has come through the New Covenant and he is able to make "us more and more like him as we are changed into his glorious image" (2 Cor 3:18).

ENDNOTES
1. Fretheim (1991:306-307) considers the question about why the earlier statements (in chs 32-33) are so uncompromising if God is forgiving by nature. He responds helpfully that they were (1) to reveal apostasy for what it is, (2) to reveal the genuine character of mercy, and (3) to enable grace to truly be grace.
2. Although Aaron, his sons, and the elders had earlier accompanied Moses at least partway (24:1), this was not to be the case now.
3. They also came to form the centerpiece in later Jewish liturgy.
4. This worldview also has the appearance of toleration, since any way of manipulating the divine is presumably as good as any other. But it is a mistake to suggest that paganism is inherently tolerant (cf. Kirsch 2004). Whenever conflict between cultures came into view in the ancient world, religious toleration was the first victim.

◆ C. Report of Building the Tabernacle: Securing Yahweh's Presence in Yahweh's Way (35:1–40:38)
   1. Instructions for the Sabbath and a call for material and skills for the Tabernacle (35:1–36:7)

Then Moses called together the whole community of Israel and told them, "These are the instructions the LORD has commanded you to follow. ²You have six days each week for your ordinary work, but the seventh day must be a Sabbath day of complete rest, a holy day dedicated to the LORD. Anyone who works on that day must be put to death. ³You must not even light a fire in any of your homes on the Sabbath."

⁴Then Moses said to the whole community of Israel, "This is what the LORD has commanded: ⁵Take a sacred offering for the LORD. Let those with generous hearts present the following gifts to the LORD:

gold, silver, and bronze;
⁶blue, purple, and scarlet thread;
   fine linen and goat hair for cloth;
⁷tanned ram skins and fine goatskin leather;
acacia wood;
⁸olive oil for the lamps;
   spices for the anointing oil and the fragrant incense;
⁹onyx stones, and other gemstones to be set in the ephod and the priest's chestpiece.

¹⁰"Come, all of you who are gifted craftsmen. Construct everything that the LORD has commanded:

¹¹the Tabernacle and its sacred tent, its covering, clasps, frames, crossbars, posts, and bases;
¹²the Ark and its carrying poles; the Ark's cover—the place of atonement;
   the inner curtain to shield the Ark;
¹³the table, its carrying poles, and all its utensils;
   the Bread of the Presence;
¹⁴for light, the lampstand, its accessories, the lamp cups, and the olive oil for lighting;

15 the incense altar and its carrying poles;
the anointing oil and fragrant incense;
the curtain for the entrance of the Tabernacle;
16 the altar of burnt offering;
the bronze grating of the altar and its carrying poles and utensils;
the washbasin with its stand;
17 the curtains for the walls of the courtyard;
the posts and their bases;
the curtain for the entrance to the courtyard;
18 the tent pegs of the Tabernacle and courtyard and their ropes;
19 the beautifully stitched garments for the priests to wear while ministering in the Holy Place—the sacred garments for Aaron the priest, and the garments for his sons to wear as they minister as priests."

20 So the whole community of Israel left Moses and returned to their tents. 21 All whose hearts were stirred and whose spirits were moved came and brought their sacred offerings to the LORD. They brought all the materials needed for the Tabernacle,* for the performance of its rituals, and for the sacred garments. 22 Both men and women came, all whose hearts were willing. They brought to the LORD their offerings of gold—brooches, earrings, rings from their fingers, and necklaces. They presented gold objects of every kind as a special offering to the LORD. 23 All those who owned the following items willingly brought them: blue, purple, and scarlet thread; fine linen and goat hair for cloth; and tanned ram skins and fine goatskin leather. 24 And all who had silver and bronze objects gave them as a sacred offering to the LORD. And those who had acacia wood brought it for use in the project.

25 All the women who were skilled in sewing and spinning prepared blue, purple, and scarlet thread, and fine linen cloth. 26 All the women who were willing used their skills to spin the goat hair into yarn. 27 The leaders brought onyx stones and the special gemstones to be set in the ephod and the priest's chestpiece. 28 They also brought spices and olive oil for the light, the anointing oil, and the fragrant incense. 29 So the people of Israel—every man and woman who was eager to help in the work the LORD had given them through Moses—brought their gifts and gave them freely to the LORD.

30 Then Moses told the people of Israel, "The LORD has specifically chosen Bezalel son of Uri, grandson of Hur, of the tribe of Judah. 31 The LORD has filled Bezalel with the Spirit of God, giving him great wisdom, ability, and expertise in all kinds of crafts. 32 He is a master craftsman, expert in working with gold, silver, and bronze. 33 He is skilled in engraving and mounting gemstones and in carving wood. He is a master at every craft. 34 And the LORD has given both him and Oholiab son of Ahisamach, of the tribe of Dan, the ability to teach their skills to others. 35 The LORD has given them special skills as engravers, designers, embroiderers in blue, purple, and scarlet thread on fine linen cloth, and weavers. They excel as craftsmen and as designers.

CHAPTER 36

"The LORD has gifted Bezalel, Oholiab, and the other skilled craftsmen with wisdom and ability to perform any task involved in building the sanctuary. Let them construct and furnish the Tabernacle, just as the LORD has commanded."

2 So Moses summoned Bezalel and Oholiab and all the others who were specially gifted by the LORD and were eager to get to work. 3 Moses gave them the materials donated by the people of Israel as sacred offerings for the completion of the sanctuary. But the people continued to bring additional gifts each morning. 4 Finally the craftsmen who were working on the sanctuary left their work. 5 They went to Moses and reported, "The people have given more than enough materials to

complete the job the LORD has commanded us to do!"

⁶So Moses gave the command, and this message was sent throughout the camp: "Men and women, don't prepare any more gifts for the sanctuary. We have enough!" So the people stopped bringing their sacred offerings. ⁷Their contributions were more than enough to complete the whole project.

35:21 Hebrew *Tent of Meeting.*

NOTES

35:3 *fire.* Cassuto (1967:454-455) suggests this prohibition may have arisen because certain pagan festivals emphasized the lighting of fires.

35:22 *a special offering.* Lit., "a wave offering." Evidently, this referred to an offering that was ceremonially lifted up before God as a sign of giving it into his ownership.

35:25 *women.* There was no gender specificity in who could contribute their skills to the service of Yahweh. See also 35:29.

COMMENTARY

The final segment of the book of Exodus leads us to the climax. The Israelites will have finally found "the way out" of their bondage, their spiritual darkness, and their alienation from God when Yahweh takes up his residence in their midst (40:34-38). Of course, this was only the beginning of a road that would extend over more than a thousand years until the full meaning of the Lord's glory filling the Tabernacle (40:34) would be brought to realization in the coming of the Holy Spirit. Nevertheless, in that moment, when God's instructions were carried out in his way,[1] the essential foundations for God's deliverance were fully laid. The fact that the book jumps directly over the other events of the six months that intervened between Moses's return from his second stint on the mountain to the completion of the Tabernacle (40:1) underscores the theological program of the book of Exodus: Deliverance is only truly realized when it results in God's residing among a worshiping and obedient people.

Instructions for the Sabbath (35:1-3). Just as the instructions for the Tabernacle and its service ended with commands relating to the Sabbath (31:12-18), so this report begins with that topic. Moses made it clear to the people that the sanctity of time and the sanctity of space are directly related. Sadly, these commands came to be a burden to a people who became obsessed with the minutiae of what was permissible and what was not permissible. Jesus made it plain that, just as Moses had said, these commands were not for God's sake but for theirs (Deut 10:13; Mark 2:27). The Sabbath was meant to relieve them of the heavy load of having to supply their own needs.[2]

A Call for Material and Skills for the Tabernacle (35:4-36:7). The list of materials here (35:4-9) corresponds to that in 25:3-7 but is expanded with a list of the objects that should be built (35:10-19), as well as a record of the variety of offerings that were brought for the work (35:20-29). The passage continues with Moses's report that Bezalel had been filled with the Spirit of God for the work and that he and

Oholiab would be enabled to teach their skills to others (35:30–36:1). The segment concludes with the report of how Moses got the work underway (36:2-7).

There are clearly three themes running through this unit, and all three set it in direct contrast with the account of the golden calf. The first is that this was the Lord's work and no one else's. Four times it is emphasized that this work is what "the LORD has commanded" (35:4, 10; 36:1, 5). Furthermore, it was being accomplished through the skills he had given (35:31-35; 36:1-2). The second theme grows directly out of this one: The work was done by many different people who had been specifically chosen and gifted by the Lord, who in turn were able to empower other people as well. The third theme is that everyone had something to give, not so much to the building project, but to the Lord (35:22, 24). They did not give at the command of Aaron in order to get something back from a god they had brought into being. Neither were they giving to a building project. Rather, they gave because they wanted to express worship for God. We can well imagine that there was a welter of emotions present: relief that they were still alive, gratitude that God was willing to go on with them, awe at the danger of treating this God inappropriately, and wonder at the radiance of Moses's face. All of these, when mingled together, meant that their "hearts were stirred" and their "spirits were moved" (35:21), and they gave abundantly and not grudgingly. Ultimately, they even had to be restrained because they were giving more than could be used (36:3-7). The giving was contagious because it was spiritually motivated. It was expressed in great variety, according to the various gifts and abilities of all involved. It was for the Lord and not for a project. It was accomplished by persons especially gifted who were able to involve many people in the task, and not merely by religious professionals.

ENDNOTES
1. The statement that the work was done "as the Lord commanded" occurs more than 25 times in these six chapters. God's presence can only be a reality in our lives when it is on his terms.
2. The question of the death penalty in this case and others is not an easy one to answer. When a particular point is made of the execution of the man who gathered sticks on the Sabbath in Num 15:32-36, one has the feeling that this was not the carrying out of a regular judicial sentence, a normal event, but a particular example, much like that of Ananias and Sapphira in Acts 5:1-11. Perhaps the pronouncement here and elsewhere in the Torah was primarily to underscore the importance of what was being said rather than to prescribe what was necessary in every case.

◆ ## 2. Building the Tabernacle (36:8–39:43)
a. Constructing the sanctuary (36:8-38)

⁸The skilled craftsmen made ten curtains of finely woven linen for the Tabernacle. Then Bezalel* decorated the curtains with blue, purple, and scarlet thread and with skillfully embroidered cherubim. ⁹All ten curtains were exactly the same size— 42 feet long and 6 feet wide.* ¹⁰Five of these curtains were joined together to

make one long curtain, and the other five were joined to make a second long curtain. ¹¹He made fifty loops of blue yarn and put them along the edge of the last curtain in each set. ¹²The fifty loops along the edge of one curtain matched the fifty loops along the edge of the other curtain. ¹³Then he made fifty gold clasps and fastened the long curtains together with the clasps. In this way, the Tabernacle was made of one continuous piece.

¹⁴He made eleven curtains of goat-hair cloth to serve as a tent covering for the Tabernacle. ¹⁵These eleven curtains were all exactly the same size—45 feet long and 6 feet wide.* ¹⁶Bezalel joined five of these curtains together to make one long curtain, and the other six were joined to make a second long curtain. ¹⁷He made fifty loops for the edge of each large curtain. ¹⁸He also made fifty bronze clasps to fasten the long curtains together. In this way, the tent covering was made of one continuous piece. ¹⁹He completed the tent covering with a layer of tanned ram skins and a layer of fine goatskin leather.

²⁰For the framework of the Tabernacle, Bezalel constructed frames of acacia wood. ²¹Each frame was 15 feet high and 27 inches wide,* ²²with two pegs under each frame. All the frames were identical. ²³He made twenty of these frames to support the curtains on the south side of the Tabernacle. ²⁴He also made forty silver bases—two bases under each frame, with the pegs fitting securely into the bases. ²⁵For the north side of the Tabernacle, he made another twenty frames, ²⁶with their forty silver bases, two bases under each frame. ²⁷He made six frames for the rear—the west side of the Tabernacle—²⁸along with two additional frames to reinforce the rear corners of the Tabernacle. ²⁹These corner frames were matched at the bottom and firmly attached at the top with a single ring, forming a single corner unit. Both of these corner units were made the same way. ³⁰So there were eight frames at the rear of the Tabernacle, set in sixteen silver bases—two bases under each frame.

³¹Then he made crossbars of acacia wood to link the frames, five crossbars for the north side of the Tabernacle ³²and five for the south side. He also made five crossbars for the rear of the Tabernacle, which faced west. ³³He made the middle crossbar to attach halfway up the frames; it ran all the way from one end of the Tabernacle to the other. ³⁴He overlaid the frames with gold and made gold rings to hold the crossbars. Then he overlaid the crossbars with gold as well.

³⁵For the inside of the Tabernacle, Bezalel made a special curtain of finely woven linen. He decorated it with blue, purple, and scarlet thread and with skillfully embroidered cherubim. ³⁶For the curtain, he made four posts of acacia wood and four gold hooks. He overlaid the posts with gold and set them in four silver bases.

³⁷Then he made another curtain for the entrance to the sacred tent. He made it of finely woven linen and embroidered it with exquisite designs using blue, purple, and scarlet thread. ³⁸This curtain was hung on gold hooks attached to five posts. The posts with their decorated tops and hooks were overlaid with gold, and the five bases were cast from bronze.

36:8 Hebrew *he*; also in 36:16, 20, 35. See 37:1. 36:9 Hebrew *28 cubits* [12.9 meters] *long and 4 cubits* [1.8 meters] *wide*. 36:15 Hebrew *30 cubits* [13.8 meters] *long and 4 cubits* [1.8 meters] *wide*. 36:21 Hebrew *10 cubits* [4.6 meters] *high and 1.5 cubits* [69 centimeters] *wide*.

NOTES

36:8 *skilled.* Lit., "wise of heart." This imagery underscores again that "heart" in the OT is not primarily the center of raw emotion but rather the core of the personality, encompassing intellect, feeling, and will. True skill involves all of these.

COMMENTARY

Unlike the instructions, which were organized more topically (e.g., ch 30; the instructions for the washbasin and the incense altar were included with directions to the priests) and theologically (25:9-10; beginning with the Ark of the Covenant), this report is organized in a logical fashion, moving from the construction of the sanctuary to the construction of the furnishings of both the sanctuary (37:1-29) and the courtyard (38:1-8) to the construction of the courtyard itself (38:9-20). Then, before moving on, there is an inventory of the materials used for the entire structure (38:21-31). Exodus 39:1-31 is devoted to a report of how the clothing for the priests was made. This is followed by a report of all the elements that Moses inspected and found acceptable (39:32-43). The instructions for the ordination of the priests and the miscellaneous instructions for their service (29:1-45; 30:11-16, 22-38) are not included here because these were only carried out after the Tabernacle was erected. There is also a brief statement that the anointing oil and incense were made (37:29).

On the design of the tent, see the commentary on 26:1-33, 36-37.

◆   b. Constructing the furniture for the sanctuary (37:1-29)

Next Bezalel made the Ark of acacia wood—a sacred chest 45 inches long, 27 inches wide, and 27 inches high.* ²He overlaid it inside and outside with pure gold, and he ran a molding of gold all around it. ³He cast four gold rings and attached them to its four feet, two rings on each side. ⁴Then he made poles from acacia wood and overlaid them with gold. ⁵He inserted the poles into the rings at the sides of the Ark to carry it.

⁶Then he made the Ark's cover—the place of atonement—from pure gold. It was 45 inches long and 27 inches wide.* ⁷He made two cherubim from hammered gold and placed them on the two ends of the atonement cover. ⁸He molded the cherubim on each end of the atonement cover, making it all of one piece of gold. ⁹The cherubim faced each other and looked down on the atonement cover. With their wings spread above it, they protected it.

¹⁰Then Bezalel* made the table of acacia wood, 36 inches long, 18 inches wide, and 27 inches high.* ¹¹He overlaid it with pure gold and ran a gold molding around the edge. ¹²He decorated it with a 3-inch border* all around, and he ran a gold molding along the border. ¹³Then he cast four gold rings for the table and attached them at the four corners next to the four legs. ¹⁴The rings were attached near the border to hold the poles that were used to carry the table. ¹⁵He made these poles from acacia wood and overlaid them with gold. ¹⁶Then he made special containers of pure gold for the table—bowls, pans, jars, and pitchers—to be used in pouring out liquid offerings.

¹⁷Then Bezalel made the lampstand of pure, hammered gold. He made the entire lampstand and its decorations of one piece—the base, center stem, lamp cups, buds, and petals. ¹⁸The lampstand had six branches going out from the center stem, three on each side. ¹⁹Each of the six branches had three lamp cups shaped like almond blossoms, complete with buds and petals. ²⁰The center stem of the lampstand was crafted with four lamp cups shaped like almond blossoms, complete with buds and petals. ²¹There was an almond bud beneath each pair of branches where the six branches extended from the

center stem, all made of one piece. ²²The almond buds and branches were all of one piece with the center stem, and they were hammered from pure gold.

²³He also made seven lamps for the lampstand, lamp snuffers, and trays, all of pure gold. ²⁴The entire lampstand, along with its accessories, was made from seventy-five pounds* of pure gold.

²⁵Then Bezalel made the incense altar of acacia wood. It was 18 inches square and 36 inches high,* with horns at the corners carved from the same piece of wood as the altar itself. ²⁶He overlaid the top, sides, and horns of the altar with pure gold, and he ran a gold molding around the entire altar. ²⁷He made two gold rings and attached them on opposite sides of the altar below the gold molding to hold the carrying poles. ²⁸He made the poles of acacia wood and overlaid them with gold.

²⁹Then he made the sacred anointing oil and the fragrant incense, using the techniques of a skilled incense maker.

37:1 Hebrew *2.5 cubits* [115 centimeters] *long, 1.5 cubits* [69 centimeters] *wide, and 1.5 cubits high.* 37:6 Hebrew *2.5 cubits* [115 centimeters] *long and 1.5 cubits* [69 centimeters] *wide.* 37:10a Hebrew *he;* also in 37:17, 25. 37:10b Hebrew *2 cubits* [92 centimeters] *long, 1 cubit* [46 centimeters] *wide, and 1.5 cubits* [69 centimeters] *high.* 37:12 Hebrew *a border of a handbreadth* [8 centimeters]. 37:24 Hebrew *1 talent* [34 kilograms]. 37:25 Hebrew *1 cubit* [46 centimeters] *long and 1 cubit wide, a square, and 2 cubits* [92 centimeters] *high.*

COMMENTARY

Much of this material duplicates material in 25:10-40 and 30:1-6; see the commentary on those sections. For a discussion of the significance of the duplication, see the opening paragraphs of the commentary on 25:1–27:19.

◆ c. Constructing the courtyard and its equipment (38:1-20)

Next Bezalel* used acacia wood to construct the square altar of burnt offering. It was 7½ feet wide, 7½ feet long, and 4½ feet high.* ²He made horns for each of its four corners so that the horns and altar were all one piece. He overlaid the altar with bronze. ³Then he made all the altar utensils of bronze—the ash buckets, shovels, basins, meat forks, and firepans. ⁴Next he made a bronze grating and installed it halfway down the side of the altar, under the ledge. ⁵He cast four rings and attached them to the corners of the bronze grating to hold the carrying poles. ⁶He made the poles from acacia wood and overlaid them with bronze. ⁷He inserted the poles through the rings on the sides of the altar. The altar was hollow and was made from planks.

⁸Bezalel made the bronze washbasin and its bronze stand from bronze mirrors donated by the women who served at the entrance of the Tabernacle.*

⁹Then Bezalel made the courtyard, which was enclosed with curtains made of finely woven linen. On the south side the curtains were 150 feet long.* ¹⁰They were held up by twenty posts set securely in twenty bronze bases. He hung the curtains with silver hooks and rings. ¹¹He made a similar set of curtains for the north side—150 feet of curtains held up by twenty posts set securely in bronze bases. He hung the curtains with silver hooks and rings. ¹²The curtains on the west end of the courtyard were 75 feet long,* hung with silver hooks and rings and supported by ten posts set into ten bases. ¹³The east end, the front, was also 75 feet long.

¹⁴The courtyard entrance was on the east end, flanked by two curtains. The curtain on the right side was 22½ feet long* and was supported by three posts set into three bases. ¹⁵The curtain on the

left side was also 22½ feet long and was supported by three posts set into three bases. ¹⁶All the curtains used in the courtyard were made of finely woven linen. ¹⁷Each post had a bronze base, and all the hooks and rings were silver. The tops of the posts of the courtyard were overlaid with silver, and the rings to hold up the curtains were made of silver.

¹⁸He made the curtain for the entrance to the courtyard of finely woven linen, and he decorated it with beautiful embroidery in blue, purple, and scarlet thread. It was 30 feet long, and its height was 7½ feet,* just like the curtains of the courtyard walls. ¹⁹It was supported by four posts, each set securely in its own bronze base. The tops of the posts were overlaid with silver, and the hooks and rings were also made of silver.

²⁰All the tent pegs used in the Tabernacle and courtyard were made of bronze.

38:1a Hebrew *he*; also in 38:8, 9.   38:1b Hebrew *5 cubits* [2.3 meters] *wide, 5 cubits long, a square, and 3 cubits* [1.4 meters] *high*.   38:8 Hebrew *Tent of Meeting*; also in 38:30.   38:9 Hebrew *100 cubits* [46 meters]; also in 38:11.   38:12 Hebrew *50 cubits* [23 meters]; also in 38:13.   38:14 Hebrew *15 cubits* [6.9 meters]; also in 38:15.   38:18 Hebrew *20 cubits* [9.2 meters] *long and 5 cubits* [2.3 meters] *high*.

NOTES

38:8 *women who served.* The only other reference to such women is in 1 Sam 2:22. Sarna (1991:230) suggests that they were menial laborers; he says their inclusion here is a way of saying that even the least of the people had something to offer to the work. Cassuto (1967:467) disagrees; he says that the phrase should be translated "women who stood in array" indicating that they stood in a long line to contribute their "bronze mirrors" to the work. The word (*tsaba'* [TH6633, ZH7371]) only occurs 13 times in the OT and the primary meaning is "to assemble," so Cassuto may be more correct.

COMMENTARY

This section repeats material found in Exodus 27:1-19; 30:17-21. See the commentary on each of those sections. For a discussion of the significance of the duplication, see the opening paragraphs of the commentary on 25:1–27:19.

◆ d. Inventory of materials (38:21-31)

²¹This is an inventory of the materials used in building the Tabernacle of the Covenant.* The Levites compiled the figures, as Moses directed, and Ithamar son of Aaron the priest served as recorder. ²²Bezalel son of Uri, grandson of Hur, of the tribe of Judah, made everything just as the LORD had commanded Moses. ²³He was assisted by Oholiab son of Ahisamach, of the tribe of Dan, a craftsman expert at engraving, designing, and embroidering with blue, purple, and scarlet thread on fine linen cloth.

²⁴The people brought special offerings of gold totaling 2,193 pounds,* as measured by the weight of the sanctuary shekel. This gold was used throughout the Tabernacle.

²⁵The whole community of Israel gave 7,545 pounds* of silver, as measured by the weight of the sanctuary shekel. ²⁶This silver came from the tax collected from each man registered in the census. (The tax is one beka, which is half a shekel,* based on the sanctuary shekel.) The tax was collected from 603,550 men who had reached their twentieth birthday. ²⁷The hundred bases for the frames of the sanctuary walls and for the posts supporting the inner curtain required 7,500 pounds of silver, about 75 pounds for each base.* ²⁸The remaining 45 pounds* of silver was

used to make the hooks and rings and to overlay the tops of the posts.

²⁹The people also brought as special offerings 5,310 pounds* of bronze, ³⁰which was used for casting the bases for the posts at the entrance to the Tabernacle, and for the bronze altar with its bronze grating and all the altar utensils. ³¹Bronze was also used to make the bases for the posts that supported the curtains around the courtyard, the bases for the curtain at the entrance of the courtyard, and all the tent pegs for the Tabernacle and the courtyard.

38:21 Hebrew *the Tabernacle, the Tabernacle of the Testimony.* **38:24** Hebrew *29 talents and 730 shekels* [994 kilograms]. Each shekel weighed about 0.4 ounces. **38:25** Hebrew *100 talents and 1,775 shekels* [3,420 kilograms]. **38:26** Or *0.2 ounces or 6 grams.* **38:27** Hebrew *100 talents* [3,400 kilograms] *of silver, 1 talent* [34 kilograms] *for each base.* **38:28** Hebrew *1,775 shekels* [20.2 kilograms]. **38:29** Hebrew *70 talents and 2,400 shekels* [2,407 kilograms].

NOTES

38:21 Ithamar. This is the fourth of Aaron's sons who are named in the text, the others being Nadab, Abihu, and Eleazar. After the deaths of Nadab and Abihu, Eleazar became the leader, and after Aaron's death, he became the high priest (Num 26:63), whereas Ithamar seems to have been in charge of the Levites who cared for the structures of the Tabernacle complex (Num 4:28-33). Yet Eli, the high priest in Shiloh (1 Sam 1), was clearly of the line of Ithamar (Ahimelech was a descendent of Ithamar, 1 Chr 24:3; Abiathar was the son of Ahimelech, 1 Sam 22:20; and Abiathar was a descendent of Eli, 1 Kgs 2:27). When that line fell under a curse because of the sins of Eli's sons, the line of Eleazar came to the fore again. What happened during the Judges period to explain these shifts is lost to us now.

38:24 the sanctuary shekel. See note on 30:13. The weight of a shekel that could be given as ransom money in a census was pegged at a fixed amount. This suggests that in a society where there were no coins and payment was made in weights of metal, there may have been discounted standards in use. These could not be used in this case.

38:26 603,550 men. This figure agrees with that of the census reported in Num 1:46. Cassuto (1967:470-471) notes that there is a problem here since the census which was apparently the basis on which the silver was collected did not occur until after the Tabernacle was erected. He concludes that what is reported in Num 1:2 was only the final tallying up of a process which had begun much earlier.

COMMENTARY

When presented with the kind of detailed information contained in this section, we are forced to one of two conclusions: Either these events took place as recorded, and this information has come down to us as part of what took place there; or someone has gone to immense trouble to make us *think* that these events took place. For instance, it is often said that the Tabernacle is a fictional creation on the pattern of Solomon's Temple. (For a lengthy treatment on the supposed origins of the Tabernacle accounts, see Houtman 2000:3.306-335.) But what about the calculation of the weight of the silver bases for the frames and the posts (38:27), for which there was no parallel in the Temple? If, as many scholars believe, this entire account is a fictional creation by priests in the postexilic era designed to validate their theological program, one wonders why it was necessary to go to these lengths. Of course, if that conclusion is correct, the reason for studying this material at all is thoroughly undercut: To make us believe their theology is "true," the priests felt it necessary to construct a completely fictional "historical" origin for the theology.

But true theology does not spring from false history. If these events did not occur, then the theology is not inspired and is simply one more fascinating yet useless tidbit from the past.

But, in fact, it is these kinds of details that argue for the historicity of these events. While it is hard to imagine people writing a fiction going to the trouble to try to imagine what details would make the account look historical and then setting about to create those details, it is quite believable that Moses, recognizing the critical importance of everything surrounding the giving of the covenant and having been required to write down its terms, would have directed the recording of details like these.

◆ ### e. Making the clothing for the priests (39:1-31)

The craftsmen made beautiful sacred garments of blue, purple, and scarlet cloth—clothing for Aaron to wear while ministering in the Holy Place, just as the LORD had commanded Moses.

²Bezalel* made the ephod of finely woven linen and embroidered it with gold and with blue, purple, and scarlet thread. ³He made gold thread by hammering out thin sheets of gold and cutting it into fine strands. With great skill and care, he worked it into the fine linen with the blue, purple, and scarlet thread.

⁴The ephod consisted of two pieces, front and back, joined at the shoulders with two shoulder-pieces. ⁵The decorative sash was made of the same materials: finely woven linen embroidered with gold and with blue, purple, and scarlet thread, just as the LORD had commanded Moses. ⁶They mounted the two onyx stones in settings of gold filigree. The stones were engraved with the names of the tribes of Israel, just as a seal is engraved. ⁷He fastened these stones on the shoulder-pieces of the ephod as a reminder that the priest represents the people of Israel. All this was done just as the LORD had commanded Moses.

⁸Bezalel made the chestpiece with great skill and care. He made it to match the ephod, using finely woven linen embroidered with gold and with blue, purple, and scarlet thread. ⁹He made the chestpiece of a single piece of cloth folded to form a pouch nine inches* square. ¹⁰They mounted four rows of gemstones* on it. The first row contained a red carnelian, a pale-green peridot, and an emerald. ¹¹The second row contained a turquoise, a blue lapis lazuli, and a white moonstone. ¹²The third row contained an orange jacinth, an agate, and a purple amethyst. ¹³The fourth row contained a blue-green beryl, an onyx, and a green jasper. All these stones were set in gold filigree. ¹⁴Each stone represented one of the twelve sons of Israel, and the name of that tribe was engraved on it like a seal.

¹⁵To attach the chestpiece to the ephod, they made braided cords of pure gold thread. ¹⁶They also made two settings of gold filigree and two gold rings and attached them to the top corners of the chestpiece. ¹⁷They tied the two gold cords to the rings on the chestpiece. ¹⁸They tied the other ends of the cords to the gold settings on the shoulder-pieces of the ephod. ¹⁹Then they made two more gold rings and attached them to the inside edges of the chestpiece next to the ephod. ²⁰Then they made two more gold rings and attached them to the front of the ephod, below the shoulder-pieces, just above the knot where the decorative sash was fastened to the ephod. ²¹They attached the bottom rings of the chestpiece to the rings on the ephod with blue cords. In this way, the chestpiece was held securely to the ephod above the

decorative sash. All this was done just as the LORD had commanded Moses.

²²Bezalel made the robe that is worn with the ephod from a single piece of blue woven cloth, ²³with an opening for Aaron's head in the middle of it. The opening was reinforced with a woven collar* so it would not tear. ²⁴They made pomegranates of blue, purple, and scarlet yarn, and attached them to the hem of the robe. ²⁵They also made bells of pure gold and placed them between the pomegranates along the hem of the robe, ²⁶with bells and pomegranates alternating all around the hem. This robe was to be worn whenever the priest ministered before the LORD, just as the LORD had commanded Moses.

²⁷They made tunics for Aaron and his sons from fine linen cloth. ²⁸The turban and the special head coverings were made of fine linen, and the undergarments were also made of finely woven linen. ²⁹The sashes were made of finely woven linen and embroidered with blue, purple, and scarlet thread, just as the LORD had commanded Moses.

³⁰Finally, they made the sacred medallion—the badge of holiness—of pure gold. They engraved it like a seal with these words: HOLY TO THE LORD. ³¹They attached the medallion with a blue cord to Aaron's turban, just as the LORD had commanded Moses.

39:2 Hebrew *He;* also in 39:8, 22. **39:9** Hebrew *1 span* [23 centimeters]. **39:10** The identification of some of these gemstones is uncertain. **39:23** The meaning of the Hebrew is uncertain.

NOTES

39:3 gold thread. The discussion of the making of gold thread is unique to this report, not having occurred in the instructions. Sarna (1991:232) says the process is typically Egyptian.

39:30 the badge of holiness. Heb. *nezer haqqodesh* [TH5145/1886.1/6924, ZH5694/2021/7731] (the holy crown). The exact significance of this phrase is unclear. It occurs in apposition to "medallion," as the NLT has it, and thus it seems unlikely that "crown" is to be taken literally. The parallel in 28:37-38 says that the "medallion" was to be suspended from the front of the high priest's turban so that it rested on his forehead. The NLT's "badge" presents *nezer* as connoting not so much a particular type of headdress as an indicator of office, which could take a variety of forms.

COMMENTARY

This report is laid out in the same order as the instructions, beginning with detailed descriptions of the workmanship of the ephod and the chestpiece (39:2-21) and then continuing with more cursory descriptions of the remaining articles of clothing. It is significant that no less than five times in these 31 verses it is specified that the work was done "just as the LORD had commanded Moses" (39:1, 7, 21, 26, 31). Perhaps this was because sacred garments such as these might be considered useful for magical purposes, and these comments were designed to forestall such thinking (in contrast, note Judg 8:25-27). For additional comments on this account, see the commentary on 28:1-43.

◆   **f. Moses inspects the work (39:32-43)**

³²And so at last the Tabernacle* was finished. The Israelites had done everything just as the LORD had commanded Moses.

³³And they brought the entire Tabernacle to Moses:

the sacred tent with all its furnishings, clasps, frames, crossbars, posts, and bases;
34 the tent coverings of tanned ram skins and fine goatskin leather;
the inner curtain to shield the Ark;
35 the Ark of the Covenant* and its carrying poles;
the Ark's cover—the place of atonement;
36 the table and all its utensils;
the Bread of the Presence;
37 the pure gold lampstand with its symmetrical lamp cups, all its accessories, and the olive oil for lighting;
38 the gold altar;
the anointing oil and fragrant incense;
the curtain for the entrance of the sacred tent;
39 the bronze altar;
the bronze grating and its carrying poles and utensils;
the washbasin with its stand;
40 the curtains for the walls of the courtyard;
the posts and their bases;
the curtain for the entrance to the courtyard;
the ropes and tent pegs;
all the furnishings to be used in worship at the Tabernacle;
41 the beautifully stitched garments for the priests to wear while ministering in the Holy Place—the sacred garments for Aaron the priest, and the garments for his sons to wear as they minister as priests.

42 So the people of Israel followed all of the LORD's instructions to Moses. 43 Then Moses inspected all their work. When he found it had been done just as the LORD had commanded him, he blessed them.

39:32 Hebrew *the Tabernacle, the Tent of Meeting;* also in 39:40.   39:35 Or *Ark of the Testimony.*

NOTES

39:37 *its symmetrical lamp cups.* Lit., "its lamps, an arrangement of lamps." Perhaps this refers to the ranks of lamps on each side of the central stem (see commentary on 25:31-40).

39:39 *the bronze altar.* In 35:16 it is specified that this was the altar of burnt offering.

39:40 *all the furnishings . . . Tabernacle.* This phrase does not appear in the list in ch 35. Here it functions to remind the reader what all of this finery is meant for. The Hebrew adds "for the Tent of Meeting," a further reminder that this was the place God had chosen to meet with his people.

COMMENTARY

This list is virtually identical to the one in Exodus 35:10-19, which describes the beginning of the construction process. Almost certainly the duplication serves the same purpose that the overall duplication of the instructions (25:1–31:18) does in the report (35:1–39:43). This time the attempt to secure God's presence was done in God's way, not in a humanly contrived way. So here, each thing that Moses had listed to be made was made (as he had been instructed by God). This fact is underscored by the opening and closing verses: "The Israelites had done everything just as the LORD had commanded Moses" (39:32); "When he found it had been done just as the LORD had commanded him, he blessed them" (39:43).

Throughout the Pentateuch to this point (and not merely in the context of covenant), a recurring issue has been that of blessing and curse. In Genesis 1, the climax of creation was God's blessing on the man and woman he had created (Gen 1:28). But in Genesis 3, that blessing was tragically changed to curse as Adam and Eve, distrusting God, refused to believe that what he said was true and disobeyed. The rest of the first 11 chapters of Genesis narrate the outcome of that curse. But God was unwilling to leave that the world under a curse; so, as recorded in Genesis 12-22, he started humanity on the way back to blessing, promising undeserved blessings to Abraham and Sarah. It is not accidental that this way back was through trust (Gen 12), belief (Gen 15), and obedience (Gen 22). Neither is it accidental that on Mount Moriah, after an ultimate act of obedience on Abraham's part, God gave Abraham a formal blessing (Gen 22:17). The remainder of the book replays these themes through the lives of Isaac, Jacob, and Joseph, demonstrating in a variety of ways that whenever humans attempt to secure blessing in their own strength, all they end up getting for themselves is a curse; whereas, when they are willing to lay aside fear and distrust and to abandon themselves to God, they find blessing showering down around them.[1] In Exodus that theme is formalized in the covenant, with its promises of blessing for those who keep it and curse for those who break it. The theme is then actualized in the golden calf incident, when human efforts to secure divine blessing actually receive divine curse. Once the people had abandoned their own efforts and carefully followed God's instructions, Moses was able to pronounce the blessing of God upon them.

ENDNOTE

1. It is no accident that the Jacob narrative, which began in all the discord caused by human efforts to secure blessing, ends with the blessings that the patriarch, surrendered to God (as reported in Gen 32), dispensed to his sons (Gen 49:28).

3. The Tabernacle completed (40:1-38)
a. Setting up the Tabernacle (40:1-33)

Then the LORD said to Moses, ²"Set up the Tabernacle* on the first day of the new year.* ³Place the Ark of the Covenant* inside, and install the inner curtain to enclose the Ark within the Most Holy Place. ⁴Then bring in the table, and arrange the utensils on it. And bring in the lampstand, and set up the lamps.

⁵"Place the gold incense altar in front of the Ark of the Covenant. Then hang the curtain at the entrance of the Tabernacle. ⁶Place the altar of burnt offering in front of the Tabernacle entrance. ⁷Set the washbasin between the Tabernacle* and the altar, and fill it with water. ⁸Then set up the courtyard around the outside of the tent, and hang the curtain for the courtyard entrance.

⁹"Take the anointing oil and anoint the Tabernacle and all its furnishings to consecrate them and make them holy. ¹⁰ Anoint the altar of burnt offering and its utensils to consecrate them. Then the altar will become absolutely holy. ¹¹Next anoint the washbasin and its stand to consecrate them.

¹²"Present Aaron and his sons at the entrance of the Tabernacle, and wash them with water. ¹³Dress Aaron with the sacred garments and anoint him, consecrating him to serve me as a priest. ¹⁴Then present his sons and dress them in their tunics.

¹⁵Anoint them as you did their father, so they may also serve me as priests. With their anointing, Aaron's descendants are set apart for the priesthood forever, from generation to generation."
¹⁶Moses proceeded to do everything just as the LORD had commanded him. ¹⁷So the Tabernacle was set up on the first day of the first month of the second year. ¹⁸Moses erected the Tabernacle by setting down its bases, inserting the frames, attaching the crossbars, and setting up the posts. ¹⁹Then he spread the coverings over the Tabernacle framework and put on the protective layers, just as the LORD had commanded him.
²⁰He took the stone tablets inscribed with the terms of the covenant and placed them* inside the Ark. Then he attached the carrying poles to the Ark, and he set the Ark's cover—the place of atonement—on top of it. ²¹Then he brought the Ark of the Covenant into the Tabernacle and hung the inner curtain to shield it from view, just as the LORD had commanded him.
²²Next Moses placed the table in the Tabernacle, along the north side of the Holy Place, just outside the inner curtain. ²³And he arranged the Bread of the Presence on the table before the LORD, just as the LORD had commanded him. ²⁴He set the lampstand in the Tabernacle across from the table on the south side of the Holy Place. ²⁵Then he lit the lamps in the LORD's presence, just as the LORD had commanded him. ²⁶He also placed the gold incense altar in the Tabernacle, in the Holy Place in front of the inner curtain. ²⁷On it he burned the fragrant incense, just as the LORD had commanded him.
²⁸He hung the curtain at the entrance of the Tabernacle, ²⁹and he placed the altar of burnt offering near the Tabernacle entrance. On it he offered a burnt offering and a grain offering, just as the LORD had commanded him.
³⁰Next Moses placed the washbasin between the Tabernacle and the altar. He filled it with water so the priests could wash themselves. ³¹Moses and Aaron and Aaron's sons used water from it to wash their hands and feet. ³²Whenever they approached the altar and entered the Tabernacle, they washed themselves, just as the LORD had commanded Moses.
³³Then he hung the curtains forming the courtyard around the Tabernacle and the altar. And he set up the curtain at the entrance of the courtyard. So at last Moses finished the work.

40:2a Hebrew *the Tabernacle, the Tent of Meeting;* also in 40:6, 29. **40:2b** Hebrew *the first day of the first month.* This day of the ancient Hebrew lunar calendar occurred in March or April. **40:3** Or *Ark of the Testimony;* also in 40:5, 21. **40:7** Hebrew *Tent of Meeting;* also in 40:12, 22, 24, 26, 30, 32, 34, 35. **40:20** Hebrew *He placed the Testimony;* see note on 25:16.

NOTES

40:2 *Tabernacle.* See the NLT mg here and also on 40:7. Throughout this passage the Tabernacle is referred to as "the Tent of Meeting," emphasizing the function of the complex as not merely the "residence" of God among his people but even more importantly, the point of contact between him and them.

the new year. Cf. 40:17 which specifies that this was on the first day of the second year after the departure from Egypt. The setting up of the Tabernacle occurred on the exact first anniversary of Passover and two weeks shy of a year from the crossing of the sea.

40:3 *curtain.* The word *paroketh* [TH6532, ZH7267] from the root *prk* (to bar) is consistently used for the veil that separated the Holy Place from the Most Holy Place, whereas *masak* [TH4539, ZH5009] (from *sakak* [TH5526, ZH6114], "to screen, cover") is regularly used for the curtains at the openings of the Tabernacle and the courtyard (40:5, 8). In 40:21 both terms are used for the veil; the NLT translates it as "inner curtain."

40:9 consecrate. Note that words having to do with holiness (from the root *qadash* [TH6942, ZH7727], like this one) occur eight times in 40:9-13, emphasizing the nature of God and of all that which was to be associated with him.

40:15 set apart . . . generation. Although the general sense of this verse is clear enough, it is virtually impossible to create a literal translation of the Hebrew that is smooth English. The NLT captures the sense effectively.

40:20 the stone tablets. This rendering is possible, but not certain. The Hebrew says that Moses "put the testimony into the Ark." It seems likely that the two stone tablets together comprised "the testimony" to the covenant (see 34:29 and NLT mg).

the Ark's cover. See the comments on this object in 25:17-22.

40:23 Bread of the Presence. Lit., "the arrangement of bread."

40:31 used water from it. The NLT properly clarifies (with "from") that Moses and the others did not wash *in* "the washbasin" (40:30).

COMMENTARY

Once again (as in 25:1–31:18 and 35:1–39:43) we have divine instructions set parallel to the human fulfillment of those instructions (40:1-33). God told Moses to set up the Tabernacle in certain ways (40:1-15), and "Moses proceeded to do everything just as the LORD had commanded him" (40:16-33). And that phrase, "just as the LORD had commanded him," occurs no less than seven additional times between verses 19 and 32. If God is to live in us, to share his holy presence with us, it must be on his terms alone.

As in chapters 35–39, the general order is from inner to outer, concluding with the clothing of the priests (40:14-15). The exception is that in the report (40:16-33) there is no mention of the priests' clothing. It may be that this was a matter that was to be deferred until after Yahweh's filling of the Tabernacle with his glory (see Lev 9:1ff). However, we are told that as Moses set up the various elements, he did inaugurate their use. So the table (40:23), the lamps (40:25), the incense altar (40:27), the altar of burnt offering (40:29), and the washbasin (40:30) were all put into service by Moses. If the order of setting up is actually as it is given here, with the "curtains forming the courtyard" (40:33) being hung last, it is interesting to think of all of this being done in the awed sight of the people.

◆ b. The Lord's glory fills the Tabernacle (40:34-38)

³⁴Then the cloud covered the Tabernacle, and the glory of the LORD filled the Tabernacle. ³⁵Moses could no longer enter the Tabernacle because the cloud had settled down over it, and the glory of the LORD filled the Tabernacle.

³⁶Now whenever the cloud lifted from the Tabernacle, the people of Israel would set out on their journey, following it. ³⁷But if the cloud did not rise, they remained where they were until it lifted. ³⁸The cloud of the LORD hovered over the Tabernacle during the day, and at night fire glowed inside the cloud so the whole family of Israel could see it. This continued throughout all their journeys.

NOTES

40:34 *filled.* This Hebrew form could be a participle. If so, the connotation would be of continuous filling.

40:35 *settled down.* The verb is *shakan* [TH7931, ZH8905], meaning "to take up residence." This is the same root that appears in the term translated "Tabernacle": *mishkan* [TH4908, ZH5438]. In later Judaism, the glory of God is referred to as the "Shekinah" (i.e., "the residing thing"), taken from the same root.

COMMENTARY

With this chapter we reach the climax of everything from chapter 25 onward, and indeed of everything in the book. What is the goal of salvation in the Bible? It is that God should take up residence in the dwelling of human hearts, filling them with himself (Eph 3:17-19). That goal is beautifully symbolized in the Tabernacle. Furthermore, the crisis associated with that goal being realized is powerfully symbolized in the incident of the golden calf. Will we experience the blessing of the presence of God in our lives by doing our wills, or by doing his will? If there remained any question by this point in the reading, it should surely be settled once and for all here.

Here is the climax of the climax. Everything in the book realizes its purpose in the moment when "the cloud covered the Tabernacle, and the glory of the LORD filled the Tabernacle" (40:34). Yahweh had been moving toward this point from the moment Adam and Eve left the Garden of Eden, from the moment when he first addressed Abram, from the moment when he spoke to Moses from the bush, from the moment when he directed Moses to extend his staff over the sea. This moment of God's taking up residence among his people in the fullness of his glory, yet without destroying them, was the reason why God had revealed himself in all those previous movements. That Yahweh was immediately present among them in the cloud and fire did not signal the slightest diminution of his holy glory. In fact, that glory was so real here in the Tabernacle that Moses, who had walked into the glory on the mountaintop, was unable to enter it. By means of the people's wholehearted commitment to the covenant and the continuous atonement that is discussed in the immediately following segment (Lev 1–9, 16), the holy God had established a way to come home to his people.

The people had cried to Aaron for "gods who can lead us" (32:1), trying to provide for their needs themselves. In these last verses of the book (40:36-38) we see conclusively how God had been planning all the time to take care of that need, doing so in more dramatic and powerful ways than they could have ever imagined. God is the only true supplier of human needs, and for those who will trust, believe, and obey him, he will do it in infinitely satisfying ways. Under the snake's questioning, Adam and Eve had come to doubt that. Now, finally, Yahweh had demonstrated the foolishness of such doubt once and for all. To be sure, the ultimate revelation of that truth could come only when the incarnate Second Person of the Trinity would come to take up residence on earth:

> So the Word became human and made his home [tabernacled] among us. He was full of unfailing love and faithfulness [cf. Ex 34:6]. And we have seen his glory, the glory of the Father's one and only Son. (John 1:14)

And the final realization of this truth came when by means of the Third Person of the Trinity, Christ took up ownership of the hearts of those wholly surrendered to him:

> But the Holy Spirit produces this kind of fruit in our lives: love, joy, peace, patience, kindness, goodness, faithfulness, gentleness, and self-control. There is no law against these things! Those who belong to Christ Jesus have nailed the passions and desires of their sinful nature to his cross and crucified them there. Since we are living by the Spirit, let us follow the Spirit's leading in every part of our lives. (Gal 5:22-25)

Thus it can be said in the book of Revelation (Rev 21:22) that there will be no temple in the New Jerusalem. There, the "the Lord God Almighty and the Lamb" will take the place of the temple, being immediately present for all believers. The symbolism of the earthly Tabernacle and Temple will have served its ultimate purpose.

BIBLIOGRAPHY

Alexander, T. D.
1998 *From Paradise to Promised Land*. Grand Rapids: Baker.

Alter, Robert
1981 *The Art of Biblical Narrative*. New York: Basic Books.

Arnold, Bill and Bryan Beyer
2002 *Readings from the Ancient Near East*. Grand Rapids: Baker.

Baly, Dennis
1957 *The Geography of the Bible: A Study in Historical Geography*. New York: Harper & Row.

Beckwith, R. T.
1985 *The Old Testament Canon of the New Testament Church and Its Background in Early Judaism*. Grand Rapids: Eerdmans.

Bimson, John
1978 *Redating the Exodus and Conquest*. Journal of Old Testament Studies Supplement 5. Sheffield: University of Sheffield.

Cassuto, Umberto
1967 *A Commentary on the Book of Exodus*. Translator, Israel Abrahams. Jerusalem: Magnes.

Childs, Brevard
1974 *The Book of Exodus. A Critical, Theological Commentary*. Old Testament Library. Philadelphia: Westminster.

Clements, Ronald
1972 *Exodus*. The Cambridge Bible Commentary. Cambridge: Cambridge University Press.

Clines, David
1978 *The Theme of the Pentateuch*. Journal of Old Testament Studies Supplement 10. Sheffield: University of Sheffield Press.

Dumbrell, W.
1984 *Covenant and Creation: An Old Testament Covenantal Theology*. Exeter: Paternoster.

Durham, John I.
1987 *Exodus*. Word Biblical Commentary 3. Waco: Word.

Ellison, H. L.
1982 *Exodus*. Philadelphia: Westminster.

Enns, Peter
2000 *The NIV Application Commentary: Exodus*. Grand Rapids: Zondervan.

Finkelstein, Israel, and Neil Asher Silberman
2001 *The Bible Unearthed: Archeology's New Vision of Ancient Israel and the Origin of Its Sacred Texts*. New York: Free Press.

Fretheim, Terence E.
1991 *Exodus*. Interpretation. Louisville: John Knox.

Friedman, Richard E.
1980 The Tabernacle in the Temple. *Biblical Archaeologist* 43:241-248.

1987 *Who Wrote the Bible?* New York: Summit Books.

Gardiner, Sir Alan
1966 *Egypt of the Pharaohs*. New York: Oxford.

Gesenius, W., E. Kautzsch, and A. E. Cowley
1963 *Gesenius' Hebrew Grammar*. Oxford: Clarendon.

Gordon, C.
1962 *Before the Bible*. London: Collins.

1965 *The Common Background of Greek and Hebrew Civilizations*. New York: Norton.

Hamilton, Gordon J.
2006 *The Origins of the West Semitic Alphabet in Egyptian Scripts*. Catholic Biblical Quarterly Monograph Series 40. Washington, DC: Catholic Biblical Association.

Haran, Menahem
1978 *Temples and Temple-Service in Ancient Israel*. Oxford: Clarendon.

BIBLIOGRAPHY

Harrison, R. K.
1969 *Introduction to the Old Testament*. Grand Rapids: Eerdmans.

Hoffmeier, James
1996 *Israel in Egypt: The Evidence for the Authenticity of the Exodus Tradition*. Oxford: Oxford University Press.

Houtman, Cornelis
1993–2000 *Exodus*. Historical Commentary on the Old Testament. 3 vols. Leuven: Peeters.

Hyatt, J. Philip
1971 *Exodus*. New Century Bible Commentary. Grand Rapids: Eerdmans.

Kaufmann, Yehezkel
1960 *The Religion of Israel: From Its Beginnings to the Babylonian Exile*. Translator, M. Greenberg. Chicago: University of Chicago Press.

Kirsch, J.
2004 *God against the Gods*. New York: Viking Compass.

Kitchen, Kenneth A.
1964 *Ancient Orient and Old Testament*. London: Tyndale Press.
2003 *On the Reliability of the Old Testament*. Grand Rapids: Eerdmans.

Knight, George A. F.
1976 *Theology as Narration: A Commentary on the Book of Exodus*. Grand Rapids: Eerdmans.

Levenson, J.
1988 *Creation and the Persistence of Evil: the Jewish Drama of Divine Omnipotence*. New York: Harper Collins.

McCarthy, D. J.
1972 *Old Testament Covenant*. Richmond: John Knox.

Motyer, J. Alec
2005 *The Message of Exodus: The Days of Our Pilgrimage*. The Bible Speaks Today. Downers Grove: InterVarsity.

Orr, James
1909 *The Problem of the Old Testament*. New York: C. Scribner's Sons.

Oswalt, John
1973 The Golden Calves and the Egyptian Concept of Deity. *Evangelical Quarterly* 45:13-20.

Quick, Daryl E.
1990 *The Healing Journey for Adult Children of Alcoholics*. Downers Grove: InterVarsity.

Redford, Donald B.
2002 *The Ancient Gods Speak: A Guide to Egyptian Religion*. New York: Oxford.

Rice, Judith
2007 Israel? *The Jewish Magazine*, 117 (Sept-Oct 2007), accessed at http://www.jewishmag.com/117mag/timemachine/timemachine.htm.

Sarna, Nahum M.
1991 *Exodus: The Traditional Hebrew Text with the New JPS Translation*. The JPS Torah Commentary. Philadelphia: Jewish Publication Society.

Shaw, Ian
2000 *The Oxford History of Ancient Egypt*. New York: Oxford.

Waltke, B. and M. O'Connor
1990 *An Introduction to Biblical Hebrew Syntax*. Winona Lake, IN: Eisenbrauns.

Walton, John
1989 *Ancient Israelite Literature in Its Cultural Context*. Grand Rapids: Zondervan.

Westermann, Claus
1967 *Basic Forms of Prophetic Speech*. Translator, H. C. White. Philadelphia: Westminster.
1981 *Praise and Lament in the Psalms*. Translators, K. Crim and R. Soulen. Atlanta: John Knox.

Williams, R. J.
1976 *Hebrew Syntax: An Outline*. 2nd ed. Toronto: University of Toronto Press.